Western Literature

I

Western Literature

I

The Ancient World

Edited by

Heinrich von Staden

YALE UNIVERSITY

Under the General Editorship of

A. Bartlett Giamatti

YALE UNIVERSITY

HARCOURT BRACE JOVANOVICH, INC.

NEW YORK   CHICAGO   SAN FRANCISCO   ATLANTA

ISBN: 0–15–595276–5

Library of Congress Catalog Card Number: 75–152578

Printed in the United States of America

ACKNOWLEDGMENTS

BASIL BLACKWELL & MOTT LTD. for C. J. Billson's translation from Pindar's *Odes of Victory: the Olympian and Pythian Odes.* Reprinted by permission of the publishers.

THE UNIVERSITY OF CHICAGO PRESS for Homer's *Iliad,* translated by Richmond Lattimore, copyright 1951, The University of Chicago Press. Reprinted by permission of the publisher.

FABER AND FABER LIMITED for *The Agamemnon of Aeschylus,* translated by Louis MacNeice. Reprinted by permission of Faber and Faber Ltd.

HARVARD UNIVERSITY PRESS for Lucretius' *De Rerum Natura,* translated by W. H. D. Rouse. Reprinted by permission of the publishers and The Loeb Classical Library. Published 1937.

DAVID MC KAY COMPANY, INC. for Aristophanes' *Lysistrata,* translated by Charles T. Murphy, from *Greek Literature in Translation,* edited by W. J. Oates and C. T. Murphy (Longmans, Green & Company: 1944). Reprinted by permission of David McKay Company, Inc.

THE UNIVERSITY OF MICHIGAN PRESS for *The Satyricon,* by Petronius, translated by William Arrowsmith. Copyright 1959, William Arrowsmith. Reprinted by permission of the University of Michigan Press. "The Works and Days," by Hesiod, translated by Richmond Lattimore. Copyright 1959, University of Michigan Press. Reprinted by permission of the University of Michigan Press.

OXFORD UNIVERSITY PRESS for *Oedipus the King,* from *Three Theban Plays of Sophocles,* translated by Theodore Howard Banks. Copyright 1956 by Theodore Howard Banks. Reprinted by permission of Oxford University Press, Inc.

CHARLES SCRIBNER'S SONS for *The Aeneid of Virgil.* Reprinted by permission of Charles Scribner's Sons from *The Aeneid of Virgil* translated by Rolfe Humphries. Copyright 1951 by Charles Scribner's Sons.

Contents

v

General Introduction

The three volumes of *Western Literature* are intended to provide the student with a broad view of the literature of the Western world. The volume on the Ancient World contains some of the best representative examples of the Hebraic and Greco-Roman traditions and of the origins of Christian writing. The second volume, covering the Middle Ages, Renaissance, and Enlightenment, opens with a troubadour's lyric to a faraway love and ends with Voltaire's satire on complacent optimism. The third volume, devoted to the Modern World, traces the contemporary spirit from Rousseau to two current masters of the Americas.

Certain principles have guided the editors, both individually and collectively, in their selections. An effort has been made to include, wherever possible, complete works or at least substantial excerpts of large works. This has not always been possible, and in a very few cases it has meant not including an author when no representative work of manageable length could be found. The underlying assumption here is that the artistic integrity of a literary work has primary importance.

The editors have tried to include translations of continental poetry by other notable poets—for example, John Milton's translation of Horace or Ezra Pound's of Cavalcanti—in order to provide the reader not only with distinguished renderings but also with instances of the critical operation of one poetic sensibility on another. The editors have also been guided by their sense of the wholeness of literature, by their conviction that literature is the expression of a fundamental human activity, the urge to order memory and desire by making a new world with the imagination. Finally, if there is one overriding principle that informs the selections in these three volumes, it is that what man has written about himself over the centuries is our best indication of where we are, and who we are.

A. B. GIAMATTI

GENERAL EDITOR

The Old Testament

Perhaps the most remarkable achievement of the ancient Hebrews is a collection of books known as the Old Testament. It represents an enormously varied literary production, extending from the tenth or ninth century B.C. down to the late second century B.C., when the Old Testament more or less reached its present form.

The Old Testament is usually divided into three groups. The first is the Pentateuch, or "Five Books," traditionally ascribed to Moses. It includes the Book of Genesis, from which the following accounts of the Creation, the Fall of Man, and the Flood are drawn. The Pentateuch probably reached its final form about 400 B.C., although much of the material in it is considerably older. Thus the Book of Genesis, which was compiled by various scribes, is widely believed to be based on three main sources: a "J," or Judaean, source, dating from the ninth or tenth century B.C.; an "E," or Ephraimite, source, somewhat later; and a "P," or Priestly, source, from approximately the fifth century B.C. The material in these sources was probably composed from still older traditions.

A second group of books, those of the Prophets, reached its present form about 200 B.C. The third collection of sacred writings in the Old Testament includes, among others, the Book of Job, the Book of Psalms, and the Song of Songs, from which selections follow. It reached its present form about 132 B.C., although most of its materials are also considerably older.

The works in all three groups in course of time acquired canonical status; that is, they were granted religious authority and thus became the basis of an entire culture. Despite the variety of their authors, dates, and subjects, they present a coherent system of belief because they are characterized by a relatively uniform view of the universe and of its creation and government by a single, all-powerful divinity.

The Old Testament

The Creation*

Genesis, or "The Book of Origins" opens with an account of the beginning of the world and man. The story of the creation is told in the myths of many cultures, including those of ancient Greece and Rome. The Hebrew version bears a strikingly close resemblance to earlier Babylonian myths about the creation and flood. Most of the myths treat the creation as a divine act of material construction or physical evolution. In contrast, the following account shows the distinctively Hebrew emphasis on creation as the act of speech—the world coming into being through the power of divine words.

In the beginning God created the heaven and the earth. And the earth was without form, and void; and darkness was upon the face of the deep.[1] And the Spirit of God moved upon the face of the waters. And God said, Let there be light: and there was light. And God saw the light, that it was good: and God divided the light from the darkness. And God called the light Day, and the darkness he called Night. And the evening and the morning were the first day.

And God said, Let there be a firmament in the midst of the waters, and let it divide the waters from the waters. And God made the firmament,[2] and divided the waters which were under the firmament from the waters which were above the firmament: and it was so. And God called the firmament Heaven. And the evening and the morning were the second day.

And God said, Let the waters under the heaven be gathered together unto one place, and let the dry land appear: and it was so. And God called the dry land Earth; and the gathering together of the waters called the Seas: and God saw that it was good. And God said, Let the earth bring forth grass,[3]

---

[1] A primordial subterranean ocean, on which the earth was supposed to rest.   [2] The "dome" of the sky.   [3] More accurately, "vegetation."   * Gen. 1:1–2:7.

the herb yielding seed, and the fruit tree yielding fruit after his kind, whose seed is in itself, upon the earth: and it was so. And the earth brought forth grass, and herb yielding seed after his kind, and the tree yielding fruit, whose seed was in itself, after his kind: and God saw that it was good. And the evening and the morning were the third day.

And God said, Let there be lights in the firmament of the heaven to divide the day from the night; and let them be for signs, and for seasons, and for days, and years: And let them be for lights in the firmament of the heaven to give light upon the earth: and it was so.[4] And God made two great lights; the greater light to rule the day, and the lesser light to rule the night: he made the stars also. And God set them in the firmament of the heaven to give light upon the earth, and to rule over the day and over the night, and to divide the light from the darkness: and God saw that it was good. And the evening and the morning were the fourth day.

And God said, Let the waters bring forth abundantly the moving creature that hath life, and fowl [5] that may fly above the earth in the open firmament of heaven. And God created great whales, and every living creature that moveth, which the waters brought forth abundantly, after their kind, and every winged fowl after his kind: and God saw that it was good. And God blessed them, saying, Be fruitful, and multiply, and fill the waters in the seas, and let fowl multiply in the earth. And the evening and the morning were the fifth day.

And God said, Let the earth bring forth the living creature after his kind, cattle,[6] and creeping thing, and beast[7] of the earth after his kind: and it was so. And God made the beast of the earth after his kind, and cattle after their kind, and every thing that creepeth upon the earth after his kind: and God saw that it was good.

And God said, Let us[8] make man in our image, after our likeness: and let them have dominion over the fish of the sea, and over the fowl of the air, and over the cattle, and over all the earth, and over every creeping thing that creepeth upon the earth. So God created man in his own image, in the image of God created he him; male and female created he them. And God blessed them, and God said unto them, Be fruitful, and multiply, and replenish the earth, and subdue it: and have dominion over the fish of the sea, and over the fowl of the air, and over every living thing that moveth upon the earth.

And God said, Behold, I have given you every herb bearing seed, which

---

[4] Most mythologies interpret the stars and planets as deities to be worshiped. However, in Hebrew culture they were merely lights fixed in the "dome" by God. [5] Birds. [6] Domestic animals. [7] Wild animals. [8] The plural conveys dignity and majesty (as often in Hebrew); the Hebraic word for God in this chapter is *Elohim,* a plural word, the exact interpretation of which is under considerable scholarly discussion. Elohim, with the Tetragrammaton, YHVH, is the chief name of God appearing in the Old Testament.

is upon the face of all the earth, and every tree, in the which is the fruit of a tree yielding seed; to you it shall be for meat. And to every beast of the earth, and to every fowl of the air, and to every thing that creepeth upon the earth, wherein there is life, I have given every green herb for meat: and it was so. And God saw every thing that he had made, and, behold, it was very good. And the evening and the morning were the sixth day.

Thus the heavens and the earth were finished, and all the host of them. And on the seventh day God ended his work which he had made; and he rested [9] on the seventh day from all his work which he had made. And God blessed the seventh day, and sanctified it: because that in it he had rested from all his work which God created and made.

These are the generations of the heavens and of the earth when they were created, in the day that the Lord God made the earth and the heavens,[10] and every plant of the field before it was in the earth, and every herb of the field before it grew: for the Lord God had not caused it to rain upon the earth, and there was not a man to till the ground. But there went up a mist from the earth, and watered the whole face of the ground. And the Lord God formed man of the dust of the ground, and breathed into his nostrils the breath of life; and man became a living soul.

The Fall of Man*

The Fall of Man is an archetypal account of the crisis that occurs when the divine and the human dash against each other. In the Old Testament, God's concern for man and man's deficient comprehension of God's design are incompatible. As soon as the original, ordered relationship between God and man is disrupted by man's fall from innocence, man must be expelled from the paradisial garden, which was a manifestation of the physical world as God's original design had intended it. The concept of man's fall or degeneration from a more perfect state also occurs in other ancient cultures. For example, in Greek and Roman literature, it can be found in Hesiod, Ovid, and Lucretius.

[9] The Hebrew word translated as "rested" is *shabath*: "cease, desist." Our word "Sabbath" is derived from it. [10] Here the compiler of Genesis begins another account of the Creation, which emphasizes the origins of things more strongly. * Gen. 2:8–3:24.

And the Lord God planted a garden eastward in Eden;[11] and there he put the man whom he had formed. And out of the ground made the Lord God to grow every tree that is pleasant to the sight, and good for food; the tree of life also in the midst of the garden, and the tree of knowledge of good and evil. . . .

And the Lord God commanded the man, saying, Of every tree of the garden thou mayest freely eat: but of the tree of the knowledge of good and evil, thou shalt not eat of it: for in the day that thou eatest thereof thou shalt surely die.

And the Lord God said, It is not good that the man should be alone; I will make him an help meet for him. And out of the ground the Lord God formed every beast of the field, and every fowl of the air; and brought them unto Adam[12] to see what he would call them: and whatsoever Adam called every living creature, that was the name thereof. And Adam gave names to all cattle, and to the fowl of the air, and to every beast of the field; but for Adam there was not found an help meet for him. And the Lord God caused a deep sleep to fall upon Adam, and he slept: and he took one of his ribs, and closed up the flesh instead thereof; and the rib, which the Lord God had taken from man, made he a woman, and brought her unto the man. And Adam said, This is now bone of my bones, and flesh of my flesh: she shall be called Woman, because she was taken out of Man. Therefore shall a man leave his father and his mother, and shall cleave unto his wife: and they shall be one flesh. And they were both naked, the man and his wife, and were not ashamed.

Now the serpent[13] was more subtil than any beast of the field which the Lord God had made. And he said unto the woman, Yea, hath God said, Ye shall not eat of every tree of the garden? And the woman said unto the serpent, We may eat of the fruit of the trees of the garden: but of the fruit of the tree which is in the midst of the garden, God hath said, Ye shall not eat of it, neither shall ye touch it, lest ye die. And the serpent said unto the woman, Ye shall not surely die: for God doth know that in the day ye eat thereof, then your eyes shall be opened, and ye shall be as gods, knowing good and evil. And when the woman saw that the tree was good for food, and that it was pleasant to the eyes, and a tree to be desired to make one wise, she took of the fruit thereof, and did eat, and gave also unto her husband with her; and he did eat. And the eyes of them both were opened, and they knew that they were naked; and they sewed fig leaves together, and made themselves aprons.[14] And they heard the voice of the Lord God walking in the garden in the cool of the day: and Adam and his wife hid them-

[11] Literally, "delight."　[12] Adam is Hebrew for "man."　[13] In the religions of many Near Eastern cultures, the serpent was considered a god and a possessor of wisdom, especially insidious and sinister wisdom.　[14] Loin coverings or girdles.

selves from the presence of the Lord God amongst the trees of the garden. And the Lord God called unto Adam, and said unto him, Where art thou? And he said, I heard thy voice in the garden, and I was afraid, because I was naked; and I hid myself. And he said, Who told thee that thou wast naked? Hast thou eaten of the tree, whereof I commanded thee that thou shouldest not eat? And the man said, The woman whom thou gavest to be with me, she gave me of the tree, and I did eat. And the Lord God said unto the woman, What is this that thou hast done? And the woman said, The serpent beguiled me, and I did eat. And the Lord God said unto the serpent, Because thou hast done this, thou art cursed above all cattle, and above every beast of the field; upon thy belly shalt thou go, and dust shalt thou eat all the days of thy life: And I will put enmity between thee and the woman, and between thy seed and her seed; it shall bruise thy head, and thou shalt bruise his heel. Unto the woman he said, I will greatly multiply thy sorrow and thy conception; in sorrow thou shalt bring forth children; and thy desire shall be to thy husband, and he shall rule over thee. And unto Adam he said, Because thou has hearkened unto the voice of thy wife, and hast eaten of the tree, of which I commanded thee, saying, Thou shalt not eat of it: cursed is the ground for thy sake; in sorrow shalt thou eat of it all the days of thy life; thorns also and thistles shall it bring forth to thee; and thou shalt eat the herb of the field; in the sweat of thy face shalt thou eat bread, till thou return unto the ground; for out of it wast thou taken: for dust thou art, and unto dust shalt thou return. And Adam called his wife's name Eve; because she was the mother of all living.[15] Unto Adam also and to his wife did the Lord God make coats of skins, and clothed them.

And the Lord God said, Behold, the man is become as one of us,[16] to know good and evil: and now, lest he put forth his hand, and take also of the tree of life, and eat, and live for ever: therefore the Lord God sent him forth from the garden of Eden, to till the ground from whence he was taken. So he drove out the man; and he placed at the east of the garden of Eden Cherubims,[17] and a flaming sword which turned every way, to keep the way of the tree of life.

---

[15] In Hebrew, the name *Eve* resembles the word for "living" or "life."   [16] The tree of life, as the source of human immortality, was a common mythological motif throughout the ancient Near East. One of the famous variants is the "herb of life" sought and lost by the Mesopotamian epic hero, Gilgamesh.   [17] Superhuman, angelic beings.   In the pagan art of Syria-Palestine, they are depicted as winged lions with human heads, guarding the tree of life.

The Flood *

The God of the Hebrews not only exacts retributive justice for man's defection, but He is also merciful. When man's rebellion against God had reached such dimensions that virtually the entire human race was corrupt, God decided on a cataclysmic destruction of humanity as the only appropriate form of justice. Yet, in His grief, He provided for the survival of a just man so that the end of one age could coincide with the beginning of another. The following Hebrew account of this event is similar, in many details, to one that was current in Babylonia considerably earlier. But the Hebrew version is distinguished by its clear emphasis on God's mercy, symbolized by the rainbow. A similar story also occurs in Greco-Roman mythology, as the selection from Ovid demonstrates.

. . . And God saw that the wickedness of man was great in the earth, and that every imagination of the thoughts of his heart was only evil continually. And it repented the Lord that he had made man on the earth, and it grieved him at his heart. And the Lord said, I will destroy man whom I have created from the face of the earth; both man, and beast, and the creeping thing, and the fowls of the air; for it repenteth me that I have made them. But Noah[18] found grace in the eyes of the Lord.

These are the generations of Noah: Noah was a just man and perfect in his generations, and Noah walked with God. And Noah begat three sons, Shem, Ham, and Japheth. The earth also was corrupt before God, and the earth was filled with violence. And God looked upon the earth, and, behold, it was corrupt; for all flesh had corrupted his way upon the earth. And God said unto Noah, the end of all flesh is come before me; for the earth is filled with violence through them; and, behold, I will destroy them with the earth.

Make thee an ark of gopher[19] wood; rooms shalt thou make in the ark, and shalt pitch it within and without with pitch. And this is the fashion which thou shalt make it of: The length of the ark shall be three hundred cubits,[20] the breadth of it fifty cubits, and the height of it thirty cubits. A window shalt thou make to the ark, and in a cubit shalt thou finish it above; and the door of the ark shalt thou set in the side thereof; with lower, second, and third stories shalt thou make it. And, behold, I, even I, do bring a flood of waters upon the earth, to destroy all flesh, wherein is the breath of life, from under heaven; and every thing that is in the earth shall die. But with

---

[18] The name means "rest" and perhaps refers to the respite God granted to mankind through Noah.   [19] A resinous tree.   [20] A cubit is about eighteen inches ("length of a forearm").   * Gen. 6:5–8:22.

thee will I establish my covenant; and thou shalt come into the ark, thou, and thy sons, and thy wife, and thy sons' wives with thee. And of every living thing of all flesh, two of every sort shalt thou bring into the ark, to keep them alive with thee; they shall be male and female. Of fowls after their kind, and of cattle after their kind, of every creeping thing of the earth after his kind, two of every sort shall come unto thee, to keep them alive. And take thou unto thee of all food that is eaten, and thou shalt gather it to thee; and it shall be for food for thee, and for them. Thus did Noah according to all that God commanded him, so did he.

And the Lord said unto Noah, Come thou and all thy house into the ark; for thee have I seen righteous before me in this generation. Of every clean beast thou shalt take to thee by sevens, the male and his female: and of beasts that are not clean by two, the male and his female. Of fowls also of the air by sevens, the male and the female; to keep seed alive upon the face of all the earth. For yet seven days, and I will cause it to rain upon the earth forty days and forty nights; and every living substance that I have made will I destroy from off the face of the earth. And Noah did according unto all that the Lord commanded him. And Noah was six hundred years old when the flood of waters was upon the earth.

And Noah went in, and his sons, and his wife, and his sons' wives with him, into the ark, because of the waters of the flood. Of clean beasts, and of beasts that are not clean, and of fowls, and of every thing that creepeth upon the earth, There went in two and two unto Noah into the ark, the male and the female, as God had commanded Noah. And it came to pass after seven days, that the waters of the flood were upon the earth.

In the six hundredth year of Noah's life, in the second month, the seventeenth day of the month, the same day were all the fountains of the great deep broken up,[21] and the windows of heaven were opened. And the rain was upon the earth forty days and forty nights. In the selfsame day entered Noah, and Shem, and Ham, and Japheth, the sons of Noah, and Noah's wife, and the three wives of his sons with them, into the ark; they, and every beast after his kind, and all the cattle after their kind, and every creeping thing that creepeth upon the earth after his kind, and every fowl after his kind, every bird of every sort. And they went in unto Noah into the ark, two and two of all flesh, wherein is the breath of life. And they that went in, went in male and female of all flesh, as God had commanded him: and the Lord shut him in. And the flood was forty days upon the earth; and the waters increased, and bare up the ark, and it was lift up above the earth.

[21] Rivers and springs were believed to rise from a single, large, freshwater source deep under the surface of the earth. Heaven, or the firmament, was conceived as separating the water in the atmosphere from the water in the "deep" which encircled the earth.

And the waters prevailed, and were increased greatly upon the earth; and the ark went upon the face of the waters. And the waters prevailed exceedingly upon the earth; and all the high hills, that were under the whole heaven, were covered. Fifteen cubits upward did the waters prevail; and the mountains were covered. And all flesh died that moved upon the earth, both of fowl, and of cattle, and of beast, and of every creeping thing that creepeth upon the earth, and every man: all in whose nostrils was the breath of life, of all that was in the dry land, died. And every living substance was destroyed which was upon the face of the ground, both man, and cattle, and the creeping things, and the fowl of the heaven; and they were destroyed from the earth: and Noah only remained alive, and they that were with him in the ark. And the waters prevailed upon the earth an hundred and fifty days.

And God remembered Noah, and every living thing, and all the cattle that was with him in the ark: and God made a wind to pass over the earth, and the waters assuaged; the fountains also of the deep and the windows of heaven were stopped, and the rain from heaven was restrained; and the waters returned from off the earth continually: and after the end of the hundred and fifty days the waters were abated. And the ark rested in the seventh month, on the seventeenth day of the month, upon the mountains of Ararat.[22] And the waters decreased continually until the tenth month: in the tenth month, on the first day of the month, were the tops of the mountains seen.

And it came to pass at the end of forty days, that Noah opened the window of the ark which he had made: and he sent forth a raven, which went forth to and fro, until the waters were dried up from off the earth. Also he sent forth a dove from him, to see if the waters were abated from off the face of the ground; but the dove found no rest for the sole of her foot, and she returned unto him into the ark, for the waters were on the face of the whole earth: then he put forth his hand, and took her, and pulled her in unto him into the ark. And he stayed yet other seven days; and again he sent forth the dove out of the ark; And the dove came in to him in the evening; and, lo, in her mouth was an olive leaf pluckt off: so Noah knew that the waters were abated from off the earth. And he stayed yet other seven days; and sent forth the dove; which returned not again unto him any more.

And it came to pass in the six hundredth and first year, in the first month, the first day of the month, the waters were dried up from off the earth: and Noah removed the covering of the ark, and looked, and, behold, the face of the ground was dry. And in the second month, on the seven and twentieth day of the month, was the earth dried.

And God spake unto Noah, saying, go forth of the ark, thou, and thy

22 Probably Armenia.

wife, and thy sons, and thy sons' wives with thee. Bring forth with thee every living thing that is with thee, of all flesh, both of fowl, and of cattle, and of every creeping thing that creepeth upon the earth; that they may breed abundantly in the earth, and be fruitful, and multiply upon the earth. And Noah went forth, and his sons, and his wife, and his sons' wives with him: every beast, every creeping thing, and every fowl, and whatsoever creepeth upon the earth, after their kinds, went forth out of the ark.

And Noah builded an altar unto the Lord; and took of every clean beast, and of every clean fowl, and offered burnt offerings on the altar. And the Lord smelled a sweet savour;[23] and the Lord said in his heart, I will not again curse the ground any more for man's sake; for the imagination of man's heart is evil from his youth; neither will I again smite any more every thing living, as I have done. While the earth remaineth, seedtime and harvest, and cold and heat, and summer and winter, and day and night shall not cease.[24]

The Book of Job

The Book of Job is a brilliant Hebrew poem of uncertain date and authorship. Although the story is an old one, perhaps dating from before 1000 B.C., its language and literary allusions indicate that it probably reached its present form sometime between the seventh and fourth centuries B.C. Its theme is human suffering, of which it takes a more pessimistic view than the stories of the Fall and the Flood. Not only does Job lose his relatives, his wealth, and his reputation in a series of brutal blows, not only does he contract a repugnant disease, but he also cannot discover the reason for his suffering. His three friends give the traditional answer for his despair, suggesting that his misery must be the result of his own wickedness. Job knows, however, that his agony is undeserved. Nevertheless, without diminishing his faith, he finally accepts the tormenting paradox that the good and just can suffer undeservedly.

CHAPTER I

There was a man in the land of Uz,[25] whose name was Job; and that man was perfect and upright, and one that feared God, and eschewed evil. And there were born unto him seven sons and three daughters. His sub-

---

[23] That is, he accepted the sacrifice. The belief that the gods delighted in sacrificial odors was also widespread in pagan religions. [24] Seasonal changes, on which man is dependent for his livelihood, will not be interrupted or suspended. [25] The exact location of Uz is uncertain; probably east or northwest of Palestine.

stance also was seven thousand sheep, and three thousand camels,[26] and five hundred yoke of oxen, and five hundred she asses, and a very great household; so that this man was the greatest of all the men of the east. And his sons went and feasted in their houses, every one his day; and sent and called for their three sisters to eat and to drink with them. And it was so, when the days of their feasting were gone about, that Job sent and sanctified them, and rose up early in the morning, and offered burnt offerings according to the number of them all: for Job said, It may be that my sons have sinned, and cursed God in their hearts. Thus did Job continually.

Now there was a day when the sons[27] of God came to present themselves before the Lord, and Satan came also among them.[28] And the Lord said unto Satan, Whence comest thou? Then Satan answered the Lord, and said, From going to and fro in the earth, and from walking up and down in it. And the Lord said unto Satan, Hast thou considered my servant Job, that there is none like him in the earth, a perfect and an upright man, one that feareth God, and escheweth evil? Then Satan answered the Lord, and said, Doth Job fear God for nought? Host not thou made an hedge about him, and about his house, and about all that he hath on every side? Thou hast blessed the work of his hands, and his substance is increased in the land. But put forth thine hand now, and touch all that he hath, and he will curse thee to thy face. And the Lord said unto Satan, Behold, all that he hath is in thy power; only upon himself put not forth thine hand. So Satan went forth from the presence of the Lord.

And there was a day when his sons and his daughters were eating and drinking wine in their eldest brother's house: and there came a messenger unto Job, and said, The oxen were plowing, and the asses feeding beside them: and the Sabeans[29] fell upon them, and took them away; yea, they have slain the servants with the edge of the sword; and I only am escaped alone to tell thee. While he was yet speaking, there came also another, and said, The fire of God [30] is fallen from heaven, and hath burned up the sheep, and the servants, and consumed them; and I only am escaped alone to tell thee. While he was yet speaking, there came also another, and said, The Chaldeans[31] made out three bands,[32] and fell upon the camels, and have carried them away, yea, and slain the servants with the edge of the sword; and I only am escaped alone to tell thee. While he was yet speaking, there came also another, and said, Thy sons and thy daughters were eating and drinking wine in their eldest brother's house: and, behold, there came a great wind from the wilderness, and smote the four corners of the house, and it fell

[26] The numbers 7 and 3 had considerable mystic significance in the ancient Near East.   [27] The angels.   [28] "Satan" means "the adversary," one who opposes or accuses man before God.   [29] Originally a people from southern Arabia.   [30] Lightning.   [31] Raiders related to the tribes that inhabited southern Babylonia (between Babylon and the Persian Gulf).   [32] Divided into three gangs.

upon the young men, and they are dead; and I only am escaped alone to tell thee. Then Job arose, and rent his mantle, and shaved his head, and fell down upon the ground, and worshipped, and said, Naked came I out of my mother's womb, and naked shall I return thither: the Lord gave, and the Lord hath taken away; blessed be the name of the Lord. In all this Job sinned not, nor charged God foolishly.

CHAPTER 2

Again there was a day when the sons of God came to present themselves before the Lord, and Satan came also among them to present himself before the Lord. And the Lord said unto Satan, From whence comest thou? And Satan answered the Lord, and said, From going to and fro in the earth, and from walking up and down in it. And the Lord said unto Satan, Hast thou considered my servant Job, that there is none like him in the earth, a perfect and an upright man, one that feareth God, and escheweth evil? And still he holdeth fast his integrity, although thou movedst me against him, to destroy him without cause. And Satan answered the Lord, and said, Skin for skin, yea, all that a man hath will he give for his life. But put forth thine hand now, and touch his bone and his flesh, and he will curse thee to thy face. And the Lord said unto Satan, Behold, he is in thine hand; but save his life.

So went Satan forth from the presence of the Lord, and smote Job with sore boils from the sole of his foot unto his crown. And he took him a potsherd to scrape himself withal;[33] and he sat down among the ashes.

Then said his wife unto him, Dost thou still retain thine integrity? Curse God, and die. But he said unto her, Thou speakest as one of the foolish women speaketh. What? shall we receive good at the hand of God, and shall we not receive evil? In all this did not Job sin with his lips.

Now when Job's three friends heard of all this evil that was come upon him, they came every one from his own place; Eliphaz the Temanite, and Bildad the Shuhite, and Zophar the Naamathite: for they had made an appointment together to come to mourn with him and to comfort him. And when they lifted up their eyes afar off, and knew him not, they lifted up their voice, and wept; and they rent every one his mantle, and sprinkled dust upon their heads toward heaven.[34] So they sat down with him upon the ground seven days and seven nights, and none spake a word unto him: for they saw that his grief was very great.

[33] With it. [34] "rent . . . heaven": signs of mourning.

CHAPTER 3

After this opened Job his mouth, and cursed his day. And Job spake, and
said, Let the day perish wherein I was born, and the night in which it was
said, There is a man child conceived. Let that day be darkness; let not God
regard it from above, neither let the light shine upon it. Let darkness and
the shadow of death stain it; let a cloud dwell upon it; let the blackness of
the day terrify it. As for that night, let darkness seize upon it; let it not be
joined unto the days of the year, let it not come into the number of the
months. Lo, let that night be solitary, let no joyful voice come therein. Let
them curse it that curse the day, who are ready to raise up their mourning.
Let the stars of the twilight thereof be dark; let it look for light, but have
none; neither let it see the dawning of the day: because it shut not up the
doors of my mother's womb, nor hid sorrow from mine eyes.

Why died I not from the womb? Why did I not give up the ghost when
I came out of the belly? Why did the knees prevent me? or why the breasts
that I should suck? For now should I have lain still and been quiet, I should
have slept: then had I been at rest, with kings and counselors of the earth,
which built desolate places for themselves; or with princes that had gold, who
filled their houses with silver: or as an hidden untimely birth I had not been;
as infants which never saw light. There the wicked cease from troubling;
and there the weary be at rest. There the prisoners rest together; they hear
not the voice of the oppressor. The small and great are there; and the servant
is free from his master.

Wherefore is light given to him that is in misery, and life unto the bitter
in soul; which long for death, but it cometh not; and dig for it more than for
hid treasures; which rejoice exceedingly, and are glad, when they can find
the grave? Why is light given to a man whose way is hid, and whom God
hath hedged in? For my sighing cometh before I eat, and my roarings are
poured out like the waters. For the thing which I greatly feared is come
upon me, and that which I was afraid of is come unto me. I was not in
safety, neither had I rest, neither was I quiet; yet trouble came.

CHAPTER 4

Then Eliphaz the Temanite answered and said, if we assay to commune
with thee, wilt thou be grieved? But who can withhold himself from speaking? Behold, thou has instructed many, and thou hast strengthened the weak
hands. Thy words have upholden him that was falling, and thou hast
strengthened the feeble knees. But now it is come upon thee, and thou
faintest; it toucheth thee, and thou art troubled. Is not this[35] thy fear, thy

---

[35] "Your reverence for God."

confidence, thy hope, and the uprightness of thy ways? Remember, I pray thee, who ever perished, being innocent? Or where were the righteous cut off? Even as I have seen, they that plow iniquity, and sow wickedness, reap the same. By the blast of God they perish, and by the breath of his nostrils are they consumed. The roaring of the lion, and the voice of the fierce lion, and the teeth of the young lions, are broken. The old lion perisheth for lack of prey, and the stout lion's whelps are scattered abroad. Now a thing was secretly brought to me, and mine ear received a little thereof. In thoughts from the visions of the night, when deep sleep falleth on men, fear came upon me, and trembling, which made all my bones to shake. Then a spirit passed before my face; the hair of my flesh stood up: it stood still, but I could not discern the form thereof: an image was before mine eyes, there was silence, and I heard a voice, saying, Shall mortal man be more just than God? shall a man be more pure than his maker? Behold, he put no trust in his servants; and his angels he charged with folly: how much less in them that dwell in houses of clay, whose foundation is in the dust, which are crushed before the moth? They are destroyed from morning to evening: they perish for ever without any regarding it. Doth not their excellency which is in them go away? They die, even without wisdom.

CHAPTER 5

Call now, if there be any that will answer thee; and to which of the saints wilt thou turn? For wrath killeth the foolish man, and envy slayeth the silly one. I have seen the foolish taking root: but suddenly I cursed his habitation. His children are far from safety, and they are crushed in the gate, neither is there any to deliver them. Whose harvest the hungry eateth up, and taketh it even out of the thorns, and the robber swalloweth up their substance. Although affliction cometh not forth of the dust, neither doth trouble spring out of the ground; yet man is born unto trouble, as the sparks fly upward.

I would seek unto God, and unto God would I commit my cause: which doeth great things and unsearchable; marvelous things without number: who giveth rain upon the earth, and sendeth waters upon the fields: to set up on high those that be low; that those which mourn may be exalted to safety. He disappointeth the devices of the crafty, so that their hands cannot perform their enterprise. He taketh the wise in their own craftiness: and the counsel of the froward is carried headlong. They meet with darkness in the daytime, and grope in the noonday as in the night. But he saveth the poor from the sword, from their mouth, and from the hand of the mighty. So the poor hath hope, and iniquity stoppeth her mouth.

Behold, happy is the man whom God correcteth: therefore despise not thou the chastening of the Almighty: for he maketh sore, and bindeth up: he woundeth, and his hands make whole. He shall deliver thee in six troubles: yea, in seven there shall no evil touch thee. In famine he shall redeem thee from death: and in war from the power of the sword. Thou shalt be hid from the scourge of the tongue: neither shalt thou be afraid of destruction when it cometh. At destruction and famine thou shalt laugh: neither shalt thou be afraid of the beasts of the earth. For thou shalt be in league with the stones of the field: and the beasts of the field shall be at peace with thee. And thou shalt know that thy tabernacle[36] shall be in peace; and thou shalt visit thy habitation, and shalt not sin. Thou shalt know also that thy seed shall be great, and thine offspring as the grass of the earth. Thou shalt come to thy grave in a full age, like as a shock of corn cometh in in his season. Lo this, we have searched it, so it is; hear it, and know thou it for thy good.

CHAPTER 6

But Job answered and said, Oh that my grief were thoroughly weighed, and my calamity laid in the balances together! For now it would be heavier than the sand of the sea: therefore my words are swallowed up. For the arrows of the Almighty are within me, the poison whereof drinketh up my spirit: the terrors of God do set themselves in array against me. Doth the wild ass bray when he hath grass? or loweth the ox over his fodder? Can that which is unsavoury be eaten without salt? or is there any taste in the white of an egg? The things that my soul refused to touch are as my sorrowful meat.[37] Oh that I might have my request; and that God would grant me the thing that I long for! Even that it would please God to destroy me; that he would let loose his hand, and cut me off! Then should I yet have comfort; yea, I would harden myself in sorrow: let him not spare; for I have not concealed [38] the words of the Holy One.

What is my strength, that I should hope? and what is mine end, that I should prolong my life? Is my strength the strength of stones? or is my flesh of brass? Is not my help in me? and is wisdom driven quite from me? To him that is afflicted pity should be shewed from his friend; but he forsaketh the fear of the Almighty.[39] My brethren have dealt deceitfully as a brook, and as the stream of brooks they pass away; which are blackish by reason of the ice, and wherein the snow is hid: what time they wax warm, they

36 Tent.   37 The Hebrew is somewhat obscure, but it seems to mean: "My appetite refuses to be attracted to my friends' statements, which are like loathsome food to me." 38 More accurately, "denied." 39 Perhaps more clearly: "To him who despairs, kindness is due from his friend, even to him who abandons the fear of the Almighty."

vanish: when it is hot, they are consumed out of their place. The paths of their way are turned aside; they go to nothing, and perish. The troops of Tema[40] looked, the companies[41] of Sheba[42] waited for them. They were confounded because they had hoped;[43] they came thither, and were ashamed. For now ye are nothing; ye see my casting down, and are afraid. Did I say, Bring unto me? or, Give a reward for me of your substance? Or, Deliver me from the enemy's hand? or, Redeem me from the hand of the mighty? Teach me, and I will hold my tongue: and cause me to understand wherein I have erred.

How forcible are right words! but what doth your arguing reprove? Do ye imagine to reprove words, and the speeches of one that is desperate, which are as wind? Yea, ye overwhelm the fatherless, and ye dig a pit for your friend. Now therefore be content, look upon me; for it is evident unto you if I lie. Return, I pray you, let it not be iniquity; yea, return again, my righteousness is in it. Is there iniquity in my tongue? Cannot my taste discern perverse things?

CHAPTER 7

Is there not an appointed time to man upon earth? Are not his days also like the days of an hireling? As a servant earnestly desireth the shadow,[44] and as an hireling looketh for the reward of his work: so am I made to possess months of vanity, and wearisome nights are appointed to me. When I lie down, I say, When shall I arise, and the night be gone? and I am full of tossings to and fro unto the dawning of the day. My flesh is clothed with worms and clods of dust; my skin is broken, and become loathsome. My days are swifter than a weaver's shuttle, and are spent without hope. O remember that my life is wind: mine eye shall no more see good. The eye of him that hath seen me shall see me no more: thine eyes are upon me, and I am not. As the cloud is consumed and vanisheth away: so he that goeth down to the grave shall come up no more. He shall return no more to his house, neither shall his place know him any more. Therefore I will not refrain my mouth; I will speak in the anguish of my spirit; I will complain in the bitterness of my soul.

Am I a sea, or a whale,[45] that thou settest a watch over me? When I say,

---

[40] The town from which Eliphas originally came, a trading center in the Arabian desert. [41] "Troops . . . companies": their trading caravans. [42] A kingdom on the southern tip of the Arabian peninsula. [43] When the caravans reached the springs which they had been counting on for water, they found them dry. [44] Evening, as at the end of a working day. [45] According to some scholars, in the original Hebrew: "Am I the sea, or a sea serpent." This is interpreted as an allusion to the Babylonian myth in which the primordial ocean, personified as a sea serpent named T'iamat, is conquered by the god of light, Marduk.

My bed shall comfort me, my couch shall ease my complaint; then thou scarest me with dreams, and terrifiest me through visions: so that my soul chooseth strangling, and death rather than my life. I loath it; I would not live alway: let me alone; for my days are vanity.

What is man, that thou shouldest magnify him? And that thou shouldest set thine heart upon him? And that thou shouldest visit him every morning, and try him every moment? How long wilt thou not depart from me, nor let me alone till I swallow down my spittle? I have sinned; what shall I do unto thee, O thou preserver of men? Why hast thou set me as a mark[46] against thee, so that I am a burden to myself? And why dost thou not pardon my transgression, and take away mine iniquity? For now shall I sleep in the dust; and thou shalt seek me in the morning, but I shall not be.

CHAPTER 8

Then answered Bildad the Shuhite and said, How long wilt thou speak these things? And how long shall the words of thy mouth be like a strong wind? Doth God pervert judgment? Or doth the Almighty pervert justice? If thy children have sinned against him, and he have cast them away for their transgression; if thou wouldest seek unto God betimes, and make thy supplication to the Almighty; if thou wert pure and upright; surely now he would awake for thee, and make the habitation of thy righteousness prosperous. Though thy beginning was small, yet thy latter end should greatly increase. For enquire, I pray thee, of the former age, and prepare thyself to the search of their fathers: (for we are but of yesterday, and know nothing, because our days upon earth are a shadow:) Shall not they teach thee, and tell thee, and utter words out of their heart? Can the rush grow up without mire? Can the flag grow without water? Whilst it is yet in his greenness, and not cut down, it withereth before any other herb.[47]

So are the paths of all that forget God; and the hypocrite's hope shall perish: whose hope shall be cut off, and whose trust shall be a spider's web. He shall lean upon his house, but it shall not stand: he shall hold it fast, but it shall not endure. He is green before the sun, and his branch shooteth forth in his garden. His roots are wrapped about the heap, and seeth the place of stones. If he destroy him from his place, then it shall deny him, saying I have not seen thee.

Behold, this is the joy of his way, and out of the earth shall others grow. Behold, God will not cast away a perfect man, neither will he help the evil doers: till he fill thy mouth with laughing, and thy lips with rejoicing. They

[46] Target.   [47] These water plants grow rapidly when a river is high, but wither immediately when the water subsides.

that hate thee shall be clothed with shame; and the dwelling place of the wicked shall come to nought.

CHAPTER 9

Then Job answered and said, I know it is so of a truth: but how should man be just with God? If he will contend with him, he cannot answer him one of a thousand. He is wise in heart, and mighty in strength: who hath hardened himself against him, and hath prospered? Which removeth the mountains, and they know not: which overturneth them in his anger. Which shaketh the earth out of her place, and the pillars thereof tremble. Which commandeth the sun, and it riseth not; and sealeth up the stars. Which alone spreadeth out the heavens, and treadeth upon the waves of the sea.[48] Which maketh Arcturus, Orion, and Pleiades, and the chambers of the south. Which doeth great things past finding out; yea, and wonders without number.

Lo, he goeth by me, and I see him not: he passeth on also, but I perceive him not. Behold, he taketh away, who can hinder him? Who will say unto him, What doest thou? If God will not withdraw his anger, the proud helpers do stoop under him.

How much less shall I answer him, and choose out my words to reason with him? Whom, though I were righteous, yet would I not answer, but I would make supplication to my judge. If I had called, and he had answered me; yet would I not believe that he had hearkened unto my voice. For he breaketh me with a tempest, and multiplieth my wounds without cause. He will not suffer me to take my breath, but filleth me with bitterness. If I speak of strength, lo, he is strong: and if of judgment, who shall set me a time to plead? If I justify myself, mine own mouth shall condemn me: if I say, I am perfect, it shall also prove me perverse. Though I were perfect, yet would I not know my soul: I would despise my life. This is one thing, therefore I said it, He destroyeth the perfect and the wicked. If the scourge slay suddenly, he will laugh at the trial of the innocent. The earth is given into the hand of the wicked: he covereth the faces of the judges thereof; if not, where, and who is he?

Now my days are swifter than a post:[49] they flee away, they see no good. They are passed away as the swift ships: as the eagle that hasteth to the prey. If I say, I will forget my complaint, I will leave off my heaviness, and comfort myself: I am afraid of all my sorrows, I know that thou wilt not hold me innocent. If I be wicked, why then labour I in vain? If I wash myself with snow water, and make my hands never so clean: yet shalt thou plunge

---

[48] Or, "trampled the back of the sea dragon."   [49] Messenger, courier.

me in the ditch, and mine own clothes shall abhor me. For he is not a man, as I am, that I should answer him, and we should come together in judgment. Neither is there any daysman[50] betwixt us, that might lay his hand upon us both. Let him take his rod away from me, and let not his fear terrify me: then would I speak, and not fear him: but it is not so with me.

CHAPTER 10

My soul is weary of my life; I will leave my complaint upon myself;[51] I will speak in the bitterness of my soul. I will say unto God, Do not condemn me; shew me wherefore thou contendest with me. Is it good unto thee that thou shouldest oppress, that thou shouldest despise the work of thine hands, and shine upon the counsel of the wicked? Hast thou eyes of flesh? Or seest thou as man seeth? Are thy days as the days of man? Are thy years as man's days, that thou enquirest after mine iniquity, and searchest after my sin? Thou knowest that I am not wicked; and there is none that can deliver out of thine hand. Thine hands have made me and fashioned me together round about; yet thou dost destroy me. Remember, I beseech thee, that thou hast made me as the clay; and wilt thou bring me into dust again? Hast thou not poured me out as milk, and curdled me like cheese? Thou hast clothed me with skin and flesh, and hast fenced me with bones and sinews. Thou hast granted me life and favour, and thy visitation hath preserved my spirit. And these things hast thou hid in thine heart: I know that this is with thee.[52]

If I sin, then thou markest me, and thou wilt not acquit me from mine iniquity. If I be wicked, woe unto me; and if I be righteous, yet will I not lift up my head. I am full of confusion; therefore see thou mine affliction; for it increaseth. Thou huntest me as a fierce lion: and again thou shewest thyself marvelous upon me. Thou renewest thy witnesses against me, and increasest thine indignation upon me; changes and war are against me.

Wherefore then hast thou brought me forth out of the womb? Oh that I had given up the ghost, and no eye had seen me! I should have been as though I had not been; I should have been carried from the womb to the grave. Are not my days few? Cease then, and let me alone, that I may take comfort a little, before I go whence I shall not return, even to the land of darkness and the shadow of death; a land of darkness, as darkness itself; and of the shadow of death, without any order, and where the light is as darkness.

[50] Referee, arbitrator.   [51] "I will give free rein to my complaint in behalf of myself."   [52] "I know that my destruction is your purpose."

CHAPTER 11

Then answer Zophar the Naamathite, and said, Should not the multitude of words be answered? And should a man full of talk be justified? Should thy lies make men hold their peace? And when thou mockest, shall no man make thee ashamed? For thou hast said, My doctrine is pure, and I am clean in thine eyes. But oh that God would speak, and open his lips against thee; and that he would shew thee the secrets of wisdom, that they are double to that which is! Know therefore that God exacteth of thee less than thine iniquity deserveth. Canst thou by searching find out God? Canst thou find out the Almighty unto perfection? It is as high as heaven; what canst thou do? Deeper than hell; what canst thou know? The measure thereof is longer than the earth, and broader than the sea. If he cut off, and shut up, or gather together, then who can hinder him? For he knoweth vain men: he seeth wickedness also; will he not then consider it? For vain man would be wise, though man be born like a wild ass's colt.[53] If thou prepare thine heart, and stretch out thine hands toward him; if iniquity be in thine hand, put it far away, and let not wickedness dwell in thy tabernacles. For then shalt thou lift up thy face without spot; yea, thou shalt be stedfast, and shalt not fear: because thou shalt forget thy misery, and remember it as waters that pass away: and thine age shall be clearer than the noonday; thou shalt shine forth, thou shalt be as the morning. And thou shalt be secure, because there is hope; yea, thou shalt dig about thee, and thou shalt take thy rest in safety. Also thou shalt lie down, and none shall make thee afraid; yea, many shall make suit unto thee. But the eyes of the wicked shall fail, and they shall not escape, and their hope shall be as the giving up of the ghost.

CHAPTER 12

And Job answered and said, No doubt but ye are the people, and wisdom shall die with you. But I have understanding as well as you; I am not inferior to you: yea, who knoweth not such things as these? I am as one mocked of his neighbour, who calleth upon God, and he answereth him: the just upright man is laughed to scorn. He that is ready to slip with his feet is as a lamp despised in the thought of him that is at ease. The tabernacles of robbers prosper, and they that provoke God are secure; into whose hands God bringeth abundantly.

But ask now the beasts, and they shall teach thee; and the fowls of the air, and they shall tell thee: or speak to the earth, and it shall teach thee:

[53] More accurately: "A hollow man who has no understanding will get understanding when a wild donkey's colt is born as a man."

and the fishes of the sea shall declare unto thee. Who knoweth not in all these that the hand of the Lord hath wrought this? In whose hand is the soul of every living thing, and the breath of all mankind. Doth not the ear try words? and the mouth taste his meat? With the ancient is wisdom; and in length of days understanding. With him is wisdom and strength, he hath counsel and understanding. Behold, he breaketh down, and it cannot be built again: he shutteth up a man, and there can be no opening. Behold, he withholdeth the waters, and they dry up: also he sendeth them out, and they overturn the earth. With him is strength and wisdom: the deceived and the deceiver are his. He leadeth counselors away spoiled, and maketh the judges fools. He looseth the bond of kings, and girdeth their loins with a girdle. He leadeth princes away spoiled, and overthroweth the mighty. He removeth away the speech of the trusty, and taketh away the understanding of the aged. He poureth contempt upon princes, and weakeneth the strength of the mighty. He discovereth deep things out of darkness, and bringeth out to light the shadow of death. He increaseth the nations, and destroyeth them: he enlargeth the nations, and straineth[54] them again. He taketh away the heart of the chief of the people of the earth, and causeth them to wander in a wilderness where there is no way. They grope in the dark without light, and he maketh them to stagger like a drunken man.

CHAPTER 13

Lo, mine eye hath seen all this, mine ear hath heard and understood it. What ye know, the same do I know also: I am not inferior unto you. Surely I would speak to the Almighty, and I desire to reason with God. But ye are forgers of lies, ye are all physicians of no value. O that ye would altogether hold your peace! and it should be your wisdom.

Hear now my reasoning, and hearken to the pleadings of my lips. Will ye speak wickedly for God? and talk deceitfully for him? Will ye accept his person? Will ye contend for God? Is it good that he should search you out? or as one man mocketh another, do ye so mock him? He will surely reprove you, if ye do secretly accept persons.[55] Shall not his excellency make you afraid? and his dread fall upon you? Your remembrances[56] are like unto ashes, your bodies to bodies of clay. Hold your peace, let me alone, that I may speak, and let come on me what will. Wherefore do I take my flesh in my teeth, and put my life in mine hand? Though he slay me, yet will I trust in him: but I will maintain mine own ways before him. He also shall be my salvation: for an hypocrite shall not come before him.

Hear diligently my speech, and my declaration with your ears. Behold

54 Narrows; makes smaller.   55 Respect or honor people for one's personal gain.
56 Utterances worth remembering.

now, I have ordered my cause; I know that I shall be justified. Who is he that will plead with me? [57] for now, if I hold my tongue, I shall give up the ghost. Only do not two things unto me: then will I not hide myself from thee.[58] Withdraw thine hand far from me: and let not thy dread make me afraid. Then call thou, and I will answer: or let me speak, and answer thou me. How many are mine iniquities and sins? make me to know my transgression and my sin. Wherefore hidest thou thy face, and holdest me for thine enemy? Wilt thou break a leaf driven to and fro? and wilt thou pursue the dry stubble? For thou writest bitter things against me, and makest me to possess the iniquities of my youth. Thou puttest my feet also in the stocks, and lookest narrowly unto all my paths; thou settest a print upon the heels of my feet. And he,[59] as a rotten thing, consumeth, as a garment that is moth eaten.

CHAPTER 14

Man that is born of a woman is of few days, and full of trouble. He cometh forth like a flower, and is cut down: he fleeth also as a shadow, and continueth not. And dost thou open thine eyes upon such an one, and bringest me into judgment with thee? Who can bring a clean thing out of an unclean? not one. Seeing his days are determined, the number of his months are with thee, thou hast appointed his bounds that he cannot pass; turn from him, that he may rest, till he shall accomplish, as an hireling, his day. For there is hope of a tree, if it be cut down, that it will sprout again, and that the tender branch thereof will not cease. Though the root thereof wax old in the earth, and the stock thereof die in the ground; yet through the scent of water it will bud, and bring forth boughs like a plant. But m' dieth, and wasteth away: yea, man giveth up the ghost, and where is As the waters fail from the sea, and the flood decayeth and drieth u' man lieth down, and riseth not: till the heavens be no more, they sh' awake, nor be raised out of their sleep.

O that thou wouldest hide me in the grave, that thou woul' me secret, until thy wrath be past, that thou wouldest appoin' time, and remember me! If a man die, shall he live again? [60] All my appointed time will I wait, till my change come. Thou sh' will answer thee: thou wilt have a desire to the work of th' now thou numberest my steps: dost thou not watch ov' transgression is sealed up in a bag, and thou sewest up m surely the mountain falling cometh to nought, and the r of his place. The waters wear the stones: thou wasb

[57] Accuse me.   [58] This is addressed directly to God.   [59]
tioning reference to a possible life beyond the grave.

which grow out of the dust of the earth; and thou destroyest the hope of man. Thou prevailest for ever against him, and he passeth: thou changest his countenance, and sendest him away. His sons come to honour, and he knoweth it not; and they are brought low, but he perceiveth it not of them. But his flesh upon him shall have pain, and his soul within him shall mourn.

In Chapters 15–28, Job's three friends condemn him for his excessive pride and rehearse again the traditional pieties concerning the punishment of the wicked by a just God. Job replies that his friends lack both pity and perception, pointing out that the wicked prosper even though they deny God. Moreover, Job continues, God's judgment seems arbitrary and falls heavily on the virtuous. Yet, despite God's indifference, or cruelty, Job asserts his continuing faith.

CHAPTER 29

Moreover Job continued his parable, and said, Oh that I were as in months past, as in the days when God preserved me; when his candle shined upon my head, and when by his light I walked through darkness; as I was in the days of my youth, when the secret of God was upon my tabernacle; when the Almighty was yet with me, when my children were about me; when I washed my steps with butter, and the rock poured me out rivers of oil; when I went out to the gate[61] through the city, when I prepared my seat in the street! The young men saw me, and hid themselves: and the aged arose, and stood up. The princes refrained talking, and laid their hand on their mouth. The nobles held their peace, and their tongue cleaved to the roof of their mouth. When the ear heard me, then it blessed me; and when the eye saw me, it gave witness to me: because I delivered the poor that cried, and the fatherless, and him that had none to help him. The blessing of him that was ready to perish came upon me: and I caused the widow's heart to sing for joy. I put on righteousness, and it clothed me: my judgment was as a robe and a diadem. I was eyes to the blind, and feet was I to the lame. I was a father to the poor: and the cause which I knew not I searched out. And I brake the jaws of the wicked, and plucked the spoil out of his teeth. Then I said, I shall die in my nest, and I shall multiply my days as the sand. My root was spread out by the waters, and the dew lay all night upon my branch. My glory was fresh in me, and my bow was renewed in my and. Unto me men gave ear, and waited, and kept silence at my counsel. fter my words they spake not again; and my speech dropped upon them. d they waited for me as for the rain; and they opened their mouth wide

he popular meeting square and the court were just inside the gate of the

as for the latter rain. If I laughed on them, they believed it not; and the light of my countenance they cast not down. I chose out their way, and sat chief, and dwelt as a king in the army, as one that comforteth the mourners.

CHAPTER 30

But now they that are younger than I have me in derision, whose fathers I would have disdained to have set with the dogs of my flock. Yea, whereto might the strength of their hands profit me, in whom old age was perished? For want and famine they were solitary; fleeing into the wilderness in former time desolate and waste. Who cut up mallows by the bushes, and juniper roots for their meat. They were driven forth from among men, (they cried after them as after a thief;) to dwell in the cliffs of the valleys, in caves of the earth, and in the rocks. Among the bushes they brayed; under the nettles they were gathered together. They were children of fools, yea, children of base men: they were viler than the earth. And now am I their song, yea, I am their byword.

They abhor me, they flee far from me, and spare not to spit in my face. Because he hath loosed my cord, and afflicted me, they have also let loose the bridle before me. Upon my right hand rise the youth; they push away my feet, and they raise up against me the ways of their destruction. They mar my path, they set forward my calamity, they have no helper. They came upon me as a wide breaking in of waters: in the desolation they rolled themselves upon me. Terrors are turned upon me: they pursue my soul as the wind: and my welfare passeth away as a cloud. And now my soul is poured out upon me;[62] the days of affliction have taken hold upon me. My bones are pierced in me in the night season: and my sinews take no rest. By the great force of my disease is my garment changed: it bindeth me about as the collar of my coat. He hath cast me into the mire, and I am become like dust and ashes. I cry unto thee, and thou dost not hear me: I stand up, and thou regardest me not. Thou art become cruel to me: with thy strong hand thou opposest thyself against me. Thou liftest me up to the wind; thou causest me to ride upon it, and dissolvest my substance. For I know that thou wilt bring me to death, and to the house appointed for all living.

Howbeit he will not stretch out his hand to the grave, though they cry in his destruction. Did not I weep for him that was in trouble? Was not my soul grieved for the poor? When I looked for good, then evil came unto me: and when I waited for light, there came darkness. My bowels boiled, and rested not: the days of affliction prevented me.[63] I went mourning without the sun: I stood up, and I cried in the congregation. I am a brother to

62 Within me.   63 Met me; came upon me.

dragons, and a companion to owls. My skin is black upon me, and my bones are burned with heat. My harp also is turned to mourning, and my organ[64] into the voice of them that weep.

CHAPTER 31

I made a covenant with mine eyes; why then should I think upon a maid? For what portion of God is there from above? And what inheritance of the Almighty from on high? Is not destruction to the wicked? and a strange punishment to the workers of iniquity? Doth not he see my ways, and count all my steps? If I have walked with vanity, or if my foot hath hasted to deceit; let me be weighed in an even balance, that God may know mine integrity. If my step hath turned out of the way, and mine heart walked after mine eyes, and if any blot hath cleaved to mine hands; then let me sow, and let another eat; yea, let my offspring be rooted out. If mine heart have been deceived by a woman, or if I have laid wait at my neighbour's door; then let my wife grind unto another, and let others bow down upon her. For this is an heinous crime; yea, it is an iniquity to be punished by the judges. For it is a fire that consumeth to destruction, and would root out all mine increase. If I did despise the cause of my manservant or of my maidservant, when they contended with me; what then shall I do when God riseth up? And when he visiteth, what shall I answer him? Did not he that made me in the womb make him? And did not one fashion us in the womb? If I have withheld the poor from their desire, or have caused the eyes of the widow to fail; or have eaten my morsel myself alone, and the fatherless hath not eaten thereof; (for from my youth he was brought up with me, as with a father, and I have guided her from my mother's womb;) if I have seen any perish for want of clothing, or any poor without covering; if his loins have not blessed me, and if he were not warmed with the fleece of my sheep; if I have lifted up my hand against the fatherless, when I saw my help in the gate:[65] then let mine arm fall from my shoulder blade, and mine arm be broken from the bone.

For destruction from God was a terror to me, and by reason of his highness I could not endure. If I have made gold my hope, or have said to the fine gold, Thou art my confidence; if I rejoiced because my wealth was great, and because mine hand had gotten much; if I beheld the sun when it shined, or the moon walking in brightness; and my heart hath been secretly enticed, or my mouth hath kissed my hand;[66] this also were an iniquity to be punished by the judge: for I should have denied the God that is above.

[64] "Lyre" and (musical) "pipe" are more accurate than "harp" and "organ."
[65] "When I exercised influence in the court."   [66] So as to throw a kiss to the sun or moon, in an act of worship, as though they were divinities.

If I rejoiced at the destruction of him that hated me, or lifted up myself when evil found him: neither have I suffered my mouth to sin by wishing a curse to his soul. If the men of my tabernacle said not, Oh that we had of his flesh! we cannot be satisfied.[67] The stranger did not lodge in the street: but I opened my doors to the traveler. If I covered my transgressions as Adam, by hiding mine iniquity in my bosom: did I fear a great multitude, or did the contempt of families terrify me, that I kept silence, and went not out of the door?

Oh that one would hear me! Behold, my desire is, that the Almighty would answer me, and that mine adversary had written a book. Surely I would take it upon my shoulder, and bind it as a crown to me. I would declare unto him the number of my steps; as a prince would I go near unto him. If my land cry against me, or that the furrows likewise thereof complain: if I have eaten the fruits thereof without money, or have caused the owners thereof to lose their life: let thistles grow instead of wheat, and cockle instead of barley. The words of Job are ended.

Chapters 32–37 introduce a new figure into the debate. The young man, Elihu the Buzite, enters the discussion and chastizes Job and his friends. He then attempts to justify the ways of God to Job. Job does not reply.

CHAPTER 38

Then the LORD answered [68] Job out of the whirlwind, and said, Who is this that darkeneth counsel by words without knowledge? Gird up now thy loins like a man; for I will demand of thee, and answer thou me. Where wast thou when I laid the foundations of the earth? Declare, if thou hast understanding. Who hath laid the measures thereof, if thou knowest? Or who hath stretched the line upon it? Whereupon are the foundations thereof fastened? Or who laid the corner stone thereof; when the morning stars sang together, and all the sons of God shouted for joy? Or who shut up the sea with doors, when it brake forth, as if it had issued out of the womb? When I made the cloud the garment thereof, and thick darkness a swaddling-band for it, and brake up for it my decreed place, and set bars and doors,[69] and said Hitherto shalt thou come, but no further: and here shall thy proud waves be stayed? Hast thou commanded the morning since thy days; and caused the dayspring[70] to know his place; that it might take hold of the ends

---

[67] The statement of the men of his tent ("tabernacle") more accurately reads, "Who is there that has not been filled with his meat?" That is, with meat from his flocks. [68] The long-awaited appearance of God now occurs in response to the repeated requests by Job. [69] Coastlines. [70] Dawn.

of the earth, that the wicked might be shaken out of it? It is turned as clay to the seal; and they stand as a garment.[71] And from the wicked their light is withholden, and the high arm shall be broken. Hast thou entered into the springs of the sea? Or hast thou walked in the search of the depth? Have the gates of death been opened unto thee? Or hast thou seen the doors of the shadow of death? Hast thou perceived the breadth of the earth? Declare if thou knowest it all. Where is the way where light dwelleth? And as for darkness, where is the place thereof. That thou shouldest take it to the bound thereof, and that thou shouldest know the paths to the house thereof? Knowest thou it, because thou wast then born? Or because the number of thy days is great? Hast thou entered into the treasures of the snow? Or hast thou seen the treasures of the hail, which I have reserved against the time of trouble, against the day of battle and war? By what way is the light parted, which scattereth the east wind upon the earth? Who hath divided a watercourse for the overflowing of waters, or a way for the lightning of thunder; to cause it to rain on the earth, where no man is; on the wilderness, wherein there is no man; to satisfy the desolate and waste ground; and to cause the bud of the tender herb to spring forth? Hath the rain a father? Or who hath begotten the drops of dew? Out of whose womb came the ice? and the hoary frost of heaven, who hath gendered it? The waters are hid as with a stone, and the face of the deep is frozen. Canst thou bind the sweet influences of Pleiades, or loose the bands of Orion? Canst thou bring forth Mazzaroth[72] in his season? Or canst thou guide Arcturus with his sons? Knowest thou the ordinances of heaven? Canst thou set the dominion thereof in the earth? Canst thou lift up thy voice to the clouds, that abundance of waters may cover thee? Canst thou send lightnings, that they may go, and say unto thee, Here we are? Who hath put wisdom in the inward parts? Or who hath given understanding to the heart? Who can number the clouds in wisdom? Or who can stay the bottles of heaven, when the dust groweth into hardness, and the clods cleave fast together? Wilt thou hunt the prey for the lion? Or fill the appetite of the young lions, when they couch in their dens, and abide in the covert to lie in wait? Who provideth for the raven his food? when his young ones cry unto God, they wander for lack of meat.

CHAPTER 39

Knowest thou the time when the wild goats of the rock bring forth? Or canst thou mark when the hinds do calve? Canst thou number the months that they fulfil? Or knowest thou the time when they bring forth? They bow themselves, they bring forth their young ones, they cast out their sor-

[71] "All things created by God are like the clothing of the universe."   [72] Obscure meaning; perhaps it designates a sign, or all the signs, of the zodiac.

rows. Their young ones are in good liking, they grow up with corn; they go forth, and return not unto them. Who hath sent out the wild ass free? or who hath loosed the bands of the wild ass? Whose house I have made the wilderness, and the barren land his dwellings. He scorneth the multitude of the city, neither regardeth he the crying of the driver. The range of the mountains is his pasture, and he searcheth after every green thing. Will the unicorn[73] be willing to serve thee, or abide by thy crib? Canst thou bind the unicorn with his band in the furrow? Or will he harrow the valleys after thee? Wilt thou trust him, because his strength is great? Or wilt thou leave thy labour to him? Wilt thou believe him, that he will bring home thy seed, and gather it into thy barn? Gavest thou the goodly wings unto the peacocks? or wings and feathers unto the ostrich? Which leaveth her eggs in the earth, and warmeth them in dust, and forgetteth that the foot may crush them, or that the wild beast may break them. She is hardened against her young ones, as though they were not her's: her labour is in vain without fear; because God hath deprived her of wisdom, neither hath he imparted to her understanding. What time she lifteth up herself on high, she scorneth the horse and his rider. Hast thou given the horse strength? Hast thou clothed his neck with thunder? [74] Canst thou make him afraid as a grasshopper? The glory of his nostrils is terrible. He paweth in the valley, and rejoiceth in his strength: he goeth on to meet the armed men. He mocketh at fear, and is not affrighted; neither turneth he back from the sword. The quiver rattleth against him, the glittering spear and the shield. He swalloweth the ground with fierceness and rage: neither believeth he that it is the sound of the trumpet. He saith among the trumpets, Ha, ha; and he smelleth the battle afar off, the thunder of the captains, and the shouting. Doth the hawk fly by thy wisdom, and stretch her wings toward the south? Doth the eagle mount up at thy command, and make her nest on high? She dwelleth and abideth on the rock, upon the crag of the rock, and the strong place. From thence she seeketh the prey, and her eyes behold afar off. Her young ones also suck up blood: and where the slain are, there is she.

CHAPTER 40

Moreover the Lord answered Job, and said, shall he that contendeth with the Almighty instruct him? He that reproveth God, let him answer it.

Then Job answered the Lord, and said, Behold, I am vile; what shall I answer thee? I will lay mine hand upon my mouth. Once have I spoken; but I will not answer: yea, twice; but I will proceed no further.

Then answered the Lord unto Job out of the whirlwind, and said, Gird up thy loins now like a man: I will demand of thee, and declare thou unto

[73] In Hebrew, simply, "wild ox." [74] Hebrew obscure.

me. Wilt thou also disannul my judgment? Wilt thou condemn me, that thou mayest be righteous? Hast thou an arm like God? Or canst thou thunder with a voice like him? Deck thyself now with majesty and excellency; and array thyself with glory and beauty. Cast abroad the rage of thy wrath: and behold every one that is proud, and abase him. Look on every one that is proud, and bring him low; and tread down the wicked in their place. Hide them in the dust together; and bind their faces in secret. Then will I also confess unto thee that thine own right hand can save thee. Behold now behemoth,[75] which I made with thee; he eateth grass as an ox. Lo now, his strength is in his loins, and his force is in the navel of his belly. He moveth his tail like a cedar: the sinews of his stones[76] are wrapped together. His bones are as strong pieces of brass; his bones are like bars of iron. He is the chief of the ways of God: he that made him can make his sword to approach unto him. Surely the mountains bring him forth food, where all the beasts of the field play. He lieth under the shady trees, in the covert of the reed, and fens. The shady trees cover him with their shadow; the willows of the brook compass him about. Behold, he drinketh up a river, and hasteth not: he trusteth that he can draw up Jordan into his mouth. He taketh it with his eyes: his nose pierceth through snares.

CHAPTER 41

Canst thou draw out leviathan[77] with an hook? or his tongue with a cord which thou lettest down? Canst thou put an hook into his nose? or bore his jaw through with a thorn? Will he make many supplications unto thee? Will he speak soft words unto thee? Will he make a covenant with thee? Wilt thou take him for a servant for ever? Wilt thou play with him as with a bird? Or wilt thou bind him for thy maidens? Shall the companions make a banquet of him? Shall they part him among the merchants? Canst thou fill his skin with barbed irons? or his head with fish spears? Lay thine hand upon him, remember the battle, do no more.[78] Behold, the hope of him is in vain: shall not one be cast down even at the sight of him? None is so fierce that dare stir him up: who then is able to stand before me? Who hath prevented me,[79] that I should repay him? Whatsoever is under the whole heaven is mine. I will not conceal his parts, nor his power, nor his comely

[75] Behemoth is unknown outside the Bible. It is presumably a mythical monster in pagan folklore, often identified with the hippopotamus. [76] More accurately, "thighs." [77] A mythical monster, conceived of as a dragon with the body of a snake and with seven heads. It sometimes embodies the chaos that was destroyed at the creation when God formed an ordered world. Here it is portrayed particularly as a monster that man cannot control. [78] "Lay your hand on him, and you will never do it again." [79] "Given me something first."

proportion. Who can discover the face of his garment? [80] Or who can come
to him with his double bridle? Who can open the doors of his face? his
teeth are terrible round about. His scales are his pride, shut up together as
with a close seal. One is so near to another, that no air can come between
them. They are joined one to another, they stick together, that they cannot
be sundered. By his neesings[81] a light doth shine, and his eyes are like the
eyelids of the morning. Out of his mouth go burning lamps, and sparks of
fire leap out. Out of his nostrils goeth smoke, as out of a seething pot or
caldron. His breath kindleth coals, and a flame goeth out of his mouth. In
his neck remaineth strength, and sorrow is turned into joy before him. The
flakes of his flesh are joined together: they are firm in themselves; they cannot be moved. His heart is as firm as a stone; yea, as hard as a piece of the
nether millstone. When he raiseth up himself, the mighty are afraid: by
reason of breakings they purify themselves.[82] The sword of him that layeth
at him cannot hold: the spear, the dart, nor the habergeon.[83] He esteemeth
iron as straw, and brass as rotten wood. The arrow cannot make him flee:
slingstones are turned with him into stubble. Darts are counted as stubble:
he laugheth at the shaking of a spear. Sharp stones are under him: he
spreadeth sharp pointed things upon the mire. He maketh the deep to boil
like a pot: he maketh the sea like a pot of ointment. He maketh a path to
shine after him; one would think the deep to be hoary.[84] Upon earth there is
not his like, who is made without fear. He beholdeth all high things: he is a
king over all the children of pride.

CHAPTER 42

Then Job answered the Lord, and said, I know that thou canst do every
thing, and that no thought can be witholden from thee. Who is he that
hideth counsel without knowledge? Therefore have I uttered that I understood not; things too wonderful for me, which I knew not. Hear, I beseech
thee, and I will speak: I will demand of thee, and declare thou unto me.
I have heard of thee by the hearing of the ear: but now mine eye seeth thee.
Wherefore I abhor myself, and repent in dust and ashes.
And it was so, that after the Lord had spoken these words unto Job, the
Lord said to Eliphaz the Temanite. My wrath is kindled against thee, and
against thy two friends: for ye have not spoken of me the thing that is right,
as my servant Job hath. Therefore take unto you now seven bullocks and
seven rams, and go to my servant Job, and offer up for yourselves a burnt

---

[80] "Who can strip off his outer hide (his scales)?"   [81] Breath, as the fiery breath
of a dragon.   [82] Probably, "at the crashing noise they are beside themselves with
fear and consternation."   [83] A short coat of mail. The Hebrew is obscure.
[84] White with the frothy wake that he churns up in the sea.

offering; and my servant Job shall pray for you: for him will I accept: lest I deal with you after your folly, in that ye have not spoken of me the thing which is right, like my servant Job.

So Eliphaz the Temanite and Bildad the Shuhite and Zophar the Naamathite went, and did according as the Lord commanded them: the Lord also accepted Job. And the Lord turned the captivity of Job, when he prayed for his friends: also the Lord gave Job twice as much as he had before.

Then came there unto him all his brethren, and all his sisters, and all they that had been of his acquaintance before, and did eat bread with him in his house: and they bemoaned him, and comforted him over all the evil that the Lord had brought upon him: every man also gave him a piece of money, and every one an earring of gold. So the Lord blessed the latter end of Job more than his beginning: for he had fourteen thousand sheep, and six thousand camels, and a thousand yoke of oxen, and a thousand she asses. He had also seven sons and three daughters. And he called the name of the first, Jemima; and the name of the second, Kezia; and the name of the third, Kerenhappuch. And in all the land were no women found so fair as the daughters of Job: and their father gave them inheritance among their brethren. After this lived Job an hundred and forty years, and saw his sons, and his sons' sons, even four generations. So Job died, being old and full of days.

Psalms

Psalms are lyrical songs that were usually accompanied by a musical instrument, particularly the harp. About half of the one hundred and fifty songs collected in the book known as *The Psalms of David* are explicitly, if not always correctly, ascribed to King David, a brilliant political and religious figure of the tenth century B.C. But the Book of Psalms probably did not reach its present form until the third century B.C. The distinguishing feature of the Psalms is their devotional character. Whether their subject is historical, prophetic, practical, or moral, they all take the form of a lyrical eulogy or a prayer to God. Personal history is often included, but usually as an illustration of a larger aspect of Hebrew beliefs.

PSALM 8

To the chief Musician upon Gittith,
A Psalm of David.

O Lord our Lord,[85] how excellent is thy name[86] in all the earth! who hast set thy glory above the heavens.

2. Out of the mouth of babes and sucklings hast thou ordained strength because of thine enemies, that thou mightest still the enemy and the avenger.

3. When I consider thy heavens, the work of thy fingers, the moon and the stars, which thou hast ordained;

4. What is man, that thou art mindful of him? and the son of man, that thou visitest him? [87]

5. For thou hast made him a little lower than the angels,[88] and hast crowned him with glory and honour.

6. Thou madest him to have dominion over the works of thy hands; thou hast put all things under his feet:

7. All sheep and oxen, yea, and the beasts of the field;

8. The fowl of the air, and the fish of the sea, and whatsoever passeth through the paths of the seas.

9. O Lord our Lord, how excellent is thy name in all the earth!

PSALM 22

To the chief Musician upon Aijeleth Shahar,
A Psalm of David.

My God, my God, why hast thou forsaken me? why art thou so far from helping me, and from the words of my roaring?

2. O my God, I cry in the daytime, but thou hearest not; and in the night season, and am not silent.

3. But thou art holy, O thou that inhabitest the praises of Israel.

4. Our fathers trusted in thee: they trusted, and thou didst deliver them.

5. They cried unto thee, and were delivered: they trusted in thee, and were not confounded.

6. But I am a worm,[89] and no man; a reproach of men, and despised of the people.

---

[85] The God of the covenant revealed to Israel.   [86] As symbol of his entire being.
[87] The theme is not amazement at God's glory in nature or as Creator, but at his choice of deficient man as his representative on earth.   [88] The original says *Elohim,* which can mean "gods" or "angels" but here probably, as usual, refers to God himself, who made man in his own image.   [89] "I am ridiculed by others because God has not delivered me."

7. All they that see me laugh me to scorn: they shoot out the lip, they shake the head, saying,

8. He trusted on the Lord that he would deliver him: let him deliver him, seeing he delighted in him.

9. But thou art he that took me out of the womb: thou didst make me hope when I was upon my mother's breasts.

10. I was cast upon thee from the womb: thou art my God from my mother's belly.

11. Be not far from me; for trouble is near; for there is none to help.

12. Many bulls have compassed me: strong bulls of Bashan[90] have beset me round.

13. They gaped upon me with their mouths, as a ravening and a roaring lion.

14. I am poured out like water, and all my bones are out of joint:[91] my heart is like wax; it is melted in the midst of my bowels.

15. My strength is dried up like a potsherd; and my tongue cleaveth to my jaws; and thou hast brought me into the dust of death.

16. For dogs have compassed me: the assembly of the wicked have inclosed me: they pierced my hands and my feet.

17. I may tell all my bones: they look and stare upon me.

18. They part my garments among them, and cast lots upon my vesture.[92]

19. But be not thou far from me, O Lord: O my strength, haste thee to help me.

20. Deliver my soul from the sword; my darling[93] from the power of the dog.

21. Save me from the lion's mouth: for thou hast heard me from the horns of the unicorns.[94]

22. I will declare thy name unto my brethren: in the midst of the congregation will I praise thee.

23. Ye that fear the Lord, praise him; all ye the seed of Jacob, glorify him; and fear him, all ye the seed of Israel.

24. For he hath not despised nor abhorred the affliction of the afflicted; neither hath he hid his face from him; but when he cried unto him, he heard.

25. My praise shall be of thee in the great congregation: I will pay my vows[95] before them that fear him.

26. The meek[96] shall eat and be satisfied: they shall praise the Lord that seek him: your heart shall live for ever.

---

[90] Wild bulls known for ferocity and strength.   [91] "I am in disruption and agony."
[92] It was customary for executioners to receive the clothes of the condemned.
[93] Literally, "my only one." That is, "my life."   [94] In the original, "wild oxen."
[95] Peace offerings.   [96] Afflicted, poor.

27. All the ends of the world shall remember and turn unto the Lord: and all the kindreds of the nations shall worship before thee.

28. For the kingdom is the Lord's: and he is the governor among the nations.

29. All they that be fat upon earth shall eat and worship: all they that go down to the dust shall bow before him: and none can keep alive his own soul.

30. A seed shall serve him; it shall be accounted to the Lord for a generation.

31. They shall come, and shall declare his righteousness unto a people that shall be born, that he hath done this.

PSALM 23

A Psalm of David.

The Lord is my shepherd; I shall not want.

2. He maketh me to lie down in green pastures: he leadeth me beside the still waters.

3. He restoreth my soul: he leadeth me in the paths of righteousness for his name's sake.

4. Yea, though I walk through the valley of the shadow of death,[97] I will fear no evil: for thou art with me; thy rod [98] and thy staff [99] they comfort me.

5. Thou preparest a table before me in the presence of mine enemies: thou anointest my head with oil; my cup runneth over.

6. Surely goodness and mercy shall follow me all the days of my life: and I will dwell in the house of the Lord for ever.

PSALM 137

By the rivers of Babylon,[100] there we sat down, yea, we wept, when we remembered Zion.

2. We hanged our harps upon the willows in the midst thereof.

3. For there they that carried us away captive required of us a song; and they that wasted us required of us mirth, saying, Sing us one of the songs of Zion.

[97] More accurately, "deep darkness." [98] Club. [99] Shepherd's crook. [100] In 587–86 B.C. the Babylonians sacked Jerusalem and took the Jews into captivity to Babylon. There they remained until the Persian king Cyrus conquered Babylon in 539 B.C. and allowed the Jews to return to Jerusalem. The Psalmist, shortly after his return, recalls the sorrow of the exiles.

4. How shall we sing the Lord's song in a strange land?

5. If I forget thee, O Jerusalem, let my right hand forget her cunning.

6. If I do not remember thee, let my tongue cleave to the roof of my mouth; if I prefer not Jerusalem above my chief joy.

7. Remember, O Lord, the children of Edom[101] in the day of Jerusalem; who said, Rase it, rase it, even to the foundation thereof.

8. O daughter of Babylon, who art to be destroyed; happy shall he be, that rewardeth thee as thou hast served us.

9. Happy shall he be, that taketh and dasheth thy little ones against the stones.

The Song of Songs

In antiquity this lyric poem about the mystery of love was known as "The Song of Solomon" from its opening words. Although it is possible that King Solomon—whose court in Jerusalem was a center of cultural activity in the tenth century B.C.—composed parts of the poem in early life, its present form must, on linguistic and stylistic grounds, be assigned to the fourth century B.C. The poem, which nowhere mentions the name of God or offers explicit religious instruction, seems to deal allegorically with love by introducing a variety of seemingly disparate characters to represent the lover and the beloved in a series of narrative sequences. Some critics have interpreted the poem to be about the love between God and Israel.

CHAPTER I

The song of songs, which is Solomon's.

2. Let him kiss me with the kisses of his mouth: for thy love is better than wine.

3. Because of the savour of thy good ointments thy name is as ointment poured forth, therefore do the virgins love thee.

4. Draw me, we will run after thee: the king hath brought me into his chambers: we will be glad and rejoice in thee, we will remember thy love more than wine: the upright love thee.

5. I am black, but comely, O ye daughters of Jerusalem, as the tents of Kedar,[102] as the curtains of Solomon.

6. Look not upon me, because I am black, because the sun hath looked

---

[101] The Edomites helped the Babylonians to capture Jerusalem. Edom is an area southeast of the Dead Sea.   [102] Semidesert area east of the Jordan river.

upon me: my mother's children were angry with me; they made me the keeper of the vineyards; but mine own vineyard have I not kept.

7. Tell me, O thou whom my soul loveth, where thou feedest, where thou makest thy flock to rest at noon: for why should I be as one that turneth aside by the flocks of thy companions?

8. If thou know not, O thou fairest among women, go thy way forth by the footsteps of the flock, and feed thy kids beside the shepherd's tents.

9. I have compared thee, O my love, to a company of horses in Pharaoh's chariots.

10. Thy cheeks are comely with rows of jewels, thy neck with chains of gold.

11. We will make thee borders of gold with studs of silver.

12. While the king sitteth at his table, my spikenard [103] sendeth forth the smell thereof.

13. A bundle of myrrh is my well-beloved unto me; he shall lie all night betwixt my breasts.

14. My beloved is unto me as a cluster of camphire in the vineyards of Engedi.[104]

15. Behold, thou art fair, my love; behold, thou art fair; thou hast doves' eyes.

16. Behold, thou art fair, my beloved, yea, pleasant: also our bed is green.

17. The beams of our house are cedar, and our rafters of fir.

CHAPTER 2

I am the rose of Sharon,[105] and the lily of the valleys.

2. As the lily among thorns, so is my love among the daughters.

3. As the apple tree among the trees of the wood, so is my beloved among the sons. I sat down under his shadow with great delight, and his fruit was sweet to my taste.

4. He brought me to the banqueting house, and his banner over me was love.

5. Stay me with flagons,[106] comfort me with apples: for I am sick of love.

6. His left hand is under my head, and his right hand doth embrace me.

7. I charge you, O ye daughters of Jerusalem, by the roes, and by the hinds of the field, that ye stir not up, nor awake my love, till he please.

---

[103] An aromatic plant used as an ointment.   [104] Village on the west bank of the Dead Sea.   [105] Palestinian coastal plain between Joppa and Caeserea.   [106] In the Hebrew, "raisins."

8. The voice of my beloved! behold, he cometh leaping upon the mountains, skipping upon the hills.

9. My beloved is like a roe or a young hart: behold, he standeth behind our wall, he looketh forth at the windows, shewing himself through the lattice.

10. My beloved spake, and said unto me, Rise up, my love, my fair one, and come away.

11. For, lo, the winter is past, the rain is over and gone;

12. The flowers appear on the earth; the time of the singing of birds is come, and the voice of the turtle is heard in our land;

13. The fig tree putteth forth her green figs, and the vines with the tender grape give a good smell. Arise, my love, my fair one, and come away.

14. O my dove, that art in the clefts of the rock, in the secret places of the stairs, let me see thy countenance, let me hear thy voice; for sweet is thy voice, and thy countenance is comely.

15. Take us the foxes, the little foxes, that spoil the vines: for our vines have tender grapes.

16. My beloved is mine, and I am his: he feedeth among the lilies.

17. Until the day break, and the shadows flee away, turn, my beloved, and be thou like a roe or a young hart upon the mountains of Bether.

CHAPTER 3

By night on my bed I sought him whom my soul loveth: I sought him, but I found him not.

2. I will rise now, and go about the city in the streets, and in the broad ways I will seek him whom my soul loveth: I sought him, but I found him not.

3. The watchmen that go about the city found me: to whom I said, Saw ye him whom my soul loveth?

4. It was but a little that I passed from them, but I found him whom my soul loveth: I held him, and would not let him go, until I had brought him into my mother's house, and into the chamber of her that conceived me.

5. I charge you, O ye daughters of Jerusalem, by the roes, and by the hinds of the field, that ye stir not up, nor awake my love, till he please.

6. Who is this that cometh out of the wilderness like pillars of smoke, perfumed with myrrh and frankincense, with all powders of the merchant?

7. Behold his bed, which is Solomon's; threescore valiant men are about it, of the valiant of Israel.

8. They all hold swords, being expert in war: every man hath his sword upon his thigh because of fear in the night.

9. King Solomon made himself a chariot of the wood of Lebanon.

10. He made the pillars thereof of silver, the bottom thereof of gold, the covering of it of purple, the midst thereof being paved with love,[107] for the daughters of Jerusalem.

11. Go forth, O ye daughters of Zion, and behold king Solomon with the crown wherewith his mother crowned him in the day of his espousals, and in the day of the gladness of his heart.

CHAPTER 4

Behold, thou art fair, my love; behold, thou art fair; thou hast doves eyes within thy locks: thy hair is as a flock of goats, that appear from mount Gilead.[108]

2. Thy teeth are like a flock of sheep that are even shorn, which came up from the washing; whereof everyone bear twins, and none is barren among them.

3. Thy lips are like a thread of scarlet, and thy speech is comely: thy temples are like a piece of a pomegranate within thy locks.

4. Thy neck is like the tower of David builded for an armoury, whereon there hang a thousand bucklers, all shields of mighty men.

5. Thy two breasts are like two young roes that are twins, which feed among the lilies.

6. Until the day break, and the shadows flee away, I will get me to the mountain of myrrh, and to the hill of frankincense.

7. Thou art all fair, my love; there is no spot in thee.

8. Come with me from Lebanon, my spouse, with me from Lebanon: look from the top of Amana,[109] from the top of Shenir[110] and Hermon, from the lions' dens, from the mountains of the leopards.

9. Thou hast ravished my heart, my sister, my spouse; thou hast ravished my heart with one of thine eyes, with one chain of thy neck.

10. How fair is thy love, my sister, my spouse! how much better is thy love than wine! and the smell of thine ointments than all spices!

11. Thy lips, O my spouse, drop as the honeycomb: honey and milk are under thy tongue; and the smell of thy garments is like the smell of Lebanon.

12. A garden inclosed is my sister, my spouse; a spring shut up, a fountain sealed.

13. Thy plants are an orchard of pomegranates, with pleasant fruits; camphire, with spikenard,

---

[107] "the midst . . . with love": missing in the Hebrew text (restored on the basis of early translations into Greek and Syriac).   [108] Mountain on the east bank of the Jordan.   [109] High mountain in what is now western Syria.   [110] "Shenir" (or Senir) is often identified with Mount Hermon, which lies between Damascus and the Jordan river.

14. Spikenard and saffron; calamus and cinnamon, with all trees of frankincense; myrrh and aloes, with all the chief spices:

15. A fountain of gardens, a well of living waters, and streams from Lebanon.

16. Awake, O north wind; and come, thou south; blow upon my garden, that the spices thereof may flow out. Let my beloved come into his garden, and eat his pleasant fruits.

CHAPTER 5

I am come into my garden, my sister, my spouse: I have gathered my myrrh with my spice; I have eaten my honeycomb with my honey; I have drunk my wine with my milk: eat, O friends; drink, yea, drink abundantly, O beloved.

2. I sleep, but my heart waketh: it is the voice of my beloved that knocketh, saying, Open to me, my sister, my love, my dove, my undefiled: for my head is filled with dew, and my locks with the drops of the night.

3. I have put off my coat; how shall I put it on? I have washed my feet; how shall I defile them?

4. My beloved put in his hand by the hole of the door, and my bowels were moved for him.

5. I rose up to open to my beloved; and my hands dropped with myrrh, and my fingers with sweet smelling myrrh, upon the handles of the lock.

6. I opened to my beloved; but my beloved had withdrawn himself, and was gone: my soul failed when he spake: I sought him, but I could not find him; I called him, but he gave me no answer.

7. The watchmen that went about the city found me, they smote me, they wounded me; the keepers of the walls took away my veil from me.

8. I charge you, O daughters of Jerusalem, if ye find my beloved, that ye tell him, that I am sick of love.

9. What is thy beloved more than another beloved, O thou fairest among women? what is thy beloved more than another beloved, that thou dost so charge us?

10. My beloved is white and ruddy, the chiefest among ten thousand.

11. His head is as the most fine gold, his locks are bushy, and black as a raven.

12. His eyes are as the eyes of doves by the rivers of waters, washed with milk, and fitly set.

13. His cheeks are as a bed of spices, as sweet flowers: his lips like lilies, dropping sweet smelling myrrh.

14. His hands are as gold rings set with the beryl: his belly is as bright ivory overlaid with sapphires.

15. His legs are as pillars of marble, set upon sockets of fine gold: his countenance is as Lebanon, excellent as the cedars.

16. His mouth is most sweet: yea, he is altogether lovely. This is my beloved, and this is my friend, O daughters of Jerusalem.

CHAPTER 6

Whither is thy beloved gone, O thou fairest among women? whither is thy beloved turned aside? that we may seek him with thee.

2. My beloved is gone down into his garden, to the beds of spices, to feed in the gardens, and to gather lilies.

3. I am my beloved's, and my beloved is mine: he feedeth among the lilies.

4. Thou art beautiful, O my love, as Tirzah, comely as Jerusalem, terrible as an army with banners.

5. Turn away thine eyes from me, for they have overcome me: thy hair is as a flock of goats that appear from Gilead.

6. Thy teeth are as a flock of sheep which go up from the washing, whereof every one beareth twins, and there is not one barren among them.

7. As a piece of a pomegranate are thy temples within thy locks.

8. There are threescore queens, and fourscore concubines, and virgins without number.

9. My dove, my undefiled is but one; she is the only one of her mother, she is the choice one of her that bare her. The daughters saw her, and blessed her; yea, the queens and the concubines, and they praised her.

10. Who is she that looketh forth as the morning, fair as the moon, clear as the sun, and terrible as an army with banners?

11. I went down into the garden of nuts to see the fruits of the valley, and to see whether the vine flourished, and the pomegranates budded.

12. Or ever I was aware, my soul made me like the chariots of Amminadib.[111]

13. Return, return, O Shulamite; return, return, that we may look upon thee. What will ye see in the Shulamite? As it were the company of [112] two armies.

CHAPTER 7

How beautiful are they feet with shoes, O prince's daughter! the joints of thy thighs are like jewels, the work of the hands of a cunning workman.

[111] The meaning of the Hebrew is uncertain.   [112] More accurately, "dance before."

2. Thy navel is like a round goblet, which wanteth not liquor: thy belly is like an heap of wheat set about with lilies.

3. Thy two breasts are like two young roes that are twins.

4. Thy neck is as a tower of ivory; thine eyes like the fishpools in Heshbon,[113] by the gate of Bathrabbim: thy nose is as the tower of Lebanon which looketh toward Damascus.

5. Thine head upon thee is like Carmel,[114] and the hair of thine head like purple; the king is held in the galleries.

6. How fair and how pleasant art thou, O love, for delights!

7. This thy stature is like to a palm tree, and thy breasts to clusters of grapes.

8. I said, I will go up to the palm tree, I will take hold of the boughs thereof: now also thy breasts shall be as clusters of the vine, and the smell of thy nose like apples;

9. And the roof of thy mouth like the best wine for my beloved, that goeth down sweetly, causing the lips of those that are asleep to speak.[115]

10. I am my beloved's, and his desire is toward me.

11. Come, my beloved, let us go forth into the field; let us lodge in the villages.

12. Let us get up early to the vineyards; let us see if the vine flourish, whether the tender grape appear, and the pomegranates bud forth: there will I give thee my loves.

13. The mandrakes give a smell, and at our gates are all manner of pleasant fruits, new and old, which I have laid up for thee, O my beloved.

CHAPTER 8

O that thou wert as my brother, that sucked the breasts of my mother! when I should find thee without, I would kiss thee; yea, I should not be despised.

2. I would lead thee, and bring thee into my mother's house, who would instruct me: I would cause thee to drink of spiced wine of the juice of my pomegranate.

3. His left hand should be under my head, and his right hand should embrace me.

4. I charge you, O daughters of Jerusalem, that ye stir not up, nor awake my love, until he please.

5. Who is this that cometh up from the wilderness, leaning upon her

---

[113] Town northeast of the Dead Sea.   [114] Mountain in northern Palestine on the coast of Galilea.   [115] The ancient Greek, Syriac, and Vulgate (Latin) translations read "gliding over lips and teeth."

beloved? I raised thee up under the apple tree: there thy mother brought thee forth: there she brought thee forth that bare thee.

6. Set me as a seal upon thine heart, as a seal upon thine arm: for love is strong as death; jealousy is cruel as the grave: the coals thereof are coals of fire, which hath a most vehement flame.

7. Many waters cannot quench love, neither can the floods drown it: if a man would give all the substance of his house for love, it would utterly be contemned.

8. We have a little sister, and she hath no breasts: what shall we do for our sister in the day when she shall be spoken for?

9. If she be a wall, we will build upon her a palace of silver: and if she be a door, we will inclose her with boards of cedar.

10. I am a wall, and my breasts like towers: then was I in his eyes as one that found favour.

11. Solomon had a vineyard at Baalhamon; he let out the vineyard unto keepers; every one for the fruit thereof was to bring a thousand pieces of silver.

12. My vineyard, which is mine, is before me: thou, O Solomon, must have a thousand, and those that keep the fruit thereof two hundred.

13. Thou that dwellest in the gardens, the companions hearken to thy voice: cause me to hear it.

14. Make haste, my beloved, and be thou like to a roe or to a young hart upon the mountains of spices.

Homer

FROM *The Iliad* AND
The Odyssey

Homer

HOMER IS THE NAME TRADITIONALLY GIVEN TO THE AUTHOR OR authors of two brilliant epic poems, *The Iliad* and *The Odyssey*. The poems were probably composed on the west coast of Asia Minor (in what is now Turkey) in about the eighth century B.C. Although Greek literature begins with these two poems, they are probably the culmination of a long and ancient tradition of oral epic. Both *The Iliad* and *The Odyssey* were composed to be sung to their audiences by a bard and both employ rather striking devices derived from an old oral tradition. These devices, which are common to all oral epic but which might seem alien or even disturbing to a modern reader, include the use of very elaborate similes and the frequent repetition of traditional epithets, of formulaic phrases and sentences, and of typical scenes.

The action of both poems is set in the world of mythical Greek heroes and gods in a remote past. Numerous archeological discoveries have shown that some of the more plausible details in the Homeric poems are, in fact, a fictionalized residue of history. There are also clear indications that early Greek audiences believed that they were hearing their own history in some of the Homeric myths, and this "historical" content reinforced the authoritative status which the poems acquired in Greek culture.

Although *The Iliad* and *The Odyssey* share the same epic techniques— the heroic development of the fate of a single man, the use of many of the same myths, gods, and heroic characters as a frame of reference—yet they represent vastly different worlds. *The Iliad* primarily concerns a tragic event firmly located in the heroic world of aristocratic warriors, whereas *The Odyssey* encompasses more social strata—ranging from kings to swineherds— and the larger world of fantastic adventures. Moreover, the two Homeric epics display some important differences as well as similarities in their interpretation of the gods. In both poems the same anthropomorphic gods appear, and in both the poet constantly interweaves human and divine will as the forces that motivate the poetic action. But the gods of *The Iliad* are marked by uninhibited, often brutal partisanship and an arbitrary, irresponsible use of power; in contrast, those in *The Odyssey,* with few exceptions, are considerably more reserved and protective of mankind. These and other differences have often led to speculation that *The Odyssey* is considerably later in composition than *The Iliad*. On the basis of linguistic evidence, it is clear that *The Iliad* is somewhat older. Yet the two poems have so much in common that the ancient tradition of assigning the name "Homer" to the poet or poets of both epics will probably continue to survive—with good reason.

The Iliad

TRANSLATED BY RICHMOND LATTIMORE *

The Iliad, generally agreed to be the earlier of the two epics, is set
in the tenth year of a war between the Greeks and the Trojans on
a battlefield in front of Troy, a walled city just south of the Dardanelles. The war was triggered by a Trojan prince, Paris, who ran
off with Helen, the wife of a Greek king, Menelaus. The main
theme of the poem is the anger, withdrawal, and tragic violence of
the strongest and bravest of the Greek warriors, Achilles. The
poem opens with the scene that led to Achilles' anger.

BOOK I

Sing, goddess,° the anger of Peleus'° son Achilleus
and its devastation, which put pains thousandfold upon the Achaians,°
hurled in their multitudes to the house of Hades strong souls
of heroes, but gave their bodies to be the delicate feasting
of dogs, of all birds, and the will of Zeus° was accomplished
since that time when first there stood in division of conflict
Atreus' son° the lord of men and brilliant Achilleus.
What god was it then set them together in bitter collision?

* Since the translator has used transliterations of most Greek proper names—rather
than the Latinized versions which have become traditional in English—some well-
known names might at first seem unfamiliar. Thus "Achilleus" is used for Achilles;
"Achaians," for Achaeans; "Atreides," for son of Atreus; "Patroklos," for Patroclus;
"Klytaimnestra," for Clytemnestra; "Aiakides," for descendant of Aeacus (Achilles), and so on.
1. _goddess:_ the muse, who gives the bard his poetic inspiration. _Peleus:_ king of the
Myrmidons (a tribe of northern Greece) and father of Achilles by a sea nymph,
Thetis. Too old to accompany Achilles to Troy, he survived his son. 2. _Achaians:_
the Greeks. 5. _Zeus:_ a Greek god, superior in strength to all other gods.
7. _Atreus' son:_ Agamemnon, leader of the Greeks.

Zeus' son and Leto's,° Apollo,° who in anger at the king drove
the foul pestilence along the host, and the people perished,   10
since Atreus' son had dishonored Chryses, priest of Apollo,
when he came beside the fast ships of the Achaians to ransom
back his daughter, carrying gifts beyond count and holding
in his hands wound on a staff of gold the ribbons of Apollo
who strikes from afar, and supplicated all the Achaians,
but above all Atreus' two sons,° the marshals of the people:
"Sons of Atreus and you other strong-greaved ° Achaians,
to you may the gods grant who have their homes on Olympos
Priam's° city to be plundered and a fair homecoming thereafter,
but may you give me back my own daughter and take the ransom,   20
giving honor to Zeus' son who strikes from afar, Apollo."
    Then all the rest of the Achaians cried out in favor
that the priest be respected and the shining ransom be taken;
yet this pleased not the heart of Atreus' son Agamemnon,
but harshly he drove him away with a strong order upon him:
"Never let me find you again, old sir, near our hollow
ships, neither lingering now nor coming again hereafter,
for fear your staff and the god's ribbons help you no longer.
The girl I will not give back; sooner will old age come upon her
in my own house, in Argos,° far from her own land, going   30
up and down by the loom and being in my bed as my companion.
So go now, do not make me angry; so you will be safer."
    So he spoke, and the old man in terror obeyed him
and went silently away beside the murmuring sea beach.
Over and over the old man prayed as he walked in solitude
to King Apollo, whom Leto of the lovely hair bore: "Hear me,
lord of the silver bow who set your power about Chryse°
and Killa° the sacrosanct, who are lord in strength over Tenedos,°
Smintheus,° if ever it pleased your heart that I built your temple,
if ever it pleased you that I burned all the rich thigh pieces   40

9. *Leto*: a goddess always persecuted by Zeus' wife Hera, since Zeus had slept
with Leto and thus sired Apollo and the goddess Artemis. *Apollo*: a god, who generally supports the Trojans in this war.   16. *Atreus' two sons*: Agamemnon and his
brother Menelaus.   17. *strong-greaved*: A greave is a piece of armor that fits over
the entire lower leg.   19. *Priam*: the king of Troy.   30. *Argos*: part of the Greek
Peloponnesus of which Agamemnon was ruler. (Mycenae is situated in this area.)
37–38. *Chryse, Killa*: cities near Troy. Apollo's priest Chryses lived in Chryse.
Tenedos: island off the Trojan coast.   39. *Smintheus*: cult name of Apollo, probably in reference either to his role as destroyer of mice (Greek, *sminthos*: mouse)
or to his cult in the town Sminthe near Troy.

of bulls, of goats, then bring to pass this wish I pray for:
let your arrows make the Danaans° pay for my tears shed."

So he spoke in prayer, and Phoibos° Apollo heard him,
and strode down along the pinnacles of Olympos,° angered
in his heart, carrying across his shoulders the bow and the hooded
quiver; and the shafts clashed on the shoulders of the god walking
angrily. He came as night comes down and knelt then
apart and opposite the ships and let go an arrow.
Terrible was the clash that rose from the bow of silver.
First he went after the mules and the circling hounds, then let go   50
a tearing arrow against the men themselves and struck them.
The corpse fires burned everywhere and did not stop burning.

Nine days up and down the host ranged the god's arrows,
but on the tenth Achilleus called the people to assembly;
a thing put into his mind by the goddess of the white arms, Hera,°
who had pity upon the Danaans when she saw them dying.
Now when they were all assembled in one place together,
Achilleus of the swift feet stood up among them and spoke forth:
"Son of Atreus, I believe now that straggling backwards
we must make our way home if we can even escape death,   60
if fighting now must crush the Achaians and the plague likewise.
No, come, let us ask some holy man, some prophet,
even an interpreter of dreams, since a dream also
comes from Zeus, who can tell why Phoibos Apollo is so angry,
if for the sake of some vow, some hecatomb° he blames us,
if given the fragrant smoke of lambs, of he goats, somehow
he can be made willing to beat the bane aside from us."

He spoke thus and sat down again, and among them stood up
Kalchas,° Thestor's son, far the best of the bird interpreters,
who knew all things that were, the things to come and the things past,   70
who guided into the land of Ilion° the ships of the Achaians
through that seercraft of his own that Phoibos Apollo gave him.
He in kind intention toward all stood forth and addressed them:
"You have bidden me, Achilleus beloved of Zeus, to explain to
you this anger of Apollo the lord who strikes from afar. Then
I will speak; yet make me a promise and swear before me

42. *Danaans:* the Greeks.   43. *Phoibos:* a traditional epithet of Apollo; literally,
"the Bright, the Pure." His maternal grandmother was Phoibe.   44. *Olympos:*
high mountain in northern Greece; mythical home of the gods.   55. *Hera:* goddess
hostile to the Trojans; wife and sister of Zeus.   65. *hecatomb:* public sacrifice of
animals to a god (literally, "hundred cattle").   69–72. *Kalchas . . . gave him:*
Kalchas interpreted omens that led the Greeks to attack Troy.   71. *Ilion:* Troy.

readily by word and work of your hands to defend me,
since I believe I shall make a man angry who holds great kingship
over the men of Argos, and all the Achaians obey him.
For a king when he is angry with a man beneath him is too strong,   80
and suppose even for the day itself he swallow down his anger,
he still keeps bitterness that remains until its fulfillment
deep in his chest. Speak forth then, tell me if you will protect me."
     Then in answer again spoke Achilleus of the swift feet:
"Speak, interpreting whatever you know, and fear nothing.
In the name of Apollo beloved of Zeus to whom you, Kalchas,
make your prayers when you interpret the gods' will to the Danaans,
no man so long as I am alive above earth and see daylight
shall lay the weight of his hands on you beside the hollow ships,
not one of all the Danaans, even if you mean Agamemnon,   90
who now claims to be far the greatest of all the Achaians."
     At this the blameless seer took courage again and spoke forth:
"No, it is not for the sake of some vow or hecatomb he blames us,
but for the sake of his priest whom Agamemnon dishonored
and would not give him back his daughter nor accept the ransom.
Therefore the archer° sent griefs against us and will send them
still, nor sooner thrust back the shameful plague from the Danaans
until we give the glancing-eyed girl back to her father
without price, without ransom, and lead also a blessed hecatomb
to Chryse; thus we might propitiate and persuade him."   100
     He spoke thus and sat down again, and among them stood up
Atreus' son the hero wide-ruling Agamemnon
raging, the heart within filled black to the brim with anger
from beneath, but his two eyes showed like fire in their blazing.
First of all he eyed Kalchas bitterly and spoke to him:
"Seer of evil: never yet have you told me a good thing.
Always the evil things are dear to your heart to prophesy,
but nothing excellent have you said nor ever accomplished.
Now once more you make divination to the Danaans, argue
forth your reason why he who strikes from afar afflicts them,   110
because I for the sake of the girl Chryseis° would not take
the shining ransom; and indeed I wish greatly to have her
in my own house; since I like her better than Klytaimestra
my own wife, for in truth she is no way inferior,
neither in build nor stature nor wit, not in accomplishment.
Still I am willing to give her back, if such is the best way.
I myself desire that my people be safe, not perish.
Find me then some prize that shall be my own, lest I only

96. *archer:* Apollo.   111. *Chryseis:* daughter of the priest Chryses.

among the Argives° go without, since that were unfitting;
you are all witnesses to this thing, that my prize goes elsewhere." 120
   Then in answer again spoke brilliant swift-footed Achilleus:
"Son of Atreus, most lordly, greediest for gain of all men,
how shall the great-hearted Achaians give you a prize now?
There is no great store of things lying about I know of.
But what we took from the cities by storm has been distributed;
it is unbecoming for the people to call back things once given.
No, for the present give the girl back to the god; we Achaians
thrice and four times over will repay you, if ever Zeus gives
into our hands the strong-walled citadel of Troy to be plundered."
   Then in answer again spoke powerful Agamemnon: 130
"Not that way, good fighter though you be, godlike Achilleus,
strive to cheat, for you will not deceive, you will not persuade me.
What do you want? To keep your own prize and have me sit here
lacking one? Are you ordering me to give this girl back?
Either the great-hearted Achaians shall give me a new prize
chosen according to my desire to atone for the girl lost,
or else if they will not give me one I myself shall take her,
your own prize, or that of Aias,° or that of Odysseus,°
going myself in person; and he whom I visit will be bitter.
Still, these are things we shall deliberate again hereafter. 140
Come, now, we must haul a black ship down to the bright sea,
and assemble rowers enough for it, and put on board it
the hecatomb, and the girl herself, Chryseis of the fair cheeks,
and let there be one responsible man in charge of her,
either Aias or Idomeneus° or brilliant Odysseus,
or you yourself, son of Peleus, most terrifying of all men,
to reconcile by accomplishing sacrifice the archer."
   Then looking darkly at him Achilleus of the swift feet spoke:
"O wrapped in shamelessness, with your mind forever on profit,
how shall any one of the Achaians readily obey you 150
either to go on a journey or to fight men strongly in battle?
I for my part did not come here for the sake of the Trojan
spearmen to fight against them, since to me they have done nothing.
Never yet have they driven away my cattle or my horses,
never in Phthia° where the soil is rich and men grow great did they
spoil my harvest, since indeed there is much that lies between us,
the shadowy mountains and the echoing sea; but for your sake,

119. Argives: the Greeks; literally, "those from Argos." *138. Aias:* the most
competent Greek fighter after Achilles, normally written "Ajax." *Odysseus:* the
most inventive, crafty, and articulate of the Greeks. *145. Idomeneus:* a powerful
Greek hero from the island of Crete. *155. Phthia:* home of Achilles in northern
Greece.

o great shamelessness, we followed, to do you favor,
you with the dog's eyes, to win your honor° and Menelaos'
from the Trojans. You forget all this or else you care nothing.   160
And now my prize you threaten in person to strip from me,
for whom I labored much, the gift of the sons of the Achaians.
Never, when the Achaians sack some well-founded citadel
of the Trojans, do I have a prize that is equal to your prize.
Always the greater part of the painful fighting is the work of
my hands; but when the time comes to distribute the booty
yours is far the greater reward, and I with some small thing
yet dear to me go back to my ships when I am weary with fighting.
Now I am returning to Phthia, since it is much better
to go home again with my curved ships, and I am minded no longer   170
to stay here dishonored and pile up your wealth and your luxury."
   Then answered him in turn the lord of men Agamemnon:
"Run away by all means if your heart drives you. I will not
entreat you to stay here for my sake. There are others with me
who will do me honor, and above all Zeus of the counsels.
To me you are the most hateful of all the kings whom the gods love.
Forever quarreling is dear to your heart, and wars and battles;
and if you are very strong indeed, that is a god's gift.
Go home then with your own ships and your own companions,
be king over the Myrmidons.° I care nothing about you.   180
I take no account of your anger. But here is my threat to you.
Even as Phoibos Apollo is taking away my Chryseis.
I shall convey her back in my own ship, with my own
followers; but I shall take the fair-cheeked Briseis,
your prize, I myself going to your shelter, that you may learn well
how much greater I am than you, and another man may shrink back
from likening himself to me and contending against me."
   So he spoke. And the anger came on Peleus' son, and within
his shaggy breast the heart was divided two ways, pondering
whether to draw from beside his thigh the sharp sword, driving   190
away all those who stood between and kill the son of Atreus,
or else to check the spleen within and keep down his anger.
Now as he weighed in mind and spirit these two courses
and was drawing from its scabbard the great sword, Athene° descended
from the sky. For Hera the goddess of the white arms sent her,
who loved both men equally in her heart and cared for them.

<hr>

159. *honor:* the purpose of the Greek expedition against Troy was to recover the
wife of Menelaus, Helen, who had been abducted by Priam's son, Paris.   180.
Myrmidons: Achilles' men.   194. *Athene* (Athena): a goddess who, like Hera,
supported the Greeks in the war; daughter of Zeus; particularly well-disposed to
Odysseus.

The goddess standing behind Peleus' son caught him by the fair hair,
appearing to him only, for no man of the others saw her.
Achilleus in amazement turned about, and straightway
knew Pallas° Athene and the terrible eyes shining.   200
He uttered winged words and addressed her: "Why have you come
            now,
o child of Zeus of the aegis,° once more? Is it that you may see
the outrageousness of the son of Atreus Agamemnon?
Yet will I tell you this thing, and I think it shall be accomplished.
By such acts of arrogance he may even lose his own life."
    Then in answer the goddess gray-eyed Athene spoke to him:
"I have come down to stay your anger—but will you obey me?—
from the sky; and the goddess of the white arms Hera sent me,
who loves both of you equally in her heart and cares for you.
Come then, do not take your sword in your hand, keep clear of fighting, 210
though indeed with words you may abuse him, and it will be that way.
And this also will I tell you and it will be a thing accomplished.
Some day three times over such shining gifts shall be given you
by reason of this outrage. Hold your hand then, and obey us."
    Then in answer again spoke Achilleus of the swift feet:
"Goddess, it is necessary that I obey the word of you two,
angry though I am in my heart. So it will be better.
If any man obeys the gods, they listen to him also."
    He spoke, and laid his heavy hand on the silver sword hilt
and thrust the great blade back into the scabbard nor disobeyed   220
the word of Athene. And she went back again to Olympos
to the house of Zeus of the aegis with the other divinities.
    But Peleus' son once again in words of derision
spoke to Atreides, and did not yet let go of his anger:
"You winesack, with a dog's eyes, with a deer's heart. Never
once have you taken courage in your heart to arm with your people
for battle, or go into ambuscade with the best of the Achaians.
No, for in such things you see death. Far better to your mind
is it, all along the widespread host of the Achaians
to take away the gifts of any man who speaks up against you.   230
King who feed on your people, since you rule nonentities;
otherwise, son of Atreus, this were your last outrage.
But I will tell you this and swear a great oath upon it:
in the name of this scepter, which never again will bear leaf nor
branch, now that it has left behind the cut stump in the mountains,

200. *Pallas*: cult name of Athene, which probably means either "brandisher" (of her traditional spear) or "young girl; virgin." 202. *aegis*: an impregnable skin shield of Zeus, sometimes lent to Athene to frighten humans; originally perhaps the thunder cloud as an emblem of Zeus.

nor shall it ever blossom again, since the bronze blade stripped
bark and leafage, and now at last the sons of the Achaians
carry it in their hands in state when they administer
the justice of Zeus. And this shall be a great oath before you:
some day longing for Achilleus will come to the sons of the Achaians,   240
all of them. Then stricken at heart though you be, you will be able
to do nothing, when in their numbers before man-slaughtering Hektor°
they drop and die. And then you will eat out the heart within you
in sorrow, that you did no honor to the best of the Achaians."

    Thus spoke Peleus' son and dashed to the ground the scepter
studded with golden nails, and sat down again. But Atreides°
raged still on the other side, and between them Nestor
the fair-spoken rose up, the lucid speaker of Pylos,
from whose lips the streams of words ran sweeter than honey.
In his time two generations of mortal men had perished,   250
those who had grown up with him and they who had been born to
these in sacred Pylos, and he was king in the third age.
He in kind intention toward both stood forth and addressed them:
"Oh, for shame. Great sorrow comes on the land of Achaia.
Now might Priam and the sons of Priam in truth be happy,
and all the rest of the Trojans be visited in their hearts with gladness,
were they to hear all this wherein you two are quarreling,
you, who surpass all Danaans in council, in fighting.
Yet be persuaded. Both of you are younger than I am.
Yes, and in my time I have dealt with better men than   260
you are, and never once did they disregard me. Never
yet have I seen nor shall see again such men as these were,
men like Peirithoös, and Dryas, shepherd of the people, . . .
or Theseus, Aigeus' son, in the likeness of the immortals.
These were the strongest generation of earth-born mortals,
the strongest, and they fought against the strongest, the beast
    men. . . .
Do you also obey, since to be persuaded is better.
You, great man that you are, yet do not take the girl away
but let her be, a prize as the sons of the Achaians gave her
first. Nor, son of Peleus, think to match your strength with   270
the king, since never equal with the rest is the portion of honor
of the sceptered king to whom Zeus gives magnificence. Even
though you are the stronger man, and the mother° who bore you was
    immortal,

---

242. *Hektor:* best fighter among the Trojans; son of King Priam.   246. *Atreides:*
Agamemnon, son of Atreus.   273. *the mother:* Achilles' mother was a sea nymph,
Thetis.

yet is this man greater who is lord over more than you rule.
Son of Atreus, give up your anger; even I entreat you
to give over your bitterness against Achilleus, he who
stands as a great bulwark of battle over all the Achaians."
    Then in answer again spoke powerful Agamemnon:
"Yes, old sir, all this you have said is fair and orderly.
Yet here is a man who wishes to be above all others,   280
who wishes to hold power over all, and to be lord of
all, and give them their orders, yet I think one will not obey him.
And if the everlasting gods have made him a spearman,
yet they have not given him the right to speak abusively."
    Then looking at him darkly brilliant Achilleus answered him:
"So must I be called of no account and a coward
if I must carry out every order you may happen to give me.
Tell other men to do these things, but give me no more
commands, since I for my part have no intention to obey you.
And put away in your thoughts this other thing I tell you.   290
With my hands I will not fight for the girl's sake, neither
with you nor any other man, since you take her away who gave her.
But of all the other things that are mine beside my fast black
ship, you shall take nothing away against my pleasure.
Come, then, only try it, that these others may see also;
instantly your own black blood will stain my spearpoint."
    So these two after battling in words of contention
stood up, and broke the assembly beside the ships of the Achaians.
Peleus' son went back to his balanced ships and his shelter
with Patroklos, Menoitios' son, and his own companions.   300
But the son of Atreus drew a fast ship down to the water
and allotted into it twenty rowers and put on board it
the hecatomb for the god and Chryseis of the fair cheeks
leading her by the hand. And in charge went crafty Odysseus.
    These then putting out went over the ways of the water
while Atreus' son told his people to wash off their defilement.
And they washed it away and threw the washings into the salt sea.
Then they accomplished perfect hecatombs to Apollo,
of bulls and goats along the beach of the barren salt sea.
The savour of the burning swept in circles up to the bright sky.   310
    Thus these were busy about the army. But Agamemnon
did not give up his anger and the first threat he made to Achilleus,
but to Talthybios he gave his orders and Eurybates
who were heralds and hard-working henchmen to him: "Go now
to the shelter of Peleus' son Achilleus, to bring back
Briseis of the fair cheeks leading her by the hand. And if he

will not give her, I must come in person to take her
with many men behind me, and it will be the worse for him."
  He spoke and sent them forth with this strong order upon them.
They went against their will beside the beach of the barren   320
salt sea, and came to the shelters and the ships of the Myrmidons.
The man himself they found beside his shelter and his black ship
sitting. And Achilleus took no joy at all when he saw them.
These two terrified and in awe of the king stood waiting
quietly, and did not speak a word at all nor question him.
But he knew the whole matter in his own heart, and spoke first:
"Welcome, heralds, messengers of Zeus and of mortals.
Draw near. You are not to blame in my sight, but Agamemnon
who sent the two of you here for the sake of the girl Briseis.
Go then, illustrious Patroklos, and bring the girl forth   330
and give her to these to be taken away. Yet let them be witnesses
in the sight of the blessed gods, in the sight of mortal
men, and of this cruel king, if ever hereafter
there shall be need of me to beat back the shameful destruction
from the rest. For surely in ruinous heart he makes sacrifice
and has not wit enough to look behind and before him
that the Achaians fighting beside their ships shall not perish."
  So he spoke, and Patroklos obeyed his beloved companion.
He led forth from the hut Briseis of the fair cheeks and gave her
to be taken away; and they walked back beside the ships of the
        Achaians,   340
and the woman all unwilling went with them still. But Achilleus
weeping went and sat in sorrow apart from his companions
beside the beach of the gray sea looking out on the infinite water.
Many times stretching forth his hands he called on his mother:
"Since, my mother, you bore me to be a man with a short life,
therefore Zeus of the loud thunder on Olympos should grant me
honor at least. But now he has given me not even a little.
Now the son of Atreus, powerful Agamemnon,
has dishonored me, since he has taken away my prize and keeps it."
  So he spoke in tears and the lady his mother heard him   350
as she sat in the depths of the sea at the side of her aged father,
and lightly she emerged like a mist from the gray water.
She came and sat beside him as he wept, and stroked him
with her hand and called him by name and spoke to him: "Why then,
child, do you lament? What sorrow has come to your heart now?
Tell me, do not hide it in your mind, and thus we shall both know."
  Sighing heavily Achilleus of the swift feet answered her:
"You know; since you know why must I tell you all this?" . . .

Thetis answered him then letting the tears fall: "Ah me,
my child. Your birth was bitterness. Why did I raise you?   360
If only you could sit by your ships untroubled, not weeping,
since indeed your lifetime is to be short, of no length.
Now it has befallen that your life must be brief and bitter
beyond all men's. To a bad destiny I bore you in my chambers.
But I will go to cloud-dark Olympos and ask this
thing of Zeus who delights in the thunder. Perhaps he will do it.
Do you therefore continuing to sit by your swift ships
be angry at the Achaians and stay away from all fighting.
For Zeus went to the blameless Aithiopians at the Ocean°
yesterday to feast, and the rest of the gods went with him.   370
On the twelfth day he will be coming back to Olympos,
and then I will go for your sake to the house of Zeus, bronze-founded,
and take him by the knees and I think I can persuade him."
    So speaking she went away from that place and left him
sorrowing in his heart for the sake of the fair-girdled woman
whom they were taking by force against his will. But Odysseus
meanwhile drew near to Chryse conveying the sacred hecatomb.
These when they were inside the many-hollowed harbor
took down and gathered together the sails and stowed them in the
        black ship,
let down mast by the forestays, and settled it into the mast crutch   380
easily, and rowed her in with oars to the mooring.
They threw over the anchor stones and made fast the stern cables
and themselves stepped out on to the break of the sea beach,
and led forth the hecatomb to the archer Apollo,
and Chryseis herself stepped forth from the seagoing vessel.
Odysseus of the many designs guided her to the altar
and left her in her father's arms and spoke a word to him:
"Chryses, I was sent here by the lord of men Agamemnon
to lead back your daughter and accomplish a sacred hecatomb
to Apollo on behalf of the Danaans,° that we may propitiate   390
the lord who has heaped unhappiness and tears on the Argives." °
    He spoke, and left her in his arms. And he received gladly
his beloved child. And the men arranged the sacred hecatomb
for the god in orderly fashion around the strong-founded altar.
Next they washed their hands and took up the scattering barley.
Standing among them with lifted arms Chryses prayed in a great voice:
"Hear me, lord of the silver bow, who set your power about

369. *Ocean:* a river that in Greek mythology encircles the entire world; at the edge
of this world live the Ethiopians.   390–91. *Danaans, Argives:* interchangeable
terms for the Greeks.

Chryse and Killa the sacrosanct, who are lord in strength over
Tenedos; if once before you listened to my prayers
and did me honor and smote strongly the host of the Achaians,   400
so one more time bring to pass the wish that I pray for.
Beat aside at last the shameful plague from the Danaans."
    So he spoke in prayer, and Phoibos Apollo heard him.
And when all had made prayer and flung down the scattering barley
first they drew back the victims' heads and slaughtered them and
       skinned them,
and cut away the meat from the thighs and wrapped them in fat,
making a double fold, and laid shreds of flesh upon them.
The old man burned these on a cleft stick and poured the gleaming
wine over, while the young men with forks in their hands stood about
       him.
But when they had burned the thigh pieces and tasted the vitals,   410
they cut all the remainder into pieces and spitted them
and roasted all carefully and took off the pieces.
Then after they had finished the work and got the feast ready
they feasted, nor was any man's hunger denied a fair portion.
But when they had put away their desire for eating and drinking,
the young men filled the mixing bowls with pure wine, passing
a portion to all, when they had offered drink in the goblets.
All day long they propitiated the god with singing,
chanting a splendid hymn to Apollo, these young Achaians,
singing to the one who works from afar, who listened in gladness. . . .   420
    But that other still sat in anger beside his swift ships,
Peleus' son divinely born, Achilleus of the swift feet.
Never now would he go to assemblies where men win glory,
never more into battle, but continued to waste his heart out
sitting there, though he longed always for the clamor and fighting.
    But when the twelfth dawn after this day appeared, the gods who
live forever came back to Olympos all in a body
and Zeus led them; nor did Thetis forget the entreaties
of her son, but she emerged from the sea's waves early
in the morning and went up to the tall sky and Olympos.   430
She found Kronos' broad-browed son° apart from the others
sitting upon the highest peak of rugged Olympos.
She came and sat beside him with her left hand embracing
his knees,° but took him underneath the chin with her right hand
and spoke in supplication to lord Zeus son of Kronos:
"Father Zeus, if ever before in word or action

431. *Kronos' . . . son:* Zeus. 433–34. *She . . . knees:* the typical posture of
a Greek suppliant. Zeus is the archprotector of suppliants.

I did you favor among the immortals, now grant what I ask for.
Now give honor to my son short-lived beyond all other
mortals. Since even now the lord of men Agamemnon
dishonors him, who has taken away his prize and keeps it.   440
Zeus of the counsels, lord of Olympos, now do him honor.
So long put strength into the Trojans, until the Achaians
give my son his rights, and his honor is increased among them."
     She spoke thus. But Zeus who gathers the clouds made no answer
but sat in silence a long time. And Thetis, as she had taken
his knees, clung fast to them and urged once more her question:
"Bend your head and promise me to accomplish this thing,
or else refuse it, you have nothing to fear, that I may know
by how much I am the most dishonored of all gods."
     Deeply disturbed Zeus who gathers the clouds answered her: 450
"This is a disastrous matter when you set me in conflict
with Hera, and she troubles me with recriminations.
Since even as things are, forever among the immortals
she is at me and speaks of how I help the Trojans in battle.
Even so, go back again now, go away, for fear she
see us. I will look to these things that they be accomplished.
See then, I will bend my head that you may believe me.
For this among the immortal gods is the mightiest witness
I can give, and nothing I do shall be vain nor revocable
nor a thing unfulfilled when I bend my head in assent to it."   460
     He spoke, the son of Kronos, and nodded his head with the dark
          brows,
and the immortally anointed hair of the great god
swept from his divine head, and all Olympos was shaken.
     So these two who had made their plans separated, and Thetis
leapt down again from shining Olympos into the sea's depth,
but Zeus went back to his own house, and all the gods rose up
from their chairs to greet the coming of their father, not one had courage
to keep his place as the father advanced, but stood up to greet him.
Thus he took his place on the throne; yet Hera was not
ignorant, having seen how he had been plotting counsels   470
with Thetis the silver-footed, the daughter of the sea's ancient,°
and at once she spoke revilingly to Zeus Son of Kronos:
"Treacherous one, what god has been plotting counsels with you?
Always it is dear to your heart in my absence to think of
secret things and decide upon them. Never have you patience
frankly to speak forth to me the thing that you purpose."

471. *sea's ancient:* the marine deity Nereus, a wise old man who lived in the
Aegean Sea; father of sea nymphs.

Then to her the father of gods and men made answer:
"Hera, do not go on hoping that you will hear all my
thoughts, since these will be too hard for you, though you are my wife.
Any thought that it is right for you to listen to, no one   480
neither man nor any immortal shall hear it before you.
But anything that apart from the rest of the gods I wish to
plan, do not always question each detail nor probe me."
      Then the goddess the ox-eyed lady Hera answered:
"Majesty, son of Kronos, what sort of thing have you spoken?
Truly too much in time past I have not questioned nor probed you,
but you are entirely free to think out whatever pleases you.
Now, though, I am terribly afraid you were won over
by Thetis the silver-footed, the daughter of the sea's ancient.
For early in the morning she sat beside you and took your   490
knees, and I think you bowed your head in assent to do honor
to Achilleus, and to destroy many beside the ships of the Achaians."
      Then in return Zeus who gathers the clouds made answer:
"Dear lady, I never escape you, you are always full of suspicion.
Yet thus you can accomplish nothing surely, but be more
distant from my heart than ever, and it will be the worse for you.
If what you say is true, then that is the way I wish it.
But go then, sit down in silence, and do as I tell you,
for fear all the gods, as many as are on Olympos, can do nothing
if I come close and lay my unconquerable hands upon you."   500
      He spoke, and the goddess the ox-eyed lady Hera was frightened
and went and sat down in silence wrenching her heart to obedience,
and all the Uranian° gods in the house of Zeus were troubled.
Hephaistos° the renowned smith rose up to speak among them,
to bring comfort to his beloved mother, Hera of the white arms:
"This will be a disastrous matter and not endurable
if you two are to quarrel thus for the sake of mortals
and bring brawling among the gods. There will be no pleasure
in the stately feast at all, since vile things will be uppermost.
And I entreat my mother, though she herself understands it,   510
to be ingratiating toward our father Zeus, that no longer
our father may scold her and break up the quiet of our feasting.
For if the Olympian who handles the lightning should be minded
to hurl us out of our places, he is far too strong for any.
Do you therefore approach him again with words made gentle,

---

503. *Uranian:* "of heaven" or "of the sky." Greek, *uranos:* sky, heaven; one of the
earliest gods, from whom most others descend.   504. *Hephaistos:* god of fire and
patron god of workers in metal; son of Zeus and Hera. He was born lame and was
famous for his limp.

and at once the Olympian will be gracious again to us."

    He spoke, and springing to his feet put a two-handled goblet
into his mother's hands and spoke again to her once more:
"Have patience, my mother, and endure it, though you be saddened,
for fear that, dear as you are, I see you before my own eyes   520
struck down, and then sorry though I be I shall not be able
to do anything. It is too hard to fight against the Olympian.
There was a time once before now I was minded to help you,
and he caught me by the foot and threw me from the magic threshold,
and all day long I dropped helpless, and about sunset
I landed in Lemnos,° and there was not much life left in me.
After that fall it was the Sintian° men who took care of me."

    He spoke, and the goddess of the white arms Hera smiled at him,
and smiling she accepted the goblet out of her son's hand.
Thereafter beginning from the left he poured drinks for the other   530
gods, dipping up from the mixing bowl the sweet nectar.°
But among the blessed immortals uncontrollable laughter
went up as they saw Hephaistos bustling about the palace.

    Thus thereafter the whole day long until the sun went under
they feasted, nor was anyone's hunger denied a fair portion,
nor denied the beautifully wrought lyre in the hands of Apollo
nor the antiphonal sweet sound of the Muses singing.

    Afterwards when the light of the flaming sun went under
they went away each one to sleep in his home where
for each one the far-renowed strong-handed Hephaistos   540
had built a house by means of his craftsmanship and cunning.
Zeus the Olympian and lord of the lightning went to
his own bed, where always he lay when sweet sleep came on him.
Going up to the bed he slept and Hera of the gold throne beside him.

*In spite of Achilleus' withdrawal from the war, the Greeks continue to
exercise severe pressure against the Trojans in battles on the plain in front
of Troy. After the Trojans suffer a number of setbacks, the Trojan leader
Hektor returns inside the city walls to urge the Trojans to offer sacrifices
and prayers for victory to their gods. In the city Hektor has successive
encounters with his mother, his brother Paris, and Helen. The visit is
climaxed, in the following scene, by his encounter with his wife and his
young son.*

526. *Lemnos:* an Aegean island, west of Troy.   527. *Sintian:* inhabitant of
Lemnos.   531. *nectar:* a mythical drink of the gods.

From BOOK VI

. . . As he had come to the gates on his way through the great city,
the Skaian gates,° whereby he would issue into the plain, there
at last his own generous wife came running to meet him,
Andromache, the daughter of high-hearted Eëtion;°
Eëtion, who had dwelt underneath wooded Plakos,°
in Thebe below Plakos, lord over the Kilikian° people.   550
It was his daughter who was given to Hektor of the bronze helm.
She came to him there, and beside her went an attendant carrying
the boy in the fold of her bosom, a little child, only a baby,
Hektor's son, the admired, beautiful as a star shining,
whom Hektor called Skamandrios,° but all of the others
Astyanax°—lord of the city; since Hektor alone saved Ilion.
Hektor smiled in silence as he looked on his son, but she,
Andromache, stood close beside him, letting her tears fall,
and clung to his hand and called him by name and spoke to him:
        "Dearest,
your own great strength will be your death, and you have no pity   560
on your little son, nor on me, ill-starred, who soon must be your widow;
for presently the Achaians, gathering together,
will set upon you and kill you; and for me is would be far better
to sink into the earth when I have lost you, for there is no other
consolation for me after you have gone to your destiny—
only grief; since I have no father, no honored mother.
It was brilliant Achilleus who slew my father, Eëtion,
when he stormed the strong-founded citadel of the Kilikians,
Thebe of the towering gates. He killed Eëtion
but did not strip his armor, for his heart respected the dead man,   570
but burned the body in all its elaborate war-gear
and piled a grave mound over it, and the nymphs of the mountains,
daughters of Zeus of the aegis, planted elm trees about it.
And they who were my seven brothers in the great house all went
upon a single day down into the house of the death god,
for swift-footed brilliant Achilleus slaughtered all of them
as they were tending their white sheep and their lumbering oxen;
and when he had led my mother, who was queen under wooded Plakos,

546. *Skaian gates:* a main entrance (in the city wall) to Troy. Hektor is still inside
the city, but he is about to return to the battle on the plain in front of Troy.
548. *Eëtion:* king of Thebe, a city in Trojan territory (not to be confused with the
Greek city Thebes, of which Oedipus was king). 549. *Plakos:* a mountain rising
above the city of Thebe; elsewhere, of Cilicia, a district in southeastern Asia Minor.
550. *Kilikian:* Theban. 555. *Skamandrios:* after Skamandros, the largest river
of the Trojan plain. 556. *Astyanax:* compound of *asty*, "city," and *anax*, "lord,
ruler."

here, along with all his other possessions, Achilleus
released her again, accepting ransom beyond count, but Artemis° 580
of the showering arrows struck her down in the halls of her father.
Hektor, thus you are father to me, and my honored mother,
you are my brother, and you it is who are my young husband.
Please take pity upon me then, stay here on the rampart,
that you may not leave your child an orphan, your wife a widow,
but draw your people up by the fig tree, there where the city
is openest to attack, and where the wall may be mounted.
Three times their bravest came that way, and fought there to storm it
about the two Aiantes° and renowned Idomeneus,
about the two Atreidai ° and the fighting son of Tydeus.° 590
Either some man well skilled in prophetic arts had spoken,
or the very spirit within themselves had stirred them to the onslaught."
    Then tall Hektor of the shining helm answered her: "All these
things are in my mind also, lady; yet I would feel deep shame
before the Trojans, and the Trojan women with trailing garments,
if like a coward I were to shrink aside from the fighting;
and the spirit will not let me, since I have learned to be valiant
and to fight always among the foremost ranks of the Trojans,
winning for my own self great glory, and for my father.
For I know this thing well in my heart, and my mind knows it: 600
there will come a day when sacred Ilion shall perish,
and Priam, and the people of Priam of the strong ash spear.
But it is not so much the pain to come of the Trojans
that troubles me, not even of Priam the king nor Hekabe,
not the thought of my brothers who in their numbers and valor
shall drop in the dust under the hands of men who hate them,
as troubles me the thought of you, when some bronze-armored
Achaian leads you off, taking away your day of liberty,
in tears, and in Argos you must work at the loom of another,
and carry water from the spring Messeis or Hypereia,° 610
all unwilling, but strong will be the necessity upon you;
and some day seeing you shedding tears a man will say of you:
'This is the wife of Hektor, who was ever the bravest fighter
of the Trojans, breakers of horses, in the days when they fought about
       Ilion.'

580. *Artemis:* twin sister of Apollo; daughter of Zeus and Leto; patron goddess of virginity. She was known for giving women painless death. 589. *Aiantes:* two Greek warriors called Aias (Ajax). 590. *Atreidai:* the sons of Atreus, Agamemnon, and Menelaus. *son of Tydeus:* a Greek leader from Argos, Diomedes, who had just demonstrated his fighting skill with disastrous consequences for the Trojans. 610. *Messeis or Hypereia:* springs in Greece.

So will one speak of you; and for you it will be yet a fresh grief,
to be widowed of such a man who could fight off the day of your slavery.
But may I be dead and the piled earth hide me under before I
hear you crying and know by this that they drag you captive."
    So speaking glorious Hektor held out his arms to his baby,
who shrank back to his fair-girdled nurse's bosom   620
screaming, and frightened at the aspect of his own father,
terrified as he saw the bronze and the crest with its horsehair,
nodding dreadfully, as he thought, from the peak of the helmet.
Then his beloved father laughed out, and his honored mother,
and at once glorious Hektor lifted from his head the helmet
and laid it in all its shining upon the ground. Then taking
up his dear son he tossed him about in his arms, and kissed him,
and lifted his voice in prayer to Zeus and the other immortals:
"Zeus, and you other immortals, grant that this boy, who is my son,
may be as I am, preeminent among the Trojans,   630
great in strength, as am I, and rule strongly over Ilion;
and some day let them say of him: 'He is better by far than his father,'
as he comes in from the fighting; and let him kill his enemy
and bring home the blooded spoils, and delight the heart of his mother."
    So speaking he set his child again in the arms of his beloved
wife, who took him back again to her fragrant bosom
smiling in her tears; and her husband saw, and took pity upon her,
and stroked her with his hand, and called her by name and spoke to
        her:
"Poor Andromache! Why does your heart sorrow so much for me?
No man is going to hurl me to Hades,° unless it is fated,   640
but as for fate, I think that no man yet has escaped it
once it has taken its first form, neither brave man nor coward.
Go therefore back to our house, and take up your own work,
the loom and the distaff, and see to it that your handmaidens
ply their work also; but the men must see to the fighting,
all men who are the people of Ilion, but I beyond others."
    So glorious Hektor spoke and again took up the helmet
with its crest of horsehair, while his beloved wife went homeward,
turning to look back on the way, letting the live tears fall.
And as she came in speed into the well-settled household   650
of Hektor the slayer of men, she found numbers of handmaidens
within, and her coming stirred all of them into lamentation.
So they mourned in his house over Hektor while he was living

640. *Hades:* god of the underworld, where the dead exist. His kingdom is also
called "Hades."

still, for they thought he would never again come back from the fighting
alive, escaping the Achaian hands and their violence.
    But Paris in turn did not linger long in his high house,
but when he had put on his glorious armor with bronze elaborate
he ran in the confidence of his quick feet through the city.
As when some stalled horse who has been cornfed at the manger
breaking free of his rope gallops over the plain in thunder   660
to his accustomed bathing place in a sweet-running river
and in the pride of his strength holds high his head, and the mane
      floats
over his shoulders; sure of his glorious strength, the quick knees
carry him to the loved places and the pasture of horses;
so from uttermost Pergamos° came Paris,° the son of
Priam, shining in all his armor of war as the sun shines,
laughing aloud, and his quick feet carried him; suddenly thereafter
he came on brilliant Hektor, his brother, where he yet lingered
before turning away from the place where he had talked with his lady.
It was Alexandros° the godlike who first spoke to him: 670
"Brother, I fear that I have held back your haste, by being
slow on the way, not coming in time, as you commanded me."
    Then tall Hektor of the shining helm spoke to him in answer:
"Strange man! There is no way that one, giving judgment in fairness,
could dishonor your work in battle, since you are a strong man.
But of your own accord you hang back, unwilling. And my heart
is grieved in its thought, when I hear shameful things spoken about you
by the Trojans, who undergo hard fighting for your sake.
Let us go now; some day hereafter we will make all right
with the immortal gods in the sky, if Zeus ever grant it,   680
setting up to them in our houses the wine-bowl of liberty
after we have driven out of Troy the strong-greaved Achaians." . . .

*Under Hektor's rallying leadership, the Trojans took the offensive and
drove the Greeks back to the rather fragile fortifications which they had
built around their ships on the beach. The Greeks were struck by panic and
terror. Their leader, Agamemnon, first counseled them to desert the war and
return home but then withdrew his advice and was persuaded to send a
delegation to Achilleus to offer a generous reconciliation in return for his*

665. *Pergamos:* the citadel inside Troy. *Paris:* Hektor's brother, who was resented
by his fellow Trojans as the cause of the war. Shortly before this scene Hektor had
reprimanded him severely for not doing his share of the fighting; Paris had previously withdrawn from the battle after his defeat in a duel with Menelaus. 670.
Alexandros (also, Alexander): frequently used as an alternate name for Paris.

resumption of fighting. Achilleus refused stubbornly. The situation worsened rapidly for the Greeks, and finally Patroklos tried to persuade Achilleus to reenter the battle. He only succeeded, however, in getting permission for himself to lead Achilleus' men—the Myrmidons—back to fight and, very significantly, to dress himself in Achilleus' own armor. Patroklos drove the Trojans back to their city walls, but was killed there by Hektor with the aid of the god Apollo, who intervened on behalf of the Trojans. Hektor stripped Achilleus' armor from Patroklos' corpse, but the Greeks managed to get Patroklos' body back to their own camp.

From BOOK XVIII

. . . Now as he was pondering this in his heart and his spirit,
meanwhile the son of stately Nestor was drawing near him
and wept warm tears, and gave Achilleus his sorrowful message:
"Ah me, son of valiant Peleus; you must hear from me
the ghastly message of a thing I wish never had happened.
Patroklos has fallen, and now they are fighting over his body
which is naked. Hektor of the shining helm has taken his armor."
He spoke, and the black cloud of sorrow closed on Achilleus.   690
In both hands he caught up the grimy dust, and poured it
over his head and face, and fouled his handsome countenance,
and the black ashes were scattered over his immortal tunic.
And he himself, mightily in his might, in the dust lay
at length, and took and tore at his hair with his hands, and defiled it.
And the handmaidens Achilleus and Patroklos had taken
captive, stricken at heart cried out aloud, and came running
out of doors about valiant Achilleus, and all of them
beat their breasts with their hands, and the limbs went slack in each of
        them.
On the other side Antilochos mourned with him, letting the tears fall,   700
and held the hands of Achilleus as he grieved in his proud heart,
fearing Achilleus might cut his throat with the iron. He cried out
terribly, aloud, and the lady his mother° heard him
as she sat in the depth of the sea at the side of her aged father,
and she cried shrill in turn, and the goddesses° gathered about her. . . .
. . . Now these, when they came to the generous Troad,
followed each other out on the seashore, where close together
the ships of the Myrmidons were hauled up about swift Achilleus.

703. *mother:* Achilles' mother, Thetis.   705. *goddesses:* Thetis' sisters, the daughters of Nereus or Nereids, who were all, like Thetis, sea nymphs.

There as he sighed heavily the lady his mother stood by him
and cried out shrill and aloud, and took her son's head in her arms,
then 710
sorrowing for him she spoke to him in winged words: "Why then,
child, do you lament? What sorrow has come to your heart now?
Speak out, do not hide it. These things are brought to accomplishment
through Zeus: in the way that you lifted your hands and prayed for,
that all the sons of the Achaians be pinned on their grounded vessels
by reason of your loss, and suffer things that are shameful."
  Then sighing heavily Achilleus of the swift feet answered her:
"My mother, all these things the Olympian° brought to accomplish-
    ment.
But what pleasure is this to me, since my dear companion has perished,
Patroklos, whom I loved beyond all other companions, 720
as well as my own life. I have lost him, and Hektor, who killed him,
has stripped away that gigantic armor, a wonder to look on
and splendid, which the gods gave Peleus, a glorious present,
on that day they drove you to the marriage bed of a mortal.°
I wish you had gone on living then with the other goddesses
of the sea, and that Peleus had married some mortal woman.
As it is, there must be on your heart a numberless sorrow
for your son's death, since you can never again receive him
won home again to his country; since the spirit within does not drive me
to go on living and be among men, except on condition 730
that Hektor first be beaten down under my spear, lose his life
and pay the price for stripping Patroklos, the son of Menoitios."
  Then in turn Thetis spoke to him, letting the tears fall:
"Then I must lose you soon, my child, by what you are saying,
since it is decreed your death must come soon after Hektor's."
  Then deeply disturbed Achilleus of the swift feet answered her:
"I must die soon, then; since I was not to stand by my companion
when he was killed. And now, far away from the land of his fathers,
he has perished, and lacked my fighting strength to defend him.
Now, since I am not going back to the beloved land of my fathers, 740
since I was no light of safety to Patroklos, nor to my other
companions, who in their numbers went down before glorious Hektor,
but sit here beside my ships, a useless weight on the good land,
I, who am such as no other of the bronze-armored Achaians
in battle, though there are others also better in council—
why, I wish that strife would vanish away from among gods and mortals,

718. Olympian: Zeus, as the supreme god on Mount Olympus. 724. mortal:
Achilles' father, Peleus, is a mortal; Peleus' wife, Thetis, is a deity.

and gall, which makes a man grow angry for all his great mind,
that gall of anger that swarms like smoke inside of a man's heart
and become a thing sweeter to him by far than the dripping of honey.
So it was here that the lord of men Agamemnon angered me.   750
Still, we will let all this be a thing of the past, and for all our
sorrow beat down by force the anger deeply within us.
Now I shall go, to overtake that killer of a dear life,
Hektor; then I will accept my own death, at whatever
time Zeus wishes to bring it about, and the other immortals.
For not even the strength of Herakles° fled away from destruction,
although he was dearest of all to lord Zeus, son of Kronos,
but his fate beat him under, and the wearisome anger of Hera.
So I likewise, if such is the fate which has been wrought for me,
shall lie still, when I am dead. Now I must win excellent glory,   760
and drive some one of the women of Troy, or some deep-girdled
Dardanian° woman, lifting up to her soft cheeks both hands
to wipe away the close bursts of tears in her lamentation,
and learn that I stayed too long out of the fighting. Do not
hold me back from the fight, though you love me. You will not per-
           suade me."
     In turn the goddess Thetis of the silver feet answered him:
"Yes, it is true, my child, this is no cowardly action,
to beat aside sudden death from your afflicted companions.
Yet, see now, your splendid armor, glaring and brazen,
is held among the Trojans, and Hektor of the shining helmet   770
wears it on his own shoulders, and glories in it. Yet I think
he will not glory for long, since his death stands very close to him.
Therefore do not yet go into the grind of the war god,
not before with your own eyes you see me come back to you.
For I am coming to you at dawn and as the sun rises
bringing splendid armor to you from the lord Hephaistos." . . .
     So her feet carried her to Olympos; meanwhile the Achaians
with inhuman clamor before the attack of manslaughtering Hektor
fled until they were making for their own ships and the Hellespont;
nor could the strong-greaved Achaians have dragged the body   780
of Patroklos, henchman of Achilleus, from under the missiles,
for once again the men and the horses came over upon him,
and Hektor, Priam's son, who fought like a flame in his fury.

---

756. *Herakles* (Hercules): a favorite son of Zeus by a human mother (Alcmena).
He was persecuted by Zeus's resentful wife, the goddess Hera, ultimately dying
from wounds caused by a poisoned cloak.   762. *Dardanian*: Trojan. Dardanus, a
legendary son of Zeus, was an ancestor of Priam and, through the Trojan warrior
Aineias (Aeneas), progenitor of the Romans.

Three times from behind glorious Hektor caught him
by the feet, trying to drag him, and called aloud on the Trojans.
Three times the two Aiantes with their battle-fury upon them
beat him from the corpse, but he, steady in the confidence of his great
    strength,
kept making, now a rush into the crowd, or again at another time
stood fast, with his great cry, but gave not a bit of ground backward.
And as herdsmen who dwell in the fields are not able to frighten   790
a tawny lion in his great hunger away from a carcass,
so the two Aiantes, marshals of men, were not able
to scare Hektor, Priam's son, away from the body.
And now he would have dragged it away and won glory forever
had not swift wind-footed Iris° come running from Olympos
with a message for Peleus' son to arm. She came secretly
from Zeus and the other gods, since it was Hera who sent her.
She came and stood close to him and addressed him in winged words:
"Rise up, son of Peleus, most terrifying of all men.
Defend Patroklos, for whose sake the terrible fighting   800
stands now in front of the ships. They are destroying each other;
the Achaians fight in defence over the fallen body
while the others, the Trojans, are rushing to drag the corpse off
to windy Ilion, and beyond all glorious Hektor
rages to haul it away, since the anger within him is urgent
to cut the head from the soft neck and set it on sharp stakes.
Up, then, lie here no longer; let shame come into your heart, lest
Patroklos become sport for the dogs of Troy to worry,
your shame, if the body goes from here with defilement upon it."
    Then in turn Achilleus of the swift feet answered her: 810
"Divine Iris, what god sent you to me with a message?"
    Then in turn swift wind-footed Iris spoke to him:
"Hera sent me, the honored wife of Zeus; but the son of
Kronos, who sits on high, does not know this, nor any other
immortal, of all those who dwell by the snows of Olympos."
    Then in answer to her spoke Achilleus of the swift feet:
"How shall I go into the fighting? They have my armor.
And my beloved mother told me I must not be armored,
not before with my own eyes I see her come back to me.
She promised she would bring magnificent arms from Hephaistos.   820
Nor do I know of another whose glorious armor I could wear
unless it were the great shield of Telamonian° Aias.
But he himself wears it, I think, and goes in the foremost

795. *Iris:* a messenger of the gods, especially of Zeus and Hera; divine embodiment
of the rainbow. 822. *Telamonian:* Aias (Ajax), the son of Telamon.

of the spear-fight over the body of fallen Patroklos."
    Then in turn swift wind-footed Iris spoke to him:
"Yes, we also know well how they hold your glorious armor.
But go to the ditch, and show yourself as you are to the Trojans,
if perhaps the Trojans might be frightened, and give way
from their attack, and the fighting sons of the Achaians get wind
again after hard work. There is little breathing space in the fighting."   830
    So speaking Iris of the swift feet went away from him;
but Achilleus, the beloved of Zeus, rose up, and Athene
swept about his powerful shoulders the fluttering aegis;
and she, the divine among goddesses, about his head circled
a golden cloud, and kindled from it a flame far-shining.
As when a flare goes up into the high air from a city
from an island far away, with enemies fighting about it
who all day long are in the hateful division of Ares°
fighting from their own city, but as the sun goes down signal
fires blaze out one after another, so that the glare goes   840
pulsing high for men of the neighboring islands to see it,
in case they might come over in ships to beat off the enemy;
so from the head of Achilleus the blaze shot into the bright air.
He went from the wall and stood by the ditch, nor mixed with the other
Achaians, since he followed the close command of his mother.
There he stood, and shouted, and from her place Pallas Athene
gave cry, and drove an endless terror upon the Trojans.
As loud as comes the voice that is screamed out by a trumpet
by murderous attackers who beleaguer a city,
so then high and clear went up the voice of Aiakides.°   850
But the Trojans, when they heard the brazen voice of Aiakides,
the heart was shaken in all, and the very floating-maned horses
turned their chariots about, since their hearts saw the coming afflictions.
The charioteers were dumbfounded as they saw the unwearied dangerous
        gerous
fire that played above the head of great-hearted Peleion°
blazing, and kindled by the goddess gray-eyed Athene.
Three times across the ditch brilliant Achilleus gave his great cry,
and three times the Trojans and their renowned companions were
        routed.
There at that time twelve of the best men among them perished
upon their own chariots and spears. Meanwhile the Achaians   860
gladly pulled Patroklos out from under the missiles

838. Ares: the god of warlike spirit and destruction. 850. Aiakides: Achilles;
literally, "descendant of Aiakos," who was Achilles' grandfather. 855. Peleion:
Achilles, son of Peleus.

and set him upon a litter, and his own companions about him
stood mourning, and along with them swift-footed Achilleus
went, letting fall warm tears as he saw his steadfast companion
lying there on a carried litter and torn with the sharp bronze,
the man he had sent off before with horses and chariot
into the fighting; who never again came home to be welcomed.
  Now the lady Hera of the ox eyes drove the unwilling
weariless sun god to sink in the depth of the Ocean,
and the sun went down, and the brilliant Achaians gave over   870
their strong fighting, and the doubtful collision of battle.
  The Trojans on the other side moved from the strong encounter
in their turn, and unyoked their running horses from under the chariots,
and gathered into assembly before taking thought for their supper.
They stood on their feet in assembly, nor did any man have the patience
to sit down, but the terror was on them all, seeing that Achilleus
had appeared, after he had stayed so long from the difficult fighting.
First to speak among them was the careful Poulydamas,°
Panthoös' son, who alone of them looked before and behind him.
He was companion to Hektor, and born on the same night with him,   880
but he was better in words, the other with the spear far better.
He in kind intention toward all stood forth and addressed them:
"Now take careful thought, dear friends; for I myself urge you
to go back into the city and not wait for the divine dawn
in the plain beside the ships. We are too far from the wall now.
While this man was still angry with great Agamemnon,
for all that time the Achaians were easier men to fight with.
For I also used then to be one who was glad to sleep out
near their ships, and I hoped to capture the oarswept vessels.
But now I terribly dread the swift-footed son of Peleus.   890
So violent is the valor in him, he will not be willing
to stay here in the plain, where now Achaians and Trojans
from either side sunder between them the wrath of the war god.
With him, the fight will be for the sake of our city and women.
Let us go into the town; believe me; thus it will happen.
For this present, immortal night has stopped the swift-footed
son of Peleus, but if he catches us still in this place
tomorrow, and drives upon us in arms, a man will be well
aware of him, be glad to get back into sacred Ilion,
the man who escapes; there will be many Trojans the vultures   900
and dogs will feed on. But let such a word be out of my hearing!
If all of us will do as I say, though it hurts us to do it,

878. *Poulydamas:* a Trojan warrior and prophet—hence "before and behind," i.e.,
future and past, in the next line. He frequently opposed Hektor's rash strategies.

this night we will hold our strength in the marketplace, and the great
    walls
and the gateways, and the long, smooth-planed, close-joined gate tim-
    bers
that close to fit them shall defend our city. Then, early
in the morning, under dawn, we shall arm ourselves in our war-gear
and take stations along the walls. The worse for him, if he endeavors
to come away from the ships and fight us here for our city.
Back he must go to his ships again, when he wears out the strong
    necks
of his horses, driving them at a gallop everywhere by the city.   910
His valor will not give him leave to burst in upon us
nor sack our town. Sooner the circling dogs will feed on him."
    Then looking darkly at him Hektor of the shining helm spoke:
"Poulydamas, these things that you argue please me no longer
when you tell us to go back again and be cooped in our city.
Have you not all had your glut of being fenced in our outworks?
There was a time when mortal men would speak of the city
of Priam as a place with much gold and much bronze. But now
the lovely treasures that lay away in our houses have vanished,
and many possessions have been sold and gone into Phrygia°   920
and into Maionia° the lovely, when great Zeus was angry.
But now, when the son of devious-devising Kronos has given
me the winning of glory by the ships, to pin the Achaians
on the sea, why, fool, no longer show these thoughts to our people.
Not one of the Trojans will obey you. I shall not allow it.
Come, then, do as I say and let us all be persuaded.
Now, take your supper by positions along the encampment,
and do not forget your watch, and let every man be wakeful.
And if any Trojan is strongly concerned about his possessions,
let him gather them and give them to the people, to use them in com-
    mon.   930
It is better for one of us to enjoy them than for the Achaians.
In the morning, under dawn, we shall arm ourselves in our war gear
and waken the bitter god of war by the hollow vessels.
If it is true that brilliant Achilleus is risen beside their
ships, then the worse for him if he tries it, since I for my part
will not run from him out of the sorrowful battle, but rather
stand fast, to see if he wins the great glory, or if I can win it.
The war god is impartial. Before now he has killed the killer."
    So spoke Hektor, and the Trojans thundered to hear him;

920–21. *Phrygia, Maionia:* territories to the east of Troy; allied with the Trojans.

fools, since Pallas Athene had taken away the wits from them.   940
They gave their applause to Hektor in his counsel of evil,
but none to Poulydamas, who had spoken good sense before them.
They took their supper along the encampment. Meanwhile the Achaians
mourned all night in lamentation over Patroklos.
Peleus' son led the thronging chant of their lamentation,
and laid his manslaughtering hands over the chest of his dear friend
with outbursts of incessant grief. As some great bearded lion
when some man, a deer hunter, has stolen his cubs away from him
out of the close wood; the lion comes back too late, and is anguished,
and turns into many valleys quartering after the man's trail   950
on the chance of finding him, and taken with bitter anger;
so he, groaning heavily, spoke out to the Myrmidons:
"Ah me. It was an empty word I cast forth on that day
when in his halls I tried to comfort the hero Menoitios.
I told him I would bring back his son in glory to Opous°
with Ilion sacked, and bringing his share of war spoils allotted.
But Zeus does not bring to accomplishment all thoughts in men's minds.
Thus it is destiny for us both to stain the same soil
here in Troy; since I shall never come home, and my father,
Peleus the aged rider, will not welcome me in his great house,   960
nor Thetis my mother, but in this place the earth will receive me.
But seeing that it is I, Patroklos, who follow you underground,
I will not bury you till I bring to this place the armor
and the head of Hektor, since he was your great-hearted murderer. . . .

*Achilleus' mother, Thetis, inspired in him a desire to resume fighting and
provided him with a shield made by the god Hephaistos. His return filled
the Trojans with terror; he killed every Trojan that crossed his path, raging
like a forest fire. But Apollo diverted him through a camouflage, while all
the Trojans except Hektor took refuge in their walled city. After a dramatic
duel Achilleus killed Hektor, tied the corpse to his chariot, and dragged it
through the dust back to the Greek camp as cries of pain and despair arose in
Troy. Through a prophecy Achilleus knew that he would die shortly after
Hektor's death; from this moment, the tragic nature of his violence becomes
particularly clear. After killing Hektor, Achilleus buried Patroklos, and the
Greeks celebrated Patroklos' fame with athletic games, for which Achilleus
gave costly prizes.*

955. *Opous:* city on the Greek mainland; home of Patroklos' father.

From BOOK XXIV

And the games broke up, and the people scattered to go away, each
    man
to his fast-running ship, and the rest of them took thought of their
    dinner
and of sweet sleep and its enjoyment; only Achilleus
wept still as he remembered his beloved companion, nor did sleep
who subdues all come over him, but he tossed from one side to the
    other
in longing for Patroklos, for his manhood and his great strength 970
and all the actions he had seen to the end with him, and the hardships
he had suffered; the wars of men; hard crossing of the big waters.
Remembering all these things he let fall the swelling tears, lying
sometimes along his side, sometimes on his back, and now again
prone on his face; then he would stand upright, and pace turning
in distraction along the beach of the sea, nor did dawn rising
escape him as she brightened across the sea and the beaches.
Then, when he had yoked running horses under the chariot
he would fasten Hektor behind the chariot, so as to drag him,
and draw him three times around the tomb of Menoitios' fallen 980
son,° then rest again in his shelter, and throw down the dead man
and leave him to lie sprawled on his face in the dust. But Apollo
had pity on him, though he was only a dead man, and guarded
the body from all ugliness, and hid all of it under the golden
aegis, so that it might not be torn when Achilleus dragged it.
    So Achilleus in his standing fury outraged great Hektor.
The blessed gods as they looked upon him were filled with compassion
and kept urging clear-sighted Argeïphontes° to steal the body.
There this was pleasing to all the others, but never to Hera
nor Poseidon,° nor the girl of the gray eyes,° who kept still 990
their hatred for sacred Ilion as in the beginning,
and for Priam and his people, because of the delusion° of Paris
who insulted the goddesses when they came to him in his courtyard
and favored her who supplied the lust that led to disaster. . . .

980–81. Menoitios' . . . son: Patroklos. *988. Argeïphontes:* an obscure title of
Hermes, a son of Zeus and Maia. He was the messenger of Zeus, famous for his
cunning and inventiveness. *990. Poseidon:* god of the sea and of earthquakes;
consistently pro-Greek in the Trojan War. *girl of the gray eyes:* Athene, also pro-
Greek in the war. *992–94. delusion . . . disaster:* Paris (Alexandros) was the
judge in a beauty contest between the goddesses Aphrodite (goddess of love and
beauty), Hera, and Athene. All three offered him attractive bribes, but Aphrodites'
offer to give him Helen, the wife of Menelaus, led Paris to declare Aphrodite the
winner.

The father of gods and men began the discourse among them:
"You have come to Olympos, divine Thetis, for all your sorrow,
with an unforgotten grief in your heart. I myself know this.
But even so I will tell you why I summoned you hither.
For nine days there has risen a quarrel among the immortals
over the body of Hektor, and Achilleus, stormer of cities.   1000
They keep urging clear-sighted Argeïphontes to steal the body,
but I still put upon Achilleus the honor that he has, guarding
your reverence and your love for me into time afterwards. Go then
in all speed to the encampment and give to your son this message:
tell him that the gods frown upon him, that beyond all other
immortals I myself am angered that in his heart's madness
he holds Hektor beside the curved ships and did not give him
back. Perhaps in fear of me he will give back Hektor.
Then I will send Iris to Priam of the great heart, with an order
to ransom his dear son, going down to the ships of the Achaians   1010
and bringing gifts to Achilleus which might soften his anger."
    He spoke and the goddess silver-foot Thetis did not disobey him
but descended in a flash of speed from the peaks of Olympos
and made her way to the shelter of her son, and there found him
in close lamentation, and his beloved companions about him
were busy at their work and made ready the morning meal, and there
stood a great fleecy sheep being sacrificed in the shelter.
His honored mother came close to him and sat down beside him,
and stroked him with her hand and called him by name and spoke to
        him:
"My child, how long will you go on eating your heart out in sorrow   1020
and lamentation, and remember neither your food nor going
to bed? It is a good thing even to lie with a woman
in love. For you will not be with me long, but already
death and powerful destiny stand closely above you.
But listen hard to me, for I come from Zeus with a message.
He says that the gods frown upon you, that beyond all other
immortals he himself is angered that in your heart's madness
you hold Hektor beside the curved ships and did not redeem him.
Come, then, give him up and accept ransom for the body."
    Then in turn Achilleus of the swift feet answered her: 1030
"So be it. He can bring the ransom and take off the body,
if the Olympian himself so urgently bids it."
    So, where the ships were drawn together, the son and his mother
conversed at long length in winged words. But the son of Kronos
stirred Iris to go down to sacred Ilion. . . .
    He spoke, and storm-footed Iris swept away with the message

and came to the house of Priam. There she found outcry and mourning.
The sons sitting around their father inside the courtyard
made their clothes sodden with their tears, and among them the old man
sat veiled, beaten into his mantle. Dung lay thick   1040
on the head and neck of the aged man, for he had been rolling
in it, he had gathered and smeared it on with his hands. And his
     daughters
all up and down the house and the wives of his sons were mourning
as they remembered all those men in their numbers and valor
who lay dead, their lives perished at the hands of the Argives.
The messenger of Zeus stood beside Priam and spoke to him
in a small voice, and yet the shivers took hold of his body:
"Take heart, Priam, son° of Dardanos, do not be frightened.
I come to you not eyeing you with evil intention
but with the purpose of good toward you. I am a messenger   1050
of Zeus, who far away cares much for you and is pitiful.
The Olympian orders you to ransom Hektor the brilliant,
to bring gifts to Achilleus which may soften his anger:
alone, let no other man of the Trojans go with you, but only
let one elder herald attend you, one who can manage
the mules and the easily running wagon, so he can carry
the dead man, whom great Achilleus slew, back to the city.
Let death not be a thought in your heart, you need have no fear,
such an escort shall go with you to guide you, Argeïphontes
who will lead you till he brings you to Achilleus. And after   1060
he has brought you inside the shelter of Achilleus, neither
will the man himself kill you but will hold back all the others;
for he is no witless man nor unwatchful, nor is he wicked
but will in all kindness spare one who comes to him as a suppliant."
    So Iris the swift-footed spoke and went away from him.
Thereupon he ordered his sons to make ready the easily rolling
mule wagon, and to fasten upon it the carrying basket.
He himself went into the storeroom, which was fragrant
and of cedar, and high-ceilinged, with many bright treasures inside it.
He called out to Hekabe his wife,° and said to her: 1070
"Dear wife, a messenger came to me from Zeus on Olympos,
that I must go to the ships of the Achaians and ransom my dear son,
bringing gifts to Achilleus which may soften his anger.
Come then, tell me. What does it seem best to your own mind
for me to do? My heart, my strength are terribly urgent
that I go there to the ships within the wide army of the Achaians."

1048. son: more accurately, "descendant." *1070. Hekabe his wife:* mother of
Hektor and Paris.

So he spoke, and his wife cried out aloud, and answered him:
"Ah me, where has that wisdom gone for which you were famous
in time before, among outlanders and those you rule over?
How can you wish to go alone to the ships of the Achaians   1080
before the eyes of a man who has slaughtered in such numbers
such brave sons of yours? The heart in you is iron. For if
he has you within his grasp and lays eyes upon you, that man
who is savage and not to be trusted will not take pity upon you
nor have respect for your rights. Let us sit apart in our palace
now, and weep for Hektor, and the way at the first strong Destiny
spun with his life line when he was born, when I gave birth to him,
that the dogs with their shifting feet should feed on him, far from his
        parents, . . ."
    In turn the aged Priam, the godlike, answered her saying:
"Do not hold me back when I would be going, neither yourself be   1090
a bird of bad omen in my palace. You will not persuade me.
If it had been some other who ordered me, one of the mortals,
one of those who are soothsayers, or priests, or diviners,
I might have called it a lie and we might rather have rejected it.
But now, for I myself heard the god and looked straight upon her,
I am going, and this word shall not be in vain. If it is my destiny
to die there by the ships of the bronze-armored Achaians,
then I wish that. Achilleus can slay me at once, with my own son
caught in my arms, once I have my fill of mourning above him."
    He spoke, and lifted back the fair covering of his clothes-chest   1100
and from inside took out twelve robes surpassingly lovely
and twelve mantles to be worn single, as many blankets,
as many great white cloaks, also the same number of tunics.
He weighed and carried out ten full talents of gold, and brought forth
two shining tripods, and four cauldrons, and brought out a goblet
of surpassing loveliness that the men of Thrace° had given him
when he went to them with a message, but now the old man spared not
even this in his halls, so much was it his heart's desire
to ransom back his beloved son. But he drove off the Trojans
all from his cloister walks, scolding them with words of revilement: 1110
"Get out, you failures, you disgraces. Have you not also
mourning of your own at home that you come to me with your sorrows?
Is it not enough that Zeus, son of Kronos, has given me sorrow
in losing the best of my sons? You also shall be aware of this
since you will be all the easier for the Achaians to slaughter
now he is dead. But, for myself, before my eyes look

1106. *Thrace:* a Balkan territory bordering on the northeast Aegean Sea.

upon this city as it is destroyed and its people are slaughtered,
my wish is to go sooner down to the house of the death god."
 He spoke, and went after the men with a stick, and they fled outside
before the fury of the old man. He was scolding his children   1120
and cursing Helenos, and Paris, Agathon the brilliant,
Pammon and Antiphonos, Polites of the great war cry,
Deïphobos and Hippothoös and proud Dios. There were nine
sons to whom now the old man gave orders and spoke to them
   roughly. . . .
Then they carried out and piled into the smooth-polished mule wagon
all the unnumbered spoils to be given for the head of Hektor,
then yoked the powerful-footed mules who pulled in the harness
and whom the Mysians° gave once as glorious presents to Priam;
but for Priam they led under the yoke those horses the old man
himself had kept, and cared for them at his polished manger.   1130
 Now in the high house the yoking was done for the herald
and Priam, men both with close counsels in their minds. And now came
Hekabe with sorrowful heart and stood close beside them
carrying in her right hand the kind, sweet wine in a golden
goblet, so that before they went they might pour a drink-offering.
She stood in front of the horses, called Priam by name and spoke to
   him:
"Here, pour a libation to Zeus father, and pray you may come back
home again from those who hate you, since it seems the spirit
within you drives you upon the ships, though I would not have it.
Make your prayer then to the dark-misted, the son of Kronos   1140
on Ida,° who looks out on all the Troad, and ask him
for a bird of omen, a rapid messenger, which to his own mind
is dearest of all birds and his strength is the biggest, one seen
on the right, so that once your eyes have rested upon him
you can trust in him and go to the ships of the fast-mounted Danaans.
But if Zeus of the wide brows will not grant you his own messenger,
then I, for one, would never urge you on nor advise you
to go to the Argive ships, for all your passion to do it."
 Then in answer to her again spoke Priam the godlike:
"My lady, I will not disregard this wherein you urge me.   1150
It is well to lift hands to Zeus and ask if he will have mercy."
 The old man spoke, and told the housekeeper who attended them
to pour unstained water over his hands. She standing beside them
and serving them held the washing bowl in her hands, and a pitcher.
He washed his hands and took the cup from his wife. He stood up

1128. *Mysians:* Trojan allies from a territory to the east of Troy. 1141. *Ida:* a
mountain range east of Troy. *Troad:* the region of which Troy was the chief city.

in the middle of the enclosure, and prayed, and poured the wine out
looking up into the sky, and gave utterance and spoke, saying:
"Father Zeus, watching over us from Ida, most high, most honored:
grant that I come to Achilleus for love and pity; but send me
a bird of omen, a rapid messenger which to your own mind   1160
is dearest of all birds and his strength is the biggest, one seen
on the right, so that once my eyes have rested upon him
I may trust in him and go to the ships of the fast-mounted Danaans."
   So he spoke in prayer, and Zeus of the counsels heard him.
Straightway he sent down the most lordly of birds, an eagle,
the dark one, the marauder, called as well the black eagle.
And as big as is the build of the door to a towering chamber
in the house of a rich man, strongly fitted with bars, of such size
was the spread of his wings on either side. He swept through the city
appearing on the right hand, and the people looking upon him   1170
were uplifted and the hearts made glad in the breasts of all of them.
   Now in urgent haste the old man mounted into his chariot
and drove out through the forecourt and the thundering close. Before
       him
the mules hauled the wagon on its four wheels, Idaios°
the sober-minded driving them, and behind him the horses
came on as the old man laid the lash upon them and urged them
rapidly through the town, and all his kinsmen were following
much lamenting, as if he went to his death. When the two men
had gone down through the city, and out, and come to the flat land,
the rest of them turned back to go to Ilion   1180
   Now when the two had driven past the great tomb of Ilos°
they stayed their mules and horses to water them in the river,
for by this time darkness had descended on the land; and the herald °
made out Hermes, who was coming toward them at a short distance.
He lifted his voice and spoke aloud to Priam: "Take thought,
son of Dardanos. Here is work for a mind that is careful.
I see a man; I think he will presently tear us to pieces.
Come then, let us run away with our horses, or if not, then
clasp his knees and entreat him to have mercy upon us."
   So he spoke, and the old man's mind was confused, he was badly   1190
frightened, and the hairs stood up all over his gnarled body
and he stood staring, but the kindly god himself coming closer
took the old man's hand, and spoke to him and asked him a question:

1174. *Idaios:* Priam's herald (and here his chariot driver).   1181. *Ilos:* Priam's
grandfather. Troy was probably named "Ilios" and "Ilion" after him; the *Iliad* in
turn derives its name from "Ilion," i.e., "The Poem About Ilion."   1183. *herald:*
Priam's herald, Idaios.

"Where, my father, are you thus guiding your mules and horses
through the immortal night while other mortals are sleeping?
Have you no fear of the Achaians whose wind is fury,
who hate you, who are your enemies, and are near? For if one
of these were to see you, how you are conveying so many
treasures through the swift black night, what then could you think of?
You are not young yourself, and he who attends you is aged   1200
for beating off any man who might pick a quarrel with you.
But I will do you no harm myself, I will even keep off
another who would. You seem to me like a beloved father." . . .
    The kind god spoke, and sprang up behind the horses and into
the chariot, and rapidly caught in his hands the lash and the guide
      reins,
and breathed great strength into the mules and horses. Now after
they had got to the fortifications about the ships, and the ditch, there
were sentries, who had just begun to make ready their dinner,
but about these the courier Argeïphontes drifted
sleep, on all, and quickly opened the gate, and shoved back   1210
the door-bars, and brought in Priam and the glorious gifts on the wagon.
But when they had got to the shelter of Peleus' son: a towering
shelter the Myrmidons had built for their king, hewing
the timbers of pine, and they made a roof of thatch above it
shaggy with grass that they had gathered out of the meadows;
and around it made a great courtyard for their king, with hedgepoles
set close together; the gate was secured by a single door-piece
of pine, and three Achaians could ram it home in its socket
and three could pull back and open the huge door-bar; three other
Achaians, that is, but Achilleus all by himself could close it.   1220
At this time Hermes, the kind god, opened the gate for the old man
and brought in the glorious gifts for Peleus' son, the swift-footed,
and dismounted to the ground from behind the horses, and spoke forth:
"Aged sir, I who came to you am a god immortal,
Hermes. My father sent me down to guide and go with you.
But now I am going back again, and I will not go in
before the eyes of Achilleus, for it would make others angry
for an immortal god so to face mortal men with favor.
But go you in yourself and clasp the knees of Peleion
and entreat him in the name of his father, the name of his mother   1230
of the lovely hair, and his child, and so move the spirit within him."
    So Hermes spoke, and went away to the height of Olympos,
but Priam vaulted down to the ground from behind the horses
and left Idaios where he was, for he stayed behind, holding

in hand the horses and mules. The old man made straight for the
    dwelling
where Achilleus the beloved of Zeus was sitting. He found him
inside, and his companions were sitting apart, as two only,
Automedon° the hero and Alkimos,° scion of Ares,
were busy beside him. He had just now got through with his dinner,
with eating and drinking, and the table still stood by. Tall Priam   1240
came in unseen by the other men and stood close beside him
and caught the knees of Achilleus in his arms, and kissed the hands
that were dangerous and manslaughtering and had killed so many
of his sons. As when dense disaster closes on one who has murdered
a man in his own land, and he comes to the country of others,
to a man of substance, and wonder seizes on those who behold him,
so Achilleus wondered as he looked on Priam, a godlike
man, and the rest of them wondered also, and looked at each other.
But now Priam spoke to him in the words of a suppliant:
"Achilleus like the gods, remember your father, one who   1250
is of years like mine, and on the doorsill of sorrowful old age.
And they who dwell nearby encompass him and afflict him,
nor is there any to defend him against the wrath, the destruction.
Yet surely he, when he hears of you and that you are still living,
is gladdened within his heart and all his days he is hopeful
that he will see his beloved son come home from the Troad.°
But for me, my destiny was evil. I have had the noblest
of sons in Troy, but I say not one of them is left to me.
Fifty were my sons, when the sons of the Achaians came here.
Nineteen were born to me from the womb of a single mother,   1260
and other women bore the rest in my palace; and of these
violent Ares broke the strength in the knees of most of them,
but one was left me who guarded my city and people, that one
you killed a few days since as he fought in defense of his country,
Hektor; for whose sake I come now to the ships of the Achaians
to win him back from you, and I bring you gifts beyond number.
Honor then the gods, Achilleus, and take pity upon me
remembering your father, yet I am still more pitiful;
I have gone through what no other mortal on earth has gone through;
I put my lips to the hands of the man who has killed my children."   1270
    So he spoke, and stirred in the other a passion of grieving
for his own father. He took the old man's hand and pushed him
gently away, and the two remembered, as Priam sat huddled

1238. *Automedon:* charioteer of Achilleus and Patroklos; outstanding Greek
warrior. *Alkimos:* a favorite companion of Achilleus; one of the Myrmidons.

at the feet of Achilleus and wept close for manslaughtering Hektor
and Achilleus wept now for his own father, now again
for Patroklos. The sound of their mourning moved in the house. Then
when great Achilleus had taken full satisfaction in sorrow
and the passion for it had gone from his mind and body, thereafter
he rose from his chair, and took the old man by the hand, and set him
on his feet again, in pity for the gray head and the gray beard,   1280
and spoke to him and addressed him in winged words: "Ah, unlucky,
surely you have had much evil to endure in your spirit.
How could you dare to come alone to the ships of the Achaians
and before my eyes, when I am one who have killed in such numbers
such brave sons of yours? The heart in you is iron. Come, then,
and sit down upon this chair, and you and I will even let
our sorrows lie still in the heart for all our grieving. There is not
any advantage to be won from grim lamentation.
Such is the way the gods spun life for unfortunate mortals,
that we live in unhappiness, but the gods themselves have no sorrows.   1290
There are two urns that stand on the doorsill of Zeus. They are unlike
for the gifts they bestow: an urn of evils, an urn of blessings.
If Zeus who delights in thunder mingles these and bestows them
on man, he shifts, and moves now in evil, again in good fortune.
But when Zeus bestows from the urn of sorrows, he makes a failure
of man, and the evil hunger drives him over the shining
earth, and he wanders respected neither of gods nor mortals.
Such were the shining gifts given by the gods to Peleus
from his birth, who outshone all men beside for his riches
and pride of possession, and was lord over the Myrmidons. Thereto   1300
the gods bestowed an immortal wife on him, who was mortal.
But even on him the god piled evil also. There was not
any generation of strong sons born to him in his great house
but a single all-untimely child he had, and I give him
no care as he grows old, since far from the land of my fathers
I sit here in Troy, and bring nothing but sorrow to you and your
     children.
And you, old sir, we are told you prospered once; for as much
as Lesbos,° Makar's hold, confines to the north above it
and Phrygia from the north confines, and enormous Hellespont,°
of these, old sir, you were lord once in your wealth and your children.   1310

1308–09. *Lesbos . . . Hellespont:* an area ranging from the Aegean island of
Lesbos (southwest of Troy) to the western Anatolian plain east of Troy, and to the
north as far as the Dardanelles.   1309. *Hellespont:* now known as the Dardanelles, a strait just north of Troy.

But now the Uranian gods brought us, an affliction upon you,
forever there is fighting about your city, and men killed.
But bear up, nor mourn endlessly in your heart, for there is not
anything to be gained from grief for your son; you will never
bring him back; sooner you must go through yet another sorrow."
    In answer to him again spoke aged Priam the godlike:
"Do not, beloved of Zeus, make me sit on a chair while Hektor
lies yet forlorn among the shelters; rather with all speed
give him back, so my eyes may behold him, and accept the ransom
we bring you, which is great. You may have joy of it, and go back   1320
to the land of your own fathers, since once you have permitted me
to go on living myself and continue to look on the sunlight."
    Then looking darkly at him spoke swift-footed Achilleus:
"No longer stir me up, old sir. I myself am minded
to give Hektor back to you. A messenger came to me from Zeus,
my mother, she who bore me, the daughter of the sea's ancient.
I know you, Priam, in my heart, and it does not escape me
that some god led you to the running ships of the Achaians.
For no mortal would dare come to our encampment, not even
one strong in youth. He could not get by the pickets, he could not   1330
lightly unbar the bolt that secures our gateway. Therefore
you must not further make my spirit move in my sorrows,
for fear, old sir, I might not let you alone in my shelter,
suppliant as you are; and be guilty before the god's orders."
    He spoke, and the old man was frightened and did as he told him.
The son of Peleus bounded to the door of the house like a lion,
nor went alone, but the two henchmen followed attending,
the hero Automedon and Alkimos, those whom Achilleus
honored beyond all companions after Patroklos dead. These two
now set free from under the yoke the mules and the horses,   1340
and led inside the herald, the old king's crier, and gave him
a chair to sit in, then from the smooth-polished mule wagon
lifted out the innumerable spoils for the head of Hektor,
but left inside it two great cloaks and a finespun tunic
to shroud the corpse in when they carried him home. Then Achilleus
called out to his serving maids to wash the body and anoint it
all over; but take it first aside, since otherwise Priam
might see his son and in the heart's sorrow not hold in his anger
at the sight, and the deep heart in Achilleus be shaken to anger;
that he might not kill Priam and be guilty before the god's orders.   1350
Then when the serving maids had washed the corpse and anointed it
with olive oil, they threw a fair great cloak and a tunic

about him, and Achilleus himself lifted him and laid him
on a litter, and his friends helped him lift it to the smooth-polished
mule wagon. He groaned then, and called by name on his beloved
     companion:
"Be not angry with me, Patroklos, if you discover,
though you be in the house of Hades, that I gave back great Hecktor
to his loved father, for the ransom he gave me was not unworthy.
I will give you your share of the spoils, as much as is fitting."

So spoke great Achilleus and went back into the shelter   1360
and sat down on the elaborate couch from which he had risen,
against the inward wall, and now spoke his word to Priam:
"Your son is given back to you, aged sir, as you asked it.
He lies on a bier. When dawn shows you yourself shall see him
as you take him away. Now you and I must remember our supper.
For even Niobe,° she of the lovely tresses, remembered
to eat, whose twelve children were destroyed in her palace,
six daughters, and six sons in the pride of their youth, whom Apollo
killed with arrows from his silver bow, being angered
with Niobe, and shaft-showering Artemis killed the daughters;   1370
because Niobe likened herself to Leto of the fair coloring
and said Leto had borne only two, she herself had borne many;
but the two, though they were only two, destroyed all those others.
Nine days long they lay in their blood, nor was there anyone
to bury them, for the son of Kronos made stones out of
the people; but on the tenth day the Uranian gods buried them.
But she remembered to eat when she was worn out with weeping.
And now somewhere among the rocks, in the lonely mountains,
in Sipylos, where they say is the resting place of the goddesses
who are nymphs, and dance beside the waters of Acheloios,   1380
there, stone still, she broods on the sorrows that the gods gave her.
Come then, we also, aged magnificent sir, must remember
to eat, and afterwards you may take your beloved son back
to Ilion, and mourn for him; and he will be much lamented."

So spoke fleet Achilleus and sprang to his feet and slaughtered
a gleaming sheep, and his friends skinned it and butchered it fairly,
and cut up the meat expertly into small pieces, and spitted them,
and roasted all carefully and took off the pieces.
Automedon took the bread and set it out on the table

1366. *Niobe:* a daughter of Tantalus, the ancestor of Agamemnon and Menelaus.
She was so proud of the large number of her children that she thought herself
superior to the goddess Leto, mother of Apollo and Artemis. After the destruction
of Niobe's children by Artemis and Apollo, Zeus changed her into a rock on
Mount Sipylus in Lydia, east of Troy, which shed tears in the summer.

in fair baskets, while Achilleus served the meats. And thereon   1390
they put their hands to the good things that lay ready before them.
But when they had put aside their desire for eating and drinking,
Priam, son of Dardanos, gazed upon Achilleus, wondering
at his size and beauty, for he seemed like an outright vision
of gods. Achilleus in turn gazed on Dardanian Priam
and wondered, as he saw his brave looks and listened to him talking.
But when they had taken their fill of gazing one on the other,
first of the two to speak was the aged man, Priam the godlike:
"Give me, beloved of Zeus, a place to sleep presently, so that
we may even go to bed and take the pleasure of sweet sleep.   1400
For my eyes have not closed underneath my lids since that time
when my son lost his life beneath your hands, but always
I have been grieving and brooding over my numberless sorrows
and wallowed in the muck about my courtyard's enclosure.
Now I have tasted food again and have let the gleaming
wine go down my throat. Before, I had tasted nothing."
     He spoke, and Achilleus ordered his serving maids and companions
to make a bed in the porch's shelter and to lay upon it
fine underbedding of purple, and spread blankets above it
and fleecy robes to be an overall covering. The maidservants   1410
went forth from the main house, and in their hands held torches,
and set to work, and presently had two beds made. Achilleus
of the swift feet now looked at Priam and said, sarcastic:
"Sleep outside, aged sir and good friend, for fear some Achaian
might come in here on a matter of counsel, since they keep coming
and sitting by me and making plans; as they are supposed to.
But if one of these come through the fleeting black night should notice
          you,
he would go straight and tell Agamemnon, shepherd of the people,
and there would be delay in the ransoming of the body.
But come, tell me this and count off for me exactly   1420
how many days you intend for the burial of great Hektor.
Tell me, so I myself shall stay still and hold back the people."
     In answer to him again spoke aged Priam the godlike:
"If you are willing that we accomplish a complete funeral
for great Hektor, this, Achilleus, is what you could do and give
me pleasure. For you know surely how we are penned in our city,
and wood is far to bring in from the hills, and the Trojans are fright-
          ened
badly. Nine days we would keep him in our palace and mourn him,
and bury him on the tenth day, and the people feast by him,
and on the eleventh day we would make the grave-barrow for him,

and on the twelfth day fight again; if so we must do."
Then in turn swift-footed brilliant Achilleus answered him:
"Then all this, aged Priam, shall be done as you ask it.
I will hold off our attack for as much time as you bid me."
So he spoke, and took the aged king by the right hand
at the wrist, so that his heart might have no fear. Then these two,
Priam and the herald who were both men of close counsel,
slept in the place outside the house, in the porch's shelter;
but Achilleus slept in the inward corner of the strong-built shelter,
and at his side lay Briseis of the fair coloring.   1440
Now the rest of the gods and men who were lords of chariots
slept nightlong, with the easy bondage of slumber upon them,
only sleep had not caught Hermes the kind god, who pondered
now in his heart the problem of how to escort King Priam
from the ships and not be seen by the devoted gate-wardens.
He stood above his head and spoke a word to him, saying:
"Aged sir, you can have no thought of evil from the way
you sleep still among your enemies now Achilleus has left you
unharmed. You have ransomed now your dear son and given much for
          him.
But the sons you left behind would give three times as much ransom   1450
for you, who are alive, were Atreus' son Agamemnon
to recognize you, and all the other Achaians learn of you."
He spoke, and the old man was afraid, and wakened his herald,
and lightly Hermes harnessed for them the mules and the horses
and himself drove them through the encampment. And no man knew
          of them.
But when they came to the crossing-place of the fair-running river,
of whirling Xanthos,° a stream whose father was Zeus the immortal,
there Hermes left them and went away to the height of Olympos,
and dawn, she of the yellow robe, scattered over all earth,
and they drove their horses on to the city with lamentation   1460
and clamor, while the mules drew the body. Nor was any other
aware of them at the first, no man, no fair-girdled woman,
only Kassandra,° a girl like Aphrodite the golden,
who had gone up to the height of the Pergamos. She saw
her dear father standing in the chariot, his herald and crier
with him. She saw Hektor drawn by the mules on a litter.
She cried out then in sorrow and spoke to the entire city:
"Come, men of Troy and Trojan women; look upon Hektor

1457. *Xanthos:* another name for the river Skamandros.   1463. *Kassandra:* Hektor's sister, a daughter of Priam and Hekabe, and a Trojan prophetess.

if ever before you were joyful when you saw him come back living
from battle; for he was a great joy to his city, and all his people." 1470
    She spoke, and there was no man left there in all the city
nor woman, but all were held in sorrow passing endurance.
They met Priam beside the gates as he brought the dead in.
First among them were Hektor's wife and his honored mother
who tore their hair, and ran up beside the smooth-rolling wagon,
and touched his head. And the multitude, wailing, stood there about
        them.
And now and there in front of the gates they would have lamented
all day till the sun went down and let fall their tears for Hektor,
except that the old man spoke from the chariot to his people:
"Give me way to get through with my mules; then afterwards 1480
you may sate yourselves with mourning, when I have him inside the
        palace."
    So he spoke, and they stood apart and made way for the wagon.
And when they had brought him inside the renowned house, they laid
        him
then on a carved bed, and seated beside him the singers
who were to lead the melody in the dirge, and the singers
chanted the song of sorrow, and the women were mourning beside
        them.
Andromache of the white arms led the lamentation
of the women, and held in her arms the head of manslaughtering
        Hektor:
"My husband, you were lost young from life, and have left me
a widow in your house, and the boy is only a baby 1490
who was born to you and me, the unhappy. I think he will never
come of age, for before then head to heel this city
will be sacked, for you, its defender, are gone, you who guarded
the city, and the grave wives, and the innocent children,
wives who before long must go away in the hollow ships,
and among them I shall also go, and you, my child, follow
where I go, and there do much hard work that is unworthy
of you, drudgery for a hard master; or else some Achaian
will take you by hand and hurl you from the tower into horrible
death,° in anger because Hektor once killed his brother, 1500
or his father, or his son; there were so many Achaians
whose teeth bit the vast earth, beaten down by the hands of Hektor.
Your father was no merciful man in the horror of battle.

1499–1500. *hurl . . . death:* After the Greeks captured Troy, Astyanax was
thrown to death from the city walls.

Therefore your people are grieving for you all through their city,
Hektor, and you left for your parents mourning and sorrow
beyond words, but for me passing all others is left the bitterness
and the pain, for you did not die in bed, and stretch your arms to me,
nor tell me some last intimate word that I could remember
always, all the nights and days of my weeping for you."

So she spoke in tears, and the women were mourning about her.   1510
Now Hekabe led out the thronging chant of their sorrow:
"Hektor, of all my sons the dearest by far to my spirit;
while you still lived for me you were dear to the gods, and even
in the stage of death they cared about you still. There were others
of my sons whom at times swift-footed Achilleus captured,
and he would sell them as slaves far across the unresting salt water
into Samos, and Imbros, and Lemnos in the gloom of the mists. You,
when he had taken your life with the thin edge of the bronze sword,
he dragged again and again around his beloved companion's
tomb, Patroklos', whom you killed, but even so did not   1520
bring him back to life. Now you lie in the palace, handsome
and fresh with dew, in the likeness of one whom he of the silver
bow, Apollo, has attacked and killed with his gentle arrows."

So she spoke, in tears, and wakened the endless mourning.
Third and last Helen led the song of sorrow among them:
"Hektor, of all my lord's brothers dearest by far to my spirit:
my husband is Alexandros, like an immortal, who brought me
here to Troy; and I should have died before I came with him;
and here now is the twentieth year upon me since I came
from the place where I was, forsaking the land of my fathers. In this
          time   1530
I have never heard a harsh saying from you, nor an insult.
No, but when another, one of my lord's brothers or sisters, a fair-robed
wife of some brother, would say a harsh word to me in the palace,
or my lord's mother—but his father was gentle always, a father
indeed—then you would speak and put them off and restrain them
by your own gentleness of heart and your gentle words. Therefore
I mourn for you in sorrow of heart and mourn myself also
and my ill luck. There was no other in all the wide Troad
who was kind to me, and my friend; all others shrank when they saw
          me."

So she spoke in tears, and the vast populace grieved with her.   1540
Now Priam the aged king spoke forth his word to his people:
"Now, men of Troy, bring timber into the city, and let not
your hearts fear a close ambush of the Argives. Achilleus
promised me, as he sent me on my way from the black ships,

that none should do us injury until the twelfth dawn comes."
    He spoke, and they harnessed to the wagons their mules and their
        oxen
and presently were gathered in front of the city. Nine days
they spent bringing in an endless supply of timber. But when
the tenth dawn had shone forth with her light upon mortals,
they carried out bold Hektor, weeping, and set the body   1550
aloft a towering pyre for burning. And set fire to it.
    But when the young dawn showed again with her rosy fingers,
the people gathered around the pyre of illustrious Hektor.
But when all were gathered to one place and assembled together,
first with gleaming wine they put out the pyre that was burning,
all where the fury of the fire still was in force, and thereafter
the brothers and companions of Hektor gathered the white bones
up, mourning, as the tears swelled and ran down their cheeks. Then
they laid what they had gathered up in a golden casket
and wrapped this about with soft robes of purple, and presently   1560
put it away in the hollow of the grave, and over it
piled huge stones laid close together. Lightly and quickly
they piled up the grave-barrow, and on all sides were set watchmen
for fear the strong-greaved Achaians might too soon set upon them.
They piled up the grave-barrow and went away, and thereafter
assembled in a fair gathering and held a glorious
feast within the house of Priam, king under God's hand.
    Such was their burial of Hektor, breaker of horses.

The Odyssey

TRANSLATED BY GEORGE HERBERT PALMER

The second, and perhaps slightly later, Homeric epic *The Odyssey*, deals with the prolonged return of Odysseus to his home on Ithaca, an island off the western coast of Greece, after an absence of ten years in the Trojan war. His hazardous journey lasted another ten years and was constantly obstructed by physical dangers, emotional trials, and sexual temptations. The *Odyssey* is set in a period of about six weeks of the tenth year but, as in the *Iliad*, the past and future are frequently introduced into the narrative. The opening scene of the poem is on Ithaca, where Odysseus' wife, Penelope, and his son, Telemachus, are faithfully awaiting him.

BOOK I

Speak to me, Muse, of the adventurous man who wandered long after he sacked the sacred citadel of Troy. Many the men whose towns he saw, whose ways he proved; and many a pang he bore in his own breast at sea while struggling for his life and his men's safe return. Yet even so, by all his zeal, he did not save his men; for through their own perversity they perished— fools! who devoured the kine[1] of the exalted Sun. Wherefore he took away the day of their return. Of this, O goddess, daughter of Zeus,[2] beginning where thou wilt, speak to us also.

Now all the others who were saved from utter ruin were at home, safe both from war and sea. Him only, longing for his home and wife, the potent nymph Calypso, a heavenly goddess, held in her hollow grotto, desiring him to be her husband. Nay, when the time had come in the revolving years at which the gods ordained his going home to Ithaca, even then, among his kin,

---

[1] Cattle. The men accompanying Odysseus on his journey from Troy slaughtered some cattle of the Sun although they had been warned beforehand against doing so. In retaliation, the Sun killed them in an incident described below (Book XII p. 106.).   [2] The Muse, who speaks through the poet.

he was not freed from trouble. Yet the gods felt compassion, all save Poseidon,[3] who steadily strove with godlike Odysseus till he reached his land.

But Poseidon now was with the far-off Ethiopians,[4] the remotest of mankind, who form two tribes, one at the setting of the Exalted one,[5] one at his rising; awaiting there a sacrifice of bulls and rams. So sitting at the feast he took his pleasure. The other gods, meanwhile, were gathered in the halls of Zeus upon Olympus, and thus began the father of men and gods; for in his mind he mused of gentle Aegisthus, whom Agamemnon's far-famed son, Orestes, slew.[6] Mindful of him, he thus addressed the immortals:

"Lo, how men blame the gods! From us, they say, spring troubles. But through their own perversity, and more than is their due, they meet with sorrow; even as now Aegisthus, pressing beyond his due, married the lawful wife of the son of Atreus and slew her husband on his coming home. Yet he well knew his own impending ruin; for we ourselves forewarned him, dispatching Hermes, our clear-sighted Speedy-comer, and told him not to slay the man nor woo the wife. 'For because of the son of Atreus shall come vengeance from Orestes when he is grown and longs for his own land.' This Hermes said, but did not turn the purpose of Aegisthus by his kindness. And now Aegisthus makes atonement for it all."

Then answered him the goddess, clear-eyed Athene: "Our father, son of Kronos, most high above all rulers, that man assuredly lies in befitting ruin. So perish all who do such deeds! Yet is my heart distressed for wise Odysseus,[7] hapless man, who, long cut off from friends, is meeting hardship upon a sea-girt island, the navel of the sea.[8] Woody the island is, and there a goddess[9] dwells, daughter of wizard Atlas who knows the depths of every sea and through his power holds the tall pillars which keep earth and sky asunder.[10] It is his daughter who detains this hapless, sorrowing man, ever with tender and insistent words enticing to forgetfulness of Ithaca. And still Odysseus, through longing but to see the smoke spring from his land, desires to die. Nevertheless, your heart turns not, Olympian one. Did not Odysseus seek your favor beside the Argive ships and offer sacrifice upon the plain of Troy? Why then are you so wroth against him, Zeus?"

Then answered her cloud-gathering Zeus, and said: "My child, what

---

[3] Poseidon is the god of the sea and of earthquakes. [4] The Ethiopians were believed to live at the end of the world. [5] Hyperion, i.e., the Sun. [6] Orestes, the son of Agamemnon and Clytemnestra, avenged his father's death by killing his uncle, Aegisthus, the lover of his mother. A somewhat different version of the myth than the one given here by Homer is dramatized in Aeschylus' *Agamemnon*. [7] Already in the *Iliad* Odysseus was Athene's favorite. [8] Ogygia, an island in the central Mediterranean. [9] The nymph Calypso. [10] Atlas (literally, "The Sustainer") was a divinity who had been inhospitable to another god and was therefore turned into Mount Atlas in northwest Africa and condemned to bear the heavens on his head and hands.

word has passed the barrier of your teeth? How could I possibly forget princely Odysseus, who is beyond all mortal men in wisdom, beyond them too in giving honor to the immortal gods, who hold the open sky? Nay, but Poseidon, the girder of the land, is ceaselessly enraged because Odysseus blinded of his eye the Cyclops, godlike Polyphemus, who of all Cyclops has the greatest power.[11] A nymph, Thoösa, bore him, daughter of Phorcys,[12] lord of the barren sea, for she within the hollow caves united with Poseidon. And since that day the earth-shaking Poseidon does not indeed destroy Odysseus, but ever drives him wandering from his land. Come then, let us all here plan for his turning home. So shall Poseidon lay by his anger, unable, in defiance of us all, to strive with the immortal gods alone."

Then answered him the goddess, clear-eyed Athene: "Our father, son of Kronos, most high above all rulers, if it now please the blessed gods that wise Odysseus shall return to his own home, let us send Hermes forth— the Guide, the Speedy-comer—into the island of Ogygia, straightway to tell the fair-haired nymph our steadfast purpose, that hardy Odysseus shall set forth upon his homeward way. I in the meanwhile go to Ithaca, to rouse his son[13] yet more and to put vigor in his breast; that, summoning to an assembly the long-haired Achaeans, he may denounce the troop of suitors, men who continually butcher his thronging flocks and swing-paced, crook-horned oxen. And I will send him to Sparta[14] and to sandy Pylos,[15] to try to learn of his dear father's coming, and so to win a good report among mankind."

Saying this, under her feet she bound her beautiful sandals, immortal, made of gold, which carry her over the flood and over the boundless land swift as a breath of wind. She took her ponderous spear, tipped with sharp bronze, thick, long, and strong, with which she vanquishes the ranks of men —of heroes, even—when this daughter of a mighty sire is roused against them. Then she went dashing down the ridges of Olympus and in the land of Ithaca stood at Odysseus' gate, on the threshold of his court. Holding in hand a brazen spear, she seemed the stranger Mentes, the Taphian leader.[16] Here then she found the haughty suitors. They were amusing themselves with games of draughts before the palace door, seated on hides of oxen which they themselves had slain. Their pages and busy squires were near; some mixing wine and water in the bowls, others with porous sponges washing and laying tables, while others still carved them abundant meat.

[11] In the course of their wanderings, Odysseus and his companions arrived in the land of one-eyed giants called Cyclops. One of them, Polyphemus, killed some of Odysseus' companions and imprisoned the rest. Odysseus and his men drugged Polyphemus with wine and then blinded his eye with a tree-sized beam in order to escape.   [12] A marine deity, comparable to Nereus; father of sea-nymphs and monstrous divinities.   [13] Telemachus.   [14] City of Menelaus, who is already returned home from the Trojan War.   [15] City of Nestor, who had also returned.   [16] Athene's fondness for disguises and cunning parallels that of Odysseus throughout the poem. The Taphians were a people on or near the west coast of Greece.

By far the first to see Athene was princely Telemachus. For he was sitting with the suitors, sad at heart, picturing in mind his noble father—how he might come from somewhere, make a scattering of the suitors, take to himself his honors, and be master of his own. Thus thinking while he sat among the suitors, Athene met his eye. Straight to the door he went, being at heart ashamed to have a stranger stand so long before his gate. So drawing near and grasping her right hand, he took her brazen spear, and speaking in winged words he said: "Hail, stranger, here with us you shall be welcome; and by and by when you have tasted food, you shall make known your needs."

Saying this, he led the way, and Pallas Athene followed. When they were come within the lofty hall, he carried the spear to a tall pillar and set it in a well-worn rack, where also stood many a spear of hardy Odysseus. Athene herself he led to a chair and seated, spreading a linen cloth below. Good was the chair and richly wrought; upon its lower part there was a rest for feet. Beside it, for himself, he set a sumptuous seat apart from all the suitors, for fear the stranger, meeting rude men and worried by their din, might lose his taste for food; and then that he might ask him, too, about his absent father. Now water for the hands a servant brought in a beautiful pitcher made of gold, and poured it out over a silver basin for their washing, and spread a polished table by their side. And the grave housekeeper brought bread and placed before them, setting out food of many a kind, freely giving of her store. The carver, too, took platters of meat, and placed before them, meat of all kinds, and set their golden goblets ready; while a page, pouring wine, passed to and fro between them.

And now the haughty suitors entered. These soon took seats in order, on couches and on chairs. Pages poured water on their hands, maids heaped them bread in baskets, and young men brimmed the bowls with drink; and on the food spread out before them they laid hands. So after they had stayed desire for drink and food, then in their thoughts they turned to other things, the song and dance; for these attend a feast. A page put a beautiful harp into the hands of Phemius, who sang perforce among the suitors; and touching the harp, he raised his voice and sang a beautiful song. Then said Telemachus to clear-eyed Athene, his head bent close, that others might not hear:

"Good stranger, will you feel offense at what I say? These things are all their[17] care—the harp and song—an easy care when, making no amends, they eat the substance of a man[18] whose white bones now are rotting in the rain, if lying on the land, or in the sea the waters roll them round. Yet were they once to see him coming home to Ithaca, they all would pray rather for speed of foot than stores of gold and clothing. But he, instead, by some hard fate is gone, and naught remains to us of comfort—no, not if any man

---

[17] The suitors'. [18] Odysseus.

on earth shall say he still will come. Passed is his day of coming. But now declare me this and plainly tell, who are you? Of what people? Where is your town and kindred? On what ship did you come? And how did sailors bring you to Ithaca? Whom did they call themselves? For I am sure you did not come on foot. And tell me truly this, that I may know full well if for the first time now you visit here, or are you my father's friend? For many foreigners once sought our home; because Odysseus also was a rover among men."

Then said to him the goddess, clear-eyed Athene: "Well, I will very plainly tell you all: Mentes I call myself, the son of wise Anchialus, and I am lord of the oar-loving Taphians. Even now I put in a here, with ship and crew, when sailing over the wine-dark sea to men of a strange speech, to Temesè, for bronze. I carry glittering iron. Here my ship lies, just off the fields outside the town, within the bay of Reithron[19] under woody Neïon. Hereditary friends we count ourselves from early days, as you may learn if you will go and ask old lord Laërtes,[20] who, people say, comes to the town no more, but far out in the country suffers hardship, an aged woman his attendant, who supplies him food and drink whenever weariness weighs down his knees, as he creeps about his slope of garden ground. Even now I came, for I was told your father was at home. But, as I see, the gods delay his journey; for surely nowhere yet on earth has royal Odysseus died; living, he lingers somewhere still on the wide sea, upon some sea-girt island, and cruel men constrain him—some savage folk, who hold him there against his will. Nay, I will prophesy such things as the immortals bring to mind, things which I think will happen; although I am no prophet and have no skill in birds. Not long shall he be absent from his own dear land, though iron fetters bind him. Some means he will devise to come away; for many a shift has he. But now, declare me this and plainly tell, if you indeed—so tall— are the true son of Odysseus. In head and beautiful eyes you surely are much like him. So often we were together before he embarked for Troy, where others too, the bravest of the Argives, went in their hollow ships. But since that day I have not seen Odysseus, nor he me."

Then answered her discreet Telemachus: "Yes, stranger, I will plainly tell you all. My mother says I am his child; I myself do not know; for no one ever yet knew his own parentage. Yet would I were the son of some blest man on whom old age had come amongst his own possessions. But now, the man born most ill-fated of all human kind—of him they say I come, since this you ask me."

Then said to him the goddess, clear-eyed Athene: "Surely the gods meant that your house should not lack future fame, when to such a son as you Penelope gave birth. Nevertheless declare me this and truly tell, what is the

---

[19] A harbor in Ithaca.   [20] Odysseus' father.

feast? What company is this? And what is your part here? Some drinking bout or wedding? It surely is no festival at common cost. So rude they seem, and wanton, feasting about the hall. A man of sense must be indignant who comes and sees such outrage."

Then answered her discreet Telemachus: "Stranger—since now you ask of this and question me—in former days this house bade fair to be wealthy and esteemed, so long as he was here; but the hard-purposed gods then changed their minds and shut him from our knowledge more than all men beside. For were he dead, I should not feel such grief, if he had fallen among comrades in the Trojan land, or in the arms of friends when the skein of war was wound. Then would the whole Achaean host have made his grave, and for his son in after days a great name had been gained. Now, silently the robber winds have swept him off. Gone is he, past all sight and hearing, and sighs and sorrows he has left to me. Yet now I do not grieve and mourn for him alone; because the gods have brought me other sore distress. For all the nobles who bear sway among the islands—Doulichion, Same, and woody Zacynthos[21]—and they who have the power in rocky Ithaca, all woo my mother and despoil my home. She neither declines the hated suit nor has she power to end it; while they with feasting impoverish my home and soon will bring me also to destruction."

Stirred into anger, Pallas Athene spoke: "Alas! in very truth you greatly need absent Odysseus, to lay hands on the shameless suitors. What if he came even now and here before his house stood at the outer gate, with helmet, shield, and his two spears—even such as when I saw him first at my own home, drinking and making merry . . . . If as he was that day Odysseus now might meet the suitors, they all would find quick turns of fate and bitter rites of marriage. Still, in the gods' lap it lies to say if he shall come and wreak revenge within his halls; but yours it is to plan to thrust the suitors from your door. Give me your ear and heed my words. Tomorrow, summoning to an assembly the Achaean lords, announce your will to all and call the gods to witness! Bid the suitors all disperse, each to his own. And for your mother, if her heart inclines to marriage, let her return to her strong father's hall. They there shall make the wedding and provide the many gifts which should accompany a well-loved child. Then for yourself I offer sound advice, if you will hearken. Man the best ship you have with twenty oarsmen, and go and gather tidings of your long-absent father. Perhaps some man may tell you, or you may catch a rumor sent from Zeus, which oftenest carries tidings. First go to Pylos, and question royal Nestor. Then on to Sparta, to light-haired Menelaus; for he came last of all the mailed [22] Achaeans. And if you hear your father is alive and coming home, then, worn as you are, you might endure for one year more. But if you hear that he is dead—no

21 Large islands in the domain of Odysseus; off the west coast of Greece, near Ithaca.   22 Wearing defensive armor.

longer with the living—you shall at once return to your own native land, and pile his mound and pay the funeral rites, full many, as are due, and you shall give your mother to a husband. Moreover, after you have ended this and finished all, within your mind and heart consider next how you may slay the suitors in your halls, whether by stratagem or open force. You must not hold to childish ways, because you are no longer now the child you were. Have you not heard what fame royal Orestes gained with all mankind, because he slew the slayer, wily Aegisthus, who had slain his famous father? You too, my friend—for certainly I find you fair and tall—be strong, that men hereafter born may speak your praise. Now I will go to my swift ship and to my comrades, who greatly chafe at waiting. Rely upon yourself. Heed what I say."

Then answered her discreet Telemachus: "Stranger, in this you speak with kindness, even as a father to a son. Never shall I forget it. But tarry now, though eager for your journey. Bathe, and refresh your soul; then glad at heart turn to your ship, bearing a gift of value, very beautiful, to be to you a keepsake from myself, even such a thing as dear friends give to friends."

Then answered him the goddess, clear-eyed Athene: "Do not detain me longer now, when I am anxious for my journey. And any gift your heart may bid you give, give when I come again, for me to carry home. Choose one exceeding beautiful; it shall be matched in the exchange."

Saying this, clear-eyed Athene passed away, even as a bird—a sea-hawk —takes its flight. Into his heart she had brought strength and courage, turning his thoughts upon his father more even than before. As he marked this in his mind, an awe came on his heart; he knew a god was with him. Straightway he sought the suitors, godlike himself.

To them the famous bard[23] was singing, while they in silence sat and listened. He sang of the return of the Achaeans, the sad return, which Pallas Athene had appointed them on leaving Troy.

Now from her upper chamber, there heard this wondrous song the daughter of Icarius, heedful Penelope, and she descended the long stairway from her room, yet not alone; two damsels followed her. And when the royal lady reached the suitors, she stood beside a column of the strong-built roof, holding before her face her delicate wimple, the while a faithful damsel stood upon either hand. Then bursting into tears, she said to the noble bard:

"Phemius, many another tale you know to charm mankind, exploits of men and gods, which bards make famous. Sit and sing one of these. The rest drink wine in silence. But cease this song, this song of woe, which harrows evermore the soul within my breast; because on me has fallen grief that cannot be forgotten. So dear a face I miss, ever remembering one whose fame is wide through Hellas and mid-Argos."

[23] Phemius.

Then answered her discreet Telemachus: "My mother, why forbid the honored bard to cheer us in whatever way his mind is moved? The bards are not to blame, but rather Zeus, who gives to toiling men even as he wills to each. And for the bard, there is no ground for censure if he sings the Danaäns' cruel doom. The song which men most heartily applaud is that which comes the newest to their ears. Then let your heart and soul submit to listen; for not Odysseus only lost the day of his return at Troy, but many another perished also. Nay, seek your chamber and attend to matters of your own—the loom, the distaff—and bid the women ply their tasks. Words are for men, for all, especially for me; for power within this house rests here."

Amazed, she turned to her own room again, for the wise saying of her son she laid to heart. And coming to the upper chamber with her maids, she there bewailed Odysseus, her dear husband, till on her lids clear-eyed Athene caused a sweet sleep to fall.

But the suitors broke into uproar up and down the dusky hall. Each prayed to lie beside her. But thus discreet Telemachus began to speak: "You suitors of my mother, overweening in your pride, let us enjoy our feast and have no brawling now. For a pleasant thing it is to hear a bard like this, one who is like the gods in voice. But in the morning let us all take seats in the assembly, where I may unreservedly announce my will that you shall quit my halls. Seek other tables and eat what is your own, changing from house to house! Or if it seems to you more profitable and better to ruin the living of one man without amends, go wasting on! But I will call upon the gods that live forever and pray that Zeus may grant deeds of requital.[24] Then beyond all amends, here in this house you shall yourselves be ruined."

He spoke, and all with teeth set in their lips marveled because Telemachus had spoken boldly. Then said Antinoüs,[25] Eupeithes' son: "Telemachus, surely the gods themselves are training you to be a man of lofty tongue and a bold speaker. But may the son of Kronos never make you king in sea-girt Ithaca, although it is by birth your heritage!"

Then answered him discreet Telemachus: "Antinoüs, will you feel offense at what I say? This I would gladly take, if Zeus would grant it. Do you suppose the kingship is the worst fate in the world? Why, it is no bad thing to be a king! Soon the house of a king grows rich and he himself is honored more. Still, as to kings of the Achaeans, here in sea-girt Ithaca are many others young and old, some one of whom may take the place, since royal Odysseus now is dead. But I myself will be the lord of our own house and of the slaves which royal Odysseus won for me."

Then answered him Eurymachus,[26] the son of Polybus: "Telemachus, in the gods' lap it lies to say which one of the Achaeans shall be king in sea-girt

[24] As the god of hospitality, Zeus is responsible for avenging any abuse of another's home or hospitality. [25] One of the two leading suitors. [26] The other leading suitor.

Ithaca. Your substance may you keep and of your house be lord; may the man never come who, heedless of your will, shall strip you of that substance while men shall dwell in Ithaca. But, good sir, I would ask about this stranger—whence the man comes, and of what land he calls himself. Where are his kinsmen and his native fields? Does he bring tidings of your father's coming, or is he come with hope of his own gains? How hastily he went! Not waiting to be known! And yet he seemed no low-born fellow by the face."

Then answered him discreet Telemachus: "Eurymachus, as for my father's coming, that is at an end. Tidings I trust no longer, let them come whence they may. Nor do I care for divinations, such as my mother seeks, summoning a diviner to the hall. This stranger is my father's friend, a man of Taphos; Mentes he calls himself, the son of wise Anchialus, and he is lord of the oar-loving Taphians."

So spoke Telemachus, but in his mind he knew the immortal goddess. Meanwhile the suitors to dancing and the gladsome song turned merrily, and waited for the evening to come on. And on their merriment dark evening came. So then, desiring rest, they each departed homeward.

But Telemachus himself, where on the beautiful court his chamber was built high upon commanding ground, went to his bed with many doubts in mind. And walking by his side, with blazing torch, went faithful Eurycleia, daughter of Ops, Peisenor's[27] son, whom once Laërtes purchased with his substance when she was but a girl, and paid the price of twenty oxen. Her equally with his faithful wife he honored at the palace, but he never sought her bed, avoiding a wife's anger. Now she it was who bore the blazing torch beside Telemachus; for she of all the handmaids loved him most and was his nurse when little. He opened the doors of the strong chamber, sat down upon the bed, pulled his soft tunic off, and laid it in the wise old woman's hands. Folding and smoothing out the tunic, she hung it on a peg beside the well-bored bedstead, then left the chamber, and by its silver ring pulled to the door, drawing the bolt home by its strap. So there Telemachus, all the night long, wrapped in a fleece of wool, pondered in mind the course Athene counseled.

Telemachus proceeds to journey to Pylos and Sparta, where he consults Nestor and Menelaus, but he does not succeed in finding out where his father is. Odysseus, in the meantime, has been stranded for seven years on Ogygia, the far-off island of the nymph Calypso. He is the only survivor of his fleet, which was completely shipwrecked after numerous adventures in unknown seas. At last Calypso releases him and he sails away on a raft, only to be shipwrecked again on the shore of the island Scheria, where he en-

[27] Perhaps the famous herald in Ithaca.

*counters the Phaeacian princess Nausicaa. She introduces him to the king
of the Phaeacians, Alcinoüs, to whom Odysseus unintentionally reveals his
identity. Alcinoüs persuades Odysseus to tell the full story of his journey,
starting with his departure from Troy at the end of the war. He describes
his fantastic adventures, among the most famous of which are his encounters
with the Lotus-eaters, the one-eyed giant Cyclops, the beautiful witch Circe,
and the dead in Hades. At the beginning of the following selection, Odysseus' account has reached the point when he has just returned from Hades
to Circe's island, Aeaea.*

From BOOK XII

"After our ship[28] had left the current of the Ocean-stream[29] and come
into the waters of the open sea and to the island of Aeaea, where is the
dwelling of the early dawn, its dancing-ground and place of rising, as we ran
in we beached our ship among the sands, and forth we went ourselves upon
the shore; where, falling fast asleep, we awaited sacred dawn.

"But when the early rosy-fingered dawn appeared, I sent men forward to
the house of Circe[30] to fetch the body of the dead Elpenor.[31] Then hastily
cutting logs, where the coast stood out most boldly we buried him, in sadness, letting the big tears fall. After the dead was burned and the armor of
the dead man, we raised a mound, and dragged a stone upon it, and fixed
on the mound's highest point his shapely oar.

"With all this we were busied; nevertheless, our coming from the house of
Hades was not concealed from Circe, but quickly she arrayed herself and
came to meet us. Her maids bore bread and stores of meat and ruddy sparkling wine; and standing in the midst of all, the heavenly goddess said:

"'Madmen! who have gone down alive into the house of Hades, thus
twice to meet with death while others die but once, come, eat this food and
drink this wine here for today, and when tomorrow comes you shall set sail.[32]
I will myself point out the way and fully show you all; lest by unhappy lack
of skill you be distressed on sea or land and suffer harm.'

"So she spoke, and our high hearts assented. Thus all throughout the day
till setting sun we sat and feasted on abundant meat and pleasant wine; and

[28] Odysseus is the narrator in this book. The Phaeacians of Scheria—and particularly their king Alcinoüs and his daughter Nausicaa—are his audience.
[29] Oceanus carried Odysseus back to earth from his visit to the world of the dead
(Hades). [30] A mythical sorceress who had seduced and detained Odysseus for an
entire year prior to his journey to Hades. [31] Companion of Odysseus. He died
when he became drunk and fell off the roof of Circe's palace just before Odysseus
left for Hades. Odysseus met Elpenor's "soul" in Hades and promised to bury his
body upon his return to earth. [32] In a previous scene Athene had commanded
Circe to release Odysseus and his men from her island.

when the sun had set and darkness came, my men lay down to sleep by the ship's cables; but leading me by the hand apart from my good comrades, the goddess bade me sit, herself reclined beside me, and asked me for my story. So I related all the tale in its due order. Then thus spoke potent Circe:

" 'All this is ended now; but listen to what I say, and God himself shall help you to remember.' [33] . . .

"Even as she spoke, the gold-throned morning came, and up the island the heavenly goddess went her way; I turned me toward my ship, and called my crew to come on board and loose the cables. Quickly they came, took places at the pins, and sitting in order smote the foaming water with their oars. And for our aid behind our dark-bowed ship came a fair wind to fill our sail, a welcome comrade, sent us by fair-haired Circe, the mighty goddess, human of speech. When we had done our work at the several ropes about the ship, we sat us down, while wind and helmsman kept her steady.

"Now to my men, with aching heart, I said: 'My friends, it is not right for only one or two to know the oracles which Circe told, that heavenly goddess. Therefore I speak, that, knowing all, we so may die, or fleeing death and doom, we may escape. She warns us first against the marvelous Sirens,[34] and bids us flee their voice and flowery meadow. Only myself she bade to hear their song; but bind me with galling cords, to hold me firm, upright upon the mast-block—round it let the rope be wound. And if I should entreat you, and bid you set me free, then with still more fetters bind me fast.'

"Thus I, relating all my tale, talked with my comrades. Meanwhile our stanch ship swiftly neared the Sirens' island; a fair wind swept her on. On a sudden the wind ceased; there came a breathless calm; Heaven hushed the waves. My comrades, rising, furled the sail, stowed it on board the hollow ship, then sitting at their oars whitened the water with the polished blades. But I with my sharp sword cut a great cake of wax into small bits, which I then kneaded in my sturdy hands. Soon the wax warmed, forced by the powerful pressure and by the rays of the exalted Sun, the lord of all. Then one by one I stopped the ears of all my crew; and on the deck they bound me hand and foot, upright upon the mast-block, round which they wound the rope; and sitting down they smote the foaming water with their oars. But when we were as far away as one can call and driving swiftly onward, our speeding ship, as it drew near, did not escape the Sirens, and thus they lifted up their penetrating voice:

" 'Come hither, come, Odysseus, whom all praise, great glory of the Achaeans! Bring in your ship, and listen to our song. For none has ever passed us in a black-hulled ship till from our lips he heard ecstatic song,

[33] In this speech (not reprinted here) Circe accurately predicts Odysseus' encounters with the Sirens, Scylla and Charybdis, and the cattle of the Sun—all of which Odysseus himself describes in the remainder of this book.   [34] Sea nymphs, whose penetrating songs irresistibly lured sailors to destruction.

then went his way rejoicing and with larger knowledge. For we know all that on the plain of Troy Argives and Trojans suffered at the gods' behest; we know whatever happens on the bounteous earth.'

"So spoke they, sending forth their glorious song, and my heart longed to listen. Knitting my brows, I made signs to my men to set me free; but bending forward, on they rowed. And straightway Perimedes[35] and Eurylochus[36] arose and laid upon me still more cords and drew them tighter. Then, after passing by, when we could hear no more the Sirens' voice nor any singing, quickly my trusty crew removed the wax with which I stopped their ears, and set me free from bondage.

"Soon after we left the island, I observed a smoke, I saw high waves and heard a plunging sound. From the hands of my frightened men down fell the oars, and splashed against the current. There the ship stayed, for they worked the tapering oars no more. Along the ship I passed, inspiriting my men with cheering words, standing by each in turn:

"'Friends, hitherto we have not been untried in danger. Here is no greater danger than when the Cyclops penned us with brutal might in the deep cave. Yet out of that, through energy of mine, through will and wisdom, we escaped. These dangers, too, I think some day we shall remember. Come then, and what I say let us all follow. You with your oars strike the deep breakers of the sea, while sitting at the pins, and see if Zeus will set us free from present death and let us go in safety. And, helmsman, these are my commands for you; lay them to heart, for you control the rudders of our hollow ship: keep the ship off that smoke and surf and hug the crags, or else, before you know it, she may veer off that way, and you will bring us into danger.'

"So I spoke, and my words they quickly heeded. But Scylla I did not name—that hopeless horror—for fear through fright my men might cease to row, and huddle all together in the hold. I disregarded too the hard behest of Circe, when she had said I must by no means arm. Putting on my glittering armor and taking in my hands my two long spears, I went upon the ship's fore-deck, for thence I looked for the first sight of Scylla[37] of the rock, who brought my men disaster. Nowhere could I descry her; I tired my eyes with searching up and down the dusky cliff.

"So up the strait we sailed in sadness; for here lay Scylla, and there divine Charybdis[38] fearfully sucked the salt sea-water down. Whenever she belched it forth, like a kettle in fierce flame all would foam swirling up, and over-

---

[35] A companion of Odysseus.   [36] A relative of Odysseus and second-in-command of his ships.   [37] A man-eating female monster. She lives in a cave in a huge, smooth rock which juts high out from the sea. She has the voice of a dog, twelve feet, and six long necks, on each of which is a head with three rows of teeth. [38] A female monster of the sea, in the form of a whirlpool. She lives underneath a second, lower rock (close to Scylla) on which a giant fig tree grows.

head spray fell upon the tops of both the crags. But when she gulped the salt sea-water down, then all within seemed in a whirl; the rock around roared fearfully, and down below the bottom showed, dark with the sand. Pale terror seized my men; on her we looked and feared to die.

"And now it was that Scylla snatched from the hollow ship six of my comrades who were best in skill and strength. Turning my eyes toward my swift ship to seek my men, I saw their feet and hands already in the air as they were carried up. They screamed aloud and called my name for the last time, in agony of heart. As when a fisher, on a jutting rock, with long rod throws a bait to lure the little fishes, casting into the deep the horn of stall-fed ox; then, catching a fish, flings it ashore writhing; even so were these drawn writhing up the rocks. There at her door she ate them, loudly shriek-ing and stretching forth their hands in mortal pangs toward me. That was the saddest sight my eyes have ever seen, in all my toils, searching the ocean pathways.

"Now after we had passed the rocks of dire Charybdis and Scylla, straight we drew near the pleasant island of the god.[39] Here were the goodly broad-browed cattle and the many sturdy flocks of the exalted Sun. While still at sea, on the black ship, I heard the lowing of stalled [40] cattle and the bleat of sheep; and on my mind fell words of the blind prophet, Teiresias of Thebes, and of Aeaean Circe, who very strictly charged me to shun the island of the Sun, the cheerer of mankind. So to my men with aching heart I said:

" 'My suffering comrades, hearken to my words, that I may tell you of the warnings of Teiresias,[41] and of Aeaean Circe, who very strictly charged me to shun the island of the Sun, the cheerer of mankind; for there our deadliest danger lay, she said. Then past the island speed the black ship on her way.'

"As I spoke thus, their very souls were crushed within them, and in-stantly Eurylochus, with surly words, made answer: 'Headstrong are you, Odysseus; more than man's is your mettle, and your limbs never tire; and yet you must be made of nothing else than iron not to allow your comrades, worn with fatigue and sleep, to land, though on this sea-girt island we might make once more a savory supper. Instead, just as we are, night falling fast, you bid us journey on and wander from the island over the misty deep. But in the night rough winds arise, fatal to vessels; and how could any one escape from utter ruin if by some chance a sudden storm of wind should come, the south wind or the blustering west, which wreck ships oftentimes, heedless of sovereign gods? No, let us now obey the dark night's bidding, let us prepare our supper and rest by the black ship; tomorrow morning we will embark and sail the open sea.'

[39] Thrinacia, island of the Sun.   [40] Stabled.   [41] On his journey to Hades, Odys-seus encountered the dead seer Teiresias, who told Odysseus about the remainder of his voyage home and his ultimate fate.

"So spoke Eurylochus, the rest assented, and then I knew some god intended ill; and speaking in winged words I said:

" 'Eurylochus, plainly you force me, since I am only one. But come, all swear me now a solemn oath that if we find a herd of cattle or great flock of sheep, none in mad willfulness will slay a cow or sheep; but be content, and eat the food immortal Circe gave.'

"So I spoke, and they then took the oath which I required. And after they had sworn and ended all their oath, we moored our stanch ship in the rounded harbor, near a fresh stream, and my companions left the ship and busily got supper. But after they had stayed desire for drink and food, then calling to remembrance their dear comrades, they wept for those whom Scylla ate, those whom she snatched from out the hollow ship; and as they wept, on them there came a pleasant sleep. Now when it was the third watch of the night and the stars crossed the zenith, cloud-gathering Zeus sent forth a furious wind in a fierce tempest, and covered with his clouds both land and sea; night broke from heaven. And when the early rosy-fingered dawn appeared, we beached our ship, hauling her up into a hollow cave where there were pretty dancing-grounds and haunts for nymphs. Then holding a council, I said to all my men:

" 'Friends, there is food and drink enough on the swift ship; let us then spare the cattle, for fear we come to harm, for these are the herds and sturdy flocks of a dread god, the Sun, who all things oversees, all overhears.'

"So I spoke, and their high hearts assented. But all that month incessant south winds[42] blew; there came no wind except from east and south. So long as they had bread and ruddy wine, they spared the cows, because they loved their lives. But when the vessel's stores were now all spent, and roaming perforce they sought for game—for fish, for fowl, for what might come to hand, caught by their crooked hooks—and hunger pinched their bellies, then I departed by myself far up the island, to beg the gods to show my homeward way. And when by a walk across the island I had escaped my crew, I washed my hands where there was shelter from the breeze, and offered prayer to all the gods that hold Olympus. But they poured down sweet sleep upon my eyelids, while Eurylochus began his evil counsel to my crew:

" 'My suffering comrades, hearken to my words. Hateful is every form of death to wretched mortals; and yet to die by hunger, and so to meet one's doom, is the most pitiful of all. Come then, and let us drive away the best of the Sun's cattle, and sacrifice them to the immortals who hold the open sky. And if we ever come to Ithaca, our native land, we will at once build a rich temple to the exalted Sun, and put therein many fair offerings. If then the Sun, wroth for his high-horned cattle, seeks to destroy our ship, and other gods consent, for my part I would rather, open-mouthed in the sea,

---

[42] Feared by sailors; they bring fog and rainstorms.

give up my life at once than slowly let it wear away here in this desert island.'

"So spoke Eurylochus; the rest assented. Forthwith they drove away the best of the Sun's cattle out of the field close by; for not far from the dark-bowed ship the cattle were grazing, crook-horned and beautiful and broad of brow. Round them they stood and prayed the gods, stripping the tender leaves from off a lofty oak; for they had no white barley on the well-benched ship. Then after prayer, when they had cut the throats and flayed the cattle, they cut away the thighs, wrapped them in fat in double layers, and placed raw flesh thereon. They had no wine to pour upon the blazing victims, but using water for libation[43] they roasted all the entrails. So after the thighs were burned and the inward parts were tasted, they sliced the rest and stuck it on the spits.

"And now the pleasant sleep fled from my eyelids; I hastened to the swift ship and the shore. But on my way, as I drew near to the curved ship, around me came the savory smell of fat. I groaned and called aloud to the immortal gods:

"'O father Zeus, and all you other blessed gods that live forever, verily to my ruin you laid me in ruthless sleep, while my men left behind plotted a monstrous deed.'

"Soon to the exalted Sun came long-robed Lampetia,[44] bearing him word that we had slain his cattle; and straightway with an angry heart he thus invoked the immortals:

"'O father Zeus, and all you other blessed gods that live forever, avenge me on the comrades of Laërtes' son, Odysseus, who insolently slew the cattle in which I joy as I go forth into the starry sky, or as again toward earth I turn back from the sky. But if they do not make me fit atonement for the cattle, I will go down to Hades and shine among the dead.'[45]

"Then answered him cloud-gathering Zeus, and said: 'O Sun, do you shine on among the immortals and on the fruitful fields of mortal men. Soon I will smite their swift ship with a gleaming bolt, and cleave it in pieces in the middle of the wine-dark sea.'

"All this I heard from fair-haired Calypso, who said she heard it from the Guide-god Hermes.[46]

"Now when I came to the ship and to the sea, I chid my men, confronting each in turn. But no help could we find; the cattle were dead already. Soon too the gods made prodigies appear: the skins would crawl; the spitted flesh,

[43] It was customary to pour an offering of wine to the gods before roasting slaughtered animals.   [44] A nymph, daughter of the Sun. She tended her father's cattle.   [45] Hades was (and always had to remain) dark.   [46] Since Odysseus, and not the poet, is the narrator at this point, the poet lets him cite his sources of information far more meticulously than the poet himself ever does. The poet can simply claim the Muse as his own source.

both roast and raw, would moan; and sounds came forth like the lowing of cattle.

"For six days afterwards my trusty comrades feasted, for they had driven away the best of the Sun's cows; but when Zeus, the son of Kronos, brought the seventh day round, then the wind ceased to blow a gale, and we in haste embarking put forth on the open sea, setting our mast and hoisting the white sail.

"Yet when we had left the island and no other land appeared, but only sky and sea, the son of Kronos set a dark cloud over the hollow ship and the deep gloomed below. The ship ran on for no long time; for soon a shrill west wind arose, blowing a heavy gale. The storm of wind snapped both the forestays of the mast. Back the mast fell, and all its gear lay scattered in the hold. At the ship's stern it struck the helmsman on the head and crushed his skull, all in an instant; like a diver from the deck he dropped, and from his frame the strong life fled. Zeus at the same time thundered, hurling his bolt against the ship. She quivered in every part, struck by the bolt of Zeus, and filled with sulphur smoke. Out of the ship my comrades fell and then like sea-fowl were borne by the side of the black ship along the waves; God cut them off from coming home.

"I myself paced the ship until the surge tore her ribs off the keel, which the waves then carried along dismantled. The mast broke at the keel; but to it clung the backstay, made of ox-hide. With this I bound the two together, keel and mast, and getting a seat on these, I drifted before the deadly winds.

"And now the west wind ceased to blow a gale; but soon the south wind came and brought me anguish that I must measure back my way to fell Charybdis. All night I drifted on, and with the sunrise I came to Scylla's crag and dire Charybdis. She at that moment sucked the salt sea-water down;[47] and when to the tall fig tree[48] I was upward borne, I clutched and clung as a bat clings. Yet could I nowhere set my feet firmly down or climb the tree; for its roots were far away and out of reach of its branches, as if these were long and large, and overspread Charybdis. But steadily I clung, until she should disgorge my mast and keel; and as I hoped they came, though it was late. But at the hour one rises from the assembly for his supper, after deciding many quarrels of contentious men, then was it that the timbers came to light from out Charybdis. I let go feet and hands, and down I dropped by the long timbers, and getting a seat on these rowed onward with my hands. But the father of men and gods gave me no further sight of Scylla, or else I should not have escaped from utter ruin.

"Thence for nine days I drifted; on the tenth, at night, gods brought me to the island of Ogygia, where dwells Calypso, a fair-haired powerful god-

---

[47] Three times daily the whirlpool, Charybdis, sucked down the water and then spouted it up again. [48] Charybdis lived under a rock on which a fig tree grew.

dess, human of speech. She welcomed me and gave me care. Why tell the tale? [49] It was but yesterday I told it in the hall to you[50] and your good wife; and it is irksome to tell a plain-told tale a second time."

From B O O K   X I I I

As he thus ended, all were hushed to silence, held by the spell throughout the dusky hall. At length, Alcinoüs answering said: "Odysseus, having crossed the brazen threshold of my high-roofed house, you shall be aided home[51] with no more wanderings, be sure, long as you now have suffered. And this I say with earnestness to everybody here, to you who in my hall drink of the elders' sparkling wine and listen to the bard: you know that in a polished chest lie garments for the stranger, with rich-wrought gold and all the other gifts which the Phaeacian councilors have brought him hither. But let us also, each man here, give a caldron and large tripod; then gathering the cost among the people, we will repay ourselves. For one to give outright were hard indeed."

So said Alcinoüs, and his saying pleased them; and now desiring rest, they each departed homeward. But when the early rosy-fingered dawn appeared, they hastened to the ship and brought the gladdening bronze. Revered Alcinoüs, going himself aboard the vessel, stowed it all carefully beneath the benches, so that it might not incommode the crew upon the passage while they labored at the oars. Then to Alcinoüs' house they went and turned to feasting.

In their behalf revered Alcinoüs offered an ox to Zeus of the dark cloud, the son of Kronos, who is the lord of all; and having burned the thighs, they held a glorious feast and made them merry. Among them sang the sacred bard, Demodocus, beloved of all. Nevertheless Odysseus would often turn his face toward the still shining sun, eager to see its setting, because he was impatient to be gone. As a man longs for supper whose pair of tawny oxen all day long have dragged the jointed plough through the fresh field; gladly for him the sunlight sinks and sends him home to supper; stiff are his knees for walking; so gladly for Odysseus sank the sun. Straightway he turned to the oar-loving Phaeacians, and speaking to Alcinoüs especially he said:

"Mighty Alcinoüs, renowned of all, pour a libation and send me safely forth. Fare you all well! All that my heart desired is ready—escort and

---

[49] Calypso detained Odysseus as her companion and lover for seven years, eventually against his will. She treated him with affectionate generosity and even tempted him with an offer of immortality. Eventually Zeus ordered her to let Odysseus go, and three weeks later he was washed ashore in tatters on Scheria, the land of the Phaeacians, where he still is. [50] King Alcinoüs, ruler of Scheria. [51] Alcinoüs is about to provide Odysseus with a ship manned by Phaeacian sailors to take him home to Ithaca.

friendly gifts—and may the gods of heaven make them a blessing! My true wife may I find on coming home, and dear ones safe! And you who stay, may you make glad your wedded wives and children! The gods bestow all happiness, and may no ill be found among you!"

He spoke, and all approved and bade send forth the stranger, for rightly had he spoken. Then said revered Alcinoüs to the page: "Pontonoüs, mix a bowl and pass the wine to all within the hall, that with a prayer to father Zeus we may send forth the stranger to his native land."

He spoke; Pontonoüs stirred the cheering wine and served to all in turn; then to the blessed gods who hold the open sky they poured libations where they sat. But royal Odysseus rose, placed in Arete's[52] hand the double cup, and speaking in winged words he said:

"Fare you well, queen, for all the years until old age and death, which visit all, shall come. I go my way; may you within this home enjoy your children, people, and Alcinoüs the king!"

So saying, royal Odysseus crossed the threshold. With him revered Alcinoüs sent a page, to show the way to the swift ship and to the shore. Arete too sent damsels after: one with the spotless robe and tunic, one to accompany the close-packed chest, and one bore bread and ruddy wine.

Now when they came to the ship and to the sea, straight the tall seamen took the stores and laid them by within the hollow ship, even all the food and drink. Then for Odysseus they spread a rug and linen sheet on the hollow vessel's deck, so that he might sleep soundly, there at the stern; and he himself embarked and laid him down in silence. The other men took places at the pins, each one in order, and loosed the cable from the perforated stone. But now when bending to their work they tossed the water with their oars, upon Odysseus' lids deep slumber fell, sound and most pleasant, very like to death. And as upon a plain four harnessed stallions spring forward all together at the crack of whip, and lifting high their feet speed swiftly on their way; even so the ship's stern lifted, while in her wake followed a huge upheaving wave of the resounding sea. Safely and steadily she ran; no circling hawk, swiftest of winged things, could keep beside her. Running thus rapidly she cut the ocean waves, bearing a man of godlike wisdom, a man who had before met many griefs of heart, cleaving his way through wars of men and through the boisterous seas, yet here slept undisturbed, heedless of all he suffered.

As that most brilliant star arose which comes the surest herald of the light of early dawn, the sea-borne ship drew near the island.[53]

Now in the land of Ithaca there is a certain harbor sacred to Phorcys, the old man of the sea. Here two projecting jagged cliffs slope inward toward the harbor and break the heavy waves raised by wild winds without. Inside,

---

[52] The wife of Alcinoüs, queen of Phaeacia. [53] Odysseus' island, Ithaca.

without a cable ride the well-benched ships when once they reach the road-stead. Just at the harbor's head a leafy olive stands, and near it a pleasant darksome cave sacred to nymphs, called Naiads. Within the cave are bowls and jars of stone, and here bees hive their honey. Long looms of stone are here, where nymphs weave purple robes, a marvel to behold. Here are ever-flowing springs. The cave has double doors: one to the north, accessible to men; one to the south, for gods. By this, men do not pass; it is the immortals' entrance.

Here they rowed in, knowing the place of old. The ship ran up the shore full half her length, by reason of her speed; so was she driven by her rowers' arms. The men then left the timbered ship and came ashore, and straight-way took Odysseus from the hollow ship—him and his linen sheet and bright-hued rug—and set him on the sands, still sunk in sleep. They also brought the treasure out which the Phaeacian chiefs gave him at his de-parture, prompted by kind Athene, and laid it all together by the olive trunk a little off the road; for fear, before Odysseus woke, some passerby might come and harm it. Then they departed homeward. . . .

Meanwhile within his native land royal Odysseus woke from sleep, and did not know the land from which he had been gone so long; for a goddess spread a cloud around, even Pallas Athene, daughter of Zeus, that she might render him unknown and herself tell him all, and that his wife, his towns-folk, and his friends might never know him until the suitors paid the price of all their lawless deeds. Thus to its master all the land looked strange—the footpaths stretching far away, the sheltered coves, steep rocks, and spreading trees. Rising, he stood and gazed upon his land, then groaned and smote his thighs with outspread hands, saying in anguish:

"Alas! To what men's land am I come now? Lawless and savage are they, with no regard for right, or are they kind to strangers and reverent toward the gods? Where shall I leave my many goods, and whither shall I turn? Would these had stayed with the Phaeacians where they were, and I myself had found some other powerful prince who might have entertained me and sent me on my way! Now, where to store my goods I do not know; yet here I must not leave them, to fall a prey to strangers. Not at all wise and just were the Phaeacian captains and councilors in bringing me to this strange shore. They promised they would carry me to far-seen Ithaca, but that they did not do. May Zeus, the god of suppliants, reward them! For over all men watches Zeus, chastising those who sin. However, let me count my goods, and see that the Phaeacians took none away upon their hollow ship."

So saying, he counted the beautiful tripods, the caldrons, gold, and goodly woven stuffs, and none was lacking. Then sighing for his native land he paced the shore of the resounding sea in sadness. Near him Athene drew, in form of a young shepherd, yet delicate as are the sons of kings. Doubled about her shoulders she wore a fine-wrought mantle; under her shining feet

her sandals, and in her hand a spear. To see her made Odysseus glad. He
went to meet her, and speaking in winged words he said:

"Friend, since you are the first I find within this land, I bid you welcome,
and hope you come with no ill-will. Nay, save these goods and save me too!
I supplicate you as a god, and I approach your knees. And tell me truly this,
that I may know full well, what land is this? What people? What sort of
men dwell here? Is it a far-seen island, or a tongue of fertile mainland that
stretches out to sea?"

Then said to him the goddess, clear-eyed Athene: "You are simple,
stranger, or come from far away, to ask about this land. It is not quite so
nameless. Many men know it well, men dwelling toward the east and rising
sun, and those behind us also toward the darksome west. It is a rugged land,
not fit for driving horses, yet not so very poor though lacking plains. Grain
grows abundantly and wine as well; the showers are frequent and the dews
refreshing; here is good pasturage for goats and cattle; trees of all kinds are
here, and never-failing springs. So, stranger, the name of Ithaca has gone as
far as Troy, which is, they say, a long way from Achaea." [54]

She spoke, and glad was long-tried royal Odysseus, filled with delight over
his native land through what was said by Pallas Athene, daughter of aegis-
bearing Zeus; and speaking in winged words he said—yet uttered not the
truth, but turned his words awry, ever revolving in his breast some gainful
purpose:

"In lowland Crete, I heard of Ithaca far off beyond the sea, and now I
reach it—I and these goods of mine. I left an equal portion to my children
and flew away from home;[55] for I had killed the dear son of Idomeneus,[56]
Orsilochus, the runner, who on the plains of Crete beat all us toiling men in
speed of foot. The cause was this: he sought to cut me off from all the
Trojan spoil to gain which I bore grief of heart, cleaving my way through
wars of men and through the boisterous seas; and all because I did not, as
he wished, serve with his father in the land of Troy, but led my separate
men. With a brazen spear I struck him as he was coming from his farm and
I was lying with a comrade near the road. A very dark night screened the
sky; no man observed us; secretly I took his life. So after I had slain him
with my brazen pointed spear, I straightway sought a ship, asked aid of the
proud Phoenicians, and gave them from my booty what they wished. I bade
them take me on their ship and set me down at Pylos, or else at sacred Elis[57]
where the Epeians rule. But stress of wind turned them aside, though much
against their will; they meant no wrong; and missing our course, here we
arrived last night. With much ado we rowed into the port, and gave no

[54] Greece. [55] What follows is a characteristic invention by Odysseus, aimed at
concealing his identity from a stranger. In the subsequent books he invents numerous such stories. [56] Famous Greek warrior from Crete in the *Iliad*. [57] City in
the western Peloponnesus, opposite Ithaca.

thought to supper, hungry although we were, but simply disembarking from the ship, we all lay down. Then, weary as I was, sweet sleep came on me; and the Phoenicians, taking my treasure from the hollow ship, laid it upon the sands where I was lying, and they embarked and sailed away to stately Sidon.[58] So I was left behind with aching heart."

As he thus spoke, the goddess, clear-eyed Athene, smiled and patted him with her hand. Her form grew like a woman's—one fair and tall and skilled in dainty work—and speaking in winged words she said:

"Prudent and wily must one be to overreach you in craft of any kind, even though it be a god who strives to match you. Bold, shifty, and insatiate of wiles, will you not now within your land cease from the false misleading tales which from the bottom of your heart you love? But let us talk no longer thus, both being versed in wiles; for you are far the best of men in plots and tales, and I of all the gods am famed for craft and wiles. And yet you did not know me, Pallas Athene, daughter of Zeus, me who am ever near to guard you in all toil, me who have made you welcome to all Phaeacian folk! Now I am come to frame with you a scheme to hide the treasure which the Phaeacian chiefs, through my advice and prompting, gave you at your departure; and I will tell you too what griefs you must endure within your stately house. Bear them, because you must. Do not report to man or woman of them all that you are come from wandering; but silently receive all pains and bear men's buffets."

Then wise Odysseus answered her and said: "Hard is it, goddess, for a man, however wise he be, to know when you are near, because you take all forms. I very well remember how kind to me you were when all we young Achaeans were in the war at Troy. But since we overthrew the lofty town of Priam, since we went away in ships and God dispersed the Achaeans, I never once have seen you, daughter of Zeus, nor known you to draw near my ship protecting me from harm. Yet bearing ever in my breast a stricken heart, I wandered till the gods delivered me from ill, when in the rich land of the Phaeacians you cheered me by your words and led me to the city. Now I entreat you by your father's name, for I cannot think that I am come to far-seen Ithaca. No, I have strayed to some strange shore, and you in mockery, I think, have told this tale to cheat me. But tell me, have I really reached my own dear land?"

Then answered him the goddess, clear-eyed Athene: "Such thoughts as these are ever in your breast; therefore I cannot leave you even in misfortune, because you are discreet, wary, and steadfast. For any other man on coming back from wanderings would eagerly have hastened home to see his wife and children; but you have no desire to know or hear of them till you have proved your wife, who as of old sits in your hall and wearily the nights

---

[58] City of the Phoenicians, on the coast north of Palestine.

and days are wasted with her tears. But I for my part never doubted. I knew within my heart that you would come, though with the loss of all your men. But I did not wish to quarrel with Poseidon, my father's brother, who bore a grudge against you in his heart, angry because you blinded his dear son.[59] Come then, and let me point you out the parts of Ithaca, that so you may believe. Here is the port of Phorcys, the old man of the sea; here at the harbor's head the leafy olive; and near at hand the pleasant darksome cave, sacred to nymphs called Naiads; here is the arching cavern too, where oftentimes you made due sacrifices to the nymphs; and this is the wood-clad hill of Neriton."

The goddess, speaking thus, scattered the cloud, and plain the land appeared. Then glad was long-tried royal Odysseus, and he exulted in his land and kissed the bounteous earth, and straightway prayed the nymphs with outstretched hands:

"O Naiad Nymphs, daughters of Zeus, I said I should not see you any more, yet now with loving prayers I give you greeting. Gifts will we also give, even as of old, if the daughter of Zeus, the Plunderer,[60] graciously grants me life and prospers my dear son."

Then said to him the goddess, clear-eyed Athene: "Be of good courage! Let not these things vex your mind! But in a corner of the monstrous cave let us lay by the goods, instantly, now, here to remain in safety; then let us plan how all may turn out well."

So saying, the goddess entered the darksome cave, and searched about the cave for hiding-places. Odysseus too brought hither all he had, gold and enduring bronze and fair-wrought raiment, things given by the Phaeacians. All these were laid away with care, and at the entrance a stone was set by Pallas Athene, daughter of aegis-bearing Zeus. Then sitting down at the foot of the sacred olive, they planned the death of the audacious suitors; and thus began the goddess, clear-eyed Athene:

"High-born son of Laërtes, ready Odysseus, consider how to lay hands on the shameless suitors, who for three years have held dominion in your hall, wooing your matchless wife and offering bridal gifts; while she, continually mourning at heart over your coming, gives hopes to all, has promises for each, and sends each messages; but her mind has a different purpose."

Then wise Odysseus answered her and said: "Certainly here at home I too had met the evil fate of Agamemnon,[61] the son of Atreus, had you not, goddess, duly told me all. Come then, and frame a plot for me to win revenge. And do you stand beside me, inspiring hardy courage, even so as when we tore the shining crown from Troy. If you would stand as stoutly by me,

---

[59] The Cyclops, Polyphemus.   [60] An epic epithet of Athene. She was a goddess of war in addition to being the patron goddess of the crafts and the embodiment of wisdom.   [61] Upon his return to Greece, Agamemnon was murdered by his wife, Clytemnestra and her lover Aegisthus.

clear-eyed one, then I would face three hundred men, mated with you, dread goddess, with you for my strong aid."

Then answered him the goddess, clear-eyed Athene: "I surely will be with you; you shall never be forgot when we begin the work. Some too, I think, shall spatter with their blood and brains the spacious floor, some of these suitors who devour your living. But let me make you strange to all men's view. I will shrivel the fair flesh on your supple limbs, pluck from your head the yellow locks, and clothe you in such rags that they who see shall loathe the wearer. And I will blear your eyes, so beautiful before, that you may seem repulsive to all the suitors here, and even to your wife and the son you left at home. But first seek out the swineherd, the keeper of your swine; for he is loyal, loving your son and steadfast Penelope. You will find him sitting by his swine. They feed along the Raven Crag by the spring of Arethusa,[62] eating the pleasant acorns and drinking the shaded water, a food which breeds abundant fat in swine. There wait, and sitting by his side question him fully; while I go on to Sparta, the land of lovely women, to summon thence Telemachus, your son, Odysseus. He went to spacious Lacedaemon[63] to visit Menelaus, hoping to learn if you were still alive."

Then wise Odysseus answered her and said: "Why, knowing all, did you yourself not tell him? Must he too meet with sorrow, roaming the barren sea, while others eat his substance?"

Then answered him the goddess, clear-eyed Athene: "Nay, let him not too much oppress your heart. I was myself his guide, and helped him win a noble name by going thither. He meets no hardship there, but sits at ease within the palace of the son of Atreus,[64] with plenty all around. Young men, indeed, now lie in wait on their black ship and seek to cut him off before he gains his native land. Yet this I think shall never be; rather the earth shall cover some of the suitors who devour your living."

So having said, Athene touched him with her wand, shriveled the fair flesh on his supple limbs, plucked from his head the yellow locks, and made the skin of all his limbs the skin of an old man. Likewise she bleared his eyes, so beautiful before, and gave him for his clothing a wretched frock and tunic, tattered and foul and grimed with filthy smoke. Then over all she threw a swift deer's ample hide, stripped of its hair; and gave him a staff and miserable wallet, full of holes, which hung upon a cord.

So having formed their plans, they parted; and thereupon the goddess went to sacred Lacedaemon, seeking Odysseus' son.

[62] One of the Naiad nymphs, often identified with fountains. [63] Sparta. [64] Menelaus.

From B O O K X I V

But from the harbor, up the rocky path, along the woody country on the hills, Odysseus went to where Athene bade him seek the noble swineherd, who guarded his estate more carefully than any man royal Odysseus owned.

He found him sitting in his porch, by which was built a high-walled yard upon commanding ground, a handsome yard and large, with space around. With his own hands the swineherd built it for the swine after his lord was gone, without assistance from the queen[65] or old Laërtes,[66] constructing it with blocks of stone and coping it with thorn. Outside the yard he drove down stakes the whole way round, stout and close-set, of split black oak. Inside the yard he made twelve sties alongside one another, as bedding places for the swine; and fifty swine that wallow in the mire were penned in each, all of them sows for breeding; the boars, much fewer, lay outside. On these the gallant suitors feasted and kept their number small; for daily the swineherd sent away the best fat hog he had. Three hundred and sixty they were now. Hard by, four dogs, like wild beasts, always lay, dogs which the swineherd bred, the overseer. He was himself now fitting sandals to his feet, cutting therefor a well-tanned hide. The other men were gone their several ways: three with the swine to pasture; a fourth sent to the town to take to the audacious suitors, as was ordered, a hog to slay and sate their souls with meat.

But now the ever-barking dogs suddenly spied Odysseus, and baying rushed upon him; whereat Odysseus calmly sat down and from his hand let fall his staff. Yet here at his own farm he would have come to cruel grief, had not the swineherd, springing swiftly after, dashed from the door and from his hand let fall the leather. Scolding the dogs, he drove them off this way and that with showers of stones, and thus addressed his master:

"Old man, my dogs had nearly torn you to pieces here all of a sudden, and so you would have brought reproach on me. Ah well! The gods have given me other griefs and sorrows; for over my matchless master I sit and sigh and groan, and tend fat hogs for other men to eat; while he, perhaps longing for food, wanders about the lands and towns of men of alien speech—if he still lives and sees the sunshine. But follow me, old man, into the lodge; so that you too, when satisfied with food and drink, may tell where you are come from and what troubles you have borne."

So saying, to the lodge the noble swineherd led the way, and bringing Odysseus in made him a seat. Beneath, he laid thick brushwood, and on the top he spread a shaggy wild goat's great soft skin, his usual bed. Odysseus was pleased that he received him so, and spoke and thus addressed him:

"Stranger, may Zeus and the other deathless gods grant all you most desire for treating me so kindly!"

And, swineherd Eumaeus, you answered him and said "Stranger, it is not

65 Penelope, Odysseus' wife. 66 Odysseus' father.

right for me to slight a stranger, not even one in poorer plight than you; for in the charge of Zeus all strangers and beggars stand, and our small gift is welcome. But so it is with servants continually afraid when new men are their masters! Surely the gods kept him from coming who would have loved me well and given me for my own the things a generous master always allows his man—a house, a plot of ground, and a fair wife—at least when one has labored long, and God has made his work to prosper, as he makes prosper all the work I undertake. So would my master have well rewarded me, had he but grown old here. But he is gone! Would all the tribe of Helen had gone too, down on their knees! for she has made the knees of many men grow weak. Yet, he too went for Agamemnon's honor to Ilios, famed for horses, to fight the Trojans there."

So saying, he hurriedly girt his tunic with his belt, and went to the sties where droves of pigs were penned. Selecting two, he brought them in and killed them both, singed them and sliced them and stuck them on the spits, and roasting carried all the meat to offer to Odysseus, hot on the spits themselves. He sprinkled it with white barley. Then in an ivy bowl he mixed some honeyed wine, and taking a seat over against Odysseus thus cheerily began:

"Now, stranger, eat what servants have, this young pig's flesh. The fatted hogs are eaten by the suitors, who heed not in their hearts the wrath of Heaven, nor even pity. Yet reckless deeds the blessed gods love not; they honor justice and men's upright deeds. Why, evil-minded cruel men who land on a foreign shore, and Zeus allows them plunder so that they sail back home with well-filled ships—even on the hearts of such falls a great fear of heavenly wrath. But these men know of something, having heard the utterance of some god about his[67] mournful end, and therefore they are minded to woo so lawlessly, never departing to their homes, but at their ease wasting this wealth with recklessness and sparing naught. For every day and night sent us by Zeus, they slay their victims, no mere one or two; and wine they also waste with reckless draughts. Odysseus' means were vast. No noble has so much on the dark mainland or in Ithaca itself. No twenty men together have such revenues as he. I will reckon up the sum. Twelve herds upon the mainland; as many flocks of sheep; as many droves of swine; as many roving bands of goats; all shepherded by foreigners and herdsmen of his own. Then here in Ithaca graze roving bands of goats, eleven in all, along the farther shore, and trusty herdsmen watch them. Of these the herdsman every day drives up the fatted goat that seems the best. My task it is to guard and keep these swine, and picking carefully the best to send it to the suitors."

So spoke the swineherd, while his companion hungrily ate his meat and drank with eagerness his wine in silence, sowing the seeds of evil for the suitors. But after he had dined and stayed his heart with food, Eumaeus,

[67] Odysseus.

filling for his guest the cup from which he drank, gave it brimful of wine. Odysseus took it and was glad at heart, and speaking in winged words he said:

"My friend, who was the man that bought you with his wealth and was so very rich and powerful as you say? You said he died for Agamemnon's honor. Tell me. I may have known some such as he. Zeus and the other deathless gods must know if I have seen him and can give you news; but I have traveled far."

Then said to him the swineherd, the overseer: "Old man, no traveler coming here to tell of him could win his wife or son to trust the story. Lightly do vagrants seeking hospitality tell lies, and never care to speak the truth. So when a vagabond reaches the land of Ithaca, he comes and chatters cheating stories to my queen. And she receives him well and, giving entertainment, questions him closely, while from her weeping eyelids trickle tears; for that is the way with wives when husbands die afar. You too, old man, would soon be patching up a story if somebody would give you clothes, a coat and tunic. But probably already dogs and swift birds have plucked the flesh from off his bones and life has left him; or fishes devoured him in the deep, and on the land his bones are lying wrapped in a heap of sand. So he died, far away, and for his friends sorrow is left behind—for all of them, and most of all for me; for never another such kind master shall I find, go where I may, not even if I return to my father's and mother's house, where I was born and where my parents reared me. Yet nowadays for them I do not greatly grieve, much as I wish to see them and to be in my own land; but longing possesses me for lost Odysseus. Why, stranger, though he is not here I speak his name with awe; for he was very kind and loved me from his heart, and worshipful I call him even when he is away."

Then long-tried royal Odysseus answered thus: "Friend, though you wholly contradict and say he will not come, and ever unbelieving is your heart, yet I declare, not with mere words but with an oath, Odysseus will return. Give me the fee for welcome news when he arrives at home. Then clothe me in a coat and tunic, goodly garments. Before that time, however great my need, I will take nothing; for hateful as the gates of hell is he who pressed by poverty tells cheating tales. First then of all the gods be witness Zeus, and let this hospitable table and the hearth of good Odysseus whereto I come be witness: all this shall be accomplished exactly as I say. This very year Odysseus comes. As this moon wanes and as the next appears, he shall return and punish all who wrong his wife and gallant son."

And, swineherd Eumaeus, you answered him and said: "Old man, I never then shall give that fee for welcome news, nor will Odysseus reach his home. Nay, drink in peace. Let us turn to other thoughts, and do not bring such matters to remembrance. Ah, my heart aches within when one recalls my honored master! As for the oath, why let it be; yet may Odysseus come, as I desire!—I and Penelope, Laërtes the old man, and prince Telemachus. But now I have unceasing grief about Odysseus' child, Telemachus; whom when the gods had made to grow like a young sapling, and I would often say that he would stand in men's esteem no whit behind his father, glorious in form and beauty, some god or man upset the balanced mind within, and off he went for tidings of his father to hallowed Pylos. And now the lordly suitors watch for his coming home, hoping to have the race of prince Arceisius[68] blotted from Ithaca and left without a name. . . .

And now the night came on, moonless and foul. Zeus rained all night; and strong the west wind blew, a wet wind always. To his companions[69] spoke Odysseus, making trial of the swineherd to see if he would pull his own coat off and offer him, or order one of the men to give a coat, through love of him.

"Hearken, Eumaeus, and all you other men, and I will boast a bit and tell a story; for crazy wine so bids, which sets a man, even if wise, to singing loud and laughing lightly, and makes him dance and brings out stories really better left untold. But since I have begun to croak, I'll not be silent. Would I were in my prime, my vigor firm, as in the days when we went under Troy[70] and set an ambush. Odysseus was our captain, and Atreides Menelaus, and with them I was third; for so they ordered. Now when we reached the city and the lofty wall, in the thick bushes by the citadel, among some reeds and marsh-grass, curled up beneath our armor, we laid us down to sleep. An ugly night came on, although the north wind fell, and bleak it was. From overhead came snow, like hoarfrost, cold; and ice formed on the edges of our shields. Then all the other men had coats and tunics, and slept in comfort with their shields snug round their shoulders. But I at starting foolishly left my coat with my companions, because I did not think I should be cold at all; so off I came with nothing but my shield and colored doublet. But when it was the third watch of the night and the stars crossed the zenith, I spoke to Odysseus who was near, nudging him with my elbow, and readily he listened:

"'High-born son of Laërtes, ready Odysseus, I shall not be among the living long. This cold is killing me, because I have no coat. Some god beguiled me into wearing nothing but my tunic. Now there is no escape.'

"So said I, and he at once had an idea in mind—so ready was he both to plan and fight—and speaking in an undertone he said: 'Keep quiet for the present, lest some other Achaean hear.'

"Then raising his head and resting on his elbow, thus he spoke: 'Hark, friends! A dream from heaven came to me in my sleep. Yes, we have come a long way from the ships. Would there were some one here to tell Atreides

---

[68] Odysseus' grandfather.   [69] In the meantime, some younger herdsmen had joined Odysseus and Eumaeus.   [70] Continuing to conceal his identity, Odysseus had told Eumaeus that he was a Cretan veteran of the Trojan War who had come to grief in Egypt.

Agamemnon, the shepherd of the people, to send us more men hither from the fleet.'

"As he thus spoke, up Thoas sprung, Andraemon's son, who, quickly casting off his purple coat, went running to the ships. I, in his garment, lay comfortably down till gold-throned morning dawned.

"So would I now were in my prime, my vigor firm; then one of the swineherds of the farm might give a coat, through kindness and respect for a deserving man. Now they despise me for the sorry clothes I wear."

Then, swineherd Eumaeus, you answered him and said: "Old man, the boastings you have uttered are not ill. You have not spoken an improper or a silly word. Therefore you shall not lack for clothes nor anything besides which it is fit a hard-pressed suppliant should find—at least for now; tomorrow you shall wrap yourself in your own rags. There are not many coats and extra tunics here to wear, but simply one apiece But when Odysseus' son returns, he will give a coat and tunic for your clothing and send you where your heart and soul may bid you go."

So saying, he rose and placed a bed beside the fire, and threw upon it skins of sheep and goats. On this Odysseus laid him down, and over him Eumaeus threw a great shaggy coat which lay at hand as extra clothing, to put on when there came a bitter storm.

So here Odysseus slept, and by his side the young men slept, but not the swineherd. A bed here pleased him not, thus parted from his swine, but he prepared to venture forth. Glad was Odysseus that Eumaeus took such care of his estate while he was gone. And first Eumaeus slung a sharp-edged sword about his sturdy shoulders, put on his storm-proof shaggy coat, picked up the fleece of a large full-grown goat, took a sharp spear to keep off dogs and men, and went away to rest where lay the white-toothed swine under a hollow rock, sheltered from Boreas.[71]

From BOOK XV

Now to spacious Lacedaemon went Pallas Athene to seek the noble son of resolute Odysseus, wishing to call his home to mind and bid him hasten. She found Telemachus and the worthy son of Nestor[72] lying within the porch of famous Menelaus. The son of Nestor was still wrapped in gentle sleep; but to Telemachus came no welcome sleep, for through the immortal night thoughts in his heart about his father kept him awake. So clear-eyed Athene, drawing near, addressed him thus:

"Telemachus, it is not well to wander longer far from home, leaving your

[71] The north wind. [72] Peisistratus, who had accompanied Telemachus on his journey from Nestor's court at Pylus to Menelaus' palace at Sparta.

wealth behind and persons in your house so insolent as these; for they may
swallow all your wealth, sharing with one another, while you are gone a fruitless journey. Nay, with all haste urge Menelaus, good at the war cry, to send
you forth, that you may find your blameless mother still at home. Already
her father and her brothers press her to wed Eurymachus; for he excels all
suitors in his gifts and overtops their dowry. But let her not against your will
take treasure from your home. You know a woman's way: she strives to
enrich his house who marries her, while of her former children and the
husband of her youth when he is dead she thinks not, and she talks of him no
more. Go then and put your household in the charge of her among the maids
who seems the best, until the gods grant you an honored wife. And let me
tell you more; lay it to heart; by a deliberate plan the leaders of the suitors
now guard the strait twixt Ithaca and rugged Samos,[73] and seek to cut you
off before you gain your native land. Yet this I think shall never be; rather
the earth shall cover some of the suitors who devour your living. Still, keep
your stanch ship off the islands and sail both night and day; and one of the
immortals who guards and keeps you safe shall send a favoring breeze. When
then you reach the nearest shore of Ithaca, send forward to the city your
ship and all her crew, and go yourself before all else straight to the swineherd, who is the keeper of your swine and ever loyal. There rest a night, but
send the swineherd to the city to bear the news to heedful Penelope how
you are safe and how you have returned from Pylos."

So saying, Athene passed away to high Olympus. But from sweet sleep
Telemachus waked Nestor's son, touching him with his heel, and thus addressed him: "Wake, Nestor's son, Peisistratus! Bring out the strong-hoofed
horses and yoke them to the car, that we may make our journey."

Then Nestor's son, Peisistratus, made answer: "Telemachus, we cannot,
eager for the journey though we are, drive in the dusky night. It will be
morning soon. Wait then awhile until the royal son of Atreus, the spearman
Menelaus, brings his gifts, places them in the chariot, and sends us forth
with cheering words upon our way. For a guest remembers all his days the
hospitable man who showed him kindness."

He spoke, and soon the gold-throned morning came; and Menelaus, good
at the war cry, now drew near, just risen from bed by fair-haired Helen.
When the son of Odysseus spied him, in haste he girt his glossy tunic round
his body, and threw a great cloak round his sturdy shoulders. So forth he
went and drawing near thus spoke Telemachus, the son of princely Odysseus:

"O son of Atreus, heaven-descended Menelaus, leader of hosts, now at last
let me go to my own native land; for my heart longs for home."

Then answered Menelaus, good at the war cry: "Telemachus, I will not

[73] A large island next to Ithaca, past which Telemachus normally would have
sailed on his way home.

keep you longer if you desire to go. I blame a host if overkind, or overrude. Better, good sense in all things. It is an equal fault to thrust away the guest who does not care to go, and to detain the impatient. Best make the stranger welcome while he stays, and speed him when he wishes. But wait until I bring you gifts and place them in your chariot, beautiful gifts, as you yourself shall see. . . ."

. . . Then after they had stayed desire for drink and food, Telemachus and Nestor's gallant son harnessed the horses, mounted the gay chariot, and off they drove from porch and echoing portico. After them came the son of Atreus, light-haired Menelaus, in his right hand a golden cup of cheering wine, for them to pour at starting. He stopped before the horses and pledging them he said:

"A health to you, young men! And say the same to Nestor, the shepherd of the people; for he was kind to me as any father those days we young Achaeans were in the war at Troy."

Then answered him discreet Telemachus: "Even as you say, O heaven-descended prince, when we arrive we will report all these your words. And would that coming home to Ithaca I there might find Odysseus in my home, and so might say how after meeting every kindness here with you I went my way and carried many precious treasures with me!"

On his right, as he was speaking, flew an eagle, bearing in his claws a large white goose, a tame fowl from the yard. People ran shouting after, men and women. But as the bird drew near, he darted to the right before the horses. All saw it and were glad, and in their breasts their hearts grew warm.[74] And thus began Peisistratus, the son of Nestor:

"Think, heaven-descended Menelaus, leader of hosts! Is it we to whom God shows this sign, or is it you?"

He spoke and valiant Menelaus pondered, doubting what he should think and rightly answer. But long-robed Helen,[75] taking up the word, spoke thus: "Hearken and I will prophesy such things as the immortals bring to mind, things which I think will happen. As the eagle caught the goose—she, fattened in the house; he, coming from the hills where he was born and bred—so shall Odysseus, through many woes and wanderings, come home and take revenge. Even now, perhaps, he is at home, sowing the seeds of ill for all the suitors."

Then answered her discreet Telemachus: "Zeus grant it so, he the loud thunderer, husband of Hera! [76] Then would I there too, as to any god, give thanks to you."

He spoke and laid the lash upon the horses, and very quickly they started

[74] In ancient divination, which was often based on observing the flight patterns of certain birds, a turn to the right by a bird was interpreted as a good omen.   [75] After the Greek victory over the the Trojans, Menelaus brought Helen back with him to Sparta.   [76] The goddess Hera.

toward the plain, hastening through the city; and all day long they shook the yoke they bore between them.

Now the sun sank and all the ways grew dark; and the men arrived at Pherae,[77] before the house of Diocles, the son of Orsilochus, whose father was Alpheius. There for the night they rested; he gave them entertainment. Then as the early rosy-fingered dawn appeared, they harnessed the horses, mounted the gay chariot, and off they drove from porch and echoing portico. Telemachus cracked the whip to start, and not unwillingly the pair flew off, and by and by they came to the steep citadel of Pylos. Then said Telemachus to Nestor's son:

"O son of Nestor, could you give and perform the promise I shall ask? Friends from of old we call ourselves, because of our fathers' friendship. Besides, we are alike in years, and this our journey will make the tie more close. Do not then, heaven-descended prince, take me beyond my ship, but leave me there; for fear old Nestor, eager for kindness, detain me at his house against my will, when I should hasten on."

So he spoke, and the son of Nestor doubted within his heart if he could rightly give and perform the promise. Yet on reflecting thus, it seemed the better way. He turned his horses toward the swift ship and shore, took out and set by the ship's stern the goodly gifts—the clothing and the gold which Menelaus gave—and hastening Telemachus, spoke thus in winged words:

"Quickly embark and summon all your crew before I reach my home and tell old Nestor; for in my mind and heart full well I know how stern his temper is. He will not let you go; he will himself come here and call you. I tell you, too, go back he will not empty-handed; for he will be very angry, notwithstanding what you say."

So saying, he drove his full-maned horses to the town of Pylos, and quickly reached the palace. But Telemachus, inspiriting his crew, called to them thus: "Put all the gear in order, friends, on the black ship; and come aboard yourselves and let us make our journey."

So he spoke, and willingly they heeded and obeyed; quickly they came on board and took their place at the pins.

With these things he was busied, and now by the ship's stern was making prayers and offerings to Athene, when up there came a wanderer, exiled from Argos through having killed a man. He was a seer, and of the lineage of Melampus.[78] . . .

It was [Polypheides'] son drew near, named Theoclymenus, and stood before Telemachus. He found him making offerings and prayers beside the swift black ship: and speaking in winged words he said:

"Friend, since I find you offering burnt-offerings here, by these offerings and the god I will entreat you, and by your own life too, and that of those

---

[77] A town between Sparta and Pylos. [78] A famous soothsayer.

who follow: tell truly all I ask. Hold nothing back. Who are you? Of what people? Where is your town and kindred?"

Then answered him discreet Telemachus: "Well, stranger, I will plainly tell you all. By birth I am of Ithaca. My father is Odysseus—if ever such there were! But long ago he died, a mournful death; so I, with men and a black ship, am come to gather news of my long-absent father."

Then answered godlike Theoclymenus: "Like you, I too am far from home, because I killed a kinsman. He has many relatives and friends in grazing Argos, and with the Achaeans their influence is large. To shun the death and the dark doom which they would deal, I flee; for I must be a wanderer now from tribe to tribe. Set me upon your ship, a fugitive and suppliant. Let them not kill me; for I know they will pursue."

Then answered him discreet Telemachus: "I shall not thrust you forth from the trim ship against your will. Nay, follow! In our land you shall receive what we can give."

So saying he took the brazen spear from Theoclymenus and laid it on the deck of the curved ship. Telemachus himself came on the seabound ship and sat him in the stern, while by his side sat Theoclymenus. The others loosed the cables. And now Telemachus, inspiriting his men, bade them lay hold upon the tackling, and they busily obeyed. Raising the pinewood mast, they set it in the hollow socket, binding it firm with forestays, and tightened the white sail with twisted ox-hide thongs. And a favorable wind clear-eyed Athene sent, which swept with violence along the sky, so that the scudding ship might swiftly make her way through the salt ocean water, Thus on they ran, past Crouni[79] and the pleasant streams of Chalcis. The sun was setting and the ways were growing dark as the ship drew near to Pheae, driven by the breeze of Zeus; then on past sacred Elis where the Epeians rule. From here Telemachus steered for the Pointed Isles,[80] uncertain if he should escape from death or fall a prey.

Meanwhile at the lodge Odysseus and the noble swineherd were eating supper, and with them supped the others. And after they had stayed desire for drink and food, thus spoke Odysseus—making trial of the swineherd, to see if he would longer give him a hearty welcome and urge his staying at the farm, or if he would send him straightway to the town:

"Hearken, Eumaeus and all you other men! I want to go tomorrow to beg about the town, for fear I burden you and these your men. Only direct me well, and give me a trusty guide to show the way. Once in the city, I must wander by myself, and hope some man will give a cup and crust. And if I come to the house of princely Odysseus, there I will tell my tale to heedful Penelope and join the audacious suitors, who might perhaps give me a meal; since they have great abundance. Soon I could serve them well in all they

[79] This and the following names refer to places on the west coast of Greece, opposite Ithaca.   [80] Samos and Ithaca.

want. For let me tell you this, and do you mark and listen: by favor of the Guide-god, Hermes, who lends the grace and dignity to all the deeds of men, in servants' work I have no equal—in laying a fire well, splitting dry wood, carving and roasting meat, and pouring wine—indeed, in all the ways that poor men serve their betters."

Then deeply moved said you, swineherd Eumaeus: "Why, stranger, how came such a notion in your mind? You certainly must long to die that very instant when you consent to plunge into the throng of suitors, whose arrogance and outrage reach to the iron heavens. Their servants are not such as you; but younger men, well dressed in coats and tunics, ever with glossy heads and handsome faces, are they who do them service. Their polished tables are laden with bread and meat and wine. No, stay with us! Nobody is disturbed that you are here, not I myself, nor any one of these my men. And when Odysseus' son returns, he will give a coat and tunic for your clothing and send you where your heart and soul may bid you go."

Then answered him long-tried royal Odysseus: "May you, Eumaeus, be as dear to father Zeus as now to me, for having stopped my wandering and saved me bitter woe. Nothing is harder for a man than restless roaming. It is for the cursed belly's sake that men meet cruel ills when wandering, misfortune, and distresses come. Yet while you keep me here, bidding me wait your master, pray tell me of the mother of princely Odysseus, and of his father, whom when he went away he left behind on the threshold of old age. Are they still living in the sunshine, or are they now already dead and in the house of Hades?"

Then said to him the swineherd, the overseer: "Well, stranger, I will plainly tell you all. Laërtes is still living, but ever prays to Zeus to let life leave his limbs here at his home; for he mourns exceedingly his absent son and the early-wedded trusty wife whose death distressed him sorely and brought him into premature old age. In sorrow for her famous son, she pined away—a piteous death! May none die so who dwells with me, who is my friend and does me kindness. . . .

Then answering said wise Odysseus: "Swineherd Eumaeus, certainly when you were small you must have wandered far from home and kindred. Tell me about it; tell me plainly too. Was the wide-wayed city of your people sacked, the city where your father and honored mother dwelt? Or when you were alone among your sheep and cattle, did foemen take you on their ships and bring you across the sea to the palace of a man who paid a proper price?"

Then said to him the swineherd, the overseer: "Stranger, since now you ask of this and question me, quietly listen; take your ease, and sit and drink your wine. These nights are vastly long. There is time enough to sleep, and time to cheer ourselves with hearing stories. You must not go to bed till bedtime; too much sleeping harms. As for the others here, if anybody's heart and liking bids, let him go off and sleep; then early in the morning after eating, let him attend his master's swine. But let us drink and feast within the lodge and please ourselves with telling one another tales of piteous ill; for afterwards a man finds pleasure in his pains, when he has suffered long and wandered long. So I will tell you what you ask and seek to know. . . ."

Then thus replied high-born Odysseus: "Eumaeus, you have deeply stirred the heart within my breast, telling these tales of all the troubles you have borne.[81] Yet side by side with evil Zeus surely gave you good, since at the end of all your toils you reached the house of a kind man who furnishes you food and drink in plenty. A comfortable life you lead; but I come here a wanderer through many cities."

So they conversed together, then lay and slept a little while, not long; for soon came bright-throned dawn.

Meantime, approaching shore, the comrades of Telemachus slackened their sail, hastily lowered the mast, and with their oars rowed the vessel to her moorings. Here they cast anchor and made fast the cables; and going forth themselves upon the shore, prepared their dinner and mixed the sparkling wine. Then after they had stayed desire for food and drink, discreet Telemachus thus began:

"Sail the black-hulled ship, my men, straight to the town; I go to the fields and herdsmen. At evening, after looking at the farm, I too will come to town. Tomorrow I will make you payment for your voyage by a bounteous feast of meat and pleasant wine."

Then up spoke godlike Theoclymenus: "Where shall I go, my child? To whose house come, of all the men who rule in rocky Ithaca? Or shall I go directly to your mother's house and yours?"

Then answered him discreet Telemachus: "At any other time I would bid you come to us, because we have no lack of means of welcome. But for yourself it would be somewhat dreary now. I shall be gone, and my mother will not see you; for she is not often seen in the same room with the suitors, but in an upper chamber far away she tends her loom. But I will name another man to whom you well might go: Eurymachus, the illustrious son of skillful Polybus, whom nowadays the men of Ithaca look upon as a god, for he is certainly the chief man here. He much desires to wed my mother and obtain the honors of Odysseus. Nevertheless, Olympian Zeus, who dwells in the clear sky, knows whether before the wedding he will set a day of ill."

Even as he spoke, upon his right there flew a bird, a hawk, Apollo's speedy messenger. With his claws he tore the dove he held and scattered down its feathers to the ground, midway between the ship and Telemachus himself. Then Theoclymenus, calling Telemachus aside from his companions, held fast his hand and spoke and thus addressed him:

"Telemachus, not without God's warrant flew this bird upon our right. I

[81] Eumaeus has meanwhile told Odysseus about his life of hardship and suffering, which ended when he arrived in Ithaca and became Odysseus' swineherd.

knew him at a glance to be a bird of omen. There is no house in Ithaca more kingly than your own; and you shall always be the rulers here."

Then answered him discreet Telemachus: "Ah stranger, would these words of yours might be fulfilled! Soon should you know my kindness and many a gift from me, and every man you met would call you blessed."

Then turning to Peiraeus, his good comrade: "Peiraeus, son of Clytius, you always do my bidding best of all the men who followed me to Pylos; so take this stranger to your home and treat him kindly, and show him honor till the time that I shall come."

Then answered him Peiraeus, the famous spearman: "Telemachus, though you stay long, I still will entertain him; no lack of welcome shall there be."

So saying, Peiraeus went aboard the ship and called the crew to come on board and loose cables. Quickly they came and took their places at the pins. Telemachus bound to his feet his beautiful sandals and took his ponderous spear, tipped with sharp bronze, from the ship's deck. The sailors loosed the cables and thrusting off the ship sailed to the town, as they were ordered by Telemachus, the son of princely Odysseus. But him, meanwhile, his feet bore swiftly onward until he reached the court where were the countless swine with whom the trusty swineherd lodged, still faithful to his master.

BOOK XVI

Meanwhile at the lodge Odysseus and the noble swineherd prepared their breakfast in the early dawn, before the lighted fire, having already sent the herdsmen with the droves of swine forth to the fields. As Telemachus drew near, the dogs that love to bark began to wag their tails, but did not bark. Royal Odysseus noticed the dogs wagging their tails, and the sound of footsteps reached him; and straightway to Eumaeus he spoke these winged words:

"Eumaeus, certainly a friend is coming, at least a man you know; for the dogs here do not bark, but wag their tails, and I hear the tramp of feet."

The words were hardly uttered when his own son stood in the doorway. In surprise up sprang the swineherd, and from his hands the vessels fell with which he had been busied, mixing sparkling wine. He went to meet his master, and kissed his face, each of his beautiful eyes, and both his hands, letting the big tears fall. And as a loving father greets the son who comes from foreign lands, ten years away, his only child, now grown a man, for whom he long has sorrowed; even so the noble swineherd took princely Telemachus in his arms and kissed him over and over, as one escaped from death, and sobbing said to him in winged words:

"So you are here, Telemachus, my own sweet light! I said I should not see you any more after you went away by ship to Pylos. Come in then, child, and let me cheer my heart with looking at you, just come from far away. You do not often visit the farm and herdsmen. You tarry in the town; for nowadays you want to watch the wasteful throng of suitors."

Then answered him discreet Telemachus: "So be it, father! [82] It is for your sake I am here, to see you with my eyes, and hear you tell if my mother still is staying at the hall, or if at last some stranger won her, and so Odysseus' bed, empty of occupants, stands covered with foul cobwebs."

Then answered him the swineherd, the overseer: "Indeed she stays with patient heart within your hall, and wearily the nights and days are wasted with her tears."

So saying, Eumaeus took Telemachus' brazen spear, and Telemachus went in and over the stone threshold. As he drew near, his father, Odysseus, yielded him his seat; but Telemachus on his part checked him, saying:

"Be seated, stranger. Elsewhere we shall find a seat at this our farm. Here is a man will give one."

He spoke, and his father turned and sat once more; but the swineherd threw green brushwood down and on its top a fleece, on which the dear son of Odysseus took his seat. And now the swineherd brought platters of roasted meat, which those who ate the day before had left. Bustling about he heaped bread in the baskets, and in an ivy bowl mixed honeyed wine, then took a seat himself over against princely Odysseus, and on the food spread out before them they laid hands. So after they had stayed desire for drink and food, to the noble swineherd said Telemachus:

"Father, whence came this stranger? How did his sailors bring him to Ithaca? Whom did they call themselves? For I am sure he did not come on foot."

Then, swineherd Eumaeus, you answered him and said: "Well, I will tell you all the truth, my child. He calls himself by birth of lowland Crete, but says he has come to many cities in his wanderings; so Heaven ordained his lot. Lately he ran away from a ship of the Thesprotians and came to my farm here. I place him in your charge. Do what you will. He calls himself your suppliant."

Then answered him discreet Telemachus:: "Eumaeus, truly these are bitter words which you have said. How can I take a stranger home? I am myself but young and cannot trust my arm to right me with the man who wrongs me first. Moreover my mother's feeling wavers, whether to bide beside me here and keep the house, and thus revere her husband's bed and heed the public voice, or finally to follow some chief of the Achaeans who woos her in the hall with largest gifts. However, since the stranger has reached your lodging here, I will clothe him in a coat and tunic, goodly garments, give him a two-edged sword and sandals for his feet, and I will

[82] A term of endearment which Telemachus often uses when he addresses the swineherd.

send him where his heart and soul may bid him go. Or, if you like, serve him yourself and keep him at the farm; and I will send him clothing and all his food to eat, so that he may not burden you and yours. Yonder among the suitors I would not have him go; for they are full of wanton pride. So they might mock him—a cruel grief to me. Hard is it even for a powerful man to act against a crowd; because together they are far too strong."

Then said to him long-tried royal Odysseus: "Friend—for surely I too have a right to answer—my heart is sore at hearing what you say, that suitors work abomination at the palace against a man like you. But tell me, do you willingly submit, or are the people of your land adverse to you, led by some voice of God? Or have you any cause to blame your brothers, on whom a man relies for aid when bitter strifes arise? Would that, to match my spirit, I were young as you, and were the son of good Odysseus, or even Odysseus' self, come from his wanderings, as there still is room for hope; then quickly should my foe strike off my head, or I would prove the bane of all these suitors when I should cross the hall of Laërtes' son Odysseus. And should they by their number crush me, all single and alone, far rather would I die, cut down within my hall, than constantly behold disgraceful deeds, strangers abused, and damsels dragged to shame through the fair palace, wine running waste, men eating up my bread, all idly, uselessly, to win what cannot be!"

Then answered him discreet Telemachus: "Well, stranger, I will plainly tell you all. My people as a whole bear me no grudge or hate; nor yet can I blame brothers, on whom a man relies for aid when bitter strifes arise; for the son of Kronos made our race run in a single line. Arceisius begot a single son Laërtes; and he, the single son Odysseus; Odysseus left me here at home, the single son of his begetting, and of me had no joy. But bands of evil-minded men now fill my house; for all the nobles who bear sway among the islands—Doulichion, Same, and woody Zacynthus—and they who have the power in rocky Ithaca, all woo my mother and despoil my home. She neither declines the hated suit nor has she power to end it, while they with feasting impoverish my home and soon will bring me also to destruction. However, in the lap of the gods these matters lie. But, father,[83] quickly go and say to steadfast Penelope that I am safe and have returned from Pylos. I will stay here; do you come hither too; and tell your tidings to her only. Let none of the rest of the Achaeans hear; for many are they that plot against me."

Then, swineherd Eumaeus, you answered him and said: "I see, I understand; you speak to one who knows. But now declare me this and plainly say, shall I go tell Laërtes on my way, wretched Laërtes, who for a time, though grieving greatly for Odysseus, still oversaw his fields and with his men at home would drink and eat as appetite inclined; but from the day you went by ship to Pylos did never eat nor drink the same, they say, nor oversaw his

---

[83] Addressing Eumaeus, not Odysseus.

fields, but full of moans and sighs sits sorrowing, while the flesh wastes upon his bones."

Then answered him discreet Telemachus: "It is hard, but though it grieves us, we will let him be; if all that men desire were in their power, the first thing we should choose would be the coming of my father. No, give your message and return, and do not wander through the fields to find Laërtes. But tell my mother to send forthwith her housemaid thither, yet privately; for to the old man she might bear the news."

So saying, he dispatched the swineherd, who took his sandals, bound them to his feet, and went to town. Yet not unnoticed by Athene swineherd Eumaeus left the farm; but she herself drew near in likeness of a woman, one fair and tall and skilled in dainty work. By the lodge door she stood, visible to Odysseus. Telemachus did not glance her way nor notice her; for not to every one do gods appear. Odysseus saw her, and the dogs; yet the dogs did not bark, but whining slunk away across the place. With her brows she made a sign; royal Odysseus understood, came forth from the hall past the great courtyard wall, and stood before her, and Athene said:

"High-born son of Laërtes, ready Odysseus, tell now your story to your son. Hide it no longer. Then having planned the suitors' death and doom, go forward both of you into the famous city. And I myself will not be far away, for I am eager for the combat."

She spoke and with a golden wand Athene touched Odysseus. And first she laid a spotless robe and tunic on his body, and then increased his bulk and bloom. Again he grew dark-hued; his cheeks were rounded, and dark the beard became about his chin. This done, she went away; and now Odysseus entered the lodge. His son was awe-struck and reverently turned his eyes aside, fearing it was a god. Then speaking in winged words he said:

"Stranger, you seem a different person now and a while ago. Your clothes are different and your flesh is not the same. You surely are one of the gods who hold the open sky. Nay, then, be gracious! So will we give you grateful offerings and fine-wrought gifts of gold. Have mercy on us!"

Then long-tried royal Odysseus answered: "I am no god. Why liken me to the immortals? I am your father, him for whom you sighed and suffered long, enduring outrage at the hands of men."

So saying, he kissed his son and down his cheeks upon the ground let fall a tear, which always hitherto he sternly had suppressed. But Telemachus— for he did not yet believe it was his father—finding his words once more made answer thus:

"No, you are not Odysseus, not my father! Some god beguiles me, to make me weep and sorrow more. No mortal man by his own wit could work such wonders, unless a god came to his aid and by his will made him with ease a young man or an old. For lately you were old and meanly clad; now you are like the gods who hold the open sky."

Then wise Odysseus answered him and said: "Telemachus, it is not right when here your father stands, to marvel overmuch and to be so amazed. Be sure no other Odysseus ever will appear; but as you see me, it is I, I who have suffered long and wandered long, and now in the twentieth year come to my native land. This is the work of the Plunderer, Athene, who makes me what she will—for she has power—now like a beggar, now again a youth in fair attire. Easily can the gods who hold the open sky give glory to a mortal man or give him shame."

So saying, he sat down; whereat Telemachus, throwing his arms round his good father, began to sob and pour forth tears, and in them both arose a longing of lament. Loud were their cries and more unceasing than those of birds, ospreys or crook-clawed vultures, when farmers take away their young before the wings are grown: so pitifully fell the tears beneath their brows. And daylight had gone down upon their weeping, had not Telemachus suddenly addressed his father thus:

"Why, father, by what ship did sailors bring you to Ithaca? Whom did they call themselves? For I am sure you did not come on foot."

Then said to him long-tried royal Odysseus: "Well, I will tell you, child, the very truth. The Phaeacians brought me here, notable men at sea, who pilot others too who come their way. They brought me across the sea on a swift ship asleep, landed me here in Ithaca and gave me glorious gifts, much bronze and gold and woven stuff; which treasures by the gods' command are laid away in caves. Here I now am by bidding of Athene, that we may plan together the slaughter of our foes. Come tell me then the number of the suitors, that I may know how many and what sort of men they are; and so, weighing the matter in my gallant heart, I may decide if we can meet them quite alone, without allies, or whether we shall seek the aid of others."

Then answered him discreet Telemachus: "Verily, father, I have ever heard your great renown, what a warrior you are in arm and what a sage in council. But now you speak of something far too vast; I am astonished. Two could not fight a troop of valiant men. The suitors number no mere ten, nor twice ten either; many more. You shall soon learn their number. From Doulichion, two and fifty chosen youth and six attendants; four and twenty men from Same; from Zacynthus twenty young Achaeans; twelve out of Ithaca itself, all men of mark, with whom are also the page Medon and the sacred bard, besides two followers skilled in table service. If we confront all these within the hall, bitter and grievous may the vengeance be, gained by your coming. So if you possibly can think of aid, consider who will aid us now whole-heartedly."

Then said to him long-tried royal Odysseus: "Nay, let me speak, and do you mark and listen. Consider if Athene, joined with father Zeus, suffice for us, or shall I seek for other aid?"

Then answered him discreet Telemachus: "Excellent helpers are the two you name, who sit among the clouds on high. All else they govern, all man-kind and the immortal gods."

Then said to him long-tried royal Odysseus: "Not long will they be absent from the mighty fray when in my hall betwixt the suitors and ourselves the tug of war is tried. But go at early morning straightway home, and join the audacious suitors. Thereafter the swineherd shall bring me to the city, like an old and wretched beggar. And if they treat me rudely in my home, let the faithful heart within your breast endure what I must bear; yes, though they drag me through the palace by the heels and out of door, or hurl their mis-siles at me, see and be patient still. Bid them, however, cease their folly, and with gentle words dissuade. They will not heed you, for their day of doom draws near. But this I will say farther; mark it well. When wise Athene puts it in my mind, then I will nod my head, and you take note. And all the fighting gear that lies about the hall do you collect and lay in a corner of the lofty chamber, carefully, every piece. Then with soft words beguile the suitors when they, because they miss it, question you: 'I put it by out of the smoke, for it looks no longer like the armor which Odysseus left behind when he went away to Troy; it is all tarnished, where the scent of fire has come nigh. Besides, the son of Kronos brought this graver fear to mind. You might when full of wine begin a quarrel and give each other wounds, making a scandal of the feast and of your wooing. Steel itself draws men on.' Yet privily reserve two swords, two spears, two leathern shields, for us to seize—to rush and seize. And thereupon shall Pallas Athene and all-wise Zeus con-found the suitors. Nay, this I will say farther; mark it well. If you are truly mine, my very blood, then that Odysseus now is here let no man know; let not Laërtes learn it, let not the swineherd, let none of the household, nor Penelope herself. But you and I alone will test the temper of the women. And we might also try the serving-men, and see who honors and respects us in his heart, and who neglects and scorns a man like you."

Then answered him his noble son and said: "My father, you shall know my heart, believe me, by and by. No laggard thoughts are mine; and yet I think your plan will prove for neither of us gain, and so I say: Consider! Long will you vainly go, trying the different men among the farms; while undisturbed within the hall these waste your wealth with recklessness and do not spare. But I advise your finding out the women, and learning who dis-honor you and who are guiltless. As to the men about the place, I would not prove them. Let that at any rate be thought of later, when you are really sure of signs from aegis-bearing Zeus."

So they conversed together. But in the mean while on to Ithaca ran the stanch ship which brought Telemachus and all his crew from Pylos. When they had entered the deep harbor, they hauled the black-hulled ship ashore, and stately squires carried their armor and straightway bore the goodly gifts to Clytius' house. And now they sent a page to the palace of Odysseus, to tell the news to heedful Penelope—how Telemachus was at the farm, but had ordered that the ship sail to the city—lest the stately queen should be alarmed and shed a tender tear. So the two met, the herald and the noble swineherd, while on the self-same errand, bearing tidings to the queen. And when they reached the palace of the noble king, the page said to Penelope in hearing of her maids: "O queen, your son has come from Pylos." But the swineherd stood beside Penelope and so reported all that her dear son had bade him say. Then when he had delivered all his charge, he departed to his swine, and left the court and hall.

But the suitors grew dismayed and downcast in their hearts, and came forth from the hall past the great courtyard wall and there before the gate sat down to council; and first Eurymachus,[84] the son of Polybus, addressed them:

"Friends, here is a monstrous action impudently brought to pass, this journey of Telemachus. We said it should not be. Come, then, and let us launch the best black ship we have, and get together fishermen for rowers, quickly to carry tidings to our friends, and bid them sail for home with all the speed they may."

The words were hardly uttered when Amphinomus,[85] turning in his place, sighted the ship in the deep harbor, some of her crew furling the sail and some with oars in hand. Then lightly laughing, thus he called to his companions:

"No need to send a message now, for here they are. Some god has told the story; or else they saw the vessel pass and could not catch her."

He spoke, and all arose and hastened to the shore. Swiftly the black-hulled ship was hauled ashore, and stately squires carried their armor. Then men themselves went in a body to the assembly and suffered no one, either young or old, to join them there; and thus Antinoüs, Eupeithes' son, addressed them:

"Strange, how gods help this man out of danger! By day our sentries sat upon the windy heights, posted in close succession; and after sunset, we did not pass the night ashore, but sailed our swift ship on the sea, awaiting sacred dawn, lying in wait to seize and slay Telemachus. Meantime some god has brought him home. Then let us here contrive a miserable ending for Telemachus, not letting him escape; for while he lives, nothing, be sure, will prosper. He is himself shrewd in his thoughts and plans, and people here proffer us no more aid. Come then, before he gathers the Achaeans in a council. Backward he will not be, I know. He will be full of wrath, and rising he will tell to all how we contrived his instant death but could not catch him. And when men hear our evil deeds, they will not praise them; but they may cause us trouble and drive us from our country, and we may have

[84] One of the leading suitors.   [85] One of the suitors, usually more temperate than the others.

to go away into the land of strangers. Let us be quick, then, and seize him in the fields far from the city, or on the road at least; and let us take possession of his substance and his wealth, sharing all suitably among ourselves; the house, however, we might let his mother keep, or him who marries her. If this plan does not please you, and you will let him live to hold his father's fortune, then let us not devour his store of pleasant things by gathering here; but from his own abode let each man make his wooing, and press his suit with gifts. So may Penelope marry the man who gives her most and comes with fate to favor."

As he thus spoke, the rest were hushed to silence. But Amphinomus addressed them now and said—Amphinomus, the illustrious son of noble Nisus and grandson of Aretias, who from Doulichion, rich in wheat and grass, had led a band of suitors, and more than all the rest found favor with Penelope through what he said, because his heart was upright—he with good will addressed them thus and said:

"Nay, friends, I would not like to kill Telemachus. It is a fearful thing to kill a king. Let us at least first ask the gods for counsel; and if the oracles of mighty Zeus approve, I will myself share in the killing and urge the others too; but if the gods turn from us, I warn you to forbear."

So said Amphinomus, and his saying pleased them. Soon they arose and entered the hall of Odysseus, and went and took their seats on polished chairs.

Heedful Penelope, meanwhile, had planned anew to show herself among the suitors, overweening in their pride. Within the palace she learned of the intended murder of her son, for the page Medon told her, who overheard the plot; so to the hall she went with her attendant women. And when the royal lady reached the suitors, she stood beside a column of the strong-built roof, holding before her face her delicate veil; and she rebuked Antinoüs and spoke to him and said:

"Antinoüs, full of all insolence and wicked guile, in Ithaca they say you are the foremost person of your years in judgment and in speech. But such you never were. Madman! Why do you seek the death and ruin of Telemachus, and pay no heed to suppliants, though Zeus be witness for them? It is impious plotting crimes against one's fellow men. Do you not know your father once took refuge here, in terror of the people? For they were very angry because he joined the Taphian pirates and troubled the Thesprotians, men who were our allies. So the people would destroy him—would snatch his life away, and swallow all his large and pleasant living; but Odysseus held them back and stayed their madness. Yet you insultingly devour his house; you woo his wife, murder his child, and make me wholly wretched. Forbear, I charge you, and bid the rest forbear!"

Then answered her Eurymachus, the son of Polybus: "Daughter of Icarius, heedful Penelope; be of good courage! Let not these things vex your mind! The man is not alive, and never will be born, who shall lay hands upon your son, Telemachus, so long as I have life and sight on earth. For this I tell you, and it shall be done: soon the dark blood of such a man shall flow around my spear. Many a time the spoiler of towns, Odysseus, has set me on his knee, put roasted meat into my hands and given me ruddy wine. Therefore I hold Telemachus dearest of all mankind. I bid him have no fear of death, at least not from the suitors. Death from the gods can no man shun."

So he spoke, cheering her, yet was himself plotting the murder. But she, going to her bright upper chamber, bewailed Odysseus, her dear husband, till on her lids clear-eyed Athene caused a sweet sleep to fall.

At evening the noble swineherd joined Odysseus and his son. Busily they prepared their supper, having killed a yearling pig. And Athene, drawing near, touched with her wand Laërtes' son Odysseus, and made him old once more and clad him in mean clothes; for fear the swineherd looking in his face might know, and go and tell the tale to steadfast Penelope, not holding fast the secret in his heart.

Now Telemachus first addressed the swineherd, saying: "So you are come, noble Eumaeus. What news then in the town? Are the haughty suitors at home again after their ambuscade, or are they watching still for me to pass?"

Then swineherd Eumaeus, you answered him and said: "I had no mind to search and question while stumbling through the town. My inclination bade me to tell my message with all speed and hasten home. There overtook me, though, an eager newsman of your crew, a page, who told his story to your mother first. Moreover, this I know, because I saw it: I was already on the road above the town, where stands the hill of Hermes, when I saw a swift ship entering our harbor. A crowd of men were on her. Heavy she was with shields and double-pointed spears. It was they, I thought, and yet I do not know."

As he thus spoke, revered Telemachus smiled, and glancing at his father shunned the swineherd's eye.

Now ceasing from their labor of laying out the meal, they fell to feasting. There was no lack of appetite for the impartial feast. And after they had stayed desire for drink and food, they turned toward bed and took the gift of sleep.

Odysseus now goes to the city, enters his own palace disguised as a beggar, and starts plotting the destruction of Penelope's suitors, who are still occupying his palace. Only the nurse of his childhood, Eurycleia, recognizes him when she washes his feet and sees a famous scar which Odysseus had before he left for Troy. She too is sworn to silence. Penelope promises the suitors that she will marry whoever manages to shoot an arrow through twelve axe-

heads with a famous bow that Odysseus had left in the palace at his depar-
ture more than nineteen years before. After each suitor tries in vain,
Odysseus, still wearing beggar's rags, persuades the unwilling suitors to let
him try. At this point the following scene occurs.

BOOK XXI

. . . Now Odysseus already held the bow and turned it round and round, trying it here and there to see if worms had gnawed the horn while its lord was far away. And glancing at his neighbor one would say:

"A sort of fancier and a trickster with the bow this fellow is. No doubt at home he has himself a bow like that, or means to make one like it. See how he turns it in his hands this way and that, ready for mischief—rascal!"

Then would another rude youth answer thus: "Oh may he always meet with luck as good as when he is unable now to bend the bow!"

So talked the suitors. Meantime wise Odysseus, when he had handled the great bow and scanned it closely—even as one well-skilled to play the lyre and sing stretches with ease round its new peg a string, securing at each end the twisted sheep-gut; so without effort did Odysseus string the mighty bow. Holding it now with his right hand, he tried its cord; and clear to the touch it sang, voiced like the swallow. Great consternation came upon the suitors. All faces then changed color. Zeus thundered loud for signal. And glad was long-tried royal Odysseus to think the son of crafty Kronos sent an omen. He picked up a swift shaft which lay beside him on the table, drawn. Within the hollow quiver still remained the rest, which the Achaeans soon should prove. Then laying the arrow on the arch, he drew the string and arrow notches, and forth from the bench on which he sat let fly the shaft, with careful aim, and did not miss an axe's ring from first to last, but clean through all sped on the bronze-tipped arrow; and to Telemachus he said:

"Telemachus, the guest now sitting in your hall brings you no shame. I did not miss my mark, nor in the bending of the bow make a long labor. My strength is sound as ever, not what the mocking suitors here despised. But it is time for the Achaeans to make supper ready, while it is daylight still; and then for us in other ways to make them sport—with dance and lyre; for these attend a feast."

He spoke and frowned the sign. His sharp sword then Telemachus girt on, the son of princely Odysseus; clasped his right hand around his spear, and close beside his father's seat he took his stand, armed with the gleaming bronze.

BOOK XXII

Then wise Odysseus threw off his rags and sprang to the broad threshold, bow in hand and quiver full of arrows. Out he poured the swift shafts at his feet, and thus addressed the suitors:

"So the dread ordeal ends! Now to another mark I turn, to hit what no man ever hit before, will but Apollo[86] grant my prayer."

He spoke, and aimed a pointed arrow at Antinoüs. The man was in the act to raise his goodly goblet—gold it was and double-eared—and even now guided it in his hands to drink the wine. Death gave his heart no care. For who could think that in this company of feasters one of the crowd, however strong, could bring upon him cruel death and dismal doom? But Odysseus aimed an arrow and hit him in the throat; right through his tender neck the sharp point passed. He sank down sidewise; from his hand the goblet fell when he was hit, and straightway from his nose ran a thick stream of human blood. Roughly he pushed his table back, kicking it with his foot, and scattered off the food upon the floor. The bread and roasted meat were thrown away. Into a tumult broke the suitors round about the hall when they saw the fallen man. They sprang from their seats and, hurrying through the hall, peered at the massive walls on every side. But nowhere was there shield or ponderous spear to seize. Then they assailed Odysseus with indignant words:

"Stranger, to your sorrow you turn your bow on men! You never shall take part in games again. Swift death awaits you; for you have killed the leader of the noble youths of Ithaca. To pay for this, vultures shall eat you here!"

So each one spoke; they thought he had not meant to kill the man. They foolishly did not see that for them one and all destruction's cords were knotted. But looking sternly on them wise Odysseus said:

"Dogs! You have been saying all the time I never should return out of the land of Troy; and therefore you destroyed my home, outraged my women-servants, and—I alive—covertly wooed my wife, fearing no gods that hold the open sky, nor that the indignation of mankind would fall on you here-after. Now for you one and all destruction's cords are knotted!"

As he spoke thus, pale fear took hold on all. Each peered about to flee from instant death. Only Eurymachus made answer, saying:

"If you indeed be Ithacan Odysseus, now returned, justly have you described what the Achaeans have been doing—full many crimes here at the hall and many in the field. But there at last lies he who was the cause of all, Antinoüs; for it was he who set us on these deeds, not so much needing and desiring marriage, but with this other purpose—which the son of Kronos never granted—that in the settled land of Ithaca he might himself be king,

[86] As the previous book indicates, the day of this scene is a festival day sacred to Apollo. He and his sister Artemis are also the archers among the gods.

when he should treacherously have slain your son. Now he is justly slain. But spare your people, and we hereafter, making you public recompense for all we drank and ate here at the hall, will pay a fine of twenty oxen each and give you bronze and gold enough to warm your heart. Till this is done, we cannot blame your wrath."

But looking sternly on him, wise Odysseus said: "Eurymachus, if you would give me all your father's goods, and all your own, and all that you might gather elsewhere, I would not stay my hands from slaying until the suitors paid the price of all their lawless deeds. It lies before you then to fight or flee, if any man will save himself from death and doom. But some here will not flee, I think, from instant death."

As he spoke thus, their knees grew feeble and their very souls; but Eurymachus called out a second time: "Come, friends, the man will not hold back his ruthless hands; but having got possession of a polished bow and quiver, he will shoot from the smooth threshold until he kills us all. Let us then turn to fighting. Draw swords, and hold the tables up against his deadly arrows! Have at him all together! Perhaps we may dislodge him from the threshold and the door, then reach the town and quickly raise the alarm. So would the fellow soon have shot his last."

So saying, he drew his sharp two-edged bronze sword and sprang upon Odysseus with a fearful cry. But on the instant royal Odysseus shot an arrow and hit him in the breast beside the nipple, fixing the swift bolt in his liver. Out of his hand his sword dropped to the ground, and he himself, sprawling across the table, bent and fell, spilling the food and double cup upon the floor. With his brow he beat the pavement in his agony of heart, and with his kicking shook the chair. Upon his eyes gathered the mists of death.

Then Amphinomus assaulted glorious Odysseus, and dashing headlong forward drew his sharp sword, hoping to make Odysseus yield the door. But Telemachus was quick and struck him with his brazen spear upon the back, between the shoulders, and drove the spear-point through his chest. He fell with a thud and struck the ground flat with his forehead. Telemachus sprang back and left the long spear sticking in Amphinomus; for he feared if he should draw the long spear out, an Achaean might attack him, rushing on him with his sword, and as he stooped might stab him. So off he ran and hastily went back to his dear father; and standing close beside him, he said in winged words:

"Now, father, I will fetch a shield and pair of spears, and a brazen helmet also, fitted to your brow. And I will go and arm myself, and give some armor to the swineherd and to the neatherd too; for to be armed is better."

Then wise Odysseus answered him and said: "Run! Bring the arms while I have arrows to defend me, or they will drive me from the door when I am left alone."

He spoke, and Telemachus heeded his dear father, and hastened to the chamber where the glittering armor lay. Out of the store he chose four shields, eight spears, and four bronze helmets having horsehair plumes. These he bore off and hastily went back to his dear father. Telemachus first girt his body with the bronze, then the two servants likewise girt themselves in goodly armor, and so all took their stand by Odysseus, keen and crafty.

He, just as he had arrows to defend him, shot down a suitor in the hall with every aim, and side by side they fell. Then when his arrows failed the princely bowman, he leaned the bow against the doorpost of the stately room, letting it stand beside the bright face-wall, and he too slung a four-fold shield about his shoulders, put on his sturdy head a shapely helmet, horsehair-plumed—grimly the crest above it nodded—and took in hand two ponderous spears pointed with bronze.

Now in the solid wall there was a postern-door; and level with the upper threshold of the stately hall, an opening to a passage, closed with jointed boards. Odysseus ordered the noble swineherd to guard this postern-door and in its neighborhood to take his stand, since this was the only exit. But to the suitors said Agelaüs,[87] speaking his words to all:

"Friends, could not one of you climb by the postern-door and tell our people, and quickly raise the alarm? So would the fellow soon have shot his last."

Then said to him Melanthius[88] the goatherd: "No, heaven-descended Agelaüs, that may in no wise be; for the good courtyard door is terribly near at hand, and the mouth of the passageway is narrow. One person there, if resolute, could bar the way for all. Yet I will fetch you from the chamber arms to wear; for there, I think, and nowhere else, Odysseus stored the armor —he and his gallant son."

So having said, Melanthius, the goatherd, climbed to the chambers of Odysseus through the vent-holes of the hall. Out of the store he chose twelve shields, as many spears, and just as many brazen helmets having horsehair plumes; then turning back, he brought them very quickly and gave them to the suitors. And now did Odysseus' knees grow feeble and his very soul, when he saw them donning arms and waving in their hands long spears. Large seemed his task; and straightway to Telemachus he spoke these winged words:

"Surely, Telemachus, a woman of the house aids the hard fight against us; or else it is Melanthius."

Then answered him discreet Telemachus: "Father, the fault is mine; no other is to blame; for I it was who opened the chamber's tight-shut door and left it open. Their watchman was too good. But, noble Eumaeus, go and close

---

[87] One of the suitors.   [88] Melanthius sided with the suitors and, in a previous scene, had insulted and kicked Odysseus. Among the servants of Odysseus, he serves as Eumaeus' foil.

the chamber-door, and see if any woman has a hand in this, or if—as I suspect—it is the son of Dolius, Melanthius."

So they conversed together. And now Melanthius, the goatherd, went to
the room again to fetch more goodly armor. The noble swineherd[89] spied
him, and quickly to Odysseus, standing near, he said:

"High-born son of Laërtes, ready Odysseus, there is the knave whom we
suspected, just going to the chamber. Speak plainly; shall I kill him if I
prove the better man, or shall I bring him here to pay for all the crimes he
plotted in your house?"

Then wise Odysseus answered him and said: "Here in the hall Telemachus and I will hold the lordly suitors, rage as they may. You two tie the
man's feet and hands and drag him within the chamber; there fasten boards
upon his back, and lashing a twisted rope around him hoist him aloft, up
the tall pillar, and bring him to the beams, that he may keep alive there
long and suffer grievous torment."

So he spoke, and willingly they heeded and obeyed. They hastened to the
chamber, unseen of him within. He was engaged in searching after armor in
a corner of the room, while the pair stood beside the door-posts, one on either
hand, and waited. Soon as Melanthius the goatherd crossed the threshold,
in one hand bearing a goodly helmet and in the other a broad old shield
beflecked with mould—the shield of lord Laërtes, which he carried in his
youth, now laid away, its strap-seams parted—then on him sprang the two
and dragged him by the hair within the door, threw him all horror-stricken
to the ground, bound hands and feet together with a galling cord, which
tight and fast they tied, as they were ordered by Laërtes' son, long-tried royal
Odysseus; then they lashed a twisted rope around and hoisted him aloft, up
the tall pillar, and brought him to the beams; and mocking him said you,
swineherd Eumaeus:

"Now then, Melanthius, you shall watch the whole night long, stretched
out on such a comfortable bed as suits you well. The early dawn out of the
Ocean-stream shall not in golden splendor slip unheeded by, when you
should drive goats for the suitors at the hall to make their meal."

Thus was he left there, fast in deadly bonds. The pair put on their armor,
closed the shining door and went to join Odysseus, keen and crafty. Here
they stood, breathing fury, four of them on the threshold, although within
the hall were many men of might. But near them came Athene, the daughter
of Zeus, likened to Mentor[90] in her form and voice. To see her made Odysseus glad, and thus he spoke:

"Mentor, save us from ruin! Remember the good comrade who often aided
you. You are of my own years."

[89] Eumaeus. [90] An Ithacan friend of Odysseus, to whom he entrusted his household when he went to Troy; frequently impersonated by the goddess Athene.

He said this, though he understood it was Athene, the summoner of hosts. But the suitors shouted from the other side, down in the hall; and foremost in abuse was Agelaüs, son of Damastor:

"Mentor, do not let Odysseus lure you by his words to fight the suitors and to lend him aid; for I am sure even then we still shall work our will. And after we have slain these men, father and son, you too shall die beside them for deeds you thought to do within the hall. Here with your head you shall make due amends. And when with the sword we have cut short your power, whatever goods you have, within doors and without, we will confound with the possessions of Odysseus. We will not let your sons and daughters live at home, nor let your true wife linger in the town of Ithaca."

As he spoke thus, Athene grew more wroth in spirit and chid Odysseus with these angry words: "Odysseus, you have no longer such firm power and spirit as when for the sake of white-armed high-born Helen you fought the Trojans nine years long unflinchingly, and vanquished many men in mortal combat, and by your wisdom Priam's wide-wayed city fell. Why, now returned to home and wealth and here confronted with the suitors, do you shrink from being brave? Nay, nay, good friend, stand by my side, watch what I do, and see how, in the presence of the foe, Mentor, the son of Alcimus, repays a kindness."

She spoke, but gave him not quite yet the victory in full. Still she made trial of the strength and spirit both of Odysseus and his valiant son. Up to the roof-beam of the smoky hall she darted like a swallow, resting there.

Now the suitors were led by Agelaüs, son of Damastor, by Eurynomus, Amphimedon, and Demoptolemus, by Peisander, son of Polyctor, and wise Polybus; for these in manly excellence were quite the best of all who still were living, fighting for their lives. The rest the bow and storm of arrows had laid low. So to these men said Agelaüs, speaking his words to all:

"Now, friends, at last the man shall hold his ruthless hands; for Mentor has departed after uttering idle boasts, and the men at the front door are left alone. So hurl your long spears, but not all together! Now then, six let fly first; and see if Zeus allows Odysseus to be hit and us to win an honor. No trouble about the rest when he is down!"

He said, and all to whom he spoke let fly their spears with power. Athene made all vain. One struck the doorpost of the stately hall; one the tight-fitting door; another's ashen shaft, heavy with bronze, crashed on the wall. And when the men were safe from the suitors' spears, then thus began long-tried royal Odysseus:

"Friends, let me give the word at last to our side too. Let fly your spears into the crowd of suitors, men who seek to slay and strip us, adding this to former wrongs!"

He spoke, and all with careful aim let fly their pointed spears. Odysseus struck down Demoptolemus; Telemachus, Euryades; the swineherd, Elatus;

and the herdsman of the cattle, Peisander. All these together bit the dust of the broad floor, the other suitors falling back from hall to deep recess. Odysseus' men sprang forward and from the bodies of the dead pulled out the spears.

And now the suitors again let fly their pointed spears with power. Athene made them for the most part vain. One struck the doorpost of the stately hall; one the tight-fitting door; another's ashen shaft, heavy with bronze, crashed on the wall. But Amphimedon wounded Telemachus on the wrist of the right hand, though slightly; the metal tore the outer skin. And Ctesippus[91] with his long spear grazed Eumaeus on the shoulder which showed above his shield; the spear flew past and fell upon the ground.

Once more the men beside Odysseus, keen and crafty, let fly their sharp spears on the crowd of suitors. And now by Odysseus, the spoiler of cities, Eurydamas was hit; by Telemachus, Amphimedon; by the swineherd, Polybus; and afterwards the herdsman of the cattle hit Ctesippus in the breast and cried in triumph:

"Ha, son of Polytherses, ready mocker, never again give way to folly and big words! Leave boasting to the gods; they are stronger far than you. This gift offsets the hoof you gave to great Odysseus a little while ago, when in his house he played the beggar man."

So spoke the herdsman of the crook-horned kine. Then Odysseus wounded Damastor's son[92] with his long spear, when fighting hand to hand. Telemachus wounded Evenor's son, Leiocritus, with a spear-thrust in the middle of the waist, and drove the point clean through. He fell on his face and struck the ground flat with his forehead. And now Athene from the roof above stretched forth her murderous aegis.[93] Their souls were panic-stricken. They scurried through the hall like herded cows, on whom the glancing gadfly falls and maddens them, in springtime when the days are long. And as the crook-clawed hook-beaked vultures, descending from the hills, dart at the birds which fly the clouds and skim the plain, while the vultures pounce and kill them; defense they have not and have no escape, and men are merry at their capture; so the four chased the suitors down the hall and smote them right and left. There went up moans, a dismal sound, as skulls were crushed and all the pavement ran with blood.

But Leiodes,[94] rushing forward, clasped Odysseus by the knees, and spoke imploringly these winged words: "I clasp your knees, Odysseus! Oh, respect and spare me! For I protest I never harmed a woman of the house by wicked word or act. No! and I used to try to stop the rest—the suitors—when one of them would do such deeds. But they were never ready to hold their hands from wrong. So through their own perversity they met a dismal doom; and I,

[91] A particularly insolent and violent suitor who had thrown a cow's hoof at Odysseus in an earlier scene.   [92] Agelaüs.   [93] The shield often carried by Athene.
[94] A reasonably well-meaning but weak suitor; he posesssed prophetic skill.

their soothsayer, although I did no ill, must also fall. There is no gratitude for good deeds done!"

Then looking sternly on him wise Odysseus said: "If you avow yourself their soothsayer, many a time you must have prayed within the hall that the issue of a glad return might be delayed for me, while my dear wife should follow you and bear you children. Therefore you shall not now avoid a shameful death."

So saying, he seized in his sturdy hand a sword that lay near by, a sword which Agelaüs had dropped upon the ground when he was slain, and drove it through the middle of Leiodes' neck. While he yet spoke, his head rolled in the dust.

But the bard, the son of Terpes, still had escaped dark doom—Phemius, who sang perforce among the suitors. He stood, holding the tuneful lyre in his hands, close to the postern-door; and in his heart he doubted whether to hasten from the hall to the massive altar of great Zeus, guardian of courts, and take his seat where oftentimes Laërtes and Odysseus had burned the thighs of beeves; or whether he should run and clasp Odysseus by the knees. Reflecting thus, it seemed the better way to touch the knees of Laërtes' son, Odysseus. He laid his hollow lyre upon the ground, midway between the mixer and the silver-studded chair, ran forward to Odysseus, clasped his knees, and spoke imploringly these winged words:

"I clasp your knees, Odysseus! Oh, respect and spare me! To you yourself hereafter grief will come, if you destroy a bard who sings to gods and men. Self-taught am I; God planted in my heart all kinds of song; and I had thought to sing to you as to a god. Then do not seek to slay me. Telemachus, your own dear son, will say how not through will of mine, nor seeking gain, I lingered at your palace, singing to the suitors at their feasts; for being more and stronger men than I, they brought me here by force."

What he had said revered Telemachus heard, and he quickly called to his father who was standing near: "Hold! For the man is guiltless. Do not stab him with the sword! And let us also spare Medon, the page, who here at home used to have charge of me while I was still a child—unless indeed Philoetius[95] or the swineherd slew him, or he encountered you as you stormed along the hall."

What he was saying Medon, that man of understanding, heard; for he lay crouching underneath a chair, wrapped in a fresh-flayed ox's hide, seeking to shun dark doom. Straightway he rose from underneath the chair, quickly cast off the hide, sprang forward to Telemachus, clasped his knees, and cried imploringly in winged words:

"Friend, stay your hand! It is I! And speak to your father, or exulting in his sharp sword he will destroy me out of indignation at the suitors, who

---

[95] The oxherd who remained loyal to Odysseus.

wasted the possessions in his halls and in their folly paid no heed to you."

But wise Odysseus, smiling, said: "Be of good cheer, for he has cleared and saved you; that in your heart you may perceive and may report to others how much more safe is doing good than ill. But both of you leave the hall and sit outside, out of this bloodshed, in the court—you and the full-voiced bard—till I have accomplished in the house all that I still must do."

Even as he spoke, the pair went forth and left the hall, and both sat down by the altar of great Zeus, peering about on every side as still expecting death. Odysseus too peered round his hall to see if any living man were lurking there, seeking to shun dark doom. He found them all laid low in blood and dust, and in such numbers as the fish which fishermen draw to the shelving shore out of the foaming sea in meshy nets; these all, sick for the salt sea wave, lie heaped upon the sands, while the resplendent sun takes life away; so lay the suitors, heaped on one another. And now to Telemachus said wise Odysseus:

"Telemachus, go call nurse Eurycleia, that I may speak to her the thing I have in mind."

He spoke, and Telemachus heeded his dear father and, shaking the door, said to nurse Eurycleia: "Up! aged woman, who have charge of all the damsels in our hall! Come hither! My father calls and now will speak with you."

Such were his words; unwinged, they rested with her. Opening the doors of the stately hall, he entered. Telemachus led the way. And there among the bodies of the slain she found Odysseus, dabbled with blood and gore, like a lion come from feeding on some stall-fed ox; its whole breast and its cheeks on either side are bloody; terrible is the beast to see; so dabbled was Odysseus, feet and hands. And when she saw the bodies and the quantity of blood, she was ready to cry aloud at the sight of the mighty deed. But Odysseus held her back and stayed her madness, and speaking in winged words he said:

"Woman, be glad within; but hush, and make no cry. It is not right to glory in the slain. The gods' doom and their reckless deeds destroyed them; for they respected nobody on earth, bad man or good, who came among them. So through their own perversity they met a dismal doom. But name me now the women of the hall, and tell me who dishonor me and who are guiltless."

Then said to him his dear nurse Eurycleia: "Then I will tell you, child, the very truth. You have fifty women-servants at the hall whom we have taught their tasks, to card the wool and bear the servant's lot. Out of these women, twelve in all have gone the way of shame, paying no heed to me nor even to Penelope. It is but lately Telemachus has come to manhood, and his mother has never suffered him to rule the maids. But let me go above, to the bright upper chamber, and tell your wife, whom a god has laid asleep."

Then wise Odysseus answered her and said: "Do not wake her yet; tell those women to come here who in the past behaved unworthily."

So he spoke, and through the hall forth the old woman went, to give the message to the maids and bid them come with speed. Meanwhile Odysseus, calling to his side Telemachus, the neatherd, and the swineherd, spoke to them thus in winged words:

"Begin to carry off the dead, and bid the women aid you; then let them clean the goodly chairs and tables with water and porous sponges. And when you have set in order all the house, lead forth these serving-maids out of the stately hall to a spot between the round-house and the neat courtyard wall, and smite them with your long swords till you take life from all; that so they may forget the love they had among the suitors, when they would meet them unobserved."

He spoke, and the women came, trooping along together, in bitter lamentation, letting the big tears fall. First they carried out the bodies of the dead and laid them by the portico of the fenced court, piling them there one on another. Odysseus gave the orders and hastened on the work, and only because compelled, the maids bore off the bodies. Then afterwards they cleaned the goodly chairs and tables with water and porous sponges. Telemachus, the neatherd, and the swineherd with shovels scraped the pavement of the strong-built room, and the maids took up the scrapings and threw them out of doors. And when they had set in order all the hall, they led the serving-maids out of the stately hall to a spot between the round-house and the neat courtyard wall, and there they penned them in a narrow space whence there was no escape. Then thus began discreet Telemachus:

"By no honorable death would I take away the lives of those who poured reproaches on my head and on my mother and were the suitors' comrades."

He spoke, and tied the cable of a dark-bowed ship to a great pillar, then lashed it to the round-house, stretching it high across, too high for one to touch the feet upon the ground. And as the wide-winged thrushes or the doves strike on a net set in the bushes; and when they think to go to roost a cruel bed receives them; even so the women held their heads in line, and around every neck a noose was laid, that they might die most vilely. They twitched their feet a little, but not long.

Then forth they led Melanthius across the porch and yard. With rustless sword they lopped his nose and ears, pulled out his bowels to be eaten raw by dogs, and in their rage cut off his hands and feet.

Afterwards washing clean their own hands and their feet, they went to meet Odysseus in the house, and all the work was done. But to his dear nurse Eurycleia said Odysseus: "Woman, bring sulphur, a protection against harm, and bring me fire to fumigate the hall. And bid Penelope come hither with her women, and order all the maids throughout the house to come."

Then said to him his dear nurse Eurycleia: "Truly, my child, in all this you speak rightly. Yet let me fetch you clothes, a coat and tunic. And do not, with this covering of rags on your broad shoulders, stand in the hall. That would be cause for blame."

But wise Odysseus answered her and said: "First let a fire be lighted in the hall."

At these his words, his dear nurse Eurycleia did not disobey, but brought the fire and sulphur. Odysseus fumigated all the hall, the buildings, and the court.

And now the old woman passed through the goodly palace of Odysseus to take his message to the maids and bid them come with speed. Out of their room they came, with torches in their hands. They gathered round Odysseus, hailing him with delight. Fondly they kissed his face and neck, and held him by the hand. Glad longing fell upon him to weep and cry aloud. All these he knew were true.

BOOK XXIII

So the old woman, full of glee, went to the upper chamber to tell her mistress her dear lord was in the house. Her knees grew strong; her feet outran themselves. By Penelope's head she paused, and thus she spoke:

"Awake, Penelope, dear child, to see with your own eyes what you have hoped to see this many a day! Here is Odysseus! He has come at last, and slain the haughty suitors—the men who vexed his house, devoured his substance, and oppressed his son."

Then heedful Penelope said to her: "Dear nurse, the gods have crazed you. They can befool one who is very wise, and often they have set the simple in the paths of prudence. They have confused you; you were soberminded heretofore. Why mock me when my heart is full of sorrow, telling wild tales like these? And why arouse me from the sleep that sweetly bound me and kept my eyelids closed? I have not slept so soundly since Odysseus went away to see accursed Ilios[96]—name never to be named. Nay then, go down, back to the hall. If any other of my maids had come and told me this and waked me out of sleep, I would soon have sent her off in sorry wise into the hall once more. This time age serves you well."

Then said to her the good nurse Eurycleia: "Dear child, I do not mock you. In very truth it is Odysseus; he is come, as I have said. He is the stranger whom everybody in the hall has set at naught. Telemachus knew long ago that he was here, but out of prudence hid his knowledge of his father till he should have revenge from these bold men for wicked deeds."

So spoke she; and Penelope was glad, and, springing from her bed, fell on the woman's neck, and let the tears burst from her eyes; and, speaking in

[96] Troy.

winged words, she said: "Nay, tell me, then, dear nurse, and tell me truly; if he is really come as you declare, how was it he laid hands upon the shameless suitors, being alone, while they were always here together?"

Then answered her the good nurse Eurycleia: "I did not see; I did not ask; I only heard the groans of dying men. In a corner of our protected chamber we sat and trembled—the doors were tightly closed—until your son Telemachus called to me from the hall; for his father bade him call. And there among the bodies of the slain I found Odysseus standing. All around, covering the trodden floor, they lay, one on another. It would have warmed your heart to see him, like a lion, dabbled with blood and gore. Now all the bodies are collected at the courtyard gate, while he is fumigating the fair house by lighting a great fire. He sent me here to call you. Follow me, then, that you may come to gladness in your true hearts together, for sorely have you suffered. Now the long hope has been at last fulfilled. He has come back alive to his own hearth, and found you still, you and his son, within his hall; and upon those who did him wrong, the suitors, on all of them here in his home he has obtained revenge."

Then heedful Penelope said to her: "Dear nurse, be not too boastful yet, nor filled with glee. You know how welcome here the sight of him would be to all, and most to me and to the son we had. But this is no true tale you tell. Nay, rather some immortal slew the lordly suitors, in anger at their galling insolence and wicked deeds; for they respected nobody on earth, bad man or good, who came among them. So for their sins they suffered. But Odysseus, far from Achaea, lost the hope of coming home; nay, he himself was lost."

Then answered her the good nurse Eurycleia: "My child, what word has passed the barrier of your teeth, to say your husband, who is now beside your hearth, will never come! Your heart is always doubting. Come, then, and let me name another sign most sure—the scar the boar dealt long ago with his white tusk. I found it as I washed him, and I would have told you then; but he laid his hand upon my mouth, and in his watchful wisdom would not let me speak. But follow me. I stake my very life; if I deceive you, slay me by the vilest death."

Then heedful Penelope answered her: "Dear nurse, 't is hard for you to trace the counsels of the everlasting gods, however wise you are. Nevertheless, let us go down to meet my son, and see the suitors who are dead, and him who slew them."

So saying, she went from her chamber to the hall, and much her heart debated whether aloof to question her dear husband, or to draw near and kiss his face and take his hand. But when she entered, crossing the stone threshold, she sat down opposite Odysseus, in the firelight, beside the farther wall. He sat by a tall pillar, looking down, waiting to hear if his stately wife would speak when she should look his way. But she sat silent long; amazement filled her heart. Now she would gaze with a long look upon his face, and now she would not know him for the mean clothes that he wore. But Telemachus rebuked her, and spoke to her and said:

"Mother, hard mother, of ungentle heart, why do you hold aloof so from my father, and do not sit beside him, plying him with words and questions? There is no other woman of such stubborn spirit to stand off from the husband who, after many grievous toils, comes in the twentieth year home to his native land. Your heart is always harder than a stone!"

Then said to him heedful Penelope: "My child, my soul within is dazed with wonder. I cannot speak to him, nor ask a question, nor look him in the face. But if this is indeed Odysseus, come at last, we certainly shall know each other better than others know; for we have signs which we two understand, signs hidden from the rest."

As she, long tried, spoke thus, royal Odysseus smiled, and said to Telemachus forthwith in winged words: "Telemachus, leave your mother in the hall to try my truth. She soon will know me better. Now, because I am foul and dressed in sorry clothes, she holds me in dishonor, and says I am not he. But you and I have yet to plan how all may turn out well. For whoso kills one man among a tribe, though the man leaves few champions behind, becomes an exile, quitting king and country. We have destroyed the pillars of the state, the very noblest youths of Ithaca. Form, then, a plan, I pray."

Then answered him discreet Telemachus: "Look you to that, dear father. Your wisdom is, they say, the best among mankind. No mortal man can rival you. Zealously will we follow, and not fail, I think, in daring, so far as power is ours."

Then wise Odysseus answered him and said: "Then I will tell you what seems best to me. First wash and put on tunics, and bid the maids about the house array themselves. Then let the sacred bard with tuneful lyre lead us in sportive dancing, that men may say, hearing us from without. 'It is a wedding,' whether such men be passersby or neighboring folk; and so broad rumor may not reach the town about the suitors' murder till we are gone to our well-wooded farm. There will we plan as the Olympian shall grant us wisdom."

So he spoke, and willingly they heeded and obeyed. For first they washed themselves and put on tunics, and the women also put on their attire. And then the noble bard took up his hollow lyre, and in them stirred desire for merry music and the gallant dance; and the great house resounded to the tread of lusty men and gay-girt women. And one who heard the dancing from without would say, "Well, well! some man has married the long-courted queen. Hard-hearted! For the husband of her youth she would not guard her great house to the end, till he should come." So they would say, but knew not how things were.

Meanwhile within the house Eurynome, the housekeeper, bathed resolute

Odysseus and anointed him with oil, and on him put a goodly robe and tunic. Upon his face Athene cast great beauty; she made him taller than before, and stouter to behold, and made the curling locks to fall around his head as on the hyacinth flower. As when a man lays gold on silver—some skillful man whom Hephaestus and Pallas Athene have trained in every art, and he fashions graceful work; so did she cast a grace upon his head and shoulders. Forth from the bath he came, in bearing like the immortals, and once more took the seat from which he first arose, facing his wife, and spoke to her these words:

"Lady, a heart impenetrable beyond the sex of women the dwellers on Olympus gave to you. There is no other woman of such stubborn spirit to stand off from the husband who, after many grievous toils, comes in the twentieth year home to his native land. Come, then, good nurse, and make my bed, that I may lie alone. For certainly of iron is the heart within her breast."

Then said to him heedful Penelope: "Nay, sir, I am not proud, nor contemptuous of you, nor too much dazed with wonder. I very well remember what you were when you went upon your long-oared ship away from Ithaca. However, Eurycleia, make up his massive bed outside that stately chamber which he himself once built. Move the massive frame out there,[97] and throw the bedding on—the fleeces, robes, and bright-hued rugs."

She said this in the hope to prove her husband; but Odysseus spoke in anger to his faithful wife: "Woman, these are bitter words which you have said! Who set my bed elsewhere? A hard task that would be for one, however skilled—unless a god should come and by his will set it with ease upon some other spot; but among men no living being, even in his prime, could lightly shift it; for a great token is inwrought into its curious frame. I built it; no one else. There grew a thick-leaved olive shrub inside the yard, full-grown and vigorous, in girth much like a pillar. Round this I formed my chamber, and I worked till it was done, building it out of close-set stones, and roofing it over well. Framed and tight-fitting doors I added to it. Then I lopped the thick-leaved olive's crest, cutting the stem high up above the roots, neatly and skillfully smoothed with my axe the sides, and to the line I kept all true to shape my post, and with an auger I bored it all along. Starting with this, I fashioned me the bed till it was finished, and I inlaid it well with gold, with silver, and with ivory. On it I stretched a thong of ox-hide, gay with purple. This is the token I now tell. I do not know whether the bed still stands there, wife, or whether somebody has set it elsewhere, cutting the olive trunk."

As he spoke thus, her knees grew feeble and her very soul, when she recognized the tokens which Odysseus truly told. Then bursting into tears,

---

[97] Penelope knows that Odysseus' bed cannot be moved.

she ran straight toward him, threw her arms round Odysseus' neck and kissed his face, and said:

"Odysseus, do not scorn me! Ever before, you were the wisest of mankind. The gods have sent us sorrow, and grudged our staying side by side to share the joys of youth and reach the threshold of old age. But do not be angry with me now, nor take it ill that then when I first saw you I did not greet you thus; for the heart within my breast was always trembling. I feared some man might come and cheat me with his tale. Many a man makes wicked schemes for gain. Nay, Argive Helen, the daughter of Zeus, would not have given herself to love a stranger if she had known how warrior sons of the Achaeans would bring her home again, back to her native land. And yet it was a god prompted her deed of shame. Before, she did not cherish in her heart such sin, such grievous sin, from which began the woe which stretched to us. But now, when you have clearly told the tokens of our bed, which no one else has seen, but only you and I and the single servant, Actoris, whom my father gave me on my coming here to keep the door of our closed chamber—you make even my ungentle heart believe."

So she spoke, and stirred still more his yearning after tears; and he began to weep, holding his loved and faithful wife. As when the welcome land appears to swimmers, whose sturdy ship Poseidon wrecked at sea, confounded by the winds and solid waters; a few escape the foaming sea and swim ashore; thick salt foam crusts their flesh; they climb the welcome land, and are escaped from danger; so welcome to her gazing eyes appeared her husband. From round his neck she never let her white arms go. And rosy-fingered dawn had found them weeping, but a different plan the goddess formed, clear-eyed Athene. She checked the long night in its passage, and at the Ocean-stream she stayed the gold-throned dawn, and did not suffer it to yoke the swift-paced horses which carry light to men. Lampus and Phaëton which bear the dawn. And now to his wife said wise Odysseus:

"O wife, we have not reached the end of all our trials yet. Hereafter comes a task immeasurable, long and severe, which I must needs fulfill; for so the spirit of Teiresias told me, that day when I descended to the house of Hades to learn about the journey of my comrades and myself. But come, my wife, let us to bed, that there at last we may refresh ourselves with pleasant sleep."

Then said to him heedful Penelope: "The bed shall be prepared whenever your heart wills, now that the gods have let you reach your stately house and native land. But since you speak of this, and God inspires your heart, come, tell that trial. In time to come, I know, I shall experience it. To learn about it now, makes it no worse."

Then wise Odysseus answered her and said: "Lady, why urge me so insistently to tell? Well, I will speak it out; I will not hide it. Yet your heart will feel no joy; I have no joy myself; for Teiresias bade me go to many a peopled town, bearing in hand a shapely oar, till I should reach the men that know no sea and do not eat food mixed with salt. These, therefore, have no knowledge of the red-cheeked ships, nor of the shapely oars which are the wings of ships. And this was the sign, he said, easy to be observed. I will not hide it from you. When another traveler, meeting me, should say I had a winnowing-fan on my white shoulder, there in the ground he bade me fix my oar and make fit offerings to lord Poseidon—a ram, a bull, and the sow's mate, a boar—and, turning homeward, to offer sacred hectacombs to the immortal gods who hold the open sky, all in the order due. And on myself death from the sea shall very gently come and cut me off, bowed down with hale old age. Round me shall be a prosperous people. All this, he said, should be fulfilled."

Then said to him heedful Penelope: "If gods can make old age the better time, then there is hope there will be rest from trouble."

So they conversed together. Meanwhile Eurynome and the nurse prepared their bed with clothing soft, under the light of blazing torches. And after they had spread the comfortable bed, with busy speed, the old woman departed to her room to rest; while the chamber-servant, Eurynome, with torch in hand, brought them to their chamber and then went her way. So they came gladly to their bed of early days. And now Telemachus, the neatherd and the swineherd stayed their feet from dancing and bade the women stay, and all betook themselves to rest throughout the dusky halls.

But while the pair joyed in their new-found love, they joyed in talking too, each one relating: she, the royal lady, what she endured at home, watching the wasteful throng of suitors, who, making excuse of her, slew many cattle, beeves, and sturdy sheep, and stores of wine were drained from out the casks; he, high-born Odysseus, what miseries he brought on other men and what he bore himself in anguish—all he told, and she was glad to listen. No sleep fell on her eyelids till he had told her all.

He began with how at first he conquered the Ciconians,[98] and came thereafter to the fruitful land of Lotus-eaters;[99] then what Cyclops did, and how he took revenge for the brave comrades whom the Cyclops ate and never pitied; then how he came to Aeolus,[100] who gave him hearty welcome and sent him on his way; but it was fated that he should not reach his dear land yet, for a sweeping storm bore him once more along the swarming sea, loudly

---

[98] A reference to Odysseus' first adventure after he left Troy. He raided the city of the Ciconians, but they collected a force while Odysseus' men were drinking and eating and drove off Odysseus, who barely escaped with his life.   [99] A mysterious people who gave some of Odysseus' men lotus to taste. Those who tasted the lotus forgot the way home and lost all desire to return to Ithaca.   [100] A king in charge of the winds, who generously entertained Odysseus and his men for an entire month and then gave Odysseus a bag stuffed with all the winds as a parting gift. Odysseus' companions opened the bag when he fell asleep; the winds escaped, causing an enormous storm.

lamenting; how he came to Telephylus in Laestrygonia,[101] where the men destroyed his ships and his mailed comrades, all of them; Odysseus fled in his black ship alone. He told of Circe, too, and all her crafty guile; and how on a ship of many oars he came to the mouldering house of Hades, there to consult the spirit of Teiresias of Thebes; how he looked on all his comrades, and on the mother who had borne him and cared for him when little; how he had heard the full-voiced Sirens' song; how he came to the Wandering Rocks, to dire Charybdis and to Scylla, past whom none goes unharmed; how then his crew slew the Sun's kine; how Zeus with a blazing bolt smote his swift ship—Zeus, thundering from on high—and his good comrades perished, utterly, all, while he escaped their evil doom; how he came to the island of Ogygia and to the nymph Calypso, who held him in her hollow grotto, wishing him to be her husband, cherishing him, and saying she would make him an immortal, young forever, but she never beguiled the heart within his breast; how then he came through many toils to the Phaeacians, who honored him exceedingly, as if he were a god, and brought him on his way to his own native land, giving him stores of bronze and gold and clothing. This was the latest tale he told, when pleasant sleep fell on him, easing his limbs and from his heart removing care.

[101] A country populated by cannibals the size of mountains, who seized some of Odysseus' companions.

Herodotus

FROM THE *History*

TRANSLATED BY GEORGE RAWLINSON

Herodotus (484 B.C.?–425 B.C.?)

HERODOTUS, THE FIRST GREAT EUROPEAN HISTORIAN, ESTAB-
lished narrative prose as a new literary form of recording heroic events.
Although his *History* retained a large number of epic elements and, like
the *Iliad* and *Odyssey*, was probably intended for oral recitation, it clearly
distinguished itself from epic poetry by manifesting an inchoate spirit of
rational inquiry. The emphasis on a rational—but still religious—view of
human events had been introduced by Greek philosophers to western Asia
Minor, where Herodotus was born, and to Athens, where he lived for a
while after his travels through Greece, Asia Minor, the Near East, and
Egypt.

The comprehensive theme of Herodotus' work is the conflict between East
and West. The *History,* which is divided into nine "books," reports this conflict from the war against the Trojans down to the defeat of the Persians in
Herodotus' early childhood. The powerful Persians, already masters of an
enormous Middle Eastern empire, invaded Europe twice in the years 490–
479 B.C. with a vast army and navy, only to be defeated by small and politically weak Greek city-states under the leadership of Athens and Sparta.

The Greek victory was widely interpreted as the triumph of Greek democracy over Oriental tyranny, of the modest humaneness of free men over
the insolent blindness of Persian despots. This view underlies large parts of
the *History* of Herodotus. He develops it in terms of a tragic moral sequence which was prominent in popular thought: prosperity and success
lead to *hubris* (blind, presumptive, and often violent overconfidence or
pride), which in turn leads to ruin or self-destruction. This ruin is brought
about by a god—usually Zeus—who "with his lightning smites the bigger
animal" and who "allows no one to have high thoughts but himself."

Herodotus' *History* concludes with the massive, but disastrously unsuccessful, amphibious operation launched against Greece in 480 B.C. by the
Persian king, Xerxes. Xerxes is portrayed as a man who did not recognize his
human limitations, who inexorably overstepped his natural bounds, and
whose tragic destruction finally resulted from his insistent imperialism. His
fundamental blindness, as portrayed by Herodotus, rendered him incapable
of grasping that a small but patriotic army and navy could defeat the huge
military forces, greater wealth, and superior equipment of the Persian invaders.

History

These are the researches[1] of Herodotus of Halicarnassus, which he publishes, in the hope of thereby preserving from decay the remembrance of what men have done, and of preventing the great and wonderful actions of the Greeks and the Barbarians[2] from losing their due meed of glory; and withal to put on record what were their grounds of feud. . . .

Solon and Croesus

Croesus,[3] . . . in the course of many years, brought under his sway almost all the nations to the west of the Halys.[4] . . .

When all these conquests had been added to the Lydian empire, and the prosperity of Sardis[5] was now at its height, there came thither, one after another, all of the sages of Greece living at the time, and among them Solon,[6] the Athenian. He was on his travels, having left Athens to be absent ten years, under the pretence of wishing to see the world, but really to avoid being forced to repeal any of the laws which, at the request of the Athenians, he had made for them. Without his sanction the Athenians could not repeal them, as they had bound themselves under a heavy curse to be governed for ten years by the laws which should be imposed on them by Solon.

On this account, as well as to see the world, Solon set out upon his travels, in the course of which he went to Egypt to the court of Amasis,[7] and also came on a visit to Croesus at Sardis.[8] Croesus received him as his guest, and lodged him in the royal palace. On the third or fourth day after, he bade his servants conduct Solon over his treasuries, and show him all their greatness

---

[1] Greek, *historie*. [2] Non-Greeks. [3] Croesus, king of Lydia on the western coast of Asia Minor (now Turkey), had systematically expanded his kingdom by conquering numerous Greek and other tribes in western and central Asia Minor. His legendary wealth grew through these conquests and vast commercial enterprises. He ruled in the middle of the sixth century B.C. [4] River in central Asia Minor. [5] Capital of Lydia. [6] Brilliant Athenian legislator, social reformer, philosopher, poet; lived from the late seventh century B.C. to the middle of the sixth century B.C. [7] Amasis' rule began in 569 B.C. [8] The historical truth of this visit is open to dispute, but Solon's wide travels are attested to by Plato and others.

and magnificence. When he had seen them all, and, so far as time allowed, inspected them, Croesus addressed this question to him, "Stranger of Athens, we have heard much of your wisdom and of your travels through many lands, from love of knowledge and a wish to see the world. I am curious therefore to inquire of you, whom, of all the men that you have seen, you consider the most happy?" This he asked because he thought himself the happiest of mortals: but Solon answered him without flattery, according to his true sentiments, "Tellus of Athens, sire." Full of astonishment at what he heard, Croesus demanded sharply, "And wherefore do you deem Tellus happiest?" To which the other replied, "First, because his country was flourishing in his days, and he himself had sons both beautiful and good, and he lived to see children born to each of them, and these children all grew up; and further because, after a life spent in what our people look upon as comfort, his end was surpassingly glorious. In a battle between the Athenians and their neighbors near Eleusis, he came to the assistance of his countrymen, routed the foe, and died upon the field most gallantly. The Athenians gave him a public funeral on the spot where he fell, and paid him the highest honors."

Thus did Solon admonish Croesus by the example of Tellus, enumerating the manifold particulars of his happiness. When he had ended, Croesus inquired a second time, who after Tellus seemed to him the happiest, expecting that, at any rate, he would be given the second place. "Cleobis and Bito," Solon answered, "they were of Argive race: their fortune was enough for their wants, and they were besides endowed with so much bodily strength that they had both gained prizes at the Games. Also this tale is told of them: There was a great festival in honor of the goddess Juno at Argos,[9] to which their mother must needs to be taken in a car. Now the oxen did not come home from the field in time: so the youth, fearful of being too late, put the yoke on their own necks, and themselves drew the car in which their mother rode. Five and forty furlongs[10] they drew her, and stopped before the temple. This deed of theirs was witnessed by the whole assembly of worshippers, and then their life closed in the best possible way. Herein, too, God showed forth most evidently, how much better a thing for man death is than life. For the Argive men stood thick around the car and extolled the vast strength of the youths; and the Argive women extolled the mother who was blessed with such a pair of sons; and the mother herself, overjoyed at the deed and at the praises it had won, standing straight before the image, besought the goddess to bestow on Cleobis and Bito, the sons who had so mightily honored her, the highest blessing to which mortals can attain. Her prayer ended, they offered sacrifice, and partook of the holy banquet, after which the two

[9] The Greek goddess Hera (Latin, Juno) was the chief deity of Argos. As a priestess of Hera, the mother of Cleobis and Bito had to be transported to the temple in a processional chariot used at the cult festival.   [10] 5 to 6 miles.

youths fell asleep in the temple. They never woke more, but so passed from
the earth. The Argives, looking on them as among the best of men, caused
statues of them to be made, which they gave the shrine at Delphi."

When Solon had thus assigned these youths the second place, Croesus
broke in angrily, "What, stranger of Athens, is my happiness,[11] then, valued
so little by you, that you do not even put me on a level with private men?"

"Croesus," replied the other, "you asked a question concerning the condition of man, of one who knows that the power above us is full of jealousy,[12]
and fond of troubling our lot. A long life gives one to witness much, and
experience much oneself, that one would not choose. Seventy years I regard
as the limit of the life of man. In these seventy years are contained, without
reckoning intercalary months, 25,200 days. Add an intercalary month to
every other year, that the seasons may come round at the right time, and
there will be, besides the seventy years, thirty-five such months, making an
addition of 1,050 days. The whole number of the days contained in the
seventy years will thus be 26,250,[13] whereof not one but will produce events
unlike the rest. Hence man is wholly accident. For yourself, Croesus, I see
that you are wonderfully rich, and the lord of many nations; but with respect
to your question, I have no answer to give, until I hear that you have closed
your life happily. For assuredly he who possesses great store of riches is no
nearer happiness than he who has what suffices for his daily needs, unless
luck attend upon him, and so he continue in the enjoyment of all his good
things to the end of life. For many of the wealthiest men have been un-
favored of fortune, and many whose means were moderate, have had excellent luck. Men of the former class excel those of the latter but in two respects; these last excel the former in many. The wealthy man is better able
to content his desires, and to bear up against a sudden buffet of calamity.
The other has less ability to withstand these evils (from which, however, his
good luck keeps him clear), but he enjoys all these following blessings: he is
whole of limb, a stranger to disease, free from misfortune, happy in his
children, and comely to look upon. If, in addition to all this, he end his life
well, he is of a truth the man of whom you are in search, the man who may
rightly be termed happy. Call him, however, until he die, not happy but
fortunate. Scarcely, indeed, can any man unite all these advantages: as there
is no country which contains within it all that it needs, but each, while it
possesses some things, lacks others, and the best country is that which contains the most; so no single human being is complete in every respect—

---

[11] Throughout the history of Greek thought, "happiness" (usually *eudaimonia,*
the manifest possession of a fortunate *daimon*) is considered an unquestionable and
legitimate human ideal.   [12] One of the chief moral conclusions of Herodotus'
"researches" is that god is envious (*phthoneros*) of excessive human prosperity.
[13] Nowhere else does Herodotus make this error of calculating the solar year to
average 375 days.

something is always lacking. He who unites the greatest number of advantages, and retaining them to the day of his death, then dies peaceably, that man alone, sire, is, in my judgment, entitled to bear the name of 'happy.' But in every matter we must mark well the end; for oftentimes God gives men a gleam of happiness, and then plunges them into ruin."

Such was the speech which Solon addressed to Croesus, a speech which brought him neither largess nor honor. The king saw him depart with much indifference, since he thought that a man must be an arrant fool who made no account of present good, but bade men always wait and mark the end.

After Solon had gone away a dreadful vengeance, sent of God, came upon Croesus, to punish him, it is likely, for considering himself the happiest of men. First he had a dream in the night, which foreshowed him truly the evils that were about to befall him in the person of his son. For Croesus had two sons, one blasted by a natural defect, being deaf and dumb; the other, distinguished far above all his mates in every pursuit. The name of the last was Atys. It was this son concerning whom he dreamed a dream, that he would die by the blow of an iron weapon. When he woke, he considered earnestly with himself, and, greatly alarmed at the dream, instantly made his son take a wife, and whereas in former years the youth had been wont to command the Lydian forces in the field, he now would not suffer him to accompany them. All the spears and javelins, and weapons used in the wars, he removed out of the male apartments, and laid them in heaps in the chambers of the women, fearing lest perhaps one of the weapons that hung against the wall might fall and strike him. . . .

Herodotus continues to describe how Croesus' son, Atys, was killed in spite of every reasonable precaution and how his empire and his capital, Sardis, were captured by the Persian king Cyrus—thus confirming Solon's view that it would have been premature to call Croesus "happy" because of his wealth and power. Croesus is the first of several examples in Herodotus' History of a man's success leading to presumptuous confidence, which in turn leads to ruin.

Xerxes

. . . Now Xerxes,[14] on first mounting the throne, was coldly disposed towards the Grecian war, and made it his business to collect an army against Egypt.[15] But Mardonius, the son of Gobryas, who was at the court, and had more influence with him than any of the other Persians, being his own

[14] King of Persia 485–465 B.C.   [15] A rebellion against Persian rule had started in Egypt during the reign of King Darius.

cousin, the child of a sister of Darius, plied him with discourses like the following:

"Master, it is not fitting that they of Athens escape scot-free, after doing the Persians such great injury.[16] Complete the work which you have in hand, and then, when the pride of Egypt is brought down, lead an army against Athens. So shall you have good report among men, and others shall fear hereafter to attack your country."

Thus far it was of vengeance that he spoke, but sometimes he would vary the theme, and observe by the way that Europe was a beautiful region, rich in all kinds of cultivated trees, and the soil excellent: no one, save the king, was worthy to own such a land.

All this he said, because he longed for adventures, and hoped to become Satrap[17] of Greece under the king; and after a while he had his way, and persuaded Xerxes to do according to his desires. . . .

After Egypt was subdued, Xerxes, being about to take in hand the expedition against Athens, called together an assembly of the noblest Persians, to learn their opinions, and to lay before them his own designs. So, when the men were met, the king spoke thus to them:

"Persians, I shall not be the first to bring in among you a new custom—I shall but follow one which has come down to us from our forefathers. Never yet, as our old men assure me, has our race reposed itself, since the time when Cyrus overcame Astyages, and so we Persians wrested the sceptre from the Medes.[18] Now in all this God guides us, and we, obeying his guidance, prosper greatly. What need have I to tell you of the deeds of Cyrus and Cambyses,[19] and my own father Darius,[20] how many nations they conquered, and added to our dominions? You know right well what great things they achieved. But for myself, I will say, that from the day on which I mounted the throne, I have not ceased to consider by what means I may rival those who have preceded me in this post of honor, and increase the power of Persia as much as any of them. And truly I have pondered upon this, until at last I have found out a way whereby we may at once win glory, and likewise get possession of a land which is as large and as rich as our own —nay, which is even more varied in the fruits its bears—while at the same time we obtain satisfaction and revenge. For this cause I have now called you

[16] The Athenians had helped the Ionian Greeks (on the west coast of Asia Minor) when they revolted against Persian rule in 499 B.C.; they also defeated the invading Persian army in 490 B.C. [17] Viceroy; provincial governor. [18] Cyrus the Great, the founder of the Persian Empire, overthrew the empire of the Medes in 549 B.C., the Lydian Empire of Croesus in 546 B.C., the western seaboard of Asia Minor (which was mostly Greek) soon thereafter, and Babylon in 539 B.C. [19] Son and successor of King Cyrus. He conquered Egypt and ruled from 528 to 522 B.C. [20] King of Persia, 522–485 B.C. Darius' army invaded Greece but was defeated at Marathon by a small Greek force of Athenians (and some Plataeans, from a neighboring city) in the famous battle of 490 B.C.

together, that I may make known to you what I design to do. My intent is to
throw a bridge over the Hellespont[21] and march an army through Europe
against Greece, that thereby I may obtain vengeance from the Athenians for
the wrongs committed by them against the Persians and against my father.
Your own eyes saw the preparations of Darius against these men; but death
came upon him, and balked his hopes of revenge. In his behalf, therefore,
and in behalf of all the Persians, I undertake the war, and pledge myself not
to rest till I have taken and burnt Athens, which has dared, unprovoked, to
injure me and my father. . . . For these reasons, therefore, I am bent upon
this war; and I see likewise therewith united no few advantages. Once let
us subdue this people, and those neighbors of theirs who hold the land of
Pelops[22] the Phrygian,[23] and we shall extend the Persian territory as far as
God's heaven reaches. The sun will then shine on no land beyond our
borders; for I will pass through Europe from one end to the other, and with
your aid make of all the lands which it contains one country. For thus, if
what I hear be true, affairs stand: The nations whereof I have spoken, once
swept away, there is no city, no country left in all the world, which will venture so much as to withstand us in arms. By this course then we shall bring
all mankind under our yoke, alike those who are guilty and those who are
innocent of doing us wrong. For yourselves, if you wish to please me, do as
follows: When I announce the time for the army to meet together, hasten to
the muster with a good will, every one of you; and know that to the man
who brings with him the most gallant array I will give the gifts which our
people consider the most honorable. This then is what you have to do. But
to show that I am not self-willed in this matter I lay the business before you,
and give you full leave to speak your minds upon it openly."

Xerxes, having so spoken, held his peace.

Whereupon Mardonius took the word, and said:

"Of a truth, my lord, you surpass, not only all living Persians, but likewise
those yet unborn. Most true and right is each word that you have now
uttered; but best of all your resolve, not to let the Ionians[24] who live in
Europe—a worthless crew—mock us any more. It were indeed a monstrous
thing if, after conquering and enslaving the Sacae,[25] the Indians, the Ethiopians, the Assyrians, and many other mighty nations, not for any wrong
that they had done us, but only to increase our empire, we should then
allow the Greeks, who have done us such wanton injury, to escape our
vengeance. What is it that we fear in them?—not surely their numbers?—

---

[21] Dardanelles.   [22] "Land of Pelops": the Peloponnesus. Pelops was a son of
Tantalus and a brother of Niobe.   [23] After growing up in Asia Minor—Herodotus
says in Phrygia, others in Lydia—Pelops was expelled and went to the western
Peloponnesus, where he became king.   [24] A Greek (Hellenic) ethnic group which,
in Herodotus' time, mostly inhabited a narrow strip of land on the west coast of
Asia Minor.   [25] Probably the Scythians, inhabitants of what is now southern
Russia.

not the greatness of their wealth? We know the manner of their battle—we know how weak their power is. . . . And yet, I am told, these very Greeks are wont to wage wars against one another in the most foolish way, through sheer perversity and doltishness. . . . Nevertheless let us spare no pains; for nothing comes without trouble, but all that men acquire is got by painstaking."

When Mardonius had in this way softened the harsh speech of Xerxes, he too held his peace.

The other Persians were silent, for all feared to raise their voice against the plan proposed to them. But Artabanus,[26] the son of Hystaspes, and uncle of Xerxes, trusting to his relationship, was bold to speak:

"O king, it is impossible, if no more than one opinion is uttered, to make choice of the best: a man is forced then to follow whatever advice may have been given him; but if opposite speeches are delivered, then choice can be exercised. In like manner pure gold is not recognized by itself; but when we test it along with baser ore, we perceive which is the better. I counseled your father, Darius, who was my own brother, not to attack the Scyths, a race of people who had no town in their whole land. He thought however to subdue those wandering tribes, and would not listen to me, but marched an army against them, and before he returned home lost many of his bravest warriors. You are about, O king, to attack a people far superior to the Scyths, a people distinguished above others both by land and sea. It is fit therefore that I should tell you what danger you incur hereby. You say that you will bridge the Hellespont, and lead your troops through Europe against Greece. Now suppose some disaster befall you by land or sea, or by both. It may be even so, for the men are reputed valiant. Indeed one may measure their prowess from what they have already done; for when Datis and Artaphernes[27] led their huge army against Attica, the Athenians singly defeated them. . . .

"Think then no more of incurring so great a danger when no need presses, but follow the advice I tender. Break up this meeting, and when you have well considered the matter with yourself, and settled what you will do, declare to us your resolve. I know not of aught in the world that so profits a man as taking good counsel with himself; for even if things fall out against one's hopes, still one has counseled well, though fortune has made the counsel of no effect: whereas if a man counsels ill and luck follows, he has gotten a windfall, but his counsel is none the less silly. See how god with his lightning always smites the bigger animals, and will not suffer them to wax insolent, while those of a lesser bulk chafe him not. How likewise his bolts fall ever on the highest houses and the tallest trees? So plainly does he love to bring down everything that exalts itself. Thus often a mighty host is discomfited by a few men, when god in his jealousy sends fear or storm from

[26] A brother of Darius. [27] Commanders of the Persian army defeated in the battle of Marathon; Artaphernes was a cousin of Xerxes.

heaven, and they perish in a way unworthy of them. For god allows no one
to have high thoughts but himself. Again, hurry always brings about disasters, from which huge sufferings are wont to arise; but in delay lie many
advantages, not apparent (it may be) at first sight, but such as in course of
time are seen of all. Such then is my counsel, O king. . . ."

Thus Artabanus spoke. But Xerxes, full of wrath, replied to him:

"Artabanus, you are my father's brother—that shall save you from receiving the proper reward for your silly words. One shame however I will lay
upon you, coward and faint-hearted as you are—you shall not come with
me to fight these Greeks, but shall tarry here with the women. Without your
aid I will accomplish all of which I spoke. For let me not be thought the
child of Darius, the son of Hystaspes, the son of Arsames, the son of Ariaram-
nes, the son of Teispes, nor of Cyrus, the son of Cambyses, the son of
Teispes, the son of Achaemenes,[28] if I take not vengeance on the Athenians.
Full well I know that, were we to remain at rest, yet would not they, but
would most certainly invade our country, if at least it be right to judge from
what they have already done; for, remember, it was they who fired Sardis
and attacked Asia.[29] So now retreat is on both sides impossible, and the
choice lies between doing and suffering injury; either our empire must pass
under the dominion of the Greeks,[30] or their land become the prey of the
Persians; for there is no middle course left in this quarrel. It is right then
that we, who have in times past received wrong, should now avenge it, and
that I should thereby discover, what that great risk is, which I run in march-
ing against these men—men whom Pelops the Phrygian, a vassal of my forefathers, subdued so utterly, that to this day both the land, and the people
who dwell therein, alike bear the name[31] of the conqueror."

*Xerxes went ahead with his invasion in spite of numerous warning visions
and contrary advice. He built his bridge of boats over the Hellespont, constructed a canal for his ships straight through Mount Athos, defeated a Greek
force at Thermopylae, and destroyed Athens almost entirely. Then, however,
his massive fleet was completely defeated by the Greeks in the famous battle
of Salamis (480 B.C.), and he hastily retreated in fear and humiliation, leaving behind Mardonius to be defeated at Plataea with a large army in 479
B.C. After some sordid affairs (including one with his brother's wife) and
further manifestations of his unbridled self-confidence and self-indulgence,
he was assassinated in 465 B.C.*

[28] Catalogues of ancestral names are used alike by Greek epic poets, in Greek
drama and historiography, and by Hebrew poets and historical writers to establish
the illustrious historical or mythological identity of a character.   [29] That is, when
the Athenians intervened on the side of the Ionian Greeks in their revolt against
Persian oppression in 499 B.C.   [30] Xerxes is conjuring up a nonexistent threat.
[31] That is, Peloponnesus.

Aeschylus

Agamemnon

TRANSLATED BY LOUIS MAC NEICE

Aeschylus (525 B.C.–456 B.C.)

The earliest representative of tragic drama in western literature, Aeschylus, was not only a poet but, like many other members of the Athenian aristocracy, also a soldier who experienced the momentous political events of his time at first hand. He fought against the Persians in the battle of Marathon and probably against Xerxes' invading forces in 480–479 B.C., and he dramatized the tragic ruin of Xerxes in his earliest surviving play, *The Persians*.

The tragedies of Aeschylus and the other Greek tragedians were first performed in an annual dramatic contest at a spring festival in honor of the god Dionysus in Athens. Although the subject matter of these tragedies only rarely had anything to do with the cult of Dionysus, it seems reasonably sure that tragedy originally developed out of choral dances and songs which were performed in his honor. Ancient sources assume that a decisive step in the evolution of tragedy out of these choral songs was the introduction of a dialogue, possibly sung but more probably spoken, between the chorus and a single "answerer" or "interpreter." This development contained enormous dramatic potential, since it not only made dialogue possible but also emphasized the individual and permitted his active development, with the chorus as a more or less passive foil. Up to the very end of the history of Greek tragedy these two elements—the individual and the chorus—remained its foundation.

Aeschylus increased the dialogue by the addition of a second actor, and his younger contemporary Sophocles soon added a third. Each actor played several roles in a play, using a different mask for each role; but the dramatically significant fact is that there were never more than two (or, after Sophocles' innovation, three) actors on the stage simultaneously in the tragedies of Aeschylus. Only seven of his more than seventy tragedies still exist: *The Persians, The Seven Against Thebes, The Suppliant Women, Prometheus Bound,* and the *Oresteia,* which is a trilogy consisting of *Agamemnon, The Libation Bearers,* and *The Eumenides.*

The *Oresteia* trilogy was first performed at a festival of Dionysus in 458 B.C., barely two years before Aeschylus died. The first play of this trilogy, *Agamemnon,* is based on a myth which had already been treated often in Greek literature and was well known to the audience. The myth concerns a vicious cycle of crimes in the family of a king from the Peloponnesus, Atreus. The cycle could apparently be terminated only by abolishing the principle of retaliation. But Zeus, in this first play of the trilogy, still supported the archaic code of retributive justice, and the violent crimes continued. It is one part of this cycle of retribution that Aeschylus masterfully dramatized in the following play.

Agamemnon

THE WATCHMAN, *a guard at King Agamemnon's palace in Argos.*

A CHORUS *of older men of Argos.*

CLYTEMNESTRA, *wife of King Agamemnon.*

A HERALD.

AGAMEMNON, *King of Argos; son of Atreus; commander of the Greeks in the Trojan war.*

CASSANDRA, *a Trojan princess with prophetic vision, brought home by King Agamemnon as part of his spoils of war.*

AEGISTHUS, *Clytemnestra's lover during Agamemnon's absence; son of Atreus' brother Thyestes and cousin of Agamemnon.*

SILENT CHARACTERS:

ATTENDANTS *of Clytemnestra and Agamemnon;* BODYGUARD *of Aegisthus.*

While the son of Atreus, Agamemnon, was commanding the
Greeks at Troy, his wife, Clytemnestra, commited adultery in his
palace at Argos with his cousin Aegisthus, who was the son of
Atreus' brother Thyestes. As the play opens, rumors have reached
Argos that Troy has been conquered and that Agamemnon might
return home soon.

SCENE. *A space in front of the palace of* AGAMEMNON *in*
    Argos. Night. A WATCHMAN *on the roof of the palace.*
WATCHMAN. The gods it is I ask to release me from this watch
  A year's length now, spending my nights like a dog,
  Watching on my elbow on the roof of the sons of Atreus°
  So that I have come to know the assembly of the nightly stars
  Those which bring storm and those which bring summer to men,
  The shining Masters riveted in the sky—
  I know the decline and rising of those stars.
  And now I am waiting for the sign of the beacon,°
  The flame of fire that will carry the report from Troy,
  News of her taking. Which task has been assigned me   10
  By a woman of sanguine heart but a man's mind.
  Yet when I take my restless rest in the soaking dew,
  My night not visited with dreams—
  For fear stands by me in the place of sleep
  That I cannot firmly close my eyes in sleep—
  Whenever I think to sing or hum to myself
  As an antidote to sleep, then every time I groan
  And fall to weeping for the fortunes of this house
  Where not as before are things well ordered now.
  But now may a good chance fall, escape from pain,   20
  The good news visible in the midnight fire.
    [*Pause. A light appears, gradually increasing, the light of*
          the beacon.]
  Ha! I salute you, torch of the night whose light
  Is like the day, an earnest of many dances
  In the city of Argos, celebration of Peace.

---

3. *sons of Atreus:* Agamemnon and Menelaus. 8–11. *beacon . . . mind:* Clytemnestra has ordered the watchman to look for the light of a relay chain of fire
signals (beacons) which would reach Troy across the Aegean islands to Argos; by
this signal Agamemnon had arranged to inform her of the capture of Troy.

I call to Agamemnon's wife; quickly to rise
Out of her bed and in the house to raise
Clamor of joy in answer to this torch
For the city of Troy is taken—
Such is the evident message of the beckoning flame.
And I myself will dance my solo first   30
For I shall count my master's fortune mine
Now that this beacon has thrown me a lucky throw.
And may it be when he comes, the master of this house,
That I grasp his hand in my hand.
As to the rest, I am silent. A great ox, as they say,
Stands on my tongue. The house itself, if it took voice,
Could tell the case most clearly. But I will only speak
To those who know. For the others I remember nothing.
        [*Enter* CHORUS OF OLD MEN. *During the following chorus
                the day begins to dawn.*]
CHORUS. The tenth year it is since Priam's high
        Adversary, Menelaus the king°   40
        And Agamemnon, the double-throned and sceptered
        Yoke of the sons of Atreus
        Ruling in fee from God,
        From this land gathered an Argive army
        On a mission of war a thousand ships,
        Their hearts howling in boundless bloodlust
        In eagles' fashion who in lonely
        Grief for nestlings above their homes hang
        Turning in cycles
        Beating the air with the oars of their wings,   50
                Now to no purpose
                Their love and task of attention.

        But above there is One,
        Maybe Pan,° maybe Zeus or Apollo,
        Who hears the harsh cries of the birds
        Guests° in his kingdom,
        Wherefore, though late, in requital
        He sends the Avenger.
        Thus Zeus our master

39–40. Priam's . . . king: Priam's son Paris abducted Helen, the wife of Menelaus, thus bringing the Greek king in opposition to the Trojan.   _54. Pan:_ a Greek
god associated with the woods, rustic areas, and wild life.   _56. guests:_ the sky is
Zeus' sphere, thus the birds are his guests.

Guardian of guest and of host°   60
Sent against Paris the sons of Atreus
For a woman of many men°
Many the dog-tired wrestlings
Limbs and knees in the dust pressed—
    For both the Greeks and Trojans
    An overture of breaking spears.

Things are where they are, will finish
In the manner fated and neither
Fire beneath nor oil above can soothe
The stubborn anger of the unburnt offering.   70
As for us, our bodies are bankrupt,
The expedition left us behind
And we wait supporting on sticks
Our strength—the strength of a child;
For the marrow that leaps in a boy's body
Is no better than that of the old
For the War God is not in his body
While the man who is very old
And his leaf withering away
Goes on the three-foot° way   80
No better than a boy, and wanders
A dream in the middle of the day.

But you, daughter of Tyndareus,
Queen Clytemnestra,°
What is the news, what is the truth, what have you learnt,
On the strength of whose word have you thus
Sent orders for sacrifice round?
All the gods, the gods of the town,
Of the worlds of Below and Above,
By the door, in the square,   90
Have their altars ablaze with your gifts,
From here, from there, all sides, all corners,
Sky-high leap the flame-jets fed
By gentle and undeceiving

---

60. *Guardian . . . host:* As god of guests and strangers, Zeus punishes violations
of the human code of hospitality, such as the abduction of Helen by Paris while
Paris was a guest of her husband, Menelaus. 62. *woman of many men:* Helen,
who had accepted Paris as her new husband, is here charged with promiscuity. In
post-Homeric legend she was married to a number of men in addition to Menelaus
and Paris. 80. *three-foot:* two feet and a cane. 84. *Clytemnestra:* she has just
entered. She leaves again in silence after line 104.

Persuasion of sacred unguent,
Oil from the royal stores.
Of these things tell
That which you can, that which you may,
Be healer of this our trouble
Which at times torments with evil   100
Though at times by propitiations
A shining hope repels
The insatiable thought upon grief
Which is eating away our hearts.
Of the omen° which powerfully speeded
That voyage of strong men, by God's grace even I
Can tell; my age can still
Be galvanized to breathe the strength of song,
To tell how the kings of all the youth of Greece
Two-throned but one in mind   110
Were launched with pike and punitive hand
Against the Trojan shore by angry birds.
Kings of the birds° to our kings came,
One with a white rump, the other black,
Appearing near the palace on the spear-arm side
Where all could see them,
Tearing a pregnant hare with the unborn young
Foiled of their courses.
      Cry, cry upon Death; but may the good prevail.

But the diligent prophet° of the army seeing the sons   120
Of Atreus twin in temper knew
That the hare-killing birds were the two
Generals, explained it thus—
"In time this expedition sacks the town
Of Troy before whose towers
By Fate's force the public
Wealth will be wasted.
Only let not some spite from the gods benight the bulky bat-
      talions,

105. *Of the omen:* The chorus here describes an omen at the departure of the
Greek army from Aulis, their embarkation port, for Troy ten years previously: two
eagles seized and killed a pregnant hare. Calchas interpreted this to mean that two
Greek kings—Agamemnon and Menelaus—would destroy the city of Troy, including her future generations of unborn Trojans. 113. *kings of the birds:* eagles,
as "bird kings" sacred to the "king" of the gods, Zeus. The flight patterns of eagles
were often observed for the purposes of divination. 120. *the diligent prophet:*
Calchas.

The bridle of Troy, nor strike them untimely;
For the goddess° feels pity, is angry   130
With the winged dogs of her father
Who killed the cowering hare with her unborn young;
Artemis hates the eagles' feast."
     Cry, cry upon Death; but may the good prevail.

"But° though you are so kind, goddess,
To the little cubs of lions
And to all the sucking young of roving beasts
In whom your heart delights,
Fulfill us the signs of these things,
The signs which are good but open to blame,   140
And I call on Apollo the Healer
That his sister raise not against the Greeks
Unremitting gales to balk their ships,
Hurrying on another kind° of sacrifice, with no feasting,
Barbarous building of hates and disloyalties
Grown on the family. For anger grimly returns
Cunningly haunting the house, avenging the death of a child,
     never forgetting its due."°
So cried the prophet—evil and good together,
Fate that the birds foretold to the king's house.
In tune with this   150
     Cry, cry upon Death; but may the good prevail.

Zeus, whoever He is, if this
Be a name acceptable,
By this name I will call him.
There is no one comparable
When I reckon all of the case
Excepting Zeus, if ever I am to jettison
The barren care which clogs my heart.

---

130. *goddess:* Artemis. As protectress of wild life and dispenser of painless birth, she is enraged that the eagles have killed a pregnant animal.   *135–149. But . . . house:* Calchas addresses a prayer to Artemis. He foresees that the goddess, in anger at the hare's death, will use unfavorable winds to prevent the Greeks from sailing for Troy until Agamemnon's daughter Iphigenia is sacrificed in compensation for the hare's death (i.e., as the price for favorable winds).   *144. another kind:* an allusion to a "sacrifice" of human flesh which has previously taken place. Agamemnon's father, Atreus, tricked his brother, Thyestes, into eating all of his own children except Aegisthus, whereupon Thyestes cursed the entire family. *147. Cunningly . . . due:* A prophecy which, as the audience knew, would be fulfilled by Clytemnestra, the mother of Iphegenia.

Not° He who formerly was great
With brawling pride and mad for broils   160
Will even be said to have been.
And He who was next has met
His match and is seen no more,
But Zeus is the name to cry in your triumph-song
And win the prize for wisdom.
Who setting us on the road
Made this a valid law—
        "That men must learn by suffering."
Drop by drop in sleep upon the heart
Falls the laborious memory of pain,   170
Against one's will comes wisdom;
The grace of the gods is forced on us
        Throned inviolably.

So at that time the elder
Chief° of the Greek ships
Would not blame any prophet
Nor face the flail of fortune;
For unable to sail, the people
Of Greece were heavy with famine,
Waiting in Aulis where the tides   180
        Flow back, opposite Chalcis.

But the winds that blew from the Strymon,°
Bringing delay, hunger, evil harborage,
Crazing men, rotting ships and cables,
By drawing out the time
Were shredding into nothing the flower of Argos,
When the prophet screamed a new
Cure for that bitter tempest
And heavier still for the chiefs,
Pleading the anger of Artemis so that the sons of Atreus   190
Beat the ground with their scepters and shed tears.

Then the elder king found voice and answered:
"Heavy is my fate, not obeying,
And heavy it is if I kill my child, the delight of my house,
And with a virgin's blood upon the altar

159–165. Not . . . wisdom: A reference to the myths about the overthrow of the
first supreme god (Uranos) by his son Cronos and the latter's overthrow by Zeus,
who symbolized order. 174–5. elder chief: Agamemnon. 182. Strymon: river
in Thrace; represents the wild and little known northeast Aegean source of the
wind.

Make foul her father's hands.
Either alternative is evil.
How can I betray the fleet
And fail the allied army?
It is right they should passionately cry for the winds to be lulled   200
By the blood of a girl. So be it. May it be well."

But when he had put on the halter of Necessity
Breathing in his heart a veering wind of evil
Unsanctioned, unholy, from that moment forward
He changed his counsel, would stop at nothing.
For the heart of man is hardened by infatuation,
A faulty adviser, the first link of sorrow.
Whatever the cause, he brought himself to slay
His daughter, an offering to promote the voyage
To a war for a runaway wife.   210
Her prayers and her cries of father,
Her life of a maiden,
Counted for nothing with those militarists;
But her father, having duly prayed, told the attendants
To lift her, like a goat, above the altar
With her robes falling about her,
To lift her boldly, her spirit fainting,
And hold back with a gag upon her lovely mouth
By the dumb force of a bridle
The cry which would curse the house.   220
Then dropping on the ground her saffron dress,
Glancing at each of her appointed
Sacrificers a shaft of pity,
Plain as in a picture she wished
To speak to them by name, for often
At her father's table where men feasted
She had sung in celebration for her father
With a pure voice, affectionately, virginally,
The hymn for happiness at the third° libation.
The sequel to this I saw not and tell not   230
But the crafts of Calchas gained their object.
To learn by suffering is the equation of Justice; the Future
Is known when it comes, let it go till then.
To know in advance is to sorrow in advance.
The facts will appear with the shining of the dawn.

---

229. *third:* Three offerings of wine (libations) were usually poured at cult banquets—the last to Zeus "the Savior," while his eulogy was sung.

[*Enter* CLYTEMNESTRA.]

But may good, at the least, follow after
As the queen here wishes, who stands
Nearest the throne, the only
    Defense of the land of Argos.

LEADER OF THE CHORUS.

    I have come, Clytemnestra, reverencing your authority.   240
For it is right to honor our master's wife
When the man's own throne is empty.
But you, if you have heard good news for certain, or if
You sacrifice on the strength of flattering hopes,
I would gladly hear. Though I cannot cavil at silence.

CLYTEMNESTRA. Bearing good news, as the proverb says, may Dawn
Spring from her mother Night.
You will hear something now that was beyond your hopes.
The men of Argos have taken Priam's city.

LEADER. What! I cannot believe it. It escapes me.   250
CLYTEMNESTRA. Troy in the hands of the Greeks. Do I speak plain?
LEADER. Joy creeps over me, calling out my tears.
CLYTEMNESTRA. Yes. Your eyes proclaim your loyalty.
LEADER. But what are your grounds? Have you a proof of it?
CLYTEMNESTRA. There is proof indeed—unless God has cheated us.
LEADER. Perhaps you believe the inveigling shapes of dreams?
CLYTEMNESTRA. I would not be credited with a dozing brain!
LEADER. Or are you puffed up by Rumor, the wingless flyer?
CLYTEMNESTRA. You mock my common sense as if I were a child.
LEADER. But at what time was the city given to sack?   260
CLYTEMNESTRA. In this very night that gave birth to this day.
LEADER. What messenger could come so fast?
CLYTEMNESTRA. Hephaestus,° launching a fine flame from Ida,°
Beacon forwarding beacon, dispatch-riders of fire,
Ida relayed to Hermes' cliff in Lemnos
And the great glow from the island was taken over third
By the height of Athos that belongs to Zeus,
And towering then to straddle over the sea
The might of the running torch joyfully tossed
The gold gleam forward like another sun,   270

---

263. *Hephaestus:* (god of) fire. *Ida:* a mountain range east of Troy. The place names which follow represent the relay stations for the chain of beacon fires. This speech demonstrates the ambiguity and irony that characterize most of Clytemnestra's statements: to the chorus the light means Agamemnon's return, the expulsion of Clytemnestra's lover Aegisthus, and the return to Argos of order; to Clytemnestra it means the return of Agamemnon to death at her hands.

Herald of light to the heights of Mount Macistus,
And he without delay, nor carelessly by sleep
Encumbered, did not shirk his intermediary role,
His farflung ray reached the Euripus' tides
And told Messapion's watchers, who in turn
Sent on the message further
Setting a stack of dried-up heather on fire.
And the strapping flame, not yet enfeebled, leapt
Over the plain of Asopus like a blazing moon
And woke on the crags of Cithaeron   280
Another relay in the chain of fire.
The light that was sent from far was not declined
By the look-out men, who raised a fiercer yet,
A light which jumped the water of Gorgopis
And to Mount Aegiplanctus duly come
Urged the reveille of the punctual fire.
So then they kindle it squanderingly and launch
A beard of flame big enough to pass
The headland that looks down upon the Saronic gulf,
Blazing and bounding till it reached at length   290
The Arachnaean steep, our neighboring heights;
And leaps in the latter end on the roof of the sons of Atreus
Issue and image of the fire on Ida.
Such was the assignment of my torch-racers,
The task of each fulfilled by his successor,
And victor is he who ran both first and last.
Such is the proof I offer you, the sign
My husband sent me out of Troy.
LEADER. To the gods, queen, I shall give thanks presently.
But I would like to hear this story further,   300
To wonder at it in detail from your lips.
CLYTEMNESTRA. The Greeks hold Troy upon this day.
The cries in the town I fancy do not mingle.
Pour oil and vinegar into the same jar,
You would say they stand apart unlovingly;
Of those who are captured and those who have conquered
Distinct are the sounds of their diverse fortunes,
For *these* having flung themselves about the bodies
Of husbands and brothers, or sons upon the bodies
Of aged fathers from a throat no longer   310
Free, lament the fate of their most loved.
But *those* a night's marauding after battle
Sets hungry to what breakfast the town offers

Not billeted duly in any barracks order
But as each man has drawn his lot of luck.
So in the captive homes of Troy already
They take their lodging, free of the frosts
And dews of the open. Like happy men
They will sleep all night without sentry.
But if° they respect duly the city's gods,   320
Those of the captured land and the sanctuaries of the gods,
They need not, having conquered, fear reconquest.
But let no lust fall first upon the troops
To plunder what is not right, subdued by gain,
For they must still, in order to come home safe,
Get round the second lap of the doubled course.
So if they return without offense to the gods°
The grievance of the slain may learn at last
A friendly talk—unless some fresh wrong falls.
Such are the thoughts you hear from me, a woman.   330
But may the good prevail for all to see.
We have much good. I only ask to enjoy it.
LEADER. Woman, you speak with sense like a prudent man.
I, who have heard your valid proofs, prepare
To give the glory to God.
Fair recompense is brought us for our troubles.
            [CLYTEMNESTRA *goes back into the palace.*]
CHORUS. O Zeus our king and Night our friend
Donor of glories,
Night who cast on the towers of Troy
A close-clinging net so that neither the grown   340
Nor any of the children can pass
The enslaving and huge
Trap of all-taking destruction.
Great Zeus, guardian of host and guest,
I honor who has done his work and taken
A leisured aim at Paris so that neither
Too short nor yet over the stars
      He might shoot to no purpose.

From Zeus is the blow they can tell of,
This at least can be established,   350
They have fared according to his ruling. For some

320–27. *But if . . . gods:* According to myths known to the audience, Agamemnon and his Greek army had, in fact, acted with irreverence to gods and humans
at the fall of Troy.

Deny that the gods deign to consider those among men
Who trample on the grace of inviolate things;
It is the impious man says this,
For Ruin is revealed the child
Of not to be attempted actions
When men are puffed up unduly
And their houses are stuffed with riches.
Measure° is the best. Let danger be distant,
This should suffice a man   360
With a proper part of wisdom.
For a man has no protection
Against the drunkenness of riches
Once he has spurned from his sight
The high altar of Justice.

Somber Persuasion compels him,
Intolerable child of calculating Doom;
All cure is vain, there is no glozing it over
But the mischief shines forth with a deadly light
And like bad coinage   370
By rubbings and frictions
He stands discolored and black
Under the test—like a boy
Who chases a winged bird
He has branded his city for ever.
His prayers are heard by no god;
Who makes such things his practice
The gods destroy him.
    This way came Paris
    To the house of the sons of Atreus   380
    And outraged the table of friendship
    Stealing the wife of his host.

Leaving to her countrymen clanging of
Shields and of spears and
Launching of warships
And bringing instead of a dowry destruction to Troy
Lightly she was gone through the gates daring
Things undared. Many the groans
Of the palace spokesmen on this theme—
"O the house, the house, and its princes,   390
O the bed and the imprint of her limbs;
One can see him crouching in silence

359. *Measure:* the moderate mean.

Dishonored and unreviling."
Through desire for her who is overseas, a ghost
Will seem to rule the household.
  And now her husband hates
  The grace of shapely statues;
  In the emptiness of their eyes
  All their appeal is departed.

But appearing in dreams persuasive   400
Images come bringing a joy that is vain,
Vain for when in fancy he looks to touch her—
Slipping through his hands the vision
Rapidly is gone
Following on wings the walks of sleep.
Such are his° griefs in his house on his hearth,
Such as these and worse than these,
But everywhere through the land of Greece which men have left
Are mourning women with enduring hearts
To be seen in all houses; many   410
Are the thoughts which stab their hearts;
  For those they sent to war
  They know, but in place of men
  That which comes home to them
  Is merely an urn and ashes.

But the money-changer War, changer of bodies,
Holding his balance in the battle
Home from Troy refined by fire
Sends back to friends the dust
That is heavy with tears, stowing   420
A man's worth of ashes
In an easily handled jar.
And they wail speaking well of the men how that one
Was expert in battle, and one fell well in the carnage—
But for another man's wife.
Muffled and muttered words;
And resentful grief creeps up against the sons
Of Atreus and their cause.
  But others there by the wall
  Entombed in Trojan ground   430
  Lie, handsome of limb,
  Holding and hidden in enemy soil.

406. *his*: Menelaus', the husband of Helen.

Heavy is the murmur of an angry people
Performing the purpose of a public curse;
There is something cowled in the night
That I anxiously wait to hear.
For the gods are not blind to the
Murderers of many and the black
Furies° in time
When a man prospers in sin   440
By erosion of life reduce him to darkness,
Who, once among the lost, can no more
Be helped. Over-great glory
Is a sore burden. The high peak
Is blasted by the eyes of Zeus.

     I prefer an unenvied fortune,
     Not to be a sacker of cities
     Nor to find myself living at another's
     Ruling, myself a captive.

AN OLD MAN. From the good news' beacon a swift   450
    Rumor is gone through the town.
    Who knows if it be true
    Or some deceit of the gods?

ANOTHER OLD MAN. Who is so childish or broken in wit
    To kindle his heart at a new-fangled message of flame
    And then be downcast
    At a change of report?

ANOTHER OLD MAN. It fits the temper of a woman
    To give her assent to a story before it is proved.

ANOTHER OLD MAN. The over-credulous passion of women expands   460
    In swift conflagration but swiftly declining is gone
    The news that a woman announced.

LEADER OF THE CHORUS.
    Soon we shall know about the illuminant torches,
    The beacons and the fiery relays,
    Whether they were true or whether like dreams
    That pleasant light came here and hoaxed our wits.
    Look: I see, coming from the beach, a herald
    Shadowed with olive shoots;° the dust upon him,
    Mud's thirsty sister and colleague, is my witness
    That he will not give dumb news nor news by lighting   470
    A flame of fire with the smoke of mountain timber;
    In words he will either corroborate our joy—

---

439. *Furies:* avenging deities.   468. *shadowed . . . shoots:* with an olive wreath.

But the opposite version I reject with horror.
To the good appeared so far may good be added.
ANOTHER SPEAKER. Whoever makes other prayers for this our city,
  May he reap himself the fruits of his wicked heart.
    [*Enter the* HERALD, *who kisses the ground before speaking.*]
HERALD. Earth of my fathers, O the earth of Argos,
  In the light of the tenth year I reach you thus
  After many shattered hopes achieving one,
  For never did I dare to think that here in Argive land   480
  I should win a grave in the dearest soil of home;
  But now hail, land, and hail, light of the sun,
  And Zeus high above the country and the Pythian king—°
  May he no longer shoot his arrows at us
  (Implacable long enough beside Scamander)
  But now be savior to us and be healer,
  King Apollo. And all the Assembly's gods
  I call upon, and him my patron, Hermes,°
  The dear herald whom all heralds adore,
  And the Heroes who sped our voyage, again with favor   490
  Take back the army that has escaped the spear.
  O cherished dwelling, palace of royalty,
  O august thrones and gods facing the sun,
  If ever before, now with your bright eyes
  Gladly receive your king after much time,
  Who comes bringing light to you in the night time,
  And to all these as well—King Agamemnon.
  Give him a good welcome as he deserves,
  Who with the axe of judgment-awarding God
  Has smashed Troy and levelled the Trojan land;   500
  The altars are destroyed, the seats of the gods,
  And the seed of all the land is perished from it.
  Having cast this halter round the neck of Troy
  The King, the elder son of Atreus, a blessed man,
  Comes, the most worthy to have honor of all
  Men that are now. Paris nor his guilty city
  Can boast that the crime was greater than the atonement.
  Convicted in a suit for rape and robbery
  He has lost his stolen goods and with consummate ruin
  Mowed down the whole country and his father's house.   510
  The sons of Priam have paid their account with interest.
LEADER OF THE CHORUS. Hail and be glad, herald of the Greek army.

483. *Pythian king:* Apollo.   488. *Hermes:* the messenger of Zeus, and the patron
deity of messengers and heralds.

HERALD. Yes. Glad indeed! So glad that at the gods' demand
　　I should no longer hesitate to die.
LEADER: Were you so harrowed by desire for home?°
HERALD. Yes. The tears come to my eyes for joy.
LEADER. Sweet then is the fever which afflicts you.
HERALD. What do you mean? Let me learn your drift.
LEADER. Longing for those whose love came back in echo.
HERALD. Meaning the land was homesick for the army?　　　　520
LEADER. Yes. I would often groan from a darkened heart.
HERALD. This sullen hatred—how did it fasten on you?
LEADER. I cannot say. Silence is my stock prescription.
HERALD. What? In your masters' absence were there some you feared?
LEADER. Yes. In your phrase, death would now be a gratification.
HERALD. Yes, for success is ours. These things have taken time.
　　Some of them we could say have fallen well,
　　While some we blame. Yet who except the gods
　　Is free from pain the whole duration of life?
　　If I were to tell of our labors, our hard lodging,　　　　530
　　The sleeping on crowded decks, the scanty blankets,
　　Tossing and groaning, rations that never reached us—
　　And the land too gave matter for more disgust,
　　For our beds lay under the enemy's walls.
　　Continuous drizzle from the sky, dews from the marshes,
　　Rotting our clothes, filling our hair with lice.
　　And if one were to tell of the bird-destroying winter
　　Intolerable from the snows of Ida
　　Or of the heat when the sea slackens at noon
　　Waveless and dozing in a depressed calm—　　　　540
　　But why make these complaints? The weariness is over;
　　Over indeed for some who never again
　　Need even trouble to rise.
　　Why make a computation of the lost?
　　Why need the living sorrow for the spites of fortune?
　　I wish to say a long goodbye to disasters.
　　For us, the remnant of the troops of Argos,
　　The advantage remains, the pain can not outweigh it;
　　So we can make our boast to this sun's light,
　　Flying on words above the land and sea:　　　　550
　　"Having taken Troy the Argive expedition
　　Has nailed up throughout Greece in every temple
　　These spoils, these ancient trophies."

515–25. *Were . . . gratification:* The chorus of old men attempts to obliquely
warn the herald that danger lurks for Agamemnon in his own city.

Those who hear such things must praise the city
And the generals. And the grace of God be honored
Which brought these things about. You have the whole story.
LEADER. I confess myself convinced by your report.
    Old men are always young enough to learn.
             [*Enter* CLYTEMNESTRA *from the palace.*]
    This news belongs by right first to the house
    And Clytemnestra—though I am enriched also.   560
CLYTEMNESTRA. Long before this I shouted at joy's command
    At the coming of the first night-messenger of fire
    Announcing the taking and capsizing of Troy.
    And people reproached me saying, "Do mere beacons
    Persuade you to think that Troy is already down?
    Indeed a woman's heart is easily exalted."
    Such comments made me seem to be wandering but yet
    I began my sacrifices and in the women's fashion
    Throughout the town they raised triumphant cries
    And in the gods' enclosures   570
    Lulling the fragrant, incense-eating flame.
    And now what need is there for you to tell me more?
    From the King himself I shall learn the whole story.
    But how the best to welcome my honored lord
    I shall take pains when he comes back—For what
    Is a kinder light for a woman to see than this,
    To open the gates to her man come back from war
    When God has saved him? Tell this to my husband,
    To come with all speed, the city's darling;
    May he returning find a wife as loyal   580
    As when he left her, watchdog of the house,
    Good to *him* but fierce to the ill-intentioned,
    And in all other things as ever, having destroyed
    No seal or pledge at all in the length of time.
    I know no pleasure with another man, no scandal,
    More than I know how to dye metal red.
    Such is my boast, bearing a load of truth,
    A boast that need not disgrace a noble wife.   [*Exit.*]
LEADER. Thus has she spoken; if you take her meaning,
    Only a specious tale to shrewd interpreters.   590
    But do you, herald, tell me; I ask after Menelaus°
    Whether he will, returning safe preserved,
    Come back with you, our land's loved master.

591. *I ask after Menelaus:* This and the following questions establish that Menelaus' absence will facilitate Agamemnon's murder.

HERALD. I am not able to speak the lovely falsehood
    To profit you, my friends, for any stretch of time.
LEADER. But if only the true tidings could be also good!
    It is hard to hide a division of good and true.
HERALD. The prince is vanished out of the Greek fleet,
    Himself and ship. I speak no lie.
LEADER. Did he put forth first in the sight of all from Troy,   600
    Or a storm that troubled all sweep him apart?
HERALD. You have hit the target like a master archer,
    Told succinctly a long tale of sorrow.
LEADER. Did the rumors current among the remaining ships
    Represent him as alive or dead?
HERALD. No one knows so as to tell for sure
    Except the sun who nurses the breeds of earth.
LEADER. Tell me how the storm came on the host of ships
    Through the divine anger, and how it ended.
HERALD. Day of good news should not be fouled by tongue   610
    That tells ill news. To each god his season.
    When, despair in his face, a messenger brings to a town
    The hated news of a fallen army—
    One general wound to the city and many men
    Outcast, outcursed, from many homes
    By the double whip which War is fond of,
    Doom with a bloody spear in either hand,
    One carrying such a pack of grief could well
    Recite this hymn of the Furies at your asking.
    But when our cause is saved and a messenger of good   620
    Comes to a city glad with festivity,
    How am I to mix good news with bad, recounting
    The storm that meant God's anger on the Greeks?
    For they swore together, those inveterate enemies,
    Fire and sea, and proved their alliance, destroying
    The unhappy troops of Argos.
    In night arose ill-waved evil,
    Ships on each other the blasts from Thrace
    Crashed colliding, which butting with horns in the violence
    Of big wind and rattle of rain were gone   630
    To nothing, whirled all ways by a wicked shepherd.
    But when there came up the shining light of the sun
    We saw the Aegean sea flowering with corpses
    Of Greek men and their ships' wreckage.
    But for us, our ship was not damaged,
    Whether someone snatched it away or begged it off,

Some god, not a man, handling the tiller;
And Saving Fortune was willing to sit upon our ship
So that neither at anchor we took the tilt of waves
Nor ran to splinters on the crag-bound coast.   640
But then having thus escaped death on the sea,
In the white day, not trusting our fortune,
We pastured this new trouble upon our thoughts,
The fleet being battered, the sailors weary,
And now if any of *them* still draw breath,
They are thinking no doubt of us as being lost
And we are thinking of them as being lost.
May the best happen. As for Menelaus
The first guess and most likely is a disaster.
But still—if any ray of sun detects him   650
Alive, with living eyes, by the plan of Zeus
Not yet resolved to annul the race completely,
There is some hope then that he will return home.
So much you have heard. Know that it is the truth.   [*Exit.*]
CHORUS. Who was it named her thus
    In all ways appositely°
    Unless it was Someone whom we do not see,
    Foreknowing fate
    And plying an accurate tongue?
    Helen, bride of spears and conflict's   660
    Focus, who as was befitting
    Proved a hell to ships and men,
    Hell to her country, sailing
    Away from delicately-sumptuous curtains,
    Away on the wind of a giant Zephyr,
    And shielded hunters mustered many
    On the vanished track of the oars,
    Oars beached on the leafy
    Banks of a Trojan river
    For the sake of bloody war.   670

    But on Troy was thrust a marring marriage
    By the Wrath that working to an end exacts
    In time a price from guests
    Who dishonored their host
    And dishonored Zeus of the Hearth,°
    From those noisy celebrants

655–56. *named . . . appositely:* Helen's name suggests a Greek root, *hele-,* which
means "to kill, to destroy."   675. *Hearth:* Zeus is the god of hospitality.

Of the wedding hymn which fell
To the brothers of Paris
To sing upon that day.
But learning this, unlearning that,   680
Priam's ancestral city now
Continually mourns, reviling
Paris the fatal bridegroom.
The city has had much sorrow,
Much desolation in life,
From the pitiful loss of her people.

So in his house a man might rear
A lion's cub caught from the dam
In need of suckling,
In the prelude of its life   690
Mild, gentle with children,
For old men a playmate,
Often held in the arms
Like a new-born child,
Wheedling the hand,
Fawning at belly's bidding.
But matured by time he showed
The temper of his stock and payed
Thanks for his fostering
With disaster of slaughter of sheep   700
Making an unbidden banquet
And now the house is a shambles,
Irremediable grief to its people,
Calamitous carnage:
For the pet they had fostered was sent
By God as a priest of Ruin.

So I would say there came
To the city of Troy
A notion of windless calm,
Delicate adornment of riches,   710
Soft shooting of the eyes and flower
Of desire that stings the fancy.
But swerving aside she achieved
A bitter end to her marriage,
Ill guest and ill companion,
Hurled upon Priam's sons, convoyed
By Zeus, patron of guest and host,
Dark angel dowered with tears.

Long current among men an old saying
Runs that a man's prosperity   720
When grown to greatness
Comes to the birth, does not die childless—
His good luck breeds for his house
Distress that shall not be appeased.
I only, apart from the others,
Hold that the unrighteous action
Breeds true to its kind,
Leaves its own children behind it.
But the lot of a righteous house
Is a fair offspring always.   730

Ancient self-glory is accustomed
To bear to light in the evil sort of men
A new self-glory and madness,
Which sometime or sometime finds
The appointed hour for its birth,
And born therewith is the Spirit, intractable, unholy, irresistible,
The reckless lust that brings black Doom upon the house,
A child that is like its parents.

But Honest Dealing is clear
Shining in smoky° homes,   740
Honors the god-fearing life.
Mansions gilded by filth of hands she leaves,
Turns her eyes elsewhere, visits the innocent house,
Not respecting the power
Of wealth misstamped with approval,
But guides all to the goal.
      [*Enter* AGAMEMNON *and* CASSANDRA *on chariots.*]
CHORUS. Come then my King, stormer of Troy,
Offspring of Atreus,
How shall I hail you, how give you honor
Neither overshooting nor falling short   750
    Of the measure of homage?
There° are many who honor appearance too much
Passing the bounds that are right.
To condole with the unfortunate man
Each one is ready but the bite of the grief
    Never goes through to the heart.
And they join in rejoicing, affecting to share it,

740. *smoky:* poor.   752–62. *There . . . friendship:* The chorus here is trying to
warn Agamemnon to be suspicious of a warm welcome.

Forcing their face to a smile.
But he who is shrewd to shepherd his sheep
Will fail not to notice the eyes of a man   760
Which seem to be loyal but lie,
    Fawning with watery friendship.
Even you, in my thought, when you marshaled the troops
For Helen's sake, I will not hide it,
Made a harsh and ugly picture,
Holding badly the tiller of reason,
Paying with the death of men
    Ransom for a willing whore.
But now, not unfriendly, not superficially,
I offer my service, well-doers' welcome.   770
In time you will learn by inquiry
Who has done rightly, who transgressed
    In the work of watching the city.
AGAMEMNON. First to Argos and the country's gods
My fitting salutations, who have aided me
To return and in the justice which I exacted
From Priam's city. Hearing the unspoken case
The gods unanimously had cast their vote
Into the bloody urn° for the massacre of Troy;
But to the opposite urn   780
Hope came, dangled her hand, but did no more.
Smoke marks even now the city's capture.
Whirlwinds of doom are alive, the dying ashes
Spread on the air the fat savor of wealth.
For these things we must pay some memorable return
To Heaven, having exacted enormous vengeance
For wife-rape; for a woman
The Argive monster ground a city to powder,
Sprung from a wooden horse,° shield-wielding folk,
Launching a leap at the setting of the Pleiads,°   790
Jumping the ramparts, a ravening lion,
Lapped its fill of the kingly blood.
To the gods I have drawn out this overture
But as for your concerns, I bear them in my mind
And say the same, you have me in agreement.
To few of men does it belong by nature
To congratulate their friends unenviously,

---

779. *urn:* an allusion to the Greek practice of voting by putting pebbles into different urns.   789. *horse:* the wooden horse with which the Greeks gained secret
entry into Troy.   790. *setting of the Pleiads:* in the late autumn.

For a sullen poison fastens on the heart,
Doubling the pain of a man with this disease;
He feels the weight of his own griefs and when   800
He sees another's prosperity he groans.
I speak with knowledge, being well acquainted
With the mirror of comradeship—ghost of a shadow
Were those who seemed to be so loyal to me.
Only Odysseus, who sailed against his will,°
Proved, when yoked with me, a ready tracehorse;
I speak of him not knowing if he is alive.
But for what concerns the city and the gods
Appointing public debates in full assembly
We shall consult. That which is well already   810
We shall take steps to ensure it remain well.
But where there is need of medical remedies,
By applying benevolent cautery or surgery
We shall try to deflect the dangers of disease.
But now, entering the halls where stands my hearth,
First I shall make salutation to the gods
Who sent me a far journey and have brought me back.
And may my victory not leave my side.
    [*Enter* CLYTEMNESTRA, *followed by women slaves carrying
                purple tapestries.*]

CLYTEMNESTRA. Men of the city, you the aged of Argos,
I shall feel no shame to describe to you my love   820
Towards my husband.° Shyness in all of us
Wears thin with time. Here are the facts first hand.
I will tell you of my own unbearable life
I led so long as this man was at Troy.
For first that the woman separate from her man
Should sit alone at home is extreme cruelty,
Hearing so many malignant rumors—First
Comes one, and another comes after, bad news to worse,
Clamor of grief to the house. If Agamemnon
Had had so many wounds as those reported   830
Which poured home through the pipes of hearsay, then—
Then he would be gashed fuller than a net has holes!
And if only he had died . . . as often as rumor told us,

---

805. *against his will:* Odysseus at first pretended that he was insane in order to avoid going to Troy with the Greeks.   820–21. *my love . . . husband:* As the audience, but not Agamemnon, recognized, the Greek is ambiguous and could also mean "the love I have for men" (i.e., such as Aegisthus). This kind of ambiguity occurs throughout her speech.

He would be like the giant° in the legend,
Three-bodied. Dying once for every body,
He should have by now three blankets of earth above him—
All that above him; I care not how deep the mattress under!
Such are the malignant rumors thanks to which
They have often seized me against my will and undone
The loop of a rope from my neck.   840
And this is why our son is not standing here,
The guarantee of your pledges and mine,
As he should be, Orestes. Do not wonder;
He is being brought up by a friendly ally and host,
Strophius the Phocian, who warned me in advance
Of dubious troubles, both your risks at Troy
And the anarchy of shouting mobs that might
Overturn policy, for it is born in men
To kick the man who is down.
This is not a disingenuous excuse.   850
For me the outrushing wells of weeping are dried up,
There is no drop left in them.
My eyes are sore from sitting late at nights
Weeping for you and for the baffled beacons,
Never lit up. And, when I slept, in dreams
I have been waked by the thin whizz of a buzzing
Gnat, seeing more horrors fasten on you
Than could take place in the mere time of my dream.
Having endured all this, now, with unsorrowed heart
I would hail this man as the watchdog of the farm,   860
Forestay that saves the ship, pillar that props
The lofty roof, appearance of an only son
To a father or of land to sailors past their hope,
The loveliest day to see after the storm,
Gush of well-water for the thirsty traveler.
Such are the metaphors I think befit him,
But envy be absent. Many misfortunes already
We have endured. But now, dear head, come down
Out of that car, not placing upon the ground
Your foot, O King, the foot that trampled Troy.   870
Why are you waiting, slaves, to whom the task is assigned
To spread the pavement of his path with tapestries?
At once, at once let his way be strewn with purple°

834. *giant:* Geryon; in Greek myth a giant with three heads and six arms.   873.
purple: that is, crimson, an extremely expensive color (the dye was made from
shellfish), but also the color of blood; another example of Clytemnestra's irony.

That Justice lead him toward his unexpected home.
The rest a mind, not overcome by sleep
Will arrange rightly, with God's help, as destined.
AGAMEMNON. Daughter of Leda,° guardian of my house,
You have spoken in proportion to my absence.
You have drawn your speech out long. Duly to praise me,
That is a duty to be performed by others.   880
And further—do not by women's methods make me
Effeminate nor in barbarian° fashion
Gape ground-groveling acclamations at me
Nor strewing my path with cloths make it invidious.
It is° the gods should be honored in this way.
But being mortal to tread embroidered beauty
For me is no way without fear.
I tell you to honor me as a man, not god.
Footcloths are very well—Embroidered stuffs
Are stuff for gossip. And not to think unwisely   890
Is the greatest gift of God. Call happy only him
Who has ended his life in sweet prosperity.
I have spoken. This thing I could not do with confidence.
CLYTEMNESTRA. Tell me now, according to your judgment.
AGAMEMNON. I tell you you shall not override my judgment.
CLYTEMNESTRA. Supposing you had feared something . . . .
Could you have vowed to God to do this thing?
AGAMEMNON. Yes. If an expert had prescribed that vow.
CLYTEMNESTRA. And how would Priam have acted in your place?
AGAMEMNON. He would have trod the cloths, I think, for certain.   900
CLYTEMNESTRA. Then do not flinch before the blame of men.
AGAMEMNON. The voice of the multitude is very strong.
CLYTEMNESTRA. But the man none envy is not enviable.
AGAMEMNON. It is not a woman's part to love disputing.
CLYTEMNESTRA. But it is a conqueror's part to yield upon occasion.
AGAMEMNON. You think such victory worth fighting for?
CLYTEMNESTRA. Give way. Consent to let me have the mastery.
AGAMEMNON. Well, if such is your wish, let someone quickly loose
My vassal sandals, underlings of my feet,
And stepping on these sea-purples may no god   910
Shoot me from far with the envy of his eye.

---

877. *Daughter of Leda:* Clytemnestra was a daughter of Leda and thus a sister of
Helen.   882. *barbarian:* a reference to the luxury, effeminacy, and despotism at
the Persian court.   885–87. *It is . . . fear:* Here Agamemnon is suggesting that
to tread the purple is an act of hubris, which in turn would call down the envy
and anger of the gods.

Great shame it is to ruin my house and spoil
The wealth of costly weavings with my feet.
But of this matter enough. This stranger woman° here
Take in with kindness. The man who is a gentle master
God looks on from far off complacently.
For no one of his will bears the slave's yoke.
This woman, of many riches being the chosen
Flower, gift of the soldiers, has come with me.
But since I have been prevailed on by your words   920
I will go to my palace home, treading on purples.

> [He dismounts from the chariot and begins to walk up the
> tapestried path. During the following speech he enters the
> palace.]

CLYTEMNESTRA. There is the sea and who shall drain it dry? It breeds
Its wealth in silver of plenty of purple gushing°
And ever-renewed, the dyeings of our garments.
The house has its store of these by God's grace, King.
This house is ignorant of poverty
And I would have vowed a pavement of many garments
Had the palace oracle enjoined that vow
Thereby to contrive a ransom for his life.
For while there is root, foliage comes to the house   930
Spreading a tent of shade against the Dog Star.
So now that you have reached your hearth and home
You prove a miracle—advent of warmth in winter;
And further this—even in the time of heat
When God is fermenting wine from the bitter grape,
Even then it is cool in the house if only
Its master walk at home, a grown man, ripe.
O Zeus the Ripener, ripen these my prayers;
Your part it is to make the ripe fruit fall. [She enters the palace.]
CHORUS. Why, why at the doors   940
Of my foreseeing heart
Does this terror keep beating its wings?
And my song play the prophet
Unbidden, unhired—

914. *stranger woman:* Hector's sister, Cassandra. She was so beautiful that Apollo
fell in love with her and conferred the gift of prophecy on her. But when she denied him sexual gratification, the god ordained that no one would believe her until
it was too late. She foretold the fall of Troy, but was not believed by her com-
patriots. After the fall of the city she was raped by Ajax and taken as one of the
spoils of war by Agamemnon.   923. *purple gushing:* In characteristically suggestive language, this both refers to the crimson dye and foreshadows the "gushing" forth of Agamemnon's blood when Clytemnestra kills him.

Which I cannot spit out
Like the enigmas of dreams
Nor plausible confidence
Sit on the throne of my mind?
It is long time since
The cables let down from the stern   950
Were chafed by the sand when the seafaring army started for
    Troy.

And I learn with my eyes
And witness myself their return;
But the hymn without lyre goes up,
The dirge of the Avenging Fiend,
In the depths of my self-taught heart
Which has lost its dear
Possession of the strength of hope.
But my guts and my heart
Are not idle which seethe with the waves   960
Of trouble nearing its hour.
But I pray that these thoughts
May fall out not as I think
    And not be fulfilled in the end.

Truly when health grows much
It respects not limit; for disease,
Its neighbor in the next door room,
Presses upon it.
A man's life, crowding sail,
Strikes on the blind reef: 970
But if caution° in advance
Jettison part of the cargo
With the derrick of due proportion,
The whole house does not sink,
Though crammed with a weight of woe
The hull does not go under.
The abundant bounty of God
And his gifts from the year's furrows
Drive the famine back.

But when upon the ground there has fallen once   980
The black blood of a man's death,

971–79. *caution . . . back:* According to a popular Greek belief, a successful and prosperous man could avert the fatal jealousy of the gods by intentionally and voluntarily dispossessing himself of part of his fortune.

Who shall summon it back by incantations?
Even Asclepius° who had the art
To fetch the dead to life, even to him
Zeus put a provident end.
But, if of the heaven-sent fates
One did not check the other,
Cancel the other's advantage,
My heart would outrun my tongue
In pouring out these fears.   990
But now it mutters in the dark,
Embittered, no way hoping
To unravel a scheme in time
  From a burning mind.
   [CLYTEMNESTRA *appears in the door of the palace.*]
CLYTEMNESTRA. Go in too, you; I speak to you, Cassandra,
  Since God in his clemency has put you in this house
  To share our holy water,° standing with many slaves
  Beside the altar that protects the house,
  Step down from the car there, do not be overproud.
  Heracles° himself they say was once   1000
  Sold, and endured to eat the bread of slavery.
  But should such a chance inexorably fall,
  There is much advantage in masters who have long been rich.
  Those who have reaped a crop they never expected
  Are in all things hard on their slaves and overstep the line.
  From us you will have the treatment of tradition.
LEADER OF CHORUS. You, it is you she has addressed, and clearly.
  Caught as you are in these predestined toils
  Obey her if you can. But should you disobey . . . .
CLYTEMNESTRA. If she has more than the gibberish of the swallow,   1010
  An unintelligible barbaric speech,
  I hope to read her mind, persuade her reason.
LEADER. As things now stand for you, she says the best.
  Obey her; leave that car and follow her.
CLYTEMNESTRA. I have no leisure to waste out here, outside the door.
  Before the hearth in the middle of my house
  The victims stand already, wait the knife.

---

983. *Asclepius:* the mythical physician (and, later, god of medicine). He was
killed with a thunderbolt by Zeus when his medical skill became so extraordinary
that he could even restore a dead man to life.   997. *holy water:* lustral or purificatory water which will be used in a sacrifice to celebrate Agamemnon's safe return.
1000. *Heracles:* He had extraordinary strength but nevertheless at one time was
forced to be a slave to an Oriental queen (Omphale).

You, if you will obey me, waste no time.
But if you cannot understand my language—
                    [*to* CHORUS LEADER]
You make it plain to her with the brute and voiceless hand.   1020
LEADER. The stranger seems to need a clear interpreter.
    She bears herself like a wild beast newly captured.
CLYTEMNESTRA. The fact is she is mad, she listens to evil thoughts,
    Who has come here leaving a city newly captured
    Without experience how to bear the bridle
    So as not to waste her strength in foam and blood.
    I will not spend more words to be ignored.
                    [*She reenters the palace.*]
CHORUS. But I, for I pity her, will not be angry.
    Obey, unhappy woman. Leave this car.
    Yield to your fate. Put on the untried yoke.   1030
CASSANDRA. Apollo! Apollo!°
CHORUS. Why do you cry like this upon Apollo?
    He is not the kind of god that calls for dirges.
CASSANDRA. Apollo! Apollo!
CHORUS. Once more her funereal cries invoke the god
    Who has no place at the scene of lamentation.
CASSANDRA. Apollo! Apollo!
    God of the Ways!° My destroyer!°
    Destroyed again—and this time utterly!
CHORUS. She seems about to predict her own misfortunes.   1040
    The gift of the god endures, even in a slave's mind.
CASSANDRA. Apollo! Apollo!
    God of the Ways! My destroyer!
    Where? To what house? Where, where have you brought me?
CHORUS. To the house of the sons of Atreus. If you do not know it,
    I will tell you so. You will not find it false.
CASSANDRA. No, no, but to a god-hated, but to an accomplice
    In much kin-killing, murdering nooses,
    Man-shambles, a floor asperged with blood.°
CHORUS. The stranger seems like a hound with a keen scent,   1050
    Is picking up a trail that leads to murder.
CASSANDRA. Clues! I have clues! Look! They are these.
    These wailing, these children, butchery of children;

1031. *Apollo:* Cassandra calls on him as the patron god of prophecies and visions.
1038. *God of the Ways:* a cult name of Apollo, whose statue was often placed at
the gate of a house. *destroyer:* a popular pun on Apollo's name. (In Greek, the
compound stem *ap-ol-* means "to destroy utterly.") 1049. *asperged with blood:*
Cassandra foresees, in her inspired vision, Agamemnon murdered by Clytemnestra.

Roasted flesh,° a father sitting to dinner.
CHORUS. Of your prophetic fame we have heard before
   But in this matter prophets are not required.
CASSANDRA. What is she° doing? What is she planning?
   What is this new great sorrow?
   Great crime . . . within here . . . planning
   Unendurable to his folk, impossible   1060
   Ever to be cured. For help
      Stands far distant.°
CHORUS. This reference I cannot catch. But the children
   I recognized; that refrain is hackneyed.
CASSANDRA. Damned, damned, bringing this work to completion—
   Your husband who shared your bed
   To bathe him, to cleanse him, and then—
   How shall I tell of the end?
   Soon, very soon, it will fall.
      The end comes hand over hand   1070
      Grasping in greed.
CHORUS. Not yet do I understand. After her former riddles
   Now I am baffled by these dim pronouncements.
CASSANDRA. Ah God, the vision! God, God, the vision!
   A net, is it? Net of Hell!
   But herself is the net; shared bed; shares murder.
   O let the pack ever-hungering after the family°
   Howl for the unholy ritual, howl for the victim.
CHORUS. What black Spirit is this you call upon the house—
   To raise aloft her cries? Your speech does not lighten me.   1080
   Into my heart runs back the blood
   Yellow as when for men by the spear fallen
   The blood ebbs out with the rays of the setting life
      And death strides quickly.
CASSANDRA. Quick! Be on your guard! The bull—
   Keep him clear of the cow.
   Caught with a trick, the black horn's point,
   She strikes. He falls; lies in the water.
   Murder; a trick in a bath. I tell what I see.
CHORUS. I would not claim to be expert in oracles   1090

1054. *roasted flesh*: Cassandra here links the past murders of Thyestes' children with the murder which is about to take place.   1057. *she*: Clytemnestra, who is about to murder Agamemnon in his bath inside the palace.   1062. *distant*: Agamemnon's brother, Menelaus, is not yet home from Troy and Agamemnon's son, Orestes, is neither at home nor old enough to rescue his father.   1077. *pack . . . family*: the avenging deities that perpetuate the cycle of murders in the house of Atreus.

But these, as I deduce, portend disaster.
Do men ever get a good answer from oracles?
No. It is only through disaster
That their garrulous craft brings home
The meaning of the prophet's panic.

CASSANDRA. And for me also, for me, chance ill-destined!
My own now I lament, pour into the cup my own.
Where is this you have brought me in my misery?
Unless to die as well. What else is meant?

CHORUS. You are mad, mad, carried away by the god,   1100
Raising the dirge, the tuneless
Tune, for yourself. Like the tawny
Unsatisfied singer from her luckless heart
Lamenting "Itys,° Itys," the nightingale
Lamenting a life luxuriant with grief.

CASSANDRA. Oh the lot of the songful nightingale!
The gods enclosed her in a winged body,
Gave her a sweet and tearless passing.
But for me remains the two-edged cutting blade.

CHORUS. From whence these rushing and God-inflicted   1110
Profitless pains?
Why shape with your sinister crying
The piercing hymn—fear-piercing?
How can you know the evil-worded landmarks
    On the prophetic path?

CASSANDRA. Oh the wedding,° the wedding of Paris—death to his
        people!
O river Scamander,° water drunk by my fathers!
When I was young, alas, upon your beaches
I was brought up and cared for.
But now it is the River of Wailing° and the banks of Hell   1120
That shall hear my prophecy soon.

CHORUS. What is this clear speech, too clear?
A child could understand it.
I am bitten with fangs that draw blood
By the misery of your cries,
Cries harrowing the heart.

1104. *Itys:* The son of Tereus, Itys, was killed and served to his father as a meal by the sisters, Philomela and Procne, because Tereus had raped Philomela. Philomela, in turn, was changed into a nightingale who always had to mourn Itys. The "Itys" is an imitation of the nightingale's sound.   1116. *wedding:* to Helen, wife of Menelaus.   1117. *Scamander:* Trojan river.   1120. *River of Wailing:* Cocytus, a river in the underworld. Cassandra here foresees her own murder by Clytemnestra.

CASSANDRA. Oh trouble on trouble of a city lost, lost utterly!
 My father's sacrifices before the towers,
 Much killing of cattle and sheep,
 No cure—availed not at all   1130
 To prevent the coming of what came to Troy,
 And I, my brain on fire, shall soon enter the trap.
CHORUS. This speech accords with the former.
 What god, malicious, overheavy, persistently pressing,
 Drives you to chant of these lamentable
 Griefs with death their burden?
 But I cannot see the end.
    [CASSANDRA *now steps down from the car.*]
CASSANDRA. The oracle now no longer from behind veils
 Will be peeping forth like a newly-wedded bride;
 But I can feel it like a fresh wind swoop   1140
 And rush in the face of the dawn and, wavelike, wash
 Against the sun a vastly greater grief
 Than this one. I shall speak no more conundrums.
 And bear me witness, pacing me, that I
 Am trailing on the scent of ancient wrongs.
 For this house here a choir° never deserts,
 Chanting together ill. For they mean ill,
 And to puff up their arrogance they have drunk
 Men's blood, this band of revelers that haunts the house,
 Hard to be rid of, fiends that attend the family.   1150
 Established in its rooms they hymn their hymn
 Of that original sin, abhor in turn
 The adultery° that proved a brother's ruin.
 A miss? Or do my arrows hit the mark?
 Or am I a quack prophet who knocks at doors, a babbler?
 Give me your oath, confess I have the facts,
 The ancient history of this house's crimes.
LEADER. And how could an oath's assurance, however finely assured,
 Turn out a remedy? I wonder, though, that you
 Being brought up overseas, of another tongue,   1160
 Should hit on the whole tale as if you had been standing by.
CASSANDRA. Apollo the prophet set me to prophesy.
LEADER. Was he, although a god, struck by desire?
CASSANDRA. Till now I was ashamed to tell that story.
LEADER. Yes. Good fortune keeps us all fastidious.

1146. *choir:* of Furies; they are the mythical embodiment of the principle of revenge. 1153. *adultery:* Thyestes seduced Atreus' wife and thereby set in motion
the direct sequence of murders.

CASSANDRA. He wrestled hard upon me, panting love.
LEADER. And did you come, as they do, to child-getting?
CASSANDRA. No. I agreed to him. And I cheated him.
LEADER. Were you already possessed by the mystic art?
CASSANDRA. Already I was telling the townsmen all their future suf-
    fering.   1170
LEADER. Then how did you escape the doom of Apollo's anger?
CASSANDRA. I did not escape. No one ever believed me.
LEADER. Yet to us your words seem worthy of belief.
CASSANDRA. Oh misery, misery!
    Again comes on me the terrible labor of true
    Prophecy, dizzying prelude; distracts . . . .
    Do you see these who sit before the house,
    Children,° like the shapes of dreams?
    Children who seem to have been killed by their kinsfolk,
    Filling their hands with meat, flesh of themselves,   1180
    Guts and entrails, handfuls of lament—
    Clear what they hold—the same their father tasted.
    For this I declare someone° is plotting vengeance—
    A lion? Lion but coward, that lurks in bed,
    Good watchdog truly against the lord's return—
    My lord, for I must bear the yoke of serfdom.
    Leader of the ships, overturner of Troy.
    He does not know what plots the accursed hound°
    With the licking tongue and the pricked-up ear will plan
    In the manner of a lurking doom, in an evil hour.   1190
    A daring criminal! Female murders male.
    What monster could provide her with a title?
    An amphisbaena° or hag of the sea who dwells
    In rocks to ruin sailors—
    A raving mother of death who breathes against her folk
    War to the finish. Listen to her shout of triumph,
    Who shirks no horrors, like men in a rout of battle.
    And yet she poses as glad at their return.
    If you distrust my words, what does it matter?
    That which will come will come. You too will soon stand here   1200
    And admit with pity that I spoke too truly.
LEADER. Thyestes' dinner of his children's meat
    I understood and shuddered, and fear grips me

1178. *Children:* Thyestes' children. 1183. *someone:* Aegisthus, the only child of
Thyestes that survived the murder committed by Atreus. 1188. *hound:* Clytemnestra. 1193. *amphisbaena* (literally, "going both ways"): mythical giant snake
with a head at both ends of its body.

To hear the truth, not framed in parables.
But hearing the rest I am thrown out of my course.

CASSANDRA. It is Agamemnon's death I tell you you shall witness.

LEADER. Stop! Provoke no evil. Quiet your mouth!

CASSANDRA. The god who gives me words is here no healer.

LEADER. Not if this shall be so. But may some chance avert it.

CASSANDRA. *You* are praying. But others are busy with murder.   1210

LEADER. What man is he promotes this terrible thing?

CASSANDRA. Indeed you have missed my drift by a wide margin!

LEADER. But I do not understand the assassin's method.

CASSANDRA. And yet too well I know the speech of Greece!

LEADER. So does Delphi but the replies are hard.°

CASSANDRA. Ah what a fire it is! It comes upon me.
      Apollo, Wolf-Destroyer, pity, pity . . . .
      It is the two-foot lioness who beds
      Beside a wolf, the noble lion away,
      It is she will kill me. Brewing a poisoned cup   1220
      She will mix my punishment too in the angry draught
      And boasts, sharpening the dagger for her husband,
      To pay back murder for my bringing here.
      Why then do I wear these mockeries of myself,
      The wand and the prophet's garland round my neck?
      My hour is coming—but you shall perish first.
      Destruction! Scattered thus you give me my revenge;
      Go and enrich some other woman with ruin.
      See: Apollo himself is stripping me
      Of my prophetic gear, who has looked on   1230
      When in this dress I have been a laughing-stock
      To friends and foes alike, and to no purpose;
      They called me crazy, like a fortune-teller,
      A poor starved beggar-woman—and I bore it.
      And now the prophet undoing his prophetess
      Has brought me to this final darkness.
      Instead of my father's altar the executioner's block
      Waits me the victim, red with my hot blood.
      But the gods will not ignore me as I die.
      One° will come after to avenge my death,   1240
      A matricide, a murdered father's champion.

1215. *replies are hard:* The replies of the Delphic oracle of Apollo were notorious for their ambiguity and enigmatic style.   1240–44. *One . . . home:* a reference to Agamemnon's son, Orestes, who (in the next play of this trilogy, *The Libation Bearers*) returns home to kill Clytemnestra and Aegisthus in revenge for Agamemnon's murder.

Exile and tramp and outlaw he will come back
To gable the family house of fatal crime;
His father's outstretched corpse shall lead him home.
Why need I then lament so pitifully?
For now that I have seen the town of Troy
Treated as she was treated, while her captors
Come to their reckoning thus by the gods' verdict,
I will go in and have the courage to die.
Look, these gates are the gates of Death. I greet them.   1250
And I pray that I may meet a deft and mortal stroke
So that without a struggle I may close
My eyes and my blood ebb in easy death.

LEADER. Oh woman very unhappy and very wise,
   Your speech was long. But if in sober truth
   You know your fate, why like an ox that the gods
   Drive, do you walk so bravely to the altar?

CASSANDRA. There is no escape, strangers. No; not by postponement.

LEADER. But the last moment has the privilege of hope.

CASSANDRA. The day is here. Little should I gain by flight.   1260

LEADER. This patience of yours comes from a brave soul.

CASSANDRA. A happy man is never paid that compliment.

LEADER. But to die with credit graces a mortal man.

CASSANDRA. Oh my father! You and your noble sons!

   [*She approaches the door, then suddenly recoils.*]

LEADER. What is it? What is the fear that drives you back?

CASSANDRA. Faugh.

LEADER. Why faugh? Or is this some hallucination?

CASSANDRA. These walls breathe out a death that drips with blood.

LEADER. Not so. It is only the smell of the sacrifice.

CASSANDRA. It is like a breath out of a charnel-house.   1270

LEADER. You think our palace burns odd incense then!

CASSANDRA. But I will go to lament among the dead
   My lot and Agamemnon's. Enough of life!
   Strangers,
   I am not afraid like a bird afraid of a bush
   But witness you my words after my death
   When a woman dies in return for me a woman
   And a man falls for a man with a wicked wife.
   I ask this service, being about to die.

LEADER. Alas, I pity you for the death you have foretold.   1280

CASSANDRA. One more speech I have; I do not wish to raise
   The dirge for my own self. But to the sun I pray
   In face of his last light that my avengers

May make my murderers pay for this my death,
Death of a woman slave, an easy victim.

[She enters the palace.]

LEADER. Ah the fortunes of men! When they go well
A shadow sketch would match them, and in ill-fortune
The dab of a wet sponge destroys the drawing.
It is not myself but the life of man I pity.

CHORUS. Prosperity in all men cries   1290
For more prosperity. Even the owner
Of the finger-pointed-at palace never shuts
His door against her, saying "Come no more."
So to our king the blessed gods had granted
To take the town of Priam, and heaven-favored
He reaches home. But now if for former bloodshed
        He must pay blood
And dying for the dead shall cause
        Other deaths in atonement
What man could boast he was born   1300
        Secure, who heard this story?

AGAMEMNON [*within*]. Oh! I am struck a mortal blow—within!

LEADER. Silence! Listen. Who calls out, wounded with a mortal stroke?

AGAMEMNON. Again—the second blow—I am struck again.

LEADER. You heard the king cry out. I think the deed is done.
Let us see if we can concert some sound proposal.

SECOND OLD MAN. Well, I will tell you my opinion—
Raise an alarm, summon the folk to the palace.

THIRD OLD MAN. I say burst in with all speed possible,
Convict them of the deed while still the sword is wet.   1310

FOURTH OLD MAN. And I am partner to some such suggestion.
I am for taking some course. No time to dawdle.

FIFTH OLD MAN. The case is plain. This is but the beginning.
They are going to set up dictatorship in the state.

SIXTH OLD MAN. We are wasting time. The assassins tread to earth
The decencies of delay and give their hands no sleep.

SEVENTH OLD MAN. I do not know what plan I could hit on to propose.
The man who acts is in the position to plan.

EIGHTH OLD MAN. So I think, too, for I am at a loss
To raise the dead man up again with words.   1320

NINTH OLD MAN. Then to stretch out our life shall we yield thus
To the rule of these profaners of the house?

TENTH OLD MAN. It is not to be endured. To die is better.
Death is more comfortable than tyranny.

ELEVENTH OLD MAN. And are we on the evidence of groans
    Going to give oracle that the prince is dead?
TWELFTH OLD MAN. We must know the facts for sure and *then* be
       angry.
    Guesswork is not the same as certain knowledge.
LEADER. Then all of you back me and approve this plan—
    To ascertain how it is with Agamemnon.   1330
       [*The doors of the palace open, revealing the bodies of*
      AGAMEMNON and CASSANDRA. CLYTEMNESTRA *stands*
          above them.]
CLYTEMNESTRA. Much having been said before to fit the moment,
    To say the opposite now will not outface me.
    How else could one serving hate upon the hated,
    Thought to be friends, hang high the nets of doom
    To preclude all leaping out?
    For me I have long been training for this match,
    I tried a fall and won—a victory overdue.
    I stand here where I struck, above my victims;
    So I contrived it—this I will not deny—
    That he could neither fly nor ward off death;   1340
    Inextricable like a net for fishes
    I cast about him a vicious wealth of raiment
    And struck him twice and with two groans he loosed
    His limbs beneath him, and upon him fallen
    I deal him the third° blow to the God beneath the earth,
    To the safe keeper of the dead a votive gift,
    And with that he spits his life out where he lies
    And smartly spouting blood he sprays me with
    The somber drizzle of bloody dew and I
    Rejoice no less than in God's gift of rain   1350
    The crops are glad when the ear of corn gives birth.
    These things being so, you, elders of Argos,
    Rejoice if rejoice you will. Mine is the glory.
    And if I could pay this corpse his due libation
    I should be right to pour it and more than right;
    With so many horrors this man mixed and filled
    The bowl—and, coming home, has drained the draught himself.
LEADER. Your speech astonishes us. This brazen boast
    Above the man who was your king and husband!
CLYTEMNESTRA. You challenge me as a woman without foresight   1360
    But I with unflinching heart to you who know

1345. *third:* an allusion to the third pouring of a wine offering.

Speak. And you, whether you will praise or blame,
It makes no matter. Here lies Agamemnon,
My husband, dead, the work of this right hand,
An honest workman. There you have the facts.

CHORUS. Woman, what poisoned
Herb of the earth have you tasted
Or potion of the flowing sea
To undertake this killing and the people's curses?
You threw down, you cut off—The people will cast you out,   1370
Black abomination to the town.

CLYTEMNESTRA. Now your verdict—in my case—is exile
And to have the people's hatred, the public curses,
Though then in no way you opposed this man
Who carelessly, as if it were a head of sheep
Out of the abundance of his fleecy flocks,
Sacrificed his own daughter,° to me the dearest
Fruit of travail, charm for the Thracian winds.
He was the one to have banished from this land,
Pay off the pollution. But when you hear what I   1380
Have done, you judge severely. But I warn you—
Threaten me on the understanding that I am ready
For two alternatives—Win by force the right
To rule me, but, if God brings about the contrary,
Late in time you will have to learn self-discipline.

CHORUS. You are high in the thoughts,
You speak extravagant things,
After the soiling murder your crazy heart
Fancies your forehead with a smear of blood.
Unhonored, unfriended, you must   1390
Pay for a blow with a blow.

CLYTEMNESTRA. Listen then to this—the sanction of my oaths:
By the Justice totting up my child's atonement,
By the Avenging Doom and Fiend to whom I killed this man,
For me hope walks not in the rooms of fear
So long as my fire is lit upon my hearth
By Aegisthus, loyal to me as he was before.
The man who outraged me lies here,
The darling of each courtesan at Troy,
And here with him is the prisoner clairvoyante,   1400
The fortune-teller that he took to bed,

1377. *daughter:* Iphigenia. Clytemnestra mentions the same motivation for her murder in lines 1393–94 and elsewhere, but never actually mentions her daughter's name.

Who shares his bed as once his bench on shipboard,
A loyal mistress. Both have their deserts.
He lies so; and she who like a swan
Sang her last dying lament
Lies his lover, and the sight contributes
An appetizer to my own bed's pleasure.
CHORUS. Ah would some quick death come not overpainful,
      Not overlong on the sickbed,
      Establishing in us the ever-   1410
      Lasting unending sleep now that our guardian
      Has fallen, the kindest of men,
      Who suffering much for a woman
      By a woman has lost his life.
            O Helen, insane, being one
            One to have destroyed so many
            And many souls under Troy,
            Now is your work complete, blossomed not for oblivion,
            Unfading stain of blood. Here now, if in any home,
            Is Discord, here is a man's deep-rooted ruin.   1420
CLYTEMNESTRA. Do not pray for the portion of death
      Weighed down by these things, do not turn
      Your anger on Helen as destroyer of men,
      One woman destroyer of many
      Lives of Greek men,
            A hurt that cannot be healed.
CHORUS. O Evil Spirit, falling on the family,
      On the two sons of Atreus and using
      Two sisters° in heart as your tools,
      A power that bites to the heart—   1430
      See on the body
      Perched like a raven he gloats
      Harshly croaking his hymn.
CLYTEMNESTRA. Ah, now you have amended your lips' opinion,
      Calling upon this family's three times° gorged
      Genius—demon who breeds
      Blood-hankering lust in the belly:

1429. Two sisters: Helen and Clytemnestra.   *1435. three times:* probably (1)
Tantalus' murder of his son Pelops, (2) Atreus' murder of his brother Thyestes'
children, and (3) Clytemnestra's murder of her husband. Tantalus, the progenitor
of the house of Atreus, served the gods the boiled flesh of his son Pelops, but they
were not deceived into eating it, and they recreated Pelops, who became the father
of Atreus and Thyestes. Atreus in turned served Thyestes the cooked flesh of his
dismembered children. The entire myth suggests a turning away from ritual can-
nibalism.

Before the old sore heals, new pus collects.
CHORUS. It is a great spirit—great—
    You tell of, harsh in anger,   1440
    A ghastly tale, alas,
    Of unsatisfied disaster
    Brought by Zeus, by Zeus,
    Cause and worker of all.
    For without Zeus what comes to pass among us?
    Which of these things is outside Providence?
        O my king, my king,
        How shall I pay you in tears,
        Speak my affection in words?
        You lie in that spider's web,   1450
        In a desecrating death breathe out your life,
        Lie ignominiously
        Defeated by a crooked death
        And the two-edged cleaver's stroke.
CLYTEMNESTRA. You say this is *my* work—mine?
    Do not cozen yourself that I am Agamemnon's wife.
    Masquerading as the wife
    Of the corpse there the old sharp-witted Genius
    Of Atreus who gave the cruel banquet
    Has paid with a grown man's life   1460
    The due for children dead.
CHORUS. That you are not guilty of
    This murder who will attest?
    No, but you may have been abetted
    By some ancestral Spirit of Revenge.
    Wading a millrace of the family's blood
    The black Manslayer forces a forward path
    To make the requital at last
    For the eaten children, the blood-clot cold with time.
        O my king, my king,   1470
        How shall I pay you in tears,
        Speak my affection in words?
        You lie in that spider's web,
        In a desecrating death breathe out your life,
        Lie ignominiously
        Defeated by a crooked death
        And the two-edged cleaver's stroke.
CLYTEMNESTRA. Did he not, too, contrive a crooked
    Horror for the house? My child by him,
    Shoot that I raised, much-wept-for Iphigeneia,   1480

He treated her like this;
So suffering like this he need not make
Any great brag in Hell having paid with death
Dealt by the sword for work of his own beginning.
CHORUS. I am at a loss for thought, I lack
All nimble counsel as to where
To turn when the house is falling.
I fear the house-collapsing crashing
Blizzard of blood—of which these drops are earnest.
Now is Destiny sharpening her justice   1490
On other whetstones for a new infliction.
O earth, earth, if only you had received me
Before I saw this man lie here as if in bed
In a bath lined with silver.
Who will bury him? Who will keen him?
Will you, having killed your own husband,
Dare now to lament him
And after great wickedness make
Unamending amends to his ghost?
And who above this godlike hero's grave   1500
Pouring praises and tears
Will grieve with a genuine heart?
CLYTEMNESTRA. It is not your business to attend to that.
By my hand he fell low, lies low and dead,
And I shall bury him low down in the earth,
And his household need not weep him
For Iphigeneia his daughter
Tenderly, as is right,
Will meet her father at the rapid ferry of sorrows,
Put her arms round him and kiss him!   1510
CHORUS. Reproach answers reproach,
It is hard to decide,
The catcher is caught, the killer pays for his kill.
But the law abides while Zeus abides enthroned
That the wrongdoer suffers. That is established.
Who could expel from the house the seed of the Curse?
The race is soldered in sockets of Doom and Vengeance.
CLYTEMNESTRA. In this you say what is right and the will of God.
But for my part I am ready to make a contract
With the Evil Genius of the House of Atreus   1520
To accept what has been till now, hard though it is,
But that for the future he shall leave this house
And wear away some other stock with deaths

Imposed among themselves. Of my possessions
A small part will suffice if only I
Can rid these walls of the mad exchange of murder.
           [*Enter* AEGISTHUS, *followed by soldiers.*]
AEGISTHUS. O welcome light of a justice-dealing day!
    From now on I will say that the gods, avenging men,
    Look down from above on the crimes of earth,
    Seeing as I do in woven robes of the Furies   1530
    This man lying here—a sight to warm my heart—
    Paying for the crooked violence of his father.
    For his father Atreus, when he ruled the country,
    Because his power was challenged, hounded out
    From state and home his own brother Thyestes.
    My father—let me be plain—was this Thyestes,
    Who later came back home a suppliant,
    There, miserable, found so much asylum
    As not to die on the spot, stain the ancestral floor.
    But to show his hospitality godless Atreus   1540
    Gave him an eager if not a loving welcome,
    Pretending a day of feasting and rich meats
    Served my father with his children's flesh.
    The hands and feet, fingers and toes, he hid
    At the bottom of the dish. My father sitting apart
    Took unknowing the unrecognizable portion
    And ate of a dish that has proved, as you see, expensive.
    But when he knew he had eaten worse than poison
    He fell back groaning, vomiting their flesh,
    And invoking a hopeless doom on the sons of Pelops   1550
    Kicked over the table to confirm his curse—
    So may the whole race perish!
    Result of this—you see this man lie here.
    I stitched this murder together; it was my title.
    Me the third son he left, an unweaned infant,
    To share the bitterness of my father's exile.
    But I grew up and Justice brought me back,
    I grappled this man while still beyond his door,
    Having pieced together the program of his ruin.
    So now would even death be beautiful to me   1560
    Having seen Agamemnon in the nets of Justice.
LEADER. Aegisthus. I cannot respect brutality in distress.
    You claim that you deliberately killed this prince
    And that you alone planned this pitiful murder.
    Be sure that in your turn your head shall not escape

The people's volleyed curses mixed with stones.
AEGISTHUS. Do you speak so who sit at the lower oar
While those on the upper bench control the ship?
Old as you are, you will find it is a heavy load
To go to school when old to learn the lesson of tact.   1570
For old age, too, jail and hunger are fine
Instructors in wisdom, second-sighted doctors.
You have eyes. Cannot you see?
Do not kick against the pricks. The blow will hurt you.
LEADER. You woman waiting in the house for those who return from
          battle
While you seduce their wives! Was it you devised
The death of a master of armies?
AEGISTHUS. And these words, too, prepare the way for tears.
Contrast your voice with the voice of Orpheus:° he
Led all things after him bewitched with joy, but you   1580
Having stung me with your silly yelps shall be
Led off yourself, to prove more mild when mastered.
LEADER. Indeed! So you are now to be king of Argos,
You who, when you had plotted the king's death,
Did not even dare to do that thing yourself!
AEGISTHUS. No. For the trick of it was clearly woman's work.
I was suspect, an enemy of old.
But now I shall try with Agamemnon's wealth
To rule the people. Any who is disobedient
I will harness in a heavy yoke, no tracehorse work for him   1590
Like barley-fed colt, but hateful hunger lodging
Beside him in the dark will see his temper soften.
LEADER. Why with your cowardly soul did you yourself
Not strike this man but left that work to a woman
Whose presence pollutes our country and its gods?
But Orestes—does he somewhere see the light
That he may come back here by favor of fortune
And kill this pair and prove the final victor?
AEGISTHUS [summoning his guards]. Well, if such is your design in
deeds and words, you will quickly learn—
Here my friends, here my guards, there is work for you at hand.   1600
LEADER. Come then, hands on hilts, be each and all of us prepared.
          [The old men and the guards threaten each other.]
AEGISTHUS. Very well! I too am ready to meet death with sword in
          hand.

1579. Orpheus: legendary poet and musician, who enthralled not only men and
beasts, but even trees and rocks with a lyre given to him by Apollo.

LEADER. We are glad you speak of dying. We accept your words for
    luck.
CLYTEMNESTRA. No, my dearest, do not so. Add no more to the train
    of wrong.
To reap these many present wrongs is harvest enough of misery.
Enough of misery. Start no more. Our hands are red.
But do you, and you old men, go home and yield to fate in time,
In time before you suffer. We have acted as we had to act.
If only our afflictions now could prove enough, we should agree—
We who have been so hardly mauled in the heavy claws of the
    evil god.   1610
So stands my word, a woman's, if any man thinks fit to hear.
AEGISTHUS. But to think that these should thus pluck the blooms of an
    idle tongue
And should throw out words like these, giving the evil god his
    chance,
And should miss the path of prudence and insult their master so!
LEADER. It is not the Argive way to fawn upon a cowardly man.
AEGISTHUS. Perhaps. But I in later days will take further steps with
    you.
LEADER. Not if the god who rules the family guides Orestes to his
    home.
AEGISTHUS. Yes. I know that men in exile feed themselves on barren
    hopes.
LEADER. Go on, grow fat defiling justice . . . while you have your
    hour.
AEGISTHUS. Do not think you will not pay me a price for your stu-
    pidity.   1620
LEADER. Boast on in your self-assurance, like a cock beside his hen.
CLYTEMNESTRA. Pay no heed, Aegisthus, to these futile barkings. You
    and I,
Masters of this house, from now shall order all things well.
            [*They enter the palace.*]

Thucydides

FROM *The History of*
the Peloponnesian War

TRANSLATED BY BENJAMIN JOWETT

Thucydides (460 B.C.?–399 B.C.?)

ONE OF THE MOST REMARKABLE PERIODS OF CREATIVITY IN THE history of Greek culture was both initiated by a war and terminated by a war. The victory of the Greeks over the Persians inaugurated a period of relative political stability and an explosion of intellectual and artistic activity, particularly in Athens. This "Golden Age" of Athens collapsed, however, by the end of the century in the degrading fury of a prolonged war between the Athenians and the Spartans with their respective allies. This war, which is known as the "Peloponnesian War" but actually ranged far beyond the Peloponnesus, is described and analyzed by the first scientific historian of antiquity, Thucydides.

Like Aeschylus and Sophocles, Thucydides seems to have had a close association with the political life of Athens. He became commander of an Athenian naval squadron in the early years of the Peloponnesian War, but when he was found guilty of a military blunder in 424 B.C. he was banished from the city. During his exile he traveled widely to collect information for his history from both parties to the war and spent some time in Thrace, where he possessed gold mines. Only after the war, when the Athenians granted him amnesty in 404 B.C., did he return to Athens. He died before completing his history, which stops dramatically in mid-sentence.

The following three selections from Thucydides' history—the first a monologue, the second an analytic description, the third a dialogue—illustrate some of the characteristic features of his style and thought. The first is a speech that was made by Pericles, perhaps the most outstanding Athenian politician of the fifth century B.C., at the public burial of Athenians who had died in the first year of the Peloponnesian War (431–430 B.C.). The speech does not say much about the dead, but it contains the most eloquent ancient description of the forces that made the Athenian community a brilliant cultural center in the mid-fifth century. The second selection provides a disturbing contrast to the first. It deals with the atmosphere in Greece barely three years after Pericles' eulogy of Athenian democracy and reveals an inferno of power politics and suspicion. It demonstrates Thucydides' constant effort to describe even his most jarring observations with near scientific detachment and to understand political phenomena in terms of causes and effects. He introduces the laws of human behavior, as he understands them, to provide a pathology of war. The third selection is the famous "Melian Dialogue," a debate that took place eleven years later, in 416 B.C., between the Athenians and the inhabitants of Melos, a small, insignificant Aegean island. This dialogue not only unmasks the political cynicism into which some Athenians had fallen and the forms of rationalistic argumentation that had become current in the last half of the century, but it also shows Thucydides as a master of dramatic narrative.

The History of the Peloponnesian War

Thucydides, an Athenian, wrote the history of the war in which the Peloponnesians and the Athenians fought against one another. He began to write when they first took up arms, believing that it would be great and memorable above any previous war. For he argued that both states were then at the full height of their military power, and he saw the rest of the Hellenes either siding or intending to side with one or other of them. No movement ever stirred Hellas more deeply than this; it was shared by many of the Barbarians, and might be said even to affect the world at large. The character of the events which preceded, whether immediately or in more remote antiquity, owing to the lapse of time cannot be made out with certainty. But, judging from the evidence which I am able to trust after most careful enquiry, I should imagine that former ages were not great either in their wars or in anything else. . . .

The Funeral Speech of Pericles

During the same winter,[1] in accordance with an old national custom, the funeral of those who first fell in this war was celebrated by the Athenians at the public charge. The ceremony is as follows: Three days before the celebration they erect a tent in which the bones of the dead are laid out, and every one brings to his own dead any offering which he pleases. At the time of the funeral the bones are placed in chests of cypress wood, which are conveyed on hearses; there is one chest for each tribe.[2] They also carry a single empty litter decked with a pall for all whose bodies are missing, and cannot be recovered after the battle. The procession is accompanied by any one who chooses, whether citizen or stranger, and the female relatives of the deceased are present at the place of interment and make lamentation. The public sepulcher is situated in the most beautiful spot outside the walls; there they always bury those who fall in war; only after the battle of Marathon[3] the

---

[1] At the end of the first year of the Peloponnesian War, in the winter of 431–430 B,C.   [2] There were ten "tribes," to one of which every Athenian citizen belonged.   [3] The famous battle of 490 B.C., in which the Athenians defeated the Persians.

dead, in recognition of their preeminent valor, were interred on the field. When the remains have been laid in the earth, some man of known ability and high reputation, chosen by the city, delivers a suitable oration over them; after which the people depart. Such is the manner of interment; and the ceremony was repeated from time to time throughout the war. Over those who were the first buried Pericles[4] was chosen to speak. At the fitting moment he advanced from the sepulcher to a lofty stage, which had been erected in order that he might be heard as far as possible by the multitude, and spoke as follows:

"Most of those who have spoken here before me have commended the lawgiver who added this oration to our other funeral customs; it seemed to them a worthy thing that such an honor should be given at their burial to the dead who have fallen on the field of battle. But I should have preferred that, when men's deeds have been brave, they should be honored in deed only, and with such an honor as this public funeral, which you are now witnessing. Then the reputation of many would not have been imperiled on the eloquence or want of eloquence of one, and their virtues believed or not as he spoke well or ill. For it is difficult to say neither too little nor too much; and even moderation is apt not to give the impression of truthfulness. The friend of the dead who knows the facts is likely to think that the words of the speaker fall short of his knowledge and of his wishes; another who is not so well informed, when he hears of anything which surpasses his own powers, will be envious and will suspect exaggeration. Mankind are tolerant of the praises of others so long as each hearer thinks that he can do as well or nearly as well himself, but, when the speaker rises above him, jealousy is aroused and he begins to be incredulous. However, since our ancestors have set the seal of their approval upon the practice, I must obey, and to the utmost of my power shall endeavor to satisfy the wishes and beliefs of all who hear me.

"I will speak first of our ancestors, for it is right and seemly that now, when we are lamenting the dead, a tribute should be paid to their memory. There has never been a time when they did not inhabit this land,[5] which by their valor they have handed down from generation to generation, and we have received from them a free state. But if they were worthy of praise, still more were our fathers, who added to their inheritance, and after many a struggle transmitted to us their sons this great empire.[6] And we ourselves

---

[4] Pericles (about 490–429 B.C.), the most outstanding statesman and politician of his generation, was the leader of the democratic party in Athens.   [5] The Athenians made much of the claim that they were direct descendants of the original inhabitants of Athens or Attica.   [6] Following the defeat of Xerxes' Persians in 480–479 B.C., the Athenians established a Greek defense league under their own leadership as a protection against any future Persian attack. The members of the league included the Greek islands and Greek cities on the west coast of Asia Minor. Gradually the Athenians converted this league, known as the Delian League, into their own empire and made its members their subjects.

assembled here today, who are still most of us in the vigor of life, have carried the work of improvement further, and have richly endowed our city with all things, so that she is sufficient for herself both in peace and war. Of the military exploits by which our various possessions were acquired, or of the energy with which we or our fathers drove back the tide of war, Hellenic or Barbarian,[7] I will not speak; for the tale would be long and is familiar to you. But before I praise the dead, I should like to point out by what principles of action we rose to power, and under what institutions and through what manner of life our empire became great. For I conceive that such thoughts are not unsuited to the occasion, and that this numerous assembly of citizens and strangers may profitably listen to them.

"Our form of government does not enter into rivalry with the institutions of others. We do not copy our neighbors, but are an example to them. It is true that we are called a democracy, for the administration is in the hands of the many and not of the few.[8] But while the law secures equal justice to all alike in their private disputes, the claim of excellence is also recognized; and when a citizen is in any way distinguished, he is preferred to the public service, not as a matter of privilege, but as the reward of merit. Neither is poverty a bar, but a man may benefit his country whatever be the obscurity of his condition. There is no exclusiveness in our public life, and in our private intercourse we are not suspicious of one another, nor angry with our neighbor if he does what he likes; we do not put on sour looks at him which, though harmless, are not pleasant. While we are thus unconstrained in our private intercourse, a spirit of reverence pervades our public acts; we are prevented from doing wrong by respect for the authorities and for the laws, having an especial regard to those which are ordained for the protection of the injured as well as to those unwritten laws which bring upon the transgressor of them the reprobation of the general sentiment.

"And we have not forgotten to provide for our weary spirits many relaxations from toil; we have regular games and sacrifices throughout the year; our homes are beautiful and elegant; and the delight which we daily feel in all these things helps to banish melancholy. Because of the greatness of our city the fruits of the whole earth flow in upon us; so that we enjoy the goods of other countries as freely as of our own.

"Then, again, our military training is in many respects superior to that of our adversaries. Our city is thrown open to the world, and we never expel a foreigner or prevent him from seeing or learning anything of which the secret if revealed to an enemy might profit him.[9] We rely not upon management or trickery, but upon our own hearts and hands. And in the matter of

[7] Greek or non-Greek (especially Persian). [8] A reference to the original meaning of "democracy," which is a compound of *dēmos*, "people," and *kratos*, "power." [9] The Athenians were proud of their "open society," and they proudly contrasted it with Sparta, which was notoriously xenophobic. The Spartans gave aliens only limited access—usually only for official transactions—and shadowed them assiduously.

education, whereas they[10] from early youth are always undergoing laborious exercises which are to make them brave, we live at ease, and yet are equally ready to face the perils which they face. And here is the proof. The Lacedaemonians[11] come into Attica not by themselves, but with their whole confederacy following; we go alone into a neighbor's country; and although our opponents are fighting for their homes and we on a foreign soil, we have seldom any difficulty in overcoming them. Our enemies have never yet felt our united strength; the care of a navy divides our attention, and on land we are obliged to send our own citizens everywhere. But they, if they meet and defeat a part of our army, are as proud as if they had routed us all, and when defeated they pretend to have been vanquished by us all.

"If then we prefer to meet danger with a light heart but without laborious training, and with a courage which is gained by habit and not enforced by law, are we not greatly the gainers? Since we do not anticipate the pain, although, when the hour comes, we can be as brave as those who never allow themselves to rest; and thus too our city is equally admirable in peace and in war. For we are lovers of the beautiful, yet simple in our tastes, and we cultivate the mind without loss of manliness. Wealth we employ, not for talk and ostentation, but when there is a real use for it. To avow poverty with us is no disgrace; the true disgrace is in doing nothing to avoid it. An Athenian citizen does not neglect the state because he takes care of his own household; and even those of us who are engaged in business have a very fair idea of politics. We alone regard a man who takes no interest in public affairs, not as a harmless, but as a useless character; and if few of us are originators, we are all sound judges of a policy. The great impediment to action is, in our opinion, not discussion, but the want of that knowledge which is gained by discussion preparatory to action. For we have a peculiar power of thinking before we act and of acting too, whereas other men are courageous from ignorance but hesitate upon reflection. And they are surely to be esteemed the bravest spirits who, having the clearest sense both of the pains and pleasures of life, do not on that account shrink from danger. In doing good, again, we are unlike others; we make our friends by conferring, not by receiving favors. Now he who confers a favor is the firmer friend, because he would fain by kindness keep alive the memory of an obligation; but the recipient is colder in his feelings, because he knows that in requiting another's generosity he will not be winning gratitude but only paying a debt. We alone do good to our neighbors not upon a calculation of interest, but in the confidence of freedom and in a frank and fearless spirit. To sum up: I say that Athens is the school of Hellas, and that the individual Athenian in his own person seems to have the power of adapting himself to the most varied forms of action with the utmost versatility and grace. This is no passing and idle word,

[10] The Spartans.   [11] Spartans.

but truth and fact; and the assertion is verified by the position to which these qualities have raised the state. For in the hour of trial Athens alone among her contemporaries is superior to the report of her. No enemy who comes against her is indignant at the reverses which he sustains at the hands of such a city; no subject complains that his masters are unworthy of him. And we shall assuredly not be without witnesses; there are mighty monuments of our power which will make us the wonder of this and of succeeding ages;[12] we shall not need the praises of Homer or of any other panegyrist[13] whose poetry may please for the moment, although his representation of the facts will not bear the light of day. For we have compelled every land and every sea to open a path for our valor, and have everywhere planted eternal memorials of our friendship and of our enmity. Such is the city for whose sake these men nobly fought and died; they could not bear the thought that she might be taken from them; and every one of us who survive should gladly toil on her behalf.

"I have dwelt upon the greatness of Athens because I want to show you that we are contending for a higher prize than those who enjoy none of these privileges, and to establish by manifest proof the merit of these men whom I am now commemorating. Their loftiest praise has been already spoken. For in magnifying the city I have magnified them, and men like them whose virtues made her glorious. And of how few Hellenes can it be said as of them, that their deeds when weighed in the balance have been found equal to their fame! Methinks that a death such as theirs has been gives the true measure of a man's worth; it may be the first revelation of his virtues, but is at any rate their final seal. For even those who come short in other ways may justly plead the valor with which they have fought for their country; they have blotted out the evil with the good, and have benefited the state more by their public services than they have injured her by their private actions. None of these men were enervated by wealth or hesitated to resign the pleasures of life; none of them put off the evil day in the hope, natural to poverty, that a man, though poor, may one day become rich. But, deeming that the punishment of their enemies was sweeter than any of these things, and that they could fall in no nobler cause, they determined at the hazard of their lives to be honorably avenged, and to leave the rest. They resigned to hope their unknown chance of happiness; but in the face of death they resolved to rely upon themselves alone. And when the moment came they were minded to resist and suffer, rather than to fly and save their lives; they ran away from the word of dishonor, but on the battlefield their feet stood fast, and in an instant, at the height of their fortune, they passed away from the scene, not of their fear, but of their glory.

[12] During the period in which Pericles ruled, Athens built a number of magnificent public buildings, among them the Parthenon.   [13] Eulogist.

"Such was the end of these men; they were worthy of Athens, and the living need not desire to have a more heroic spirit, although they may pray for a less fatal issue. The value of such a spirit is not to be expressed in words. Any one can discourse to you for ever about the advantages of a brave defense, which you know already. But instead of listening to him I would have you day by day fix your eyes upon the greatness of Athens, until you become filled with the love of her; and when you are impressed by the spectacle of her glory, reflect that this empire has been acquired by men who knew their duty and had the courage to do it, who in the hour of conflict had the fear of dishonor always present to them, and who, if ever they failed in an enterprise, would not allow their virtues to be lost to their country, but freely gave their lives to her as the fairest offering which they could present at her feast. The sacrifice which they collectively made was individually repaid to them; for they received again each one for himself a praise which grows not old, and the noblest of all sepulchers—I speak not of that in which their remains are laid, but of that in which their glory survives, and is proclaimed always and on every fitting occasion both in word and deed. For the whole earth is the sepulcher of famous men; not only are they commemorated by columns and inscriptions in their own country, but in foreign lands there dwells also an unwritten memorial of them, graven not on stone but in the hearts of men. Make them your examples, and, esteeming courage to be freedom and freedom to be happiness,[14] do not weigh too nicely the perils of war. The unfortunate who has no hope of a change for the better has less reason to throw away his life than the prosperous who, if he survive, is always liable to a change for the worse, and to whom any accidental fall makes the most serious difference. To a man of spirit, cowardice and disaster coming together are far more bitter than death striking him unperceived at a time when he is full of courage and animated by the general hope.

"Wherefore I do not now commiserate the parents of the dead who stand here; I would rather comfort them. You know that your life has been passed amid manifold vicissitudes; and that they may be deemed fortunate who have gained most honor, whether an honorable death like theirs, or an honorable sorrow like yours, and whose days have been so ordered that the term of their happiness is likewise the term of their life. I know how hard it is to make you feel this, when the good fortune of others will too often remind you of the gladness which once lightened your hearts. And sorrow is felt at the want of those blessings, not which a man never knew, but which were a part of his life before they were taken from him. Some of you are of an age at which they may hope to have other children, and they ought to bear their sorrow better; not only will the children who may hereafter be

[14] Pericles is here linking the three highest ideals of Greece and saying in effect that they are identical.

born make them forget their own lost ones, but the city will be doubly a gainer. She will not be left desolate, and she will be safer. For a man's counsel cannot have equal weight or worth, when he alone has no children to risk in the general danger. To those of you who have passed their prime, I say: 'Congratulate yourselves that you have been happy during the greater part of your days; remember that your life of sorrow will not last long, and be comforted by the glory of those who are gone. For the love of honor alone is ever young, and not riches, as some say, but honor is the delight of men when they are old and useless.'

"To you who are the sons and brothers of the departed, I see that the struggle to emulate them will be an arduous one. For all men praise the dead, and, however preeminent your virtue may be, hardly will you be thought, I do not say to equal, but even to approach them. The living have their rivals and detractors, but when a man is out of the way, the honor and goodwill which he receives is unalloyed. And, if I am to speak of womanly virtues to those of you who will henceforth be widows, let me sum them up in one short admonition: To a woman not to show more weakness than is natural to her sex is a great glory, and not to be talked about for good or for evil among men.

"I have paid the required tribute, in obedience to the law, making use of such fitting words as I had. The tribute of deeds has been paid in part; for the dead have been honorably interred, and it remains only that their children should be maintained at the public charge until they are grown up: this is the solid prize with which, as with a garland, Athens crowns her sons living and dead, after a struggle like theirs. For where the rewards of virtue are greatest, there the noblest citizens are enlisted in the service of the state. And now, when you have duly lamented, every one his own dead, you may depart." . . .

Human Nature and War

. . . Not long afterwards[15] the whole Hellenic world was in commotion; in every city the chiefs of the democracy and of the oligarchy[16] were struggling, the one to bring in the Athenians, the other the Lacedaemonians. Now in time of peace, men would have had no excuse for introducing either, and

[15] Thucydides is describing the atmosphere and attitudes of the year 427 B.C. in Greece; the contrast with Pericles' retrospective analysis of three years earlier is devastating.   [16] Reactionary and despotic rule by a privileged clique. (The word "oligarchy" is a compound of *olig-*, "few," and *archia*, "rule" or "sovereign power.")

no desire to do so, but when they were at war and both sides could easily obtain allies to the hurt of their enemies and the advantage of themselves, the dissatisfied party was only too ready to invoke foreign[17] aid. And revolution brought upon the cities of Hellas many terrible calamities, such as have been and always will be while human nature remains the same, but which are more or less aggravated and differ in character with every new combination of circumstances. In peace and prosperity both states and individuals are actuated by higher motives, because they do not fall under the dominion of imperious necessities; but war which takes away the comfortable provision of daily life is a hard master, and tends to assimilate men's characters to their conditions.

When troubles had once begun in the cities, those who followed carried the revolutionary spirit further and further, and determined to outdo the report of all who had preceded them by the ingenuity of their enterprises and the atrocity of their revenges. The meaning of words had no longer the same relation to things, but was changed by them as they thought proper. Reckless daring was held to be loyal courage; prudent delay was the excuse of a coward; moderation was the disguise of unmanly weakness; to know everything was to do nothing. Frantic energy was the true quality of a man. A conspirator who wanted to be safe was a recreant in disguise. The lover of violence was always trusted, and his opponent suspected. He who succeeded in a plot was deemed knowing, but a still greater master in craft was he who detected one. . . .

The cause of all these evils was the love of power, originating in avarice and ambition, and the party spirit which is engendered by them when men are fairly embarked in a contest. For the leaders on either side used specious names, the one party professing to uphold the constitutional equality of the many, the other the wisdom of an aristocracy, while they made the public interests, to which in name they were devoted, in reality their prize. Striving in every way to overcome each other, they committed the most monstrous crimes; yet even these were surpassed by the magnitude of their revenges which they pursued to the very utmost, neither party observing any definite limits either of justice or public expediency, but both alike making the caprice of the moment their law. Either by the help of an unrighteous sentence, or grasping power with the strong hand, they were eager to satiate the impatience of party spirit. Neither faction cared for religion; but any fair pretence which succeeded in effecting some odious purpose was greatly lauded. And the citizens who were of neither party fell a prey to both; either

17 The traditional autonomy of each Greek city-state (*polis*) was still a major factor in Greek political thought, in spite of the political consolidation and the League during the period after the Persian Wars. The inhabitants of each polis therefore still regarded help from another Greek city as "foreign aid."

they were disliked because they held aloof, or men were jealous of their surviving.

Thus revolution[18] gave birth to every form of wickedness in Hellas. The simplicity[19] which is so large an element in a noble nature was laughed to scorn and disappeared. An attitude of perfidious antagonism everywhere prevailed; for there was no word binding enough, nor oath terrible enough to reconcile enemies. Each man was strong only in the conviction that nothing was secure; he must look to his own safety, and could not afford to trust others. Inferior intellects generally succeeded best. For, aware of their own deficiencies, and fearing the capacity of their opponents, for whom they were no match in powers of speech, and whose subtle wits were likely to anticipate them in contriving evil, they struck boldly and at once. But the cleverer sort, presuming in their arrogance that they would be aware in time, and disdaining to act when they could think, were taken off their guard and easily destroyed. . . .

The Melian Dialogue

The Athenians next made an expedition against the island of Melos[20] with thirty ships of their own, six Chian, and two Lesbian,[21] twelve hundred hoplites[22] and three hundred archers besides twenty mounted archers of their own, and about fifteen hundred hoplites furnished by their allies in the islands. The Melians are colonists of the Lacedaemonians[23] who would not submit to Athens like the other islanders. At first they were neutral and took no part. But when the Athenians tried to coerce them by ravaging their lands, they were driven into open hostilities. The generals, Cleomedes the son of Lycomedes and Tisias the son of Tisimachus, encamped with the Athenian forces on the island. But before they did the country any harm they sent envoys to negotiate with the Melians. Instead of bringing these

---

[18] The Greek (*stasis*) is perhaps more accurately translated as "seditious partisanship." [19] Literally, "goodness of character"; in its positive use it implies both "goodness of heart" and "guilelessness." [20] An insignificant and barren Aegean island off the southeast coast of the Peloponnesus, about halfway between Athens and Crete. The attack takes place in 416 B.C., after a temporary truce in the Peloponnesian War (concluded in 421 B.C.) had fizzled out. [21] Chios and Lesbos, two islands off the west coast of Asia Minor, were at this time members of the Delian League dominated by Athens. [22] Heavy infantry. [23] Melos had been occupied in the eighth century B.C. by Dorians from Laconia (the southeastern district of the Peloponnesus, of which Sparta was the capital). It had neither joined the League formed by the Athenians nor sided with the Spartans.

envoys before the people, the Melians desired them to explain their errand to the magistrates and to the dominant class.[24] They[25] spoke as follows:

"Since we are not allowed to speak to the people, lest, forsooth, a multitude should be deceived by seductive and unanswerable arguments which they would hear set forth in a single uninterrupted oration (for we are perfectly aware that this is what you mean in bringing us before a select few), you who are sitting here may as well make assurance yet surer. Let us have no set speeches at all, but do you reply to each several statement of which you disapprove, and criticize it at once. Say first of all how you like this mode of proceeding."

The Melian representatives answered: "The quiet interchange of explanations is a reasonable thing, and we do not object to that. But your warlike movements, which are present not only to our fears but to our eyes, seem to belie your words. We see that, although you may reason with us, you mean to be our judges; and that at the end of the discussion, if the justice of our cause prevail and we therefore refuse to yield, we may expect war; if we are convinced by you, slavery."

ATHENIAN: "Nay, but if you are only going to argue from fancies about the future, or if you meet us with any other purpose than that of looking your circumstances in the face and saving your city, we have done; but if this is your intention we will proceed."

MELIAN: "It is an excusable and natural thing that men in our position should neglect no argument and no view which may avail. But we admit that this conference has met to consider the question of our preservation; and therefore let the argument proceed in the manner which you propose."

ATHENIAN: "Well, then, we Athenians will use no fine words; we will not go out of our way to prove at length that we have a right to rule, because we overthrew the Persians;[26] or that we attack you now because we are suffering any injury at your hands. We should not convince you if we did; nor must you expect to convince us by arguing that, although a colony of the Lacedaemonians, you have taken no part in their expeditions, or that you have never done us any wrong. But you and we should say what we really think, and aim only at what is possible, for we both alike know that into the discussion of human affairs the question of justice only enters where there is equal power to enforce it, and that the powerful exact what they can, and the weak grant what they must."

MELIAN: "Well, then, since you set aside justice and invite us to speak of

[24] Probably because Melos had an oligarchic form of government.   [25] The Athenians.   [26] The Athenians played a more important role than any other Greek citystate in the defeat of the massive Persian invasions from 490 B.C. to 479 B.C.

expediency,[27] in our judgment it is certainly expedient that you should respect a principle which is for the common good; that to every man when in peril a reasonable claim should be accounted a claim of right, and that any plea which he is disposed to urge, even if failing of the point a little, should help his cause. Your interest in this principle is quite as great as ours; inasmuch as you, if you fall, will incur the heaviest vengeance, and will be the most terrible example to mankind."

ATHENIAN: "The fall of our empire, if it should fall, is not an event to which we look forward with dismay; for ruling states such as Lacedaemon are not cruel to their vanquished enemies.[28] With the Lacedaemonians, however, we are not now contending; the real danger is from our many subject states, who may of their own motion rise up and overcome their masters. But this is a danger which you may leave to us. And we will now endeavor to show that we have come in the interests of our empire, and that in what we are about to say we are only seeking the preservation of your city. For we want to make you ours with the least trouble to ourselves, and it is for the interests of us both that you should not be destroyed."

MELIAN: "It may be your interest to be our masters, but how can it be ours to be your slaves?"

ATHENIAN: "To you the gain will be that by submission you will avert the worst; and we shall be all the richer for your preservation."

MELIAN: "But must we be your enemies? Will you not receive us as friends if we are neutral and remain at peace with you?"

ATHENIAN: "No, your enmity is not half so mischievous to us as your friendship; for the one is in the eyes of our subjects an argument of our power, the other of our weakness."

MELIAN: "But are your subjects really unable to distinguish between states in which you have no concern, and those which are chiefly your own colonies, and in some cases have revolted and been subdued by you?"[29]

ATHENIAN: "Why, they do not doubt that both of them have a good deal to say for themselves on the score of justice, but they think that states like

27 This is an echo of debates conducted by some of the fifth-century Sophists, professional teachers of rhetoric and philosophy. They argued that it was acceptable to appeal to the advantages of expediency rather than to accepted (or "inherently" right) moral standards and that political power and physical superiority rather than "nature" often determined what was "right."   28 "An accurate prognostication": at the end of the Peloponnesian War, in 404 B.C., the victorious Spartans (Lacedaemonians) treated their Athenian victims with what some historians have considered astounding mildness.   29 The Athenians had brutally put down revolts by subject states of her imperial Delian League. When, for example, Mytilene (the chief city of the island Lesbos) headed a revolt against Athens in 428 B.C., the Athenians put more than a thousand prisoners to death, demolished the city walls, and confiscated their fleet.

yours are left free because they are able to defend themselves, and that we do not attack them because we dare not. So that your subjection will give us an increase of security, as well as an extension of empire. For we are masters of the sea, and you who are islanders, and insignificant islanders too, must not be allowed to escape us."

MELIAN: "But do you not recognize another danger? For, once more, since you drive us from the plea of justice and press upon us your doctrine of expediency, we must show you what is for our interest, and, if it be for yours also, may hope to convince you: Will you not be making enemies of all who are now neutrals? When they see how you are treating us they will expect you some day to turn against them; and if so, are you not strengthening the enemies whom you already have, and bringing upon you others who, if they could help, would never dream of being your enemies at all?"

ATHENIAN: "We do not consider our really dangerous enemies to be any of the peoples inhabiting the mainland who, secure in their freedom, may defer indefinitely any measures of precaution which they take against us, but islanders who, like you, happen to be under no control, and all who may be already irritated by the necessity of submission to our empire—these are our real enemies, for they are the most reckless and most likely to bring themselves as well as us into a danger which they cannot but foresee."

MELIAN: "Surely then, if you and your subjects will brave all this risk, you to preserve your empire and they to be quit of it, how base and cowardly would it be in us, who retain our freedom, not to do and suffer anything rather than be your slaves."

ATHENIAN: "Not so, if you calmly reflect: for you are not fighting against equals to whom you cannot yield without disgrace, but you are taking counsel whether or no you shall resist an overwhelming force. The question is not one of honor but of prudence."

MELIAN: "But we know that the fortune of war is sometimes impartial, and not always on the side of numbers. If we yield now, all is over; but if we fight, there is yet a hope that we may stand upright."

ATHENIAN: "Hope is a good comforter in the hour of danger, and when men have something else to depend upon, although hurtful, she is not ruinous. But when her spendthrift nature has induced them to stake their all, they see her as she is in the moment of their fall, and not till then. While the knowledge of her might enable them to be ware of her, she never fails. You are weak and a single turn of the scale might be your ruin. Do not you be thus deluded; avoid the error of which so many are guilty, who, although they might still be saved if they would take the natural means, when visible grounds of confidence forsake them, have recourse to the invisible, to prophecies and oracles and the like, which ruin men by the hopes which they inspire in them."

MELIAN: "We know only too well how hard the struggle must be against your power, and against fortune, if she does not mean to be impartial. Nevertheless we do not despair of fortune; for we hope to stand as high as you in the favor of heaven, because we are righteous, and you against whom we contend are unrighteous; and we are satisfied that our deficiency in power will be compensated by the aid of our allies the Lacedaemonians; they cannot refuse to help us, if only because we are their kinsmen,[30] and for the sake of their own honor. And therefore our confidence is not so utterly blind as you suppose."

ATHENIAN: "As for the Gods, we expect to have quite as much of their favor as you: for we are not doing or claiming anything which goes beyond common opinion about divine or men's desires about human things. For of the Gods we believe, and of men we know, that by a law of their nature wherever they can rule they will. This law was not made by us, and we are not the first who have acted upon it; we did but inherit it, and shall bequeath it to all time, and we know that you and all mankind, if you were as strong as we are, would do as we do. So much for the Gods; we have told you why we expect to stand as high in their good opinion as you. And then as to the Lacedaemonians—when you imagine that out of very shame they will assist you, we admire the innocence of your idea, but we do not envy you the folly of it. The Lacedaemonians are exceedingly virtuous among themselves, and according to their national standard of morality. But, in respect of their dealings with others, although many things might be said, they can be described in few words—of all men whom we know they are the most notorious for identifying what is pleasant with what is honorable, and what is expedient with what is just. But how inconsistent is such a character with your present blind hope of deliverance!"

MELIAN: "That is the very reason why we trust them; they will look to their interest, and therefore will not be willing to betray the Melians, who are their own colonists, lest they should be distrusted by their friends in Hellas and play into the hands of their enemies."

ATHENIAN: "But do you not see that the path of expediency is safe, whereas justice and honor involve danger in practice, and such dangers the Lacedaemonians seldom care to face?"

MELIAN: "On the other hand, we think that whatever perils there may be, they will be ready to face them for our sakes, and will consider danger less dangerous where we are concerned. For if they need our aid we are close at hand, and they can better trust our loyal feeling because we are their kinsmen."

ATHENIAN: "Yes, but what encourages men who are invited to join in a conflict is clearly not the goodwill of those who summon them to their side, but a decided superiority in real power. To this no men look more keenly

[30] The Melians were ethnically related to the Lacedaemonians (Spartans).

than the Lacedaemonians; so little confidence have they in their own resources, that they only attack their neighbors when they have numerous
allies, and therefore they are not likely to find their way by themselves to an
island, when we are masters of the sea."

MELIAN: "But they may send their allies: the Cretan sea[31] is a large place;
and the masters of the sea will have more difficulty in overtaking vessels
which want to escape than the pursued in escaping. If the attempt should
fail they may invade Attica[32] itself, and find their way to allies of yours
whom Brasidas[33] did not reach: and then you will have to fight, not for the
conquest of a land in which you have no concern, but nearer home, for the
preservation of your confederacy and of your own territory."

ATHENIAN: "Help may come from Lacedaemon to you as it has come to
others, and should you ever have actual experience of it, then you will know
that never once have the Athenians retired from a siege through fear of a
foe elsewhere. You told us that the safety of your city would be your first
care, but we remark that, in this long discussion, not a word has been uttered
by you which would give a reasonable man expectation of deliverance. Your
strongest grounds are hopes deferred, and what power you have is not to be
compared with that which is already arrayed against you. Unless after we
have withdrawn you mean to come, as even now you may, to a wiser conclusion, you are showing a great want of sense. For surely you cannot dream of
flying to that false sense of honor which has been the ruin of so many when
danger and dishonor were staring them in the face. Many men with their
eyes still open to the consequences have found the word 'honor' too much
for them, and have suffered a mere name to lure them on, until it has drawn
down upon them real and irretrievable calamities; through their own folly
they have incurred a worse dishonor than fortune would have inflicted upon
them. If you are wise you will not run this risk; you ought to see that there
can be no disgrace in yielding to a great city which invites you to become her
ally on reasonable terms, keeping your own land, and merely paying tribute;
and that you will certainly gain no honor if, having to choose between two
alternatives, safety and war, you obstinately prefer the worse. To maintain
our rights against equals, to be politic with superiors, and to be moderate
towards inferiors is the path of safety. Reflect once more when we have withdrawn, and say to yourselves over and over again that you are deliberating
about your one and only country, which may be saved or may be destroyed
by a single decision."

The Athenians left the conference: the Melians, after consulting among
themselves, resolved to persevere in their refusal, and made answer as fol-

---

[31] Melos lies about seventy miles north of Crete in the Cretan Sea.   [32] Part of
Greece, of which Athens was the chief city.   [33] A distinguished Spartan general;
earlier in the war, with a small force, he had gained possession of many towns in
Thessaly (northern Greece) that were subject to the Athenians.

lows: "Men of Athens, our resolution is unchanged; and we will not in a moment surrender that liberty which our city, founded seven hundred years ago, still enjoys; we will trust to the good fortune which, by the favor of the Gods, has hitherto preserved us, and for human help to the Lacedaemonians, and endeavor to save ourselves. We are ready however to be your friends, and the enemies neither of you nor of the Lacedaemonians, and we ask you to leave our country when you have made such a peace as may appear to be in the interest of both parties."

Such was the answer of the Melians; the Athenians, as they quitted the conference, spoke as follows: "Well, we must say, judging from the decision at which you have arrived, that you are the only men who deem the future to be more certain than the present, and regard things unseen as already realized in your fond anticipation, and that the more you cast yourselves upon the Lacedaemonians and fortune and hope, and trust them, the more complete will be your ruin."

The Athenian envoys returned to the army; and the generals, when they found that the Melians would not yield, immediately commenced hostilities. They surrounded the town of Melos with a wall, dividing the work among the several contingents. They then left troops of their own and of their allies to keep guard both by land and by sea, and retired with the greater part of their army; the remainder carried on the blockade. . . .

The Melians took that part of the Athenian wall which looked towards the agora[34] by a night assault, killed a few men, and brought in as much corn and other necessaries as they could; they then retreated and remained inactive. After this the Athenians set a better watch. So the summer ended.

In the following winter . . . the Melians took another part of the Athenian wall; for the fortifications were insufficiently guarded. Whereupon the Athenians sent fresh troops, under the command of Philocrates the son of Demeas. The place was now closely invested, and there was treachery among the citizens themselves. So the Melians were induced to surrender at discretion. The Athenians thereupon put to death all who were of military age, and made slaves of the women and children. They then colonized the island, sending thither five hundred settlers of their own.

[34] Marketplace.

Sophocles

Oedipus the King

TRANSLATED BY THEODORE H. BANKS

Sophocles (496 B.C.?–405 B.C.?)

THE GREEK TRAGEDIAN SOPHOCLES WAS BORN INTO A DISTIN-
guished aristocratic family at Colonus, a suburb of Athens, where he also
died. He was very active in Athenian political and religious life: he held
priesthoods, was a high fiscal official, and in 440 B.C., at the height of the
Periclean age, he was a general. His attachment to Athens was legendary,
and as far as we know he never left the city except in its service. In contrast
to his younger contemporary, Euripides, he won and always maintained a
favorable audience for his tragedies, even at the age of ninety.

In addition to introducing a third actor, Sophocles made two important in-
novations in Greek tragedy. First, he gave the chorus an even less direct share
in the action than it had previously had, even though he raised the number of
chorus members from twelve to fifteen. Second, he produced trilogies in
which the three individual plays were unconnected in subject. Of the more
than one hundred tragedies that he wrote, only seven have survived: *Ajax*,
Antigone, *Oedipus the King*, *Electra*, *The Women of Trachis*, *Philoctetes*,
and *Oedipus at Colonus*.

Sophocles' *Oedipus the King*, which has overshadowed everything else he
wrote, was probably first performed between 430 and 428 B.C., when the
Athenian community was absorbing the initial impact of the Peloponnesian
War. The legend of Oedipus, like the myth about the house of Atreus on
which Aeschylus based his *Agamemnon*, was already well known to the
Athenians. Oedipus, a king of Thebes, did not know his true origin. Unknowingly, and against his own intentions, he broke the moral code expressed
in the divine order by killing his own father, Laius, and marrying his own
mother, Jocasta. As a result of these involuntary violations, a god inflicted a
devastating plague on Thebes. When Oedipus set out energetically to discover the reason behind the plague, he stumbled on the intolerable truth
about himself. Sophocles dramatized only that part of the myth in which
Oedipus, through his quick intelligence and deadly logic, gradually discovered who he really was and what he had done.

The poet used the familiarity of the myth to create a constant discrepancy
between the knowledge of the audience and the groping ignorance of
Oedipus, who only grasps at the end of the play what the audience has
known all along. This discrepancy, which is a source of dramatic irony, is
used to convey Sophocles' interpretation of the myth as a profound expression of the relation between man and god, of the inadequacy of man's intellect and his inability to perceive and control all the forces that operate in
human life.

Oedipus the King

OEDIPUS, *King of Thebes.*
A PRIEST OF ZEUS.
CREON, *brother-in-law of King Oedipus.*
CHORUS *of Old Men of Thebes.*
TIRESIAS, *an old, blind Theban prophet.*
JOCASTA, *wife of Oedipus and sister of Creon.*
FIRST MESSENGER.
AN OLD SHEPHERD.
SECOND MESSENGER.
SILENT CHARACTERS: A LITTLE BOY *leading Tiresias;* SERVANTS *of Jocasta and Oedipus;* ANTIGONE *and* ISMENE, *Oedipus' daughters.*

Before the doors of the palace of OEDIPUS *at Thebes. A crowd of citizens are seated next to the two altars at the sides. In front of one of the altars stands the* PRIEST OF ZEUS.

[*Enter* OEDIPUS.]

OEDIPUS. Why are you here as suppliants, my children.
You in whose veins the blood of Cadmus° flows?
What is the reason for your boughs of olive,°
The fumes of incense, the laments and prayers
That fill the city? Because I thought it wrong,
My children, to depend on what was told me,
I have come to you myself, I, Oedipus,
Renowned in the sight of all.° [*To* PRIEST.] Tell me—you are
Their natural spokesman—what desire or fear
Brings you before me? I will gladly give you   10
Such help as is in my power. It would be heartless
Not to take pity on a plea like this.
PRIEST. King Oedipus, you see us, young and old,
Gathered about your altars: some, mere fledglings
Not able yet to fly; some bowed with age;
Some, priests, and I the priest of Zeus among them;
And these, who are the flower of our young manhood.
The rest of us are seated—the whole city—
With our wreathed branches in the marketplaces,
Before the shrines of Pallas,° before the fire   20
By which we read the auguries of Apollo.°
Thebes, as you see yourself, is overwhelmed
By the waves of death that break upon her head.
No fruit comes from her blighted buds; her cattle
Die in the fields; her wives bring forth dead children.
A hideous pestilence consumes the city,
Striking us down like a god armed with fire,
Emptying the house of Cadmus, filling full

---

2. *Cadmus:* founder and first king of Thebes.   3. *boughs of olive:* A suppliant carried a branch of an olive tree and laid it on an altar until his request was granted.   8. *Renowned . . . all:* This is not arrogance (in the modern sense), but typical self-characterization by an epic hero.   20. *Pallas:* the goddess Athena. 20–21. *before . . . Apollo:* reference to a temple of Apollo where divination by burnt offerings was practiced. Apollo and his oracular shrine at Delphi figure prominently throughout the play, since it concerns the gradual revelation of a terrifying truth predicted by Apollo's oracles.

The dark of Hades with loud lamentation.
I and these children have not thronged your altars   30
Because we hold you equal to the immortals,
But because we hold you foremost among men,
Both in the happenings of daily life
And when some visitation of the gods
Confronts us. For we know that when you came here,
You freed us from our bondage, the bitter tribute
The Sphinx° wrung from us by her sorceries.
And we know too that you accomplished this
Without foreknowledge, or clue that we could furnish.
We think, indeed, some god befriended you,   40
When you renewed our lives. Therefore, great king,
Glorious in all men's eyes, we now beseech you
To find some way of helping us, your suppliants,
Some way the gods themselves have told you of,
Or one that lies within our mortal power;
For the words of men experienced in evil
Are mighty and effectual. Oedipus!
Rescue our city and preserve your honor,
Since the land hails you as her savior now
For your past service. Never let us say   50
That when you ruled us, we were lifted up
Only to be thrown down. Restore the state
And keep it forever steadfast. Bring again
The happiness and good fortune you once brought us.
If you are still to reign as you reign now,
Then it is better to have men for subjects
Than to be king of a mere wilderness,
Since neither ship nor town has any value
Without companions or inhabitants.
OEDIPUS. I pity you, my children. Well I know   60
What hopes have brought you here, and well I know
That all of you are suffering. Yet your grief,
However great, is not so great as mine.

---

37. *Sphinx* (literally, "Strangler" or "One who knots"): a winged female monster
with a lion's body and a woman's head and breasts. She terrorized the city of
Thebes by killing every passerby who could not answer her riddle ("What walks
on four feet, then on two, then on three, and has only one voice?"). Some years
before the time of this play, Oedipus had traveled to Thebes and solved the riddle
(the solution: Man, who crawls in infancy, then walks, and finally needs a cane),
whereupon the Sphinx killed herself and Oedipus was gratefully proclaimed king
of Thebes.

Each of you suffers for himself alone,
But my heart feels the heaviness of my sorrow,
Your sorrow, and the sorrow of all the others.
You have not roused me, I have not been sleeping.
No. I have wept, wept long and bitterly,
Treading the devious paths of anxious thought;
And I have taken the only hopeful course   70
That I could find. I have sent my kinsman,° Creon,
Son of Menoeceus, to the Pythian home°
Of Phoebus Apollo to find what word or deed
Of mine might save the city. He has delayed
Too long already, his absence troubles me;
But when he comes, I pledge myself to do
My utmost to obey the god's command.

PRIEST. Your words are timely, for even as you speak
They sign to me that Creon is drawing near.

OEDIPUS. O Lord Apollo! Grant he may bring to us   80
Fortune as smiling as his smiling face.

PRIEST. Surely he brings good fortune. Look! The crown
Of bay leaves that he wears is full of berries.

OEDIPUS. We shall know soon, for he is close enough
To hear us. Brother, son of Menoeceus, speak!
What news? What news do you bring us from the god?
                    [*Enter* CREON.]

CREON. Good news. If we can find the fitting way
To end this heavy scourge, all will be well.

OEDIPUS. That neither gives me courage nor alarms me.
What does the god say? What is the oracle?   90

CREON. If you wish me to speak in public, I will do so.
Otherwise let us go in and speak alone.

OEDIPUS. Speak here before everyone. I feel more sorrow
For their sakes than I feel for my own life.

CREON. Then I will give the message of Lord Phoebus:°
A plain command to drive out the pollution
Here in our midst, and not to nourish it
Till our disease has grown incurable.

---

71. *kinsman:* Throughout the play such words are, to its Athenian audience, ex-
plosive with dramatic irony: Creon is a brother of Jocasta and therefore both
Oedipus' brother-in-law (as Oedipus knows) and his uncle (unknown to Oedipus).
72. *Pythian home:* oracular shrine of Apollo at Delphi (originally called "Pytho"
after Apollo's killing of a female serpent at Delphi); his prophesying priestess there
is the "Pythia."   95. *Phoebus:* Apollo.

OEDIPUS. What rite will purge us? How are we corrupted?
CREON. We must banish a man, or have him put to death   100
    To atone for the blood he shed, for it is blood
    That has brought this tempest down upon the city.
OEDIPUS. Who is the victim whose murder is revealed?
CREON. King Laius,° who was our lord before you came
    To steer the city on its proper course.
OEDIPUS. I know his name well, but I never saw him.
CREON. Laius was killed, and now we are commanded
    To punish his killers, whoever they may be.
OEDIPUS. How can they be discovered? Where shall we look
    For the faint traces of this ancient crime?   110
CREON. In Thebes, the god said. Truth can be always found:
    Only what is neglected ever escapes.
OEDIPUS. Where was King Laius murdered? In his home,
    Out in the fields, or in some foreign land?
CREON. He told us he was journeying to Delphi.
    After he left, he was never seen again.
OEDIPUS. Was no one with King Laius who saw what happened?
    You could have put his story to good use.
CREON. The sole survivor fled from the scene in terror,
    And there was only one thing he was sure of.   120
OEDIPUS. What was it? A clue might lead us far
    Which gave us even the faintest glimmer of hope.
CREON. He said that they were violently attacked
    Not by one man but by a band of robbers.
OEDIPUS. Robbers are not so daring. Were they bribed
    To commit this crime by some one here in Thebes?
CREON. That was suspected. But in our time of trouble
    No one appeared to avenge the death of Laius.
OEDIPUS. But your King was killed! What troubles could you have had
    To keep you from searching closely for his killers?   130
CREON. We had the Sphinx. Her riddle made us turn
    From mysteries to what lay before our doors.
OEDIPUS. Then I will start fresh and again make clear

---

104. *Laius:* previous king of Thebes, former husband of Jocasta (and father of Oedipus). Laius had ordered that Oedipus be abandoned on a mountain as an infant because an oracle had prophesied that he, Laius, would die by the hand of his own son. A Corinthian shepherd found Oedipus and took him to Polybus, King of Corinth, by whom he was raised as a son. Shortly before he solved the Sphinx's riddle, Oedipus had in fact killed Laius in a scuffle at a crossroads in the country—without ever discovering whom he had killed.

Things that are dark. All honor to Apollo
And to you, Creon, for acting as you have done
On the dead King's behalf. So I will take
My rightful place beside you as your ally,
Avenging Thebes and bowing to the god.
Not for a stranger will I dispel this taint,
But for my own sake, since the murderer,   140
Whoever he is, may strike at me as well.
Therefore in helping Laius I help myself.
Come, children, come! Rise from the altar steps,
And carry away those branches. Summon here
The people° of Cadmus. Tell them I mean to leave
Nothing undone. So with Apollo's aid
We may at last be saved—or meet destruction.   [*Exit* OEDIPUS.]
PRIEST. My children, let us go. The King has promised
The favor that we sought. And may Lord Phoebus
Come to us with his oracles, assuage   150
Our misery, and deliver us from death.
                [*Exeunt. Enter* CHORUS.]
CHORUS.
The god's great word,° in whose sweetness we ever rejoice,
        To our glorious city is drawing nigh,
Now, even now, from the gold of the Delphic shrine.
        What next decree will be thine,
Apollo, thou healer, to whom in our dread we cry?
        We are anguished, racked, and beset by fears!
What fate will be ours? One fashioned for us alone,
        Or one that in ancient time was known
        That returns once more with the circling years?   160
Child of our golden hope, O speak, thou immortal voice!

Divine Athene, daughter of Zeus, O hear!
        Hear thou, Artemis! Thee we hail,
Our guardian goddess° throned in the market place.
        Apollo, we ask thy grace.
Shine forth, all three, and the menace of death will fail.
        Answer our call! Shall we call in vain?
If ever ye came in the years that have gone before,

145. *people:* represented by the chorus (elderly Theban men of noble birth),
which comes into the orchestra at this cue.   152. *great word:* oracular response
requested by the plague-ridden Thebans.   164. *guardian goddess:* A statue of
Artemis was in the marketplace of Thebes.

Return, and save us from plague once more,
Rescue our city from fiery pain!   170
Be your threefold strength our shield. Draw near to us now, draw
    near!

Death is upon us. We bear a burden of bitter grief.
There is nothing can save us now, no device that our thought can
    frame.
    No blossom, no fruit, no harvest sheaf
    Springs from the blighted and barren earth.
Women cry out in travail and bring no children to birth;
    But swift as a bird, swift as the sweep of flame,
      Life after life takes sudden flight
To the western god,° to the last, dark shore of night.

Ruin has fallen on Thebes. Without number her children are
    dead;   180
Unmourned, unattended, unpitied, they lie polluting the ground.
    Gray-haired mothers and wives new-wed
    Wail at the altars everywhere,
With entreaty, with loud lament, with clamor filling the air.
    And songs of praise to Apollo, the healer, resound.
    Athene, thou knowest our desperate need.
    Lend us thy strength. Give heed to our prayer, give heed!

Fierce Ares° has fallen upon us. He comes unarrayed for war,
Yet he fills our ears with shrieking, he folds us in fiery death.
    Grant that he soon may turn in headlong flight from our land,   190
Swept to the western deep by the fair wind's favoring breath,
    Or swept to the savage sea that washes the Thracian° shore.
We few who escape the night are stricken down in the day.
    O Zeus, whose bolts of thunder are balanced within thy hand,
Hurl down thy lightning upon him! Father, be swift to slay!

Save us, light-bringing Phoebus! The shower of thine arrows
    let fly;
Loose them, triumphant and swift, from the golden string of thy
    bow!
    O goddess, his radiant sister, roaming the Lycian glade,
Come with the flash of thy fire! Artemis, conquer our foe!

179. western god: The next world was traditionally in the west.   *188. Ares:* here god of destruction; probably identified with the plague.   *192. Thracian:* Thrace is a Balkan territory (roughly what now is Bulgaria); represents distance and remoteness.

And thou, O wine-flushed god to whom the Bacchantes° cry,   200
With thy brilliant torch ablaze amid shouts of thy maenad train,
   With thy hair enwreathed with gold, O Bacchus, we beg thine
     aid
Against our destroyer Ares, the god whom the gods disdain!
          [*Enter* OEDIPUS.]
OEDIPUS. You have been praying. If you heed my words
   And seek the remedy for your own disease,
   The gods will hear your prayers, and you will find
   Relief and comfort. I myself know nothing
   About this story, nothing about the murder,
   So that unaided and without a clue
   I could not have tracked it down for any distance.   210
   And because I have only recently been received
   Among you as a citizen, to you all,
   And to all the rest, I make this proclamation:
   Whoever knows the man who killed King Laius,
   Let him declare his knowledge openly.
   If he himself is guilty, let him confess
   And go unpunished, except for banishment.
   Or if he knows the murderer was an alien,
   Let him by speaking earn his due reward,
   And thanks as well. But if he holds his tongue,   220
   Hoping to save himself or save a friend,
   Then let him hear what I, the King, decree
   For all who live in Thebes, the land I rule.
   No one shall give this murderer shelter. No one
   Shall speak to him. No one shall let him share
   In sacrifice or prayer or lustral rites.°
   The door of every house is barred against him.
   The god has shown me that he is polluted.
   So by this edict I ally myself
   With Phoebus and the slain. As for the slayer,   230
   Whether he had accomplices or not,
   This is my solemn prayer concerning him:
   May evil come of evil; may he live
   A wretched life and meet a wretched end.
   And as for me, if I should knowingly
   Admit him as a member of my household,

---

200. *Bacchantes:* female followers of the wine-god, Dionysus (Bacchus), who was closely associated with Thebes since his mother, Semele, was a daughter of the founder of Thebes, Cadmus. 226. *lustral rites:* sprinkling participants at a sacrifice with water.

May the same fate which I invoked for others
Fall upon me. Make my words good, I charge you,
For love of me, Apollo, and our country
Blasted by the displeasure of the gods.   240
You should not have left this guilt unpurified,
Even without an oracle to urge you,
When a man so noble, a man who was your King,
Had met his death. Rather, it was your duty
To seek the truth. But now, since it is I
Who hold the sovereignty that once was his,
I who have wed his wife, who would have been
Bound to him by the tie of having children
Born of one mother, if he had had a child
To be a blessing, if fate had not struck him down—   250
Since this is so, I intend to fight his battle
As though he were my father. I will leave
Nothing undone to find his murderer,
Avenging him and all his ancestors.
And I pray the gods that those who disobey
May suffer. May their fields bring forth no harvest,
Their wives no children; may the present plague,
Or one yet worse, consume them. But as for you,
All of you citizens who are loyal to me,
May Justice, our champion, and all the gods   260
Show you their favor in the days to come.
CHORUS. King Oedipus, I will speak to avoid your curse.
    I am no slayer, nor can I point him out.
    The question came to us from Phoebus Apollo;
    It is for him to tell us who is guilty.
OEDIPUS. Yes. But no man on earth is strong enough
    To force the gods to act against their will.
CHORUS. There is, I think, a second course to follow.
OEDIPUS. If there is yet a third, let me know that.
CHORUS. Tiresias, the prophet, has the clearest vision°   270
    Next to our Lord Apollo. He is the man
    Who can do most to help us in our search.
OEDIPUS. I have not forgotten. Creon suggested it,
    And I have summoned him, summoned him twice.
    I am astonished he is not here already.
CHORUS. The only rumors are old and half-forgotten.
OEDIPUS. What are they? I must find out all I can.

270. *clearest vision:* It is a frequent theme of Greek tragedy that the blind or possessed see clearest.

CHORUS. It is said the King was killed by travelers.

OEDIPUS. So I have heard, but there is no eye-witness.

CHORUS. If fear can touch them, they will reveal themselves   280
    Once they have heard so dreadful a curse as yours.

OEDIPUS. Murderers are not terrified by words.

CHORUS. But they can be convicted by the man
    Being brought here now, Tiresias. He alone
    Is godlike in his knowledge of the truth.

                    [*Enter* TIRESIAS, *led by a* BOY.]

OEDIPUS. You know all things in heaven and earth, Tiresias:
    Things you may speak of openly, and secrets
    Holy and not to be revealed. You know,
    Blind though you are, the plague that ruins Thebes.
    And you, great prophet, you alone can save us.   290
    Phoebus has sent an answer to our question,
    An answer that the messengers may have told you,
    Saying there was no cure for our condition
    Until we found the killers of King Laius
    And banished them or had them put to death.
    Therefore, Tiresias, do not begrudge your skill
    In the voice of birds or other prophecy,
    But save yourself, save me, save the whole city,
    Save everything that the pestilence defiles.
    We are at your mercy, and man's noblest task   300
    Is to use all his powers in helping others.

TIRESIAS. How dreadful a thing, how dreadful a thing is wisdom,
    When to be wise is useless! This I knew
    But I forgot, or else I would never have come.

OEDIPUS. What is the matter? Why are you so troubled?

TIRESIAS. Oedipus, let me go home. Then you will bear
    Your burden, and I mine, more easily.

OEDIPUS. Custom entitles us to hear your message.
    By being silent you harm your native land.

TIRESIAS. You do not know when, and when not to speak.   310
    Silence will save me from the same misfortune.

OEDIPUS. If you can be of help, then all of us
    Kneel and implore you not to turn away.

TIRESIAS. I refuse to pain you. I refuse to pain myself.
    It is useless to ask me. I will tell you nothing.

OEDIPUS. You utter scoundrel! You would enrage a stone!
    Is there no limit to your stubbornness?

TIRESIAS. You blame my anger and forget your own.

OEDIPUS. No one could help being angry when he heard

How you dishonor and ignore the state.   320
TIRESIAS. What is to come will come, though I keep silent.
OEDIPUS. If it must come, your duty is to speak.
TIRESIAS. I will say no more. Rage to your heart's content.
OEDIPUS. Rage? Yes, I will rage! I will spare you nothing.
  In the plot against King Laius, I have no doubt
  That you were an accomplice, yes almost
  The actual killer. If you had not been blind,
  I would have said that you alone were guilty.
TIRESIAS. Then listen to my command! Obey the edict
  That you yourself proclaimed and never speak,   330
  From this day on, to me or any Theban.
  You are the sinner who pollutes our land.
OEDIPUS. Have you no shame? How do you hope to escape
  The consequence of such an accusation?
TIRESIAS. I have escaped. My strength is the living truth.
OEDIPUS. This is no prophecy. Who taught you this?
TIRESIAS. You did. You forced me to speak against my will.
OEDIPUS. Repeat your slander. Let me learn it better.
TIRESIAS. Are you trying to tempt me into saying more?
  I have spoken already. Have you not understood?   340
OEDIPUS. No, not entirely. Give your speech again.
TIRESIAS. I say you are the killer, you yourself.
OEDIPUS. Twice the same insult! You will pay for it.
TIRESIAS. Shall I say more to make you still more angry?
OEDIPUS. Say what you want to. It will make no sense.
TIRESIAS. You are living in shame with those most dear to you,
  As yet in ignorance of your dreadful fate.
OEDIPUS. Do you suppose that you can always use
  Language like that and not be punished for it?
TIRESIAS. Yes, I am safe, if truth has any strength.   350
OEDIPUS. Truth can save anyone excepting you,
  You with no eyes, no hearing, and no brains!
TIRESIAS. Poor fool! You taunt me, but you soon will hear
  The self-same insults heaped upon your head.
OEDIPUS. You live in endless night. What can you do
  To me or anyone else who sees the day?
TIRESIAS. Nothing. I have no hand in your destruction.
  For that, Apollo needs no help from me.
OEDIPUS. Apollo! Is this your trick, or is it Creon's?
TIRESIAS. Creon is guiltless. The evil is in you.   360
OEDIPUS. How great is the envy roused by wealth, by kingship,
  By the subtle skill that triumphs over others

In life's hard struggle! Creon, who has been
For years my trusted friend, has stealthily
Crept in upon me anxious to seize my power,
The unsought gift the city freely gave me.
Anxious to overthrow me, he has bribed
This scheming mountebank, this fraud, this trickster,
Blind in his art and in everything but money!
Your art of prophecy! When have you shown it?   370
Not when the watchdog° of the gods was here,
Chanting her riddle. Why did you say nothing,
When you might have saved the city? Yet her puzzle
Could not be solved by the first passerby.
A prophet's skill was needed, and you proved
That you had no such skill, either in birds
Or any other means the gods have given.
But I came, I, the ignorant Oedipus,°
And silenced her. I had no birds to help me.
I used my brains. And it is I you now   380
Are trying to destroy in the hope of standing
Close beside Creon's throne. You will regret
This zeal of yours to purify the land,
You and your fellow-plotter. You seem old;
Otherwise you would pay for your presumption.

CHORUS. Sir, it appears to us that both of you
Have spoken in anger. Anger serves no purpose.
Rather we should consider in what way
We best can carry out the god's command.

TIRESIAS. King though you are, I have a right to answer   390
Equal to yours. In that I too am king.
I serve Apollo. I do not acknowledge
You as my lord or Creon as my patron.
You have seen fit to taunt me with my blindness.
Therefore I tell you this: you have your eyesight
And cannot see the sin of your existence,
Cannot see where you live or whom you live with,
Are ignorant of your parents, bring disgrace
Upon your kindred in the world below

---

371. *watchdog:* the Sphinx, which had been sent by the goddess Hera (wife of
Zeus) to haunt Thebes since it was the city of a rival, Semele, with whom Zeus
had slept. 378. *ignorant Oedipus:* There is a frequent play in the original on
the similarity of sound between the first part of Oedipus' name (Greek *Oid-*) and
the Greek verb *oida,* "I know."

And here on earth. And soon the double lash   400
Of your mother's and father's curse will drive you headlong
Out of the country, blinded, with your cries
Heard everywhere, echoed by every hill
In all Cithaeron.° Then you will have learned
The meaning of your marriage, learned in what harbor,
After so fair a voyage, you were shipwrecked.
And other horrors you could never dream of
Will teach you who you are, will drag you down
To the level of your children. Heap your insults
On Creon and my message if you choose to.   410
Still no one ever will endure the weight
Of greater misery than will fall on you.

OEDIPUS. Am I supposed to endure such talk as this,
    Such talk from him? Go, curse you, go! Be quick!

TIRESIAS. Except for your summons I would never have come.

OEDIPUS. And I would never have sent for you so soon
    If I had known you would prove to be a fool.

TIRESIAS. Yes. I have proved a fool—in your opinion,
    And yet your parents thought that I was wise.

OEDIPUS. What parents? Wait! Who was my father? Tell me!   420

TIRESIAS. Today will see your birth and your destruction.

OEDIPUS. You cannot speak unless you speak in riddles!

TIRESIAS. And yet how brilliant you are in solving them!

OEDIPUS. You sneer at me for what has made me great.

TIRESIAS. The same good fortune that has ruined you.

OEDIPUS. If I have saved the city, nothing else matters.

TIRESIAS. In that case I will go. Boy, take me home.

OEDIPUS. Yes, let him take you. Here, you are in the way.
    Once you are gone, you will give no further trouble.

TIRESIAS. I will not go before I have said my say,   430
    Indifferent to your black looks. You cannot harm me.
    And I say this: the man whom you have sought,
    Whom you have threatened, whom you have proclaimed
    The killer of King Laius—he is here.
    Now thought an alien, he shall prove to be
    A native Theban, to his deep dismay.
    Now he has eyesight, now his wealth is great;
    But he shall make his way to foreign soil
    Blinded, in beggary, groping with a stick.

404. *Cithaeron:* mountain range south of Thebes, on which King Laius ordered
the infant Oedipus to be abandoned.

In his own household he shall be shown to be 440
The father of his children—and their brother,
Son to the woman who bore him—and her husband,
The killer and the bedfellow of his father.
Go and consider this; and if you find
That I have been mistaken, you can say
That I have lost my skill in prophecy.

[*Exeunt* OEDIPUS *and* TIRESIAS.]

CHORUS.

What man is this the god from the Delphic rock denounces,
  Whose deeds are too shameful to tell, whose murderous hands
    are red?
Let his feet be swifter now than hooves of horses racing
  The storm-clouds overhead 450
For Zeus's son, Apollo, leaps in anger upon him,
  Armed with lightning to strike and slay;
And the terrible Fates, unflagging, relentless,
  Follow the track of their prey.

The words of the god have flashed from the peaks of snowy
  Parnassus,°
Commanding us all to seek this killer as yet unknown.
Deep in the tangled woods, through rocks and caves he is roam-
  ing
  Like a savage bull, alone.
On his lonely path he journeys, wretched, broken by sorrow,
  Seeking to flee from the fate he fears; 460
  But the voice from the center of earth° that doomed him
  Inescapably rings in his ears.

Dreadful, dreadful those words! We can neither approve nor
  deny them.
  Shaken, confounded with fears, we know not what to say.
Nothing is clear to us, nothing—what is to come tomorrow,
  Or what is upon us today.
If the prophet seeks revenge for the unsolved murder of Laius,
  Why is Oedipus charged with crime?
  Because some deep-rooted hate divides their royal houses?

455. *Parnassus:* here a mountain just north of Delphi, sacred to Apollo and the Muses.   461. *center of earth:* The temple of Apollo at Delphi was regarded as the center of the earth; a stone in it marked the spot where eagles flying simultaneously from the extreme east and extreme west of the earth had met.

The houses of Laius and Oedipus, son of the King of
    Corinth?°   470
There is none that we know of, now, or in ancient time.

From Zeus's eyes and Apollo's no human secret is hidden;
    But man has no test for truth, no measure his wit can devise.
Tiresias, indeed, excels in every art of his office,
    And yet we too may be wise.
Though Oedipus stands accused, until he is proven guilty
      We cannot blacken his name;
    For he showed his wisdom the day the wingéd maiden° faced
      him.
He triumphed in that ordeal, saved us, and won our affection.
We can never believe he stooped to an act of shame.   480
            [Enter CREON.]
CREON. Thebans, I come here outraged and indignant,
    For I have learned that Oedipus has accused me
    Of dreadful crimes. If, in the present crisis,
    He thinks that I have wronged him in any way,
    Wronged him in word or deed, then let my life
    Come to a speedy close. I cannot bear
    The burden of such scandal. The attack
    Ruins me utterly, if my friends, and you,
    And the whole city are to call me traitor.
CHORUS. Perhaps his words were only a burst of anger,   490
    And were not meant as a deliberate insult.
CREON. He *did* say that I plotted with Tiresias?
    And that the prophet lied at my suggestion?
CHORUS. Those were his words. I cannot guess his motive.
CREON. Were his eyes clear and steady? Was his mind
    Unclouded, when he brought this charge against me?
CHORUS. I cannot say. To see what princes do
    Is not our province. Here comes the King himself.
            [Enter OEDIPUS.]
OEDIPUS. So you are here! What brought you to my door?
    Impudence? Insolence? You, my murderer!   500
    You, the notorious stealer of my crown!
    Why did you hatch this plot? What kind of man,
    By heaven, what kind of man, could you have thought me?

---

470. *son . . . Corinth:* Like Oedipus, the chorus still believes that Oedipus is
the son of the man who raised him, King Polybus of Corinth; Oedipus had left
Corinth to avoid killing Polybus, since an oracle had also told him that he would
kill his own father.   478. *maiden:* Sphinx.

A coward or a fool? Did you suppose
I would not see your trickery take shape,
Or when I saw it, would not counter it?
How stupid you were to reach for royal power
Without a troop of followers or rich friends!
Only a mob and money win a kingdom.

CREON. Sir, let me speak. When you have heard my answer,　　　510
    You will have grounds on which to base your judgment.

OEDIPUS. I cannot follow all your clever talk.
    I only know that you are dangerous.

CREON. That is the issue. Let me explain that first.

OEDIPUS. Do not explain that you are true to me.

CREON. If you imagine that a blind self-will
    Is strength of character, you are mistaken.

OEDIPUS. As you are, if you strike at your own house,
    And then expect to escape all punishment.

CREON. Yes, you are right. That would be foolishness.　　　520
    But tell me, what have I done? How have I harmed you?

OEDIPUS. Did you, or did you not, urge me to summon
    Tiresias, that revered, that holy prophet?

CREON. Yes. And I still think my advice was good.

OEDIPUS. Then answer this: how long ago was Laius—

CREON. Laius! Why how am I concerned with him?

OEDIPUS. How many years ago was Laius murdered?

CREON. So many they cannot easily be counted.

OEDIPUS. And was Tiresias just as cunning then?

CREON. As wise and honored as he is today.　　　530

OEDIPUS. At that time did he ever mention me?

CREON. Not in my hearing. I am sure of that.

OEDIPUS. And the murderer—a thorough search was made?

CREON. Yes, certainly, but we discovered nothing.

OEDIPUS. Then why did the man of wisdom hold his tongue?

CREON. I cannot say. Guessing is not my habit.

OEDIPUS. One thing at least you need not guess about.

CREON. What is it? If I know it, I will tell you.

OEDIPUS. Tiresias would not have said I murdered Laius,
    If you two had not put your heads together.　　　540

CREON. You best know what he said. But now I claim
    The right to take my turn in asking questions.

OEDIPUS. Very well, ask. You never can find me guilty.

CREON. Then answer this: my sister is your wife?

OEDIPUS. I cannot deny that fact. She is my wife.

CREON. And in your rule she has an equal share?

OEDIPUS. She has no wish that goes unsatisfied.
CREON. And as the third I stand beside you both?
OEDIPUS. True. That position proves your treachery.
CREON. No. You would see, if you thought the matter through   550
    As I have done. Consider. Who would choose
    Kingship and all the terrors that go with it,
    If, with the same power, he could sleep in peace?
    I have no longing for a royal title
    Rather than royal freedom. No, not I,
    Nor any moderate man. Now I fear nothing.
    Every request I make of you is granted,
    And yet as king I should have many duties
    That went against the grain. Then how could rule
    Be sweeter than untroubled influence?   560
    I have not lost my mind. I want no honors
    Except the ones that bring me solid good.
    Now all men welcome me and wish me joy.
    Now all your suitors ask to speak with me,
    Knowing they cannot otherwise succeed.
    Why should I throw away a life like this
    For a king's life? No one is treacherous
    Who knows his own best interests. To conspire
    With other men, or to be false myself,
    Is not my nature. Put me to the test.   570
    First, go to Delphi. Ask if I told the truth
    About the oracle. Then if you find
    I have had dealings with Tiresias, kill me.
    My voice will echo yours in passing sentence.
    But base your verdict upon something more
    Than mere suspicion. Great injustice comes
    From random judgments that bad men are good
    And good men bad. To throw away a friend
    Is, in effect, to throw away your life,
    The prize you treasure most. All this, in time,   580
    Will become clear to you, for time alone
    Proves a man's honesty, but wickedness
    Can be discovered in a single day.
CHORUS. Sir, that is good advice, if one is prudent.
    Hasty decisions always lead to danger.
OEDIPUS. When a conspiracy is quick in forming,
    I must move quickly to retaliate.
    If I sat still and let my enemy act,
    I would lose everything that he would gain.

CREON. So then, my banishment is what you want?   590
OEDIPUS. No, not your banishment. Your execution.
CREON. I think you are mad.
OEDIPUS.   I can protect myself.
CREON. You should protect me also.
OEDIPUS.   You? A traitor?
CREON. Suppose you are wrong?
OEDIPUS.   I am the King. I rule.
CREON. Not if you rule unjustly.
OEDIPUS.   Thebes! Hear that!
CREON. Thebes is my city too, as well as yours.
CHORUS. No more, no more, sirs! Here is Queen Jocasta.
      She comes in time to help make peace between you.
                        [*Enter* JOCASTA.]
JOCASTA. Oedipus! Creon! How can you be so foolish?
      What! Quarrel now about a private matter   600
      When the land is dying? You should be ashamed.
      Come, Oedipus, come in. Creon, go home.
      You make a trivial problem too important.
CREON. Sister, your husband has made dreadful threats.
      He claims the right to have me put to death
      Or have me exiled. He need only choose.
OEDIPUS. Yes. I have caught him at his treachery,
      Plotting against the person of the King.
CREON. If I am guilty, may it be my fate
      To live in misery and to die accursed.   610
JOCASTA. Believe him, Oedipus, believe him, spare him—
      I beg you by the gods—for his oath's sake,
      For my sake, for the sake of all men here.
CHORUS. Consent, O King. Be gracious. Hear us, we beg you.
OEDIPUS. What shall I hear? To what shall I consent?
CHORUS. Respect the evidence of Creon's wisdom,
      Respect the oath of innocence he has taken.
OEDIPUS. You know that this means?
CHORUS.   Yes.
OEDIPUS.   Tell me again what you ask
                                   for.
CHORUS. To yield, to relent.
      He is your friend and swears he is not guilty.   620
         Do not act in haste, convicting him out of hand.
OEDIPUS. When you ask for this, you ask for my destruction;
      You sentence me to death or to banishment.
         Be sure that you understand.

CHORUS. No, by Apollo, no!
    If such a thought has ever crossed my mind,
      Then may I never find
    A friend to love me or a god to save;
    And may dark doom pursue me to the grave.
      My country perishes, and now new woe   630
    Springs from your quarrel, one affliction more
    Has come upon us, and my heart is sore.
OEDIPUS. Let him go free, even though that destroys me.
    I shall be killed, or exiled in disgrace.
    Not his appeal but yours aroused my pity.
    I shall hate him always, no matter where he is.
CREON. You go beyond all bounds when you are angry,
    And are sullen when you yield. Natures like yours
    Inflict their heaviest torments on themselves.
OEDIPUS. Go! Go! Leave me in peace!
CREON.   Yes, I will go.   640
    You have not understood, but in the sight
    Of all these men here I am innocent.   [*Exit* CREON.]
CHORUS. Take the King with you, Madam, to the palace.
JOCASTA. When I have learned what happened, we will go.
CHORUS. The King was filled with fear and blind suspicion.
    Creon resented what he thought injustice.
JOCASTA. Both were at fault?
CHORUS.   Both.
JOCASTA.   Why was the King suspicious?
CHORUS. Do not seek to know.
    We have said enough. In a time of pain and trouble
    Inquire no further. Let the matter rest.   650
OEDIPUS. Your well meant pleading turned me from my purpose,
    And now you come to this. You fall so low
      As to think silence best.
CHORUS. I say again, O King,
    No one except a madman or a fool
      Would throw aside your rule.
    For you delivered us; your single hand
        Lifted the load from our belovéd land.
    When we were mad with grief and suffering,
        In our extremity you found a way   660
        To save the city, as you will today.
JOCASTA. But tell *me,* Oedipus, tell *me,* I beg you,
    Why you were so unyielding in your anger.
OEDIPUS. I will, Jocasta for I honor you

More than I do the elders. It was Creon's plotting.
JOCASTA. What do you mean? What was your accusation?
OEDIPUS. He says I am the murderer of King Laius.
JOCASTA. Did he speak from first-hand knowledge or from hearsay?
OEDIPUS. He did not speak at all. His lips are pure.
    He bribed Tiresias, and that scoundrel spoke.   670
JOCASTA. Then you can rid your mind of any fear
    That you are guilty. Listen to me. No mortal
    Shares in the gods' foreknowledge. I can give you
    Clear proof of that. There came once to King Laius
    An oracle—I will not say from Phoebus,
    But from his priest—saying it was his fate
    That he should be struck down by his own child,
    His child and mine. But Laius, as we know,
    Was killed by foreign robbers at a place
    Where three roads came together. As for the child,   680
    When it was only three days old, its father
    Pierced both its ankles, pinned its feet together,
    And then gave orders that it be abandoned
    On a wild mountainside. So in this case
    Phoebus did not fulfill his oracle. The child
    Was not its father's murderer, and Laius
    Was not the victim of the fate he feared,
    Death at this son's hands, although just that fate
    Was what the seer predicted. Pay no heed
    To prophecies. Whatever may be needful   690
    The god himself can show us easily.
OEDIPUS. What have you said, Jocasta? What have you said?
    The past comes back to me. How terrible!
JOCASTA. Why do you start so? What has happened to you?
OEDIPUS. It seemed to me—I thought you said that Laius
    Was struck down where three roads came together.
JOCASTA. I did. That was the story, and still is.
OEDIPUS. Where was it that this murder was committed?
JOCASTA. In Phocis, where the road from Thebes divides,
    Meeting the roads from Daulia and Delphi.   700
OEDIPUS. Is this my fate? Is this what the gods decreed?
JOCASTA. What have I said that has so shaken you?
OEDIPUS. Do not ask me yet. Tell me about King Laius.
    What did he look like? Was he young or old?
JOCASTA. His build was not unlike yours. He was tall.
    His hair was just beginning to turn gray.
OEDIPUS. I cannot bear the thought that I called down

A curse on my own head unknowingly.
JOCASTA. What is it, Oedipus? You terrify me!
OEDIPUS. I dread to think Tiresias had clear eyesight;   710
     But tell me one thing more, and I will know.
JOCASTA. And I too shrink, yet I will answer you.
OEDIPUS. How did he travel? With a few men only,
     Or with his guards and servants, like a prince?
JOCASTA. There were five of them in all, with one a herald.
     They had one carriage in which King Laius rode.
OEDIPUS. It is too clear, too clear! Who told you this?
JOCASTA. The only servant who escaped alive.
OEDIPUS. And is he still here now, still in the palace?
JOCASTA. No. When he came home and found Laius dead   720
     And you the reigning king, he pleaded with me
     To send him where the sheep were pasturing,
     As far as possible away from Thebes.
     And so I sent him. He was a worthy fellow
     And, if a slave can, deserved a greater favor.
OEDIPUS. I hope it is possible to get him quickly.
JOCASTA. Yes, that is easy. Why do you want to see him?
OEDIPUS. Because I am afraid, deadly afraid
     That I have spoken more than I should have done.
JOCASTA. He shall come. But Oedipus, have I no right   730
     To learn what weighs so heavily on your heart?
OEDIPUS. You shall learn everything, now that my fears
     Have grown so great, for who is dearer to me
     Than you, Jocasta? Whom should I speak to sooner,
     When I am in such straits? King Polybus
     Of Corinth was my father. Meropé,
     A Dorian, was my mother. I myself
     Was foremost among all the citizens,
     Till something happened, strange, but hardly worth
     My feeling such resentment. As we sat   740
     One day at dinner, a man who had drunk too much
     Insulted me by saying I was not
     My father's son. In spite of being angry,
     I managed to control myself. Next day
     I asked my parents, who were both indignant
     That he had leveled such a charge against me.
     This was a satisfaction, yet the thing
     Still rankled, for the rumor grew widespread.
     At last I went to Delphi secretly.
     Apollo gave no answer to my question   750

But sent me off, anguished and terrified,
With fearful prophecies that I was fated
To be my mother's husband, to bring forth
Children whom men could not endure to see,
And to take my father's life. When I heard this
I turned and fled, hoping to find at length
Some place where I would know of Corinth only
As a far distant land beneath the stars,
Some place where I would never have to see
The infamies of this oracle fulfilled.   760
And as I went on, I approached the spot
At which you tell me Laius met his end.
Now this, Jocasta, is the absolute truth.
When I had come to where the three roads fork,
A herald met me, walking before a carriage,
Drawn by two colts, in which a man was seated,
Just as you said. The old man and the herald
Ordered me off the road with threatening gestures.
Then as the driver pushed me to one side,
I struck him angrily. And seeing this,   770
The old man, as I drew abreast, leaned out
And brought his driver's two-pronged goad down hard
Upon my head. He paid a heavy price
For doing that. With one blow of my staff
I knocked him headlong from his chariot
Flat on his back. Then every man of them
I killed. Now if the blood of Laius flowed
In that old stranger's veins, what mortal man
Could be more wretched, more accursed than I?
I whom no citizen or foreigner   780
May entertain or shelter, I to whom
No one may speak, I, I who must be driven
From every door. No other man has cursed me,
I have brought down this curse upon myself.
The hands that killed him now pollute his bed!
Am I not vile, foul, utterly unclean?
For I must fly and never see again
My people or set foot in my own land,
Or else become the husband of my mother
And put to death my father Polybus,   790
To whom I owe my life and my upbringing.
Men would be right in thinking that such things
Have been inflicted by some cruel fate.

May the gods' high and holy majesty
Forbid that I should see that day. No! No!
Rather than be dishonored by a doom
So dreadful may I vanish from the earth.
CHORUS. Sir, these are terrible things, but there is hope
    Until you have heard what the one witness says.
OEDIPUS. That is the one remaining hope I have,   800
    To wait for the arrival of the shepherd.
JOCASTA. And when he *has* arrived, what can he do?
OEDIPUS. He can do this. If his account agrees
    With yours, I stand acquitted of this crime.
JOCASTA. Was what I said of any consequence?
OEDIPUS. You said his story was that robbers killed
    King Laius. If he speaks of the same number,
    Then I am not the murderer. One man
    Cannot be several men. But if he says
    One traveler, single-handed, did the deed,   810
    Beyond all doubt the evidence points to me.
JOCASTA. I am quite certain that was what he said.
    He cannot change now, for the whole of Thebes
    Heard it, not I alone. In any case,
    Even supposing that his story *should*
    Be somewhat different, he can never make
    Laius's death fulfill the oracle.
    Phoebus said plainly Laius was to die
    At my son's hands. However, that poor child
    Certainly did not kill him, for it died   820
    Before its father. I would not waste my time
    In giving any thought to prophecy.
OEDIPUS. Yes, you are right. And yet have someone sent
    To bring the shepherd here. Make sure of this.
JOCASTA. I will, at once. Come, Oedipus, come in.
    I will do nothing that you disapprove of.
                 [*Exeunt* OEDIPUS *and* JOCASTA.]
CHORUS.
    May piety and reverence mark my actions;
        May every thought be pure through all my days.
    May those great laws whose dwelling is in heaven
        Approve my conduct with their crown of praise: 830
    Offspring of skies that overarch Olympus,
        Laws from the loins of no mere mortal sprung,
    Unslumbering, unfailing, unforgetting,
        Filled with a godhead that is ever young.

Pride° breeds the tyrant.° Insolent presumption,°
   Big with delusive wealth and false renown,
Once it has mounted to the highest rampart
   Is headlong hurled in utter ruin down.
But pour out all thy blessings, Lord Apollo,
   Thou who alone has made and kept us great,   840
On all whose sole ambition is unselfish,
   Who spend themselves in service to the state.

Let that man be accurséd who is proud,
In act unscrupulous, in thinking base,
   Whose knees in reverence have never bowed,
In whose hard heart justice can find no place,
   Whose hands profane life's holiest mysteries,
How can he hope to shield himself for long
   From the gods' arrows that will pierce him through?
If evil triumphs in such ways as these,   850
   Why should we seek, in choric dance and song,
To give the gods the praise that is their due?

I cannot go in full faith as of old,
To sacred Delphi or Olympian vale,
   Unless men see that what has been foretold
Has come to pass, that omens never fail.
   All-ruling Zeus, if thou art King indeed,
Put forth thy majesty, make good thy word,
   Faith in these fading oracles restore!
To priest and prophet men pay little heed;   860
   Hymns to Apollo are no longer heard;
And all religion soon will be no more.°

[*Enter* JOCASTA.]
JOCASTA. Elders of Thebes, I thought that I should visit
   The altars of the gods to offer up
   These wreaths I carry and these gifts of incense.
   The King is overanxious, overtroubled.
   He is no longer calm enough to judge
   The present by the lessons of the past,

---

835. *Pride* and *Insolent presumption*: Greek, "hubris." *tyrant*: Greek, *tyrannos*,
title of Oedipus; used (1) generally of any despotic or monarchical ruler, including
gods, and (2) specifically of acquired kingship as opposed to hereditary kingship.
860–62. *To . . . more*: contemporary allusion to the popular Sophistic enlightenment, which Sophocles seems to have thought of as irreligious. It should be remembered that Sophocles held priestly office, in addition to his various political
ones.

But trembles before anyone who brings
An evil prophecy. I cannot help him.   870
Therefore, since thou art nearest, bright Apollo,
I bring these offerings to thee. O, hear me!
Deliver us from this defiling curse.
His fear infects us all, as if we were
Sailors who saw their pilot terrified.

[*Enter* MESSENGER.]

MESSENGER. Sirs, I have come to find King Oedipus.
    Where is his palace, can you tell me that?
    Or better yet, where is the King himself?
CHORUS. Stranger, the King is there, within his palace.
    This is the Queen, the mother of his children.   880
MESSENGER. May all the gods be good to you and yours!
    Madam, you are a lady richly blessed.
JOCASTA. And may the gods requite your courtesy.
    But what request or message do you bring us?
MESSENGER. Good tidings for your husband and your household.
JOCASTA. What is your news? What country do you come from?
MESSENGER. From Corinth. And the news I bring will surely
    Give you great pleasure—and perhaps some pain.
JOCASTA. What message can be good and bad at once?
MESSENGER. The citizens of Corinth, it is said,   890
    Have chosen Oedipus to be their King.
JOCASTA. What do you mean? Their King is Polybus.
MESSENGER. No, madam. Polybus is dead and buried.
JOCASTA. What! Dead! The father of King Oedipus?
MESSENGER. If I speak falsely, let me die myself.
JOCASTA [*to* ATTENDANT]. Go find the King and tell him this. Be quick!
    What does an oracle amount to now?
    This is the man whom Oedipus all these years
    Has feared and shunned to keep from killing him,
    And now we find he dies a natural death!   900

[*Enter* OEDIPUS.]

OEDIPUS. My dear Jocasta, why have you sent for me?
JOCASTA. Listen to this man's message, and then tell me
    What faith you have in sacred oracles.
OEDIPUS. Where does he come from? What has he to say?
JOCASTA. He comes from Corinth and has this to say:
    The King, your father, Polybus is dead.
OEDIPUS [*to* MESSENGER]. My father! Tell me that again yourself.
MESSENGER. I will say first what you first want to know.
    You may be certain he is dead and gone.

OEDIPUS. How did he die? By violence or sickness?   910
MESSENGER. The scales of life tip easily for the old.
OEDIPUS. That is to say he died of some disease.
MESSENGER. Yes, of disease, and merely of old age.
OEDIPUS. Hear that, Jocasta! Why should anyone
    Give heed to oracles from the Pythian shrine,
    Or to the birds that shriek above our heads? °
    They prophesied that I must kill my father.
    But he is dead; the earth has covered him.
    And I am here, I who have never raised
    My hand against him—unless he died of grief,   920
    Longing to see me. Then I might be said
    To have caused his death. But as they stand, at least,
    The oracles have been swept away like rubbish.
    They are with Polybus in Hades, dead.
JOCASTA. Long ago, Oedipus, I told you that.
OEDIPUS. You did, but I was blinded by my terror.
JOCASTA. Now you need take these things to heart no longer.
OEDIPUS. But there is still my mother's bed to fear.
JOCASTA. Why should you be afraid? Chance rules our lives,
    And no one can foresee the future, no one.   930
    We live best when we live without a purpose
    From one day to the next. Forget your fear
    Of marrying your mother. That has happened
    To many men before this in their dreams.
    We find existence most endurable
    When such things are neglected and forgotten.
OEDIPUS. That would be true, Jocasta, if my mother
    Were not alive; but now your eloquence
    Is not enough to give me reassurance.
JOCASTA. And yet your father's death is a great comfort.   940
OEDIPUS. Yes, but I cannot rest while she is living.
MESSENGER. Sir, will you tell me who it is you fear?
OEDIPUS. Queen Meropé, the wife of Polybus.
MESSENGER. What is so terrible about the Queen?
OEDIPUS. A dreadful prophecy the gods have sent us.
MESSENGER. Are you forbidden to speak of it, or not?
OEDIPUS. It may be told. The Lord Apollo said
    That I was doomed to marry my own mother,
    And shed my father's blood with my own hands.
    And so for years I have stayed away from Corinth,   950

916. *birds . . . heads:* Divination was often based on observation of birds in flight.

My native land—a fortunate thing for me,
Though it is very sweet to see one's parents.
MESSENGER. Was that the reason you have lived in exile?
OEDIPUS. Yes, for I feared my mother and my father.
MESSENGER. Then since my journey was to wish you well,
    Let me release you from your fear at once.
OEDIPUS. That would deserve my deepest gratitude.
MESSENGER. Sir, I *did* come here with the hope of earning
    Some recompense when you had gotten home.
OEDIPUS. No. I will never again go near my home.   960
MESSENGER. O son, son! You know nothing. That is clear—
OEDIPUS. What do you mean, old friend? Tell me, I beg you.
MESSENGER. If that is why you dare not come to Corinth.
OEDIPUS. I fear Apollo's word would be fulfilled.
MESSENGER. That you would be polluted through your parents?
OEDIPUS. Yes, yes! My life is haunted by that horror.
MESSENGER. You have no reason to be horrified.
OEDIPUS. I have no reason! Why? They are my parents.
MESSENGER. No. You are not the son of Polybus.
OEDIPUS. What did you say? Polybus not my father?   970
MESSENGER. He was as much your father as I am.
OEDIPUS. How can that be—my father like a stranger?
MESSENGER. But he was *not* your father, nor am I.
OEDIPUS. If that is so, why was I called his son?
MESSENGER. Because he took you as a gift, from me.
OEDIPUS. Yet even so, he loved me like a father?
MESSENGER. Yes, for he had no children of his own.
OEDIPUS. And when you gave me, had you bought or found me?
MESSENGER. I found you in the glens of Mount Cithaeron.
OEDIPUS. What could have brought you to a place like that?   980
MESSENGER. The flocks of sheep that I was tending there.
OEDIPUS. You went from place to place, hunting for work?
MESSENGER. I did, my son. And yet I saved your life.
OEDIPUS. How? Was I suffering when you took me up?
MESSENGER. Your ankles are the proof of what you suffered.
OEDIPUS. That misery! Why do you speak of that?
MESSENGER. Your feet were pinned together, and I freed them.
OEDIPUS. Yes. From my cradle I have borne those scars.
MESSENGER. They are the reason for your present name.°
OEDIPUS. Who did it? Speak! My mother, or my father?   990
MESSENGER. Only the man who gave you to me knows.

989. *name:* "Oedipus" is a compound of the stem *oid-,* "swell," and the word *pus,*
"foot."

OEDIPUS. Then you yourself did not discover me.

MESSENGER. No. A man put you in my arms, some shepherd.

OEDIPUS. Do you know who he was? Can you describe him?

MESSENGER. He was, I think, one of the slaves of Laius.

OEDIPUS. The Laius who was once the King of Thebes?

MESSENGER. Yes, that is right. King Laius was his master.

OEDIPUS. How could I see him? Is he still alive?

MESSENGER. One of his fellow Thebans would know that.

OEDIPUS. Does anyone here know who this shepherd is?   1000
  Has anyone ever seen him in the city
  Or in the fields? Tell me. Now is the time
  To solve this mystery once and for all.

CHORUS. Sir, I believe the shepherd whom he means
  Is the same man you have already sent for.
  The Queen, perhaps, knows most about the matter.

OEDIPUS. Do you, Jocasta? You know the man we summoned.
  Is he the man this messenger spoke about?

JOCASTA. Why do you care? What difference can it make?
  To ask is a waste of time, a waste of time!   1010

OEDIPUS. I cannot let these clues slip from my hands.
  I must track down the secret of my birth.

JOCASTA. Oedipus, Oedipus! By all the gods,
  If you set any value on your life,
  Give up this search! I have endured enough.

OEDIPUS. Do not be frightened. Even if my mother
  Should prove to be a slave, and born of slaves,
  This would not touch the honor of your name.

JOCASTA. Listen, I beg you! Listen! Do not do this!

OEDIPUS. I cannot fail to bring the truth to light.   1020

JOCASTA. I know my way is best for you, I know it!

OEDIPUS. I know your best way is unbearable.

JOCASTA. May you be saved from learning who you are!

OEDIPUS. Go, someone. Bring the shepherd. As for her,
  Let her take comfort in her noble birth.

JOCASTA. You are lost! Lost! That is all I can call you now!
  That is all I will ever call you, ever again! [*Exit* JOCASTA.]

CHORUS. What wild grief, sir, has driven the Queen away?
  Evil, I fear, will follow from her silence,
  A storm of sorrow that will break upon us.   1030

OEDIPUS. Then let it break upon us. I must learn
  My parentage, whatever it may be.
  The Queen is proud, far prouder than most women,
  And feels herself dishonored by my baseness.

But I shall not be shamed. I hold myself
The child of Fortune, giver of all good.
She brought me forth. And as I lived my life,
The months, my brothers, watched the ebb and flow
Of my well-being. Never could I prove
False to a lineage like that, or fail   1040
To bring to light the secret of my birth.

CHORUS. May Phoebus grant that I prove a true prophet!
    My heart foreknows what the future will bring:
    At tomorrow's full moon we shall gather, in chorus
      To hail Cithaeron, to dance and sing
    In praise of the mountain by Oedipus honored,
      Theban nurse of our Theban King.

    What long-lived nymph was the mother who bore you?
      What god whom the joys of the hills invite
    Was the god who begot you? Pan? or Apollo?   1050
      Or Hermes, Lord of Cyléné's° height?
    Or on Helicon's° slope did an oread° place you
      In Bacchus's arms for his new delight?

OEDIPUS. Elders, I think I see the shepherd coming
Whom we have sent for. Since I never met him,
I am not sure, yet he seems old enough,
And my own slaves are the men bringing him.
But you, perhaps, know more of this than I,
If any of you have seen the man before.

CHORUS. Yes, it is he. I know him, the King's shepherd,   1060
As true a slave as Laius ever had.

               [*Enter* SHEPHERD.]

OEDIPUS. I start with you, Corinthian. Is this man
The one you spoke of?

MESSENGER.   Sir, he stands before you.

OEDIPUS. Now you, old man. Come, look me in the face.
Answer my questions. You were the slave of Laius?

SHEPHERD. Yes, but not bought. I grew up in his household.

OEDIPUS. What was the work that you were given to do?

SHEPHERD. Sheep-herding. I have always been a shepherd.

OEDIPUS. Where was it that you took your sheep to pasture?

SHEPHERD. On Mount Cithaeron, or the fields near by.   1070

1051. *Cyléné* (sometimes *Cyllene*): mountain of Arcadia (central plateau of the
Peloponnesus) sacred to Hermes, who was said to have been born in a cave there.
1052. *Helicon:* mountain range in central Greece (a few miles roughly west of
Thebes) sacred to the Muses. *oread:* mountain nymph.

OEDIPUS. Do you remember seeing this man there?
SHEPHERD. What was he doing? What man do you mean?
OEDIPUS. That man beside you. Have you ever met him?
SHEPHERD. No, I think not. I cannot recollect him.
MESSENGER. Sir, I am not surprised, but I am sure
    That I can make the past come back to him.
    He cannot have forgotten the long summers
    We grazed our sheep together by Cithaeron,
    He with two flocks, and I with one—three years,
    From spring to autumn. Then, for the winter months,   1080
    I used to drive my sheep to their own fold,
    And he drove his back to the fold of Laius.
    Is that right? Did it happen as I said?
SHEPHERD. Yes, you are right, but it was long ago.
MESSENGER. Well then, do you remember you once gave me
    An infant boy to bring up as my own?
SHEPHERD. What do you mean? Why do you ask me that?
MESSENGER. Because the child you gave me stands before you.
SHEPHERD. Will you be quiet? Curse you! Will you be quiet?
OEDIPUS [to SHEPHERD]. You there! You have no reason to be angry.   1090
    You are far more to blame in this than he.
SHEPHERD. What have I done, my Lord? What have I done?
OEDIPUS. You have not answered. He asked about the boy.
SHEPHERD. Sir, he knows nothing, nothing at all about it.
OEDIPUS. And you say nothing. We must make you speak.
SHEPHERD. My Lord, I am an old man! Do not hurt me!
OEDIPUS [to GUARDS]. One of you tie his hands behind his back.
SHEPHERD. Why do you want to know these fearful things?
OEDIPUS. Did you, or did you not, give him that child?
SHEPHERD. I did. I wish I had died instead.   1100
OEDIPUS. You will die now, unless you tell the truth.
SHEPHERD. And if I speak, I will be worse than dead.
OEDIPUS. You seem to be determined to delay.
SHEPHERD. No. No! I told you that I had the child.
OEDIPUS. Where did it come from? Was it yours or not?
SHEPHERD. No, it was not mine. Someone gave it to me.
OEDIPUS. Some citizen of Thebes? Who was it? Who?
SHEPHERD. Oh! Do not ask me that! Not that, my Lord!
OEDIPUS. If I must ask once more, you are a dead man.
SHEPHERD. The child came from the household of King Laius.   1110
OEDIPUS. Was it a slave's child? Or of royal blood?
SHEPHERD. I stand on the very brink of speaking horrors.
OEDIPUS. And I of hearing horrors—but I must.

SHEPHERD. Then hear. The child was said to be the King's.
    You can best learn about this from the Queen.
OEDIPUS. The Queen! She gave it to you?
SHEPHERD.   Yes, my Lord.
OEDIPUS. Why did she do that?
SHEPHERD.   So that I should kill it.
OEDIPUS. Her own child?
SHEPHERD.   Yes, she feared the oracles.
OEDIPUS. What oracles?
SHEPHERD.   That it must kill its father.
OEDIPUS. Then why did you give it up to this old man?   1120
SHEPHERD. I pitied the poor child. I thought the man
    Would take it with him back to his own country.
    He saved its life only to have it come
    At last to this. If you should be the man
    He says you are, you were born miserable.
OEDIPUS. All true! All, all made clear! Let me no longer
    Look on the light of day. I am known now
    For what I am—I, cursed in being born,
    Cursed in my marriage, cursed in the blood I shed.
                                   [*Exit* OEDIPUS.]

CHORUS.
    Men are of little worth. Their brief lives last   1130
        A single day.
    They cannot hold elusive pleasure fast;
    It melts away.
    All laurels wither; all illusions fade;
    Hopes have been phantoms, shade on air-built shade,
        Since time began.
    Your fate, O King, your fate makes manifest
    Life's wretchedness. We can call no one blessed,
        No, not one man.

    Victorious, unerring, to their mark   1140
        Your arrows flew.
    The Sphinx with her curved claws, her riddle dark,
        Your wisdom slew.
    By this encounter you preserved us all,
    Guarding the land from death's approach, our tall,
        Unshaken tower.
    From that time, Oedipus, we held you dear,
    Great King of our great Thebes, without a peer
        In place and power.

But now what sadder story could be told?   1150
   A life of triumph utterly undone!
What fate could be more grievous to behold?
    Father and son
Both found a sheltering port, a place of rest,
    On the same breast.
Father and son both harvested the yield
    Of the same bounteous field.
How could that earth endure such dreadful wrong
    And hold its peace so long?

All-seeing time condemned your marriage lot;   1160
   In ways you least expected bared its shame—
Union wherein begetter and begot
    Were both the same.
This loud lament these tears that well and flow,
    This bitter woe
Are for the day you rescued us, O King,
    From our great suffering;
For the new life and happiness you gave
    You drag down to the grave.

           [*Enter* SECOND MESSENGER.]
SECOND MESSENGER. Most honored elders, princes of the land,   1170
   If you are true-born Thebans and still love
   The house of Labdacus,° then what a burden
   Of sorrow you must bear, what fearful things
   You must now hear and see! There is no river—
   No, not the stream of Ister° or of Phasis°—
   That could wash clean this house from the pollution
   It hides within it or will soon bring forth:
   Horrible deeds not done in ignorance,
   But done deliberately. The cruelest evils
   Are those that we embrace with open eyes.   1180
CHORUS. Those we already know of are enough
   To claim our tears. What more have you to tell?
SECOND MESSENGER. It may be briefly told. The Queen is dead.
CHORUS. Poor woman! oh, poor woman! How? What happened?
SECOND MESSENGER. She killed herself. You have been spared the
       worst,
   Not being witnesses. Yet you shall learn
   What her fate was, so far as I remember.

1172. *Labdacus:* father of Laius. 1175. *Ister:* Lower Danube. *Phasis:* a large
river of Colchis, a country at the eastern extreme of the Black Sea.

When she came in, almost beside herself,
Clutching her hair with both her hands, she rushed
Straight to her bedroom and slammed shut the doors   1190
Behind her, screaming the name of Laius—
Laius long dead, but not her memory
Of their own child, the son who killed his father,
The son by whom his mother had more children.°
She cursed the bed in which she had conceived
Husband by husband, children by her child,
A dreadful double bond. Beyond this much
I do not know the manner of her death,
For with a great cry Oedipus burst in,
Preventing us from following her fate   1200
To its dark end. On him our gaze was fixed,
As in a frenzy he ran to and fro,
Calling: "Give me a sword! Give me a sword!
Where is that wife who is no wife, that mother,
That soil where I was sower and was sown?"
And as he raved, those of us there did nothing,
Some more than mortal power directed him.
With a wild shriek, as though he had some sign,
He hurled himself against the double doors,
Forcing the bars out of their loosened sockets,   1210
And broke into his room. There was the Queen,
Hanged in a noose, still swinging back and forth.
When he saw this, the King cried out in anguish,
Untied the knotted cord in which she swung,
And laid the wretched woman on the ground.
What happened then was terrible to see.
He tore the golden brooches from her robe,
Lifted them up as high as he could reach,
And drove them with all his strength into his eyes,
Shrieking, "No more, no more shall my eyes see   1220
The horrors of my life—what I have done,
What I have suffered. They have looked too long
On those whom they ought never to have seen.°
They never knew those whom I longed to see.°
Blind, blind! Let them be blind!" With these wild words

1194. children: Oedipus and Jocasta had two sons (Eteocles and Polynices) and two daughters (Antigone and Ismene). 1222–23. *They . . . seen:* a reference to his four children by his mother-wife Jocasta. 1224. *They . . . see:* a reference to his real parents, whom he had long sought but whom his eyes never recognized when he finally did see them.

He stabbed and stabbed his eyes. At every blow,
The dark blood dyed his beard, not sluggish drops,
But a great torrent like a shower of hail.
A twofold punishment of twofold sin
Broke on the heads of husband and of wife.   1230
Their happiness was once true happiness,
But now disgrace has come upon them, death,
Sorrow, and ruin, every earthly ill
That can be named. Not one have they escaped.

CHORUS. Is he still suffering? Has he found relief?

SECOND MESSENGER. He calls for someone to unbar the doors
And show him to all Thebes, his father's killer,
His mother's—no, I cannot say the word;
It is unholy, horrible. He intends
To leave the country, for his staying here
Would bring down his own curse upon his house.   1240
He has no guide and no strength of his own.
His pain is unendurable. This too
You will see. They are drawing back the bars.
The sight is loathsome and yet pitiful.

> [*Enter* OEDIPUS.]

CHORUS.
Hideous, hideous! I have seen nothing so dreadful,
    Ever before!
    I can look no more.
Oedipus, Oedipus! What madness has come upon you?
    What malignant fate
    Has leaped with its full weight,   1250
Has struck you down with an irresistible fury,
    And borne you off as its prey?
        Poor wretch! There is much that I yearn
        To ask of you, much I would learn;
But I cannot. The sight of you fills me with horror!
    I shudder and turn away.

OEDIPUS.
Oh, Oh! What pain! I cannot rest in my anguish!
    Where am I? Where?
Where are my words? They die away as I speak them,
    Into thin air.   1260
        What is my fate to be?

CHORUS.
A fate too fearful for men to hear of, for men to see.

OEDIPUS.

Lost! Overwhelmed by the rush of unspeakable darkness!
　　It smothers me in its cloud.
　　The pain of my eyes is piercing.
The thought of my sins, the horrors that I have committed,
　　Racks me without relief.

CHORUS.

No wonder you suffer, Oedipus, no wonder you cry aloud
　　Under your double burden of pain and grief.

OEDIPUS.

My friend, my friend! How steadfast you are, how ready　　　1270
　　To help me in my great need!
　　I feel your presence beside me.
Blind as I am, I know your voice in the blackness
　　Of my long-lasting night.

CHORUS.

How could you put out your eyes, still another infamous deed?
　　What god, what demon, induced you to quench their light?

OEDIPUS.

It was Apollo,° my friends, who brought me low,
Apollo who crushed me beneath this unbearable burden;
　　But it was my hand, mine, that struck the blow.
Why should I see? What sight could have given me pleasure?　　1280

CHORUS.

These things are as you say.

OEDIPUS.

What is there now to love? What greeting can cheer me?
　　Lead me away.
Quickly, quickly! O lead me out of the country
　　To a distant land! I am beyond redemption
Accursed, beyond hope lost, the one man living
　　Whom all the gods most hate.

CHORUS.

Would we had never heard of your existence,
　　Your fruitless wisdom and your wretched fate.

OEDIPUS.

My curses be upon him, whoever freed　　　　　　　　1290
My feet from the cruel fetters, there on the mountain,
　　Who restored me from death to life, a thankless deed.

1277. *Apollo:* both as god of the Delphic oracle and as god of truth, light, and order.

My death would have saved my friends and me from anguish.
CHORUS.
    I too would have had it so.
OEDIPUS.
    Then would I never have been my father's killer.
       Now all men know
    That I am the infamous son who defiled his mother,
      That I shared the bed of the father who gave me being.
    And if there is sorrow beyond any mortal sorrow,
      I have brought it upon my head.   1300
CHORUS.
    I cannot say that you have acted wisely.
    Alive and blind? You would be better dead.

OEDIPUS. Give me no more advice, and do not tell me
    That I was wrong. What I have done is best.
    For if I still had eyesight when I went
    Down to the underworld, how could I bear
    To see my father and my wretched mother?
    After the terrible wrong I did them both,
    It would not have been punishment enough
    If I had hanged myself. Or do you think   1310
    That I could find enjoyment in the sight
    Of children born as mine were born? No! No!
    Nor in the sight of Thebes with its towered walls
    And sacred statues of the gods. For I—
    Who is so wretched?—I, the foremost Theban,
    Cut myself off from this by my own edict
    That ordered everyone to shun the man
    Polluting us, the man the gods have shown
    To be accursed, and of the house of Laius.
    Once I laid bare my shame, could I endure   1320
    To look my fellow-citizens in the face?
    Never! Never! If I had found some way
    Of choking off the fountain of my hearing,
    I would have made a prison of my body,
    Sightless and soundless. It would be sweet to live
    Beyond the reach of sorrow. Oh, Cithaeron!
    Why did you give me shelter rather than slay me
    As soon as I was given to you? Then
    No one would ever have heard of my begetting.
    Polybus, Corinth, and the ancient house   1330
    I thought my forebears'! You reared me as a child.

My fair appearance covered foul corruption,
I am impure, born of impurity.
Oh, narrow crossroad where the three paths meet!
Secluded valley hidden in the forest,
You that drank up my blood, my father's blood
Shed by my hands, do you remember all
I did for you to see? Do you remember
What else I did when I came here to Thebes?
Oh marriage rites! By which I was begotten,   1340
You then brought forth children by your own child,
Creating foulest blood-relationship:
An interchange of fathers, brothers, sons,
Brides, wives, and mothers—the most monstrous shame
Man can be guilty of. I should not speak
Of what should not be done. By all the gods,
Hide me, I beg you, hide me quickly somewhere
Far, far away. Put me to death or throw me
Into the sea, out of your sight forever.
Come to me, friends, pity my wretchedness.   1350
Let your hands touch me. Hear me. Do not fear,
My curse can rest on no one but myself.
CHORUS. Creon is coming. He is the one to act
    On your requests, or to help you with advice.
    He takes your place as our sole guardian.
OEDIPUS. Creon! What shall I say? I cannot hope
    That he will trust me now, when my past hatred
    Has proved to be so utterly mistaken.
                    [*Enter* CREON.]
CREON. I have not come to mock you, Oedipus,
    Or to reproach you for my evil-doing.   1360
    [*To* ATTENDANTS.] You there. If you have lost all your respect
    For men, revere at least the Lord Apollo,
    Whose flame supports all life. Do not display
    So nakedly pollution such as this,
    Evil that neither earth nor holy rain
    Nor light of day can welcome. Take him in,
    Take him in, quickly. Piety demands
    That only kinsmen share a kinsman's woe.
OEDIPUS. Creon, since you have proved my fears were groundless,
    Since you have shown such magnanimity   1370
    To one so vile as I, grant my petition.
    I ask you not for my sake but your own.
CREON. What is it that you beg so urgently?

OEDIPUS. Drive me away at once. Drive me far off.
Let me not hear a human voice again.
CREON. I have delayed only because I wished
To have the god reveal to me my duty.
OEDIPUS. But his command was certain: put to death
The unholy parricide. And I am he.
CREON. True. But as things are now, it would be better   1380
To find out clearly what we ought to do.
OEDIPUS. An oracle for a man so miserable?
CREON. Yes. Even you will now believe the god.
OEDIPUS. I will. Creon, I charge you with this duty.
Accept it, I entreat you. Give to her
Who lives within such burial as you wish,
For she belongs to you. You will perform
The proper obsequies. But as for me,
Let not my presence doom my father's city,
But send me to the hills, to Mount Cithaeron,   1390
My mountain, which my mother and my father
Chose for my grave. So will I die at last
By the decree of those who sought to slay me.
And yet I know I will not die from sickness
Or anything else. I was preserved from death
To meet some awful, some mysterious end.
My own fate does not matter, only my children's.
Creon, my sons need give you no concern,
For they are men, and can find anywhere
A livelihood. But Creon, my two girls!   1400
How lost, how pitiable! They always ate
Their daily bread with me, at my own table,
And had their share of everything I touched.
Take care of them! O Creon, take care of them!
And one thing more—if I could only touch them
And with them weep. O prince, prince, grant me this!
Grant it, O noble Creon! If I touched them,
I could believe I saw them once again.
What! Do I hear° my daughters? Hear them sobbing?
Has Creon had pity on me? Has he sent them,   1410
My children, my two darlings? Is it true?
CREON. Yes, I have had them brought. I knew how much
You used to love them, how you love them still.

1409. hear: Oedipus' daughters, Antigone and Ismene, enter.

OEDIPUS. May the gods bless you, Creon, for this kindness;
  And may they guard you better on your journey
  Than they have guarded me. Children, where are you?
  Come to your brother's hands, the hands that made
  Your father's clear eyes into what these are—
  Your father, who saw nothing and knew nothing,
  Begetting you where he had been conceived.   1420
  I cannot see you, but I weep for you,
  Weep for the bitter lives that you must lead
  Henceforward. Never, never will you go
  To an assembly with the citizens,
  Or to a festival, and take your part.
  You will turn back in tears. And when you come
  To the full bloom of womanhood, what man
  Will run the risk of bringing on himself
  Your shame, my daughters, and your children's shame?
  Is there one evil, one, that is not ours?   1430
  "Your father killed his father; he begot
  Children of his own mother; she who bore you
  Bore him as well." These are the taunts, the insults
  That you will hear. Who, then, will marry you?
  No one, my children. Clearly it is your fate
  To waste away in barren maidenhood.
  Creon, Creon, their blood flows in your veins.
  You are the only father left to them;
  They have lost both their parents. Do not let them
  Wander away, unmarried, destitute,   1440
  As miserable as I. Have pity on them,
  So young, so utterly forlorn, so helpless
  Except for you. You are kind-hearted. Touch me
  To tell me that I have your promise. Children,
  There is so much, so much that I would say,
  If you were old enough to understand it,
  But now I only teach you this one prayer:
  May I be given a place in which to live,
  And may my life be happier than my father's.
CREON. Come, come with us. Have done with further woe.   1450
OEDIPUS. Obedience is hard.
CREON.   No good in life endures beyond its season.
OEDIPUS. Do you know why I yield?
CREON.   When I have heard your reason I
         will know.

OEDIPUS. You are to banish me.

CREON. The gods alone can grant you that entreaty.

OEDIPUS. I am hated by the gods.

CREON. Then their response to you will not be slow.

OEDIPUS. So you consent to this?

CREON. I say no more than I have said already.

OEDIPUS. Come, then, lead me away.

CREON. Not with your children. You must let them go.

OEDIPUS. Creon, not that, not that!

CREON. You must be patient. Nothing can restore

Your old dominion. You are King no more.

[*Exeunt* CREON, OEDIPUS, ISMENE, *and* ANTIGONE.]

CHORUS. Behold him, Thebans: Oedipus, great and wise,
Who solved the famous riddle. This is he   1460
Whom all men gazed upon with envious eyes,
Who now is struggling in a stormy sea,
Crushed by the billows of his bitter woes.
Look to the end of mortal life. In vain
We say a man is happy, till he goes
Beyond life's final border, free from pain.

Euripides

Bacchae

TRANSLATED BY HENRY HART MILMAN
ADAPTED BY HEINRICH VON STADEN

Euripides (485 B.C.?–407 B.C.)

THE LAST GREAT GREEK TRAGEDIAN, EURIPIDES, DID NOT HAVE
the close ties with Athens that were characteristic of Aeschylus and Sophocles. He never fought for his city or held public office, and in his plays he did
not speak as a reverent citizen to fellow citizens but as an inquiring and outspoken social and religious critic who displayed deep intellectual restlessness.
As Athens became increasingly crazed by more than twenty years of the
Peloponnesian War, Euripides' open antagonism to the prowar party in
Athens and his probing skepticism drove him into growing isolation. In
about 408 B.C., when he was over seventy, he finally went in voluntary exile
to semibarbarian Macedonia, where he died the next year. An unpublished
play, the *Bacchae,* was found among his writings after his death.

From his vast number of plays we have eighteen of undisputed authen-
ticity. The most famous of these are *Alcestis, Medea, Hippolytus, Heracles,
Ion, The Trojan Women,* two *Iphigenia* plays, *Helen, Electra,* and *Bacchae.*

In the *Bacchae* Euripides, like the other Greek tragedians, dramatizes a
myth already well known to his audience. It concerns the punishment and
death of a Theban king, Pentheus, for his resistance to the spread of the
orgiastic cult of the god of wine and vegetation, Dionysus. By the time of
Euripides, the orgiastic aspects of the worship of Dionysus had been toned
down considerably at Athens, possibly under the influence of the cult of
Apollo and its emphasis on enlightened self-discipline. But in this play
Euripides, perhaps inspired by the orgiastic religions and irrational movements which the social stresses of the war were producing in Athens, reverts
to an earlier, more primitive stage in the worship of Dionysus. At this stage
the followers of the god performed a wild mountain dance in a rite of group
ecstasy in order to achieve communion with their god. The climactic act of
this communion consisted of tearing apart and eating the raw flesh of an
animal—perhaps originally a man—which represented the god. This act was
believed to enable the dancers to assimilate the animalistic, unrestrained
potency of a god who represented the liberation of instinctive life from the
restraint of reason and social custom. These rites are used by Euripides as the
background of his play.

Euripides frequently chose myths that concern the irrational forces in
man. In the *Bacchae* he interprets aspects of the relation between the irrational and reason. The play perhaps represents Euripides' final attempt to
understand the fundamentally two-edged nature of rationalism, as represented by Pentheus, and of the elementary emotions, as represented by
Dionysus. Both rationalism and the Dionysiac experience, the poet suggests,
can be a source of destruction and violence.

Bacchae

CHARACTERS

DIONYSUS, *a god (also called Bacchus, Iacchus, Bromius, and Evius).*

CHORUS OF ASIAN BACCHAE *(or "Bacchantes"), followers of Dionysus (also called his thiasus).*

TEIRESIAS, *a blind prophet of Thebes.*

CADMUS, *founder and first King of Thebes.*

PENTHEUS, *grandson of Cadmus and his successor as King of Thebes.*

ATTENDANT OF PENTHEUS.

FIRST MESSENGER, *a herdsman from Mount Cithaeron.*

SECOND MESSENGER *from Cithaeron.*

AGAVE, *daughter of Cadmus and mother of Pentheus.*

SILENT CHARACTERS: ATTENDANTS *of Pentheus;* THEBAN BAC-CHANTES *led by Agave;* CITIZENS *of Thebes;* ATTENDANTS *of Agave.*

The scene is before the royal palace of Pentheus in Thebes. The stage entrance on the left leads to the country, on the right to the city. The tomb of Semele, mother of Dionysus, stands in the center of the orchestra. The youthful DIONYSUS *enters in traditional Dionysiac costume: on his head a crown of ivy, in his hand his thyrsus —a fennel stick with ivy—and wrapped around his body a fawn-skin.*

DIONYSUS. To this land of Thebes I return—I, the son of Zeus,
    Dionysus; he to whom Semele, Cadmus' daughter,
    Amid the dread midwifery of lightning fire°
    Once gave birth. In a mortal form, having shed
    The appearance of a god, I stand by Dirce's stream
    And cool Ismenus' ° waters; and I survey
    My mother's grave, the thunder-slain, and the ruins
    Still smoldering of that old ancestral palace,
    The flame still living of the lightning fire—
    Hera's immortal vengeance against my mother. 10
       But I approve of Cadmus' sacred ban
    On that heaven-stricken, unapproached place,
    His daughter's tomb, which I have screened over
    With the pale green of the climbing vine.
       I have left behind the golden Lydian shores,
    The Phrygian° and the Persian sun-seared plains,
    And Bactria's° walls; the Medes' ° wild wintry land
    I have passed, and Arabia the rich, and all
    Of Asia° that along the salt sea-coast
    Lifts up her high-towered cities where the Greeks, 20
    With the barbarians mingled, dwell in peace.
    And everywhere I have founded my sacred dances, my rites

3. *dread . . . fire:* Semele, who had become pregnant by Zeus, was persuaded by Zeus' jealous wife (the goddess Hera) to request Zeus to appear to her in the same glory with which he always approached Hera. Zeus, unwillingly compliant, appeared in thunder and lightning; Semele, seized by flames, gave premature birth to a child, Dionysus. Zeus sewed him up in his thigh until he matured enough for normal birth. *5–6. Dirce, Ismenus:* rivers of Thebes. *15–16. Lydia, Phrygia:* districts in Asia Minor where the cult of Dionysus was supposed to have originated. *17. Bactria:* now northern Afghanistan and southern Uzbekistan (Russia); formerly a province of the Persian Empire. *Medes:* inhabitants of the northwest part of what is now Iran. *19–21. Of Asia . . . in peace:* the western coast of Asia Minor, where Greek colonies had been established.

And revels—I, by mankind confessed to be a god.
 But now of all the Hellenic land first here in Thebes
I have raised my revel shout, donned my fawn-skin,°
Taken in my hand my thyrsus,° ivy-crowned.
 Yet *here,* where it was least seemly, my mother's sisters
Vowed that Dionysus was no son of Zeus. They claim
That Semele, their sister, seduced by a mortal lover,
Pretended great Zeus was father of her child;   30
That the story was simply old Cadmus' lying craft.
Hence, they claim, Zeus in anger
Struck her dead—she, the bold usurper of his bed.
 So from their homes I have goaded them in frenzy;
Their wits all crazed, they wander over the mountains,°
And I have forced them to wear my wild attire.
There's not a woman of old Cadmus' race,
Whom I have not maddened out of her quiet house.
Unseemly mingled, rich and poor alike,
On the roofless rocks beneath the pale firs they sit. 40
 This recalcitrant city now must learn:
It lacks initiation in my Mysteries.
It must seek to make atonement
To me for Semele, my outraged slandered mother—
To me, the god manifest, born of Zeus.
 Old Cadmus has now given up his might and kingly rule
To Pentheus, his daughter's son,
Foe of my divinity; who repels and rejects *me,* a god,
From his rich offerings
Nor makes mention of my name   50
In holy prayer. Wherefore to him, to Thebes,
And all her men, soon will I terribly show
That I was born a god. And then I shall depart
(Once all things are well disposed here) to other lands,
Making dread revelation of myself.
 But if this Theban city in her anger
Shall seek with arms to drive off from the mountains
My Bacchae, then at my wild Maenads' ° head

25. *fawn-skin:* a traditional cloak of Dionysus and his Bacchantic women. 26. *thyrsus:* Dionysus' staff, in this instance crowned with ivy. Ivy, because of its evergreen vitality, typifies the victory of vegetation over winter and barrenness; Dionysus was sometimes worshipped as the "Ivy-Lord" (*Kissos*). 35. *mountains:* Mount Cithaeron, about eight miles south of Thebes. 58. *Maenads:* female followers of Dionysus, like the Bacchae raging with madness and enthusiasm. In this play, "Bacchae" and "Maenads" are sometimes used interchangeably.

I shall meet, and mingle in the awful war.
Hence have I taken the likeness of a man,   60
Myself transmuted into human form.
          [*He calls off stage to the* CHORUS OF ASIAN BACCHAE.]
     But you who have left Tmolus,° Lydia's strength, you,
My band of women, whom I have led
From lands barbarian, my associates here,
And fellow-pilgrims: lift up your drums,°
Familiar in your native Phrygian cities,
Made by your mother Rhea's° craft and mine;
And beat them all round Pentheus' royal palace,
Beat, till the city of Cadmus throngs to see.
I to my Bacchae in the dim glens   70
Of wild Cithaeron go to lead the dance.
          [*Exit* DIONYSUS. *The* CHORUS OF ASIAN BACCHAE *enters*
               dancing, carrying drums, flutes, and thyrsi.]
CHORUS [*sings*].
     From the Asian shore,
     And by the sacred steep of Tmolus,
     Lightly I danced with winglike feet,
     To honor god Bromius.°
     Toilless toil and labor sweet,
     Evoë! ° Away, whoever he be,
     Leave our path, our temple free!
     Seal up each silent lip in holy awe.
     But I, obedient to thy law,   80
O Dionysus, chant the choral hymn to thee.

     Blest above all of human line,
     Who, deep in mystic rites divine,
     Leads his hallowed life with us,
     Initiate in our thiasus;°
     And, purified with holiest waters,
Goes dancing over the hills with Bacchus' daughters.

62. *Tmolus:* (modern Musa Dagh in Turkey): forming the backbone of Lydia
and looming above Sardis.   65. *drums:* along with flutes, the characteristic
instruments of orgiastic cults.   67. *Rhea:* a goddess with orgiastic rites; mother
of Zeus, sometimes identified with the Near Eastern goddess Cybele. As "Great
Mother of the Gods," her worship was often combined with that of Dionysus
as "*Son* of the Great God."   75. *Bromius:* title of Dionysus (literally, "Roarer"—
as bull-god, lion-god, earthquake-god, and god with kettledrums).   77. *Evoë:* an
ecstatic exclamation honoring Dionysus.   85. *thiasus:* a religious society; the term
was also often used with reference to Dionysus' retinue.

And your dark orgies hallows he,
O mighty Mother, Cybele! °
He his thyrsus shaking round,   90
All his locks with ivy crowned,
O Dionysus! boasts of your dread dance to be.

Bacchae! away, away!
Lead your god in fleet array;
Bacchus lead, the ever young.
A god that from gods sprung.
From the Phrygian mountains down
Through every wide-squared Grecian town.

Him the Theban queen of yore
Amid Zeus' fast flashing lightnings bore;   100
In her awful travail wild
Sprung from her womb the untimely child,
While smitten with the thunder-blast
The sad mother breathed her last.

Instantly him Zeus, son of Cronus,
Received with all a mother's love;
In his secret thigh immured,
There with golden clasps secured,
Safe from Hera's jealous sight;
Then, with the Fates fulfilled, to light   110
He gave the horned° god, and wound
The living snakes° his brows around;
Whence still the wanded Maenads bear
Their serpent prey wreathed in their floating hair.

Put on your ivy crown,
O Thebes, you sacred town!
O hallowed house of dark-haired Semele!
Bloom, blossom everywhere,

---

89. *Cybele:* the mother goddess; her cult was introduced to Greece in the fifth century B.C. 111. *horned:* Dionysus, as god of fertility and animal vitality, is sometimes represented as horned; among cattle-herding Greeks, the bull was the greatest symbol of the procreative forces in nature. In a cult rite (the ōmophagia) associated with the winter dance, a bull was often torn to pieces and eaten raw, thus communicating the vital potency of the god to his worshipers. 112. *living snakes:* snake-handling was once practiced in some forms of the Dionysian cult.

With flowers and bryony° fair,
And let your frenzied steps supported be   120

   With thyrsi from the oak
   Or the green fir-tree° broke;
   Your spotted fawn-skins line with locks
   Torn from the snowy-fleeced flocks:
Shaking his wanton wand let each advance,
And all the land shall madden with the dance.

   Bromius it is that his revel rout
   To the mountain leads about;
   To the mountain leads along,
   Where awaits the female throng;   130
   Driven from shuttle, from the loom,
   Raging with the god they come.
   O mountains, wild and high,
   Where the old Curetes° lie,
   Glens of Crete, where Zeus was nursed.
   In your sunless caverns first
   The crested Corybantes° found
   The leathern drums mysterious round,
   That, mingling in harmonious strife
   With the sweet-breathed Phrygian fife,   140
   In Mother Rhea's hands they place—
   Drums with which the Bacchic song to grace.
   And the frantic Satyrs° round
   That ancient goddess leap and bound:
   And soon the biennial dances light°
Began—immortal Bacchus' chief delight.

   On the mountains wild it's sweet
   When with rapid dance faint our feet;
   Ourselves on earth all careless thrown
   With the sacred fawn-skins strewn,   150
   To quaff the goat's delicious blood,
   A strange, a rich, a savage food.

---

119. bryony: an evergreen creeper with bright red berries. *122. fir-tree:* the typical tree of Cithaeron. Dionysus is often honored as Lord of the Trees. *134. Curetes:* semidivine attendants of the infant Zeus after Rhea gave birth to him in Crete. *137. Corybantes:* attendants of Rhea, here identified with the Curetes. They invented the kettledrum to drown the cries of the infant Zeus, lest his father Cronos should find and swallow him, as he had swallowed his other children. *143. Satyrs:* half man and half beast, they are creatures of woods and mountains closely associated with Dionysus; lascivious; representatives of the vital powers in nature. *145. dances light:* the biennial orgiastic festival of Dionysus.

Then off again the revel goes
Over Phrygian, Lydian mountain brows;
Evoë! Evoë! He leads the road,
Bacchus himself the maddening god!

And flows with milk the plain, and flows with wine,
Flows with the wild bees' nectar-dews divine;
And soars, like smoke, the Syrian incense pale—
    The frantic Bacchic god,   160
    The beaconing pine-torch° on his wand
    Whirls around with rapid hand,
    And drives the wandering dance about,
    Beating time with joyous shout,
    And casts upon the breezy air
    All his rich luxuriant hair;
    Ever the burden of his song,
    "Raging, maddening, haste along
    Bacchus' daughters, pride
    Of golden Tmolus' fabled side;   170
    While your heavy cymbals ring,
    Still your 'Evoë! Evoë!' sing!"
Evoë! the Evian god rejoices
In Phrygian tones and Phrygian voices,
    When the soft holy flute is breathing sweet,
    In notes harmonious to her feet,
Who to the mountain, to the mountain speeds;
Like some young colt that by its mother feeds,
    Gladsome with many a frisking bound,
The Bacchant goes forth and treads the echoing ground.   180

TEIRESIAS. Ho! someone in the gates, call from his palace
Cadmus, Agenor's° son, who left Sidon's walls
And built up this towered city of Thebes.
Ho! someone tell him, "Teiresias is waiting for you."
He knows well why I am here; the covenant
Which I, the old man, have made with him still older,
To lift the thyrsus wand, to wear the fawn-skin,
And to crown our gray hair with the ivy-leaves.
CADMUS. Best friend, with what delight within my palace

161. *pine-torch:* the Bacchic celebrant, who is temporarily the incarnation of the god, lifts high a flaming pine-torch.   182. *Agenor:* King of Phoenicia (coastal territory north of Palestine; its chief city was Sidon). When Zeus carried off Agenor's daughter Europa, Agenor sent his son Cadmus in search of her. An oracle instructed Cadmus to follow a cow and build a town where she sank down with fatigue; this spot was Thebes.

I heard your voice, the voice of a wise man!   190
Look! I am here in the gods' sacred costume,
For we must worship the son of my own daughter—
Dionysus, now amongst men a manifest god—
Yes, we must, to the utmost of our power.
Where shall we lead the dance, plant the light foot,
And shake our gray locks. Teiresias, you
The aged lead the aged: you are wise.
Nor will I grow weary, beating the earth night and day
With my lithe thyrsus. How sweetly
Will we forget that we are old!

TEIRESIAS.   You are like me: 200
    I too grow young; I too will try the dance.
CADMUS. Shall we then go to the mountains in our chariots?
TEIRESIAS. Walking would demonstrate more honor to the god.
CADMUS. I, an old man, will lead you, an old man, like a child.
TEIRESIAS. The god will lead the two of us there without trouble.
CADMUS. Of all the men, are we alone going to dance for Bacchus?
TEIRESIAS. All the others blindly misjudge; we alone can see.
CADMUS. We are delaying too long; take hold of my arm.
TEIRESIAS. Thus true yoke-fellows join hand with hand.
CADMUS. Being mortal-born, I may not despise the gods.   210
TEIRESIAS. No wiles, no trifling with the deities!
    No subtle reasoning, even if it soared aloft
    To the height of wisdom, can overthrow
    That ancestral faith coeval with our race.
    Someone will say that I disgrace my age,
    Rapt in the dance, and ivy-crowned my head.
    The gods admit no difference: old or young,
    It behooves all to mingle in the rite.
    From all he will receive the common honor,
    Nor deign to count his countless votaries.   220
CADMUS. Since you, Teiresias, cannot see,
    I, as your Seer, must interpret what is coming.
    Here—Pentheus, hurrying homewards to his palace,
    Echion's son, to whom I have given the kingdom.
    He is strangely disturbed! What new thing will he say now?
      [Enter PENTHEUS *from the right, talking excitedly to his
               attendants.*]
PENTHEUS. I have been absent from this land and now I hear
    Of strange and evil doings in the city.
    Our women all have left their homes to join
    In feigned ecstasies. On the shadowy rocks

They sit, honoring this god of yesterday,   230
Dionysus, whoever he is, with revels
Dishonorable. In their midst
Stand full bowls of wine;° and each, stealing forth
This way and that, creeps to a bed of lawless lust;
Pretending to be a sacrificing Maenad,
But in fact serving Aphrodite more than Bacchus.
All whom I have apprehended, our officers guard
In chains in the public prison.
Those that have escaped I shall hunt off the mountains—
Ino, Agave, who bore me to Echion, and   240
Her too, Autonoë,° mother of Actaeon.°
And fettering them all in iron bonds,
I shall put an end to their mad wickedness.
It's said a stranger has appeared among us,
A wizard, sorcerer, from the land of Lydia,
Handsome with golden locks and red cheeks,
Eyes moist with Aphrodite's melting fire.
And day and night he is with young girls
To guile them into his soft inebriate rites.
But if I catch him beneath this roof, I will silence   250
The beating of his thyrsus, I will stop his locks'
Wild tossing, cutting his neck from his body.
He, they say, is the new god, Dionysus,
That was sewn up within the thigh of Zeus.
He, with his mother (who guiltily boasted that she
Was Zeus' bride), was blasted by the lightning.
Are not such impostures deserving of hanging?
Insolence heaped on insolence! Whoever this stranger may be.

> [*Only now does* PENTHEUS *notice* CADMUS *and* TEIRESIAS
> *in their Bacchic costumes.*]

But look, new wonders! Do I not see Teiresias,
The prophet, dressed in the dappled fawn-skin?   260
My mother's father too—a sight for laughter!—
Tossing his hair? Sir, I blush for you,
Seeing your old age grown so fatuous.
Will you not shake off that ivy? Free your hand
From that unseemly wand, grandfather!

233. *bowls of wine:* Dionysus is also the Greek wine-god.   240–41. *Ino, Agave
. . . Autonoë:* the three sisters of Semele referred to in lines 27–38. *bore . . .
Echion:* Agave is Pentheus' mother and Echion is his father. *Actaeon:* cousin of
Pentheus and a mighty hunter who had offended the goddess Artemis. He was torn
to pieces by his own dogs on Mount Cithaeron because, like Pentheus, he had
scorned a deity.

This is your doing, Teiresias. You wish to install
This new god amongst men, to sell new prophecies
At higher price, and to profit from well-paid offerings.
If your old age were not your safeguard, you
Would now pine in chains among the Bacchant women.   270
False teacher of new rites! For wherever among women
The grape's sweet poison mingles with the feast,
There we may expect nothing good of such worship.

CHORUS. What blasphemy! Do you not revere the gods?
Nor Cadmus who sowed° the earth-born harvest?
Echion's son, how you shame your lineage!

TEIRESIAS. It's easy to be eloquent, for one
That's skilled in speech and has a stirring theme.
You have the flowing tongue of a wise man,
But there's no wisdom in your fluent words;   280
For the bold demagogue, powerful in speech,
Is but a dangerous citizen, lacking sense.
This new deity you laugh to scorn,
I may not tell you how mighty he will be
Throughout all Hellas. Young man, for mankind
Two things are primary: first, Demeter, the goddess
(Or would you rather call her Mother Earth?),
Maintains the race of man with solid food.
He, on the other hand, the son of Semele,
Found out the grape's rich juice, and taught us mortals   290
That which makes suffering mankind forgetful
Of sorrow, when they drink the vine's rich stream.
Sleep too, and drowsy oblivion of care
He gives, all healing medicine of our woes.
And when wine offerings are poured to gods
This god of wine is poured himself,
So that thus through him mankind has rich blessings.
Him do you scorn, disbelieving that in Zeus' thigh he was
Sewn up; but this profound truth I will unfold.
When Zeus had snatched him from the lightning-fire,   300
He bore the new-born babe Dionysus to Olympus.
Stern Hera strove to thrust him out of heaven,
But Zeus encountered her with wiles divine:

---

275. *sowed:* Cadmus killed a dragon guarding a well of Ares near Thebes and, on the advice of Athena, sowed its teeth, out of which grew armed men, all but five of whom destroyed each other. These five became the ancestors of the Thebans; one of them was Echion ("Snake-Man"), the father of Pentheus.

He broke off part of the earth-encircling ether,°
And placed Dionysus there, a pleasing hostage,
Aloof from jealous Hera. So henceforth
Men said that he was cradled in Zeus' thigh
(From the assonance of the words in our old tongue
For thigh and hostage the wild fable grew).
    A prophet is our god, for Bacchic worship   310
And madness are alike mantic.°
And when the god comes down in all his power,
He makes the mad to rave of things to come.
Also of Ares he has attributes: he scatters an army
In all its firm array and serried arms
With panic, even before a lance is raised—
Dionysus causes this frenzied panic too.°
And someday we shall see him leaping even on Delphi's crags,°
With his pine-torches lighting up
The rifts of the twin-headed rock, and shouting   320
And shaking all around his Bacchic wand,
Great through all Hellas. But Pentheus, take my advice:
Do not vaunt your power over man, even if you *think*
That you are wise, for such thought of yours is diseased;
No, do not *think* it! Receive this god in your land,
Pour wine, join the dance, and crown your head with ivy.
    Dionysus° does not force our women
To Aphrodite's rites; the chaste by nature
Are not in this way robbed of their chastity.
You must consider this, for in the Bacchic company   330
The chaste woman will not be less chaste.
    Look, you are proud, when men throng the gates to greet you
And the glad city welcomes Pentheus' name;
So also he, I think, delights in being honored.
I, therefore, and old Cadmus whom you mock,

---

304. *ether:* an airy, fiery substance of which the sky—including the stars—is
made, according to numerous ancient authors.   311. *mantic:* Greek *mania,* ("madness") is etymologically connected with *mantikē,* "the art of prophecy." Apollo was
the established god of prophecy in Greece and thus Teiresias' patron god, but in
Thrace and at an oracular shrine in central Greece, Dionysus too was a god of
trance-mediumship.   314–17. *Also . . . too:* Teiresias relates Dionysus' functions
in an unusual way to those of Apollo and Ares, and thus tries to build a bridge
for the "new" god to enter the Greek religion.   318. *Delphi's crags:* Apollo's
domain.   327–29. *Dionysus' . . . chastity:* Teiresias speaks in terms popularized
by the Sophistic movement of the fifth century: nature and character (not law,
custom, or circumstance) determine conduct. Dionysus is not immoral; his cult is
amoral.

Will crown our heads with ivy and dance along—
An ancient pair, yet dance we really must.
  I will not listen to your words and war with gods.
For you are at the height of madness, there's no medicine
That can minister to disease° so deep as yours.   340
CHORUS. Old man, you certainly do not disgrace Apollo, your own god,
  And you are wise to worship that great god Bromius.
CADMUS. My boy, Teiresias has counseled you well;
  Dwell safely with us within the pale of law.
  Now you just flutter about; your sense is void of sense.
  Even if, as you declare, he were no god,
  Call him god. It would in fact be a splendid falsehood
  If Semele were thought to have borne a god;
  It would be an honor to us and to our race.
  Have you not seen Actaeon's wretched fate?   350
  The dogs he bred, who fed from his own board,
  Rent him to pieces in wrath; for he boasted
  That he was a mightier hunter than Artemis.
  Let that not happen to you: come, let me crown your head
  With ivy, and with us give the god his honor.
PENTHEUS. Keep off your hands! Away! Go rave and dance,
  And do not wipe your folly off on me.
  On Teiresias, your folly's teacher, I will wreak
  Instant relentless justice. Someone go, overthrow
  The seat from which he spies the flight of birds,   360
  That false augur, with iron forks overthrow,
  Scattering in wild confusion all abroad,
  And cast his chaplets° to the winds and storms;
  You'll gall him thus, gall to the height of bitterness.
  Now to the city! seek that stranger out,
  That womanly man,° who with this new disease
  Afflicts our women, and defiles their beds.
  Seize him, and bring him straight here in chains,
  That he may suffer stoning,° that dread death.
  Such will be his bitter revel here in Thebes.   370

---

340. *disease:* throughout the play it is suggested that sobriety of thought, logic,
and rationalism might at times be diseased insanity.   363. *chaplets:* sacred woolen
bands, hung up to consecrate his seat as a place of divination.   366. *womanly
man:* by the late fifth century B.C., Dionysus is often represented as very youthful,
with a beardless face, ruddy cheeks, and an effeminate appearance.   369. *stoning:*
an exceptional method of execution, used especially in cases of ritual atonement
for sacrilege (as here) or murder of a kinsman. The irony is that Pentheus is
planning thus to murder his own kinsman—Dionysus, who is his cousin (their
mothers, Agave and Semele, are sisters).

TEIRESIAS. O, miserable fool! you do not know what you say,
 Crazed you've been, now you're at the height of madness;
 But let us go, Cadmus, and pour forth our prayer,
 Even for this savage and ungodly man—
 And for our city, lest the god overtake us
 With some strange vengeance.
        Come with your ivy staff,
 Lean on me, and I will lean on you:
 It would be shameful for two old men to stumble; yet go
 We must, and serve great Bacchus, son of Zeus.
 What woe, O Cadmus, will this woe-named man°   380
 Bring to your house! I do not speak a prophecy
 But a plain simple fact: fools always speak folly.
     [*Exeunt all except* CHORUS.]
CHORUS [*sings*].
  Holy goddess, goddess old!
  Holy! you who the crown of gold
  In the nether realm still wear,
  Pentheus' awful speech you hear,
  Hear his insulting tone
  Against Semele's immortal son,
  Bromius, of gods the first and best.
  At every gay and flower-crowned feast,   390
  His the dance's merry boot
  And the laughter with the flute,
  Every care and grief to lull,
  When the sparkling wine-cup full
  Crowns the gods' banquets, or lets fall
 Sweet sleep on the eyes of men at mortal festival.

  For tongue unbridled without awe,
  For madness spurning holy law—
  For such Zeus-doomed is sorrow close.
  But the life of calm repose   400
  And of modest reverence holds the state
  Unbroken by disturbing fate
  And knits whole houses in the tie
  Of sweet domestic harmony.
  Beyond the range of mortal things
  Wise thoughts hold no wisdom.

380. *woe-named man:* a play on the etymological connection between "Pentheus"
and *penthos,* "grief, sorrow, mourning." Such punning is frequent in tragedy, particularly because of the deeply rooted Greek belief that the connection between a
person and his name is significant, not accidental.

Life is brief; the present clasp,
Nor after some bright glory grasp.
Such grasping were the wisdom, as I've seen
Only of frantic and ill-counseled men.   410

O, would to Cyprus I might roam,
    Soft Aphrodite's isle,°
Where the young Loves have their perennial home,
    That soothe men's hearts with tender spells;
Or to Paphos' ° shore, wherever
The hundred-mouthed barbaric river
Makes teem with wealth the showerless land!
O lead me! lead me, till I stand,
Bromius! sweet Bromius! where high swelling
Soars the Pierian Muses' dwelling°—   420
Olympus' summit white and high—
You revel-loving deity!
        For there are all the Graces,°
            And sweet Desire° is there,
        And to those hallowed places,
To lawful rites the Bacchae repair.
The deity, the son of Zeus,
        The feast is his joy,
Peace,° the wealth-giver, does he love,
        That nurse of many a noble boy.   430
Not the rich man's sole possessing,
To the poor the painless blessing
Gives he of the wine-cup bright.
Him he hates, who day and night,

412. *Aphrodite's isle:* the island Cyprus was a principal place of worship of Aphrodite, who like Dionysus is an eastern divinity. As the goddess of natural, erotic impulse and sensual emancipation, her association with the other great nature-god, Dionysus, is rooted in popular thought. (Lines 411–426 are what has been called a "Euripidean escape-prayer," i.e., a personal prayer with little dramatic relevance, best understandable as wartime lyrics). 415. *Paphos:* town on the southwest coast of Cyprus. 420. *Pierian . . . dwelling:* birthplace of the Muses, on the northern side of Mount Olympus. Dionysus is often associated with this area. The Muses inspire the tragic poetry which is performed at his festival. 423. *Graces:* companions of the Muses; their cult was early associated with that of Dionysus. 424. *Desire: Pothos,* a winged boy who accompanies the dances of Satyrs and Maenads with the flute; son of Aphrodite. 429. *Peace: Eirene,* frequently a member of Dionysus' *thiasus* ("revelrous company"), since Dionysus too gives increase and enrichment of life. The yearning for peace is frequently expressed by Euripides, who wrote a large number of his plays during the Peloponnesian War.

Gentle night, and gladsome day,
Cares not thus to while away.
Be now wisely unsevere!
Shun the stern and the austere!
    Follow the multitude;
Their customs still pursue!   440
    Their homely wisdom rude,
(Such is my belief), is both right and true.
    [PENTHEUS *reenters from the right, while his attendants,*
    leading the captured DIONYSUS, *enter from the left.*]
ATTENDANT. Pentheus! we are here! nor did we go in vain.
The prey which you commanded we have taken.
Gently our prey met us, nor turned back
His foot in flight, but held out both his hands;
Became not pale, changed not his ruddy color.
Smiling he bade us chain and lead him off,
Stood still, and made our work a work of ease.
Reverently I said, "Stranger, I arrest you not   450
Of my own will, but by the king's command."
But all the Bacchae, the ones you had seized
And bound in chains within the public prison,
All now have disappeared; released they are, leaping
In their wild orgies, hymning the god Bacchus.
Spontaneously the chains fell from their feet;
The bolts drew back untouched by mortal hand.
In truth this man comes to our city
With many miracles. But now the rest is your care.
PENTHEUS. Untie his hands! Thus in our snare,   460
He must be sharp indeed to escape us now.
    [*Pauses; stares at* DIONYSUS.]
There *is* beauty in your body, stranger,
At least for women—for whom you came to Thebes.
Your fine bright hair, not coarse like the hard athlete's,°
Is mantling over your cheek warm with desire;
And carefully you have cherished your white skin;
Not in the sun's strong beams, but in cool shade,
Wooing soft Aphrodite with your loveliness.
But tell me first, from where did your race come?
DIONYSUS. There is no need to boast. It's easy to tell this: 470
Have you perhaps heard of flowery Tmolus?
PENTHEUS. Yes; that which rings the city of Sardis.

---

464. *hard athlete:* athletes affected close-cropped hair and were sunburnt.

DIONYSUS. From there I have come, my country is Lydia.
PENTHEUS. And from whom do you bring these rites into Hellas?
DIONYSUS. Dionysus, son of Zeus, initiated me into them.
PENTHEUS. Is there a local Zeus, then, that begets new gods?
DIONYSUS. No, it was here that he slept with Semele.
PENTHEUS. Did he constrain you by night, or in the eye of day?
DIONYSUS. In open vision he revealed his rites to me.
PENTHEUS. And what, then, is your rites' solemn form?   480
DIONYSUS. That is never uttered to the uninitiate.
PENTHEUS. What benefit, then, is theirs who worship him?
DIONYSUS. You may not know—but it is worth knowing.
PENTHEUS. A cunning reply designed to make me wish to hear.
DIONYSUS. The rites of our god scorn irreverent disbelievers.
PENTHEUS. You say you saw the god. What was his form?
DIONYSUS. Whatever he would. It was not for me to choose.
PENTHEUS. Cleverly evaded my question with no answer.
DIONYSUS. He who speaks most wisely, to the fool speaks foolishness.
PENTHEUS. And did you introduce your new god here first?   490
DIONYSUS. There's no foreigner that does not adore these rites.
PENTHEUS. Because they are much less wise than we Greeks.
DIONYSUS. But in this more wise. Customs differ much.
PENTHEUS. Do you perform these rites by night or day?
DIONYSUS. Most by night—night holds more solemn awe.
PENTHEUS. A crafty rotten plot to catch our women.
DIONYSUS. Even in the day bad men can do bad deeds.
PENTHEUS. For your clever sophistries you will pay the penalty.
DIONYSUS. And you for your ignorance and irreverence towards the gods!
PENTHEUS. He's bold, this Bacchant—ready enough in words.   500
DIONYSUS. What penalty? what evil will you do to me?
PENTHEUS. First I will clip away those soft bright locks.
DIONYSUS. My locks are holy, dedicated to my god.
PENTHEUS. Next, give me that thyrsus in your hand.
DIONYSUS. Take it yourself; it's Dionysus' wand.
PENTHEUS. I will tie your body in strong iron chains.
DIONYSUS. My God himself will undo them when he wishes.
PENTHEUS. When you invoke him amid your Bacchantes.
DIONYSUS. Even now he is present; he sees me now.
PENTHEUS. Where is he then? My eyes do not see him.   510
DIONYSUS. Near me; your irreverent eyes do not discern him.
PENTHEUS. Seize him, for he insults our city Thebes!
DIONYSUS. I warn you, do not chain me; the insane, the sane.
PENTHEUS. I, stronger than you are, say I will chain you.
DIONYSUS. You do not know where you are, or what you are.

PENTHEUS. Pentheus, Agave's son, my father Echion.
DIONYSUS. You have a name whose very sound is grief.
PENTHEUS. Away! Go chain him in our royal stable,
    That he may sit in midnight gloom profound—
    There lead your dance! But those you have led here,   520
    Your guilt's accomplices, we'll sell for slaves;
    Or, silencing their noise and beating drums,
    As handmaids to the loom we'll set them down.
        [*Exit* PENTHEUS, *as his attendants tie* DIONYSUS' *hands.*]
DIONYSUS. I go. For there's no need to bear what should not be.
    The vengeance for this outrage *he* will wreak,
    Dionysus, whose being you deny.
    Outraging *me*, bind *him* in your chains!
      [PENTHEUS' *attendants leave the stage with* DIONYSUS *in*
                    chains.]
CHORUS [*sings*].
        Holy virgin-haunted water,
        Ancient Acheloüs'° daughter,
        Dirce! In your crystal wave   530
        You the child of Zeus did lave.
        You, when Zeus, his awful sire,
        Snatched him from the immortal fire
        And locked him up within his thigh,
        Said with a loud but gentle cry—
        "Come, my Dithyrambus,° come,
        Enter you the masculine womb!
        Look! To Thebes I thus proclaim,
        'Twice born!' thus your mystic name."
        Blessed Dirce! Why do you then now   540
        From your green banks repel
        Me and all my merry round
        With their ivy garlands crowned?
            Why do you fly me?
            Why deny me?
        By all the joys of wine I swear,
        Bromius still shall be my care.

        What fury, fury unforgiven,
        Manifests against high heaven
        The earth-born Pentheus, whom immortal birth   550
        Echion begot—Echion, son of earth:

529. *Acheloüs:* river-god and source of all fresh water.   536. *Dithyrambus:* name
of Dionysus; derived from the dithyramb, a Dionysiac choral performance.

Pentheus of the dragon brood,
Not of human flesh and blood,
But fiercest beast like him whose pride,
The Titan, all the gods defied.
Me, great Bromius' handmaid true,
Me, with all my festive crew,
Thralled in chains, he still would keep
In his palace dungeon deep.
    Do you see this, O son of Zeus,   560
Dionysus from above?
Your shackled prophets do you see,
At strife with dark necessity?
        The golden wand
        In your right hand
Come, come you down Olympus' side,
And quell the bloody tyrant in his pride.

Are you holding revel now
On Nysa's° wild-beast-haunted brow?
Is it your company that clambers   570
Over Corycia's° mountain-chambers?
Or on Olympus thick with wood,
With his harp where Orpheus stood
And led the forest trees along,
Led the wild beasts with his song?
        O Pieria, blessed land,
Evius° honors you, advancing,
With his wild choir's mystic dancing.
        Over rapid Axius' stand
He shall pass; over Lydias'° tide   580
Then his whirling Maenads guide.
Lydias, parent of health,
Giver to man of boundless wealth;
Washing many a sunny mead,
Where the prancing horses feed.
DIONYSUS. Ho! Listen! you Bacchae!
    Rouse and wake! your master calls.

569. Nysa: as god of processions over mountains and mountain-dances, Dionysus is associated with numerous mountains, including Nysa (location uncertain), Parnassus, Olympus, and Cithaeron. _571. Corycia:_ probably near the Corycian cave on Mount Parnassus. _577. Evius:_ cult name of Dionysus, derived from the exclamatory cries in his honor, _euhai_ or _euhoi_. _579-80. Axius, Lydias:_ Axius and Lydias are Macedonian rivers which Dionysus must cross on his way from the north (probably Thrace) to Pieria.

[DIONYSUS *shouts from off stage to the accompaniment of loud rumbles and crashes.*]

CHORUS.

Who is here? and *what* is he
  That calls upon our wandering train?

DIONYSUS.

  Ho! I call again! I,   590
The son of Zeus and Semele.

CHORUS.

  —Ho! our Lord and Master:
    Come, with footsteps fast and faster,
      Join our revel! Bromius, speed,
      Till quakes the earth beneath our tread.
        Alas! Alas!
  —Soon shall Pentheus' palace wall,
    Shake and crumble to its fall.
  —Bacchus treads the palace floor!
    Adore him!   600
  —Oh! we do adore!
  —Look! Look!
    The pillars with their weight above,
    Of ponderous marble, shake and move,
    Hear! the trembling roof within,
    Bacchus shouts his mighty din.

DIONYSUS.

  The kindling lamp of the dark lightning bring!
  Fire, fire the palace of the guilty king.
    [*A flash of lightning strikes and flames leap up from* SE-
             MELE'S *tomb.*]

CHORUS.

  Look! Look! it flames! do you not see,
  Around the sacred tomb of Semele,   610
    The blaze, that left the lightning there,
    When Zeus' red thunder fired the air?
      On the earth, supine and low,
      Your shuddering limbs, you Maenads, throw!
  The king, the Zeus-born god, destroying all,
  In widest ruin strews the palace wall.
    [*The façade of* PENTHEUS' *palace has crashed;* DIONYSUS
             enters.]

DIONYSUS. O, you foreign women, thus prostrate in dismay
  Upon the earth you've fallen! Do you not see, as you may,
  How Bacchus has shaken down Pentheus' palace in wrath?

Rise up! Rise up! Take courage; shake off that trembling swoon.   620
CHORUS. O light that goodliest shines over our mystic rite,
    In state forlorn we saw you—saw with what deep a fright!
DIONYSUS. How you yielded to despair, when I sent myself inside
    To Pentheus, as though I were about to fall into his dark traps!
CHORUS. How could I less? If you who guards us should come to woe?
    But how did you escape from your godless foe?
DIONYSUS. Myself, delivered myself—with ease and effort slight.
CHORUS. Your hands—had he not bound them, in ties strong and tight?
DIONYSUS. It was then I mocked him; he *thought* me in his chain,
    But he touched me not, nor reached me—his idle thoughts were
        vain!   630
    In the stable he found a bull, where he thought he had me bound.
    His cords round the beast's knee and cloven hoofs he wound,
    Wrath-breathing. From his body the sweat fell like a flood.
    He bit his lips in fury, while I who stood beside unrecognized
    Looked on in unmoved quiet. But at that instant
    Bacchus shook the strong palace and on his mother's tomb
    Kindled flames. Pentheus saw it—on fire the palace deeming,
    Hither he rushed, and thither, for "water, water" screaming,
    And all his slaves began to labor, but labored all in vain.
    His efforts he soon abandoned, thinking I had fled; insane   640
    He rushed into the palace; in his hand the dark sword gleamed.
    Then, as it seemed, great Bromius (but only as it seemed)
    Kindled a bright light in the hall; to that light Pentheus rushed,
        and there,
    Thinking he was slaying me in vengeance, stood stabbing the thin
        air.
    But then the avenging Bacchus wrought new calamities.
    From roof to base that palace in smoldering ruin lies,
    Avenging our imprisonment. Exhausted by the blow, Pentheus
        threw
    On earth his useless sword. Mere mortal, he had dared to do
    Against a god unholy battle. But I in quiet state,
    Unheeding Pentheus' anger came through the palace gate.   650
    It seems even now his sandal is sounding on its way;
    Soon he will be here before us—and now what will he say?
    With ease will I confront him, rage-breathing though he stand.
    It's easy for a wise man to practice self-command.
                [Enter PENTHEUS *from the ruins of his palace.*]
PENTHEUS. Strange, terrible things I have suffered. That stranger,
    Whom I had bound in iron chains, has escaped.
                [*He suddenly sees* DIONYSUS.]

What! He's here! This man! How's this? How can he stand
Before our palace, as though he's walked out?
DIONYSUS. Stay your step! Subdue your anger here.
PENTHEUS. How did you break the chains and escape? 660
DIONYSUS. Did I not say—or did you not hear—that someone would
    free me?
PENTHEUS. What one? You still speak new and strange words.
DIONYSUS. He who plants the grape-clustered vine for man.
PENTHEUS. You do well to attribute that evil to Dionysus.
    [*To his attendants.*] I order you, close and bar the tower-gates all
    around.
DIONYSUS. What! And the gods? Can *they* not overleap all walls?
PENTHEUS. Clever, clever you are—except when you should be.
DIONYSUS. Where one should be most, there I'm by nature clever.
    But listen first, and hear the words of him
    Who comes to you with tidings from the mountains. 670
    [*Enter a herdsman from Mount Cithaeron, a* MESSENGER.]
    I will stay here. Have no fear, I will not run away.
MESSENGER. Pentheus, who rules over this land of Thebes!
    I come from high Cithaeron, ever white
    With the bright glittering snow's perennial rays.
PENTHEUS. Why did you come? What is the pressing message?
MESSENGER. I have seen the frenzied Bacchae, who had fled
    On their white feet, goaded forth from the city.
    I come to tell to you and to this city
    What strange deeds they do, what powerful miracles.
    But answer first, if I should freely say 680
    All that is done there, or shorten my speech.
    For I do fear your quick temper, O king,
    Your sharp resentment and over-royal pride.
PENTHEUS. Speak freely. You will leave unharmed by me;
    Anger is not seemly against the unoffending.
    But the more terrible what you say of these
    Mad women, the more I will wreak my just revenge
    On him who has led them to their strange rites.
MESSENGER. I was driving my herds of cows, they were slowly
    Winding their way along the mountain crags 690
    As the sun pounded his full beams on the earth.
    Then I saw three bands of dancing women: one
    Autonoë led, your mother Agave led the second,
    And the third Ino. And all of them
    Quietly slept, their languid limbs stretched out:
    Some resting on the fir-trees' stem their locks;

Some with their heads thrown on the oak-leaves
Carelessly but not immodestly—not, as you think,
Drunk with the goblet; nor do they prowl with the shrill flute
In the dusk woods for lawless lust.   700
Your mother, as she heard the horned herds
Lowing deep, stood up amid the Bacchae
And shouted loud to wake them from their rest.
They, from their lids shaking the freshening sleep,
Rose up, a wonder of decent beauty to see,
The young, the old, the unmarried girls.
And first they loosed their locks over their shoulders,
Fastened their fawn-skins, wherever the clasps
Had lost their hold, and tied all the dappled furs
With serpents that licked out with lithe tongues.   710
Some in their arms held a gazelle or wild-wolf's cub,
Suckling it with their white milk,° all young mothers
Who had left their new-born babes and stood with breasts
Full swelling. And they all put on their crowns
Of ivy, oak, or flowering bryony.
One° took a thyrsus wand, and struck the rock;
There leapt forth at once a dewy mist of water;
And one plunged her rod deep in the earth, and there
The god sent up a fountain of bright wine.
And those that longed for milk   720
Lightly scraped with their finger-ends and the soil
Gave streams of exquisite milk; from the ivy wands
Dropped sweet streams of honey.
     Had you been there and seen these things,
You would have worshipped with prayer the very god you now
        revile.
     And we, herdsmen and shepherds, gathered around.
And there was strife among us in our words
About these strange things they did, these marvelous things.
One fellow, city-bred, a glib and practiced speaker,
Addressed us thus: "You that inhabit here   730
The holy mountain slopes, shall we not chase
Agave, Pentheus' mother, from the Bacchae,

---

712. *Suckling . . . milk:* this has ritual meaning: young animals are incarnations
of the eternally young god (Dionysus), and by suckling them the human mother
or Maenad becomes a foster mother of Dionysus. 716–19. *One . . . wine:*
Dionysus' generative power is transmitted to his followers when they hold his
magic rod or thyrsus.

And win the favor of the king?" To us
He seemed to speak sense; so, crouched in the thick bushes,
We lay in ambush. The Bacchae at a set hour
Shook their wild thyrsi in the Bacchic dance,
Crying "Iacchus" with one voice, "The son of Zeus,"
"Bromius." The hills danced with them;
And the wild beasts; nothing that stood was unmoved.
　　And I leapt forth, as though to seize on her,   740
Leaving the ambush where I had hidden myself.
But she shrieked out: "Ho, my swift-footed dogs!
These men are hunting us down, but follow me,
Follow me, all your hands with thyrsi armed."
We had to flee fast, or by the Bacchae
We would have been torn in pieces. They with brave hands,
Unarmed with iron, rushed on the grazing cattle.
You could see a single woman tearing a vigorous heifer
Lowing in her grasp, like prize of war.
And some were tearing apart the young calves;   750
And you might see the ribs or cloven hoofs
Hurled wildly up and down, and mangled skins
Were hanging from the fir-trees, dropping blood.
The proud bulls, violence in their tossing horns,
Fell stumbling, staggering to the ground,
Dragged down by the strong hands of thousand women.
And quicker were the entrails torn away
Than blink the lids of your royal eyeballs.
　　Like birds that skim the earth, they glide along
Over the wide plains, that by Asopus' ° streams   760
Shoot up for Thebes the rich and yellow grain;
And invading Hysie and Erythrae (that dwell low
Beneath Cithaeron's crag) like fierce foes
They confounded all with ravage, waste and wide.
They snatched infants from their sweet homes.
And what they threw across their shoulders, clung
Unfastened, nor fell down to the black ground—
Not even brass, nor heavy iron. On their locks
Was fire that burned them not. Of those they pillaged
Some in their sudden fury rushed to arms.   770
Then was a mightier miracle seen, O king:
From the Bacchae the pointed lances drew no blood.
Rather, hurling their thyrsi like javelins, the Bacchae

760. *Asopus:* river between Cithaeron and Thebes.

Drove all away and smote them as they fled.
Women drove back men, but not without the god's help.
　　Then the Bacchae returned from where they had come,
To the fountains, which the god made flow;
Washed off the blood, and from their cheeks the serpents
Licked the drops and made them bright and clean.
This god then, whoever he may be, my master,   780
Receive within our city. In other things too he is great,
But in this I hear men say he is the greatest:
That he has given sorrow-soothing wine to man;
For where wine is not, love will never be,
Nor any other joy of human life.°

　　　　　[*Exit the* SHEPHERD. *After a protracted silence, the*
　　　　　　　CHORUS *reacts to the* SHEPHERD's *report.*]

CHORUS. I am afraid to speak the words of freedom
　　Before the tyrant, yet it must be said:
　　"Inferior to no god is Dionysus."
PENTHEUS. It *is* here then, like a wild fire, burning on,
　　This Bacchic insolence, Hellas' deep disgrace!   790

　　　　　　　[PENTHEUS *addresses an* ATTENDANT.]

　　No more delay! Go to the Electrian gates°
　　And summon all that bear shields, and all
　　The cavalry on their prancing steeds,
　　And those that hurl the lance, and the archers
　　That twang the sharp string. Against these Bacchae
　　We will go to war. It were indeed too much
　　To endure from women what we endure.

　　　　　　　[*The* ATTENDANT *leaves hurriedly.*]

DIONYSUS. You will not be persuaded by my words,
　　Pentheus! Yet though at your hands I have suffered wrong,
　　I warn you, rise not up against a god.   800
　　Stay quietly. Bromius will never let
　　You drive his Bacchae from their mountain revels.
PENTHEUS. Don't start instructing me! Rather, having escaped once,
　　Now just save yourself—or shall I punish you once more?
DIONYSUS. Rather do sacrifice, than in your rage
　　Kick against necessity's goad—a mortal against a god.
PENTHEUS. I'll sacrifice (and I'll do it Cithaeron's glens,
　　As they deserve) a horde of slaughtered women.
DIONYSUS. You'll run away. It will be shameful for shields of brass

784–85. *whose . . . life:* a reference to the belief in wine as a magical source of
vitality, and particularly of sexual potency.　791. *Electrian gates:* southern entrance to Thebes, where the road from Cithaeron arrived.

To flee before the Bacchic wands of ivy. 810
PENTHEUS. I am bewildered by this dubious stranger;
Doing or suffering, he will not keep quiet.
DIONYSUS. My friend! you still might bring this to a good end.
PENTHEUS. How? by being the slave of my own slaves?
DIONYSUS. These women—without force of arms, I'll bring them back.
PENTHEUS. Alas! now he's plotting some trap against me!
DIONYSUS. But what if I could save you by my skills?
PENTHEUS. You've all conspired, that you may hold your Bacchic orgies.
DIONYSUS. I've conspired, it's true, but with the god.
PENTHEUS. Bring out my armor! And you, stop blabbering. 820
[PENTHEUS *is about to leave but* DIONYSUS *lures him back.*]
DIONYSUS. Hey! Would you like to see them seated on the mountains?
PENTHEUS. Yes! For *that* sight I'd give a thousand weight of gold.
DIONYSUS. Why have you fallen into this strange desire?
PENTHEUS. Of course, it would be sad to see them in their drunkenness.
DIONYSUS. Yet you would gladly see, what seen would grieve you.
PENTHEUS. Indeed—at least if I were seated in silence underneath
the fir-trees.
DIONYSUS. But if you go in secret they will track you down.
PENTHEUS. Then rather openly; in this you've spoken sense.
DIONYSUS. Let me then lead you—and you will dare the trip?
PENTHEUS. Lead on—and quickly! Let no time be lost now! 830
DIONYSUS. But first dress yourself in this linen dress.
PENTHEUS. What! Should I, a man, dress like women?
DIONYSUS. Else they might kill you, if you were seen *there* as a *man.*
PENTHEUS. Again you make sense, like one who was wise long ago.
DIONYSUS. Dionysus taught me all of these things.
PENTHEUS. How then can we best do what you advise?
DIONYSUS. I will enter the house—and there dress you.
PENTHEUS. In what dress? A woman's? I am ashamed to wear it.
DIONYSUS. Are you no longer eager to see the Maenads?
PENTHEUS. Well, what dress do you say I must wrap around me? 840
DIONYSUS. I will comb your hair down long on your brow for you.
PENTHEUS. What is the second part of my costume?
DIONYSUS. A dress to your feet, a bonnet on your head.
PENTHEUS [*fascinated and pleased*]. And then, in what else will you
dress me?
DIONYSUS. A thyrsus in your hand, a dappled fawn-skin.
PENTHEUS. But really, I could not possibly put on a woman's dress.
DIONYSUS. Well, then you would have bloodshed, warring on the Bac-
chae.
PENTHEUS. Right, I must first go survey the field.

DIONYSUS. It would be wiser than to hunt evil with evil.
PENTHEUS. But how will I pass through the city, without being seen
    by the Thebans? 850
DIONYSUS. We can go by deserted byways; I will lead you safely.
PENTHEUS. Anything would be better than to be mocked by these
    Bacchae.
    When we come back—well, we'll deliberate what seems best.
DIONYSUS. As you wish. I am here at your service.
PENTHEUS. I might go; for either I must go forth in arms,
    Or follow the advice you give me.
               [PENTHEUS *enters his palace.*]
DIONYSUS. Women, this man is in our net; he goes
    To find his just doom among the Bacchae.
    Dionysus, to your work! You are not far off;
    Vengeance is ours. But bereave him first of his senses, 860
    Inspire him with light-headed frenzy. For in his right mind
    He would never have put on a woman's dress;
    But now, shaken in his mind, he will wear it.
    I will make him a laughing stock to all Thebes—
    Led in a woman's dress through the wide city
    After all those fierce threats in which he was so great.
    But I must go; and so must Pentheus, wearing the clothes
    Which he will wear when (killed by his own mother's hand)
    He goes down to Hades. He will recognize
    Dionysus, son of Zeus, mightiest among the gods 870
    Yet mildest to the sons of men.
              [DIONYSUS *enters the palace.*]
CHORUS [*sings*].
    —O when, through the long night,
      With fleet foot glancing white,
    Shall I go dancing in my revelry,
      My neck cast back, and bare
      Into the dewy air
    Like sportive fawn in the green meadow's glee,
      When she escapes and in fear springs
      Over the encircling rings,
    Over the well-woven hunters' nets far off and fast, 880
      While swift along her track
      The huntsman cheers his pack,
    With panting toil and fiery storm-wind haste?
    Where down the river-bank spreads the wide meadow,
      She rejoices in the manless solitude,

Couches at length beneath the silent shadow
   Of the old hospitable wood.

—What is wisest? What is fairest,
   Of god's boons to man the rarest?
   With the conscious conquering hand   890
   Above an enemy's head to stand?
   What is fairest still is dearest.

—Slowly come, but come at length,
   In their majestic strength,
Faithful and true, the avenging deities:
   And chastening human folly,
   And the mad pride unholy,
Of those who to the gods bow not their knees.
   For hidden still and mute
   As glides their printless foot,   900
The unholy on their winding path they hound.

   For it is wrong to know,
   And it is wrong to do,
Beyond the law's inexorable bound.
It costs little in his own power sublime
   To honor divinity, whatever it may be;
And custom sanctioned by the longest time,
Is law, nature's unrepealed decree.

—What is wisest? What is fairest,
   Of god's boons to man the rarest?   910
   With the conscious conquering hand
   Above an enemy's head to stand?
   What is fairest still is dearest.

—He who has escaped the turbulent sea,
   And reached the haven, happy is he!
   Happy he whose toils are over,
   In the race of wealth and power!
   This one here, and that one there,
   Passes by, and everywhere
   Still expectant thousands over   920
   Thousand hopes are seen to hover.
Some hopes for mortals end in bliss,
   Some have already fled away:
Happiness alone is his,
   Who is happy today.

[DIONYSUS *returns from the palace, shouting over his
shoulder to* PENTHEUS, *who is still in the palace.*]

DIONYSUS. You who are eager to see that which you should not see,
    And desirous of that you should not desire,
    Pentheus, I say, come out! Let me see you
    Clothed in the Bacchic Maenads' female dress,
    To spy on your mother and her company.   930

[PENTHEUS *enters, dressed like a Bacchic woman, but with
the addition of a linen dress. He begins to show signs of
being crazed by* DIONYSUS.]

DIONYSUS. Hey, you look just like one of Cadmus' daughters!

PENTHEUS. What! Now indeed, two suns I seem to see,
    A double Thebes, two seven-gated cities;
    You, as a bull, seem to walk before me,
    And horns have grown on your head. But were you once
    A wild beast? ° For you really are a bull now.

DIONYSUS. It's the god that's here with us; unfriendly before,
    He's now at truce: now do you see what you should see?

PENTHEUS [*as he grins and imitates a female gait*].
    What do I see? Is that not the step of Ino?
    And is it not Agave there, my mother?   940

DIONYSUS. It really looks like them when I watch you.
    But, look! this lock of yours has strayed out of its place,
    No longer as I fixed it beneath your headband.

PENTHEUS. Tossing my head this way now, then that way
    In Bacchic glee, I must have shaken it from its place.

DIONYSUS. But I, whose care is to attend to you,
    Will braid it up again. Lift up your head.

PENTHEUS. Fix it as you wish; because I'm in your charge, completely.

DIONYSUS. Now your belt is loosened, and the long folds of your dress
    Droop outward, no longer concealing your ankles.   950

PENTHEUS. You're right, it seems; around my right foot at least,
    But around the other my dress sits straight and well.

DIONYSUS. Will you not think me the best of friends,
    When you see that the Bacchae are chaste, against expectation?

PENTHEUS. The thyrsus—shall I hold it in my right hand?
    Or am I more like a Bacchante this way?

DIONYSUS. In your right hand, and with your right foot raise it.
    [*Pauses.*]
    I approve of the change of mind that has come over you.

PENTHEUS [*with a crazed sense of strength*].

936. *wild beast:* Dionysus, in his aspect as a fertility god, was sometimes represented with the attributes of a bull.

Could I not now lift up on my shoulders
   Cithaeron's crag, with all the Bacchae?   960
DIONYSUS. You could if you wished. You were not in your
   Right mind before; now you are as you should be.
PENTHEUS. Shall I take crowbars, pluck it up with my hands,
   Or thrust my arm or shoulder beneath its base?
DIONYSUS. Now just don't destroy the haunts of the Nymphs,
   The seats where Pan plays his shepherd's pipes!
PENTHEUS. You make sense; it's not by force that one conquers
   These women. I'll go hide in the fir-trees.
DIONYSUS. You will be hiding in a fatal ambush,
   Stealing up like a treacherous spy on the Maenads.   970
PENTHEUS. And now I seem to see them there like mating birds,
   Couching on their soft beds among the bushes.
DIONYSUS. Well then, go there, delegated to watch over them.
   You might just seize them—if they do not seize you first.
PENTHEUS. Then lead me through the center of Thebes!
   I, only I, have dared a deed like this.
DIONYSUS. You, only you, suffer for this city; yes, you alone.
   Therefore struggles await you—struggles which must be.
   Follow me. I'll accompany you there safely;
   From there someone else will lead you back.   980
PENTHEUS. I suppose my mother.
DIONYSUS. Distinguished as everyone sees.
PENTHEUS. That's where I am going—to her.
DIONYSUS. You will return home carried . . .
PENTHEUS.   O the soft carriage!
DIONYSUS. In your mother's arms.
PENTHEUS.   You will force me into effeminate luxury!
DIONYSUS. Such luxury, indeed!
PENTHEUS. But, I deserve it.

> [PENTHEUS *starts toward the exit for Mount Cithaeron. As*
> DIONYSUS *follows, he still addresses* PENTHEUS *and then,*
> *with* PENTHEUS *off stage, he lingers for one more remark.*]

DIONYSUS. You are unusual, yes strange, and you go to strange experi-
      ences.
   Your fame will soar up to the high heavens.
   Stretch forth your hand, Agave, and you, her sisters,   990
   Daughters of Cadmus! To a terrible struggle
   I lead this youth! I myself shall be the victor,
   Bromius and I; the event will show the rest.   [*Exit* DIONYSUS.]
CHORUS [*sings*].
   —Ho! fleet dogs and furious, to the mountains, ho!

Where their mystic revels Cadmus' daughters keep.
  Rouse them goad them out
Against him, in woman's dress concealed,
Male spy on the Maenads in their dark rites unrevealed.
First his mother shall see him peering deep
From the tall tree's trunk or from the wild crag steep.   1000
    Fiercely will she shout—
"Who's this spying on the Maenads' revels here on mountain
    rocks?
To the mountain, to the mountain, Bacchae, who has come?"
  What gave birth to him? He is not of woman's blood.
  Did the lioness? Or the Libyan Gorgon's° brood?
—Come, Justice, come, display yourself,
  With your bright sword reveal yourself;
    A bloody sentence wreak
    On the dissevered neck
Of him who has neither god, nor law, or justice known,   1010
Echion's earth-born son.

—With thought unrighteous and lawless rage
  Against Bacchus and the rites of the mother,
    He still holds his frenzied strife.
He runs against the God, thinking it light
  To vanquish the invincible of might.
Such a man implacable death makes humble to the gods.
But a man of sound mind can live a smooth painless life.
I admire not, envy not, who is unsoundly overwise:
Mine is another chase—for me it's still the prize.   1020
    By night and day
  To live of the immortal gods in awe;
    Who fears them not
  Is but the outcast of all law.

—Come, Justice, come display yourself
  With your bright sword reveal yourself;
    The bloody sentence wreak
    On the dissevered neck
Of him who has neither god, nor law or justice known,
Echion's earth-born son.   1030

—Dionysus, appear! appear! either° as the stately steer
  Or many-headed dragon be,
Or the fire-breathing lion,° terrible to see.

1005. _Gorgon:_ winged female monsters with serpents in place of hair.   1031–33.
either . . . lion: For the purpose of destruction Dionysus is, as elsewhere in Greek
literature, invoked under his dangerous bestial appearance.

Come, Bacchus, come against the hunter of the Bacchae
  Even now, now as he falls
Upon the Maenads' fatal herd beneath.
  With smiling brow,
  Around him throw,
The inexorable net of death.

[*A* MESSENGER *from Mount Cithaeron enters.*]

MESSENGER. O house most prosperous once throughout all Hellas!   1040
  House of Cadmus, the Sidonian who in this land
  Sowed the dragon's serpent's earth-born harvest,
  How I mourn for you, even though I am a slave;
  For faithful slaves grieve for their master's sorrows.
CHORUS. What's this? Any news about the Bacchae?
MESSENGER. Pentheus is dead, old Echion's son.
CHORUS. King Bromius, you are indeed a mighty god!
MESSENGER. What are you saying? How is this? Do you rejoice,
  Woman, in my master's awful fate?
CHORUS. Lightly I, a stranger, chant my barbarous strains;   1050
  I cower not in fear for the menace of chains.
MESSENGER. Do you think all Thebes is so void of men that . . . .
CHORUS. O Dionysus! Dionysus! Thebes now
  Has no power over me.
MESSENGER. It's pardonable, but it is not good,
  Women, to rejoice in others' miseries.
CHORUS. Tell me, then by what fate did the unjust—
  That man, the dark contriver of injustice—die?
MESSENGER. Having left behind us the houses of this Theban city,
  And passed along Asopus' winding shore,   1060
  We began to climb Cithaeron's steep rock—
  Pentheus and I (I was my master's attendant),
  And he that led us on our quest, the stranger.
  And first we crept along a grassy glade,
  With silent footsteps, and with silent tongues,
  Slow-moving so as to see, without being seen.
  There was a rock-walled glen, watered by a streamlet,
  And shadowed over with pines; we saw the Maenads
  Sitting there, all their hands busy with pleasant tasks.
  Some were winding the leafy thyrsus, whose ivy   1070
  Had dropped away, with fresh ivy.
  Others, gamboling like fillies unharnessed from the bridle,
  Chanted Bacchic songs in response.
  Ill-fated Pentheus, since he could barely see
  That company of women, said: "Where we now stand, stranger,
  I cannot see these fake Maenads,

But if I mounted on a bank, or a tall fir-tree,
I could see their deeds of shame properly."
And then I saw that stranger do a miracle.
He seized a fir-tree's high heaven-reaching stem,   1080
And dragged it down, dragged, dragged to the low earth;
And like a bow it bent. As a curved wheel
Becomes a circle in the turner's lathe,
So did the stranger bend down that mountain fir
To the earth, a deed of more than mortal strength.
Then, seating Pentheus on the highest branches of the tree,
He let it rise upward, steadily, gently
Through his hands, careful lest it shake him off;
And slowly it rose, upright to its height,
Bearing my master seated on its ridge.°   1090
But there he was seen by the Maenads better than he saw them.
More visible he could not be, seated aloft.
The stranger now vanished from our view,
And then from the heavens a voice (most likely
Dionysus') shouted loud: "Look! I bring you,
Women, the man that mocked you and me, that scorned
Our rites; now take your vengeance."
And as he spoke, a flash of holy fire
Stood up, and blazed from earth straight up to heaven.
Silent the air, silent the wooded grove   1100
Held its still leaves: not a sound of beasts.
The Bacchae, as their ears just caught the half-heard voice,
Stood up erect, and rolled their wondering eyes.
Again he shouted. But when Cadmus' daughters
Heard clearly the god's awakening voice,
They rushed forth faster than a dove,
Their nimble feet running up and down.
Agave first, his mother, then her sisters and all
The Maenads, down the torrent's bed in the grove,
From crag to crag they leaped, maddened by the god,   1110
And first they hurled heavy stones at Pentheus,
Climbing a rock opposite his tree; and branches of fir-trees,
Like javelins, they threw through the sounding air
At Pentheus, their target. And yet they did not strike him;
His height was still greater than their eager rage.

1090. *seated on its ridge:* Perching Pentheus atop a fir-tree possibly had traditional
symbolic significance. As a representative of sexual repression and antifeminism,
Pentheus is "impaled" on the most phallic of those objects, embodying the power
of the lord of the trees and god of vegetation, Dionysus.

There sat the wretch, helpless in his despair.
Then they struck off branches of oak, as though by lightning,
And tried to pry up the roots, with the branches as wedges.
But their wild labors all were vain.
Agave spoke, "Come, all of you, and stand around the tree.   1120
Grip the tree, you Maenads, soon we will seize
The beast that rides on it, so that he will never reveal
The mysteries of our god." A thousand hands
Were on the fir-tree, and tore it from the earth:
And he that sat on top fell down, headlong, down he
Fell to the ground, with thousand piteous shrieks,
Pentheus, for he knew well his end was near.
His mother began the sacrificial slaughter
And fell on him first. He threw his bonnet from his hair
That she might know and not kill him,   1130
Poor Agave. And caressing her cheek he said:
"I am your child, your own, mother!
I'm Pentheus, whom in Echion's house you bore.
Have mercy on me, mother! Do not,
Because of my wrongs, kill your own son."
She, foaming at the mouth, her rolling eyeballs
Whirling around, in her unreasoning reason,
By Bacchus all possessed, knew and heeded nothing.
She seized his left arm at the elbow,
And, with her feet set against his side,   1140
Tore out the shoulder—not with her own strength:
The god made that cruel deed easy for her hands.
And Ino worked on the other side,
Tearing out his flesh. Also Autonoë and the rest
Pressed fiercely on, and there was one wild din—
He groaning deeply while he had breath to groan,
They shouting triumph. One carried a torn-off arm of his,
Another a sandaled foot; and both his sides
Lay open, torn. Every woman in her bloody hand
Tossed wildly to and fro dead Pentheus' limbs.   1150
His body lay all over, parts beneath the rough rocks,
Parts in the forest's thick-strewn leaves,
Not easy to be found. His mad mother seized
His grisly head in her hands and, impaling it
On a thyrsus, carried it all over Cithaeron, like a mountain lion's,
Leaving her sisters in their Maenad dance.
But now she is coming here exulting in her unfortunate hunt,
Coming inside these walls, still invoking Bacchus,

Her fellow-hunter, partner in her prey,
Her triumph—a triumph soon to end in tears!   1160
I myself fled from the sight of that dark tragedy,
Hastening here before Agave reaches the palace.
O! to be of sound mind, to revere the gods—
This is the best, and I think the wisest, course for man.

CHORUS.
             Dance and sing
             In Bacchic ring,
Shout, shout the fate, the fate of gloom,
    Of Pentheus, from the dragon born;°
    He, who a woman's dress has worn,
Following the bull, the harbinger, that led him to his doom.   1170
    O you Theban Bacchae!
Intone now the hymn victorious,
    The hymn all glorious,
To the tear, and to the groan!
    O game of glory!
To bathe the hands stained and gory,
    In the blood of her own son.
    But I see Agave, Pentheus' mother,
    Nearing the palace with distorted eyes.
    Now welcome the revelrous band of the Evian god!   1180

AGAVE. Asian Bacchae!
CHORUS. Who are you, urging us on?
AGAVE. From the mountains we are carrying
    To the palace gate
Our freshly cut wreath, our blessed quarry of the hunt.
CHORUS. I see, I see, and welcome you, our fellow-reveler.
AGAVE. Without a net, without a snare,
    The lion's cub, I took him there.
CHORUS. In the wilderness, or where?
AGAVE. Cithaeron . . .
CHORUS.   Cithaeron what?
AGAVE.   Gave him to be killed.   1190
CHORUS. Who struck him first?
AGAVE.   Mine, mine, the glorious lot.
    "Agave the blessed," I am called by the Bacchic band.
CHORUS. Who else?
AGAVE.   Cadmus' . . .
CHORUS.   Cadmus' what?

1168. *dragon horn:* descended from the dragon's teeth sown by Cadmus.

AGAVE. Cadmus' daughters° after me, after me touched
This beastly prey. What a fortunate hunt!
CHORUS [*Two lines missing in original.*]
AGAVE. Then share the feast with me!
CHORUS. What? Share, unhappy woman? Share what?
    [AGAVE *takes a crazed look at* PENTHEUS' *impaled head,*
       which she still believes to be that of a lion cub.]
AGAVE. How delicate this cub is, and young!
The thin mane has only recently sprung
  Over his forehead fair.   1200
CHORUS. At least he *looks* like a grazing beast with that hair.
AGAVE. Bacchus, hunter known to fame!
Did not he our Maenads bring
On the track of this proud game?
CHORUS. A mighty hunter is our king!
AGAVE. Do you commend me now?
CHORUS.   I do.
AGAVE. Soon the Thebans . . .
CHORUS. And certainly your son, Pentheus . . .
AGAVE. Will praise his mother, who caught as hunting prey
This lion cub.   1210
CHORUS. Prodigious prey!
AGAVE. Prodigiously caught!
CHORUS. Do you rejoice?
AGAVE. Yes, I'm happy with my great, great achievement
On this hunt—manifestly great.
CHORUS. Then, poor woman, to the citizens of Thebes
Now show the conquered prey you brought here.
    [AGAVE *raises her thyrsus with* PENTHEUS' *head, still not*
    recognizing it as her son's head, and shows it to the audi-
          ence on all sides.]
AGAVE. You who live in the high-towered Theban city
Come and gaze at our prey,
The mighty beast caught by Cadmus' daughters—   1220
Not with Thessalian sharp-pointed javelins,
Nor nets, but with the white and delicate palms
Of our own hands. Go ahead, and make your boast,
Trusting in the spear-maker's useless craft—
But we with these hands have taken our prey, and torn
The mangled limbs of this grim beast apart.
    But where is my old father? Let him come here!

1194. *Cadmus' daughters:* her sisters Autonoë and Ino.

And where is my son Pentheus? Let him mount
On a broad ladder in front of our house,
And on the gable nail this lion's head, 1230
That I have brought him from our splendid chase.
[CADMUS *enters with attendants who carry the limbs of*
PENTHEUS *on a stretcher.*]

CADMUS. Follow me, follow, bearing your sad burden,
My servants, Pentheus' body, to our house;
The body that with long and weary search
I found at length in lone Cithaeron's glens;
Thus torn, not lying in one place, but widely
Scattered amid the dark and tangled thicket.
Already, as I entered in the city
With old Teiresias, from the Bacchae
I heard about the fearful doings of my daughters. 1240
And so I rushed back to the mountain, to gather
The body of this boy, murdered by the furious Maenads.
There I saw Autonoë, who bore Actaeon to Aristaeus,
Autonoë I saw, and Ino with her
Still in the thicket, goaded with wild madness.
But someone said that on her dancing feet
Agave had come here—and indeed it's true,
For I see her now: O most unhappy sight!

AGAVE. Father, now it can be your greatest boast:
That you sired the very best of mortal women— 1250
Me—me the very best of those excellent sisters.
For I left the shuttle and the loom
For mightier deeds—to capture wild beasts with my own
Hands. Look, I carry in my arms
These glorious trophies, to be hung up high
On your house: receive them father;
Call your friends to the feast! You are blest,
Most blest, through us who have done such splendid deeds.

CADMUS. Measureless grief! No eye may gaze on it,
On the slaughter wrought by those most awful hands. 1260
O, what a sacrifice before the gods!
All Thebes, and us, you call to the feast.
Justly—too justly—has king Bromius
Destroyed us, fatal god of our own race.

AGAVE [*looking at* CADMUS' *joyless face*].
How sullen is man in his old age,
And grouchy in his mien! I hope my son will be
More like his mother, mighty in his hunting,

When he goes forth with the youth of Thebes
To hunt wild beasts. But the only thing at which he excels
Is warring against the gods. We two, father, 1270
Must counsel him against his evil wisdom,
But where is he? Who will call him out here
So he may see me in my happiness?

CADMUS. No, no! Enough! When you realize what you have done,
With what deep sorrow will you suffer. But if
To the very end you remain in your present state,
You will seem not to be unhappy—but without being happy.

AGAVE. What is not well? Is there something sad?

CADMUS. First lift your eyes up to the air around.

AGAVE. There. But why do you suggest that I look? 1280

CADMUS. Is it all still the same? Or does there appear to be a change?

AGAVE. It seems brighter, clearer than before.

CADMUS. Do you sense the same elation in your soul?

AGAVE. I do not quite know what you mean . . . but I am becoming
Conscious, my mind is changing . . . settling down.

CADMUS. Can you listen and answer me clearly?

AGAVE. Now I have forgotten, father, all that I said before.

CADMUS. To whom were you married?

AGAVE. Echion, the one they call the Dragon-born.

CADMUS. Who was the son you bore your husband? 1290

AGAVE. Pentheus.

CADMUS. And whose head are you holding in your hands?

AGAVE. A lion's; that's what my fellow-hunters said.

CADMUS. Look at it straight; it takes little effort to look.

AGAVE. What do I see? No! What's this in my hands?

CADMUS. Look at it again, more closely. Examine it clearly.

AGAVE. Oh, no! I see the greatest sorrow! Wretched me!

CADMUS. Now does it still look like a lion to you?

AGAVE. No: wretch, wretch that I am; it's . . . it's Pentheus' head!

CADMUS. Mourned even before you recognized him. 1300

AGAVE. Who murdered him? . . . How did he get into my hands?

CADMUS. Sorrowful truth! how untimely do you come!

AGAVE. Come on, speak! My heart leaps with foreboding.

CADMUS. You are the one that killed him—you and your sisters.

AGAVE. Where did he die? in his palace? where?

CADMUS. There where once the dogs tore Actaeon in pieces.

AGAVE. But why did Pentheus go to Cithaeron, ill-fated Pentheus?

CADMUS. To mock the god, to mock the revels there.

AGAVE. But how and why had we gone there?

CADMUS. In madness! The whole city was filled with Bacchic frenzy. 1310

AGAVE. Dionysus has destroyed us! How late I learn it.

CADMUS. Mocked with dread mockery; for you did not consider him a
              god.

AGAVE. Father, where's the body of my dearest son now?

CADMUS. I brought it here, only after searching out the pieces with
              great effort.

AGAVE. Are all the limbs together, sound and whole? . . .

                   [*Here a line is missing in the original.*]

        But Pentheus—why should *he* have part in my desperate fury?

CADMUS. He was like you—he blasphemed the god.

        All of us,° therefore, are wrapped up in one terrible ruin:
        You, he, in whom has perished all our house,
        And I who, with no male offspring, see   1320
        This single fruit—O miserable—of your womb
        So shamefully, so horribly killed—
        Your son, to whom our house looked up, the pride
        Of our whole palace he, my daughter's son,
        The awe of the whole city.   [CADMUS *now addressed* PENTHEUS'
              remains.]

                                None would dare
        Insult the old man when he saw
        Your face, well knowing he would pay the penalty.
        Unhonored now, I am driven out from my home;
        Cadmus the great, who sowed the whole race of Thebes
        In the earth, and reaped that harvest fair.   1330
        O best beloved of men, even though you are no more,
        Yet you still are dearest of my children.
        No more, fondling this gray beard with your hand,
        Will you call me "grandfather," no more
        Embrace me and say, "Who does not honor you,
        Old man, who troubles or afflicts your heart?
        Tell me, that I may avenge your wrong, my father!"
        Now I am the most grieved of men. You are pitiable—
        Even more pitiable your mother—and sad are her sisters.
        If there is still any man who scorns the great gods,   1340
        Let him look on this death, and know that there are gods.

*Here follows a large lacuna in the extant manuscript. Missing are probably
(1) a speech by Agave, explaining her bitter sorrow and showing her affec-*

1318. *All of us:* Cadmus foresees his banishment, knowing that a religious pollution as severe as that caused by the murder of Pentheus can only be expiated by
the expulsion of the whole guilty family.

tion for Pentheus, and (2) the return to the stage of Dionysus, who inter-
prets the murder of Pentheus in terms of divine justice, and then orders the
expulsion of Agave and her sisters from Thebes in expiation of the murder.
Dionysus next turns to Cadmus, and there the text resumes.

DIONYSUS. And you, Cadmus, father of this earth-born race,
  Will become a dragon, and your wife Harmonia,
  Daughter of Ares, will likewise be a snake.
  With your wife, leading a barbarians' host
  You will ride in a cart drawn by young bulls.
  And many cities with your countless host
  Will you destroy, but when your army dares destroy
  The shrine of Apollo, they will return home
  In shameful flight. But Ares will guard Harmonia   1350
  And you, and will bring you to the Isles of the Blest.
      This say I, of no mortal father born,
  Dionysus, son of Zeus. Had all of you only known how
  To be sound-minded when you did not wish to, Zeus' son
  Would now have been your friend; you would have been happy
      still.
CADMUS. Dionysus, we beg you! We have done wrong!
DIONYSUS. Too late your insight; when you should have known me,
      you would not.
CADMUS. We recognize that now; but you're extreme in vengeance.
DIONYSUS. Was I, a god, not outraged by you?
CADMUS. The gods should not be like men in their wrath.   1360
DIONYSUS. My father Zeus assented to all these fates long ago.
AGAVE. Alas, old man! Our exile is in fact decreed.
DIONYSUS. Why then delay the inevitable?
CADMUS. Child, to what a terrible end we have fallen,
  Miserable you, your sisters, and unhappy me.
  Also I to the barbarians must depart, although I am
  An old man. For there's a prophecy
  That Harmonia, my wife, daughter of Ares, will lead
  Against Hellas a barbaric mingled host. And transformed
  Into a dragon I, with dragon nature fierce,   1370
  Will lead the stranger spearmen against the altars
  And tombs of Hellas. Never will my woes end,
  Sad wretch! Not even when I have ferried over
  Dark Acheron, shall I exist in peace.
AGAVE. Father! Into exile I go, without you!
CADMUS. Why do you clasp me in your arms, sad child,

A drone among the bees, a swan° worn out?
AGAVE. Where shall I go, an exile from my country?
CADMUS. I do not know, my child; your father now is a feeble help.
AGAVE. Farewell, my home! Farewell, my native Thebes!　　　　　1380
　　　My bridal chamber, banished I go.
CADMUS. Go to the house of Aristaeus,° my child.
AGAVE. I grieve for you, father.
CADMUS. I for you.
　　　And for your sisters.
AGAVE. Terrible, terrible, this deep disgrace,
　　　That Dionysus has brought upon our race.
DIONYSUS. Terrible the wrong that you had done;
　　　My name was unhonored in Thebes alone.
AGAVE. Father, farewell.　　　　　　　　　　　　　　　　　　1390
CADMUS. Farewell, poor, unhappy daughter.
　　　Farewell, but you will find the journey harsh.　[*Exit* CADMUS.]
AGAVE. So lead me, attendants, to meet my sisters now,
　　　Sad fallen exiles. Let me go,
　　　Where cursed Cithaeron may never see me
　　　Nor I cursed Cithaeron see again,
　　　Where there is no memory of the thyrsus dance.
　　　Let the Bacchic revels be the care of others.
　　　　　　　　　　[*Exit* AGAVE *and her attendants.*]
CHORUS. Many are the forms of gods
　　　And many things the gods accomplish　　　　　　　　　　1400
　　　Unexpectedly. Even what is thought likely
　　　Is not fulfilled. But god has found a way
　　　For the unexpected.
　　　Such was the end of this event.

1377. *swan:* The swan is a type of filial loyalty.　1382. *Aristaeus:* a god of
agriculture, cattle breeding, and hunting; the father of Actaeon.

Aristophanes

Lysistrata

TRANSLATED BY CHARLES T. MURPHY

Aristophanes (445?–385 B.C.?)

OF THE MORE THAN FORTY COMIC POETS OF THE FIFTH CEN-
tury B.C. whose names are still known, Aristophanes alone is known through
surviving works. He was born in the days of political stability and peace,
when Pericles, Sophocles, and the Parthenon were becoming the symbols of
a remarkable Athenian community. But most of his plays were written at a
time when Athenian democracy was disintegrating because of war and internal stresses. Every one of his comedies is a testimony to his interest in the
intellectual, literary, and political developments of his day. They caricature
political and cultural figures, they castigate the educational system introduced by the Sophists, and they criticize the war between Athens and
Sparta. The most famous of these plays are *The Acharnians, The Knights,
The Clouds, The Wasps, The Peace, The Birds, Lysistrata,* and *The Frogs.*

Aristophanes' comedies, like those of all Greek comic poets, were produced in dramatic contests at festivals of the god Dionysus in Athens. Revelrous festivity in the cult of Dionysus may have been associated with the
origins of comedy. According to the most plausible theory, comedy developed
out of the obscene ridicule and bawdy choral songs which accompanied a
phallus-bearing procession. The basic choral element acquired a decisive
additional feature when the chorus, singing verses of invective, was engaged
in an improvised altercation, or *agon,* with a single actor. Most of these
early elements—a chorus, invective, obscenity, altercation—remain visible in
the comedies of Aristophanes.

Lysistrata was first produced in 411 B.C., the twentieth year of the Peloponnesian War. The plot revolves around a group of Greek women who aim
at stopping the war. Their plan is simple—to deprive all men of sexual
pleasures until they have concluded a peace—and it works. But the temporary sacrifice is portrayed, with a torrent of sexual allusions, as an extreme
hardship for both the women and the men.

It is significant that Aristophanes expressed so openly, in the midst of a
bitter war between Athens and Sparta, a strong conviction that all Greeks
could and should coexist. The general tone of conciliation which permeates
the play is reflected in the fact that the chief helper of Lysistrata (an
Athenian) is a Spartan woman, Lampito. This tone is also maintained in a
famous speech that Lysistrata addresses to the male representatives of the
two parties to the war, in which she reminds the warring Greeks of their
common heritage. In a manner characteristic of Aristophanes, this serious
theme of unity and conciliation is developed throughout the play with a
profusion of wit and obscenity.

Lysistrata

LYSISTRATA[1] ⎫
CALONICE ⎬ *Athenian women*
MYRRHINE ⎭

LAMPITO, *a Spartan woman*

CHORUS OF ATHENIAN MEN

CHORUS OF ATHENIAN WOMEN

ATHENIAN MAGISTRATE

CINESIAS, *an Athenian, husband of Myrrhine*

INFANT CHILD *of Cinesias and Myrrhine*

SPARTAN HERALD

SPARTAN AMBASSADORS

ATHENIAN AMBASSADORS

CHORUS OF SPARTANS

CHORUS OF ATHENIANS

SILENT CHARACTERS: A BOEOTIAN WOMAN; A CORINTHIAN WOMAN;
    A SCYTHIAN SLAVE-GIRL; FOUR SCYTHIAN POLICEMEN;
    CINESIAS' SLAVE.

SCENE. *in Athens, beneath the Acropolis. In the center of the stage is the Propylaea, or gateway to the Acropolis; to one side is a small grotto, sacred to Pan. The Orchestra represents a slope leading up to the gateway.*
It is early in the morning. LYSISTRATA *is pacing impatiently up and down.*

LYSISTRATA.[1] If they'd been summoned to worship the God of Wine, or Pan,[2] or to visit the Queen of Love, why, you couldn't have pushed your way through the streets for all the timbrels.[3] But now there's not a single woman here—except my neighbor; here she comes. [*Enter* CALONICE.] Good day to you, Calonice.

CALONICE. And to you, Lysistrata. [*Noticing* LYSISTRATA's *impatient air.*] But what ails you? Don't scowl, my dear; it's not becoming to you to knit your brows like that.

LYSISTRATA [*sadly*]. Ah, Calonice, my heart aches; I'm so annoyed at us women. For among men we have a reputation for sly trickery—

CALONICE. And rightly too, on my word!

LYSISTRATA. —but when they were told to meet here to consider a matter of no small importance, they lie abed and don't come.

CALONICE. Oh, they'll come all right, my dear. It's not easy for a woman to get out, you know. One is working on her husband, another is getting up the maid, another has to put the baby to bed, or wash and feed it.

LYSISTRATA. But after all, there are other matters more important than all that.

CALONICE. My dear Lysistrata, just what is this matter you've summoned us women to consider? What's up? Something big?

LYSISTRATA. Very big.

CALONICE [*interested*]. It is stout, too?

LYSISTRATA [*smiling*]. Yes indeed—both big and stout.

CALONICE. What? And the women still haven't come? [4]

[1] The names of the characters in ancient comedies often have a symbolic meaning. Thus Lysistrata, "She who dissolves armies"; Calonice, "Beautiful victory"; Myrrhine ("Myrtle"), suggests *myrton* ("myrtle-berry"), which is a colloquial expression for "female genital organs"; Lampito, a famous Spartan name, suggests "luminous brightness"; Cinesias suggests *kinein* ("to move"), which is slang for having sexual intercourse.   [2] A rural Arcadian god of lascivious and mischievous tendencies often associated with the worship of Dionysus.   [3] Used in orgiastic cults, such as that of Dionysus.   [4] Sexual allusions abound in ancient comedy and were not considered offensive by the Athenian audiences, which always saw these plays at religious festivals. Invective and obscenity were regarded as traditional elements of comedy; censorship of the plays was unknown.

LYSISTRATA. It's not what you suppose; they'd have come soon enough for *that*. But I've worked up something, and for many a sleepless night I've turned it this way and that.

CALONICE [*in mock disappointment*]. Oh, I guess it's pretty fine and slender, if you've turned it this way and that.

LYSISTRATA. So fine that the safety of the whole of Greece lies in us women.

CALONICE. In us women? It depends on a very slender reed then.

LYSISTRATA. Our country's fortunes are in our hands; and whether the Spartans shall perish—[5]

CALONICE. Good! Let them perish, by all means.

LYSISTRATA. —and the Boeotians shall be completely annihilated.

CALONICE. Not completely! Please spare the eels.[6]

LYSISTRATA. As for Athens, I won't use any such unpleasant words. But you understand what I mean. But if the women will meet here—the Spartans, the Boeotians, and we Athenians—then all together we will save Greece.

CALONICE. But what could women do that's clever or distinguished? We just sit around all dolled up in silk robes, looking pretty in our sheer gowns and evening slippers.

LYSISTRATA. These are just the things I hope will save us: these silk robes, perfumes, evening slippers, rouge, and our chiffon blouses.

CALONICE. How so?

LYSISTRATA. So never a man alive will lift a spear against the foe—

CALONICE. I'll get a silk gown at once.

LYSISTRATA. —or take up his shield—

CALONICE. I'll put on my sheerest gown!

LYSISTRATA. —or sword.

CALONICE. I'll buy a pair of evening slippers.

LYSISTRATA. Well then, shouldn't the women have come?

CALONICE. Come? Why, they should have *flown* here.

LYSISTRATA. Well, my dear, just watch: they'll act in true Athenian fashion—everything too late! And now there's not a woman here from the shore or from Salamis.[7]

CALONICE. They're coming, I'm sure; at daybreak they were laying— to their oars to cross the straits.

---

[5] The time of the play is approximately 411 B.C., at which time the Athenians and Spartans (and their respective allies) had been waging the Peloponnesian War for almost twenty years.   [6] A favorite Athenian delicacy from Copais, a lake in Boeotia (central Greece, just north of Attica). Because of the war, eels had become rare in Athenian shops; Boeotia (led by their chief city, Thebes) was the closest ally of Sparta and the most bitter enemy of Athens in the Peloponnesian War.   [7] An island to the west across the bay from Athens.

LYSISTRATA. And those I expected would be the first to come—the women of Acharnae[8]—they haven't arrived.

CALONICE. Yet the wife of Theagenes[9] means to come: she consulted Hecate about it. [*Seeing a group of women approaching.*] But look! Here come a few. And there are some more over here. Hurrah! Where do they come from?

LYSISTRATA. From Anagyra.

CALONICE. Yes indeed! We've raised up a quite a stink from Anagyra[10] anyway.

[*Enter* MYRRHINE *in haste, followed by several other women.*]

MYRRHINE [*breathlessly*]. Have we come in time, Lysistrata? What do you say? Why so quiet?

LYSISTRATA. I can't say much for you, Myrrhine, coming at this hour on such important business.

MYRRHINE. Why, I had trouble finding my girdle in the dark. But if it's so important, we're here now; tell us.

LYSISTRATA. No. Let's wait a little for the women from Boeotia and the Peloponnesus.

MYRRHINE. That's a much better suggestion. Look! Here comes Lampito now.

[*Enter* LAMPITO *with two other women.*]

LYSISTRATA. Greetings, my dear Spartan friend. How pretty you look, my dear. What a smooth complexion and well-developed figure! You could throttle an ox.

LAMPITO. Faith, yes, I think I could. I take exercises and kick my heels against my bum. [*She demonstrates with a few steps of the Spartan "bottom-kicking" dance.*]

LYSISTRATA. And what splendid breasts you have.[11]

LAMPITO. La! You handle me like a prize steer.

LYSISTRATA. And who is this young lady with you?

LAMPITO. Faith, she's an Ambassadress from Boeotia.

---

[8] A village and district a few miles north of Athens. [9] An Athenian woman so superstitious that she never left her home without consulting the statue of the goddess Hecate—usually a sculptured pillar—at her front door. Hecate is goddess of the crossroads and magic arts, who confers the blessings of daily life. [10] A village and district about twenty miles south of Athens. There is a play on (1) the *anagyros,* a bad-smelling plant from which the district had its name (the "Hurrah!" in the previous line is sometimes translated as "ugh!" since Calonice mockingly exclaims in grief at the smell of the women from Anagyra); and on (2) the Greek idiom "don't move the anagryos," which means "let sleeping dogs lie." [11] A popular Spartan dress was more or less open on one side (fastened only with a pin) and could therefore be folded back easily to expose the body.

LYSISTRATA. Oh yes, a Boeotian, and blooming like a garden too.[12]

CALONICE [*lifting up her skirt*]. My word! How neatly her garden's weeded!

LYSISTRATA. And who is the other girl?

LAMPITO. Oh, she's a Corinthian swell.

MYRRHINE [*after a rapid examination*]. Yes indeed. She swells very nicely [*pointing*] here and here.

LAMPITO. Who has gathered together this company of women?

LYSISTRATA. I have.

LAMPITO. Speak up, then. What do you want?

MYRRHINE. Yes, my dear, do tell us what this important matter is.

LYSISTRATA. Very well, I'll tell you. But before I speak, let me ask you a little question.

MYRRHINE. Anything you like.

LYSISTRATA [*earnestly*]. Tell me: don't you yearn for the fathers of your children, who are away at the wars? I know you all have husbands abroad.

CALONICE. Why, yes; mercy me! my husband's been away for five months in Thrace keeping guard on—Eucrates.[13]

MYRRHINE. And mine for seven whole months in Pylus.[14]

LAMPITO. And mine, as soon as ever he returns from the fray, readjusts his shield and flies out of the house again.

LYSISTRATA. And as for lovers, there's not even a ghost of one left. Since the Milesians revolted from us,[15] I've not even seen an eight-inch dingus to be a leather consolation for us widows. Are you willing, if I can find a way, to help me end the war?

MYRRHINE. Goodness, yes! I'd do it, even if I had to pawn my dress and—get drunk on the spot!

CALONICE. And I, even if I had to let myself be split in two like a flounder.

LAMPITO. I'd climb up Mt. Taygetus[16] if I could catch a glimpse of peace.

LYSISTRATA. I'll tell you, then, in plain and simple words. My friends,

---

[12] Compared to Athens, Boeotia seemed like a rural plain or garden.   [13] Probably the brother of Nicias, an Athenian general who was an ardent advocate of peace and who was finally put to death by the Athenians in 413 B.C. (two years before this play) because of his lack of enthusiasm for warfare and his part in the complete defeat in 413 B.C. of an Athenian expedition to Sicily.   [14] Famous old town of Nestor on the west coast of the Peloponnesus; at this time occupied by Athenian troops.   [15] The previous year the city of Miletus (on the west coast of Asia Minor), one of the earliest Athenian allies, had deserted the Athenian cause. According to an ancient papyrus, the Milesians manufactured phalluses and sold them to women.   [16] Chief mountain range of Laconia; towers over Sparta.

if we are going to force our men to make peace, we must do without—

MYRRHINE. Without what? Tell us.

LYSISTRATA. Will you do it?

MYRRHINE. We'll do it, if it kills us.

LYSISTRATA. Well then, we must do without sex altogether. [*General consternation.*] Why do you turn away? Where go you? Why turn so pale? Why those tears? Will you do it or not? What means this hesitation?

MYRRHINE. I won't do it! Let the war go on.

CALONICE. Nor I! Let the war go on.

LYSISTRATA. So, my little flounder? Didn't you say just now you'd split yourself in half?

CALONICE. Anything else you like. I'm willing, even if I have to walk through fire. Anything rather than sex. There's nothing like it, my dear.

LYSISTRATA [*to* MYRRHINE]. What about you?

MYRRHINE [*sullenly*]. I'm willing to walk through fire, too.

LYSISTRATA. Oh vile and cursed breed! No wonder they make tragedies about us: we're naught but "love affairs and bassinets." [17] But you, my dear Spartan friend, if you alone are with me, our enterprise might yet succeed. Will you vote with me?

LAMPITO. 'Tis cruel hard, by my faith, for a woman to sleep alone without her nooky; but for all that, we certainly do need peace.

LYSISTRATA. O my dearest friend! You're the only real woman here.

CALONICE [*wavering*]. Well, if we do refrain from— [*shuddering*] what you say (God forbid!), would that bring peace?

LYSISTRATA. My goodness, yes! If we sit at home all rouged and powdered, dressed in our sheerest gowns, and neatly depilated, our men will get excited and want to take us; but if you don't come to them and keep away, they'll soon make a truce.

LAMPITO. Aye; Menelaus caught sight of Helen's naked breast and dropped his sword, they say.[18]

CALONICE. What if the men give us up?

LYSISTRATA. "Flay a skinned dog," [19] as Pherecrates[20] says.

---

[17] In Sophocles' lost tragedy *Tyro*, which the same audience had recently seen, the heroine abandoned her twin infants (born out of an illicit affair with Poseidon) in a bassinet. [18] An allusion to Euripides' *Andromache* in which Menelaus, about to stab his faithless wife, is overcome by her seductive beauty and drops his sword. [19] References to (1) a proverb for laboring in vain; and (2) the supposition that the Milesian phalluses were made of dogskin. [20] Comic poet, contemporary of Aristophanes.

CALONICE. Rubbish! These make-shifts are no good. But suppose they grab us and drag us into the bedroom?

LYSISTRATA. Hold on to the door.

CALONICE. And if they beat us?

LYSISTRATA. Give in with a bad grace. There's no pleasure in it for them when they have to use violence. And you must torment them in every possibly way. They'll give up soon enough; a man gets no joy if he doesn't get along with his wife.

MYRRHINE. If this is your opinion, we agree.

LAMPITO. As for our own men, we can persuade them to make a just and fair peace; but what about the Athenian rabble? Who will persuade them not to start any more monkey-shines?

LYSISTRATA. Don't worry. We guarantee to convince them.

LAMPITO. Not while their ships are rigged so well and they have that mighty treasure in the temple of Athene.[21]

LYSISTRATA. We've taken good care for that too: we shall seize the Acropolis today. The older women have orders to do this, and while we are making our arrangements, they are to pretend to make a sacrifice and occupy the Acropolis.

LAMPITO. All will be well then. That's a very fine idea.

LYSISTRATA. Let's ratify this, Lampito, with the most solemn oath.

LAMPITO. Tell us what oath we shall swear.

LYSISTRATA. Well said. Where's our Policewoman? [To a Scythian slave.] What are you gaping at? Set a shield upside-down here in front of me, and give me the sacred meats.

CALONICE. Lysistrata, what sort of an oath are we to take?

LYSISTRATA. What oath? I'm going to slaughter a sheep over the shield, as they do in Aeschylus.[22]

CALONICE. Don't, Lysistrata! No oaths about peace over a shield.

LYSISTRATA. What shall the oath be, then?

CALONICE. How about getting a white horse somewhere and cutting out its entrails for the sacrifice?

LYSISTRATA. White horse indeed! [23]

CALONICE. Well then, how shall we swear?

---

[21] Twenty years earlier, at the outbreak of the war, Pericles set aside an enormous sum of money in the back of the Parthenon—which was sacred to Athene—for use in an emergency. [22] In Aeschylus' tragedy *The Seven Against Thebes*, the warrior heroes on the side of Polynices sanctify their mutual oath of allegiance by slaughtering a bull and letting its blood flow into the hollow of a shield. [23] The joke has three points of reference: (1) sacrifices of horses are so rare that this is an unreal suggestion; (2) "horse" (according to a later Greek source) is slang for the female genitalia and for a form of coitus; (3) Leucippus, a common male name in Athens, means "White Horse."

MYRRHINE. I'll tell you: let's place a large black bowl upside-down and then slaughter—a flask of Thasian wine.[24] And then let's swear —not to pour in a single drop of water.

LAMPITO. Lord! How I like that oath!

LYSISTRATA. Someone bring out a bowl and a flask.

[*A slave brings the utensils for the sacrifice.*]

CALONICE. Look, my friends! What a big jar! Here's a cup that 'twould give me joy to handle. [*She picks up the bowl.*]

LYSISTRATA. Set it down and put your hands on our victim. [*As* CALO- NICE *places her hands on the flask.*] O Lady of Persuasion and dear Loving Cup, graciously vouchsafe to receive this sacrifice from us women. [*She pours the wine into the bowl.*]

CALONICE. The blood has a good color and spurts out nicely.

LAMPITO. Faith, it has a pleasant smell, too.

MYRRHINE. Oh, let me be the first to swear, ladies! [25]

CALONICE. No, by our Lady! Not unless you're alloted the first turn.

LYSISTRATA. Place all your hands on the cup, and one of you repeat on behalf of all what I say. Then all will swear and ratify the oath. *I will suffer no man, be he husband or lover,*

CALONICE. *I will suffer no man, be he husband or lover,*

LYSISTRATA. *To approach me all hot and horny.* [*As* CALONICE *hesi-tates.*] Say it!

CALONICE [*slowly and painfully*]. *To approach me all hot and horny.* O Lysistrata, I feel so weak in the knees!

LYSISTRATA. *I will remain at home unmated,*

CALONICE. *I will remain at home unmated,*

LYSISTRATA. *Wearing my sheerest gown and carefully adorned,*

CALONICE. *Wearing my sheerest gown and carefully adorned,*

LYSISTRATA. *That my husband may burn with desire for me.*

CALONICE. *That my husband may burn with desire for me.*

LYSISTRATA. *And if he takes me by force against my will,*

CALONICE. *And if he takes me by force against my will,*

LYSISTRATA. *I shall do it badly and keep from moving.*

CALONICE. *I shall do it badly and keep from moving.*

LYSISTRATA. *I will not stretch my slippers toward the ceiling,*

CALONICE. *I will not stretch my slippers toward the ceiling,*

LYSISTRATA. *Nor will I take the posture of the lioness*[26] *on the knife-handle.*

---

[24] Powerful, popular wine from the north Aegean island of Thasos. Greek comic poets often allude to the drinking habits of Athenian housewives, who were in charge of domestic wine supplies.   [25] The first to have completed an oath may drink first.   [26] About to leap, as in archaic sculptures: front legs pressed down close to the earth, hind legs high.

CALONICE. Nor will I take the posture of the lioness on the knife-handle.

LYSISTRATA. If I keep this oath, may I be permitted to drink from this cup,

CALONICE. If I keep this oath, may I be permitted to drink from this cup,

LYSISTRATA. But if I break it, may the cup be filled with water.

CALONICE. But if I break it, may the cup be filled with water.

LYSISTRATA. Do you all swear to this?

ALL. I do, so help me!

LYSISTRATA. Come then, I'll just consummate this offering. [She takes a long drink from the cup.]

CALONICE [snatching the cup away]. Shares, my dear! Let's drink to our continued friendship.

[A shout is heard from off stage.]

LAMPITO. What's that shouting?

LYSISTRATA. That's what I was telling you: the women have just seized the Acropolis. Now, Lampito, go home and arrange matters in Sparta; and leave these two ladies[27] here as hostages. We'll enter the Acropolis to join our friends and help them lock the gates.

CALONICE. Don't you suppose the men will come to attack us?

LYSISTRATA. Don't worry about them. Neither threats nor fire will suffice to open the gates, except on the terms we've stated.

CALONICE. I should say not! Else we'd belie our reputation as unmanageable pests.

[LAMPITO leaves the stage. The other women retire and enter the Acropolis through the Propylaea. Enter the CHORUS OF OLD MEN, carrying fire-pots and a load of heavy sticks.]

LEADER OF MEN. Onward, Draces, step by step, though your shoulder's aching.

Cursèd logs of olive-wood, what a load you're making!

FIRST SEMICHORUS OF OLD MEN [singing].

Aye, many surprises[28] await a man who lives to a ripe old age;

For who could suppose, Strymodorus my lad, that the women we've nourished (alas!),

Who sat at home to vex our days,

---

[27] The Boeotian and the Corinthian. Like Boeotia, Corinth was a Spartan ally and a bitter enemy of Athens in this war.   [28] Critical allusion to a verse of Archilochus, a famous poet of the seventh century B.C.: "Nothing among men is unexpected."

Would seize the holy image here,[29]
And occupy this sacred shrine,
With bolts and bars, with fell design,
To lock the Propylaea?

LEADER. Come with speed, Philourgus, come! to the temple hast'ning.
There we'll heap these logs about in a circle round them,
And whoever has conspired, raising this rebellion,
Shall be roasted, scorched, and burnt, all without exception,
Doomed by one unanimous vote—but first the wife of Lycon.[30]

SECOND SEMICHORUS [singing].
No, no! by Demeter,[31] while I'm alive, no woman shall mock at
me.
Not even the Spartan Cleomenes, our citadel first to seize,
Got off unscathed;[32] for all his pride
And haughty Spartan arrogance,
He left his arms and sneaked away,
Stripped to his shirt, unkempt, unshav'd,
With six years' [33] filth still on him.

LEADER. I besieged that hero bold, sleeping at my station,
Marshaled at these holy gates sixteen deep against him.
Shall I not these cursèd pests punish for their daring,
Burning these Euripides-and-God-detested women? [34]
Aye! or else may Marathon overturn my trophy.[35]

FIRST SEMICHORUS [singing].
There remains of my road
Just this brow of the hill;
There I speed on my way.
Drag the logs up the hill, though we've got no ass to help.

---

[29] Probably a famous wooden statue of Athena "Polias" (Guardian of the Polis) in the Erechtheum, a temple on the Acropolis. Other notable shrines on the Acropolis were the Parthenon and the temple of Nike (Athena as goddess of victory). [30] According to an ancient commentator, a woman much lampooned for her licentiousness. (Lycon is probably the demagogue who became one of Socrates' prosecutors.) [31] Athenian men often swear by Demeter, the earth goddess and goddess of agriculture, whose festival of the Eleusinia they celebrated annually. [32] About a century earlier the Spartan king Cleomenes occupied the Athenian Acropolis at the end of an unsuccessful bid to prevent the installation of a democratic regime in Athens under the reform politician Cleisthenes. [33] Comic exaggeration: the occupation of the Acropolis in fact lasted only two days. [34] Euripides' realistic portrayals of women enraged Athenian society ladies and caused contemporary comic poets like Aristophanes to portray him as a misogynist, although in fact his lack of idealization is often coupled with perceptive sympathy for women. [35] In this case, a high mound covering the Athenian soldiers who died in the battle of Marathon. Again, comic exaggeration: the year is 411 B.C., and the chorus could in truth neither have fought against Cleomenes in 508 B.C. nor at Marathon in 490 B.C.

(God! my shoulder's bruised and sore!)
Onward still must we go.
Blow the fire! Don't let it go out
Now we're near the end of our road.

ALL [blowing on the fire-pots].
Whew! Whew! Drat the smoke!

SECOND SEMICHORUS [singing].
Lord, what smoke rushing forth
From the pot, like a dog
Running mad, bites my eyes!
This must be Lemnos[36]-fire. What a sharp and stinging smoke!
Rushing onward to the shrine
Aid the gods. Once for all
Show your mettle, Laches my boy!
To the rescue hastening all!

ALL [blowing on the fire-pots].
Whew! Whew! Drat the smoke!
[The chorus has now reached the edge of the orchestra
nearest the stage, in front of the Propylaea. They begin
laying their logs and fire-pots on the ground.]

LEADER. Thank heaven, this fire is still alive. Now let's first put down
these logs here and place our torches in the pots to catch; then
let's make a rush for the gates with a battering ram. If the women
don't unbar the gate at our summons, we'll have to smoke them
out.

Let me put down my load. Ouch! That hurts! [To the audience.] Would any of the generals in Samos[37] like to lend a hand
with this log? [Throwing down a log.] Well, that won't break my
back any more, at any rate. [Turning to his fire-pot.] Your job,
my little pot, is to keep those coals alive and furnish me shortly
with a red-hot torch.

O mistress Victory, be my ally and grant me to rout these
audacious women in the Acropolis.

[While the men are busy with their logs and fires, the
CHORUS OF OLD WOMEN enters, carrying pitchers of
water.]

LEADER OF WOMEN. What's this I see? Smoke and flames? Is that a
fire ablazing?
Let's rush upon them. Hurry up! They'll find us women ready.

FIRST SEMICHORUS OF OLD WOMEN [singing].
With wingèd foot onward I fly,

---

36 Volcanic Aegean island.   37 Most of the Athenian fleet was based on the
Aegean island Samos, practically the only Ionian ally left to Athens.

Ere the flames consume Neodice;
Lest Critylla[38] be overwhelmed
By a lawless, accurst herd of old men.
I shudder with fear. Am I too late to aid them?
At break of the day filled we our jars with water
Fresh from the spring, pushing our way straight through the
    crowds. Oh, what a din!
Mid crockery crashing, jostled by slave-girls,
Sped we to save them, aiding our neighbors,
Bearing this water to put out the flames.

SECOND SEMICHORUS OF OLD WOMEN [*singing*].
    Such news I've heard: doddering fools
    Come with logs, like furnace-attendants,
    Loaded down with three hundred pounds,
    Breathing many a vain, blustering threat,
    That all these abhorred sluts will be burnt to charcoal.
    O goddess, I pray never may they be kindled;
Grant them to save Greece and our men; madness and war help
    them to end.
With this as our purpose, golden-plumed Maiden,[39]
Guardian of Athens, seized we thy precinct.
Be my ally, Warrior-maiden,
'Gainst these old men, bearing water with me.

[*The women have now reached their position in the orchestra, and their* LEADER *advances toward the* LEADER OF
THE MEN.]

LEADER OF WOMEN. Hold on there! What's this, you utter scoundrels?
No decent, God-fearing citizens would act like this.

LEADER OF MEN. Oho! Here's something unexpected: a swarm of
women have come out to attack us.

LEADER OF WOMEN. What, do we frighten you? Surely you don't
think we're too many for you. And yet there are ten thousand
times more of us whom you haven't even seen.

LEADER OF MEN. What say, Phaedria?[40] Shall we let these women
wag their tongues? Shan't we take our sticks and break them over
their backs?

LEADER OF WOMEN. Let's set our pitchers on the ground; then if anyone lays a hand on us, they won't get in our way.

LEADER OF MEN. By God! If someone gave them two or three smacks

---

[38] Names of Athenian women. [39] Athene, who was born from the head of
Zeus with complete armor, is often represented as wearing a helmet with a
golden plume (or plumes). [40] Male name. More correct form: Phaedrias.

on the jaw, like Bupalus,[41] they wouldn't talk so much!

LEADER OF WOMEN. Go on, hit me, somebody! Here's my jaw! But no other bitch will bite a piece out of you before me.

LEADER OF MEN. Silence! or I'll knock out your—senility!

LEADER OF WOMEN. Just lay one finger on Stratyllis, I dare you!

LEADER OF MEN. Suppose I dust you off with this fist? What will you do?

LEADER OF WOMEN. I'll tear the living guts out of you with my teeth.

LEADER OF MEN. No poet is more clever than Euripides: "There is no beast so shameless as a woman."

LEADER OF WOMEN. Let's pick up our jars of water, Rhodippe.

LEADER OF MEN. Why have you come here with water, you detestable slut?

LEADER OF WOMEN. And why have you come with fire, you funeral vault? To cremate yourself?

LEADER OF MEN. To light a fire and singe your friends.

LEADER OF WOMEN. And I've brought water to put out your fire.

LEADER OF MEN. What? You'll put out my fire?

LEADER OF WOMEN. Just try and see!

LEADER OF MEN. I wonder: shall I scorch you with this torch of mine?

LEADER OF WOMEN. If you've got any soap, I'll give you a bath.

LEADER OF MEN. Give *me* a bath, you stinking hag?

LEADER OF WOMEN. Yes—a bridal bath!

LEADER OF MEN. Just listen to her! What crust!

LEADER OF WOMEN. Well, I'm a free citizen.

LEADER OF MEN. I'll put an end to your bawling. [*The men pick up their torches.*]

LEADER OF WOMEN. You'll never do jury duty[42] again. [*The women pick up their pitchers.*]

LEADER OF MEN. Singe her hair for her!

LEADER OF WOMEN. Do your duty, water! [*The women empty their pitchers on the men.*]

LEADER OF MEN. Ow! Ow! For heaven's sake!

LEADER OF WOMEN. Is it too hot?

LEADER OF MEN. What do you mean "hot"? Stop! What are you doing?

LEADER OF WOMEN. I'm watering you, so you'll be fresh and green.

LEADER OF MEN. But I'm all withered up with shaking.

---

[41] A sculptor so mercilessly lampooned in the satiric invective of the sixth century poet Hipponax that, according to an anecdotal tradition, he hanged himself. Several verses with a bearing on this survive. Here Aristophanes refers to: "Hold me my cloak; I'll knock Bupalus in the eye / For ambidextrous I am and knocking I miss not." [42] Remunerated jury duty was a source of income and an exercise of power.

LEADER OF WOMEN. Well, you've got a fire; why don't you dry your-self?

[*Enter an Athenian* MAGISTRATE, *accompanied by four Scythian policemen.*] [43]

MAGISTRATE. Have these wanton women flared up again with their timbrels and their continual worship of Sabazius? [44] Is this an-other Adonis dirge[45] upon the rooftops—which we heard not long ago in the Assembly? That confounded Demostratus[46] was urg-ing us to sail to Sicily, and the whirling women shouted, "Woe for Adonis!" And then Demostratus said we'd best enroll the in-fantry from Zacynthus,[47] and a tipsy woman on the roof shrieked, "Beat your breasts for Adonis!" And that vile and filthy lunatic forced his measure through. Such license do our women take.

LEADER OF MEN. What if you heard of the insolence of these women here? Besides their other violent acts, they threw water all over us, and we have to shake out our clothes just as if we'd leaked in them.

MAGISTRATE. And rightly, too, by God! For we ourselves lead the women astray and teach them to play the wanton; from these roots such notions blossom forth. A man goes into the jeweler's shop and says, "About that necklace you made for my wife, gold-smith: last night, while she was dancing, the fastening-bolt slipped out of the hole. I have to sail over to Salamis today; if you're free, do come around tonight and fit in a new bolt for her." Another goes to the shoemaker, a strapping young fellow with manly parts, and says, "See here, cobbler, the sandal-strap chafes my wife's little—toe; it's so tender. Come around during the siesta and stretch it a little, so she'll be more comfortable." Now we see the results of such treatment: here I'm a special Councillor and need money to procure oars for the galleys; and I'm locked out of the Treasury by these women.[48]

But this is no time to stand around. Bring up crow-bars there! I'll put an end to their insolence. [*To one of the policemen.*] What are you gaping at, you wretch? What are you staring at? Got an eye out for a tavern, eh? Set your crow-bars here to the

---

[43] Archers, the regular Athenian police.   [44] Nature-god from Asia Minor or Thrace recently introduced in Athens; considered an immoral force of chaos by religious conservatives; sometimes identified with Dionysus.   [45] A formal lament of women for Adonis (probably identical with the Semitic deity Tammuz), a vegetation god who spent four months a year—the winter season—in the under-world. When the fatal Athenian expedition to Sicily departed, the women were mourning the departure of Adonis for the underworld—a bad omen.   [46] One of the supporters of the expedition.   [47] Island off the west coast of Greece, near Ithaca.   [48] Cf. note 21.

gates and force them open. [*Retiring to a safe distance.*] I'll help from over here.

[*The gates are thrown open and* LYSISTRATA *comes out followed by several other women.*]

LYSISTRATA. Don't force the gates; I'm coming out of my own accord. We don't need crow-bars here; what we need is good sound common-sense.

MAGISTRATE. Is that so, you strumpet? Where's my policeman? Officer, arrest her and tie her arms behind her back.

LYSISTRATA. By Artemis, if he lays a finger on me, he'll pay for it, even if he is a public servant.

[*The policeman retires in terror.*]

MAGISTRATE. You there, are you afraid? Seize her round the waist— and you, too. Tie her up, both of you!

FIRST WOMAN [*as the second policeman approaches* LYSISTRATA]. By Pandrosus,[49] if you but touch her with your hand, I'll kick the stuffings out of you.

[*The second policeman retires in terror.*]

MAGISTRATE. Just listen to that: "kick the stuffings out." Where's another policeman? Tie *her* up first, for her chatter.

SECOND WOMAN. By the Goddess of the Light,[50] if you lay the tip of your finger on her, you'll soon need a doctor.

[*The third policeman retires in terror.*]   ·

MAGISTRATE. What's this? Where's my policeman? Seize *her* too. I'll soon stop your sallies.

THIRD WOMAN. By the Goddess of Tauros,[51] if you go near her, I'll tear out your hair until it shrieks with pain.

[*The fourth policeman retires in terror.*]

MAGISTRATE. Oh, damn it all! I've run out of policemen. But women must never defeat us. Officers, let's charge them all together. Close up your ranks!

[*The policemen rally for a mass attack.*]

LYSISTRATA. By heaven, you'll soon find out that we have four companies of warrior-women, all fully equipped within!

MAGISTRATE. [*advancing*]. Twist their arms off, men!

LYSISTRATA. [*shouting*]. To the rescue, my valiant women!

O sellers-of-barley-green-stuffs-and-eggs,

O sellers-of-garlic, ye keepers-of-taverns, and vendors-of-bread,

Grapple! Smite! Smash!

[49] Daughter of Cecrops, mythical founder of Athens; literally, "all-bedewing." [50] Greek, *Phosphoros*—Artemis in her capacity as moon-goddess. She is also the most unrelenting virgin in Greek myth.   [51] Artemis. Probably so named either because there was a famous temple of hers in Tauros (Crimea) or because she was associated with bulls.

Won't you heap filth on them? Give them a tongue-lashing!

[*The women beat off the policemen.*]

Halt! Withdraw! No looting on the field.

MAGISTRATE. Damn it! My police force has put up a very poor show.

LYSISTRATA. What did you expect? Did you think you were attacking
slaves? Didn't you know that women are filled with passion?

MAGISTRATE. Aye, passion enough—for a good strong drink!

LEADER OF MEN. O chief and leader of this land, why spend your
words in vain?

Don't argue with these shameless beasts. You know not how
we've fared:

A soapless bath they've given us; our clothes are soundly soaked.

LEADER OF WOMEN. Poor fool! You never should attack or strike a
peaceful girl.

But if you do, your eyes must swell. For I am quite content

To sit unmoved, like modest maids, in peace and cause no pain;

But let a man stir up my hive, he'll find me like a wasp.

CHORUS OF MEN [*singing*].

O God, whatever shall we do with creatures like Womankind?

This can't be endured by any man alive. Question them!

   Let us try to find out what this means.

  To what end have they seized on this shrine,

    This steep and rugged, high and holy,

      Undefiled Acropolis?

LEADER OF MEN. Come, put your questions; don't give in, and probe
her every statement.

For base and shameful it would be to leave this plot untested.

MAGISTRATE. Well then, first of all I wish to ask her this: for what
purpose have you barred us from the Acropolis?

LYSISTRATA. To keep the treasure safe, so you won't make war on account of it.

MAGISTRATE. What? Do we make war on account of the treasure?

LYSISTRATA. Yes, and you cause all our other troubles for it, too. Peisander[52] and those greedy office-seekers keep things stirred up so
they can find occasions to steal. Now let them do what they like:
they'll never again make off with any of this money.

MAGISTRATE. What will you do?

LYSISTRATA. What a question! We'll administer it ourselves.

MAGISTRATE. *You* will administer the treasure?

---

[52] A reckless leader of the Athenian prowar party who, at the time this play was
performed (411 B.C.), was intriguing successfully to overthrow the Athenian
democracy and establish in its place a hated oligarchic rule by the Council of Four
Hundred.

LYSISTRATA. What's so strange in that? Don't we administer the household money for you?

MAGISTRATE. That's different.

LYSISTRATA. How is it different?

MAGISTRATE. We've got to make war with this money.

LYSISTRATA. But that's the very first thing: you mustn't make war.

MAGISTRATE. How else can we be saved?

LYSISTRATA. We'll save you.

MAGISTRATE. *You?*

LYSISTRATA. Yes, we!

MAGISTRATE. God forbid!

LYSISTRATA. We'll save you, whether you want it or not.

MAGISTRATE. Oh! This is terrible!

LYSISTRATA. You don't like it, but we're going to do it none the less.

MAGISTRATE. Good God! it's illegal!

LYSISTRATA. We *will* save you, my little man!

MAGISTRATE. Suppose I don't want you to?

LYSISTRATA. That's all the more reason.

MAGISTRATE. What business have you with war and peace?

LYSISTRATA. I'll explain.

MAGISTRATE [*shaking his fist*]. Speak up, or you'll smart for it.

LYSISTRATA. Just listen, and try to keep your hands still.

MAGISTRATE. I can't. I'm so mad I can't stop them.

FIRST WOMAN. Then you'll be the one to smart for it.

MAGISTRATE. Croak to yourself, old hag! [*To* LYSISTRATA.] Now then, speak up.

LYSISTRATA. Very well. Formerly we endured the war for a good long time with our usual restraint, no matter what you men did. You wouldn't let us say "boo," although nothing you did suited us. But we watched you well, and though we stayed at home we'd often hear of some terribly stupid measure you'd proposed. Then, though grieving at heart, we'd smile sweetly and say, "What was passed in the Assembly today about writing on the treaty-stone?" [53] "What's that to you?" my husband would say. "Hold your tongue!" And I held my tongue.

FIRST WOMAN. But I wouldn't have—not I!

MAGISTRATE. You'd have been soundly smacked, if you hadn't kept still.

LYSISTRATA. So I kept still at home. Then we'd hear of some plan still worse than the first; we'd say, "Husband, how could you pass such a stupid proposal?" He'd scowl at me and say, "If you don't

[53] The official texts of treaties were inscribed on a stone set up in a public place.

mind your spinning, your head will be sore for weeks. *War shall be the concern of Men.*" [54]

MAGISTRATE. And he was right, upon my word!

LYSISTRATA. Why right, you confounded fool, when your proposals were so stupid and we weren't allowed to make suggestions?

"There's not a *man* left in the country," says one. "No, not one," says another. Therefore all we women have decided in council to make a common effort to save Greece. How long should we have waited? Now, if you're willing to listen to our excellent proposals and keep silence for us in your turn, we still may save you.

MAGISTRATE. We men keep silence for you? That's terrible; I won't endure it!

LYSISTRATA. Silence!

MAGISTRATE. Silence for *you,* you wench, when you're wearing a snood? I'd rather die!

LYSISTRATA. Well, if that's all that bothers you—here! Take my snood and tie it round your head. [*During the following words the women dress up the* MAGISTRATE *in women's garments.*] And *now* keep quiet! Here, take this spinning-basket, too, and card your wool with robes tucked up, munching on beans. *War shall be the concern of Women!*

LEADER OF WOMEN. Arise and leave your pitchers, girls; no time is this to falter.

We too must aid our loyal friends; our turn has come for action.

CHORUS OF WOMEN [*singing*].

I'll never tire of aiding them with song and dance; never may Faintness keep my legs from moving to and fro endlessly.

For I yearn to do all for my friends;
They have charm, they have wit, they have grace,
With courage, brains and best of virtues—
Patriotic sapience.

LEADER OF WOMEN. Come, child of manliest ancient dames, offspring of stinging nettles,

Advance with rage unsoftened; for fair breezes speed you onward.

LYSISTRATA. If only sweet Eros and the Cyprian Queen of Love[55] shed charm over our breasts and limbs and inspire our men with amorous longing and priapic spasms, I think we may soon be called Peacemakers[56] among the Greeks.

---

[54] A quote from *The Iliad* VI.   [55] Aphrodite.   [56] The Greek, *Lysimachas,* is a pun on the name of Lysistrata.

MAGISTRATE. What will you do?

LYSISTRATA. First of all, we'll stop those fellows who run madly about the Marketplace in arms.

FIRST WOMAN. Indeed we shall, by the Queen of Paphos.[57]

LYSISTRATA. For now they roam about the market, amid the pots and greenstuffs, armed to the teeth like Corybantes.[58]

MAGISTRATE. That's what manly fellows ought to do!

LYSISTRATA. But it's so silly: a chap with a Gorgon-emblazoned shield buying pickled herring.

FIRST WOMAN. Why, just the other day I saw one of those long-haired dandies who command our cavalry ride up on horseback and pour into his bronze helmet the egg-broth he'd bought from an old dame. And there was a Thracian slinger too, shaking his lance like Tereus;[59] he'd scared the life out of the poor fig-peddler and was gulping down all her ripest fruit.

MAGISTRATE. How can you stop all the confusion in the various states and bring them together?

LYSISTRATA. Very easily.

MAGISTRATE. Tell me how.

LYSISTRATA. Just like a ball of wool, when it's confused and snarled: we take it thus, and draw out a thread here and a thread there with our spindles; thus we'll unsnarl this war, if no one prevents us, and draw together the various states with embassies here and embassies there.

MAGISTRATE. Do you suppose you can stop this dreadful business with balls of wool and spindles, you nit-wits?

LYSISTRATA. Why, if *you* had any wits, you'd manage all affairs of state like our wool-working.

MAGISTRATE. How so?

LYSISTRATA. First you ought to treat the city as we do when we wash the dirt out of a fleece: stretch it out and pluck and thrash out of the city all those prickly scoundrels; aye, and card out those who conspire and stick together to gain office, pulling off their heads. Then card the wool, all of it, into one fair basket of goodwill, mingling in the aliens residing here, any loyal foreigners, and anyone who's in debt to the Treasury; and consider that all our colonies lie scattered round about like remnants; from all of these collect the wool and gather it together here, wind up a great ball, and then weave a good stout cloak for the democracy.

---

[57] Aphrodite. [58] Frenetic, armed, divine attendants of the Phrygian goddess Cybele (sometimes of Rhea). [59] Mythical king of Thrace (in the Balkan). Thracian mercenaries, notorious for their coarseness and lack of discipline, served in the Athenian army.

MAGISTRATE. Dreadful! Talking about thrashing and winding balls of wool, when you haven't the slightest share in the war!

LYSISTRATA. Why, you dirty scoundrel, we bear more than twice as much as you. First, we bear children and send off our sons as soldiers.

MAGISTRATE. Hush! Let bygones be bygones!

LYSISTRATA. Then, when we ought to be happy and enjoy our youth, we sleep alone because of your expeditions abroad. But never mind us married women: I grieve most for the maids who grow old at home unwed.

MAGISTRATE. Don't men grow old, too?

LYSISTRATA. For heaven's sake! That's not the same thing. When a man comes home, no matter how gray he is, he soon finds a girl to marry. But woman's bloom is short and fleeting; if she doesn't grasp her chance, no man is willing to marry her and she sits at home a prey to every fortune-teller.

MAGISTRATE [coarsely]. But if a man can still get it up—

LYSISTRATA. See here, you: what's the matter? Aren't you dead yet? There's plenty of room for you. Buy yourself a shroud and I'll bake you a honey-cake.[60] [Handing him a copper coin[61] for his passage across the Styx.] Here's your fare! Now get yourself a wreath. [During the following dialogue the women dress up the MAGISTRATE as a corpse.]

FIRST WOMAN. Here, take these fillets.

SECOND WOMAN. Here, take this wreath.

LYSISTRATA. What do you want? What's lacking? Get moving; off to the ferry! Charon is calling you; don't keep him from sailing.

MAGISTRATE. Am I to endure these insults? By God! I'm going straight to the magistrates to show them how I've been treated.

LYSISTRATA. Are you grumbling that you haven't been properly laid out? Well, the day after tomorrow we'll send around all the usual offerings early in the morning.

[The MAGISTRATE goes out still wearing his funeral decorations. LYSISTRATA and the women retire into the Acropolis.]

LEADER OF MEN. Wake, ye sons of freedom, wake! 'Tis no time for sleeping.
Up and at them, like a man! Let us strip for action.

[60] The dead were given a honey-cake to throw to Cerberus, the three-headed dog-like monster with the tail of a serpent who guarded the entry to Hades.   [61] To pay the fare (an obol) required by Charon, the mythical old ferryman over the Styx (a river that flows around the underworld). The coin was usually placed in the corpse's mouth before burial.

[*The* CHORUS OF MEN *remove their outer cloaks.*]
CHORUS OF MEN [*singing*].
    Surely there is something here greater than meets the eye;
    For without a doubt I smell Hippias'[62] tyranny.
    Dreadful fear assails me lest certain bands of Spartan men,
    Meeting here with Cleisthenes,[63] have inspired through treachery
    All these god-detested women secretly to seize
    Athens' treasure in the temple, and to stop that pay
        Whence I live at my ease.
LEADER OF MEN. Now isn't it terrible for them to advise the state and
    chatter about shields, being mere women?
        And they think to reconcile us with the Spartans—men who
    hold nothing sacred any more than hungry wolves. Surely this is
    a web of deceit, my friends, to conceal an attempt at tyranny.
    But they'll never lord it over me; I'll be on my guard and from
    now on,
        "The blade I bear   A myrtle spray shall wear." [64]
    I'll occupy the market under arms and stand next to Aristogei-
    ton.[65]
        Thus I'll stand beside him. [*He strikes the pose of the famous
    statue of the tyrannicides, with one arm raised.*] And here's my
    chance to take this accurst old hag and—[*striking the* LEADER OF
    WOMEN] smack her on the jaw!

LEADER OF WOMEN. You'll go home in such a state your Ma won't rec-
        ognize you!
    Ladies all, upon the ground let us place these garments.
        [*The* CHORUS OF WOMEN *remove their outer garments.*]
CHORUS OF WOMEN [*singing*].
    Citizens of Athens, hear useful words for the state.
    Rightly; for it nurtured me in my youth royally.
    As a child of seven years carried I the sacred box;

---

[62] The hated and despised last despotic ruler of Athens, expelled in 510 B.C. Fear and expectation of tyranny were persistent at this time. [63] Not the reformer mentioned earlier but a contemporary of Aristophanes, notorious for his effeminacy. This rendered him suspect both as a conspirator with Spartan soldiers (whose homosexuality was, in certain units, officially approved of as an emotionally binding force) and as a fellow-conspirator of the women. [64] From the first stanza of a popular Greek drinking song: "Hidden in a branch of myrtle I'll carry my sword / just like Harmodius and Aristogeiton / when the two of them killed the tyrant / and rendered Athens a city with equal rights for all." It refers to the assassination of the tyrant Hipparchus (brother of Hippias) in 514 B.C. by a pederastic couple, who were celebrated by subsequent generations of Athenians as patriotic saviors. [65] There were famous statues of the two assassins at the Athenian marketplace.

> Then I was a Miller-maid, grinding at Athene's shrine;
> Next I wore the saffron robe and played Brauronia's Bear;
> And I walked as Basket-bearer, wearing chains of figs,
> As a sweet maiden fair.[66]

LEADER OF WOMEN. Therefore, am I not bound to give good advice to the city?

Don't take it ill that I was born a woman, if I contribute something better than our present troubles. I pay my share; for I contribute MEN. But you miserable old fools contribute nothing, and after squandering our ancestral treasure, the fruit of the Persian Wars, you make no contribution in return. And now, all on account of you, we're facing ruin.

What, muttering, are you? If you annoy me, I'll take this hard, rough slipper and—[*striking the* LEADER OF MEN] smack you on the jaw!

CHORUS OF MEN [*singing*].
> This is outright insolence! Things go from bad to worse.
> If you're men with any guts, prepare to meet the foe.
> Let us strip our tunics off! We need the smell of male
> Vigor. And we cannot fight all swaddled up in clothes.
> [*They strip off their tunics.*]
> Come then, my comrades, on to the battle, ye who once to Leip-
> sydrion[67] came;
> Then ye were MEN. Now call back your youthful vigor.
> With light, wingèd footstep advance,
> Shaking old age from your frame.

LEADER OF MEN. If any of us give these wenches the slightest hold, they'll stop at nothing: such is their cunning.

They will even build ships and sail against us, like Artemisia.[68] Or if they turn to mounting, I count our Knights as

---

[66] These lines describe some religious duties of an aristocratic Athenian girl: (1) Semiannually four chosen girls carried Athena's sacred objects in a procession at her festival; (2) the mill-girl ground the flour for sacrificial cakes; (3) Brauronia was a festival of Artemis held every fifth year—its central myth concerned the killing of a bear sacred to Artemis and in this connection young girls represented bears; (4) in golden baskets young girls carried the sacrificial cakes in the processions at Athens' most important religious festivals, such as the Panathenaea and The Great Dionysia.   [67] A place in the mountains north of Athens, where anti-despotic Athenian exiles (ancestors of Pericles, called the Alcmaeonids) were besieged in 513 B.C. by the forces of the tyrant Hippias; symbol of the noble but lost cause. The chorus continues, in comic exaggeration, to pretend that it experienced events of a century earlier.   [68] Queen of Halicarnassus on the west coast of Asia Minor; ally of Xerxes against the Greeks.

done for: a woman's such a tricky jockey when she gets astraddle, with a good firm seat for trotting. Just look at those Amazons[69] that Micon[70] painted, fighting on horseback against men!

But we must throw them all in the pillory—[*seizing and choking the* LEADER OF WOMEN] grabbing hold of yonder neck!

CHORUS OF WOMEN [*singing*].
'Ware my anger! Like a boar 'twill rush upon you men.
Soon you'll bawl aloud for help, you'll be so soundly trimmed!
Come, my friends, let's strip with speed, and lay aside these robes;
Catch the scent of women's rage. Attack with tooth and nail!
    [*They strip off their tunics.*]
Now then, come near me, you miserable man! You'll never eat
    garlic or black beans again.
And if you utter a single hard word, in rage I will "nurse" you
    as once
    The beetle requited her foe.[71]
LEADER OF WOMEN. For you don't worry me; no, not so long as my
    Lampito lives and our Theban friend, the noble Ismenia.
You can't do anything, not even if you pass a dozen—decrees! You miserable fool, all our neighbors hate you. Why, just the other day when I was holding a festival for Hecate, I invited as playmate from our neighbors the Boeotians a charming, well-bred Copaic—eel.[72] But they refused to send me one on account of your decrees.

And you'll never stop passing decrees until I grab your foot and—[*tripping up the* LEADER OF MEN] toss you down and break your neck!

    [*Here an interval of five days is supposed to elapse.*
    LYSISTRATA *comes out from the Acropolis.*]
LEADER OF WOMEN [*dramatically*].[73] Empress of this great emprise
    and undertaking,
Why come you forth, I pray, with frowning brow?
LYSISTRATA. Ah, these cursèd women! Their deeds and female notions
    make me pace up and down in utter despair.
LEADER OF WOMEN. Ah, what sayest thou?
LYSISTRATA. The truth, alas! the truth.

[69] Mythical race of warrior-women who invaded Attica in heroic times. [70] A contemporary painter of frescoes on public buildings. [71] In an Aesopian fable, the beetle revenges itself on the eagle by breaking the latter's eggs. [72] Here Aristophanes is using the phallic suggestiveness of the eel to express the multiple deprivations of war. [73] The following passage is a caricature of tragic style.

LEADER OF WOMEN. What dreadful tale hast thou to tell thy friends?

LYSISTRATA. 'Tis shame to speak, and not to speak is hard.

LEADER OF WOMEN. Hide not from me whatever woes we suffer.

LYSISTRATA. Well then, to put it briefly, we want—laying!

LEADER OF WOMEN. O Zeus, Zeus!

LYSISTRATA. Why call on Zeus? That's the way things are. I can no longer keep them away from the men, and they're all deserting. I caught one wriggling through a hole near the grotto of Pan,[74] another sliding down a rope, another deserting her post; and yesterday I found one getting on a sparrow's[75] back to fly off to Orsilochus,[76] and had to pull her back by the hair. They're digging up all sorts of excuses to get home. Look, here comes one of them now. [A woman comes hastily out of the Acropolis.] Here you! Where are you off to in such a hurry?

FIRST WOMAN. I want to go home. My very best wool is being devoured by moths.

LYSISTRATA. Moths? Nonsense! Go back inside.

FIRST WOMAN. I'll come right back; I swear it. I just want to lay it out on the bed.

LYSISTRATA. Well, you won't lay it out, and you won't go home, either.

FIRST WOMAN. Shall I let my wool be ruined?

LYSISTRATA. If necessary, yes.

[Another woman comes out.]

SECOND WOMAN. Oh dear! Oh dear! My precious flax! I left it at home all unpeeled.

LYSISTRATA. Here's another one, going home for her "flax." Come back here!

SECOND WOMAN. But I just want to work it up a little and then I'll be right back.

LYSISTRATA. No indeed! If you start this, all the other women will want to do the same.

[A third woman comes out.]

THIRD WOMAN. O Eilithyia,[77] goddess of travail, stop my labor till I come to a lawful spot! [78]

LYSISTRATA. What's this nonsense?

THIRD WOMAN. I'm going to have a baby—right now!

LYSISTRATA. But you weren't even pregnant yesterday.

---

[74] A cave on the Acropolis sacred to Pan, outside the citadel wall.   [75] Aphrodite's bird; several of them pulled her chariot.   [76] Literally, "One who stirs beds": a brothel-keeper.   [77] Deity who assisted women in childbirth, often identified with Artemis or Hera.   [78] The Acropolis was sacred ground and would be polluted by birth or death.

THIRD WOMAN. Well, I am today. O Lysistrata, do send me home to see a midwife, right away.

LYSISTRATA. What are you talking about? [*Putting her hand on her stomach.*] What's this hard lump here?

THIRD WOMAN. A little boy.

LYSISTRATA. My goodness, what have you got there? It seems hollow; I'll just find out. [*Pulling aside her robe.*] Why, you silly goose, you've got Athene's sacred helmet there. And you said you were having a baby!

THIRD WOMAN. Well, I *am* having one, I swear!

LYSISTRATA. Then what's this helmet for?

THIRD WOMAN. If the baby starts coming while I'm still in the Acropolis, I'll creep into this like a pigeon and give birth to it there.

LYSISTRATA. Stuff and nonsense! It's plain enough what you're up to. You just wait here for the christening of this—helmet.

THIRD WOMAN. But I can't sleep in the Acropolis since I saw the sacred snake.[79]

FIRST WOMAN. And I'm dying for lack of sleep: the hooting of the owls[80] keeps me awake.

LYSISTRATA. Enough of these shams, you wretched creatures. You want your husbands, I suppose. Well, don't you think they want us? I'm sure they're spending miserable nights. Hold out, my friends, and endure for just a little while. There's an oracle that we shall conquer, if we don't split up. [*Producing a roll of paper.*] Here it is.

FIRST WOMAN. Tell us what it says.

LYSISTRATA. Listen.

"When in the length of time the Swallows shall gather together,
Fleeing the Hoopoe's amorous flight and the Cockatoo shunning,
Then shall your woes be ended and Zeus who thundres in
    heaven
Set what's below on top—"

FIRST WOMAN. What? Are we going to be on top?

LYSISTRATA. "But if the Swallows rebel and flutter away from the temple,
Never a bird in the world shall seem more wanton and worthless." [81]

FIRST WOMAN. That's clear enough, upon my word!

LYSISTRATA. By all that's holy, let's not give up the struggle now. Let's

---

[79] A snake was supposedly kept in the Erechtheum but was never seen by anyone.
[80] Sacred birds of Athene.   [81] This oracle, invented by Lysistrata, mocks the obscure ambiguity of numerous oracles that left the giver of the oracle more or less blameless regardless of the accuracy or inaccuracy of the prediction.

go back inside. It would be a shame, my dear friends, to disobey
the oracle.

[*The women all retire to the Acropolis again.*]

CHORUS OF MEN [*singing*].

> I have a tale to tell,
> Which I know full well.
> > It was told me
> > In the nursery.

> Once there was a likely lad,
> > Melanion they name him;
> The thought of marriage made him mad,
> > For which I cannot blame him.

> So off he went to mountains fair;
> > (No women to upbraid him!)
> A mighty hunter of the hare,
> > He had a dog to aid him.

> He never came back home to see
> > Detested women's faces.
> He showed a shrewd mentality.
> > With him I'd fain change places!

ONE OF THE MEN [*to one of the women*].

> Come here, old dame; give me a kiss.

WOMAN. You'll ne'er eat garlic, if you dare!

MAN. I want to kick you—just like this!

WOMAN. Oh, there's a leg with bushy hair!

MAN. Myronides and Phormio[82]

> Were hairy—and they thrashed the foe.

CHORUS OF WOMEN [*singing*].

> I have another tale,
> With which to assail
> > Your contention
> > 'Bout Melanion.

> Once upon a time a man
> > Named Timon[83] left our city,
> To live in some deserted land.
> > (We thought him rather witty.)

[82] Successful Athenian commanders.   [83] Fifth-century Athenian misanthrope.

He dwelt alone amidst the thorn;
   In solitude he brooded.
From some grim Fury he was born:
   Such hatred he exuded.

He cursed you men, as scoundrels through
   And through, till life he ended.
He couldn't stand the sight of YOU
   But women he befriended.[84]

WOMAN [*to one of the men*]. I'll smash your face in, if you like.

MAN. Oh no, please don't! You frighten me.

WOMAN. I'll lift my foot—and thus I'll strike.

MAN. Aha! Look there! What's that I see?

WOMAN. Whate'er you see, you cannot say
    That I'm not neatly trimmed today.

      [LYSISTRATA *appears on the wall of the Acropolis.*]

LYSISTRATA. Hello! Hello! Girls, come here quick!
      [*Several women appear beside her.*]

WOMAN. What is it? Why are you calling?

LYSISTRATA. I see a man coming: he's in a dreadful state. He's mad with passion. O Queen of Cyprus, Cythera,[85] and Paphos, just keep on this way!

WOMAN. Where is the fellow?

LYSISTRATA. There, beside the shrine of Demeter.

WOMAN. Oh yes, so he is. Who is he?

LYSISTRATA. Let's see. Do any of you know him?

MYRRHINE. Yes indeed. That's my husband, Cinesias.

LYSISTRATA. It's up to you, now: roast him, rack him, fool him, love him—and leave him! Do everything, except what our oath forbids.

MYRRHINE. Don't worry; I'll do it.

LYSISTRATA. I'll stay here to tease him and warm him up a bit. Off with you.
    [*The other women retire from the wall. Enter* CINESIAS *followed by a slave carrying a baby.* CINESIAS *is obviously in great pain and distress.*]

CINESIAS [*groaning*]. Oh-h! Oh-h-h! This is killing me! O God, what tortures I'm suffering!

LYSISTRATA [*from the wall*]. Who's that within our lines?

---

[84] A feature not consistent with other extant versions of Timon's life.   [85] Island off the southern Peloponnesus with a famous temple of Aphrodite.

CINESIAS. Me.

LYSISTRATA. *A man?*

CINESIAS [*pointing*]. A *man*, indeed

LYSISTRATA. Well, go away!

CINESIAS. Who are you to send me away?

LYSISTRATA. The captain of the guard.

CINESIAS. Oh, for heaven's sake, call out Myrrhine for me.

LYSISTRATA. Call Myrrhine? Nonsense! Who are you?

CINESIAS. Her husband, Cinesias of Paionidai.[86]

LYSISTRATA [*appearing much impressed*]. Oh, greetings, friend. Your
name is not without honor here among us. Your wife is always
talking about you, and whenever she takes an egg or an apple,
she says, "Here's to my dear Cinesias!"

CINESIAS [*quivering with excitement*]. Oh, ye gods in heaven!

LYSISTRATA. Indeed she does! And whenever our conversations turn
to men, your wife immediately says, "All others are mere rubbish
compared with Cinesias."

CINESIAS [*groaning*]. Oh! Do call her for me.

LYSISTRATA. Why should I? What will you give me?

CINESIAS. Whatever you want. All I have is yours—and you see what
I've got!

LYSISTRATA. Well then, I'll go down and call her. [*She descends.*]

CINESIAS. And hurry up! I've had no joy of life ever since she left
home. When I go in the house, I feel awful: everything seems so
empty and I can't enjoy my dinner. I'm in such a state all the
time!

MYRRHINE [*from behind the wall*]. I *do* love him so. But he won't let
me love him. No, no! Don't ask me to see him!

CINESIAS. O my darling, O Myrrhine honey, why do you do this to
to me? [MYRRHINE *appears on the wall.*] Come down here!

MYRRHINE. No, I won't come down.

CINESIAS. Won't you come, Myrrhine, when *I* call you?

MYRRHINE. No; you don't want me.

CINESIAS. *Don't want you?* I'm in agony!

MYRRHINE. I'm going now.

CINESIAS. Please don't! At least, listen to your baby. [*To the baby.*]
Here you, call your mamma! [*Pinching the baby.*]

BABY. Ma-ma! Ma-ma! Ma-ma!

CINESIAS [*to* MYRRHINE]. What's the matter with you? Have you no
pity for your child, who hasn't been washed or fed for five whole
days?

[86] A district near Athens; here the name suggests the Greek verb *paio,* "I strike,"
which is slang for sexual intercourse.

MYRRHINE. Oh, poor child; your father pays no attention to you.

CINESIAS. Come down then, you heartless wretch, for the baby's sake.

MYRRHINE. Oh, what it is to be a mother! I've got to come down, I suppose. [*She leaves the wall and shortly reappears at the gate.*]

CINESIAS [*to himself*]. She seems much younger, and she has such a sweet look about her. Oh, the way she teases me! And her pretty, provoking ways make me burn with longing.

MYRRHINE [*coming out of the gate and taking the baby*]. O my sweet little angel. Naughty papa! Here, let Mummy kiss you, Mamma's little sweetheart! [*She fondles the baby lovingly.*]

CINESIAS [*in despair*]. You heartless creature, why do you do this? Why follow these other women and make both of us suffer so? [*He tries to embrace her.*]

MYRRHINE. Don't touch me!

CINESIAS. You're letting all our things at home go to wrack and ruin.

MYRRHINE. I don't care.

CINESIAS. You don't care that your wool is being plucked to pieces by the chickens?

MYRRHINE. Not in the least.

CINESIAS. And you haven't celebrated the rites of Aphrodite for ever so long. Won't you come home?

MYRRHINE. Not on your life, unless you men make a truce and stop the war.

CINESIAS. Well then, if that pleases you, we'll do it.

MYRRHINE. Well then, if that pleases *you*, I'll come home—afterwards! Right now I'm on oath not to.

CINESIAS. Then just lie down here with me for a moment.

MYRRHINE. No—[*in a teasing voice*] and yet, I won't say I don't love you.

CINESIAS. You love me? Oh, do lie down here, Myrrhine dear!

MYRRHINE. What, you silly fool in front of the baby?

CINESIAS [*hastily thrusting the baby at the slave*]. Of course not. Here—home! Take him, Manes! [*The slave goes off with the baby.*] See, the baby's out of the way. Now won't you lie down?

MYRRHINE. But where, my dear?

CINESIAS. Where? The grotto of Pan's a lovely spot.

MYRRHINE. How could I purify myself before returning to the shrine?

CINESIAS. Easily: just wash here in the Clepsydra.[87]

MYRRHINE. And then, shall I go back on my oath?

CINESIAS. On my head be it! Don't worry about the oath.

MYRRHINE. All right, then. Just let me bring out a bed.

CINESIAS. No, don't. The ground's all right.

[87] A spring on the Acropolis.

MYRRHINE. Heavens, no! Bad as you are, I won't let you lie on the bare ground. [*She goes into the Acropolis.*]

CINESIAS. Why, she really loves me; it's plain to see.

MYRRHINE [*returning with a bed*]. There! Now hurry up and lie down. I'll just slip off this dress. But—let's see: oh yes, I must fetch a mattress.

CINESIAS. Nonsense! No mattress for me.

MYRRHINE. Yes indeed! It's not nice on the bare springs.

CINESIAS. Give me a kiss.

MYRRHINE [*giving him a hasty kiss*]. There! [*She goes.*]

CINESIAS [*in mingled distress and delight*]. Oh-h! Hurry back!

MYRRHINE [*returning with a mattress*]. Here's the mattress; lie down on it. I'm taking my things off now—but—let's see: you have no pillow.

CINESIAS. I don't *want* a pillow!

MYRRHINE. But I do. [*She goes.*]

CINESIAS. Cheated again, just like Heracles and his dinner! [88]

MYRRHINE [*returning with a pillow*]. Here, lift your head. [*To herself, wondering how else to tease him.*] Is that all?

CINESIAS. Surely that's all! Do come here, precious!

MYRRHINE. I'm taking off my girdle. But remember: don't go back on your promise about the truce.

CINESIAS. Hope to die, if I do.

MYRRHINE. You don't have a blanket.

CINESIAS [*shouting in exasperation*]. *I don't want one!* I WANT TO—

MYRRHINE. Sh-h! There, there, I'll be back in a minute. [*She goes.*]

CINESIAS. She'll be the death of me with these bedclothes.

MYRRHINE [*returning with a blanket*]. Here, get up.

CINESIAS. I've got *this* up!

MYRRHINE. Would you like some perfume?

CINESIAS. Good heavens, no! I won't have it!

MYRRHINE. Yes, you shall, whether you want it or not. [*She goes.*]

CINESIAS. O lord! Confound all perfumes anyway!

MYRRHINE [*returning with a flask*]. Stretch out your hand and put some on.

CINESIAS [*suspiciously*]. By God, I don't much like this perfume. It smacks of shilly-shallying, and has no scent of the marriage-bed.

MYRRHINE. Oh dear! This is Rhodian perfume I've brought.

CINESIAS. It's quite all right, dear. Never mind.

MYRRHINE. Don't be silly! [*She goes out with the flask.*]

---

[88] In the Greek Cinesias compares his male organ to Heracles at a dinner-table—a reference to the mythical glutton hero who, in comedies, is often raving with hunger but never gets enough from his hosts.

CINESIAS. Damn the man who first concocted perfumes!

MYRRHINE [*returning with another flask*]. Here, try this flask.

CINESIAS. I've got another one all ready for you. Come, you wretch, lie down and stop bringing me things.

MYRRHINE. All right; I'm taking off my shoes. But, my dear, see that you vote for peace.

CINESIAS [*absently*]. I'll consider it. [MYRRHINE *runs away to the Acropolis.*] I'm ruined! The wench has skinned me and run away! [*Chanting, in tragic style.*] Alas! Alas! Deceived, deserted by this fairest of women, whom shall I—lay? Ah, my poor little child, how shall I nurture thee? Where's Cynalopex? [89] I needs must hire a nurse!

LEADER OF MEN [*chanting*]. Ah, wretched man, in dreadful wise beguiled, betrayed, thy soul is sore distressed. I pity thee, alas! alas! What soul, what loins, what liver could stand this strain? How firm and unyielding he stands, with naught to aid him of a morning.

CINESIAS. O lord! O Zeus! What tortures I endure!

LEADER OF MEN. This is the way she's treated you, that vile and cursèd wanton.

LEADER OF WOMEN. Nay, not vile and cursèd, but sweet and dear.

LEADER OF MEN. Sweet, you say? Nay, hateful, hateful!

CINESIAS. Hateful indeed! O Zeus, Zeus!
    Seize her and snatch her away,
    Like a handful of dust, in a mighty,
    Fiery tempest! Whirl her aloft, then let her drop
    Down to the earth, with a crash, as she falls—
    On the point of this waiting
        Thingummybob!   [*He goes out.*]
    [*Enter a Spartan* HERALD, *in an obvious state of excitement, which he is doing his best to conceal.*]

HERALD. Where can I find the Senate or the Pyrtanes? [90] I've got an important message. [*The Athenian* MAGISTRATE *enters.*]

MAGISTRATE. Say there, are you a man or Priapus? [91]

HERALD [*in annoyance*]. I'm a herald, you lout! I've come from Sparta about the truce.

MAGISTRATE. Is that a spear you've got under your cloak?

HERALD. No, of course not!

---

[89] A pimp or brothel-keeper (literally, "Dog-fox mongrel").   [90] Members of a 50-man organizational committee that operated the 500-man representative Council of Athens.   [91] A phallic god of fruitfulness, worshiped as protector of vineyards and gardens, where his statues—a phallus alone or a human deformity with enlarged genitals—were often set up; son of Dionysus and Aphrodite.

MAGISTRATE. Why do you twist and turn so? Why hold your cloak in
    front of you? Did you rupture yourself on the trip?
HERALD. By gum, the fellow's an old fool.
MAGISTRATE [*pointing*]. Why, you dirty rascal, you're all excited.
HERALD. Not at all. Stop this tom-foolery.
MAGISTRATE. Well, what's that I see?
HERALD. A Spartan message-staff.[92]
MAGISTRATE. Oh, certainly! That's just the kind of message-staff I've
    got. But tell me the honest truth: how are things going in Sparta?
HERALD. All the land of Sparta is up in arms—and our allies are up,
    too. We need Pellene.[93]
MAGISTRATE. What brought this trouble on you? A sudden Panic?
HERALD. No, Lampito started it and then all the other women in
    Sparta with one accord chased their husbands out of their beds.
MAGISTRATE. How do you feel?
HERALD. Terrible. We walk around the city bent over like men light-
    ing matches in a wind. For our women won't let us touch them
    until we all agree and make peace throughout Greece.
MAGISTRATE. This is a general conspiracy of the women; I see it now.
    Well, hurry back and tell the Spartans to send ambassadors here
    with full powers to arrange a truce. And I'll go tell the Council
    to choose ambassadors from here; I've got a little something here
    that will soon persuade them!
HERALD. I'll fly there; for you've made an excellent suggestion.
            [*The* HERALD *and the* MAGISTRATE *depart on opposite
                        sides of the stage.*]
LEADER OF MEN. No beast or fire is harder than womankind to tame,
    Nor is the spotted leopard so devoid of shame.
LEADER OF WOMEN. Knowing this, you dare provoke us to attack?
    I'd be your steady friend, if you'd but take us back.
LEADER OF MEN. I'll never cease my hatred keen of womankind.
LEADER OF WOMEN. Just as you will. But now just let me help you
            find
    That cloak you threw aside. You look so silly there
    Without your clothes. Here, put it on and don't go bare.
LEADER OF MEN. That's very kind, and shows you're not entirely bad.
    But I threw off my things when I was good and mad.
LEADER OF WOMEN. At last you seem a man, and won't be mocked, my
            lad.

[92] A cryptographic device. A strip of leather or papyrus was wrapped round a
tapered rod, then inscribed and unwound; it could only be deciphered by wrapping
it round an exactly similar rod.   [93] A double-barreled reference to 1) a city in
Achaea held by Athenians and claimed by Spartans and (2) a name of an
Athenian prostitute.

If you'd been nice to me, I'd take this little gnat
That's in your eye and pluck it out for you, like that.
LEADER OF MEN. So that's what's bothered me and bit my eye so long!
Please dig it out for me. I own that I've been wrong.
LEADER OF WOMEN. I'll do so, though you've been a most ill-natured
            brat.
Ye gods! See here! A huge and monstrous little gnat!
LEADER OF MEN. Oh, how that helps! For it was digging wells in me.
            And now it's out, my tears can roll down hard and free.
LEADER OF WOMEN. Here, let me wipe them off, although you're such
            a knave,
And kiss me.
LEADER OF MEN.   No!
LEADER OF WOMEN.   Whate'er you say, a kiss I'll have.

                                          [*She kisses him.*]

LEADER OF MEN. Oh, confound these women! They've a coaxing way
            about them.
He was wise and never spoke a truer word, who said,
"We can't live with women, but we cannot live without them."
Now I'll make a truce with you. We'll fight no more; instead,
    I will not injure you if you do me no wrong.
    And now let's join our ranks and then begin a song.

COMBINED CHORUS [*singing*].
            Athenians, we're not prepared,
            To say a single ugly word
            About our fellow citizens.
    Quite the contrary: we desire but to say and to do
    Naught but good. Quite enough are the ills now on hand.

            Men and women, be advised:
                If anyone requires
            Money—minae[94] two or three—,
                We've got what he desires.

            My purse is yours, on easy terms:
                When Peace shall reappear,
            Whate'er you've borrowed will be due.
                So speak up without fear.

            You needn't pay me back, you see,
            If you can get a cent from me!

            We're about to entertain
                Some foreign gentlemen;

[94] Greek denomination of money.

We've soup and tender, fresh-killed pork.
Come round to dine at ten.

Come early; wash and dress with care,
And bring the children, too.
Then step right in, no "by your leave."
We'll be expecting you.

Walk in as if you owned the place.
You'll find the door—shut in your face!

[*Enter a group of Spartan* AMBASSADORS; *they are in the
same desperate condition as the* HERALD *in the previous
scene.*]

LEADER OF CHORUS. Here come the envoys from Sparta, sprouting
long beards and looking for all the world as if they were carrying
pigpens in front of them.

Greetings, gentlemen of Sparta. Tell me, in what state have
you come?

SPARTAN. Why waste words? You can plainly see what state we've
come in!

LEADER OF CHORUS. Wow! You're in a pretty high-strung condition,
and it seems to be getting worse.

SPARTAN. It's indescribable. Won't someone please arrange a peace for
us—in any way you like.

LEADER OF CHORUS. Here comes our own, native ambassadors, crouching like wrestlers and holding their clothes in front of them; this
seems an athletic kind of malady.

[*Enter several Athenian* AMBASSADORS.]

ATHENIAN. Can anyone tell us where Lysistrata is? You see our condition.

LEADER OF CHORUS. Here's another case of the same complaint. Tell
me, are the attacks worse in the morning?

ATHENIAN. No, we're always afflicted this way. If someone doesn't
soon arrange this truce, you'd better not let me get my hands on
—Cleisthenes! [95]

LEADER OF CHORUS. If you're smart, you'll arrange your cloaks so none
of the fellows who smashed the Hermae[96] can see you.

---

[95] The notorious homosexual.   [96] Small busts of Hermes mounted on ithyphallic
pillars, which stood in almost every doorway in Athens as guardians against thieves.
Just before the Athenian expedition to Sicily sailed in 415 B.C., many of these
"Herms" were smashed, perhaps by oligarchic conspirators opposed to the expedition.

ATHENIAN. Right you are; a very good suggestion.

SPARTAN. Aye, by all means. Here, let's hitch up our clothes.

ATHENIAN. Greetings, Spartan. We've suffered dreadful things.

SPARTAN. My dear fellow, we'd have suffered still worse if one of those fellows had seen us in this condition.

ATHENIAN. Well, gentlemen, we must get down to business. What's your errand here?

SPARTAN. We're ambassadors about peace.

ATHENIAN. Excellent; so are we. Only Lysistrata can arrange things for us; shall we summon her?

SPARTAN. Aye, and Lysistratus too, if you like.

LEADER OF CHORUS. No need to summon her, it seems. She's coming out of her own accord.

> [*Enter* LYSISTRATA *accompanied by a statue of a nude female figure, which represents Reconciliation.*]

Hail, noblest of women; now must thou be
A judge shrewd and subtle, mild and severe,
Be sweet yet majestic: all manners employ.
The leaders of Hellas, caught by thy love-charms,
Have come to thy judgment, their charges submitting.

LYSISTRATA. This is no difficult task, if one catch them still in amorous passion, before they've resorted to each other. But I'll soon find out. Where's Reconciliation? Go, first bring the Spartans here, and don't seize them rudely and violently, as our tactless husbands used to do, but as befits a woman, like an old, familiar friend; if they won't give you their hands, take them however you can. Then go fetch these Athenians here, taking hold of whatever they offer you. Now then, men of Sparta, stand here beside me, and you Athenians on the other side, and listen to my words.

I am a woman, it is true, but I have a mind; I'm not badly off in native wit, and by listening to my father and my elders, I've had a decent schooling.

Now I intend to give you a scolding which you both deserve. With one common font you worship at the same altars, just like brothers, at Olympia, at Thermopylae, at Delphi—how many more might I name, if time permitted;—and the Barbarians stand by waiting with their armies; yet you are destroying the men and towns of Greece.

ATHENIAN. Oh, this tension is killing me!

LYSISTRATA. And now, men of Sparta—to turn to you—don't you remember how the Spartan Pericleidas came here once as a suppliant, and sitting at our altar, all pale with fear in his crimson cloak, begged us for an army? [97] For all Messene[98] had attacked you and the god sent an earthquake too? Then Cimon went forth with four thousand hoplites and saved all Lacedaemon. Such was the aid you received from Athens, and now you lay waste the country which once treated you so well.

ATHENIAN [*hotly*]. They're in the wrong, Lysistrata, upon my word, they are!

SPARTAN [*absently, looking at the statue of Reconciliation*]. We're in the wrong. What hips! How lovely they are!

LYSISTRATA. Don't think I'm going to let you Athenians off. Don't you remember how the Spartans came in arms when you were wearing the rough, sheepskin cloak of slaves and slew the host of Thessalians, the comrades and allies of Hippias? [99] Fighting with you on that day, alone of all the Greeks, they set you free and instead of a sheepskin gave your folk a handsome robe to wear.

SPARTAN [*looking at* LYSISTRATA]. I've never seen a more distinguished woman.

ATHENIAN [*looking at Reconciliation*]. I've never seen a more voluptuous body!

LYSISTRATA. Why then, with these many noble deeds to think of, do you fight each other? Why don't you stop this villainy? Why not make peace? Tell me, what prevents it?

SPARTAN [*waving vaguely at Reconciliation*]. We're willing, if you're willing to give up your position on yonder flank.

LYSISTRATA. What position, my good man?

SPARTAN. Pylus; we've been panting for it for ever so long.

ATHENIAN. No, by God! You shan't have it!

LYSISTRATA. Let them have it, my friend.

ATHENIAN. Then what shall we have to rouse things up?

LYSISTRATA. Ask for another place in exchange.

ATHENIAN. Well, let's see: first of all [*pointing to various parts of*

---

[97] In 464 B.C., after a devastating earthquake, Spartan rule was endangered by a rebellion of their serfs. The Athenians sent a force under the famous Athenian commander, Cimon, to help the Spartan rulers.   [98] Southwest Peloponnesus, conquered by the Spartans in the eighth and seventh centuries B.C. The inhabitants were reduced to the condition of Spartan serfs (helots).   [99] Hippias allowed exiled democrats to return, but they had to wear sheepskins as readily visible identification "tags." Partially with the help of Spartan soldiers, these exiles and their Athenian supporters finally expelled Hippias and his Thessalian mercenaries from Athens.

Reconciliation's anatomy] give us Echinus here, this Maliac Inlet
in back there, and these two Megarian legs.[100]

SPARTAN. No, by heavens! You can't have *everything*, you crazy fool!

LYSISTRATA. Let it go. Don't fight over a pair of legs.

ATHENIAN [*taking off his cloak*]. I think I'll strip and do a little plant-
ing now.

SPARTAN [*following suit*]. And I'll just do a little fertilizing, by gosh!

LYSISTRATA. Wait until the truce is concluded. Now if you've decided
on this course, hold a conference and discuss the matter with your
allies.

ATHENIAN. Allies? Don't be ridiculous! They're in the same state we
are. Won't all our allies want the same thing we do—to jump in
bed with their women?

SPARTAN. Ours will, I know.

ATHENIAN. Especially the Carystians,[101] by God!

LYSISTRATA. Very well. Now purify yourselves, that your wives may
feast and entertain you in the Acropolis; we've provisions by the
basketfull. Exchange your oaths and pledges there, and then each
of you may take his wife and go home.

ATHENIAN. Let's go at once.

SPARTAN. Come on, where you will.

ATHENIAN. For God's sake, let's hurry!
                    [*They all go into the Acropolis.*]

CHORUS [*singing*].
      Whate'er I have of coverlets
         And robes of varied hue
    And golden trinklets—without stint
      I offer them to you.

    Take what you will and bear it home,
      Your children to delight,
  Or if your girl's a Basket-maid;
      Just choose whate'er's in sight.

[100] Like Pylus on "yonder flank" these names operate with double meaning,
referring both to disputed territories and to physical parts of the statue of Reconciliation. Echinus is a town in Thessaly as well as the word for "hedgehog"—slang
for the female genitalia. The Maliac Inlet is a gulf just south of Echinus, but also
a pun on Greek words for breasts (in the dialect of Sparta *mala*, "apples") and
bosom or womb (*kolpos*, "gulf" or "bay"). Megara is a famous city-state between
Athens and Corinth, and *megaron* sometimes means "bedroom." [101] From the
town of Carystus, an Athenian ally, on Euboea (the largest island of the Aegean).
Their reputation for savagery and lechery was connected with their descent from
pre-Hellenic stock.

There's naught within so well secured
    You cannot break the seal
And bear it off; just help yourselves;
    No hesitation feel.

But you'll see nothing, though you try,
Unless you've sharper eyes than I!

If anyone needs bread to feed
    A growing family,
I've lots of wheat and full-grown loaves;
    So just apply to me.

Let every poor man who desires
    Come round and bring a sack
To fetch the grain; my slave is there
    To load it on his back.

But don't come near my door, I say:
Beware the dog, and stay away!

> [*An* ATHENIAN *enters carrying a torch; he knocks at the
> gate.*]

ATHENIAN. Open the door! [*To the* CHORUS, *which is clustered around
the gate.*] Make way, won't you! What are you hanging around
for? Want me to singe you with this torch? [*To himself.*] No; it's
a stale trick, I won't do it! [*To the audience.*] Still, if I've got to
do it to please *you,* I suppose I'll have to take the trouble.

> [*A second* ATHENIAN *comes out of the gate.*]

SECOND ATHENIAN. And I'll help you.

FIRST ATHENIAN. [*waving his torch at the* CHORUS]. Get out! Go bawl
your heads off! Move on there, so the Spartans can leave in peace
when the banquet's over.

> [*They brandish their torches until the* CHORUS *leaves the
> Orchestra.*]

SECOND ATHENIAN. I've never seen such a pleasant banquet:[102] the
Spartans are charming fellows, indeed they are! And we Athenians are very witty in our cups.

FIRST ATHENIAN. Naturally: for when we're sober we're never at our
best. If the Athenians would listen to me, we'd always get a little
tipsy on our embassies. As things are now, we go to Sparta when
we're sober and look around to stir up trouble. And then we don't
hear what they say—and as for what they *don't* say, we have all

---

[102] At Athenian banquets each guest in turn had to sing an appropriate drinking
song, which would fit and at least equal that of the previous singer.

sort of suspicions. And then we bring back varying reports about the mission. But this time everything is pleasant; even if a man should sing the Telamon[103]-song when he ought to sing "Cleitagoras," [104] we'd praise him and swear it was excellent.

[*The two* CHORUSES *return, as a* CHORUS OF ATHENIANS *and a* CHORUS OF SPARTANS.]

Here they come back again. Go to the devil, you scoundrels!

SECOND ATHENIAN. Get out, I say! They're coming out from the feast.

[*Enter the Spartan and Athenian envoys, followed by* LYSISTRATA *and all the women.*]

SPARTAN [*to one of his fellow envoys*]. My good fellow, take up your pipes; I want to do a fancy two-step and sing a jolly song for the Athenians.

ATHENIAN. Yes, do take your pipes, by all means. I'd love to see you dance.

SPARTAN [*singing and dancing with the* CHORUS OF SPARTANS].

These youths inspire
To song and dance, O Memory;
Stir up my Muse, to tell how we
And Athens' men, in your galleys clashing
At Artemisium,[105] 'gainst foemen dashing
In godlike ire,
Conquered the Persian and set Greece free.

Leonidas[106]
Led on his valiant warriors
Whetting their teeth like angry boars.
Abundant foam on their lips was flow'ring,
A stream of sweat from their limbs was show'ring.
The Persian was
Numberless as the sand on the shores.

O Huntress[107] who slayest the beasts in the glade,
O Virgin divine, hither come to our truce,
Unite us in bonds which all time will not loose.
Grant us to find in this treaty, we pray,
An unfailing source of true friendship today,

---

[103] Mythical king of Salamis (brother of Peleus and father of Ajax). [104] Name of a less heroic, coarser drinking song which celebrated looting and the violence of war. [105] Site of an inconclusive naval battle against the Persians off the coast of Euboea in 480 B.C., at the time of the battle of Thermopylae. [106] Spartan king who led the Greek forces at Thermopylae and died there. [107] Artemis, worshiped in Athens and Sparta alike.

And all of our days, helping us to refrain
From weaseling tricks which bring war in their train.
  Then hither, come hither! O huntress maid.

LYSISTRATA. Come then, since all is fairly done, men of Sparta, lead away your wives, and you, Athenians, take yours. Let every man stand beside his wife, and every wife beside her man, and then, to celebrate our fortune, let's dance. And in the future, let's take care to avoid these misunderstandings.

CHORUS OF ATHENIANS [*singing and dancing*].
 Lead on the dances, your graces revealing.
 Call Artemis hither, call Artemis' twin,
 Leader of dances, Apollo the Healing,
 Kindly God—hither! let's summon him in!

   Nysian Bacchus call,
 Who with his Maenads, his eyes flashing fire,
  Dances, and last of all
 Zeus of the thunderbolt flaming, the Sire,
   And Hera in majesty,
   Queen of prosperity.

  Come, ye Powers who dwell above
  Unforgetting, our witnesses be
 Of Peace with bonds of harmonious love—
 The Peace which Cypris[108] has wrought for me.
   Alleluia! Io Paean!
   Leap in joy—hurrah! hurrah!
   'Tis victory—hurrah! hurrah!
   Euoi! Euoi! Euai! Euai!

LYSISTRATA [*to the Spartans*]. Come now, sing a new song to cap ours.

CHORUS OF SPARTANS [*singing and dancing*].
 Leaving Taygetus fair and renown'd,
 Muse of Laconia,[109] hither come:
 Amyclae's[110] god in hymns resound,
 Athene of the Brazen Home,[111]
 And Castor and Pollux,[112] Tyndareus' sons,
 Who sport where Eurotas[113] murmuring runs.

[108] Aphrodite. [109] Southeastern Peloponnesian region of which Sparta was capital. [110] Town just south of Sparta, famous for a colossal statue of Apollo. [111] Bronze-plated temple of Athene in Sparta. [112] Dioscuri, brothers of Helen and Clytemnestra; Sparta was the center of their cult. [113] River of Sparta and Amyclae.

On with the dance! Heia! Ho!
    All leaping along,
Mantles a-swinging as we go!
    Of Sparta our song.
There the holy chorus ever gladdens,
There the beat of stamping feet,
As our winsome fillies, lovely maidens,
Dance, beside Eurotas' banks a-skipping,—
    Nimbly go to and fro
Hast'ning, leaping feet in measures tripping,
Like the Bacchae's revels, hair a-streaming.
Leda's child, divine and mild,
Leads the holy dance, her fair face beaming.
    On with the dance! As your hand
      Presses the hair
   Streaming away unconfined.
      Leap in the air
  Light as the deer; footsteps resound
  Aiding our dance, beating the ground.
Praise Athene, Maid divine, unrivaled in her might,
Dweller in the Brazen Home, unconquered in the fight.
           [All go out singing and dancing.]

Plato

Apology AND

FROM *Phaedo*

TRANSLATED BY BENJAMIN JOWETT

Plato (427 B.C.?–347 B.C.)

FEW FIGURES IN THE HISTORY OF FIFTH CENTURY ATHENS ILLUStrate the uncertainties of the last decades of the century as clearly and tragically as the stonemason and philosopher Socrates. Born at Athens about 469 B.C., Socrates grew to manhood at a time when the "golden" Periclean age of creative and intellectual freedom was approaching its zenith; his life ended ignominiously in 399 B.C., when a jury of Athenian citizens found him guilty of "irreverence" to the gods and of "corrupting the youth" (presumably by encouraging them critically to examine accepted values, including those of the existing order).

Since Socrates himself did not record his discussions, all of our knowledge about him is filtered through intermediaries such as his follower Plato, Plato's younger contemporary Xenophon, and the comic poet Aristophanes, who caricatured Socrates in his play *The Clouds* in 423 B.C. Plato's *Apology,* probably written not too long after Socrates' death, is believed to give us one of the most accurate representations of Socrates' thought, manner, and method of inquiry. It reflects the radical and insistent nature of his examination of justice and other norms of human conduct and his profound awareness of man's limitations. Although his speech in court is fatally defiant, his tone is motivated neither by deliberate martyrdom nor by political shortsightedness, but rather by his refusal to compromise and by his principled denial of conventional standards.

This behavior is also observed when Socrates later refused to avail himself of plans made for his escape from prison. The major theme of the *Phaedo,* a later dialogue in which Plato describes Socrates' last hours and death, is the immortality of the human "soul" in contrast to the mortality of all physical things, and the consequences this must have for man's behavior.

Plato was the brilliant creator of a new literary genre, the prose dialogue. The epic poets, tragedians, writers of comedy, and even historians had relied on dialogue as a dramatic device, but Plato—inspired by the Socratic method of relentless cross-examination—transformed it into a literary instrument of rational inquiry.

Throughout his writings Plato retained much of his Socratic heritage: the anthropocentric emphasis, the problem of moral norms, the concern with ethical conflicts. But in his twenty-five extant dialogues he increasingly amplified this heritage and connected it with his own examination of other questions, such as the nature of reality and knowledge, cosmology, and political and educational philosophy. Perhaps the most brilliant example of this later extension of the Socratic heritage is Plato's *Republic*.

*Apology**

How you, O Athenians, have been affected by my accusers, I cannot tell; but I know that they almost made me forget who I was—so persuasively did they speak; and yet they have hardly uttered a word of truth. But of the many falsehoods told by them, there was one which quite amazed me;—I mean when they said that you should be upon your guard and not allow yourselves to be deceived by the force of my eloquence. To say this, when they were certain to be detected as soon as I opened my lips and proved myself to be anything but a great speaker, did indeed appear to me most shameless —unless by the force of eloquence they mean the force of truth; for if such is their meaning, I admit that I am eloquent. But in how different a way from theirs! Well, as I was saying, they have scarcely spoken the truth at all; but from me you shall hear the whole truth: not, however, delivered after their manner in a set oration duly ornamented with words and phrases. No, by heaven! but I shall use the words and arguments which occur to me at the moment; for I am confident in the justice of my cause: at my time of life I ought not to be appearing before you, O men of Athens, in the character of a juvenile orator—let no one expect it of me. And I must beg of you to grant me a favor: If I defend myself in my accustomed manner, and you hear me using the words which I have been in the habit of using in the agora[1] at the tables of the money-changers, or anywhere else, I would ask you not to be surprised, and not to interrupt me on this account. For I am more than seventy years of age, and appearing now for the first time in a court of law, I am quite a stranger to the language of the place; and therefore I would have you regard me as if I were really a stranger, whom you would excuse if he spoke in his native tongue, and after the fashion of his country: Am I making an unfair request of you? Never mind the manner, which may or may not be good; but think only of the truth of my words, and give heed to that: let the speaker speak truly and the judge decide justly.

And first, I have to reply to the older charges and to my first accusers,[2]

* *Apology* means "defense." Socrates delivered the following speech at his own trial after the prosecution had argued the case against him.   [1] The Athenian marketplace. Lying northwest of the Acropolis, it was the center of public and commercial life.   [2] Without regard for correct legal procedure, Socrates will first deal with old ("first") prejudices and criticisms which really provoked the formal charges against him, rather than beginning with the charges themselves.

and then I will go on to the later ones. For of old I have had many accusers, who have accused me falsely to you during many years; and I am more afraid of them than of Anytus³ and his associates, who are dangerous, too, in their own way. But far more dangerous are the others, who began when you were children, and took possession of your minds with their falsehoods, telling of one Socrates, a wise man, who speculated about the heaven above, and searched into the earth beneath, and made the worse appear the better cause.⁴ The disseminators of this tale are the accusers whom I dread; for their hearers are apt to fancy that such enquirers do not believe in the existence of the gods. And they are many, and their charges against me are of ancient date, and they were made by them in the days when you were more impressible than you are now—in childhood, or it may have been in youth—and the cause when heard went by default, for there was none to answer. And hardest of all, I do not know and cannot tell the names of my accusers; unless in the chance case of a Comic poet.⁵ All who from envy and malice have persuaded you—some of them having first convinced themselves—all this class of men are most difficult to deal with; for I cannot have them up here, and cross-examine them, and therefore I must simply fight with shadows in my own defence, and argue when there is no one who answers. I will ask you then to assume with me, as I was saying, that my opponents are of two kinds; one recent, the other ancient: and I hope that you will see the propriety of my answering the latter first, for these accusations you heard long before the others, and much oftener.

Well, then, I must make my defense, and endeavor to clear away in a short time, a slander which has lasted a long time. May I succeed, if to succeed be for my good and yours, or likely to avail me in my cause! The task is not an easy one; I quite understand the nature of it. And so leaving the event with God, in obedience to the law I will now make my defense.

I will begin at the beginning, and ask what is the accusation which has given rise to the slander of me, and in fact has encouraged Meletus⁶ to prefer this charge against me. Well, what do the slanderers say? They shall be my prosecutors, and I will sum up their words in an affidavit: "Socrates is an evil-doer, and a curious person, who searches into things under the earth and in heaven, and he makes the worse appear the better cause; and he teaches the aforesaid doctrines to others." Such is the nature of the accusation: it is just what you have yourselves seen in the comedy of Aristophanes, who has introduced a man whom he calls Socrates, going about and saying that he

³ A prominent politician; one of Socrates' prosecutors in this trial.   ⁴ Some opponents accused Socrates of disseminating antireligious and materialistic explanations of the universe.   ⁵ Aristophanes' *The Clouds* (produced in 423 B.C.) contained a caricature of Socrates and his associates as bizarre eggheads without ethical scruples.   ⁶ Main prosecutor.

walks in air, and talking a deal of nonsense concerning matters of which I do not pretend to know either much or little—not that I mean to speak disparagingly of any one who is a student of natural philosophy. I should be very sorry if Meletus could bring so grave a charge against me. But the simple truth is, O Athenians, that I have nothing to do with physical speculations. Very many of those here present are witnesses to the truth of this, and to them I appeal. Speak then, you who have heard me, and tell your neighbors whether any of you have ever known me hold forth in few words or in many upon such matters. . . . You hear their answer. And from what they say of this part of the charge you will be able to judge of the truth of the rest.

As little foundation is there for the report that I am a teacher, and take money; this accusation has no more truth in it than the other.[7] Although, if a man were really able to instruct mankind, to receive money for giving instruction would, in my opinion, be an honor to him. There is Gorgias of Leontium, and Prodicus of Ceos, and Hippias of Elis,[8] who go the round of the cities, and are able to persuade the young men to leave their own citizens by whom they might be taught for nothing, and come to them whom they not only pay, but are thankful if they may be allowed to pay them. There is at this time a Parian[9] philosopher residing in Athens, of whom I have heard; and I came to hear of him in this way: I came across a man who has spent a world of money on the Sophists, Callias, the son of Hipponicus, and knowing that he had sons, I asked him: "Callias," I said, "if your two sons were foals or calves, there would be no difficulty in finding some one to put over them; we should hire a trainer of horses, or a farmer probably, who would improve and perfect them in their own proper virtue and excellence; but as they are human beings, whom are you thinking of placing over them? Is there any one who understands human and political virtue? You must have thought about the matter, for you have sons; is there any one?" "There is," he said. "Who is he?" said I; "and of what country? and what does he charge?" "Evenus the Parian," he replied; "he is the man, and his charge is five minae." Happy is Evenus, I said to myself, if he really has this wisdom,

---

[7] The professional teachers (Sophists) made fortunes selling "knowledge" and rhetorical skills, whereas Socrates pursued his quest for truth without any regular income.   [8] Famous Sophists. Leontium is in Sicily, Ceos an Aegean island, Elis in the Peloponnesus. Gorgias (about 485 B.C.–395 B.C.) was particularly famous as the inventor of an influential prose style, and is the principal speaker in Plato's dialogue *Gorgias*. Prodicus (about 465 B.C.–395 B.C.) gave extensive lecture courses. Hippias (about 450 B.C.–385 B.C.) rose from poverty to luxurious wealth, which he proudly displayed.   [9] From Paros, an island in the central Aegean. Evenus, to whom Socrates here refers, is known to have written a didactic poem on rhetoric, as well as shorter poems, in a setting of drinking parties with serious discussion (*symposia*).

and teaches at such a moderate charge. Had I the same, I should have been
very proud and conceited; but the truth is that I have no knowledge of the
kind.

I dare say, Athenians, that some one among you will reply, "Yes, Socrates,
but what is the origin of these accusations which are brought against you;
there must have been something strange which you have been doing? All
these rumors and this talk about you would never have arisen if you had
been like other men: tell us, then, what is the cause of them, for we should
be sorry to judge hastily of you." Now I regard this as a fair challenge, and I
will endeavor to explain to you the reason why I am called wise and have
such an evil fame. Please to attend then. And although some of you may
think that I am joking, I declare that I will tell you the entire truth. Men of
Athens, this reputation of mine has come of a certain sort of wisdom which I
possess. If you ask me what kind of wisdom, I reply, wisdom such as may
perhaps be attained by man, for to that extent I am inclined to believe
that I am wise; whereas the persons of whom I was speaking have a
superhuman wisdom, which I may fail to describe, because I have it not
myself; and he who says that I have, speaks falsely, and is taking away my
character. And here, O men of Athens, I must beg you not to interrupt me,
even if I seem to say something extravagant. For the word which I will speak
is not mine. I will refer you to a witness who is worthy of credit; that witness shall be the God of Delphi [10]—he will tell you about my wisdom, if I
have any, and of what sort it is. You must have known Chaerephon;[11] he
was early a friend of mine, and also a friend of yours, for he shared in the
recent exile of the people, and returned with you.[12] Well, Chaerephon, as
you know, was very impetuous in all his doings, and he went to Delphi and
boldly asked the oracle to tell him whether—as I was saying, I must beg you
not to interrupt—he asked the oracle to tell him whether any one was wiser
than I was, and the Pythian prophetess answered, that there was no man
wiser. Chaerephon is dead himself; but his brother, who is in court, will
confirm the truth of what I am saying.

Why do I mention this? Because I am going to explain to you why I have
such an evil name. When I heard the answer, I said to myself, What can
the god mean? and what is the interpretation of his riddle? for I know that I
have no wisdom, small or great. What then can he mean when he says that
I am the wisest of men? And yet he is a god, and cannot lie; that would be
against his nature. After long consideration, I thought of a method of trying

[10] Apollo's oracle.   [11] Loyal follower of Socrates; also caricatured in *The Clouds*.
[12] When the Peloponnesian War ended in 404 B.C., the Spartans imposed on the
Athenians a regime known as the Thirty Tyrants. They exercised an oligarchic
reign of terror and forced all the outspoken defenders of democracy into exile.
After a brief period democracy was restored when the returning exiles defeated
and deposed the Thirty.

the question. I reflected that if I could only find a man wiser than myself, then I might go to the god with a refutation in my hand. I should say to him, "Here is a man who is wiser than I am; but you said that I was the wisest." Accordingly I went to one who had the reputation of wisdom, and observed him—his name I need not mention; he was a politician whom I selected for examination—and the result was as follows: When I began to talk with him, I could not help thinking that he was not really wise, although he was thought wise by many, and still wiser by himself; and thereupon I tried to explain to him that he thought himself wise, but was not really wise; and the consequence was that he hated me, and his enmity was shared by several who were present and heard me. So I left him, saying to myself, as I went away: Well, although I do not suppose that either of us knows anything really beautiful and good, I am better off than he is—for he knows nothing, and thinks that he knows; I neither know nor think that I know. In this latter particular, then, I seem to have slightly the advantage of him. Then I went to another who had still higher pretensions to wisdom, and my conclusion was exactly the same. Whereupon I made another enemy of him, and of many others besides him.

Then I went to one man after another, being not unconscious of the enmity which I provoked, and I lamented and feared this: but necessity was laid upon me—the word of God, I thought, ought to be considered first. And I said to myself, Go I must to all who appear to know, and find out the meaning of the oracle. And I swear to you, Athenians, by the dog I swear! [13] —for I must tell you the truth—the result of my mission was just this: I found that the men most in repute were all but the most foolish; and that others less esteemed were really wiser and better. I will tell you the tale of my wanderings and of the "Herculean" labors, as I may call them, which I endured only to find at last the oracle irrefutable. After the politicians, I went to the poets; tragic, dithyrambic,[14] and all sorts. And there, I said to myself, you will be instantly detected; now you will find out that you are more ignorant than they are. Accordingly, I took them some of the most elaborate passages in their own writings, and asked what was the meaning of them—thinking that they would teach me something. Will you believe me? I am almost ashamed to confess the truth, but I must say that there is hardly a person present who would not have talked better about their poetry than they did themselves. Then I knew that not by wisdom do poets write poetry, but by a sort of genius and inspiration; they are like diviners or soothsayers who also say many fine things, but do not understand the meaning of them. The poets appeared to me to be much in the same case; and I further ob-

---

[13] A mild Greek oath.   [14] Dithyramb is a short narrative choral song in the cult of Dionysus. It maintained itself as a literary form beside tragedy throughout the fifth century.

served that upon the strength of their poetry they believed themselves to be the wisest of men in other things in which they were not wise. So I departed, conceiving myself to be superior to them for the same reason that I was superior to the politicians.

At last I went to the artisans. I was conscious that I knew nothing at all, as I may say, and I was sure that they knew many fine things; and here I was not mistaken, for they did know many things of which I was ignorant, and in this they certainly were wiser than I was. But I observed that even the good artisans fell into the same error as the poets;—because they were good workmen they thought that they also knew all sorts of high matters, and this defect in them overshadowed their wisdom; and therefore I asked myself on behalf of the oracle, whether I would like to be as I was, neither having their knowledge nor their ignorance, or like them in both; and I made answer to myself and to the oracle that I was better off as I was.

This inquisition has led to my having many enemies of the worst and most dangerous kind, and has given occasion also to many calumnies. And I am called wise, for my hearers always imagine that I myself possess the wisdom which I find wanting in others: but the truth is, O men of Athens, that God only is wise; and by his answer he intends to show that the wisdom of men is worth little or nothing; he is not speaking of Socrates, he is only using my name by way of illustration, as if he said, He, O men, is the wisest, who, like Socrates, knows that his wisdom is in truth worth nothing. And so I go about the world, obedient to the god, and search and make enquiry into the wisdom of any one, whether citizen or stranger, who appears to be wise; and if he is not wise, then in vindication of the oracle I show him that he is not wise; and my occupation quite absorbs me, and I have no time to give either to any public matter of interest or to any concern of my own, but I am in utter poverty by reason of my devotion to the god.

There is another thing:—young men of the richer classes, who have not much to do, come about me of their own accord; they like to hear the pretenders examined, and they often imitate me, and proceed to examine others; there are plenty of persons, as they quickly discover, who think that they know something, but really know little or nothing; and then those who are examined by them instead of being angry with themselves are angry with me: This confounded Socrates, they say; this villainous misleader of youth!— and then if somebody asks them, Why, what evil does he practice or teach? they do not know, and cannot tell; but in order that they may not appear to be at a loss, they repeat the ready-made charges which are used against all philosophers about teaching things up in the clouds and under the earth, and having no gods, and making the worse appear the better cause; for they do not like to confess that their pretense of knowledge has been detected— which is the truth; and as they are numerous and ambitious and energetic, and are drawn up in battle array and have persuasive tongues, they have filled your ears with their loud and inveterate calumnies. And this is the reason why my three accusers, Meletus and Anytus and Lycon, have set upon me; Meletus, who has a quarrel with me on behalf of the poets; Anytus, on behalf of the craftsmen and politicians; Lycon, on behalf of the rhetoricians: and as I said at the beginning, I cannot expect to get rid of such a mass of calumny all in a moment. And this, O men of Athens, is the truth and the whole truth; I have concealed nothing, I have dissembled nothing. And yet, I know that my plainness of speech makes them hate me, and what is their hatred but a proof that I am speaking the truth? Hence has arisen the prejudice against me; and this is the reason of it, as you will find out either in this or in any future enquiry.

I have said enough in my defense against the first class of my accusers; I turn to the second class.[15] They are headed by Meletus, that good man and true lover of his country, as he calls himself. Against these, too, I must try to make a defense: Let their affidavit be read: it contains something of this kind: It says that Socrates is a doer of evil, who corrupts the youth; and who does not believe in the gods of the state, but has other new divinities[16] of his own. Such is the charge; and now let us examine the particular counts. He says that I am a doer of evil, and corrupt the youth; but I say, O men of Athens, that Meletus is a doer of evil, in that he pretends to be in earnest when he is only in jest, and is so eager to bring men to trial from a pretended zeal and interest about matters in which he really never had the smallest interest. And the truth of this I will endeavor to prove to you.

Come hither, Meletus, and let me ask a question of you.[17] You think a great deal about the improvement of youth?

Yes, I do.

Tell the judges, then, who is their improver; for you must know, as you have taken the pains to discover their corrupter, and are citing and accusing me before them. Speak, then, and tell the judges who their improver is. Observe, Meletus, that you are silent, and have nothing to say. But is not this rather disgraceful, and a very considerable proof of what I was saying, that you have no interest in the matter? Speak up, friend, and tell us who their improver is.

The laws.

But that, my good sir, is not my meaning. I want to know who the person is, who, in the first place, knows the laws.

---

[15] Those conducting the current prosecution.   [16] Implying religious belief of some kind. Perhaps a reference to Socrates' famous *daimon* or "inner voice," which at times warned him against certain decisions but never gave him positive instructions.   [17] In Greek courts the defendant was allowed to cross-examine his accusers. Socrates, who was the master of philosophical cross-examination, thus fulfills his pledge to defend himself in the same manner that he had consistently in the marketplace in his public discussions.

The judges,[18] Socrates, who are present in court.

What, do you mean to say, Meletus, that they are able to instruct and improve youth?

Certainly they are.

What, all of them, or some only and not others?

All of them.

By the goddess Herè,[19] that is good news! There are plenty of improvers, then. And what do you say of the audience—do they improve them?

Yes, they do.

And the senators? [20]

Yes, the senators improve them.

But perhaps the members of the assembly[21] corrupt them? or do they too improve them?

They improve them.

Then every Athenian improves and elevates them; all with the exception of myself; and I alone am their corrupter? Is that what you affirm?

That is what I stoutly affirm.

I am very unfortunate if you are right. But suppose I ask you a question: How about horses? [22] Does one man do them harm and all the world good? Is not the exact opposite the truth? One man is able to do them good, or at least not many; the trainer of horses, that is to say, does them good, and others who have to do with them rather injure them? Is not that true, Meletus, of horses, or of any other animals? Most assuredly it is; whether you and Anytus say yes or no. Happy indeed would be the condition of youth if they had one corrupter only, and all the rest of the world were their improvers. But you, Meletus, have sufficiently shown that you never had a thought about the young: your carelessness is seen in your not caring about the very things which you bring against me.

And now, Meletus, I will ask you another question—by Zeus I will: Which is better, to live among bad citizens, or among good ones? Answer, friend, I say; the question is one which may be easily answered. Do not the good do their neighbors good, and the bad do them evil?

Certainly.

And is there any one who would rather be injured than benefited by those who live with him? Answer, my good friend, the law requires you to answer —does any one like to be injured?

Certainly not.

---

[18] The jury. The Athenian jury usually consisted of five hundred citizens chosen by lot.   [19] Hera.   [20] The five hundred members of the Council (*Boulē*) of Athens.   [21] The *ecclēsia*, the legislative and sovereign body according to the Athenian constitution. It was comprised of all the citizens of Athens (i.e., all male freemen over 18 years).   [22] A characteristic Socratic analogy. This kind of analogy frequently occurs in the Platonic dialogues.

And when you accuse me of corrupting and deteriorating the youth, do you allege that I corrupt them intentionally or unintentionally?

Intentionally, I say.

But you have just admitted that the good do their neighbors good, and the evil do them evil. Now, is that a truth which your superior wisdom has recognized thus early in life, and am I, at my age, in such darkness and ignorance as not to know that if a man with whom I have to live is corrupted by me, I am very likely to be harmed by him; and yet I corrupt him, and intentionally, too—so you say, although neither I nor any other human being is ever likely to be convinced by you. But either I do not corrupt them, or I corrupt them unintentionally; and on either view of the case you lie. If my offense is unintentional, the law has no cognizance of unintentional offenses: you ought to have taken me privately, and warned and admonished me; for if I had been better advised, I should have left off doing what I only did unintentionally—no doubt I should; but you would have nothing to say to me and refused to teach me. And now you bring me up in this court, which is a place not of instruction, but of punishment.

It will be very clear to you, Athenians, as I was saying, that Meletus has no care[23] at all, great or small, about the matter. But still I should like to know, Meletus, in what I am affirmed to corrupt the young. I suppose you mean, as I infer from your indictment, that I teach them not to acknowledge the gods which the state acknowledges, but some other new divinities or spiritual agencies in their stead. These are the lessons by which I corrupt the youth, as you say.

Yes, that I say emphatically.

Then, by the gods, Meletus, of whom we are speaking, tell me and the court, in somewhat plainer terms, what you mean! For I do not as yet understand whether you affirm that I teach other men to acknowledge some gods, and therefore that I do believe in gods, and am not an entire atheist—this you do not lay to my charge—but only you say that they are not the same gods which the city recognizes—the charge is that they are different gods. Or, do you mean that I am an atheist simply, and a teacher of atheism?

I mean the latter—that you are a complete atheist.[24]

What an extraordinary statement! Why do you think so, Meletus? Do you mean that I do not believe in the godhead of the sun or moon, like other men?

I assure you, judges, that he does not: for he says that the sun is stone, and the moon earth.

---

[23] A pun on Meletus' name, with the word (e)melēsen, "he cared."   [24] The most dangerous charge. Although religious skepticism is expressed frequently in early Greek literature, unqualified atheism was rare. In his original charge Meletus had ascribed some religious belief to Socrates and he is therefore contradicting himself now.

Friend Meletus, you think that you are accusing Anaxagoras:[25] and you have but a bad opinion of the judges, if you fancy them illiterate to such a degree as not to know that these doctrines are found in the books of Anaxagoras the Clazomenian,[26] which are full of them. And so, forsooth, the youth are said to be taught them by Socrates, when there are not unfrequently exhibitions of them at the theater[27] (price of admission one drachma at the most); and they might pay their money, and laugh at Socrates if he pretends to father these extraordinary views. And so, Meletus, you really think that I do not believe in any god?

I swear by Zeus that you believe absolutely in none at all.

Nobody will believe you, Meletus, and I am pretty sure that you do not believe yourself. I cannot help thinking, men of Athens, that Meletus is reckless and impudent, and that he has written this indictment in a spirit of mere wantonness and youthful bravado. Has he not compounded a riddle, thinking to try me? He said to himself: I shall see whether the wise Socrates will discover my facetious contradiction, or whether I shall be able to deceive him and the rest of them. For he certainly does appear to me to contradict himself in the indictment as much as if he said that Socrates is guilty of not believing in the gods, and yet of believing in them—but this is not like a person who is in earnest.

I should like you, O men of Athens, to join me in examining what I conceive to be his inconsistency; and do you, Meletus, answer. And I must remind the audience of my request that they would not make a disturbance[28] if I speak in my accustomed manner:

Did ever man, Meletus, believe in the existence of human things, and not of human beings? . . . I wish, men of Athens, that he would answer, and not be always trying to get up an interruption. Did ever any man believe in horsemanship, and not in horses? or in flute-playing, and not in flute-players? No, my friend; I will answer to you and to the court, as you refuse to answer for yourself. There is no man who ever did. But now please to answer the next question: Can a man believe in spiritual and divine agencies, and not in spirits or demigods?

He cannot.

How lucky I am to have extracted that answer, by the assistance of the court! But then you swear in the indictment that I teach and believe in

---

[25] A fifth century philosopher (500 B.C.–428 B.C.).He lived in Athens for thirty years and was a friend and teacher of Euripides and Pericles, but when his philosophical speculation offended the Athenians he was exiled in 433 B.C. because of "impiety."   [26] From Clazomenae, an Ionian city on the west coast of Asia Minor, where Anaxagoras was born.   [27] An allusion to the mention or reflection of Anaxagoras' doctrines in the works of comic and tragic poets.   [28] His opponents are becoming fidgety with frustration.

divine or spiritual agencies (new or old, no matter for that); at any rate, I believe in spiritual agencies—so you say and swear in the affidavit; and yet if I believe in divine beings, how can I help believing in spirits or demigods; must I not? To be sure I must; and therefore I may assume that your silence gives consent. Now what are spirits or demigods? are they not either gods or the sons of gods?

Certainly they are.

But this is what I call the facetious riddle invented by you: the demigods or spirits are gods, and you say first that I do not believe in gods, and then again that I do believe in gods; that is, if I believe in demigods. For if the demigods are the illegitimate sons of gods, whether by the nymphs or by any other mothers, of whom they are said to be the sons—what human being will ever believe that there are no gods if they are the sons of gods? You might as well affirm the existence of mules, and deny that of horses and asses. Such nonsense, Meletus, could only have been intended by you to make trial of me. You have put this into the indictment because you had nothing real of which to accuse me. But no one who has a particle of understanding will ever be convinced by you that the same men can believe in divine and superhuman things, and yet not believe that there are gods and demigods and heroes.

I have said enough in answer to the charge of Meletus: any elaborate defense is unnecessary; but I know only too well how many are the enmities which I have incurred, and this is what will be my destruction if I am destroyed; not Meletus, nor yet Anytus, but the envy and detraction of the world, which has been the death of many good men, and will probably be the death of many more; there is no danger of my being the last of them.

Some one will say: And are you not ashamed, Socrates, of a course of life which is likely to bring you to an untimely end? To him I may fairly answer: There you are mistaken: a man who is good for anything ought not to calculate the chance of living or dying; he ought only to consider whether in doing anything he is doing right or wrong—acting the part of a good man or of a bad. Whereas, upon your view, the heroes who fell at Troy were not good for much, and the son of Thetis[29] above all, who altogether despised danger in comparison with disgrace; and when he was so eager to slay Hector, his goddess mother said to him, that if he avenged his companion Patroclus, and slew Hector, he would die himself—"Fate," she said, in these or the like words, "waits for you next after Hector"; he, receiving this warning, utterly despised danger and death, and instead of fearing them, feared rather to live in dishonor, and not to avenge his friend. "Let me die forth-

---

[29] Achilles. In the following passage, Socrates is referring to a scene in *The Iliad* XVIII.

with," he replies, "and be avenged of my enemy, rather than abide here by the beaked ships, a laughing-stock and a burden of the earth." Had Achilles any thought of death and danger? For wherever a man's place is, whether the place which he has chosen or that in which he has been placed by a commander, there he ought to remain in the hour of danger; he should not think of death or of anything but of disgrace. And this, O men of Athens, is a true saying.

Strange, indeed, would be my conduct, O men of Athens, if I who, when I was ordered by the generals whom you chose to command me at Potidaea and Amphipolis and Delium,[30] remained where they placed me, like any other man, facing death—if now, when, as I conceive and imagine, God orders me to fulfill the philosopher's mission of searching into myself and other men, I were to desert my post through fear of death, or any other fear; that would indeed be strange, and I might justly be arraigned in court for denying the existence of the gods, if I disobeyed the oracle because I was afraid of death, fancying that I was wise when I was not wise. For the fear of death[31] is indeed the pretense of wisdom, and not real wisdom, being a pretense of knowing the unknown; and no one knows whether death, which men in their fear apprehend to be the greatest evil, may not be the greatest good. Is not this ignorance of a disgraceful sort, the ignorance which is the conceit that a man knows what he does not know? And in this respect only I believe myself to differ from men in general, and may perhaps claim to be wiser than they are: that whereas I know but little of the world below,[32] I do not suppose that I know: but I do know that injustice and disobedience to a better, whether God or man, is evil and dishonorable, and I will never fear or avoid a possible good rather than a certain evil. And therefore if you let me go now, and are not convinced by Anytus, who said that since I had been prosecuted I must be put to death; (or if not that I ought never to have been prosecuted at all); and that if I escape now, your sons will all be utterly ruined by listening to my words—if you say to me, Socrates, this time we will not mind Anytus, and you shall be let off, but upon one condition, that you are not to enquire and speculate in this way any more, and that if you are caught doing so again you shall die; if this was the condition on which you let me go, I should reply: Men of Athens, I honor and love you; but I shall obey God rather than you, and while I have life and strength I shall never cease from the practice and teaching of philosophy, exhorting any one whom I meet and saying to him after my manner: You, my friend—a citizen of the great and mighty and wise city of Athens—are you not ashamed of heaping up the greatest amount of money and honor and reputation, and caring so little about wisdom and truth and the greatest improvement of the

[30] Three battles of the Peloponnesian War in which Socrates fought as an Athenian soldier.   [31] Here Socrates is asserting that certain values are superior to life.   [32] The world of the dead. Hades was thought to be located beneath the earth.

soul,[33] which you never regard or heed at all? And if the person with whom I am arguing, says: Yes, but I do care; then I do not leave him or let him go at once; but I proceed to interrogate and examine and cross-examine him, and if I think that he has no virtue in him, but only says that he has, I reproach him with undervaluing the greater, and overvaluing the less. And I shall repeat the same words to every one whom I meet, young and old, citizen and alien, but especially to the citizens, inasmuch as they are my brethren. For know that this is the command of God; and I believe that no greater good has ever happened in the state than my service to the God. For I do nothing but go about persuading you all, old and young alike, not to take thought for your persons or your properties, but first and chiefly to care about the greatest improvement of the soul. I tell you that virtue is not given by money, but that from virtue comes money and every other good of man, public as well as private. This is my teaching, and if this is the doctrine which corrupts the youth, I am a mischievous person. But if any one says that this is not my teaching, he is speaking an untruth. Wherefore, O men of Athens, I say to you, do as Anytus bids or not as Anytus bids, and either acquit me or not; but whichever you do, understand that I shall never alter my ways, not even if I have to die many times.

Men of Athens, do not interrupt, but hear me; there was an understanding between us that you should hear me to the end:[34] I have something more to say, at which you may be inclined to cry out; but I believe that to hear me will be good for you, and therefore I beg that you will not cry out. I would have you know, that if you kill such an one as I am, you will injure yourselves more than you will injure me. Nothing will injure me, not Meletus nor yet Anytus—they cannot, for a bad man is not permitted to injure a better than himself. I do not deny that Anytus may, perhaps, kill him, or drive him into exile, or deprive him of civil rights; and he may imagine, and others may imagine, that he is inflicting a great injury upon him: but there I do not agree. For the evil of doing as he is doing—the evil of unjustly taking away the life of another—is greater far.

And now, Athenians, I am not going to argue for my own sake, as you may think, but for yours, that you may not sin against the God by condemning me, who am his gift to you. For if you kill me you will not easily find a successor to me, who, if I may use such a ludicrous figure of speech, am a sort of gadfly, given to the state by God; and the state is a great and noble steed who is tardy in his motions owing to his very size, and requires to be stirred into life. I am that gadfly which God has attached to the state, and all day long and in all places am always fastening upon you, arousing

33 *Psychē*, "the principle of life," which is the seat of intelligence, emotions, and desires and therefore the center of ethical activity.   34 The jury and spectators are increasingly agitated and surprised, because Socrates is not making the expected compromises and the customary plea for one's life.

and persuading and reproaching you. You will not easily find another like me, and therefore I would advise you to spare me. I dare say that you may feel out of temper (like a person who is suddenly awakened from sleep), and you think that you might easily strike me dead as Anytus advises, and then you would sleep on for the remainder of your lives, unless God in his care of you sent you another gadfly. When I say that I am given to you by God, the proof of my mission is this: if I had been like other men, I should not have neglected all my own concerns or patiently seen the neglect of them during all these years, and have been doing yours, coming to you individually like a father or elder brother, exhorting you to regard virtue; such conduct, I say, would be unlike human nature. If I had gained anything, or if my exhortations had been paid, there would have been some sense in my doing so; but now, as you will perceive, not even the impudence of my accusers dares to say that I have ever exacted or sought pay of any one; of that they have no witness. And I have a sufficient witness to the truth of what I say—my poverty.

Some one may wonder why I go about in private giving advice and busying myself with the concerns of others, but do not venture to come forward in public and advise the state. I will tell you why. You have heard me speak at sundry times and in divers places of an oracle or sign which comes to me, and is the divinity which Meletus ridicules in the indictment. This sign, which is a kind of voice, first began to come to me when I was a child; it always forbids but never commands me to do anything which I am going to do. This is what deters me from being a politician. And rightly, as I think. For I am certain, O men of Athens, that if I had engaged in politics, I should have perished long ago, and done no good either to you or to myself. And do not be offended at my telling you the truth: for the truth is, that no man who goes to war with you or any other multitude, honestly striving against the many lawless and unrighteous deeds which are done in a state, will save his life; he who will fight for the right, if he would live even for a brief space, must have a private station and not a public one.

I can give you convincing evidence of what I say, not words only, but what you value far more—actions. Let me relate to you a passage of my own life which will prove to you that I should never have yielded to injustice from any fear of death, and that "as I should have refused to yield" I must have died at once. I will tell you a tale of the courts, not very interesting perhaps, but nevertheless true. The only office of state which I ever held, O men of Athens, was that of senator:[35] the tribe Antiochis,[36] which is my

[35] One of the five hundred members of the Council (Boulē) of Athens, which consisted of fifty members (Prytanes) of each of the ten tribes into which the Athenian population was divided. Like all other Council members, Socrates was not elected but assigned by lot. [36] Each of the ten Athenian tribes was named after a hero from Greek myth.

tribe, had the presidency[37] at the trial of the generals who had not taken up the bodies of the slain after the battle of Arginusae;[38] and you proposed to try them in a body, contrary to law, as you all thought afterwards; but at the time I was the only one of the Prytanes who was opposed to the illegality, and I gave my vote against you; and when the orators threatened to impeach and arrest me, and you called and shouted, I made up my mind that I would run the risk, having law and justice with me, rather than take part in your injustice because I feared imprisonment and death. This happened in the days of the democracy. But when the oligarchy of the Thirty was in power,[39] they sent for me and four others into the rotunda,[40] and bade us bring Leon the Salaminian from Salamis, as they wanted to put him to death. This was a specimen of the sort of commands which they were always giving with the view of implicating as many as possible in their crimes; and then I showed, not in word only but in deed, that, if I may be allowed to use such an expression, I cared not a straw for death, and that my great and only care was lest I should do an unrighteous or unholy thing. For the strong arm of that oppressive power did not frighten me into doing wrong; and when we came out of the rotunda the other four went to Salamis and fetched Leon, but I went quietly home. For which I might have lost my life, had not the power of the Thirty shortly afterwards come to an end. And many will witness to my words.

Now do you really imagine that I could have survived all these years, if I had led a public life, supposing that like a good man I had always maintained the right and had made justice, as I ought, the first thing? No indeed, men of Athens, neither I nor any other man. But I have been always the same in all my actions, public as well as private, and never have I yielded any base compliance to those who are slanderously termed my disciples, or to any other. Not that I have any regular disciples. But if any one likes to come and hear me while I am pursuing my mission, whether he be young or old, he is not excluded. Nor do I converse only with those who pay; but any one, whether he be rich or poor, may ask and answer me and listen to my words; and whether he turns out to be a bad man or a good one, neither result can be justly imputed to me; for I never taught or professed to teach him anything. And if any one says that he has ever learned or heard anything from me in private which all the world has not heard, let me tell you that he is lying.

[37] The fifty-man tribal delegations to the Council of Athens acted in rotation as a standing committee of the whole Council.   [38] Famous naval victory of Athens over Sparta in 406 B.C. After the battle the ten victorious commanders were collectively charged before the Athenian Assembly (*ecclēsia*) with neglecting to rescue the crews of twelve Athenian ships that were sinking in a storm at the end of the battle. All ten were condemned to death.   [39] The Thirty Tyrants. [40] The Tholos, a building in which the Prytanes held their meetings. It was located in the marketplace.

But I shall be asked, Why do people delight in continually conversing with you? I have told you already, Athenians, the whole truth about this matter: they like to hear the cross-examination of the pretenders to wisdom; there is amusement in it. Now this duty of cross-examining other men has been imposed upon me by God; and has been signified to me by oracles, visions, and in every way in which the will of divine power was ever intimated to any one. This is true, O Athenians; or, if not true, would be soon refuted. If I am or have been corrupting the youth, those of them who are now grown up and have become sensible that I gave them bad advice in the days of their youth should come forward as accusers, and take their revenge; or if they do not like to come themselves, some of their relatives, fathers, brothers, or other kinsmen, should say what evil their families have suffered at my hands. Now is their time. Many of them I see in the court. There is Crito,[41] who is of the same age and of the same deme[42] with myself, and there is Critobulus his son, whom I also see. Then again there is Lysanias of Sphettus, who is the father of Aeschines—he is present; and also there is Antiphon of Cephisus, who is the father of Epigenes; and there are the brothers of several who have associated with me. There is Nicostratus the son of Theosdotides, and the brother of Theodotus (now Theodotus himself is dead, and therefore he, at any rate, will not seek to stop him); and there is Paralus the son of Demodocus, who had a brother Theages; and Adeimantus the son of Ariston, whose brother Plato[43] is present; and Aeantodorus, who is the brother of Apollodorus, whom I also see. I might mention a great many others, some of whom Meletus should have produced as witnesses in the course of his speech; and let him still produce them, if he has forgotten —I will make way for him. And let him say, if he has any testimony of the sort which he can produce. Nay, Athenians, the very opposite is the truth. For all these are ready to witness on behalf of the corrupter, of the injurer of their kindred, as Meletus and Anytus call me; not the corrupted youth only—there might have been a motive for that—but their uncorrupted elder relatives. Why should they too support me with their testimony? Why, indeed, except for the sake of truth and justice, and because they know that I am speaking the truth, and that Meletus is a liar.

Well, Athenians, this and the like of this is all the defense which I have to offer. Yet a word more. Perhaps there may be some one who is offended at me, when he calls to mind how he himself on a similar, or even a less serious occasion, prayed and entreated the judges with many tears, and how he produced his children in court, which was a moving spectacle, together with a host of relations and friends;[44] whereas I, who am probably in danger of my life, will do none of these things. The contrast may occur to his mind,

---

[41] Follower of Socrates.   [42] District. The demes were local units of administration in Attica.   [43] The author of the *Apology*.   [44] Socrates is referring to the customary appeal to emotion at the conclusion of a defense.

and he may be set against me, and vote in anger because he is displeased at me on this account. Now if there be such a person among you—mind, I do not say that there is—to him I may fairly reply: My friend, I am a man, and like other men, a creature of flesh and blood, and not "of wood or stone," as Homer says;[45] and I have a family, yes, and sons, O Athenians, three in number, one almost a man, and two others who are still young; and yet I will not bring any of them hither in order to petition you for an acquittal. And why not? Not from any self-assertion or want of respect for you. Whether I am or am not afraid of death is another question, of which I will not now speak. But, having regard to public opinion, I feel that such conduct would be discreditable to myself, and to you, and to the whole state. One who has reached my years, and who has a name for wisdom, ought not to demean himself. Whether this opinion of me be deserved or not, at any rate the world has decided that Socrates is in some way superior to other men. And if those among you who are said to be superior in wisdom and courage, and any other virtue, demean themselves in this way, how shameful is their conduct! I have seen men of reputation, when they have been condemned, behaving in the strangest manner: they seemed to fancy that they were going to suffer something dreadful if they died, and that they could be immortal if you only allowed them to live; and I think that such are a dishonor to the state, and that any stranger coming in would have said of them that the most eminent men of Athens, to whom the Athenians themselves give honor and command, are no better than women. And I say that these things ought not to be done by those of us who have a reputation; and if they are done, you ought not to permit them; you ought rather to show that you are far more disposed to condemn the man who gets up a doleful scene and makes the city ridiculous, than him who holds his peace.

But, setting aside the question of public opinion, there seems to be something wrong in asking a favor of a judge, and thus procuring an acquittal, instead of informing and convincing him. For his duty is, not to make a present of justice, but to give judgment; and he has sworn that he will judge according to the laws, and not according to his own good pleasure; and we ought not to encourage you, nor should you allow yourselves to be encouraged, in this habit of perjury—there can be no piety in that. Do not then require me to do what I consider dishonorable and impious and wrong, especially now, when I am being tried for impiety on the indictment of Meletus. For if, O men of Athens, by force of persuasion and entreaty I could overpower your oaths, then I should be teaching you to believe that there are no gods, and in defending should simply convict myself of the

---

[45] A reference to *The Odyssey* XIX, when Penelope says to Odysseus, whom she has not yet recognized and who is still disguised as a beggar: "But tell me about your clan, where you come from; / for not from an oak, as the old saying goes, did you spring nor from a rock."

charge of not believing in them. But that is not so—far otherwise. For I do believe that there are gods, and in a sense higher than that in which any of my accusers believe in them. And to you and to God I commit my cause, to be determined by you as is best for you and me.[46]

There are many reasons why I am not grieved, O men of Athens, at the vote of condemnation. I expected it, and am only surprised that the votes are so nearly equal; for I had thought that the majority against me would have been far larger; but now, had thirty votes gone over to the other side, I should have been acquitted. And I may say, I think, that I have escaped Meletus. I may say more; for without the assistance of Anytus and Lycon, any one may see that he would not have had a fifth part of the votes, as the law requires, in which case he would have incurred a fine of a thousand drachmae.

And so he proposes death as the penalty. And what shall I propose on my part, O men of Athens? Clearly that which is my due. And what is my due? What return shall be made to the man who has never had the wit to be idle during his whole life; but has been careless of what the many care for— wealth, and family interests, and military offices, and speaking in the assembly, and magistracies, and plots, and parties. Reflecting that I was really too honest a man to be a politician and live, I did not go where I could do no good to you or to myself; but where I could do the greatest good privately to every one of you, thither I went, and sought to persuade every man among you that he must look to himself, and seek virtue and wisdom before he looks to his private interests, and look to the state before he looks to the interests of the state; and that this should be the order which he observes in all his actions. What shall be done to such an one? Doubtless some good thing, O men of Athens, if he has his reward; and the good should be of a kind suitable to him. What would be a reward suitable to a poor man who is your benefactor, and who desires leisure that he may instruct you? There can be no reward so fitting as maintenance in the Prytaneum,[47] O men of Athens, a reward which he deserves far more than the citizen who has won the prize at Olympia in the horse or chariot race, whether the chariots were drawn by two horses or by many. For I am in want, and he has enough; and he only gives you the appearance of happiness, and I give you the reality.

---

[46] After this the jury announces a verdict of guilty by a split decision of 280 to 220 votes. The sentence must still be settled: the jury must choose between sentences now proposed and argued in turn by the prosecution and the defendant. The following speech concerns Socrates' defiant proposal about an appropriate sentence. Again, his nonconformity confounds the court's expectations.   [47] A place where the Prytanes, acting on behalf of the polis, hold their meetings and receptions for distinguished citizens and visitors. All activities in the Prytaneum were supported by public funds.

And if I am to estimate the penalty fairly, I should say that maintenance in the Prytaneum is the just return.

Perhaps you think that I am braving you in what I am saying now, as in what I said before about the tears and prayers. But this is not so. I speak rather because I am convinced that I never intentionally wronged any one, although I cannot convince you—the time has been too short; if there were a law at Athens, as there is in other cities,[48] that a capital cause should not be decided in one day, then I believe that I should have convinced you. But I cannot in a moment refute great slanders; and, as I am convinced that I never wronged another, I will assuredly not wrong myself. I will not say of myself that I deserve any evil, or propose any penalty. Why should I? Because I am afraid of the penalty of death which Meletus proposes? When I do not know whether death is a good or an evil, why should I propose a penalty which would certainly be an evil? Shall I say imprisonment? And why should I live in prison, and be the slave of the magistrates of the year— of the Eleven? [49] Or shall the penalty be a fine, and imprisonment until the fine is paid? There is the same objection. I should have to lie in prison, for money I have none, and cannot pay. And if I say exile (and this may possibly be the penalty which you will affix), I must indeed be blinded by the love of life, if I am so irrational as to expect that when you, who are my own citizens, cannot endure my discourses and words, and have found them so grievous and odious that you will have no more of them, others are likely to endure me. No indeed, men of Athens, that is not very likely. And what a life should I lead, at my age, wandering from city to city, ever changing my place of exile, and always being driven out! For I am quite sure that wherever I go, there, as here, the young men will flock to me; and if I drive them away, their elders will drive me out at their request; and if I let them come, their fathers and friends will drive me out for their sakes.

Some one will say: Yes, Socrates, but cannot you hold your tongue, and then you may go into a foreign city, and no one will interfere with you? [50] Now I have great difficulty in making you understand my answer to this. For if I tell you that to do as you say would be a disobedience to the God, and therefore that I cannot hold my tongue, you will not believe that I am serious; and if I say again that daily to discourse about virtue, and of those other things about which you hear me examining myself and others, is the greatest good of man, and that the unexamined life is not worth living, you are still less likely to believe me. Yet I say what is true, although a thing of which it is hard for me to persuade you. Also, I have never been accustomed to think that I deserve to suffer any harm. Had I money I might have esti-

---

[48] An allusion to Sparta. [49] Athenian "police commissioners" in charge of the prisons and executions. [50] According to Athenian custom, Socrates should have proposed exile as the penalty in order to save his life.

mated the offense at what I was able to pay, and not have been much the worse. But I have none, and therefore I must ask you to proportion the fine to my means. Well, perhaps I could afford a mina, and therefore I propose that penalty: Plato, Crito, Critobulus, and Apollodorus, my friends here, bid me say thirty minae, and they will be the sureties. Let thirty minae[51] be the penalty; for which sum they will be ample security to you.

Not much time will be gained, O Athenians, in return for the evil name which you will get from the detractors of the city, who will say that you killed Socrates,[52] a wise man; for they will call me wise, even although I am not wise, when they want to reproach you. If you had waited a little while, your desire would have been fulfilled in the course of nature. For I am far advanced in years, as you may perceive, and not far from death. I am speaking now not to all of you, but only to those who have condemned me to death. And I have another thing to say to them: You think that I was convicted because I had no words of the sort which would have procured my acquittal—I mean, if I had thought fit to leave nothing undone or unsaid. Not so; the deficiency which led to my conviction was not of words—certainly not. But I had not the boldness or impudence or inclination to address you as you would have liked me to do, weeping and wailing and lamenting, and saying and doing many things which you have been accustomed to hear from others, and which, as I maintain, are unworthy of me. I thought at the time that I ought not to do anything common or mean when in danger: nor do I now repent of the style of my defense; I would rather die having spoken after my manner, than speak in your manner and live. For neither in war nor yet at law ought I or any man to use every way of escaping death. Often in battle there can be no doubt that if a man will throw away his arms, and fall on his knees before his pursuers, he may escape death; and in other dangers there are other ways of escaping death, if a man is willing to say and do anything. The difficulty, my friends, is not to avoid death, but to avoid unrighteousness; for that runs faster than death. I am old and move slowly, and the slower runner has overtaken me, and my accusers are keen and quick, and the faster runner, who is unrighteousness, has overtaken them. And now I depart hence condemned by you to suffer the penalty of death—they too go their ways condemned by the truth to suffer the penalty of villainy and wrong; and I must abide by my award—let them abide by theirs. I suppose that these things may be regarded as fated—and I think that they are well.

And now, O men who have condemned me, I would fain prophesy to you;

[51] Six times the price of cheap instruction by a Sophist. A famous Sophist, Protagoras, is said to have charged a hundred minae for a course of instruction.
[52] The jury has chosen the death penalty proposed by Meletus, according to a later source, by a vote of 300 to 200.

for I am about to die, and in the hour of death men are gifted with prophetic power.[53] And I prophesy to you who are my murderers, that immediately after my departure punishment far heavier than you have inflicted on me will surely await you. Me you have killed because you wanted to escape the accuser, and not to give an account of your lives. But that will not be as you suppose: far otherwise. For I say that there will be more accusers of you than there are now; accusers whom hitherto I have restrained: and as they are younger they will be more inconsiderate with you, and you will be more offended at them. If you think that by killing men you can prevent some one from censuring your evil lives, you are mistaken; that is not a way of escape which is either possible or honorable; the easiest and the noblest way is not to be disabling others, but to be improving yourselves. This is the prophecy which I utter before my departure to the judges who have condemned me.

Friends, who would have acquitted me, I would like also to talk with you about the thing which has come to pass, while the magistrates are busy, and before I go to the place at which I must die. Stay then a little, for we may as well talk with one another while there is time. You are my friends, and I should like to show you the meaning of this event which has happened to me. O my judges—for you I may truly call judges—I should like to tell you of a wonderful circumstance. Hitherto the divine faculty of which the internal oracle is the source[54] has constantly been in the habit of opposing me even about trifles, if I was going to make a slip or error in any matter; and now as you see there has come upon me that which may be thought, and is generally believed to be, the last and worst evil. But the oracle made no sign of opposition, either when I was leaving my house in the morning, or when I was on my way to the court, or while I was speaking, at anything which I was going to say; and yet I have often been stopped in the middle of a speech, but now in nothing I either said or did touching the matter in hand has the oracle opposed me. What do I take to be the explanation of this silence? I will tell you. It is an intimation that what has happened to me is a good, and that those of us who think that death is an evil are in error. For the customary sign would surely have opposed me had I been going to evil and not to good.

Let us reflect in another way, and we shall see that there is great reason to hope that death is a good; for one of two things—either death is a state of nothingness and utter unconsciousness, or, as men say, there is a change and migration of the soul from this world to another. Now if you suppose that there is no consciousness, but a sleep like the sleep of him who is undisturbed even by dreams, death will be an unspeakable gain. For if a person were to select the night in which his sleep was undisturbed even by dreams, and were to compare with this the other days and nights of his life, and then

53 An allusion to the dying Hector's prophecy of Achilles' death in the *Iliad*.
54 His *daimon*.

were to tell us how many days and nights he had passed in the course of his life better and more pleasantly than this one, I think that any man, I will not say a private man, but even the great king will not find many such days or nights, when compared with the others. Now if death be of such a nature, I say that to die is gain; for eternity is then only a single night. But if death is the journey to another place, and there, as men say, all the dead abide, what good, O my friends and judges, can be greater than this? If indeed when the pilgrim arrives in the world below, he is delivered from the professors of justice in this world, and finds the true judges who are said to give judgment there, Minos and Rhadamanthus and Aeacus and Triptolemus,[55] and other sons of God who were righteous in their own life, that pilgrimage will be worth making. What would not a man give if he might converse with Orpheus[56] and Musaeus[57] and Hesiod [58] and Homer? Nay, if this be true, let me die again and again. I myself, too, shall have a wonderful interest in there meeting and conversing with Palamedes, and Ajax[59] the son of Telamon, and any other ancient hero who has suffered death through an unjust judgment; and there will be no small pleasure, as I think, in comparing my own sufferings with theirs. Above all, I shall then be able to continue my search into true and false knowledge; as in this world, so also in the next; and I shall find out who is wise, and who pretends to be wise, and is not. What would not a man give, O judges, to be able to examine the leader of the great Trojan expedition; or Odysseus[60] or Sisyphus,[61] or numberless others, men and women too! What infinite delight would there be in conversing with them and asking them questions! In another world they do not put a man to death for asking questions: assuredly not. For besides being happier than we are, they will be immortal, if what is said is true.

Wherefore, O judges, be of good cheer about death, and know of a certainty, that no evil can happen to a good man, either in life or after death. He and his are not neglected by the gods; nor has my own approaching end happened by mere chance. But I see clearly that the time had arrived when it was better for me to die and be released from trouble; wherefore the oracle

---

[55] The first three are sons of Zeus who were traditional models of wisdom and justice on earth and therefore became judges in Hades. Triptolemus, a mythical inventor of the plough and agriculture, is rarely associated with judgment in Hades, but he was closely associated with Demeter and Persephone, and thus also with the underworld.   [56] A legendary poet, musician, and founder of a mystical cult in which a belief in immortality following a cycle of transmigrations was prominent. [57] A semilegendary, very early Greek poet whose verses had oracular authority. [58] See Hesiod, p. 385.   [59] Palamedes, a Greek commander at Troy, was unjustly executed for treason on the basis of false evidence; Ajax (Aias) committed suicide after an unreasonable decision against him.   [60] As a representative of cunning intelligence.   [61] Notorious for his fraud and cunning. Sisyphus was condemned in Hades to the eternal task of rolling a marble block which always rolled down again just as he was reaching the top.

gave no sign. For which reason, also, I am not angry with my condemners, or with my accusers; they have done me no harm, although they did not mean to do me any good; and for this I may gently blame them.

Still I have a favor to ask of them. When my sons are grown up, I would ask you, O my friends, to punish them; and I would have you trouble them, as I have troubled you, if they seem to care about riches, or anything, more than about virtue; or if they pretend to be something when they are really nothing—then reprove them, as I have reproved you, for not caring about that for which they ought to care, and thinking that they are something when they are really nothing. And if you do this, both I and my sons will have received justice at your hands.

The hour of departure has arrived, and we go our ways—I to die, and you to live. Which is better God only knows.

Phaedo

The narrator of this dialogue is Phaedo, who was present at the execution of his friend Socrates. Phaedo gives his host Echecrates an account of Socrates' last hours. Socrates, surrounded by a number of friends, including Crito, was engaged in a philosophical argument—about his belief in the immortality of the soul—with two Theban philosophers, Simmias and Cebes. Socrates concluded his argument with an account of the next world, describing the places of reward reserved for the virtuous and those of punishment reserved for the evil. The following selection begins with the concluding remarks of this argument.

The Death of Socrates

Those[1] too who have been preeminent for holiness of life are released from this earthly prison,[2] and go to their pure home which is above, and dwell in the purer earth; and of these, such as have duly purified themselves with philosophy live henceforth altogether without the body, in mansions fairer still which may not be described, and of which the time would fail me to tell.

Wherefore, Simmias, seeing all these things, what ought not we to do that we may obtain virtue and wisdom in this life? Fair is the prize, and the hope great!

A man of sense ought not to say, nor will I be very confident, that the description which I have given of the soul and her mansions is exactly true. But I do say that, inasmuch as the soul is shown to be immortal, he may venture to think, not improperly or unworthily, that something of the kind is true. The venture is a glorious one, and he ought to comfort himself with words like these, which is the reason why I lengthen out the tale. Wherefore, I say, let a man be of good cheer about his soul, who having cast away the pleasures and ornaments of the body as alien to him and working harm rather than good, has sought after the pleasures of knowledge; and has

[1] Souls.   [2] The bodies which contain the souls.

arrayed the soul, not in some foreign attire, but in her own proper jewels, temperance, and justice, and courage, and nobility, and truth[3]—in these adorned she is ready to go on her journey to the world below, when her hour comes. You, Simmias and Cebes, and all other men, will depart at some time or other. Me already, as a tragic poet would say, the voice of fate calls. Soon I must drink the poison;[4] and I think that I had better repair to the bath first, in order that the women may not have the trouble of washing my body after I am dead.

When he had done speaking, Crito said: And have you any commands for us, Socrates—anything to say about your children, or any other matter in which we can serve you?

Nothing particular, Crito, he replied: only, as I have always told you, take care of yourselves; that is a service which you may be ever rendering to me and mine and to all of us, whether you promise to do so or not. But if you have no thought for yourselves, and care not to walk according to the rule which I have prescribed for you, not now for the first time, however much you may profess or promise at the moment, it will be of no avail.

We will do our best, said Crito: And in what way shall we bury you?

In any way that you like; but you must get hold of me, and take care that I do not run away from you. Then he turned to us, and added with a smile: I cannot make Crito believe that I am the same Socrates who have been talking and conducting the argument; he fancies that I am the other Socrates whom he will soon see, a dead body—and he asks, How shall he bury me? And though I have spoken many words in the endeavor to show that when I have drunk the poison I shall leave you and go to the joys of the blessed—these words of mine, with which I was comforting you and myself, have had, as I perceive, no effect upon Crito. And therefore I want you to be surety for me to him now, as at the trial he was surety to the judges for me: but let the promise be of another sort; for he was surety for me to the judges that I would remain, and you must be my surety to him that I shall not remain, but go away and depart; and then he will suffer less at my death, and not be grieved when he sees my body being burned or buried. I would not have him sorrow at my hard lot, or say at the burial, Thus we lay out Socrates, or, Thus we follow him to the grave or bury him; for false words are not only evil in themselves, but they infect the soul with evil. Be of good cheer then, my dear Crito, and say that you are burying my body only, and do with that whatever is usual, and what you think best.

When he had spoken these words, he arose and went into a chamber to bathe; Crito followed him and told us to wait. So we remained behind, talking and thinking of the subject of discourse, and also of the greatness of our

---

3 The four Platonic "cardinal virtues" are, in Plato's most famous dialogues, temperance, justice, courage, and knowledge or wisdom.   4 Poisoning by hemlock was the usual method of official execution in Athens.

sorrow; he was like a father of whom we were being bereaved, and we were about to pass the rest of our lives as orphans. When he had taken the bath his children were brought to him—(he had two young sons and an elder one); and the women of his family also came, and he talked to them and gave them a few directions in the presence of Crito; then he dismissed them and returned to us.

Now the hour of sunset was near, for a good deal of time had passed while he was within. When he came out, he sat down with us again after his bath, but not much was said. Soon the jailer, who was the servant of the Eleven, entered and stood by him, saying: To you, Socrates, whom I know to be the noblest and gentlest and best of all who ever came to this place, I will not impute the angry feelings of other men, who rage and swear at me, when, in obedience to the authorities, I bid them drink the poison—indeed, I am sure that you will not be angry with me; for others, as you are aware, and not I, are to blame. And so fare you well, and try to bear lightly what must needs be—you know my errand. Then bursting into tears he turned away and went out.

Socrates looked at him and said: I return your good wishes, and will do as you bid. Then turning to us, he said, How charming the man is: since I have been in prison he has always been coming to see me, and at times he would talk to me, and was as good to me as could be, and now see how generously he sorrows on my account. We must do as he says, Crito; and therefore let the cup be brought, if the poison is prepared: if not, let the attendant prepare some.

Yet, said Crito, the sun is still upon the hilltops, and I know that many a one has taken the draught late, and after the announcement has been made to him, he has eaten and drunk, and enjoyed the society of his beloved; do not hurry—there is time enough.

Socrates said: Yes, Crito, and they of whom you speak are right in so acting, for they think that they will be gainers by the delay; but I am right in not following their example, for I do not think that I should gain anything by drinking the poison a little later; I should only be ridiculous in my own eyes for sparing and saving a life which is already forfeit. Please then to do as I say, and not to refuse me.

Crito made a sign to the servant, who was standing by; and he went out, and having been absent for some time, returned with the jailer carrying the cup of poison. Socrates said: You, my good friend, who are experienced in these matters, shall give me directions how I am to proceed. The man answered: You have only to walk about until your legs are heavy, and then to lie down, and the poison will act. At the same time he handed the cup to Socrates, who in the easiest and gentlest manner, without the least fear or change of color or feature, looking at the man with all his eyes, Echecrates, as his manner was, took the cup and said: What do you say about making a libation out of this cup to any god? [5] May I, or not? The man answered: We only prepare, Socrates, just so much as we deem enough. I understand, he said: but I may and must ask the gods to prosper my journey from this to the other world—even so—and so be it according to my prayer. Then raising the cup to his lips, quite readily and cheerfully he drank off the poison. And hitherto most of us had been able to control our sorrow; but now when we saw him drinking, and saw too that he had finished the draught, we could no longer forbear, and in spite of myself my own tears were flowing fast; so that I covered my face and wept, not for him, but at the thought of my own calamity in having to part from such a friend. Nor was I the first; for Crito, when he found himself unable to restrain his tears, had got up, and I followed; and at that moment, Apollodorus, who had been weeping all the time, broke out in a loud and passionate cry which made cowards of us all. Socrates alone retained his calmness: What is this strange outcry? he said. I sent away the women mainly in order that they might not misbehave in this way, for I have been told that a man should die in peace. Be quiet then, and have patience. When we heard his words we were ashamed, and refrained our tears; and he walked about until, as he said, his legs began to fail, and then he lay on his back, according to the directions, and the man who gave him the poison now and then looked at his feet and legs; and after a while he pressed his foot hard, and asked him if he could feel; and he said, No; and then his leg, and so upwards and upwards, and showed us that he was cold and stiff. And he felt them himself, and said: When the poison reaches the heart, that will be the end. He was beginning to grow cold about the groin, when he uncovered his face, for he had covered himself up, and said—they were his last words—he said: Crito, I owe a cock to Asclepius;[6] will you remember to pay the debt? The debt shall be paid, said Crito; is there anything else? There was no answer to this question; but in a minute or two a movement was heard, and the attendants uncovered him; his eyes were set, and Crito closed his eyes and mouth.

Such was the end, Echecrates, of our friend; concerning whom I may truly say, that of all the men of his time whom I have known, he was the wisest and justest and best.

---

[5] Socrates asks the jailer whether he may pour a little of the poison out as a libation or offering to the gods—as one would have done with wine before drinking it.   [6] A sacrifice to the god of medicine and healing, probably as an offering in gratitude for death without illness and for his soul being "cured" from the "illness" of physically existing on earth.

Greek and Roman
Poetry

THIS UNIT, WHICH CONTAINS A SELECTION OF SHORTER SAMPLES of Greek and Roman poetry, provides a representative view of some major poetic forms and themes. The notion that translation is "the art of the impossible" is always particularly applicable to the literary documents of an ancient or distant culture, and it can perhaps be applied with even greater validity to the lyric poetry of these cultures. Despite the difficulties presented by translation, the following lyric poems have been included as a measure of their significance in antiquity and of their influence on subsequent developments in Western literature.

The Greek poet Hesiod and the Roman poet Ovid, for example, illustrate a use of epic that is strikingly different from that of Homer or Virgil. Hesiod and Ovid, who are separated by at least six centuries, both wrote nonheroic epic poetry and, in the passages that follow, dealt with the same theme: the Ages of Man.

The group of lyric poets—from Sappho to Horace—represent a broad range in time and manner, from the seventh or sixth century B.C. in archaic and largely illiterate Greece down to the first century B.C. in highly sophisticated Augustan Rome. Despite the variety of poetic traditions they represent, most of these poets share the intense subjectivism and the relative brevity of lyric expression. Although moments of intensely personal expression occur frequently as early as the Homeric poems, they are always imbedded in and qualified by a larger mythological action. It is only with the creation of relatively short solo songs—usually accompanied by the flute or the lyre (hence *lyric*)—that direct, personal expression by the poet becomes possible. By the first century B.C., when Catullus and Horace made lyric poetry popular in Rome, poems were written primarily for recitation and reading, with the musical element reduced to quite an insignificant role, although many of the other early characteristics persisted.

Another tradition in ancient lyric poetry is the choral song, which was accompanied not only by music but also by a choral dance. This kind of poetry was frequently composed for ceremonial occasions—to celebrate an athletic victory, a wedding, or a religious festival—and combined a highly formal manner with personal observations. Its greatest representative is the Greek poet Pindar.

By the third century B.C. the rapidly increasing urbanization of ancient life inspired a new tradition: the literary idealization of the pains and pleasures of country life. Two selections in this anthology—from the Greek poet Theocritus and the Roman poet Virgil—are representatives of this tradition of pastoral poetry.

Greek and Roman Poetry

Hesiod (8th–7th century B.C.?)

Hesiod is the earliest of a large number of Greek didactic poets. He probably lived in a rural district of central Greece (Boeotia). Two poems attributed to Hesiod with reasonable certainty are *Works and Days* and *Theogony*. The first, from which a selection follows, is a poem with ethical precepts and advice on farming. It initiates a long tradition of pessimism in Greek poetry. The second poem is an attempt to systematize the legends of gods and heroes with particular reference to their genealogy.

From *Works and Days*

. . . There is no way to avoid what Zeus has intended.

. . . If you will, I will outline it for you
   in a different story,
well and knowledgeably—store it up
   in your understanding—
the beginnings of things, which were the same for gods
   as for mortals.

In the beginning,° the immortals
   who have their homes on Olympos
created the golden generation of mortal people.
These lived in Kronos' ° time, when he

5. *In the beginning:* the notion of cycles of human degeneration accompanied by cultural and technological progress is prominent in several other cultures, such as Persian, Indian, and Hebrew. Comparable themes are also found in Ovid (p. 411) and Lucretius (p. 426), as well as Virgil's *Fourth Eclogue* (p. 407).
7. *Kronos:* father of Zeus, preceded Zeus as most powerful god; ruled during the human Golden Age. He was later overthrown by Zeus, who replaced his chaotic violence among the gods with order and divine justice.

was the king in heaven.
They lived as if they were gods,
   their hearts free from all sorrow,
by themselves, and without hard work or pain;
   no miserable
old age came their way; their hands, their feet,
   did not alter.   10
They took their pleasure in festivals,
   and lived without troubles.
When they died, it was as if they fell asleep.
   All goods
were theirs. The fruitful grainland
   yielded its harvest to them
of its own accord; this was great and abundant,
   while they at their pleasure
quietly looked after their works,
   in the midst of good things
[prosperous in flocks, on friendly terms
   with the blessed immortals].

     Now that the earth has gathered over this generation,
these are called pure and blessed spirits;
   they live upon earth,
and are good, they watch over mortal men
   and defend them from evil,
they keep watch over lawsuits and hard dealings;
   they mantle   20
themselves in dark mist
   and wander all over the country;
they bestow wealth; for this right
   as of kings was given them.
     Next after these the dwellers upon Olympos created
a second generation, of silver, far worse
   than the other.
They were not like the golden ones either in shape
   or spirit.
A child was a child for a hundred years,
   looked after and playing
by his gracious mother, kept at home,
   a complete booby.
But when it came time for them to grow up
   and gain full measure,
they lived for only a poor short time;

by their own foolishness
they had troubles, for they were not able
    to keep away from   30
reckless crime against each other,
    nor would they worship
the gods, nor do sacrifice on the sacred altars
    of the blessed ones,
which is the right thing among the customs of men,
    and therefore
Zeus, son of Kronos, in anger engulfed them,
    for they paid no due
honors to the blessed gods who live on Olympos.

    But when the earth had gathered over this generation
also—and they too are called blessed spirits
    by men, though under
the ground, and secondary, but still
    they have their due worship—
then Zeus the father created the third generation
    of mortals,
the age of bronze. They were not like
    the generation of silver.   40
They came from ash spears.° They were terrible
    and strong, and the ghastly
action of Ares was theirs, and violence.
    They ate no bread,°
but maintained an indomitable and adamantine spirit.
None could come near them; their strength was big,
    and from their shoulders
the arms grew irresistible on their ponderous bodies.
The weapons of these men were bronze,°
    of bronze their houses,
and they worked as bronzesmiths. There was not yet
    any black iron.
Yet even these, destroyed beneath the hands
    of each other,
went down into the moldering domain of cold Hades;

41. *came . . . spears:* the notion that men grew out of trees or out of their products is common in myths of several cultures. The ash-tree was particularly revered by some Greek tribes; its hardness was thought to symbolize the hardness and cruelty of this Age. 42. *bread:* agriculture has not yet been taught to man by Demeter; man is still a food-gatherer and hunter. 46. *bronze:* widely used to line or decorate walls in early Greek architecture.

nameless; for all they were formidable black death   50
seized them, and they had to forsake
     the shining sunlight.

Now when the earth had gathered over this generation
also, Zeus, son of Kronos, created yet another
fourth generation° on the fertile earth,
     and these were better and nobler,
the wonderful generation of hero-men, who are also
called half-gods, the generation before our own
     on this vast earth.
But of these too, evil war and the terrible carnage
took some; some by seven-gated Thebes
     in the land of Kadmos°
as they fought together over the flocks of Oidipous;°
     others
war had taken in ships over the great gulf
     of the sea,   60
where they also fought for the sake
     of lovely-haired Helen.
There, for these, the end of death was misted
     about them.
But on others Zeus, son of Kronos, settled a living
     and a country
of their own, apart from human kind,
     at the end of the world.
And there they have their dwelling place,
     and hearts free of sorrow
in the islands of the blessed °
     by the deep-swirling stream of the ocean,
prospering heroes, on whom in every year
     three times over
the fruitful grainland bestows its sweet yield.
     These live
far from the immortals, and Kronos
     is king among them.
For Zeus, father of gods and mortals,
     set him free from his bondage,   70

54. fourth generation: the fourth generation is not associated with a specific metal.
55. Kadmos: Cadmus. *59. flocks of Oidipous:* the legendary sons of Oedipus,
Polynices and Eteocles, gathered together large armies and fought each other in a
war for the throne of Thebes. *66. islands of the blessed:* islands of the dead on
the edge of the earth, where Okeanos (Ocean) encircles the world.

although the position and the glory still belong
    to the young gods.°

After this, Zeus of the wide brows
    established yet one more
generation of men, the fifth, to be
    on the fertile earth.

And I wish that I were not any part
    of the fifth generation
of men, but had died before it came,
    or been born afterward.
For here now is the age of iron. Never by daytime
will there be an end to hard work and pain,
    nor in the night
to weariness, when the gods will send anxieties
    to trouble us.
Yet here also there shall be some good things
    mixed with the evils.
But Zeus will destroy this generation of mortals
    also,   80
in the time when children, as they are born,
    grow gray on the temples,
when the father no longer agrees with the children,
    nor children with their father,
when guest is no longer at one with host,
    nor companion to companion,
when your brother is no longer your friend,
    as he was in the old days.°

Men will deprive their parents of all rights,
    as they grow old,
and people will mock them too,
    babbling bitter words against them,
harshly, and without shame in the sight of the gods;
    not even
to their aging parents will they give back
    what once was given.
Strong of hand, one man shall seek
    the city of another.
There will be no favor for the man
    who keeps his oath, for the righteous   90

71. *young gods:* the generation of Zeus, which overthrew the gods of the generation of Kronos in a savage battle.   *84. in the old days:* prophecies characteristic
of apocalyptic literature.

and the good man, rather men shall give their praise
    to violence°
and the doer of evil. Right will be in the arm.°
    Shame will
not be. The vile man will crowd his better out,
    and attack him
with twisted accusations and swear an oath
    to his story.
The spirit of Envy, with grim face
    and screaming voice, who delights
in evil, will be the constant companion
    of wretched humanity,
and at last Nemesis and Aidos,° Decency and Respect,
    shrouding
their bright forms in pale mantles, shall go
    from the wide-wayed
earth back on their way to Olympos,
    forsaking the whole race
of mortal men, and all that will be left by them
    to mankind   100
will be wretched pain. And there shall be no defense
    against evil.

—TR. RICHMOND LATTIMORE

Sappho (7th–6th century B.C.?)

The most famous Greek poetess, Sappho, came from the eastern
Aegean island of Lesbos. She seems to have been the center of an
aristocratic group of young girls devoted to literature and religion.
This group was perhaps associated with the cult of Aphrodite—
who figures prominently in Sappho's poetry—and was probably
one of several such female associations formed in response to the
preoccupation of the male nobility with warfare and drinking.

---

91. *violence: hubris,* or wanton violence arising from pride of strength.   92.
Right . . . arm: literally, "Justice will lie in fists."   97. *Nemesis:* in Greek religion, Nemesis (here translated as "Decency") is a deified force representing the
distribution of what is due. It is often used of divine retribution, especially the
retribution exercised in righteous anger at human injustices. *Aidos:* a force representing reverence, awe, or respect, both for the feelings of others and for one's
own conscience. Hence it often designates either a sense of honor or a sense of
shame.

Sappho wrote a large number of marriage songs, but her favorite form of poetry was individual songs to the lyre, in which she sings of her personal experiences.

To Aphrodite

Glittering-throned, undying Aphrodite,
Wile-weaving daughter of high Zeus, I pray thee,
Tame not my soul with heavy woe, dread mistress,
          Nay, nor with anguish!

But hither come, if ever erst of old time°
Thou didst incline, and listenedst to my crying,
And from thy father's palace down descending,
          Camest with golden

Chariot yoked: thee fair swift-flying sparrows°
Over dark earth with multitudinous fluttering,   10
Pinion on pinion, thorough middle ether
          Down from heaven hurried.

Quickly they came° like light, and thou, blest lady,
Smiling with clear undying eyes didst ask me
What was the woe that troubled me, and wherefore
          I had cried to thee:

What thing I longed for to appease my frantic
Soul: and Whom now must I persuade, thou askedst,
Whom must entangle to thy love, and who now,
          Sappho, hath wronged thee?   20

Yea, for if now she° shun, she soon shall chase thee;
Yea, if she take not gifts, she soon shall give them;
Yea, if she love not, soon shall she begin to
          Love thee, unwilling.

Come to me now too, and from tyrannous sorrow
Free me, and all things that my soul desires to
Have done, do for me, queen, and let thyself too
          Be my great ally!

                              —TR. J. ADDINGTON SYMONDS

5. *of old time:* Sappho is asking the goddess Aphrodite to descend from heaven, as she did previously on similar occasions, to release the poetess from the agonies of unrequited love for another girl.   9. *sparrows:* birds sacred to Aphrodite. In Greek mythology they drew her chariot.   13. *they came:* the sparrows, drawing Aphrodite's chariot on a previous visit to Sappho.   21. *she:* the girl whom Sappho loves in vain.

To a Girl

Blest beyond earth's bliss, with heaven I deem him
    Blest, the man that in thy° presence near thee
Face to face may sit, and while thou speakest,
    Listening may hear thee,

And thy sweet-voiced laughter: In my bosom°
    The rapt heart so troubleth, wildly stirred:
Let me see thee, but a glimpse—and straightway
    Utterance of word

Fails me; no voice comes; my tongue is palsied;
    Thrilling fire through all my flesh hath run;   10
Mine eyes cannot see, mine ears make dinning
    Noises that stun;

The sweat streameth down—my whole frame seized with
    Shivering—and wan paleness o'er me spread,
Greener than the grass; I seem with faintness
    Almost as dead.°

                        —TR. WALTER HEADLAM

Love*

Lo, Love once more, the limb-dissolving King,
The bitter-sweet impracticable thing,
Wild-beast-like rends me with fierce quivering.
                 —TR. J. ADDINGTON SYMONDS

2. *thy:* of a girl whom Sappho loves, who is talking and laughing in the company of a man.   5–16. *In my bosom . . . dead:* the earliest description of the physical symptoms of a poet's own passion.   16. The remainder of the poem is not extant. Compare Catullus' adaptation, "To Lesbia," p. 404.   * Probably the only surviving fragment of a poem by Sappho on the ambivalent nature of love.

Pindar (522?–443 B.C.)

Pindar, perhaps the most accomplished lyric poet of ancient
Greece, came from Boeotia in central Greece. Most of his extant
poetry is choral lyric, which was often commissioned by Greek
aristocrats and rulers for ceremonial occasions. His poetry brought
him into contact with many political centers, but it was particularly his success in Sicily, where he formed a close association with
the powerful and brilliant courts of the Greek tyrants, that determined his reputation in the Greek world.

*The First Pythian Ode: To Hieron**

O dear to Leto's son,° and no less dear
  To all the dusk-haired muses, golden lyre,°
    Whose notes invite the dancer's listening feet,
  And lead the songs of the responsive choir,
    When from thy trembling strings the prelude sweet
      Of forceful strains they hear.
Thou° stay'st the eternal lightning's lance of fire,
  And lulled by thee the eagle, feathered king,
  Drooping to either side each powerful wing,
Sleeps on the scepter of Olympus' Sire.°   10

A cloudy haze of slumber, drawing close
  O'er his° bowed head, hath sweetly sealed his eyes,
    And while he yields to thy melodious sway
  On his soft back the feathers fall and rise.
    Even stern Ares throws his spears away
      And sinks in deep repose
Beneath the spell, for thy keen music flings
  A charm to hold the very gods in trance,
  When o'er the chords Apollo's fingers° glance,

---

* A choral song for—and commissioned by—Hieron, tyrant of the Greek city
Syracuse (in Sicily), to celebrate his victory in the chariot race at the Pythian
Games at Delphi in 470 B.C. The poem is composed of five stanzas, each of which
consists of a triad of strophe, antistrophe, and epode. 1. *Leto's son:* Apollo. 2.
lyre: Apollo was a god of music, and especially of the lyre. 7. *thou:* the lyre.
The Greek fusion of music and poetry is reflected in this "hymn" to the lyre. 10.
Olympus' Sire: Zeus on Mount Olympus. As "King of Birds," the eagle was sacred
to Zeus. 12. *his:* the eagle's. 19. *Apollo's fingers:* The musician, like the poet,
is merely an inspired medium of Apollo or the Muses.

Or when deep-girdled Muses sweep the strings.   20

But those whom Zeus hath loved not, when they hear
    The pure Pierian° strains on earth or sea,
        Shrink in affright, with him who cowers below,
    The hundred-headed Typhon.° Nurse was he
        In famed Cilician° grot the Immortals' foe,
            But now the sea-cliffs sheer
Of Cumae° and Sicilian earth are cast
    O'er his rude breast, and Aetna's mountain height,
    A pillar of the heavens for ever white
With year-long fostered snows, now holds him fast.   30

Founts inapproachable of purest fire°
    Well from her inmost core. With lurid gleams
        Their smoking torrents in the daytime flow,
    But all night through the red and blazing streams
        Roll down great rocks to the far sea below
            With uproar loud and dire,
While still that spawn of dragons flings on high
    The deadly jets of flame, a thing of fear
    For men to see, and even to those who hear
The din that deafens all who fare anigh.   40

Below the plain, below the mountain drear,
    His back all harrowed by its rocky bed,
        The monster lies immured by God's command.
    On us, O Zeus! on us thy love be shed,
        Lord of the mount° which fronts a fruitful land,
            Whose namesake city° near
Her founder hath upraised to glorious place,
    Since late the herald at the Pythian Games
    Proclaimed her title with the victor's names
And Hieron's triumph in the chariot race.   50

As seafarers at sailing hold most dear
    A furthering breeze, which augurs, as they say,
        The fairer voyage for their home return,

---

22. *Pierian:* from Pieria, the home of the Muses at the foot of Mount Olympus.
24. *Typhon:* a hundred-headed monster buried by Zeus in Tartarus—a part of the underworld.   25. *Cilician:* from Cilicia, a district on the southeast coast of Asia Minor, just west of Syria.   27. *Cumae:* Greek town in southern Italy (near Naples).   31. *fire:* Aetna is a volcanic mountain.   45. *mount:* Sicily.   46. *namesake city:* Hieron had founded a city called Aetna and appointed his young son Deinomenes its king.

So may his fortune with this city stay,
 And may her steeds fresh wreaths of glory earn
  With songs of festal cheer.
O lord of Lycia and of Delos,° thou
 Who lov'st Parnassus and Castalia's° rill,
 Deign, Phoebus, all her promise to fulfill,
And with brave men this goodly land endow! 60

From gods alone all human greatness flows,
 Wit, eloquence, and every doughty deed;
  And while I haste the victor's praise to sing
 Ne'er out of bounds must the keen javelin speed,
  But straight and far my song-shaft let me fling
   Beyond all rival throws.
O may he float as now, while life remains,
 On the full flood of Fortune's prospering tide,
 May wealth with him and welfare still abide,
And swift forgetfulness of all his pains. 70

Let him remember how with dauntless breast
 In battles oft he stood,° and how God heaped
  Both wealth and honor on his people's head,
 A lordlier prize than ever Greek had reaped.
  To war like Philoctetes° he was led
   When, by their need oppressed,
The proud had stooped his favor to cajole,
 As once the archer, Poeas' son,° was sought
 By godlike heroes and from Lemnos brought
For all the bitter pain that rent his soul. 80

Yet moved by Fate his feeble arm laid low
 The towers of Priam's town, and made an end
  Of all the labors of the Danaan host.
 May God to Hieron such grace extend
  Through future years, and all he covets most
   In fitting hour bestow.
And sound, O Muse, the chariot's triumph-song

---

57. *lord of Lycia and of Delos:* Apollo. 58. *Castalia:* a spring rising in a cave on Mount Parnassus; sacred to Apollo and the Muses; symbolic source of poetic inspiration. 72. *In battles . . . stood:* Hieron had famous military successes. In Syracuse he maintained a palace that was famous for its dazzling splendor. 75. *like Philoctetes:* The mythical Greek hero Philoctetes had a wound in his foot which produced such a stench that the Greeks abandoned him on an island, Lemnos, until an oracle declared that Troy could not be taken without him. Hieron was suffering from dropsy. 78. *Poeas' son:* Philoctetes.

For Aetna's king, Deinomenes, to hear,
—The father's glory to his son is dear—
Then let his praise our loving strains prolong.   90

That city Hieron for his son's abode
On Hyllus' statutes° raised divinely free;
  For Heracleidae° and Pamphylus' seed,
    Though neath Taygetus° their dwelling be,
      Keep still the fashion of their Dorian breed,
        And choose Aegimius'° code.
They ranged from Pindus,° made Amyclae theirs,
And prospered full of glory near the meads
  Where rode the Tyndarids° on snow-white steeds,
And brightly flowered the splendor of their spears.   100

All-ordering Zeus! may every tongue confess
  That king and burgher such a fate have found
    By Amenas' ° stream. O may thy love incline
King Hieron to guide his royal son,
    And make the glory of this people shine
      In peace and happiness.
Let Tuscans and Phoenicians° keep at home
  Their battle-cries unheard, who saw of late
  Their baffled navies all their pride abate,
And groaning reel amid Cumaean foam,   110

When Syracuse's lord from every prow
  Flung to the waves the flower of all their ranks,
    And Hellas spurned the shackles of the slave.

---

92. *Hyllus' statutes:* Hyllus was a son of Heracles, from whom the Dorians claimed descent. Hieron wished his new city, Aetna, to embody the ideals of the Dorian military aristocracy, so he populated it with about ten thousand Dorians from the Greek mainland and from Syracuse.   93. *Heracleidae:* descendants of Heracles, Dorians.   94. *Taygetus:* mountain looming above Sparta, the chief city of the Dorians.   96. *Aegimius:* a Dorian ancestor; friend and father-in-law of Hyllus. 97. *Pindus:* a reference to the widespread belief that the Dorians originally invaded the Peloponnesus from northern Greece (Pindus is a mountain in northwestern Greece) in prehistoric times.   99. *Tyndarids:* the Dioscuri, descendants of Tyndareus, who was restored to the Spartan throne by Heracles. The cult of the Dioscuri was established at Sparta and throughout the rest of the Dorian world. 103. *Amenas:* stream near which the city of Aetna was built.   107. *Tuscans and Phoenicians:* Hieron broke the power of Etruria (Tuscany) in Italy, and his brother, Gelon, who preceded him as tyrant of Syracuse, defeated the Carthaginians, whose city had been founded by Phoenicians.

Soon° Salamis shall earn me Athens' thanks,
   At Sparta I will hymn the battle brave
     Fought neath Cithaeron's brow,
Twain tribulations of the crook-bowed Medes;
   But to Deinomenes' strong sons is due
   This song of praise, who valiantly o'erthrew
Their stricken foes by Himera's water-reeds.   120

Speak but in season, and bind up in few
   A hundred threads, lest censure come too near,
     For surfeit dulls the edge of all desire,
    And human hearts in secret sink to hear
      The city's talk, for soon the praises tire
       Of deeds that others do.
Yet hold not back. More onerous is ruth
   Than envy. With the helm of justice steer
   Thy people nobly on their brave career,
And weld thy speech upon the forge of truth.   130

Thy lightest word hath weight: a goodly store
   Thou guardest, and for any kind of deed
     True witness hast thou. O still retain
    Thy spirit's flower of beauty, nor give heed
      Too nearly to the cost, if thou would'st gain
       Sweet homage evermore;
But like a mariner set free the sail
   To catch each breeze, and never, friend, be led
   By treasure's lure, for after men are dead
Nought but their living memory shall avail.   140

Only the voice of fame can then relate
   To scribe and poet what their fashion was.
     The charity of Croesus° shall not fade,
But he who burned men in the bull of brass,°

114–20. *Soon . . . water-reeds:* that is, just as the Athenians will thank the poet for praising their victory over the Persians at Salamis, and just as the Spartans will thank him for singing of their victory over the Persians ("Medes") at Plataea (near Mount Cithaeron), so too he will find favor with Sicilians for singing of the Carthaginians' defeat at Himera by Gelon, Hieron, and their Syracusans ("Deinomenes' strong sons"). *143. charity of Croesus:* according to some ancient authors, Croesus was saved from a burning pyre by Apollo out of gratitude for the victim's generosity to Delphi. *144. bull of brass:* Phalaris, a sixth-century tyrant of the Greek city Acragas in Sicily, died in an outbreak of popular fury against his practice of burning alive his opponents in a bronze bull.

Inhuman Phalaris, can ne'er evade
 The bruit of general hate:
No songs for him from sweet boy-voices rise
 Blent with the lyre in hall. Life's primal crown
 Is happiness; the next is good renown;
And who gains both hath won man's highest prize.   150
           —TR. C. J. BILLSON

Theocritus (310?–260 B.C.?)

Theocritus was a Greek poet from Sicily who is traditionally regarded as the creator of the pastoral or bucolic genre of poetry. His
Idylls, of which about thirty have survived, use dramatic means to
portray everyday life in city and country. They frequently have a
Sicilian setting, but he also had close connections with the Aegean
island of Cos, which forms the background of his seventh Idyll,
and with the Egyptian city of Alexandria, which was a metropoli-
tan center of Greek culture in the third to first centuries B.C.

The Harvest Feast

Once on a time did Eucritus and I °
(With us Amytas) to the riverside
Steal from the city. For Lycopeus' sons
Were that day busy with the harvest-home,°
Antigenes and Phrasidamus, sprung
(If aught thou holdest by the good old names)
By Clytia from great Chalcon—him who erst
Planted one stalwart knee against the rock,
And lo, beneath his foot Burinè's rill °
Brake forth, and at its side poplar and elm   10
Shewed aisles of pleasant shadow, greenly roofed
By tufted leaves. Scarce midway were we now,
Nor yet descried the tomb of Brasilas:°
When, thanks° be to the Muses, there drew near

1. I: Simichidas, the narrator (and an alias of the poet). *4. harvest-home:* a
harvest festival in honor of Demeter, the goddess of the earth's products (especially
grain), celebrated on the farm of Antigenes and Phrasidamus. *9. Burinè's rill:*
a spring southwest of the narrator's town. *13. Brasilas:* unknown. *14. thanks
. . . Muses:* in their capacity as the inspiring deities of song.

A wayfarer from Crete, young Lycidas.
The horned herd ° was his care: a glance might tell
So much: for every inch a herdsman he.

Slung o'er his shoulder was a ruddy hide
Torn from a he-goat, shaggy, tangle-haired,
That reeked of rennet° yet: a broad belt clasped   20
A patched cloak round his breast, and for a staff
A gnarled wild-olive bough his right hand bore.
Soon with a quiet smile he spoke—his eye
Twinkled, and laughter sat upon his lip:
"And whither ploddest thou thy weary way
Beneath the noontide sun, Simichidas?
For now the lizard sleeps upon the wall,
The crested lark folds now his wandering wing.
Dost speed, a bidden guest, to some reveler's board?
Or townward to the treading of the grape?   30
For lo! recoiling from thy hurrying feet
The pavement-stones ring out right merrily."
Then I: "Friend Lycid, all men say that none
Of haymakers or herdsmen is thy match
At piping:° and my soul is glad thereat.
Yet, to speak sooth, I think to rival thee.
Now look, this road holds holiday today:
For banded brethren solemnize a feast
To richly-dight Demeter, thanking her
For her good gifts: since with no grudging hand   40
Hath the boon goddess filled the wheaten floors.
So come: the way, the day, is thine as mine:
Try we our woodcraft—each may learn from each.
I am, as thou, a clarion-voice of song;
All hail me chief of minstrels. But I am not,
Heaven knows, o'ercredulous: no, I scarce can yet
(I think) outvie Philetas,° nor the bard
Of Samos,° champion of Sicilian° song.
They are as cicadas challenged by a frog."

---

16. horned herd: goats. *20. rennet:* curd in the stomach of an unweaned calf.
35. piping: playing on a shepherd's pipe. *47. Philetas:* a leading poet (third-
second century B.C.) and contemporary of Theocritus. *47–48. bard/of Samos:*
the Hellenistic poet Asclepiades, also a contemporary and friend of Theocritus.
48. Sicilian: Asclepiades' real name or byname was Sicelidas, "son of Sicelus."

I spake to gain mine ends; and laughing light   50
He said: "Accept this club,° as thou'rt indeed
A born truth-teller, shaped by heaven's own hand!
I hate your builders who would rear a house
High as Oromedon's° mountain-pinnacle:
I hate your song-birds° too, whose cuckoo-cry
Struggles (in vain) to match the Chian bard.°
But come, we'll sing forthwith, Simichidas,
Our woodland music: and for my part I—
List, comrade, if you like the simple air
I forged among the uplands yesterday.   60

[*Sings*] Safe be my true-love convoyed o'er the main
To Mytilenè°—though the southern blast
Chase the lithe waves, while westward slant the Kids,°
Or low above the verge Orion stand °—
If from Love's furnace she° will rescue me,
For Lycidas is parched with hot desire.
Let halcyons° lay the sea-waves and the winds,
Northwind and Westwind, that in shores far-off
Flutters the seaweed—halcyons, of all birds
Whose prey is on the waters, held most dear   70
By the green Nereids:° yea let all things smile
On her to Mytilenè voyaging,
And in fair harbor may she ride at last.
I on that day, a chaplet woven of dill
Or rose or simple violet on my brow,
Will draw the wine of Pteleas° from the cask

51. *club:* a gnarled wild-olive bough, used as a staff. The bough as a present from one poet to another is an allusion to a laurel-staff supposedly given to Hesiod by the Muses as a symbol of his poetic vocation.   54. *Oromedon:* mountain range flanking the south coast of Cos.   55. *song-birds:* boastful and urbane contemporaries, who thought their sophistication superior to the "simplicity" of Homer and of pastoral poets.   56. *Chian bard:* Homer, who was traditionally associated with the Aegean island of Chios in antiquity.   62. *Mytilene:* city on the island of Lesbos, north of Cos. Simichidas' friend is about to sail on a voyage, and the goatherd's song is a prayer for a safe return—with a condition.   63. *Kids:* the Haedi, stars close to Capella in the constellation of Auriga. Stormy weather is often associated with the rising or setting of the Kids.   64. *Or . . . stand:* that is, in late summer.   65. *she:* most scholars agree that Simichidas' friend (Ageanax) was male, not female.   67. *halcyons:* a reference to "the Halcyon days" when the sea was, according to a Greek tradition, calm while the halcyon nested and reared its young.   71. *green Nereids:* Sea nymphs were always thought to assume the color of the element in which they lived.   76. *Pteleas:* probably a place on Cos.

Stretched by the ingle.° They shall roast me beans,
And elbow-deep in thyme and asphodel
And quaintly-curling parsley shall be piled
My bed of rushes, where in royal ease 80
I sit and, thinking of my darling, drain
With steadfast lip the liquor to the dregs.
I'll have a pair of pipers, shepherds both,
This from Acharnae, from Lycopè° that;
And Tityrus° shall be near me and shall sing
How the swain Daphnis° loved the stranger-maid;
And how he ranged the fells,° and how the oaks
(Such oaks as Himera's° banks are green withal)
Sang dirges o'er him waning fast away
Like snow on Athos,° or on Haemus° high, 90
Or Rhodopè,° or utmost Caucasus.
And he shall sing me how the big chest held
(All through the maniac malice of his lord)
A living goatherd: how the round-faced bees,
Lured from their meadow by the cedar-smell,
Fed him with daintiest flowers, because the Muse
Had made his throat a well-spring of sweet song.
Happy Comatas,° this sweet lot was thine!
Thee the chest prisoned, for thee the honey-bees
Toiled, as thou slavedst out the mellowing year: 100
And oh hadst thou been numbered with the quick
In my day! I had led thy pretty goats
About the hillside, listening to thy voice:
While thou hadst lain thee down 'neath oak or pine,
Divine Comatas, warbling pleasantly."

He spake and paused; and thereupon spake I.
"I too, friend Lycid, as I ranged the fells,
Have learned much lore and pleasant from the Nymphs,

---

77. *ingle:* fireplace. *84. Acharnae:* in Attica. *Lycope:* in Aetolia (northern Greece). Theocritus is probably using these names to lend verisimilitude to imaginary characters. *85. Tityrus:* an imaginary person. *86. Daphnis:* legendary Sicilian oxherd and inventor of bucolic poetry. *87. fells:* mountains, hills. *88. Himera:* river in Sicily. *90. Athos:* mountain at southern end of the peninsula now known as Athos. *Haemus:* the Balkan Mountains, now in central Bulgaria. *91. Rhodope:* high mountain, now in western Bulgaria. *98. Comatas:* according to a famous Greek legend, a goatherd, Comatas, was locked up in a chest by his master because he frequently sacrificed animals from his master's herds to the Muses; two months later his master found him alive and the chest full of honeycomb.

Whose fame mayhap hath reached the throne of Zeus.°
But this wherewith I'll grace thee ranks the first: 110
Thou listen, since the Muses like thee well.

[*Sings*] On me the young Loves sneezed:° for hapless I
Am fain° of Myrto° as the goats of Spring.
But my best friend Aratus° inly pines
For one who loves him not. Aristis° saw—
(A wondrous seer is he, whose lute and lay
Shrinèd Apollo's self would scarce disdain)—
How love had scorched Aratus to the bone.
O Pan,° who hauntest Homolè's° fair champaign,
Bring the soft charmer, whosoe'er it be,   120
Unbid to his sweet arms—so, gracious Pan,
May ne'er thy ribs and shoulderblades be lashed
With squills by young Arcadians,° whensoe'er
They are scant of supper! But should this my prayer
Mislike thee, then on nettles mayest thou sleep,
Dinted and sore all over from their claws!
Then mayest° thou lodge amid Edonian hills
By Hebrus, in midwinter; there subsist,
The Bear thy neighbor: and, in summer, range
With the far Æthiops 'neath the Blemmyan rocks   130
Where Nile is no more seen! But O ye Loves,
Whose cheeks are like pink apples, quit your homes
By Hyetis,° or Byblis' ° pleasant rill,

109. *throne of Zeus:* an allusion to the fact that the fame of Theocritus' bucolic
poetry had reached Ptolemy Philadelphus at the Alexandrian court; Ptolemy was
frequently compared to Zeus or to a god by Theocritus and his contemporaries.
112. *sneezed:* a good omen. 113. *fain:* fond. *Myrto:* "myrtle"; flower names are
often the names of courtesans. 114. *Aratus:* a friend to whom Theocritus addresses another Idyll. 115. *Aristis:* apparently an intimate acquaintance of
Aratus. There is an allusion in the next line ("wondrous"; Greek, *aristos*) to the
meaning of his name. 119. *Pan:* god of flocks and herds; inventor of the shepherd's pipe, hence particularly associated with pastoral poetry. *Homole:* mountain
and town in Thessaly (northern Greece). Pan was particularly popular in Thessaly
and Macedonia. 123. *Arcadians:* Pan was originally a divinity of Arcadia, the
central plateau of the Peloponnesus whose inhabitants were mostly shepherds and
hunters. The rite or custom described here is otherwise unknown. 127-31. *Then
mayest . . . seen:* if he fails to grant the request, Pan is here cursed to live at the
extremes of his range in the wrong season—on Thracian mountains in midwinter,
in southern Egypt in summer. 133. *Hyetis, Byblis:* springs in Miletus (west coast
of Asia Minor), connected with a legendary Byblis who met her death as the result
of an incestuous love affair.

Or fair Dionè's° rocky pedestal,°
And strike that fair one with your arrows, strike
The ill-starred damsel ° who disdains my friend.
And lo, what is she but an o'er-ripe pear?
The girls all cry 'Her bloom is on the wane.'
We'll watch, Aratus, at that porch no more,
Nor waste shoe leather: let the morning cock   140
Crow to wake others up to numb despair!
Let Molon,° and none else, that ordeal brave:
While we make ease our study, and secure
Some witch,° to charm all evil from our door."

    I ceased. He, smiling sweetly as before,
Gave me the staff, "the Muses' parting gift,"
And leftward sloped tow'rd Pyxa. We the while,
Bent us to Phrasydame's, Eucritus and I,
And baby-faced Amyntas: there we lay
Half-buried in a couch of fragrant reed   150
And fresh-cut vineleaves, who so glad as we?
A wealth of elm and poplar shook o'erhead;
Hard by, a sacred spring flowed gurgling on
From the Nymphs' grot, and in the somber boughs
The sweet cicada chirped laboriously.
Hid in the thick thorn-bushes far away
The treefrog's note was heard; the crested lark
Sang with the goldfinch; turtles made their moan,
And o'er the fountain hung the gilded bee.
All of rich summer smacked, of autumn all: 160
Pears at our feet, and apples at our side
Rolled in luxuriance; branches on the ground
Sprawled, overweighed with damsons; while we brushed
From the cask's head the crust of four long years.
Say, ye who dwell upon Parnassian peaks,
Nymphs of Castalia, did old Chiron° e'er

---

134. Dione: usually mother of Aphrodite; here perhaps, as often in Latin poetry, used for Aphrodite herself. *rocky pedestal:* a temple of Aphrodite, built by Byblis' father not far from Miletus.   *136. damsel:* in the Greek it is Philinus, a boy, for whom Aratus pines in vain.   *142. Molon:* Aratus' rival for the boy Philinus. *144. witch:* literally, some old woman spitting. Spitting was thought to avert evil influences or forces, in particular Nemesis, who may be provoked by self-praise. *166. Chiron:* wisest of the Centaurs (half-horses and half-men); friend of Heracles.

Set before Heracles a cup so brave
In Pholus' ° cavern—did as nectarous draughts
Cause that Anapian shepherd,° in whose hand
Rocks were as pebbles, Polypheme the strong,   170
Featly to foot it o'er the cottage lawns:—
As, ladies, ye bid flow that day for us
All by Demeter's shrine at harvest-home?
Beside whose cornstacks may I oft again
Plant my broad fan: while she stands by and smiles,
Poppies and cornsheaves on each laden arm.

—TR. C. S. CALVERLEY

Catullus (84–55 B.C.?)

One of the most outstanding Roman authors of the first century
B.C. was the lyric poet Catullus, who died at an early age after an
emotionally exhausting life. The range of his moods and the versatility of his poetic skill are brilliantly reflected in his love poetry,
in his political verses (which include an attack on Julius Caesar),
in his superb imitations of the poetry of Sappho and the Hellenistic poet Callimachus, and in his poems on mythological themes.
His love poetry is addressed to "Lesbia," who is historically identified with the prominent and flamboyant Clodia (sister of a notorious Roman politician and embittered opponent of Cicero).

To Lesbia*

Equal to Jove that youth must be—
Greater than Jove he seems to me—
Who, free from Jealousy's alarms,

---

168. Pholus: a Centaur who was persuaded by Heracles to open a cask of
extraordinary wine. The fragrance attracted the other Centaurs, who besieged
Pholus' cave until Heracles drove them off—but in doing so he accidently killed
his friend Chiron and his host Pholus. *169. Anapian shepherd:* the Cyclops
Polyphemus, who was blinded by Odysseus. * A characteristic Roman adaptation
of a Greek original. In this case the model is an ode of Sappho ("To a Girl"), in
which she describes her reactions at the sight of a girl she loves talking with a man.
Catullus converts it into a description of the sensations "Lesbia" excites in him.

Securely views thy matchless charms.°
That cheek, which ever dimpling glows,
That mouth, from whence such music flows,
To him, alike, are always known,
Reserved for him, and him alone.
Ah! Lesbia, though 'tis death to me,
I cannot choose but look on thee;   10
But, at the sight, my senses fly;
I needs must gaze, but, gazing die;
Whilst trembling with a thousand fears,
Parched to the throat my tongue adheres,
My pulse beats quick, my breath heaves short,
My limbs deny their slight support,
Cold dews my pallid face o'erspread,
With deadly languor droops my head,
My ears with tingling echoes ring,
And life itself is on the wing;   20
My eyes refuse the cheering light,
Their orbs are veiled in starless night;
Such pangs my nature sinks beneath,
And feels a temporary death.°

—TR. LORD BYRON

Invitation to Love

Live we, love we, Lesbia dear,
And the stupid saws° austere,
Which your sour old dotards prate,
Let us at a farthing rate!
When the sun sets, 'tis to rise
Brighter in the morning skies;
But, when sets our little light,°
We must sleep in endless night.
Give me then a thousand kisses,
Add a hundred to my blisses,   10

4. *matchless charms:* Here and elsewhere Lord Byron's translation is somewhat free, but it superbly conveys the intensity that marked the early days of Catullus' relationship with "Lesbia." 24. In the Latin text there follows a concluding strophe that contains an abrupt moralizing soliloquy to the effect that "Your trouble, Catullus, is *otium*—not having anything to do." 2. *saws:* sayings; gossip. 7. *little light:* literally, "brief light." The shortness of life to the lover is a theme introduced in lyric poetry by a Greek poet of the seventh century B.C., and then made popular among Roman love poets by Catullus.

Then a thousand more, and then
Add a hundred once again.
Crown me with a thousand more,
Give a hundred as before,
Then kiss on without cessation,
Till ° we lose all calculation,
And no envy mar our blisses,
Hearing of such heaps of kisses.

—TR. THEODORE MARTIN

To Lesbia Kind

Dost thou, Lesbia, ask that I
   Say how many of thy kisses
Would my craving satisfy,
   Yea, would surfeit me with blisses?

Count the grains of sand besprent
   O'er Cyrene's° spicy° plain,
'Twixt old Battus' ° monument,
   And the sweltering Hammon's fane.°

Count the silent stars of night,
   That be ever watching, when   10
Lovers tasting stol'n delight
   Dream not of their silent ken.

When these numbers thou hast told,
   And hast kisses given as many,
Then I may, perchance, cry Hold!
   And no longer wish for any.

But, my love, there's no amount
   For a rage like mine too vast,
Which a curious fool may count,
   Or with tongue malignant° blast.   20

—TR. THEODORE MARTIN

16–18. Till . . . kisses: to count one's blessings is to invite Nemesis and the evil eye; *"envy"* is represented by a Latin verb which originally meant "cast the evil eye on (someone)." *6. Cyrene:* Hellenized district on the north coast of Africa (now part of Libya), here mentioned because of its association with desert sand. *spicy:* reference to a Libyan desert plant whose juice was used for medicinal purposes in antiquity. *7. Battus:* legendary founder of the city Cyrene. *8. Hammon's fane:* oracular shrine of Ammon, a Libyan and Egyptian god identified with the Greek Zeus and the Roman Jupiter, at an oasis in the Libyan desert. *20. tongue malignant:* a tongue that bewitches by casting spells or uttering curses.

To Lesbia

ON HER FALSEHOOD

Thou told'st me, in our days of love,
 That I had all that heart of thine;
That ev'n to share the couch of Jove,°
 Thou wouldst not, Lesbia, part from mine.

How purely wert thou worshipp'd then!
 Not with the vague and vulgar fires
Which Beauty wakes in soulless men,—
 But loved, as children by their sires.

That flattering dream, alas, is o'er;—
 I know thee now—and though these eyes   10
Dote on thee wildly as before,
 Yet, ev'n in doting, I despise.

Yes, sorceress—mad as it may seem—
 With all thy craft, such spells adorn thee,
That passion ev'n outlives esteem,
 And I at once adore—and scorn thee.

—TR. THOMAS MOORE

Virgil (70–19 B.C.)

Virgil's life and works are briefly discussed on p. 456. The following poem is the fourth of ten pastoral poems or *Eclogues* which he wrote some years before *The Aeneid*. In this poem Virgil creates an idealized pastoral world, through which he expresses his joy at the prospect of a recurrence of peace, of a new Golden Age which would coincide with the birth of a wonder-child.

The Fourth Eclogue

Sicilian° Muse, begin a loftier strain!
Tho' lowly shrubs, and trees that shade the plain,
Delight not all; Sicilian Muse, prepare
To make the vocal woods deserve a consul's° care.

3. *ev'n . . . Jove:* a proverbial expression derived from the numerous affairs that Jupiter (Zeus) had with human women in Greco-Roman mythology.   1. *Sicilian:* an acknowledgment of indebtedness to Theocritus, who placed the scene of many of his Idylls in Sicily.   4. *consul:* highest Roman political office.

The last great age, foretold by sacred rhymes,°
Renews its finish'd course: Saturnian° times
Roll round again; and mighty years, begun
From their first orb, in radiant circles run.
The base degenerate iron offspring ends;
A golden progeny from heav'n descends.   10
O chaste Lucina,° speed the mother's pains,
And haste the glorious birth! thy own Apollo reigns!
The lovely boy, with his auspicious face,
Shall Pollio's° consulship and triumph grace;
Majestic months set out with him to their appointed race.
The father banish'd virtue shall restore,
And crimes shall threat the guilty world no more.
The son shall lead the life of gods, and be
By gods and heroes seen, and gods and heroes see.
The jarring nations he in peace shall bind,   20
And with paternal virtues rule mankind.
Unbidden Earth shall wreathing ivy bring,
And fragrant herbs (the promises of spring),
As her first off'rings to her infant king.
The goats with strutting dugs shall homeward speed,
And lowing herds secure from lions feed.
His cradle shall with rising flow'rs be crown'd:
The serpent's brood shall die; the sacred ground
Shall weeds and pois'nous plants refuse to bear;
Each common bush shall Syrian roses wear.   30
But when heroic verse his youth shall raise,
And form it to hereditary praise,
Unlabor'd harvests shall the fields adorn,
And cluster'd grapes shall blush on every thorn;
The knotted oaks shall show'rs of honey weep,
And thro' the matted grass the liquid gold shall creep.
Yet of old fraud some footsteps shall remain:
The merchant still shall plow the deep for gain;
Great cities shall with walls be compass'd round,

5. *sacred rhymes:* the so-called Sibylline Books, which were said to have contained the oracular utterances of a sixth-century B.C. Sibyl, who predicted the end of the Iron Age—and possibly the return of a new Golden Age connected with the birth of a Wonder-Child. 6. *Saturnian:* when Saturn (Kronos) was still the supreme god; the First (or Golden) Age of Man. 11. *Lucina:* goddess of childbirth, usually identified with Juno, but here with Diana (Artemis), the twin sister of Apollo. 14. *Pollio:* poet, historian, politician; friend of Virgil; consul in 40 B.C. He was instrumental in arranging a reconciliation between Octavian and Mark Antony, which might have suggested Virgil's prophecy of a peaceful age.

And sharpen'd shares shall vex the fruitful ground;   40
Another Tiphys° shall new seas explore;
Another Argo land the chiefs upon th' Iberian shore;°
Another Helen other wars create,
And great Achilles urge the Trojan fate.
But when to ripen'd manhood he shall grow,
The greedy sailer shall the seas forego;
No keel shall cut the waves for foreign ware,
For every soil shall every product bear.
The laboring hind° his oxen shall disjoin;
No plow shall hurt the glebe, no pruning hook the vine;   50
Nor wool shall in dissembled° colors shine.
But the luxurious father of the fold,
With native purple, or unborrow'd gold,
Beneath his pompous fleece shall proudly sweat;
And under Tyrian robes° the lamb shall bleat.
The Fates, when they this happy web have spun,
Shall bless the sacred clew, and bid it smoothly run.
Mature in years, to ready honors move,
O of celestial seed! O foster son of Jove! °
See, lab'ring Nature calls thee to sustain   60
The nodding frame of heav'n, and earth, and main!
See to their base restor'd, earth, seas, and air;
And joyful ages, from behind, in crowding ranks appear.
To sing thy praise, would Heav'n my breath prolong,
Infusing spirits worthy such a song,
Not Thracian° Orpheus should transcend my lays,
Nor Linus° crown'd with never-fading bays;
Tho' each his heav'nly parent should inspire;
The Muse instruct the voice, and Phœbus tune the lyre.°
Should Pan contend in verse, and thou my theme,   70
Arcadian judges should their god condemn.
Begin, auspicious boy, to cast about

---

41. *Tiphys:* Jason's helmsman on the "Argo" in the Argonaut's famous expedition in search of the Golden Fleece. 42. *Iberian shore:* not Spain in this case, but the land of Colchis at the eastern end of the Black Sea. 49. *hind:* ploughman. 51. *dissembled:* dyed. 55. *Tyrian robes:* purple-red fleece. 59. O . . . *Jove!:* addressed to the Wonder-Child. 66. *Thracian:* The legendary poet and musician Orpheus was a son of the Thracian king Oeagrus and the Muse Calliope. 67. *Linus:* son of Apollo, who like Orpheus was said to have been such a skilled poet and musician that he could even charm trees into moving after him. 69. *Muse . . . lyre:* Orpheus was presented with the lyre by Apollo and instructed in its use by the Muses.

Thy infant eyes, and, with a smile, thy mother single out:
Thy mother well deserves that short delight,
The nauseous qualms of ten long months and travel to requite.
Then smile: the frowning infant's doom is read;
No god shall crown the board, nor goddess bless the bed.

—TR. JOHN DRYDEN

Horace (65–8 B.C.)

After Virgil, the Roman lyric poet Horace is one of the most important literary witnesses to the Augustan era of peace and cultural brilliance. The son of a southern Italian fiscal official, he became a distinguished supporter of the emperor Augustus. His surviving works include a collection of lyric poetry known as the *Odes* or *Carmina,* to which the following poem belongs. The *Odes* often lack the emotional intensity of other ancient lyric poetry, but they are almost unrivaled as examples of the most skillful verbal and metrical architectonics in Latin.

To Pyrrha

What slender Youth° bedew'd with liquid odours°
Courts thee on Roses in some pleasant Cave,
    Pyrrha° for whom bind'st thou
    In wreaths thy golden Hair,
Plain in thy neatness; O how oft shall he
On Faith and changed ° Gods complain: and Seas
    Rough with black winds and storms°
    Unwonted shall admire:
Who now enjoyes thee credulous all Gold,
Who always vacant, always amiable   10

---

1. *Youth:* Pyrrha's new lover, still unaware of her treacherous nature. *bedew'd . . . odours:* dripping with fragrant oils. 3. *Pyrrha:* Greek name of a fictitious person. It suggests (1) "The Red-blond Girl" (referring to a fashionable hair color) and (2) the name of a city on Lesbos. Possibly also Ovid's Pyrrha. 6. *changed:* first apparently favoring his love, then apparently against it. 7. *black winds and storms:* the dangerous moods of the sea here as a metaphor for love. This image recurs frequently in Hellenistic poetry, which is one of Horace's formal models.

Hopes thee;° of flattering gales
Unmindfull. Hapless they
To whom thou untry'd seem'st fair. Me° in my vow'd
Picture the sacred wall declares t' have hung
My dank and dropping weeds
To the stern God of Sea.°

—TR. JOHN MILTON

Ovid (43 B.C.–17 A.D.?)

Ovid was a prolific Roman poet of the Augustan age. He first enjoyed the favor of the emperor Augustus but then was banished to a town on the Black Sea (now in Rumania) in 9 A.D., possibly because of an affair with Augustus' granddaughter but allegedly because of his frank poem on erotic techniques, *The Art of Love*. He was a brilliant poet, particularly of love elegy, and his fascination with the theme of love is also evident in the *Metamorphoses*, his epic poem in fifteen books on the transformations of mythical characters. This poem, along with the works of Homer and Hesiod, is one of the chief sources for our knowledge of ancient mythology.

From *Metamorphoses*

Of bodies chang'd to various forms I sing:
Ye gods, from whom these miracles did spring,
Inspire my numbers with celestial heat;
Till I my long laborious work complete,
And add perpetual tenor to my rhymes,
Deduc'd from nature's birth to Caesar's times.°
    Before the seas, and this terrestrial ball,
And heav'n's high canopy, that covers all,

10–11. *Who . . . thee:* who hopes you will always remain free ("vacant") for himself and capable of being loved by him ("amiable"). 13–16. *Me . . . sea:* Sailors who survived shipwreck (here his "shipwreck" is the relationship with Pyrrha) dedicated the wet clothes ("dank . . . weeds") in which they were rescued to Neptune, God of the Sea, and commemorated this event on a votive tablet ("vow'd / Picture"). 6. *Caesar's times:* his own times. Caesar here refers to Julius Caesar, with whose death and deification the poem ends in Book XV. Ovid was born a year after Caesar's death.

One was the face of nature, if a face;
Rather a rude and indigested mass;   10
A lifeless lump, unfashion'd, and unfram'd,
Of jarring seeds, and justly Chaos° nam'd.
No sun was lighted up, the world to view;
No moon did yet her blunted horns renew:
Nor yet was earth suspended in the sky;
Nor, pois'd, did on her own foundations lie:
Nor seas about the shores their arms had thrown,
But earth and air and water were in one.
Thus air was void of light, and earth unstable,
And water's dark abyss unnavigable.   20
No certain form on any was impress'd;
All were confus'd, and each disturb'd the rest:
For hot and cold were in one body fix'd,
And soft with hard, and light with heavy mix'd.
    But God, or Nature, while they thus contend,
To these intestine discords put an end.
Then earth from air, and seas from earth were driv'n,°
And grosser air sunk from ethereal heav'n.
Thus disembroil'd, they take their proper place;
The next of kin contiguously embrace,   30
And foes are sunder'd by a larger space.
The force of fire ascended first° on high,
And took its dwelling in the vaulted sky.
Then air succeeds, in lightness next to fire;
Whose atoms from unactive earth retire.
Earth sinks beneath, and draws a numerous throng
Of ponderous, thick, unwieldy seeds along.
About her coasts unruly waters roar,
And, rising on a ridge, insult the shore.
Thus when the God, whatever God was he,   40
Had form'd the whole, and made the parts agree,

12. *Chaos:* the first god in time. In Greco-Roman mythology, his existence begins
earlier than that of Gaia (literally, "Earth"), the only other original god. Compare
the story of the Creation in the Old Testament (p. 3) and Job.   27. *earth . . .
driven:* the separation of four basic physical elements (earth, water, air, and fire)
out of an original chaos was accepted as plausible by several Greek thinkers. The
notion that there are only four basic elements was taught by a Greek philosopher
of the fifth century B.C., Empedocles, and by the Stoics (philosophers of the
Hellenistic period—third century B.C. onward—who had become very popular in
Rome by Ovid's time).   32. *ascended first:* the stars were thought of as fire
which, as the lightest of the elements, ascended highest. Earth and water, as the
heaviest elements, settled below "fire" and air.

That no unequal portions° might be found,
He molded earth into a spacious round;
Then, with a breath, he gave the winds to blow,
And bade the congregated waters flow.
He adds the running springs and standing lakes,
And bounding banks for winding rivers makes.
Some part in earth are swallow'd up, the most
In ample oceans, disimbogued, are lost.
He shades the woods, the valleys he restrains   50
With rocky mountains, and extends the plains.
    And as five zones th' ethereal regions bind,
Five, correspondent, are to earth assign'd:° . . .
    High o'er the clouds,° and empty realms of wind,
The God a clearer space for heav'n design'd;
Where fields of light, and liquid ether° flow,
Purg'd from the pond'rous dregs of earth below.
    Scarce had the pow'r distinguish'd these, when straight
The stars,° no longer overlaid with weight,
Exert their heads from underneath the mass,   60
And upward shoot, and kindle as they pass,
And with diffusive light adorn their heav'nly place.
Then, every void of nature to supply,
With forms of gods he° fills the vacant sky:
New herds of beasts he sends, the plains to share;
New colonies of birds, to people air;
And to their oozy beds the finny fish repair.
    A creature of a more exalted kind
Was wanting yet, and then was Man design'd;
Conscious of thought, of more capacious breast,°   70
For empire form'd, and fit to rule the rest:
Whether with particles of heav'nly fire°

---

42. *no unequal portions:* that is, he made equal parts of earth, water, air, and
fire.   53. *Five . . . assign'd:* the five zones in the sky correspond to the five
climatic zones on earth: the equatorial region, the arctic and antarctic, and the
two temperate zones between the equator and the poles.   54. *High o'er the clouds:*
after describing the lower regions of the atmosphere, in which storms are generated, Ovid now proceeds to a region high above the atmosphere.   56. *ether*
(aither): an airy, fiery substance, here not distinguished from the "force of fire"
of line 32.   59. *The stars:* in antiquity the stars were often thought of as living
beings with a divine nature. Even philosophers, such as the Stoics, subscribed to
this view.   64. *he:* the god.   70. *of more capacious breast:* more capable of intelligence.   72. *heav'nly fire:* fire was considered the most divine of the four
basic elements, since its region (the ether) was the highest, and therefore closest
to the gods.

The God of Nature did his soul inspire;°
Or earth, but new divided from the sky,
And pliant still, retain'd the ethereal energy;°
Which wise Prometheus° temper'd into paste,
And, mix'd with living streams, the godlike image cast.°
Thus, while the mute° creation downward bend
Their sight, and to their earthy mother tend,
Man looks aloft, and with erected eyes   80
Beholds his own hereditary skies.
From such rude principles our form began,
And earth was metamorphos'd into man.

THE GOLDEN AGE

The Golden Age was first; when man, yet new,
No rule but uncorrupted reason knew;
And, with a native bent, did good pursue.
Unforc'd by punishment, unaw'd by fear,
His words were simple, and his soul sincere:
Needless was written law, where none oppress'd;
The law of man was written in his breast;   90
No suppliant crowds before the judge appear'd;
No court erected yet, nor cause was hear'd;
But all was safe, for conscience was their guard.
The mountain trees in distant prospect please,
Ere yet the pine° descended to the seas;
Ere sails were spread, new oceans to explore;
And happy mortals, unconcern'd for more,
Confin'd their wishes to their native shore.
No walls were yet, nor fence, nor moat, nor mound;
Nor drum was heard, nor trumpet's angry sound: 100
Nor swords were forg'd; but, void of care and crime,

73. *his soul inspire:* gave him life; created him.   74. *retained . . . energy:* the
earth at first retained some elements related to those of heaven (fire or ether) since
it had only recently been separated from the fiery element.   76. *Prometheus*
(literally, "Forethought"): one of the Titans and benefactor of mankind in Greek
mythology. Against the will of Zeus, he stole fire from heaven for man, for which
Zeus punished him brutally. In some versions of the myth, Prometheus created
man.   77. *godlike image cast:* moulded man into the image of the gods. The
Greco-Roman gods were still thought of as anthropomorphic in Ovid's day, although this view had been attacked as early as the sixth century B.C., when the
poet and philosopher Xenophanes claimed that man simply created anthropomorphic gods in his own image, rather than the reverse.   78. *mute:* animals.   95.
pine: ships were made of pine wood.

The soft creation slept away their time.
The teeming earth, yet guiltless of the plow,
And unprovok'd,° did fruitful stores allow:
Content with food, which nature freely bred,
On wildings° and on strawberries they fed;
Cornels° and bramble berries gave the rest,
And falling acorns furnish'd out a feast.
The flow'rs, unsown, in fields and meadows reign'd,
And western winds immortal spring° maintain'd.   110
In following years the bearded corn ensued
From earth unask'd, nor was that earth renew'd;°
From veins of valleys milk and nectar broke,
And honey° sweating thro' the pores of oak.

THE SILVER AGE

But when good Saturn,° banish'd from above,
Was driv'n to hell, the world was under Jove.
Succeeding times a Silver Age behold,
Excelling brass, but more excell'd by gold.
Then Summer, Autumn, Winter did appear;
And Spring was but a season of the year.   120
The sun his annual course obliquely made,
Good days contracted, and enlarg'd the bad.
Then air with sultry heats began to glow;
The wings of winds were clogg'd with ice and snow;
And shivering mortals, into houses driv'n,
Sought shelter from th' inclemency of heav'n.
Those houses, then, were caves, or homely sheds,
With twining osiers° fenc'd, and moss their beds.
Then plows, for seed, the fruitful furrows broke,
And oxen labor'd first beneath the yoke.   130

---

104. *unprovok'd:* spontaneously, without any cultivation.   106. *wildings:* wild berries.   107. *Cornels:* wild cherries.   110. *immortal spring:* the notion that spring was the only "season" in the primitive world (and that the world was created in spring) recurs frequently in Greco-Roman mythology.   112. *renew'd:* filled.   113–14. *milk . . . honey:* an abundant, natural supply of milk, honey, and nectar (a drink of the gods) was often considered a feature of the ideal land.   115. *Saturn:* after Greek mythology penetrated into Italy, the early Italic god Saturn was often identified with the Greek Kronos (*Cronos*), who was the supreme god during the Golden Age of man, whereas Jupiter was identified by the Romans with the Greek god Zeus, the son and successor of Kronos.   128. *osiers:* willow shoots (often used in basketwork).

THE BRAZEN AGE

To this next came in course the Brazen° Age:
A warlike offspring, prompt to bloody rage,
Not impious yet—

THE IRON AGE

—Hard Steel succeeded then;
And stubborn as the metal were the men.
Truth, Modesty, and Shame, the world forsook;
Fraud, Avarice, and Force, their places took.
Then sails were spread to every wind that blew;
Raw were the sailors, and the depths were new:
Trees, rudely hollow'd, did the waves sustain,
Ere ships in triumph plow'd the wat'ry plain.   140
   Then landmarks limited to each his right:
For all before was common as the light.°
Nor was the ground alone requir'd to bear
Her annual income to the crooked share;°
But greedy mortals, rummaging her store,
Digg'd from her entrails first the precious ore,
Which next to hell the prudent gods had laid,
And that alluring ill to sight display'd.
Thus cursed steel, and more accursed gold,
Gave mischief birth, and made that mischief bold;   150
And double death did wretched man invade,
By steel assaulted,° and by gold betray'd.
Now (brandish'd weapons glittering in their hands)
Mankind is broken loose from moral bands;
No rights of hospitality remain:
The guest, by him who harbor'd him, is slain;
The son-in-law° pursues the father's life;
The wife her husband murders, he the wife;
The stepdame poison for the son prepares;

---

131. *Brazen:* bronze. 142. *common as the light:* just like the sunlight, everything else had previously been the common property of all men. 144. *crooked
share:* the ploughshare. 152. *By steel assaulted:* attacked with weapons made of
iron. 157. *son-in-law:* most Romans of Ovid's time would remember that Julius
Caesar was the father-in-law of Pompey, who became Caesar's arch-enemy in a
vicious civil war.

The son inquires° into his father's years.   160
Faith flies, and Piety° in exile mourns;
And Justice, here oppress'd, to heav'n returns. . . .

"Mankind's° a monster, and th' ungodly times,
Confed'rate into guilt, are sworn to crimes.
All are alike involv'd in ill, and all
Must by the same relentless fury fall." °
   Thus ended Jove; the greater gods assent,
By clamors urging his severe intent;
The less fill up the cry for punishment.
Yet still with pity they remember man,   170
And mourn as much as heav'nly spirits can.
They ask, when those were lost of human birth,°
What he would do with all this waste of earth;
If his dispeopled world he would resign
To beasts, a mute, and more ignoble line:°
Neglected altars must no longer smoke,
If none were left to worship and invoke.
To whom the Father of the Gods° replied:
"Lay that unnecessary fear aside:
Mine be the care new people to provide.   180
I will from wondrous principles ordain
A race unlike the first, and try my skill again."
   Already had he toss'd the flaming brand°
And roll'd the thunder in his spacious hand,
Preparing to discharge on seas and land;
But stopp'd, for fear, thus violently driven,
The sparks should catch his axletree of heav'n:
Rememb'ring, in the Fates, a time° when fire
Should to the battlements of heav'n aspire,
And all his blazing worlds above should burn,   190

160. *son inquires:* the son, eager for his inheritance, inquires from astrologers when his father will die.   161. *Piety:* the virtue of *pietas* (a sense of affectionate respect and duty toward the gods, one's parents, benefactors, rulers, and one's country) was considered of the highest importance by the Romans.   163–66. *Mankind's . . . fall:* in this scene Jupiter (Zeus) is addressing the other gods on the necessity of destroying the entire human race of the Iron Age since all of mankind had become morally cancerous and incurably evil.   172. *lost of human birth:* when the fury of Jupiter has destroyed all human beings.   175. *mute . . . line:* wild beasts.   178. *Father of the Gods:* Jupiter.   183. *flaming brand:* lightning, thunderbolt.   188–91. *time . . . turn:* destruction of the entire world by fire is here rejected by Jupiter as too dangerous for the gods themselves, although it will be the ultimate fate of the world. A theory about such a universal conflagra-

And all th' inferior globe to cinders turn.°
His dire artill'ry thus dismiss'd, he bent
His thoughts to some securer punishment;
Concludes to pour a wat'ry deluge down,
And, what he durst not burn, resolves to drown.
The northern breath,° that freezes floods, he binds,
With all the race of cloud-dispelling winds:
The South° he loos'd, who night and horror brings;
And fogs are shaken from his flaggy wings.
From his divided beard two streams he pours;   200
His head and rheumy eyes distil in showers;
With rain his robe and heavy mantle flow,
And lazy mists are low'ring on his brow.
Still as he swept along, with his clench'd fist
He squeez'd the clouds;° th' imprison'd clouds resist:
The skies, from pole to pole, with peals resound;
And show'rs inlarg'd come pouring on the ground.
Then, clad in colors of a various dye,
Junonian Iris° breeds a new supply.
To feed the clouds: impetuous rain descends;   210
The bearded corn beneath the burthen bends;
Defrauded clowns° deplore their perish'd grain,
And the long labors of the year are vain.
   Nor from his patrimonial heav'n alone
Is Jove content to pour his vengeance down:
Aid from his brother of the seas° he craves,
To help him with auxiliary waves.
The wat'ry tyrant calls his brooks and floods;
Who roll from mossy caves, their moist abodes,
And with perpetual urns his palace fill: 220

tion was developed by Heraclitus, an early fifth-century Greek philosopher, and
the Stoics, who influenced Ovid's cosmological views considerably. The two
classical means of universal destruction—fire and water—are often coupled in
mythology and in prophetic visions.   *196. northern breath:* the north wind is
locked up, since it brings bright, dry weather.   *198–205. The South . . . clouds:*
the south (or southwest) wind is deified in Greco-Roman mythology and was
feared because he frequently brought fog and rainstorms in winter and spring
(although in other seasons he was a dry and sultry wind). Ovid's description of
this god's appearance is the most elaborate in all of ancient poetry.   *209. Junonian
Iris:* Iris is the personification of the rainbow. She is called Junonian since she is
very often the messenger of the Roman goddess Juno (wife of Jupiter).
212. clowns: foolish farmers.   *216. brother of the seas:* Jupiter's brother, Neptune, was a Roman god of water who became more specifically god of the sea
after his identification with the Greek god Poseidon.

To whom, in brief, he thus imparts his will:
   "Small exhortation needs: your pow'rs employ,
And this bad world (so Jove requires) destroy.
Let loose the reins to all your wat'ry store;
Bear down the dams, and open every door."
   The floods, by nature enemies to land,
And proudly swelling with their new command,
Remove the living stones that stopp'd their way,
And, gushing from their source, augment the sea.
Then, with his mace,° their monarch° struck the ground: 230
With inward trembling° earth receiv'd the wound,
And rising streams a ready passage found.
Th' expanded waters gather on the plain,
They float the fields, and overtop the grain;
Then rushing onwards, with a sweepy sway,
Bear flocks, and folds, and lab'ring hinds away.
Nor safe their dwellings were; for, sapp'd by floods,
Their houses fell upon their household gods.
The solid piles, too strongly built to fall,
High o'er their heads behold a wat'ry wall: 240
Now seas and earth were in confusion lost;
A world of waters, and without a coast.
   One climbs a cliff; one in his boat is borne,
And plows above, where late he sow'd his corn.
Others o'er chimney tops and turrets row,
And drop their anchors on the meads below;
Or downward driv'n, they bruise the tender vine,
Or toss'd aloft, are knock'd against a pine;
And where of late the kids° had cropp'd the grass,
The monsters° of the deep now take their place.   250
Insulting Nereids° on the cities ride,
And wond'ring dolphins o'er the palace glide;
On leaves and masts of mighty oaks they browse,
And their broad fins entangle in the boughs.
The frighted wolf now swims amongst the sheep;
The yellow lion wanders in the deep:
His rapid force no longer helps the boar;
The stag swims faster than he ran before:°
The fowls,° long beating on their wings in vain,

230. *mace:* his trident, which was his symbol and weapon. *monarch:* Neptune.
231. *trembling:* Neptune was also the god of earthquakes. 249. *kids:* goats.
250. *monsters:* more accurately "seals." 215. *Nereids:* sea nymphs. 258. *The stag . . . before:* that is, he is swept away by rapid currents.

Despair of land, and drop into the main.   260
Now hills and vales no more distinction know,
And level'd nature lies oppress'd below.
The most of mortals perish in the flood,
The small remainder dies for want of food.
    A mountain of stupendous height there stands
Betwixt th' Athenian and Bœotian lands,
The bound of fruitful fields, while fields they were,
But then a field of waters did appear:
Parnassus° is its name; whose forky rise
Mounts thro' the clouds, and mates the lofty skies.   270
High on the summit of this dubious cliff,
Deucalion,° wafting, moor'd his little skiff.
He with his wife were only left behind
Of perish'd man; they two were humankind.
The mountain nymphs° and Themis° they adore,
And from her oracles relief implore.
The most upright of mortal men was he;
The most sincere and holy woman, she.
    When Jupiter, surveying earth from high,
Beheld it in a lake of water lie,   280
That, where so many millions lately liv'd,
But two, the best of either sex, surviv'd,
He loos'd the northern wind; fierce Boreas flies
To puff away the clouds, and purge the skies:
Serenely, while he blows, the vapors, driven,
Discover heav'n to earth, and earth to heav'n.
The billows fall, while Neptune lays his mace
On the rough sea, and smooths its furrow'd face.
Already Triton,° at his call, appears
Above the waves; a Tyrian° robe he wears,   290

259. *fowls:* birds.   269. Parnassus here refers to a twin-peaked mountain, just north of Delphi, sacred to Apollo and the Muses.   272. *Deucalion:* human son of the divinity Prometheus. His wife, Pyrrha, was a human daughter of Prometheus' brother, Epimetheus (literally, "After-Thought").   275. *mountain nymphs:* near the two peaks of Parnassus is the famous Corycian Cave which was sacred to mountain nymphs. *Themis:* a daughter of Sky (Uranus) and Earth (Gaia or Ge); the divine personification of right and of the immutable order established by custom and divine decree. As such, she also had a prophetic gift and in very early times was associated with the oracle at Delphi, near Parnassus.   289. *Triton:* a legendary son of Neptune (Poseidon), usually represented as human to the waist and dolphin below, often blowing on a conch ("crooked trumpet") to calm the seas.   290. *Tyrian:* of purple color (he is dark blue, like the sea); more accurately: "dark-blue Triton, his shoulders covered with clustering shellfish."

And in his hand a crooked trumpet bears.
The sovereign bids him peaceful sounds inspire,
And give the waves the signal to retire.
His writhen shell he takes, whose narrow vent
Grows by degrees into a large extent;
Then gives it breath: the blast, with doubling sound,
Runs the wide circuit of the world around.
The sun first heard it, in his early east,
And met the rattling echoes in the west.
The waters, list'ning to the trumpet's roar,   300
Obey the summons, and forsake the shore.
    A thin circumference of land appears;
And Earth, but not at once, her visage rears,
And peeps upon the seas from upper grounds:
The streams, but just contain'd within their bounds,
By slow degrees into their channels crawl;
And earth increases as the waters fall.
In longer time the tops of trees appear,
Which mud on their dishonor'd branches bear.
    At length the world was all restor'd to view,   310
But desolate, and of a sickly hue:
Nature beheld herself, and stood aghast;
A dismal desart,° and a silent waste.
    Which when Deucalion, with a piteous look,
Beheld, he wept, and thus to Pyrrha spoke:
"O wife, O sister,° O of all thy kind
The best and only creature left behind,
By kindred, love, and now by dangers join'd;
Of multitudes who breath'd the common air
We two remain; a species in a pair: 320
The rest the seas have swallow'd; nor have we
Ev'n of this wretched life a certainty.
The clouds are still above; and, while I speak,
A second deluge o'er our heads may break.
Should I be snatch'd from hence, and thou remain,
Without relief, or partner of thy pain,
How couldst thou such a wretched life sustain?
Should I be left, and thou be lost, the sea,
That buried her I lov'd, should bury me.

313. *desart:* desert. 316. *sister:* Pyrrha is his cousin and wife; "sister" expresses
both kinship and endearment.

O could our father° his old arts inspire,   330
And make me heir of his informing fire,
That so I might abolish'd man retrieve,°
And perish'd people in new souls might live!
But Heav'n is pleas'd, nor ought we to complain,
That we, th' examples of mankind, remain."
He said: the careful couple join their tears,
And then invoke the gods, with pious prayers.
    Thus in devotion having eas'd their grief,
From sacred oracles they seek relief:
And to Cephisus' ° brook their way pursue: 340
The stream was troubled, but the ford they knew.
With living waters in the fountain bred,
They sprinkle first their garments, and their head,°
Then took the way which to the temple led.
The roofs were all defiled with moss and mire,
The desert altars void of solemn fire.
Before the gradual prostrate they adored,
The pavement kissed; and thus the saint° implored.
"O righteous Themis, if the powers above
By prayers are bent to pity, and to love;   350
If human miseries can move their mind;
If yet they can forgive, and yet be kind;
Tell how we may restore, by second birth,
Mankind, and people desolated earth."
Then thus the gracious goddess, nodding, said:
"Depart, and with your vestments veil your head:°
And stooping lowly down, with loosened zones,°
Throw each behind your backs your mighty mother's bones."
Amazed the pair, and mute with wonder, stand,
Till Pyrrha first refused the dire command.   360
"Forbid it Heaven," said she, "that I should tear
Those holy relics from the sepulcher."

---

330. *father:* Prometheus.   332. *That . . . retrieve:* "so that thus I might recreate
man out of fiery earth and water, as once Prometheus did."   340. *Cephisus*
(Cephysus): a large river that originates on Parnassus and flows past Athens.
342–43. *With . . . head:* persons approaching a Greek temple had to purify
themselves by ablution. Here they approach the oracular shrine of Themis (later
of Apollo) at Delphi.   348. *saint:* the goddess Themis.   356. *veil your head:* so
that the sacred miracle which follows will not be desecrated by human eyes.
357. *zones:* belts; garments. In Greek myth loosening one's garments often seems
to signify a free and complete surrender to a divinity.

They pondered the mysterious words again,
For some new sense; and long they sought in vain.
At length Deucalion cleared his cloudy brow,
And said: "The dark enigma will allow
A meaning, which, if well I understand,
From sacrilege will free the god's command:
This earth our mighty mother° is, the stones
In her capacious body are her bones: 370
These we must cast behind." With hope, and fear,
The woman did the new solution hear:
The man diffides in° his own augury,°
And doubts the gods; yet both resolve to try.
Descending from the mount, they first unbind
Their vests, and, veiled, they cast the stones behind:
The stones (a miracle to mortal view,
But long tradition makes it pass for true)
Did first the rigor of their kind expel,
And suppled into softness as they fell;   380
Then swelled, and, swelling, by degrees grew warm:
And took the rudiments of human form;
Imperfect shapes, in marble such are seen;
When the rude chisel does the man begin;
While yet the roughness of the stone remains,
Without the rising muscles, and the veins.
The sappy° parts, and next resembling juice,
Were turned to moisture, for the body's use:
Supplying humors,° blood, and nourishment:
The rest, too solid to receive a bent,   390
Converts to bones; and what was once a vein,
Its former name and nature did retain.
By help of power Divine, in little space,
What the man threw assumed a manly face;
And what the wife, renewed the female race,
Hence we derive our nature, born to bear,
Laborious life, and hardened into care.
        The rest of animals from teeming earth,

---

369. *mother:* Earth (Gaia) was their great-grandmother.   373. *diffides in:* distrusts. *augury:* his interpretation of the oracle.   387. *sappy:* with residual moisture from the Flood.   389. *humors:* it was a common notion in antiquity that the body contained four basic liquids (blood, phlegm, choler or yellow bile, and melancholy or black bile); predominance of any one of these determines one's temperament and character.

Produced in various forms, received their birth.
The native moisture, in its close retreat,   400
Digested by the sun's ethereal heat,
As in a kindly womb, began to breed:
Then swelled, and quickened by the vital seed.
And some in less, and some in longer space,
Were ripened into form, and took a several face. . . .
    For heat and moisture, when in bodies joined,
The temper that results from either kind,
Conception makes; and fighting, till they mix,
Their mingled atoms in each other fix.
Thus Nature's hand the genial bed prepares   410
With friendly discord, and with fruitful wars.
    From hence the surface of the ground with mud
And slime besmeared the feces of the flood)
Received the rays of heaven; and sucking in
The seeds of heat, new creatures did begin.

—TR. JOHN DRYDEN

Lucretius

FROM *On the Nature of Things*

Lucretius (99?–55 B.C.?)

LITTLE IS KNOWN OF THE ROMAN POET LUCRETIUS, A UNIQUE literary figure of the first century B.C. According to a story popular in antiquity and frequently revived since then, Lucretius became insane after taking an aphrodisiac; in the lucid spells of his mental illness, the story claims, he wrote his epic. This anecdote was probably inspired by the hostility of Romans and Church fathers to Lucretius' thought. Nevertheless, it suggests that Lucretius' didactic poem *On the Nature of Things* (*De rerum natura*) was considered unusual and, in fact, the poem was perhaps the literary anomaly of the century for at least three reasons.[1]

First, while Catullus and other "New Poets" were popularizing lyric poetry and stressing formal perfection in shorter poetic forms, Lucretius was writing didactic poetry in an archaizing epic style. Second, he chose as his subject the scientifically intricate atomistic theory of the Greek philosopher Epicurus—a subject considered hardly suited to a poetic mold. Third, although Epicurus' emphasis on the pleasures of tranquillity and an undisturbed, "natural" existence appealed to numerous Romans, his opposition to active participation in political life and his materialistic explanation of the universe were not particularly suited to the Roman preoccupation with public duty and religious reverence.

Lucretius' poem expounds, in six books, major aspects of the philosophy of Epicurus (341 B.C.–270 B.C.) and is indeed one of the chief sources of our knowledge of this philosophy. According to the philosophy of Epicurus, not only the evolution of the universe but also all events on earth, including human decisions and emotions, are caused purely by the motions and chance combinations of atoms—not by the gods. One of the ethical conclusions drawn from these materialistic principles is that man should withdraw from the carousel of political and military life and pursue instead the Epicurean ideal of an undisturbed life in accordance with nature.

Lucretius perceived his role as that of a teacher of tranquil enlightenment. Yet his poem displays a persistent melancholy and a passionate preoccupation with fear, anxiety, doubt, and death, which not only turns a derivative philosophical argument into remarkable poetry but also suggests a subterranean anxiety and doubt within the prophet of tranquillity himself.

[1] Lucretius employs more than one poetic style. In the passages that deal with the bare facts of Epicurus' atomistic materialism, Lucretius' poetry is not much more than ingeniously versified science. On the other hand, the passages dealing with human anxiety, death, and war often reveal Lucretius' enormous poetic power. To convey at least some sense of these differences in poetic style and tone, two different translations have been chosen: a modern prose translation for expository passages and the unrivaled verse translation of the English poet John Dryden for the other.

On the Nature of Things

From BOOKS II and III

TRANSLATED BY JOHN DRYDEN

'T is pleasant, safely to behold from shore°
The rolling ship, and hear the tempest roar:
Not that another's pain is our delight;
But pains unfelt produce the pleasing sight.
'T is pleasant also to behold from far
The moving legions mingled in the war;°
But much more sweet thy lab'ring steps to guide
To virtue's heights, with wisdom well supplied,
And all the magazines of learning fortified:
From thence to look below on humankind,   10
Bewilder'd in the maze of life, and blind:
To see vain fools ambitiously contend
For wit and pow'r; their lost endeavors bend
T' outshine each other, waste their time and health
In search of honor, and pursuit of wealth.
 O wretched man! in what a mist of life,
Inclos'd with dangers and with noisy strife,
He spends his little span, and overfeeds
His cramm'd desires with more than nature needs!
For nature wisely stints our appetite,   20
And craves no more than undisturb'd delight:°
Which minds, unmix'd with cares and fears, obtain;
A soul serene, a body void of pain.
So little this corporeal frame requires;
So bounded are our natural desires,
That wanting all, and setting pain aside,

---

1. *from shore:* Epicurus considered withdrawal from the turmoil of public life to be a prerequisite for achieving the "natural" state of being, which constitutes "pleasure." 6. *war:* Lucretius, as an Epicurean, expresses his opposition to war throughout the poem. 21. *undisturb'd delight:* the highest Epicurean ideal.

With bare privation sense is satisfied.
If golden sconces hang not on the walls,
To light the costly suppers and the balls;
If the proud palace shines not with the state   30
Of burnish'd bowls, and of reflected plate;
If well-tun'd harps, nor the more pleasing sound
Of voices, from the vaulted roofs rebound;
Yet on the grass, beneath a poplar shade,
By the cool stream our careless limbs are laid;
With cheaper pleasures innocently blest,
When the warm spring with gaudy flow'rs is dress'd.
Nor will the raging fever's fire abate
With golden canopies and beds of state;
But the poor patient will as soon be sound   40
On the hard mattress, or the mother ground.
    Then since our bodies are not eas'd the more
By birth, or pow'r, or fortune's wealthy store,
'T is plain, these useless toys of every kind
As little can relieve the lab'ring mind:
Unless we could suppose the dreadful sight
Of marshal'd legions moving to the fight,
Could, with their sound and terrible array,
Expel our fears, and drive the thoughts of death away.
But, since the supposition vain appears,   50
Since clinging cares, and trains of inbred fears,
Are not with sounds to be affrighted thence,
But in the midst of pomp pursue the prince,
Not aw'd by arms, but in the presence bold,
Without respect to purple or to gold;
Why should not we these pageantries despise,
Whose worth but in our want of reason lies?
For life is all in wand'ring errors led;
And just as children are surpris'd with dread,
And tremble in the dark, so riper years   60
Ev'n in broad daylight are possess'd with fears,
And shake at shadows fanciful and vain
As those which in the breasts of children reign.
These bugbears of the mind, this inward hell,
No rays of outward sunshine can dispel;
But nature and right reason must display
Their beams abroad, and bring the darksome soul to day.

AGAINST THE FEAR OF DEATH

What has this bugbear death to frighten man,
If souls can die, as well as bodies can?
For, as before our birth we felt no pain,   70
When Punic arms° infested land and main,
When heav'n and earth were in confusion hurl'd,
For the debated empire of the world,
Which aw'd with dreadful expectation lay,
Sure to be slaves, uncertain who should sway:
So, when our mortal frame shall be disjoin'd,
The lifeless lump uncoupled from the mind,
From sense of grief and pain we shall be free;
We shall not feel, because we shall not *be*.
Tho' earth in seas, and seas in heav'n were lost,   80
We should not move, we only should be toss'd.
Nay, ev'n suppose when we have suffer'd fate,
The soul could feel in her divided state,
What's that to us? for we are only we
While souls and bodies in one frame agree.
Nay, tho' our atoms should revolve by chance,
And matter leap into the former dance;
Tho' time our life and motion could restore,
And make our bodies what they were before,
What gain to us would all this bustle bring?   90
The new-made man would be another thing.
When once an interrupting pause is made,
That individual being is decay'd.
We, who are dead and gone, shall bear no part
In all the pleasures, nor shall feel the smart
Which to that other mortal shall accrue,
Whom of our matter time shall mold anew.
For backward if you look on that long space
Of ages past, and view the changing face
Of matter, toss'd and variously combin'd   100
In sundry shapes, 't is easy for the mind
From thence t' infer, that seeds° of things have been
In the same order as they now are seen:

---

71. *Punic arms:* a reference to three prolonged and vicious wars for control of a large part of the Mediterranean between Rome and Carthage (a "Punic" or Phoenecian city on the north coast of Africa) during the period of 264–146 B.C., which ended in a Roman victory (in spite of the feats of the Carthaginian general Hannibal) but debilitated both parties.   102. *seed:* atoms.

Which yet our dark remembrance cannot trace,
Because a pause of life, a gaping space,
Has come betwixt, where memory lies dead,
And all the wand'ring motions from the sense are fled.
For whosoe'er shall in misfortunes live,
Must *be,* when those misfortunes shall arrive;
And since the man who *is* not, feels not woe,   110
(For death exempts him, and wards off the blow,
Which we, the living, only feel and bear,)
What is there left for us in death to fear?
When once that pause of life has come between,
'T is just the same as we had never been.
    And therefore if a man bemoan his lot,
That after death his mold'ring limbs shall rot,
Or flames, or jaws of beasts devour his mass,
Know, he's an unsincere, unthinking ass.
A secret sting remains within his mind;   120
The fool is to his own cast offals kind.
He boasts no sense can after death remain,
Yet makes himself a part of life again,
As if some other He could feel the pain.
If, while he live, this thought molest his head,
What wolf or vulture shall devour me dead?
He wastes his days in idle grief, nor can
Distinguish 'twixt the body and the man;
But thinks himself can still himself survive;
And, what when dead he feels not, feels alive.   130
Then he repines that he was born to die,
Nor knows in death there is no other He,
No living He remains his grief to vent,
And o'er his senseless carcass to lament.
If after death 't is painful to be torn
By birds, and beasts, then why not so to burn;
Or, drench'd in floods of honey,° to be soak'd;
Imbalm'd, to be at once preserv'd and chok'd;
Or on an airy mountain's top to lie,
Expos'd to cold and heav'n's inclemency;   140
Or crowded in a tomb to be oppress'd
With monumental marble on thy breast?
    But to be snatch'd from all thy household joys,
From thy chaste wife, and thy dear prattling boys,
Whose little arms about thy legs are cast,

137. *floods of honey:* a type of embalming favored by the rich.

And climbing for a kiss prevent their mother's haste,
Inspiring secret pleasure thro' thy breast—
All these shall be no more: thy friends oppress'd
Thy care and courage now no more shall free;
"Ah! wretch!" thou cry'st, "ah! miserable me!   150
One woful day sweeps children, friends, and wife,
And all the brittle blessings of my life!"
Add one thing more, and all thou say'st is true;
Thy want and wish of them is vanish'd too:
Which, well consider'd, were a quick relief
To all thy vain imaginary grief.
For thou shalt sleep, and never wake again,
And, quitting life, shalt quit thy living pain.
But we, thy friends, shall all those sorrows find,
Which in forgetful death thou leav'st behind;   160
No time shall dry our tears, nor drive thee from our mind.
The worst that can befall thee, measur'd right,
Is a sound slumber, and a long good-night.
Yet thus the fools, that would be thought the wits,
Disturb their mirth with melancholy fits:
When healths go round, and kindly brimmers flow,
Till the fresh garlands on their foreheads glow,
They whine, and cry: "Let us make haste to live.
Short are the joys that human life can give."
Eternal preachers, that corrupt the draught,   170
And pall the god,° that never thinks, with thought;
Idiots with all that thought, to whom the worst
Of death is want of drink, and endless thirst,
Or any fond desire as vain as these.
For ev'n in sleep, the body, wrapp'd in ease,
Supinely lies, as in the peaceful grave;
And, wanting nothing, nothing can it crave.
Were that sound sleep eternal, it were death;
Yet the first atoms then, the seeds of breath,
Are moving near to sense; we do but shake   180
And rouse that sense, and straight we are awake.
Then death to us, and death's anxiety,
Is less than nothing, if a less could be.
For then our atoms, which in order lay,
Are scatter'd from their heap, and puff'd away,
And never can return into their place,
When once the pause of life has left an empty space.

171. *the god:* Dionysus.

        And last, suppose great Nature's voice should call
To thee, or me, or any of us all:
"What dost thou mean, ungrateful wretch, thou vain,   190
Thou mortal thing, thus idly to complain,
And sigh and sob that thou shalt be no more?
For if thy life were pleasant heretofore,
If all the bounteous blessings, I could give,
Thou hast enjoy'd; if thou has known to live,
And pleasure not leak'd thro' thee like a sieve;
Why dost thou not give thanks as at a plenteous feast,
Cramm'd to the throat with life, and rise and take thy rest?
But if my blessings thou hast thrown away,
If indigested joys pass'd thro', and would not stay,   200
Why dost thou wish for more to squander still?
If life be grown a load, a real ill,
And I would all thy cares and labors end,
Lay down thy burden, fool, and know thy friend.
To please thee, I have emptied all my store;
I can invent and can supply no more,
But run the round again, the round I ran before.
Suppose thou are not broken yet with years,
Yet still the selfsame scene of things appears,
And would be ever, couldst thou ever live;   210
For life is still but life, there's nothing new to give."
What can we plead against so just a bill?
We stand convicted, and our cause goes ill.
        But if a wretch, a man oppress'd by fate,
Should beg of Nature to prolong his date,
She speaks aloud to him with more disdain:
"Be still, thou martyr fool, thou covetous of pain."
But if an old decrepit sot lament;
"What, thou," she cries, "who hast outliv'd content!
Dost thou complain, who hast enjoy'd my store?   220
But this is still th' effect of wishing more.
Unsatisfied with all that Nature brings;
Loathing the present, liking absent things;
From hence it comes, thy vain desires, at strife
Within themselves, have tantaliz'd thy life;
And ghastly death appear'd before thy sight,
Ere thou hadst gorg'd thy soul and senses with delight.
Now leave those joys, unsuiting to thy age,
To a fresh comer, and resign the stage."

Is Nature to be blam'd if thus she chide?   230
No, sure; for 't is her business to provide,
Against this ever-changing frame's decay,
New things to come, and old to pass away.
One being, worn, another being makes;
Chang'd, but not lost; for Nature gives and takes:
New matter must be found for things to come,
And these must waste like those, and follow Nature's doom.
All things, like thee, have time to rise and rot;
And from each other's ruin are begot:
For life is not confin'd to him or thee;   240
'T is given to all for use, to none for property.
   Consider former ages past and gone,
Whose circles ended long ere thine begun,
Then tell me, fool, what part in them thou hast.
Thus may'st thou judge the future by the past.
What horror see'st thou in that quiet state?
What bugbear dreams to fright thee after fate?
No ghost, no goblins, that still passage keep;
But all is there serene, in that eternal sleep.
For all the dismal tales that poets tell   250
Are verified on earth, and not in hell.
No Tantalus° looks up with fearful eye,
Or dreads th' impending rock to crush him from on high;
But fear of chance on earth disturbs our easy hours,
Or vain imagin'd wrath of vain imagin'd pow'rs.
No Tityus° torn by vultures lies in hell;
Nor could the lobes of his rank liver swell
To that prodigious mass for their eternal meal:
Not tho' his monstrous bulk had cover'd o'er
Nine spreading acres,° or nine thousand more;   260
Not tho' the globe of earth had been the giant's floor:
Nor in eternal torments could he lie,
Nor could his corpse sufficient food supply.
But he's the Tityus, who by love oppress'd,
Or tyrant passion preying on his breast,

---

252. *Tantalus:* sentenced, according to the version alluded to here, to stand eternally under an overhanging rock in Hades which was always about to fall and
crush him (from his name, the English "tantalize"). 256. *Tityus:* sentenced
for his sexual approach to the virgin goddess Artemis to lie in Tartarus while two
vultures perpetually tore out pieces of his liver. 260. *Nine . . . acres:* the legendary size of Tityus' body.

And ever-anxious thoughts, is robb'd of rest.
The Sisyphus° is he, whom noise and strife
Seduce from all the soft retreats of life,
To vex the government, disturb the laws:
Drunk with the fumes of popular applause,   270
He courts the giddy crowd to make him great,
And sweats and toils in vain, to mount the sovereign seat.
For still to aim at pow'r, and still to fail,
Ever to strive, and never to prevail,
What is it, but, in reason's true account,
To heave the stone against the rising mount?
Which urg'd, and labor'd, and forc'd up with pain,
Recoils, and rolls impetuous down, and smokes along the plain.
Then still to treat thy ever-craving mind
With ev'ry blessing, and of ev'ry kind,   280
Yet never fill thy rav'ning appetite;
Tho' years and seasons vary thy delight,
Yet nothing to be seen of all the store,
But still the wolf within thee barks for more;
This is the fable's moral, which they tell
Of fifty foolish virgins° damn'd in hell
To leaky vessels, which the liquor spill;
To vessels of their sex, which none could ever fill.
As for the Dog,° the Furies, and their snakes,
The gloomy caverns, and the burning lakes,   290
And all the vain infernal trumpery,
They neither are, nor were, nor e'er can be.
But here on earth the guilty have in view
The mighty pains to mighty mischiefs due;
Racks, prisons, poisons, the Tarpeian rock,°
Stripes, hangmen, pitch, and suffocating smoke;
And last, and most, if these were cast behind,
Th' avenging horror of a conscious mind,
Whose deadly fear anticipates the blow,
And sees no end of punishment and woe;   300
But looks for more, at the last gasp of breath:

267. *Sisyphus:* for his fraud and avarice, punished in Hades by having to roll uphill a huge marble block, which always rolled down again as soon as he neared the top.   286. *foolish virgins:* for murdering their husbands at the suggestion of Danaüs, the fifty daughters of Danaüs were punished in Hades by being compelled eternally to carry water in a leaking vessel.   289. *Dog:* Cerberus, a three-headed monster guarding the entry to Hades.   295. *Tarpeian rock:* a cliff near Rome from which condemned traitors were thrown; named after Tarpeia, a legendary Roman traitor.

This makes a hell on earth, and life a death.
   Meantime, when thoughts of death disturb thy head;
Consider, Ancus, great and good,° is dead;
Ancus, thy better far, was born to die;
And thou, dost thou bewail mortality?
So many monarchs with their mighty state,
Who rul'd the world, were overrul'd by fate.
That haughty king,° who lorded o'er the main,
And whose stupendous bridge did the wild waves restrain,   310
(In vain they foam'd, in vain they threaten'd wreck,
While his proud legions march'd upon their back,)
Him death, a greater monarch, overcame;
Nor spar'd his guards the more, for their immortal name.
The Roman chief, the Carthaginian dread,
Scipio,° the thunderbolt of war, is dead,
And, like a common slave, by fate in triumph led.
The founders of invented arts are lost;
And wits, who made eternity their boast.
Where now is Homer, who possess'd the throne?   320
Th' immortal work remains, the mortal author's gone.
Democritus,° perceiving age invade,
His body weaken'd, and his mind decay'd,
Obey'd the summons° with a cheerful face;
Made haste to welcome death, and met him half the race.
That stroke ev'n Epicurus° could not bar,
Tho' he in wit surpass'd mankind, as far
As does the midday sun the midnight star.
And thou, dost thou disdain to yield thy breath,
Whose very life is little more than death?   330
More than one half by lazy sleep possess'd;

304. *Ancus . . . good:* legendary fourth king of Rome (640–616 B.C.), said to have formed the original Roman plebs by settling inhabitants from conquered Latin towns in Rome; also credited with several public works. 309. *haughty king:* Xerxes, who built his bridge of ships over the Hellespont. 316. *Scipio:* here a famous Roman general who defeated Hannibal in 202 B.C. and thus ended the Second Punic War. 322. *Democritus:* a fifth-century B.C. Greek philosopher; one of the earliest atomists; developed the physical foundations for a number of Epicurus' theories. 324. *Obey'd the summons:* Democritus, according to an ancient tradition, committed suicide by starvation after becoming more than ninety years old. The Epicureans did not recommend suicide, as the Stoics did, but thought it permissible. 326. *Epicurus:* Lucretius' philosophical source. Epicurus too thought that a logical conclusion of his mechanistic materialism must be that the gods, who might exist, do not interfere in human life. This is the only place in the entire poem where Epicurus is mentioned by name, which indicates the importance of the argument to Lucretius.

And when awake, thy soul but nods at best,
Day-dreams and sickly thoughts revolving in thy breast.
Eternal troubles haunt thy anxious mind,
Whose cause and cure thou never hop'st to find;
But still uncertain, with thyself at strife,
Thou wander'st in the labyrinth of life.
   O, if the foolish race of man, who find
A weight of cares still pressing on their mind,
Could find as well the cause° of this unrest,   340
And all this burden lodg'd within the breast;
Sure they would change their course, nor live as now,
Uncertain what to wish or what to vow.
Uneasy both in country and in town,
They search a place to lay their burden down.
One, restless in his palace, walks abroad,
And vainly thinks to leave behind the load;
But straight returns, for he's as restless there,
And finds there's no relief in open air.
Another to his villa would retire,   350
And spurs as hard as if it were on fire;
No sooner enter'd at his country door,
But he begins to stretch, and yawn, and snore;
Or seeks the city which he left before.
Thus every man o'erworks his weary will,
To shun himself, and to shake off his ill;
The shaking fit returns, and hangs upon him still.
No prospect of repose, nor hope of ease;
The wretch is ignorant of his disease;
Which known would all his fruitless trouble spare,   360
For he would know the world not worth his care;
Then would he search more deeply for the cause;
And study nature well, and nature's laws:
For in this moment lies not the debate,
But on our future, fix'd, eternal state;
That never-changing state, which all must keep,
Whom death has doom'd to everlasting sleep.
   Why are we then so fond of mortal life,
Beset with dangers, and maintain'd with strife?
A life which all our care can never save;   370
One fate attends us, and one common grave.
Besides, we tread but a perpetual round;
We ne'er strike out, but beat the former ground,

---

340. find . . . cause: through Epicureanism.

And the same mawkish joys in the same track are found.
For still we think an absent blessing best,
Which cloys, and is no blessing when possess'd;
A new arising wish expels it from the breast.
The fev'rish thirst of life increases still;
We call for more and more, and never have our fill,
Yet know not what tomorrow we shall try,   380
What dregs of life in the last draught may lie:
Nor, by the longest life we can attain,
One moment from the length of death we gain;
For all behind belongs to his eternal reign.
When once the Fates have cut the mortal thread,
The man as much to all intents is dead,
Who dies today, and will as long be so,
As he who died a thousand years ago.

From BOOK V

TRANSLATED BY W. H. D. ROUSE

. . . In the beginning[1] the earth gave forth grasses after their kinds and bright verdure about the hills and all over the plains, and the flowering meadows shone with the color of green; then to the various kinds of trees came a mighty struggle, as they raced at full speed to grow up into the air. As feathers and hair and bristles grow on the frame of four-footed creatures or the body of birds all strong-i'-the-wing, so then the new-born earth put forth herbage and trees first, and in the next place created the generations of mortal creatures, arising in many kinds and in many ways by different processes. For animals cannot have fallen from the sky, nor can creatures of the land have come out of the salt pools. It remains, therefore, that the earth deserves the name of mother[2] which she possesses, since from the earth all things have been produced. And even now many living creatures arise from the earth, formed by the rain and the warm heat of the sun, so that it is less wonderful if then more and larger ones arose, which grew up when earth and air were young. First the race of winged things and the different birds issued from their eggs being hatched in the springtime, even as now in summer the cicadas of their own accord leave their filmy husks, to seek life and living. Then first, look you, the earth gave forth the generations of mortal creatures. For there was great abundance of heat and moisture in the

---

[1] That is, in the world's infancy. The previous argument concerned the gradual evolution of the earth, the other planets and the rest of the universe out of collisions and chance combinations of atoms.   [2] Lucretius has eliminated the sky (air) and water ("salt pools") as the generators of human life, and since he considers fire an impossible source of life, earth alone of the four traditional elements remains.

fields; therefore wherever a suitable place was found, wombs would grow, holding to the earth by roots; and when in due time the age of the infants broke the bladders, fleeing from the moisture and seeking the air, nature would direct thither pores of the earth and make it discharge from these open veins a liquid like to milk, even as now when a woman has brought forth she is filled with sweet milk, because all that rush of nourishment is directed towards the breasts. Earth gave food for the children, warmth gave the raiment, the herbage a bed with abundance of down rich and soft. But the infancy of the world produced neither hard cold nor excessive heat nor winds of great force: for all things grow and gain strength together. . . .

Many were the monsters also that the earth then tried to make, springing up with wondrous appearance and frame: the hermaphrodite, between man and woman yet neither, different from both; some without feet, others again bereft of hands; some found dumb also without a mouth, some blind without face; some bound fast with all their limbs adhering to their bodies, so that they could do nothing and go nowhere, could neither avoid mischief nor take what they might need. So with the rest of like monsters and portents that she made, it was all in vain: since nature denied them growth, and they could not attain the desired flower of age nor find food nor join by the ways of Venus. For we see that living beings need many things in conjunction, so that they may be able by procreation to forge out the chain of the generations: first there must be food, next there must be a way for the life-giving seeds to ooze through the frame and be discharged from the body, and that male and female be joined they must both have the means to exchange mutual pleasures. . . .

But the race of men at that time[3] was much hardier on the land, as was fitting inasmuch as the hard earth had made it; built up within it was with bones larger and more solid, fitted with strong sinews throughout the flesh, not such as easily to be mastered by heat or cold or strange food or any ailment of the body. Through many lusters[4] of the sun rolling through the sky they passed their lives after the wide-wandering fashion of wild beasts. No sturdy guider of the curved plough was there, none knew how to work the fields with iron, to dig new shoots into the ground, to prune off old branches from the tall trees with a sickle. What sun and rain had given, what the earth had produced of her own accord, that was a gift enough to content their minds. Amidst the acorn-laden oaks they refreshed themselves for the most part; and the arbute-berries which in winter time you now see ripen with crimson color, then the earth bore in abundance and even larger than now. Many another kind of food besides the flowering infancy of the world then produced, hard but amply sufficient for poor mortals. But to

[3] Shortly after the earth had given birth to man. See the descriptions of the Golden Age in Hesiod, Ovid, and Virgil's *Fourth Eclogue*.   [4] A period of five years (between purificatory or "lustral" sacrifices).

quench thirst, rivers and springs invited them, as now the rushing of water down from the great mountains calls loud and far to the thirsting hordes of beasts. Next as they roamed abroad they dwelt in familiar woodland precincts of the Nymphs, whence they knew that some running rivulet issued rippling over the wet rocks, rippling over the rocks in abundant flow and dripping upon the green moss, with plenty left to splash and bubble over the level plain. Not yet did they know how to work things with fire, nor to use skins and to clothe themselves in the strippings of beasts; but they dwelt in the woods and forests and mountain caves, and hid their rough bodies in the underwoods when they had to escape the beating of wind and rain. They could not look to the common good, they knew not how to govern their intercourse by custom and law. Whatever prize fortune gave to each, that he carried off, every man taught to live and be strong for himself at his own will. And Venus joined the bodies of lovers in the woods; for either the woman was attracted by some mutual desire, or caught by the man's violent force and vehement lust, or by a bribe—acorns and arbute-berries or choice pears. And by the aid of their wonderful powers of hand and foot, they would hunt the woodland tribes of beasts with volleys of stones and ponderous clubs, overpowering many, shunning but a few in their lairs; and when night overtook them, like so many bristly hogs they just cast their savage bodies naked upon the ground, rolling themselves in leaves and boughs. Nor did they go seeking the day and the sun with great outcry over the country-side, wandering panic-stricken in the shadows of night,[5] but waited quiet and buried in sleep until the sun with rosy torch spread his light over the heavens. For since they had been accustomed from childhood always to see darkness and light return in alternate sequence, it was impossible that they should ever feel wonder, or fear lest everlasting night should possess the world, the sun's light being withdrawn for ever. Rather what troubled them was that the hordes of beasts often made their rest dangerous to them: and driven from their shelter, they would flee to the rocks and caves when a foaming boar appeared or a mighty lion, and at dead of night in terror would yield their leaf-strewn beds to the savage guests.

. . . In those days again, it was lack of food that drove fainting bodies to death; now contrariwise it is the abundance that overwhelms them. In those days men often unwittingly poured poison for themselves, now more skillfully taught they give poison to others.

Next, when they had got them huts and skins, and fire, and woman mated with man was appropriated to one, [and the laws of wedlock] [6] became known, and they saw offspring born of them, then first the human race began to grow soft. For the fire saw to it that their shivering bodies were

[5] According to some ancient authors, primitive man feared that the sun would never reappear once it set; Lucretius rejects this view. [6] The words in brackets are supplied by the translator for a line missing in the original.

less able to endure cold under the canopy of heaven, and Venus sapped their strength, and children easily broke their parents' proud spirit by coaxings. Then also neighbors began eagerly to join friendship amongst themselves to do no hurt and suffer no violence, and asked protection for their children and womankind, signifying by voice and gesture with stammering tongue that it was right for all to pity the weak. Nevertheless concord could not altogether he produced, but a good part, nay the most kept the covenant unblemished, or else the race of mankind would have been even then wholly destroyed, nor would birth and begetting have been able to prolong their posterity.

But the various sounds of the tongue nature drove them to utter, and convenience pressed out of them names for things, not far otherwise than very speechlessness is seen to drive children to the use of gesture, when it makes them point with the finger at things that are before them. For each feels to what purpose he is able to use his own powers. . . . Therefore to suppose that someone then distributed names amongst things, and from him that men learnt their first words, is folly.[7] For why should he have been able to mark all things with titles and to utter the various sounds of the tongue, and at the same time others not be thought able to have done it? Besides, if others had not also used these terms in their intercourse, whence was that foreknowledge of usefulness implanted, and whence did he first gain such power, as to know what he wanted to do and to see it in his mind's eye? . . . Lastly, what is so very wonderful in this business, if the human race, having active voices and tongues, could distinguish things by varying sounds to suit varying feelings? seeing that dumb animals, seeing that even wild beasts of all kinds are wont to utter sounds different and varying when they are in fear or pain, and when now joy begins to glow. . . . Therefore if different feelings compel animals, dumb though they are, to utter different sounds, how much more natural it is that mortal men should then have been able to mark different things with one sound or another! . . .

More and more daily they were shown how to change their former life and living for new ways, by those men of goodwill who were preeminent in genius and strong in mind. Kings began to found cities and to build a citadel for their own protection and refuge; and they divided cattle and lands, and gave them to each according to beauty and strength and genius: for beauty had great power, and strength had importance, in those days. Afterwards wealth was introduced and gold was discovered, which easily robbed both the strong and the handsome of their honor; for however strong and hand-

---

[7] Lucretius here alludes to a controversy about the origin of language. Some philosophers claimed, as Lucretius does here, that it developed naturally, whereas others thought that it was "made" by consent between men. Epicurus synthesized the two theories by differentiating between a "natural" stage and a stage of conscious name-giving.

some in body, men for the most part follow the party of the richer. But if one should guide his life by true principles, man's greatest riches is to live on a little with contented mind; for a little is never lacking. Yet men desired to be famous and powerful, that their fortune might stand fast upon a firm foundation, and that being wealthy they might be able to pass a quiet life: all in vain, since in the struggle to climb to the summit of honor they made their path full of danger; and even down from the summit, nevertheless, envy strikes them oftentimes like a thunderbolt and casts them with scorn into loathly Tartarus; since envy, like the thunderbolt, usually scorches the summits and all those that are elevated above others; so that it is indeed much better to obey in peace, than to desire to hold the world in fee and to rule kingdoms. Leave them then to be weary for nought, and to sweat blood in struggling along the narrow path of ambition; since their wisdom comes from the lips of others, and they pursue things on hearsay rather than from their own feelings. And this was in the beginning, as much as it is now and shall be without end.

Kings therefore were slain; the ancient majesty of thrones and proud scepters lay overthrown in the dust; the illustrious badge of the topmost head, bloodstained beneath the feet of the mob, bewailed its lost honor: for men are eager to tread underfoot what they have once too much feared. So things came to the uttermost dregs of confusion, when each man for himself sought dominion and exaltation. Then there were some who taught them to create magistrates, and established law, that they might be willing to obey statutes. For mankind, tired of living in violence, was fainting from its feuds, and so they were readier of their own will to submit to statutes and strict rules of law. . . .

. . . Therefore[8] mankind labors always in vain and to no purpose, consuming their days in empty cares, plainly because they know not the limit of possession, and how far it is ever possible for real pleasure to grow: and this little by little has carried life out into the deep sea, and has stirred up from the bottom the great billows of war.

But those watchful sentinels sun and moon, traveling with their light around the great revolving region of heaven, have taught men well that the seasons of the year come round, and that all is done on a fixed plan and in fixed order.

Already men lived fenced in with strong towers, the earth was divided up and distributed for cultivation, already every sea was covered with sail-flying ships, men had already allies and friends under formal treaty, when poets

[8] In the intervening passage Lucretius described the development of religion through awe and fear of natural phenomena; the development of mining and commerce, of arms and war, of agriculture and clothing—all of which was accompanied by an increase in material greed and a decline in the emotional quality of life.

began to commemorate doughty deeds in verse; nor had letters been invented long time before. For this reason our age cannot look back upon what happened before, unless in any respect reasoning shows the way.

Ships and agriculture, fortifications and laws, arms, roads, clothing and all else of this kind, life's prizes, its luxuries also from first to last, poetry and pictures, the shaping of statues by the artist, all these as men progressed gradually step by step were taught by practice and the experiments of the active mind. So by degrees time brings up before us every single thing, and reason lifts it into the precincts of light. For their intellect saw one thing after another grow famous amongst the arts, until they came to their highest point.

Cicero

The Dream of Scipio

TRANSLATED BY HEINRICH VON STADEN

Cicero (106–43 B.C.)

MARCUS TULLIUS CICERO, A ROMAN STATESMAN, ORATOR, philosopher, and man of letters, was perhaps one of the most influential authors in the history of antiquity. After studying oratory and law in Rome and philosophy in Athens and Rhodes, he became a successful lawyer and soon was prominent in politics. In 63 B.C. he was elected to the consulate, the highest Roman political office at the time, but later a reaction against his policies caused him to leave Rome. Eventually he returned to the city several times, but after Julius Caesar's murder in 44 B.C. Mark Antony, whom Cicero opposed, ordered his execution. In 43 B.C. Cicero—aged 64—was cornered by soldiers; his slaves were ready to defend him with their lives, but he told them to desist and surrendered. His head and hands were immediately cut off and taken to Rome, where, by order of Mark Antony, they were nailed to a public platform.

As a man and citizen Cicero may have been vain and fickle, but as an author he created a classical model for Latin prose. Fifty-six of his legal and political speeches survive, which have served as both fortunate and unfortunate models for Western writers. Also extant are works on rhetoric, a collection of more than eight hundred private letters that give a remarkable picture of his times and about ten philosophical works. In the latter he made available to the Latin-speaking world—including, subsequently, the medieval Latin world—the theories of Greek philosophers, particularly those of Plato and the philosophers of the Hellenistic period, such as Epicurus and the Stoics. Although Cicero was a philosophical eclectic, he was influenced more by the Stoics than by any other school of philosophy.

One of Cicero's most interesting philosophical works is *On the Commonwealth* or *The Republic,* of which large parts were rediscovered only in the nineteenth century. In addition to a design of a model state it includes analyses of the Roman constitution, of other forms of government, and of the ideal ruler and citizen. Much of it is based on Plato's *Republic,* but Cicero combined some of Plato's views with Stoic and other theories and, characteristically, transposed the entire discussion into the practical sphere of the Roman republic. The work concludes with the "Dream of Scipio."

The Dream of Scipio

The following account forms the concluding scene of a fictitious
dialogue set in the year 129 B.C. The only speaker in this part of
the dialogue is a famous Roman general and statesman, Publius
Cornelius Scipio Africanus the Younger. He tells about a conversation that took place between himself and his equally famous grandfather in a dream which he had twenty years previously.

Now when I had arrived in Africa[1] to serve, as you know, in the capacity
of military tribune,[2] there was nothing I wanted to do more than meet King
Masinissa who, for excellent reasons, was a close friend of my family.[3] When
I went to him, the old king embraced me and burst into tears. After a while
he looked up at the sky and said: "Highest Sun and you other heavenly
powers, I thank you that before I leave this life I may see, here in my own
kingdom and in this very house, Publius Cornelius Scipio, the sound of
whose name alone already restores me. Indeed, never did the memory of that
outstanding and invincible man, whose name he shares,[4] fade from my
mind!" Then I proceeded to question him about his Kingdom and he me
about our Republic and soon the whole day was over, spent in lengthy discussion.

Afterwards, when I had been entertained with regal sumptuousness, we
continued our conversation deep into the night while the old king spoke
about nothing but Africanus,[5] recollecting not only his deeds but also his
words. Later when we had parted to go to bed, an unusually deep sleep
overwhelmed me, because I was tired from the journey and because I had
been awake so late into the night. In my sleep Africanus himself appeared

[1] Scipio the Younger (the speaker) had gone to Africa in 149 B.C. to fight in the
third and last of three major wars (the "Punic Wars") between Rome and the
North African city of Carthage. This third war lasted from 149 B.C. to 146 B.C.
[2] Primarily an administrative officer. Six tribunes were normally attached to a
legion of 4,500 soldiers. [3] Scipio the Elder, grandfather of the present speaker,
restored and enlarged Masinissa's North African domain (Numidia) as a reward
for his active support of the Romans in the Second Punic War (218–201 B.C.).
[4] Scipio the Elder and his adopted grandson, Scipio the Younger, shared the same
name: Publius Cornelius Scipio Africanus. [5] Scipio the Elder.

to me. (I think probably because the king and I had talked about him; for it often happens that one's thoughts and conversations evoke something like them in one's dreams—just as Ennius[6] writes that Homer, about whom he used to think and speak very frequently, appeared to him in a dream.) In any case, Africanus stood before me in this dream with an appearance which was more familiar to me from pictures and statues of him than from his person. As soon as I recognized him, I shuddered, but he said: "Keep your presence of mind; do not be afraid, Scipio, and imprint my words on your memory.

"Do you see that city[7] over there which, though I compelled it to obey the Roman people, is now resuming its old war against us and cannot stay quiet and subdued?" As he said this, he pointed to Carthage from a highly elevated, bright and clear place which teemed with stars.[8] "I mean that city which you, as a soldier, have come here to besiege. Within two years you, as consul,[9] will destroy it, thus through your own achievement obtaining the byname which up to now you have possessed only through inheritance from me.[10] But after you have destroyed Carthage, celebrated your triumph, been censor,[11] and visited Egypt, Syria, Asia and Greece as an ambassador, you will be elected consul a second time in your absence, and bring to conclusion a very great war: you will obliterate Numantia![12] When you have been driven in triumph up to the Capitol in a processional chariot, however, you will find the state in turmoil because of the intrigues of one of my grandsons.[13]

"Then, Africanus, you will have to exhibit the clear light of your intellect, your ability, your cleverness. With regard to that time I foresee as it were a double way[14] determined for you by the fates. For when your life has run the course of seven annual revolutions of the sun eight different

[6] An early Roman poet (239 B.C.–169 B.C.) whose epic poem on the history of Rome, the *Annales,* lent him the status of "father of Latin poetry." In the first book of his poem he describes how Homer appeared to him in a dream. [7] Carthage. [8] Scipio the Elder is speaking to Scipio the Younger from heaven. [9] The highest Roman political office at the time; held by Scipio the Younger in 147 B.C. and again in 134 B.C. [10] Scipio the Elder received the last name "Africanus" in recognition of his victory over the Carthaginian general Hannibal in the Second Punic War; Scipio the Younger inherited the name when he became the elder Scipio's grandson by adoption, but now will deserve it through his own victories in the Third Punic War. [11] A Roman magistrate elected to regulate public morals, particularly of senators, and to supervise the quinquennial census. Scipio the Younger was censor in 142 B.C. His grandfather here is "predicting" a career that was well known to Cicero's contemporaries. [12] A center of resistance to the Roman conquest of Spain; destroyed by Scipio the Younger after a prolonged, massive siege in 133 B.C. [13] Tiberius Gracchus, whose land reforms offended wealthy and conservative Romans and inaugurated a century of civil discord. It was rumored that partisans of Gracchus had a hand in the death of Scipio the Younger. [14] On the one hand opposition from kinsmen such as Gracchus, on the other hand spectacular political successes.

times, and when these two numbers—seven and eight, each of which is considered perfect for a different reason—have completed this sum allotted to you in a natural cycle,[15] then the whole state will turn to you alone and to your name. To you the senate will look, and all the patriotic citizens, all our allies, all of the Latin race. And on you alone the safety of the state will depend. To make it brief: once you have escaped from the irreverent hands of your relatives, it will be your task to restore order to the republic as dictator." [16]

At this point Laelius[17] interrupted Scipio's account of his dream with an impatient exclamation, and the rest of the group groaned rather heavily, but Scipio smiled at them lightly and said: "Hush! Please do not wake me out of my dream yet; just listen for a little while to the rest of it."

"But so that you may be even more keen, Africanus,[18] to protect our state, take account of this: all those who have preserved, aided and extended their own country are assigned a definite, secure place in heaven, where they may enjoy an eternal life in happiness. For there is nothing in the realm of earth that is as pleasing to the highest god who rules the entire universe, as communities and groups of human beings associated and united by law—those groups which we call 'states.' And the men who direct and preserve these states come from heaven and return there."

At this point I was terrified through fear not so much of death as of my own treacherous relatives. Nevertheless I inquired whether he himself and my father Paulus and others whom we thought dead were actually alive.

"But of course," he said, "everybody is alive who has escaped from the bondage of his body as from a prison. In fact, it is your so-called life that is really death. Do you not see your father Paulus? Look, he is coming to you now!"

As soon as I caught sight of my father I burst into a flood of tears, but he embraced and kissed me, telling me to stop weeping. After I had suppressed my tears and was able to speak again, I said: "Please tell me, venerable and very best father, since this here in heaven is life, as I just heard Africanus say, why should I still linger on earth? Why not hasten up here to all of you?"

"That is not quite the way things work," my father replied. "For unless that god, whose temple[19] all of this is that you now see, has freed you from the bondage of your body, the entrance to this place cannot possibly be

---

[15] In 129 B.C., at the time of this dialogue, Scipio the Younger was almost 56 years old. The numbers eight and seven played a significant role in Greek and Roman religion and philosophy. [16] A constitutional magistrate, usually appointed for six months as an autocratic ruler to deal with a military, civil, or judiciary crisis. [17] A friend of the younger Scipio and participant in this dialogue. [18] Scipio the Younger, still addressed in heaven by his grandfather. [19] In Latin, *templum* originally designated an area of the sky that was marked off for divination by an official augur. In this dialogue it designates the entire universe, as the celestial temple of a supreme god and of divine planets and stars.

accessible to you. For human beings were generated with the condition that they protect the spherical body which you can see in the center of this temple, the one called earth. And the soul [20] given to humans was taken from these eternal fires which you call planets and stars, these spherical and round fires (which in turn are given life through divine souls and complete their cycles and revolutions at an amazing speed). Consequently, Publius, you and all reverent and good men must keep your souls in the custody of your bodies, and must not leave human life against the will of the god who gave you your souls—lest you might seem to have shirked the very duty assigned to man by god. Instead of leaving earth, in other words, Scipio, you should follow the example of your grandfather here and of me, your father, and cultivate justice and respectful duty, which are important in relations both with one's parents and relatives and, in particular, with one's country. It is such a life that leads to heaven, to this gathering up here of those who have already completed their lives and, having been released from their bodies, live in the place you now see."

A sphere that was shining with a brighter blaze than the various other fires then caught my eye, and he said: "What you see there is the one which you on earth call the Milky Circle,[21] a term borrowed from Greek."

As I stared around thoughtfully from there everything else seemed brightly clear and astonishingly beautiful. There were, for example, stars which we have never seen from down here on earth, and the sizes of the stars were such as we have never suspected. The smallest of them was the one furthest from heaven and closest to earth, the one which always shines with light from a source outside itself.[22] Those stars easily beat the size of the earth; in fact, the earth itself seemed so small to me that I was almost ashamed of our empire which, as it were, only scratches a little dot on the earth's surface.

When I gazed down more intently at the earth Africanus said: "Please, how long will you keep your mind glued to the ground? Do you not even notice into what temples you have come? Look, here are the nine circles or rather spherical bodies by which everything is joined together. One of them is the heavenly sphere, the outermost one which encircles all the rest and is itself the highest god, enclosing and containing the rest. To it the eternally revolving courses of the stars are attached. And placed beneath this outermost sphere you see seven other spherical bodies, which revolve with a motion and direction opposite to that of the heavenly sphere. The highest of these belongs to the planet which people on earth call Saturn. Next there is that bright light belonging to what it called Jupiter, favorable and beneficent to mankind. Then comes what you call Mars, reddish and terrifying

[20] "Soul" here refers primarily to the principle of life, which enters the body at birth but, being eternal, survives the death of the body.   [21] The Milky Way.
[22] The Moon, which gets its light from the Sun.

for those on earth. Below Mars, the middle of the entire universal region is occupied by the Sun, the leader, sovereign and director of the other star-lights.[23] As the mind and ordering principle of the universe the Sun is of such a huge size that it illuminates and floods all things with its light. Like companions the orbits of Venus and Mercury attend the Sun, and in the lowest of these seven circles revolves the Moon, lit by the rays of the Sun. But whereas everything above the Moon is eternal, already just below the Moon there are only mortal and frail, perishable things—with the exception, of course, of the souls which have been given to mankind as a gift from the gods. For what lies in the center of the universe, as a ninth sphere, namely the earth, on the one hand does not move and on the other is the very lowest sphere, so that all masses tend towards it through their natural downward inclination."

I looked at these things in a daze and, once I composed myself again, asked him: "What is that? There, listen! What is this loud and pleasant sound flooding my ears?"

"That," he replied, "is the sound which arises from the rush and motion of the spheres themselves; its distinctness comes from the distances or intervals between the spheres which, though unequal, are differentiated according to definitely regulated proportions. By mingling in due proportion the high tones of some spheres with the low tones of others, it produces various consistent harmonies. You see, such vast motions as those of the spheres cannot take place in silence, and nature brings it about that an extreme on one side sounds high tones and on another low tones. Thus it happens that the highest orbit (that of the star-bearing heaven itself), whose revolution is faster than that of the others, moves with a high, sharp sound, whereas the lowest sphere (the lunar sphere) moves with the deepest sound. For the earth, though as the ninth sphere it is lower than the Moon, remains unmoved and is always stuck to one single place, embracing the center of the universe. But the eight revolving planets, of which two have the same speed, produce seven sounds of different pitch (and this number seven is the unifying bond between virtually all things). By imitating the proportions of these harmonies on string instruments and in songs, educated men have opened up for themselves a kind of return to this place of celestial harmony; just as others, endowed with outstanding intelligence, have cultivated the study of these divine things in their human life. But when the sound of these spheres flooded the ears of human beings, they grew deaf and now, in fact, you humans have no duller sense than that of hearing—just as the inhabitants of the place where the Nile thunders down from very high

---

[23] The concept of a heliocentric universe was not unknown in antiquity, but Cicero, while conceding a special place to the sun, here follows the more popular notion of a geocentric universe. Most of his ideas about astronomy are derived from Plato's *Republic* in this work.

mountains to the cataract you call Catadupa have lost their hearing because of the enormous noise. So great is the noise produced by the extremely rapid revolutions of the universe that human ears cannot perceive it, just as you cannot stare directly at the sun without your sharp eyesight and vision being overcome by its rays."

Although I was admiring these things with awe, I continually turned my eyes back to the earth.

"I notice," Africanus then said, "that you are still fixing your eyes on the seat and home of mankind. Should it seem small to you—as indeed it really is—then always look at the heavenly region and despise human things. For what prestige could you gain from the talk of men or what fame that is really worth striving for? You yourself see that the earth is inhabited only thinly, in a few limited places, and that there are vast deserted areas intervening between the few inhabited 'stains.' And you also notice that the inhabitants of the earth are not only so separated from each other that no communication can really flow between them from one group to another, but that some of them also stand at an oblique angle to you, others at cross angles, and still others diametrically on the opposite side of earth.[24] Surely you could not expect any fame from these people?

"Moreover, you notice that the earth is bound and encircled with 'belts,' of which two are at opposite ends from each other. These two 'belts' or zones, propped against the poles of the sky on either side, have become congealed with ice, whereas the central and largest belt is scorched by the glowing heat of the Sun. Two belts are habitable. One is southern (where people stand and press their tracks exactly opposite to yours) and has no direct relation to your nation at all. The other is this one, situated in the north, which you inhabit—but look what a slim portion of it you occupy! For the whole land area in which you live,[25] narrow from north to south and wider from west to east, is really only a kind of island surrounded by the sea which you on earth call the 'Atlantic' or the 'Great Sea' or 'Oceanus' but which, for all its great names, is really small, as you can see from here.

"Now did your name or that of any of us ever go beyond these cultivated and well-known parts of the earth, and either traverse the Caucasus mountains, which you see over here, or cross the Ganges river over there? Who will ever hear about you at the other extremes of the earth, where the sun rises or sets, or in the far north or south? When these are sliced off and subtracted, you can see right away in what narrow confines your fame would like to inflate itself. And even those very people who now talk about us—how long will they continue to do so?

[24] That is, because of the round shape of the earth, people on various parts of its surface stand at varying angles to one another. Cicero interprets this as proof of the unbridgeable isolation of nations from each other.   [25] That is, not just Italy, but the entire Roman Empire.

"Yes, even if the offspring of future generations of men, having heard eulogies of each of us from their fathers, should desire to transmit such praise to posterity—even then we could not attain durable, let alone eternal, fame. For floods and cosmic conflagrations[26] will always recur on earth at given intervals. But what difference would it make anyway whether those who live after you mention you, if those who lived before you never did? Men of previous generations certainly were not fewer and, in fact, they were better. What difference does it all make then, particularly since not one of the people who can now hear mention of you is able to remember the events even of a single year. For people like to measure a year only by the revolution of the Sun, that is of a *single* star only; but in reality one can only speak of 'the course of a year' when *all* the stars have returned to their starting point and have, at long intervals, restored their original appearance throughout the sky. I scarcely dare say how many generations of men would be contained in such a cosmic year,[27] but let me give you an example of it. Since it once appeared to men that the sun was fading and becoming extinguished—namely at the time when the soul of Romulus[28] entered into these very sanctuaries up here—therefore you should recognize that a cosmic year will only have been completed when the Sun, once again, is eclipsed at the same place and the same time, after all the constellations and stars have been recalled to their initial position. But you should know that not even a twentieth of this cosmic year has yet passed.

"Consequently, if you despair of ever returning here to this celestial region, in which there is every reward for great and outstanding men, then of what small value, after all, is that fame among men, which can barely last a fractional part of a single year! If therefore you wish to look up high and contemplate this eternal home, you should not yield to the talk of the masses nor place any expectation concerning your affairs in rewards from human beings. Instead, excellence itself, through its own allurements, should draw you to true honor. Let it be the concern of others what they want to say about you—for talk they will in any case. But all their talk will be confined by the narrow limits of those regions you see, nor did talk about anyone ever last eternally; it dies with the death of men and is extinguished in the oblivion of posterity."

After these words of his I said: "Africanus, if indeed the passage to heaven lies open for men who have earned it by service to their country, then—now that such a remarkable reward has been revealed—I shall strive for it much more vigilantly than before, even though from my earliest youth

---

[26] The Stoic philosophers taught that a cosmic fire destroys the universe periodically. [27] In antiquity astronomers calculated that a cosmic year lasts anywhere from 12,000 to 15,000 years. [28] A legendary hero who founded Rome, supposedly in 753 B.C. He was believed to have died in 716 B.C., almost 570 years before the date of Scipio's vision.

I have followed in the tracks of my father and in yours, and have not been indifferent to the honor you won."

"Make every effort," he replied, "and take into account that only this body of yours is mortal, not you yourself. For you are not really what your outward appearance suggests; but rather, each person's mind [29] is his real self— not that physical shape to which one can point. Recognize then that you are a 'god,' if indeed that which possesses the vital power of life is a 'god,' that which feels, remembers, foresees, and which rules, directs and moves the body of which it is in charge, even as a sovereign god directs this universe. And just as the eternal god himself moves a universe which is in part perishable, so too man's eternal mind moves his frail and transitory body.

"You see, that which always continues moving is eternal. But that which imparts motion to something else and is itself in turn moved by something else must necessarily end its life when its motion ends. Accordingly, only that which moves itself never ceases to be moved, since it never deserts itself. In fact, that which moves itself is also the fountain and primary cause of motion for all others that are moved. A primary cause,[30] however, has no origin, since everything arises from the primary cause, and it cannot itself be born out of any other thing. Nor could something be a primary cause if it were born out of another source; and if the primary cause never had a beginning in time, then indeed it also will never have an end. For a primary cause, once extinguished, could not itself be reborn from another cause nor could it create another out of itself, if indeed all things must arise from a primary cause. So it follows that the beginning of motion is rooted in that which is moved by itself and can neither be born nor die. Otherwise the whole sky and all nature would have to collapse and come to a halt, and could obtain no power from which it might get an initial impulse for motion again.

"Consequently, since it is now transparently clear that whatever is self-moved is also eternal, who could possibly deny that this essential power has been assigned to souls? For everything that is set in motion by an external impulse is lifeless (that is, without soul), whereas whatever is alive is moved by an internal motion of its own. And this is the very essence and power of the soul: to move itself! If then the soul alone, of all things, is self-moving, surely it has no beginning and is eternal. Therefore train it for the highest purposes! Of these surely the best are those that have to do with the security and well-being of one's country. A soul which is engaged and trained in such concerns will fly more rapidly to this place, its proper abode and home. And it will speed here all the more rapidly if, while it is still enclosed in the body, it already extends outside the body; and if, by fixing its gaze on things

[29] The "mind" or intellect is here conceived of as the dominating part of the "soul" or principle of life. [30] The word here used for "primary cause" also has strong connotations of "principle" and "beginning."

beyond, it detaches itself as much as possible from the body. The souls of those, however, who have surrendered to sensual pleasures, who have offered themselves as 'attendants' to these pleasures, and who have violated the laws of gods and men at the prompting of those desires that serve physical pleasures, flutter around the earth after escaping from their bodies, and do not return here to this celestial place until they have been harassed and tormented for many ages."

He left me then; I awoke from my sleep.

Virgil

FROM *The Aeneid*

TRANSLATED BY ROLFE HUMPHRIES

Virgil (70–19 B.C.)

Publius Vergilius Maro, better known as Virgil, was born in the northern Italian town of Mantua. He was educated in Cremona, Milan, and Rome, and then attached himself to an Epicurean circle in Naples. In his early manhood he established a wide reputation as a gifted poet, and because of this he was introduced to Octavian—who was to become the emperor Augustus—and to the famous patron of the arts, Maecenas. They remained his friends and supporters to the end of his life.

The earliest work that is attributed to Virgil with certainty is the *Eclogues* ("Selections"), a collection of pastoral poems. These were followed by his most polished work, the *Georgics,* a didactic poem on farming. During the last eleven years of his life Virgil worked on *The Aeneid,* the national epic of the Romans. The emperor Augustus took an active interest in the growth of the poem, and in Roman literary circles enthusiastic expectations were voiced frequently. Although the poem had soon been completed in outline, Virgil never finished it and on his deathbed tried to prevent its publication. After his death, however, the unfinished poem was published at the order of Augustus.

The Aeneid tells the story of a mythical Trojan hero, Aeneas, who survived the capture of Troy by the Greeks and set out to find a new home in the "West" (Italy). His voyage, like that of Odysseus, was beset by storms, adventures, temptations, and constant delays. At length, after seven years' wandering, he landed in Italy, where the king of the Latins gave Aeneas his daughter in marriage. But the marriage was opposed by some of the native Italians, and only after numerous battles (modeled after those in the *Iliad*) did Aeneas finally defeat their leader, Turnus, in a decisive duel. At this point *The Aeneid* ends; but it was common knowledge in Rome that the Julian clan, of which the emperor Augustus was a member, traced its origin to Aeneas' son Iulus. It was also recognized that Virgil characterized Aeneas as a prefiguration of the ideal Roman ruler, who possesses the self-sacrificial devotion to public duty which Cicero had described in his *Republic* and which, the poem implies, characterized Augustus.

The Aeneid, in other words, sets out to reveal the story of those seeds of Roman history that had come to full flowering under the emperor Augustus. After decades of civil wars, Augustus inaugurated a period of peace, apparent stability, and generous cultural patronage. Virgil tried to show the significance of these developments in a larger mythological and historical context. Despite a persistent undercurrent of pessimism, he seemed to interpret the emperor Augustus as a descendant, in every sense, of the mythical founder of the Roman race, Aeneas, and the Augustan age as the fulfillment of the promise that the gods had made Aeneas when he sacrificed some of his own inclinations in order to found a new city in Italy.

The Aeneid

Arms and the man° I sing, the first who came,
Compelled by fate, an exile out of Troy,
To Italy and the Lavinian° coast,
Much buffeted on land and on the deep
By violence of the gods, through that long rage,
That lasting hate, of Juno's.° And he suffered
Much, also, in war, till he should build his town
And bring his gods to Latium, whence, in time,
The Latin race, the Alban° fathers, rose
And the great walls of everlasting Rome.   10
    Help me, O Muse, recall the reasons: why,
Why did the queen of heaven° drive a man
So known for goodness, for devotion, through
So many toils and perils? Was there slight,
Affront, or outrage? Is vindictiveness
An attribute of the celestial mind?
    There was an ancient city, Carthage, once
Founded by Tyrians,° facing Italy
And Tiber's° mouth, far-off, a wealthy town,

---

1. the man: Aeneas, son of the goddess Venus and the Trojan Anchises; partici-
pant in the Trojan War and a leader of the surviving Trojans.   *3. Lavinian:* in
the region of Lavinium, the city founded by Aeneas on the coast of Latium (a
district south of Rome).   *6. Juno:* often identified with the Greek Hera. In the
Iliad, she was hostile to the Trojans because Paris judged her inferior to Venus
(Aphrodite) in beauty. In this poem she is not only anti-Trojan but also pro-
Carthaginian.   *9. Alban:* reference to Alba Longa, a Latin city founded on the
Alban Hills southeast of Rome by Aeneas' son Ascanius or Iulus. From it came
Romulus and Remus, the legendary founders of Rome.   *12. queen of heaven:*
Juno, as wife of the supreme god, Jupiter, is "queen."   *18. Tyrians:* Phoenecians
from Tyro. The North African city Carthage was their chief colony in the western
Mediterranean. In *The Aeneid* Tyrians more specifically means Carthaginians.
19. Tiber: river in central Italy; Rome was built on its southern bank. Its mouth
faces southwest.

War-loving, and aggressive; and Juno held   20
Even her precious Samos° in less regard.
Here were her arms, her chariot, and here,
Should fate at all permit, the goddess burned
To found the empire of the world forever.
But, she had heard, a Trojan race would come,
Some day, to overthrow the Tyrian towers,
A race would come, imperious people, proud
In war, with wide dominion, bringing doom
For Libya.° Fate willed it so. And Juno
Feared, and remembered: there was the old war   30
She fought at Troy for her dear Greeks; her mind
Still fed on hurt and anger; deep in her heart
Paris' decision rankled, and the wrong
Offered her slighted beauty; and the hatred
Of the whole race; and Ganymede's° honors—
All that was fuel to fire; she tossed and harried
All over the seas, wherever she could, those Trojans
Who had survived the Greeks and fierce Achilles,
And so they wandered over many an ocean,
Through many a year, fate-hounded. Such a struggle   40
It was to found the race of Rome! . . .

*In the following passage Virgil describes how Juno used a storm to batter
Aeneas' fleet and separate him from his companions, until he found refuge
on the Carthaginian coast. Juno's storm is comparable to the storms created
by Poseidon to delay Odysseus in* The Odyssey.

*Aeneas and his friend, Achates, left their ship after the storm to explore
the strange country. Aeneas' mother, Venus, intervened to reassure him
that his ships were safe and to guide him to the city of Carthage, which had
recently been founded by the queen of Carthage, Dido.*

And they went on, where the little pathway led them
To rising ground; below them lay the city,
Majestic buildings now, where once were hovels,
A wonder to Aeneas, gates and bustle
And well-paved streets, the busy Tyrians toiling

21. *Samos:* Aegean island off the west coast of Asia Minor, well-known as a center
of the worship of Hera or Juno. 29. *Libya:* that is, as part of Africa. In *The
Aeneid* it is often identified specifically with the area around Carthage. 35.
Ganymede: a Trojan boy, taken up into heaven by Jupiter. This further incited
Juno's hatred of the Trojans.

With stones for walls and citadel, or marking
Foundations for their homes, drainage and furrow,
All under ordered process. They dredge harbors,
Set cornerstones, quarry the rock, where someday   50
Their theater will tower. They are like bees
In early summer over the country flowers
When the sun is warm, and the young of the hive emerge,
And they pack the molten honey, bulge the cells
With the sweet nectar, add new loads, and harry
The drones away from the hive, and the work glows,
And the air is sweet with bergamot and clover.
"Happy the men whose walls already rise!"
Exclaims Aeneas, gazing on the city,
And enters there, still veiled in cloud °—a marvel!—   60
And walks among the people, and no one sees him.
    There was a grove in the middle of the city,
Most happy in its shade; this was the place
Where first the Tyrians, tossed by storm and whirlwind,
Dug up the symbol royal Juno showed them,
The skull of a war-horse,° a sign the race to come
Would be supreme in war and wealth, for ages,
And Dido here was building a great temple
In Juno's honor, rich in gifts, and blessed
With the presence of the goddess. Lintel and rafter   70
Were bronze above bronze stairways, and bronze portals
Swung on bronze hinges. Here Aeneas first
Dared hope for safety, find some reassurance
In hope of better days: a strange sight met him,
To take his fear away. Waiting the queen,
He stood there watching, under the great temple,
Letting his eyes survey the city's fortune,
The artist's workmanship, the craftsman's labor,
And there, with more than wonder, he sees the battles
Fought around Troy, and the wars whose fame had traveled   80
The whole world over; there is Agamemnon,
Priam, and Menelaus, and Achilles,
A menace to them all. He is moved to tears.
"What place in all the world," he asks Achates,
"Is empty of our sorrow? There is Priam!

60. *cloud:* Venus surrounded Aeneas and Achates with a mist to render them invisible to the Carthaginians.   66. *skull of a war-horse:* a sign that was interpreted to mean that (1) the Carthaginians would live in a rich land, which could support horses, and (2) they would be skilled at warfare.

Look! even here there are rewards for praise,
There are tears for things, and what men suffer touches
The human heart. Dismiss your fear; this story
Will bring some safety to you." Sighing often,
He could not turn his gaze away; it was only   90
A picture on a wall, but the sight afforded
Food for the spirit's need. He saw the Greeks,
Hard-pressed, in flight, and Trojans coming after,
Or, on another panel, the scene reversed,
Achilles in pursuit, his own men fleeing;
He saw, and tears came into his eyes again,
The tents of Rhesus, snowy-white, betrayed
In their first sleep by bloody Diomedes
With many a death, and the fiery horses driven
Into the camp, before they ever tasted   100
The grass of Troy, or rank from Xanthus' river.°
Another scene showed Troilus,° poor youngster,
Running away, his arms flung down; Achilles
Was much too good for him; he had fallen backward
Out of his car, but held the reins, and the horses
Dragged him along the ground, his hair and shoulders
Bounding in dust, and the spear making a scribble.
And there were Trojan women, all in mourning,
With streaming hair, on their way to Pallas' temple,
Bearing, as gift, a robe, but the stern goddess   110
Kept her gaze on the ground. Three times Achilles
Had dragged the body of Hector around the walls,
And was selling it for money. What a groan
Came from Aeneas' heart, seeing that spoil,
That chariot, and helpless Priam reaching
His hands, unarmed, across the broken body!
And he saw himself there, too, fighting in battle
Against Greek leaders, he saw the Eastern columns,
And swarthy Memnon's arms.° Penthesilea,°
The Amazon, blazes in fury, leading   120
Her crescent-shielded thousands, a golden buckle

101. *Xanthus' river*: an oracle predicted that Troy would not be captured if the
horses of the Thracian king Rhesus—a Trojan ally who arrived just prior to the
end of the war—ate Trojan grass and drank the water of the Trojan river Xanthus.
In a secret attack at night, Diomedes and Odysseus killed the king and stole his
horses.   102. *Troilus*: young son of Priam, killed by Achilles.   119. *Memnon's
arms*: an Ethiopian ally of the Trojans against the Greeks; his arms were made by
a god. *Penthesilea*: queen of the Amazons (mythical women warriors who fought
on the Trojan side); killed by Achilles.

Below her naked breast, a soldieress
Fighting with men.
                            And as he watched these marvels
In one long fascinated stare of wonder,
Dido, the queen, drew near; she came to the temple
With a great train, all majesty, all beauty,
As on Eurotas' ° riverside, or where
Mount Cynthus° towers high, Diana leads
Her bands of dancers, and the Oreads° follow
In thousands, right and left, the taller goddess,   130
The quiver-bearing maiden, and Latona°
Is filled with secret happiness, so Dido
Moved in her company, a queen, rejoicing,
Ordering on her kingdom's rising glory.
At Juno's portal, under the arch of the temple,
She took her throne, a giver of law and justice,
A fair partitioner of toil and duty,
And suddenly Aeneas, from the crowd,
Saw Trojan men° approaching, brave Cloanthus,
Sergestus, Antheus, and all those others   140
Whom the black storm had driven here and yonder.
This he cannot believe, nor can Achates,
Torn between fear and joy. They burn with ardor
To seek their comrades' handclasp, but confusion
Still holds them in the cloud: what can have happened?
They watch from the cover of mist: men still were coming
From all the ships, chosen, it seemed, as pleaders
For graciousness before the temple, calling
Aloud: what fortune had been theirs, he wonders,
Where had they left the ships; why were they coming?   150
They were given audience; Ilioneus,°
Senior to all, began: "O Queen, whom Jove
Has given the founding of a great new city,
Has given to bridle haughty tribes with justice,
We, pitiful Trojans, over every ocean
Driven by storm, make our appeal: keep from us
The terrible doom of fire; protect our vessels;

127. *Eurotas:* river in the Peloponnesus; flows near Sparta, which was a center of the cult of Artemis (Latin, Diana).   128. *Mount Cynthus:* on the island of Delos, traditional birthplace of Diana or Artemis.   129. *Oreads:* mountain nymphs. 131. *Latona:* mother of Diana and Apollo; often identified with the Greek goddess Leto.   139. *Trojan men:* commanders of Aeneas' ships, from whom Juno's storm had separated him.   151. *Ilioneus:* an old and respected Trojan traveling with Aeneas.

Have mercy on a decent race; consider
Our lot with closer interest. We have not come
To ravish Libyan homes, or carry plunder　　　　　　160
Down to the shore. We lack the arrogance
Of conquerors; there is no aggression in us.
There is a place which Greeks have given a name,
The Land in the West; it is powerful in arms,
Rich in its soil; Oenotrians° used to live there,
And now, the story goes, a younger people
Inhabit it, calling themselves Italians
After their leader's name.° We were going there
When, big with storm and cloud, Orion rising
Drove us on hidden quicksands, and wild winds　　　170
Scattered us over the waves, by pathless rocks
And the swell of the surge. A few of us have drifted
Here to your shores. What kind of men are these,
What barbarous land permits such attitudes?
We have been denied the welcome of the beach,
Forbidden to set foot on land; they rouse
All kinds of war against us. You despise,
It may be, human brotherhood, and arms
Wielded by men. But there are gods, remember,
Who care for right and wrong. Our king Aeneas　　180
May be alive; no man was ever more just,
More decent ever, or greater in war and arms.
If fate preserves him still, if he still breathes
The welcome air, above the world of shadows,
Fear not; to have treated us with kindly service
Need bring you no repentance. We have cities
In Sicily as well, and King Acestes°
Is one of us, from Trojan blood. We ask you
To let us beach our battered fleet, make ready
Beams from the forest timber, mend our oarage,　　190
Seek Italy and Latium, glad at knowing
Our king and comrades rescued. But if safety
Is hopeless for him now, and Libyan water
Has been his grave, and if his son Iulus
Is desperate, or lost, grant us permission
At least to make for Sicily, whence we came here,

---

165. *Oenotrians:* legendary original inhabitants of southwest Italy.　168. *leader's name:* Italus.　187. *King Acestes:* king of Trojan descent; settled in Sicily before Aeneas's arrival.

Where King Acestes has a dwelling for us."
The Trojans, as he ended, all were shouting,
And Dido, looking down, made a brief answer:
"I am sorry, Trojans; put aside your care,   200
Have no more fear. The newness of the kingdom
And our strict need compel to me such measures—
Sentries on every border, far and wide.
But who so ignorant as not to know
The nation of Aeneas, manly both
In deeds and people, and the city of Troy?
We are not as dull as that, we folk from Carthage;
The sun shines on us here. Whether you seek
The land in the west, the sometime fields of Saturn,°
Or the Sicilian realms and king Acestes,   210
I will help you to the limit; should you wish
To settle here and share this kingdom with me,
The city I found is yours; draw up your ships;
Trojan and Tyrian I treat alike.
Would, also, that your king were here, Aeneas,
Driven by that same wind. I will send good men
Along the coast to seek him, under orders
To scour all Libya; he may be wandering
Somewhere, in woods or town, surviving shipwreck."
    Aeneas and Achates both were eager   220
To break the cloud;° the queen inspired their spirit
With her address. Achates asked Aeneas:
"What do we do now, goddess-born? You see
They all are safe, our vessels and our comrades,
Only one missing, and we saw him drowning,
Ourselves, beneath the waves; all other things
Confirm what Venus told us." And as he finished,
The cloud around them broke, dissolved in air,
Illumining Aeneas, like a god,
Light radiant around his face and shoulders,   230
And Venus gave him all the bloom of youth,
Its glow, its liveliness, as the artist adds
Luster to ivory, or sets in gold
Silver or marble. No one saw him coming
Until he spoke: "You seek me; here I am,
Trojan Aeneas, saved from the Libyan waves.

209. *Saturn*: the god was frequently associated positively with Italy ("Land of the West" or "Hesperia"), particularly as the god who ruled in Italy during the Golden Age of man. 221. *cloud*: the mist in which Venus had shrouded them.

Worn out by all the perils of land and sea,
In need of everything, blown over the great world,
The means to thank our only pitier   240
A remnant left by the Greeks, Dido, we lack
For offer of a city and a home.
If there is justice anywhere, if goodness
Means anything to any power, if gods
At all regard good people, may they give
The great rewards you merit. Happy the age,
Happy the parents who have brought you forth!
While rivers run to sea, while shadows move
Over the mountains, while the stars burn on,
Always, your praise, your honor, and your name,
Whatever land I go to, will endure."   250
His hand went out to greet his men, Serestus,
Gyas, Cloanthus, Ilioneus,
The others in their turn. And Dido marveled
At his appearance, first, and all that trouble
He had borne up under; there was a moment's silence
Before she spoke: "What chance, what violence,
O goddess-born, has driven you through danger,
From grief to grief? Are you indeed that son
Whom Venus bore Anchises? I remember
When Teucer° came to Sidon,° as an exile   260
Seeking new kingdoms, and my father helped him,
My father, Belus, conqueror of Cyprus.
From that time on I have known about your city,
Your name, and the Greek kings, and the fall of Troy
Even their enemies would praise the Trojans,
Or claim descent from Teucer's° line. I bid you
Enter my house. I, too, am fortune-driven
Through many sufferings; this land at last
Has brought me rest. Not ignorant of evil,
I know one thing, at least—to help the wretched."   270
And so she led Aeneas to the palace,
Proclaiming sacrifice at all the temples
In honor of his welcome, and sent presents
To his comrades at the shore, a score of bullocks,

260. *Teucer:* here a legendary Greek hero who, after being exiled from Salamis,
wandered until he founded a city on Cyprus. *Sidon:* Phoenician city from which
Dido came.   266. *Teucer:* here a different Teucer, an ancestor of the kings of
Troy; the Trojans are therefore often called "Teucrians." Dido, however, confuses
the two Teucers.

A hundred swine, a hundred ewes and lambs
In honor of the joyous day. The palace,
Within, is made most bright with pomp and splendor,
The halls prepared for feasting. Crimson covers
Are laid, with fine embroidery, and silver
Is heavy on the tables; gold, engraven,   280
Recalls ancestral prowess, a tale of heroes
From the race's first beginnings. . . .

*Dido, at the ensuing banquet for Aeneas, requested him to tell her about
the fall of Troy and about his travels and adventures in search of a new
country. Like Odysseus at the banquet of the Phaeacians, Aeneas complied
by relating these events in vivid detail. As he did so Dido—who had sworn
an oath of lifelong fidelity to her dead husband—fell increasingly in love
with Aeneas. For different reasons the goddesses Venus and Juno, the one
his mother, the other his arch-enemy, encouraged this passion. The poet here
resumes just after Aeneas completed his narration.*

From BOOK IV

But the queen finds no rest. Deep in her veins
The wound is fed; she burns with hidden fire.
His manhood, and the glory of his race
Are an obsession with her, like his voice,
Gesture and countenance. On the next morning,
After a restless night, she sought her sister:
"I am troubled, Anna, doubtful, terrified,
Or am I dreaming? What new guest is this   290
Come to our shores? How well he talks, how brave
He seems in heart and action! I suppose
It must be true; he does come from the gods.
Fear proves a bastard spirit. He has been
So buffeted by fate. What endless wars
He told of! Sister, I must tell you something:
Were not my mind made up, once and for all,
Never again to marry, having been
So lost when Sychaeus° left me for the grave,
Slain by my murderous brother at the altar,   300
Were I not sick forever of the torch

299. *Sychaeus:* Dido's first husband, who was murdered by her brother Pygmalion,
king of the Phoenician seaport Tyre.

And bridal bed, here is the only man
Who has moved my spirit, shaken my weak will.
I might have yielded to him. I recognize
The marks of an old fire. But I pray, rather,
That earth engulf me, lightning strike me down
To the pale shades and everlasting night
Before I break the laws of decency.
My love has gone with Sychaeus; let him keep it,
Keep it with him forever in the grave."   310
She ended with a burst of tears. "Dear sister,
Dearer than life," Anna replied, "why must you
Grieve all your youth away in loneliness,
Not know sweet children, or the joys of love?
Is that what dust demands, and buried shadows?
So be it. You have kept your resolution
From Tyre to Libya, proved it by denying
Iarbas° and a thousand other suitors
From Africa's rich kingdoms. Think a little.
Whose lands are these you settle in? Getulians,°   320
Invincible in war, the wild Numidians,°
Unfriendly Syrtes,° ring us round, and a desert
Barren with drought, and the Barcaean° rangers.
Why should I mention Tyre, and wars arising
Out of Pygmalion's threats? And you, my sister,
Why should you fight against a pleasing passion?
I think the gods have willed it so, and Juno
Has helped to bring the Trojan ships to Carthage.
What a great city, sister, what a kingdom
This might become, rising on such a marriage!   330
Carthage and Troy together in arms, what glory
Might not be ours? Only invoke the blessing
Of the great gods, make sacrifice, be lavish
In welcome, keep them here while the fierce winter
Rages at sea, and cloud and sky are stormy,
And ships still wrecked and broken."
                                         So she fanned
The flame of the burning heart; the doubtful mind

---

318. *Iarbus:* Dido's chief suitor in North Africa.   320. *Getulians:* North African people, often identified with the Berbers.   321. *Numidians:* North African nomads who rode their horses without bridles; politically powerful.   322. *Syrtes:* tribe from the west and east of Carthage.   323. *Barcaean:* a tribe from Barca, a North African city east of Carthage, hear Cyrene.

Was given hope, and the sense of guilt was lessened.
And first of all they go to shrine and altar
Imploring peace; they sacrifice to Ceres,°   340
Giver of law, to Bacchus, to Apollo,°
And most of all to Juno, in whose keeping
The bonds of marriage rest.° In all her beauty
Dido lifts up the goblet, pours libation
Between the horns of a white heifer, slowly,
Or, slowly, moves to the rich altars, noting
The proper gifts to mark the day, or studies
The sacrificial entrails° for the omens.
Alas, poor blind interpreters! What woman
In love is helped by offerings or altars?   350
Soft fire consumes the marrow-bones, the silent
Wound grows, deep in the heart.
Unhappy Dido burns, and wanders, burning,
All up and down the city, the way a deer
With a hunter's careless arrow in her flank
Ranges the uplands, with the shaft still clinging
To the hurt side. She takes Aeneas with her
All through the town, displays the wealth of Sidon,
Buildings projected; she starts to speak, and falters,
And at the end of the day renews the banquet,   360
Is wild to hear the story, over and over,
Hangs on each word, until the late moon, sinking,
Sends them all home. The stars die out, but Dido
Lies brooding in the empty hall, alone,
Abandoned on a lonely couch. She hears him,
Sees him, or sees and hears him in Iulus,
Fondles the boy, as if that ruse might fool her,
Deceived by his resemblance to his father.
The towers no longer rise, the youth are slack

340. *Ceres:* like the Greek Demeter, goddess of grain crops. 340–41. *Ceres . . .
Apollo:* Ceres, Bacchus, and Apollo are the gods associated with the founding of
new cities. One of the reasons is suggested by Teiresias in Euripides' *Bacchae:*
Ceres and Bacchus represent the basic livelihood (grain and grape products) of
colonists in a new land. 342–43. *to Juno . . rest:* Just as Dido prays to the
founder deities as she contemplates relinquishing her role as a founder, so too she
prays to the goddess of the marriage covenant as she is on the verge of breaking
her vow of loyalty to Sychaeus. 348. *sacrificial entrails:* in Rome divination was
based not only on the flight patterns of birds but also on the appearance of a
sacrificial victim's entrails. The former, called "augury," formed part of the state
religion; the latter (*haruspicium*) was often considered a pseudoscience.

In drill for arms, the cranes and derricks rusting,   370
Walls halt halfway to heaven.
                              And Juno saw it,
The queen held fast by this disease, this passion
Which made her good name meaningless. In anger
She rushed to Venus: "Wonderful!—the trophies,
The praise, you and that boy of yours are winning!
Two gods outwit one woman—splendid, splendid!
What glory for Olympus! I know you fear me,
Fear Carthage, and suspect us. To what purpose?
What good does all this do? Is there no limit?
Would we not both be better off, to sanction   380
A bond of peace forever, a formal marriage?
You have your dearest wish; Dido is burning
With love, infected to her very marrow.
Let us—why not?—conspire to rule one people
On equal terms; let her serve a Trojan husband;
Let her yield her Tyrian people as her dowry."
    This, Venus knew, was spoken with a purpose,
A guileful one, to turn Italian empire
To Libyan shores:° not without reservation
She spoke in answer: "Who would be so foolish   390
As to refuse such terms, preferring warfare,
If only fortune follows that proposal?
I do not know, I am more than a little troubled
What fate permits: will Jupiter allow it,
One city for the Tyrians and Trojans,
This covenant, this mixture? You can fathom
His mind, and ask him, being his wife. I follow
Wherever you lead." And royal Juno answered:
"That I will tend to. Listen to me, and learn
How to achieve the urgent need. They plan,   400
Aeneas, and poor Dido, to go hunting
When sunlight floods the world tomorrow morning.
While the rush of the hunt is on, and the forest shaken
With beaters and their nets, I will pour down
Dark rain and hail, and make the whole sky rumble
With thunder and threat. The company will scatter,
Hidden or hiding in the night and shadow,
And Dido and the Trojan come for shelter

388–89. *to turn . . . shores:* that is, to prevent Aeneas from founding Lavinium and his descendants from founding Rome, by diverting him permanently to Carthage through marriage to Dido.

To the same cave. I will be there and join them
In lasting wedlock; she will be his own,   410
His bride, forever; this will be their marriage."
Venus assented, smiling, not ungracious—
The trick was in the open.

    Dawn, rising, left the ocean, and the youth
Come forth from all the gates, prepared for hunting,
Nets, toils, wide spears, keen-scented coursing hounds,
And Dido keeps them waiting; her own charger
Stands bright in gold and crimson; the bit foams,
The impatient head is tossed. At last she comes,
With a great train attending, gold and crimson,   420
Quiver of gold, and combs of gold, and mantle
Crimson with golden buckle. A Trojan escort
Attends her, with Iulus, and Aeneas
Comes to her side, more lordly than Apollo
Bright along Delos' ° ridges in the springtime
With laurel in his hair and golden weapons
Shining across his shoulders. Equal radiance
Is all around Aeneas, equal splendor.

    They reach the mountain heights, the hiding places
Where no trail runs; wild goats from the rocks are started,   430
Run down the ridges; elsewhere, in the open
Deer cross the dusty plain, away from the mountains.
The boy Ascanius,° in the midst of the valley,
Is glad he has so good a horse, rides, dashing
Past one group or another: deer are cowards
And wild goats tame; he prays for some excitement,
A tawny lion coming down the mountain
Or a great boar with foaming mouth.
                    The heaven
Darkens, and thunder rolls, and rain and hail
Come down in torrents. The hunt is all for shelter,   440
Trojans and Tyrians and Ascanius dashing
Wherever they can; the streams pour down the mountains.
To the same cave go Dido and Aeneas,
Where Juno, as a bridesmaid, gives the signal,
And mountain nymphs wail high their incantations,
First day of death, first cause of evil. Dido
Is unconcerned with fame, with reputation,

425. *Delos:* Aegean island, birthplace of Apollo and sacred to him. 433. *Ascanius:* another name of Iulus, son of Aeneas and his deceased wife Creusa. (She died on the night of the fall of Troy, before Aeneas left for Italy.)

With how it seems to others. This is marriage
For her, not hole-and-corner guilt; she covers
Her folly with this name.
                    Rumor goes flying   450
At once, through all the Libyan cities, Rumor
Than whom no other evil was ever swifter.
She thrives on motion and her own momentum;
Tiny at first in fear, she swells, colossal
In no time, walks on earth, but her head is hidden
Among the clouds. . . .
    And Jove . . . turned his eyes to Carthage and the lovers
Forgetful of their better reputation.
He summoned Mercury:° "Go forth, my son,
Descend on wing and wind to Tyrian Carthage,   460
Speak to the Trojan leader, loitering there
Unheedful of the cities given by fate.
Take him my orders through the rapid winds:
It was not for this his lovely mother saved him
Twice from Greek arms;° she promised he would be
A ruler, in a country loud with war,
Pregnant with empire; he would sire a race
From Teucer's noble line; he would ordain
Law for the world. If no such glory moves him,
If his own fame and fortune count as nothing,   470
Does he, a father, grudge his son the towers
Of Rome to be? What is the fellow doing?
With what ambition wasting time in Libya?
Let him set sail. That's all; convey the message."
    Before he ended, Mercury made ready
To carry out the orders of his father;
He strapped the golden sandals on, the pinions
To bear him over sea and land, as swift
As the breath of the wind; he took the wand, which summons
Pale ghosts from Hell, or sends them there,° denying   480
Or giving sleep, unsealing dead men's eyes,
Useful in flight through wind and stormy cloud,
And so came flying till he saw the summit
And towering sides of Atlas,° rugged giant

459. *Mercury:* Latin version of Hermes, messenger of Jupiter (Jove) and Juno.
465. *Twice . . . arms:* during the capture of Troy, Venus intervened twice to
save Aeneas from almost certain death in the burning city. 479–80. *he . . .
there:* one of Mercury's cult titles was *Psychopompus,* "Guide of Souls" (to or
from Hades). 484. *Atlas:* mountain range in Mauretania (northwest Africa),
sometimes personified as holding up the heavens on his head and hands.

With heaven on his neck, whose head and shoulders
Are dark with fir, ringed with black cloud, and beaten
With wind and rain, and laden with the whiteness
Of falling snow, with rivers running over
His agèd chin, and the rough beard ice-stiffened.
Here first on level wing the god paused briefly,   490
Poised, plummeted to ocean, like a bird
That skims the water's surface, flying low
By shore and fishes' rocky breeding ground,
So Mercury darted between earth and heaven
To Libya's sandy shore, cutting the wind
From the home of Maia's° father.
Soon as the winged sandals skim the rooftops,
He sees Aeneas founding towers, building
New homes for Tyrians; his sword is studded
With yellow jasper; he wears across his shoulders   500
A cloak of burning crimson, and golden threads
Run through it, the royal gift of the rich queen.
Mercury wastes no time: "What are you doing,
Forgetful of your kingdom and your fortunes,
Building for Carthage? Woman-crazy fellow,
The ruler of the gods, the great compeller
Of heaven and earth, has sent me from Olympus
With no more word than this: what are you doing,
With what ambition wasting time in Libya?
If your own fame and fortune count as nothing,   510
Think of Ascanius at least, whose kingdom
In Italy, whose Roman land, are waiting
As promise justly due." He spoke, and vanished
Into thin air. Appalled, amazed, Aeneas
Is stricken dumb; his hair stands up in terror,
His voice sticks in his throat. He is more than eager
To flee that pleasant land, awed by the warning
Of the divine command. But how to do it?
How get around that passionate queen? What opening
Try first? His mind runs out in all directions,   520
Shifting and veering. Finally, he has it,
Or thinks he has: he calls his comrades to him,
The leaders, bids them quietly prepare
The fleet for voyage, meanwhile saying nothing
About the new activity; since Dido
Is unaware, has no idea that passion

496. *Maia:* daughter of Atlas and mother of Hermes.

As strong as theirs is on the verge of breaking,
He will see what he can do, find the right moment
To let her know, all in good time. Rejoicing,
The captains move to carry out the orders.　　　　　　　　530
　　Who can deceive a woman in love? The queen
Anticipates each move, is fearful even
While everything is safe, foresees this cunning,
And the same trouble-making goddess, Rumor,
Tells her the fleet is being armed, made ready
For voyaging. She rages through the city
Like a woman mad, or drunk, the way the Maenads
Go howling through the nighttime on Cithaeron
When Bacchus' cymbals summon with their clashing.
She waits no explanation from Aeneas;　　　　　　　　540
She is the first to speak: "And so, betrayer,
You hoped to hide your wickedness, go sneaking
Out of my land without a word? Our love
Means nothing to you, our exchange of vows,
And even the death of Dido could not hold you.
The season is dead of winter, and you labor
Over the fleet; the northern gales are nothing—
You must be cruel, must you not? Why, even,
If ancient Troy remained, and you were seeking
Not unknown homes and lands, but Troy again,　　　　550
Would you be venturing Troyward in this weather?
I am the one you flee from: true? I beg you
By my own tears, and your right hand—(I have nothing
Else left my wretchedness)—by the beginnings
Of marriage, wedlock, what we had, if ever
I served you well, if anything of mine
Was ever sweet to you, I beg you, pity
A falling house; if there is room for pleading
As late as this, I plead, put off that purpose.
You are the reason I am hated; Libyans,　　　　　　　560
Numidians, Tyrians, hate me; and my honor
Is lost, and the fame I had, that almost brought me
High as the stars, is gone. To whom, O guest—
I must not call you husband any longer—
To whom do you leave me? I am a dying woman;
Why do I linger on? Until Pygmalion,
My brother, brings destruction to this city?
Until the prince Iarbas leads me captive?
At least if there had been some hope of children

Before your flight, a little Aeneas playing 570
Around my courts, to bring you back, in feature
At least, I would seem less taken and deserted."
    There was nothing he could say. Jove bade him keep
Affection from his eyes, and grief in his heart
With never a sign. At last, he managed something:
"Never, O Queen, will I deny you merit
Whatever you have strength to claim; I will not
Regret remembering Dido, while I have
Breath in my body, or consciousness of spirit.
I have a point or two to make. I did not, 580
Believe me, hope to hide my flight by cunning;
I did not, ever, claim to be a husband,
Made no such vows. If I had fate's permission
To live my life my way, to settle my troubles
At my own will, I would be watching over
The city of Troy, and caring for my people,
Those whom the Greeks had spared, and Priam's palace
Would still be standing; for the vanquished people
I would have built the town again. But now
It is Italy I must seek, great Italy, 590
Apollo orders, and his oracles
Call me to Italy. There is my love,
There is my country. If the towers of Carthage,
The Libyan citadels, can please a woman
Who came from Tyre, why must you grudge the Trojans
Ausonian° land? It is proper for us also
To seek a foreign kingdom. I am warned
Of this in dreams: when the earth is veiled in shadow
And the fiery stars are burning, I see my father,
Anchises,° or his ghost, and I am frightened; 600
I am troubled for the wrong I do my son,
Cheating him out of his kingdom in the west,
And lands that fate assigns him. And a herald,
Jove's messenger—I call them both to witness—
Has brought me, through the rush of air, his orders;
I saw the god myself, in the full daylight,
Enter these walls, I heard the words he brought me.
Cease to inflame us both with your complainings;
I follow Italy not because I want to."
    Out of the corner of her eye she watched him 610

596. *Ausonian:* Italian.   600. *Anchises:* Aeneas' aged father had died in Sicily,
shortly prior to Aeneas' journey to Carthage.

During the first of this, and her gaze was turning
Now here, now there; and then, in bitter silence,
She looked him up and down; then blazed out at him:
"You treacherous liar! No goddess was your mother,
No Dardanus° the founder of your tribe,
Son of the stony mountain-crags, begotten
On cruel rocks, with a tigress for a wet-nurse!
Why fool myself, why make pretense? what is there
To save myself for now? When I was weeping
Did he so much as sigh? Did he turn his eyes,   620
Ever so little, toward me? Did he break at all,
Or weep, or give his lover a word of pity?
What first, what next? Neither Jupiter nor Juno
Looks at these things with any sense of fairness.
Faith has no haven anywhere in the world.
He was an outcast on my shore, a beggar,
I took him in, and, like a fool, I gave him
Part of my kingdom; his fleet was lost, I found it,
His comrades dying, I brought them back to life.
I am maddened, burning, burning: now Apollo   630
The prophesying god, the oracles
Of Lycia,° and Jove's herald, sent from heaven,
Come flying through the air with fearful orders—
Fine business for the gods, the kind of trouble
That keeps them from their sleep.° I do not hold you,
I do not argue, either. Go. And follow
Italy on the wind, and seek the kingdom
Across the water. But if any gods
Who care for decency have any power,
They will land you on the rocks; I hope for vengeance,   640
I hope to hear you calling the name of Dido
Over and over, in vain. Oh, I will follow
In blackest fire, and when cold death has taken
Spirit from body, I will be there to haunt you,
A shade, all over the world. I will have vengeance,
And hear about it; the news will be my comfort
In the deep world below." She broke it off,
Leaving the words unfinished; even light
Was unendurable; sick at heart, she turned

615. *Dardanus:* here the mythical founder of Troy.   632. *Lycia:* a district in
southwest Asia Minor, where there was a famous oracular shrine of Apollo.
635. *keeps . . . sleep:* an allusion to the Epicurean view of the gods' passivity
toward humans.

And left him, stammering, afraid, attempting   650
To make some kind of answer. And her servants
Support her to her room, that bower of marble,
A marriage chamber once; here they attend her,
Help her lie down.
             And good Aeneas, longing
To ease her grief with comfort, to say something
To turn her pain and hurt away, sighs often,
His heart being moved by this great love, most deeply,
And still—the gods give orders, he obeys them;
He goes back to the fleet. And then the Trojans
Bend, really, to their work, launching the vessels   660
All down the shore. The tarred keel swims in the water,
The green wood comes from the forest, the poles are lopped
For oars, with leaves still on them. All are eager
For flight; all over the city you see them streaming,
Bustling about their business, a black line moving
The way ants do when they remember winter
And raid a hill of grain, to haul and store it
At home, across the plain, the column moving
In thin black line through grass, part of them shoving
Great seeds on little shoulders, and part bossing   670
The job, rebuking laggards, and all the pathway
Hot with the stream of work.
                And Dido saw them
With who knows what emotion: there she stood
On the high citadel, and saw, below her,
The whole beach boiling, and the water littered
With one ship after another, and men yelling,
Excited over their work, and there was nothing
For her to do but sob or choke with anguish.
There is nothing to which the hearts of men and women
Cannot be driven by love. Break into tears,   680
Try prayers again, humble the pride, leave nothing
Untried, and die in vain: "Anna, you see them
Coming from everywhere; they push and bustle
All up and down the shore: the sails are swelling,
The happy sailors garlanding the vessels.
If I could hope for grief like this, my sister,
I shall be able to bear it. But one service
Do for me first, dear Anna, out of pity.
You were the only one that traitor trusted,
Confided in; you know the way to reach him,   690

The proper time and place. Give him this message,
Our arrogant enemy: tell him I never
Swore with the Greeks at Aulis° to abolish
The Trojan race, I never sent a fleet
To Pergamus,° I never desecrated
The ashes or the spirit of Anchises:
Why does he, then, refuse to listen to me?
What is the hurry? Let him give his lover
The one last favor: only wait a little,
Only a little while, for better weather   700
And easy flight. He has betrayed the marriage,
I do not ask for that again; I do not
Ask him to give up Latium and his kingdom.
Mere time is all I am asking, a breathing space,
A brief reprieve, until my luck has taught me
To reconcile defeat and sorrow. This
Is all I ask for, sister; pity and help me:
If he grants me this, I will pay it ten times over
After my death." And Anna, most unhappy,
Over and over, told her tears, her pleading;   710
No tears, no pleading, move him; no man can yield
When a god stops his ears. As northern winds
Sweep over Alpine mountains, in their fury
Fighting each other to uproot an oak-tree
Whose ancient strength endures against their roaring
And the trunk shudders and the leaves come down
Strewing the ground, but the old tree clings to the mountain,
Its roots as deep toward hell as its crest toward heaven,
And still holds on—even so, Aeneas, shaken
By storm-blasts of appeal, by voices calling   720
From every side, is tossed and torn, and steady.
His will stays motionless, and tears are vain.
     Then Dido prays for death at last; the fates
Are terrible, her luck is out, she is tired
Of gazing at the everlasting heaven.
The more to goad her will to die, she sees—
Oh terrible!—the holy water blacken,
Libations turn to blood, on ground and altar,
When she makes offerings. But she tells no one,
Not even her sister. From the marble shrine,   730
Memorial to her former lord, attended,

---

693. *Aulis*: port of departure at which the Greek forces assembled to sail against
Troy. 695. *Pergamus*: the citadel of Troy.

Always, by her, with honor, fleece and garland,
She hears his voice, his words, her husband calling
When darkness holds the world, and from the house-top
An owl sends out a long funereal wailing,
And she remembers warnings of old seers,
Fearful, foreboding. In her dreams Aeneas
Appears to hunt her down; or she is going
Alone in a lost country, wandering
Trying to find her Tyrians, mad as Pentheus,°   740
Or frenzied as Orestes,° when his mother
Is after him with whips of snakes, or firebrands,
While the Avengers menace at the threshold.
    She was beaten, harboring madness, and resolved
On dying; alone, she plotted time and method;
Keeping the knowledge from her sorrowing sister,
She spoke with calm composure: "I have found
A way (wish me good luck) to bring him to me
Or set me free from loving him forever.
Near Ocean and the west there is a country,   750
The Ethiopian land, far-off, where Atlas
Turns on his shoulders the star-studded world;
I know a priestess there; she guards the temple
Of the daughters of the Evening Star; she feeds
The dragon° there, and guards the sacred branches,
She sprinkles honeydew, strews drowsy poppies,
And she knows charms to free the hearts of lovers
When she so wills it, or to trouble others;
She can reverse the wheeling of the planets,
Halt rivers in their flowing; she can summon   760
The ghosts of nighttime; you will see earth shaking
Under her tread, and trees come down from mountains.
Dear sister mine, as heaven is my witness,
I hate to take these arts of magic on me!
Be secret, then; but in the inner courtyard,
Raise up a funeral pyre, to hold the armor
Left hanging in the bower, by that hero,
That good devoted man, and all his raiment,

740. *Pentheus:* the king of Thebes, driven mad by Dionysus. 741. *Orestes:*
Orestes, after killing his mother Clytemnestra, is pursued relentlessly by hideous
avenging deities, the Furies. In other versions of this myth he is haunted by his
mother's spirit. Virgil alludes to both versions. 755. *dragon:* a dragon or serpent
guarded the golden fruit in the garden of the "daughters of the Evening Star"
(Hesperides).

And add the bridal bed, my doom: the priestess
Said to do this, and it will be a pleasure   770
To see the end of all of it, every token
Of that unspeakable knave."
                         And so, thought Anna,
Things are no worse than when Sychaeus perished.
She did not know the death these rites portended,
Had no suspicion, and carried out her orders.

   The pyre is raised in the court; it towers high
With pine and holm-oak, it is hung with garlands
And funeral wreaths, and on the couch she places
Aeneas' sword, his garments, and his image,
Knowing the outcome. Round about are altars,   780
Where, with her hair unbound, the priestess calls
On thrice a hundred gods, Erebus,° Chaos,°
Hecate,° queen of Hell, triple Diana.°
Water is sprinkled, from Avernus° fountain,
Or said to be, and herbs are sought, by moonlight
Mown with bronze sickles, and the stem-ends running
With a black milk, and the caul of a colt, new-born.
Dido, with holy meal and holy hands,
Stands at the altar, with one sandal loosened
And robes unfastened, calls the gods to witness,   790
Prays to the stars that know her doom, invoking,
Beyond them, any powers, if there are any,
Who care for lovers in unequal bondage.

   Night: and tired creatures over all the world
Were seeking slumber; the woods and the wild waters
Were quiet, and the silent stars were wheeling
Their course half over; every field was still;
The beasts of the field, the brightly colored birds,
Dwellers in lake and pool, in thorn and thicket,
Slept through the tranquil night, their sorrows over,   800
Their troubles soothed. But no such blessèd darkness
Closes the eyes of Dido; no repose
Comes to her anxious heart. Her pangs redouble,

---

782. *Erebus:* primordial darkness, often used to refer to part of the underworld.
Chaos: original god, the father of Erebus, and sometimes associated with the
underworld. 783. *Hecate:* sometimes a goddess of the underworld; associated
with the night and with sorcery. *triple Diana* (Artemis): she has three forms:
in the sky she is Phoebe (the Moon), on earth she is the goddess of hunting and
virginity, and in the underworld she is Hecate or Trivia as goddess of night and
magic rites. 784. *Avernus:* lake near Naples, in antiquity thought to be an
entrance to the underworld; the modern Lago di Averno.

Her love swells up, surging, a great tide rising
Of wrath and doubt and passion. "What do I do?
What now? Go back to my Numidian suitors,
Be scorned by those I scorned? Pursue the Trojans?
Obey their orders? They were grateful to me,
Once, I remember. But who would let them take me?
Suppose I went. They hate me now; they were always   810
Deceivers: is Laomedon° forgotten,
Whose blood runs through their veins? What then? Attend them,
Alone, be their companion, the loud-mouthed sailors?
Or with my own armada follow after,
Wear out my sea-worn Tyrians once more
With vengeance and adventure? Better die.
Die; you deserve to; end the hurt with the sword.
It is your fault, Anna; you were sorry for me,
Won over by my tears; you put this load
Of evil on me. It was not permitted,   820
It seems, for me to live apart from wedlock,
A blameless life. An animal does better.
I vowed Sychaeus faith. I have been faithless."
So, through the night, she tossed in restless torment.
    Meanwhile Aeneas, on the lofty stern,
All things prepared, sure of his going, slumbers
As Mercury comes down once more to warn him,
Familiar blond young god: "O son of Venus,
Is this a time for sleep? The wind blows fair,
And danger rises all around you. Dido,   830
Certain to die, however else uncertain,
Plots treachery, harbors evil. Seize the moment
While it can still be seized, and hurry, hurry!
The sea will swarm with ships, the fiery torches
Blaze, and the shore rankle with fire by morning.
Shove off, be gone! A shifty, fickle object
Is woman, always." He vanished into the night.
And, frightened by that sudden apparition,
Aeneas started from sleep, and urged his comrades:
"Hurry, men, hurry; get to the sails and benches,   840
Get the ships under way. A god from heaven
Again has come to speed our flight, to sever
The mooring ropes. O holy one, we follow,

811. *Laomedon:* former king of Troy and father of Priam; notorious for his failure
to give promised rewards to Apollo, Neptune (Poseidon), and Hercules (Heracles)
for services they had performed for him.

Whoever you are, we are happy in obeying.
Be with us, be propitious; let the stars
Be right in heaven!" He drew his sword; the blade
Flashed, shining, at the hawser; and all the men
Were seized in the same restlessness and rushing.
They have left the shore, they have hidden the sea water
With the hulls of the ships; the white foam flies, the oars   850
Dip down in dark-blue water.
     And Aurora°
Came from Tithonus' saffron couch to freshen
The world with rising light, and from her watch tower
The queen saw day grow whiter, and the fleet
Go moving over the sea, keep pace together
To the even spread of the sail; she knew the harbors
Were empty of sailors now; she struck her breast
Three times, four times; she tore her golden hair,
Crying, "God help me, will he go, this stranger,
Treating our kingdom as a joke? Bring arms,   860
Bring arms, and hurry! follow from all the city,
Haul the ships off the ways, some of you! Others,
Get fire as fast as you can, give out the weapons,
Pull oars! What am I saying? Or where am I?
I must be going mad. Unhappy Dido,
Is it only now your wickedness strikes home?
The time it should have was when you gave him power.
Well, here it is, look at it now, the honor,
The faith of the hero who, they tell me, carries
With him his household gods,° who bore on his shoulders   870
His agèd father! ° Could I not have seized him,
Torn him to pieces, scattered him over the waves?
What was the matter? Could I not have murdered
His comrades, and Iulus, and served the son
For a dainty at the table of his father?
But fight would have a doubtful fortune. It might have,
What then? I was going to die; whom did I fear?
I would have, should have, set his camp on fire,
Filled everything with flame, choked off the father,
The son, the accursèd race, and myself with them.   880
Great Sun, surveyor of all the works of earth,

851. *Aurora:* goddess of dawn, married to a mythical human hero named
Tithonus. 870. *household gods:* divinities of the threshold and the home.
Aeneas rescued them from the flames at the fall of Troy. 871. *father:* Aeneas
saved Anchises' life on the night of the fall of Troy by carrying him through the
burning city.

Juno, to whom my sorrows are committed,
Hecate, whom the crossroads of the cities
Wail to by night,° avenging Furies, hear me,
Grant me divine protection, take my prayer
If he must come to harbor, then he must,
If Jove ordains it, however vile he is,
False, and unspeakable. If Jove ordains,
The goal is fixed. So be it. Take my prayer.°
Let him be driven by arms and war, an exile   890
Let him be taken from his son Iulus,
Let him beg for aid, let him see his people dying
Unworthy deaths, let him accept surrender
On unfair terms, let him never enjoy the kingdom,
The hoped-for light, let him fall and die, untimely,
Let him lie unburied on the sand. Oh, hear me,
Hear the last prayer, poured out with my last blood!
And you, O Tyrians, hate, and hate forever
The Trojan stock. Offer my dust this homage.
No love, no peace, between these nations, ever!   900
Rise from my bones, O great unknown avenger,°
Hunt them with fire and sword, the Dardan° settlers,
Now, then, here, there, wherever strength is given.
Shore against shore, wave against wave, and war,
War after war, for all the generations."
    She spoke, and turned her purpose to accomplish
The quickest end to the life she hated. Briefly
She spoke to Barce, Sychaeus' nurse; her own
Was dust and ashes in her native country:
"Dear nurse, bring me my sister, tell her to hurry,   910
Tell her to sprinkle her body with river water,
To bring the sacrificial beast and offerings,
And both of you cover your temples with holy fillets.
I have a vow to keep; I have made beginning
Of rites to Stygian° Jove, to end my sorrows,
To burn the litter of that Trojan leader."
Barce, with an old woman's fuss and bustle,

883–84. *Hecate . . . night:* the goddess was believed to visit crossroads at night accompanied by ghosts and hell-dogs. 889. *prayer:* the following prayer—Dido's last—contains an accurate vision of the difficulties that Aeneas will encounter after reaching Italy. 901. *avenger:* the poet, retrospectively, lets Dido make a prophetic allusion to the famous Carthaginian general Hannibal, who invaded Italy with great initial success during the Second Punic War. 902. *Dardan:* Trojan. 915. *Stygian:* of the underworld. Styx is one of the rivers of the underworld.

Went hurrying out of sight; but Dido, trembling,
Wild with her project, the blood-shot eyeballs rolling,
Pale at the death to come, and hectic color   920
Burning the quivering cheeks, broke into the court,
Mounted the pyre in madness, drew the sword,
The Trojan gift, bestowed for no such purpose,
And she saw the Trojan garments, and the bed
She knew so well, and paused a little, weeping,
Weeping, and thinking, and flung herself down on it,
Uttering her last words:
"Spoils that were sweet while gods and fate permitted,
Receive my spirit, set me free from suffering.
I have lived, I have run the course that fortune gave me,   930
And now my shade, a great one, will be going
Below the earth. I have built a noble city,
I have seen my walls, I have avenged a husband,
Punished a hostile brother. I have been
Happy, I might have been too happy, only
The Trojans made their landing." She broke off,
Pressed her face to the couch, cried: "So, we shall die,
Die unavenged; but let us die. So, so—
I am glad to meet the darkness. Let his eyes
Behold this fire across the sea, an omen   940
Of my death going with him."
                                        As she spoke,
Her handmaids saw her, fallen on the sword,
The foam of blood on the blade, and blood on the hands.
A scream rings through the house; Rumor goes reeling,
Rioting, through the shaken town; the palace
Is loud with lamentation, women sobbing,
Wailing and howling, and the vaults of heaven
Echo the outcry, as if Tyre or Carthage
Had fallen to invaders,° and the fury
Of fire came rolling over homes and temples.   950
Anna, half lifeless, heard in panic terror,
Came rushing through them all, beating her bosom,
Clawing her face: "Was it for this, my sister?
To trick me so? The funeral pyre, the altars,
Prepared this for me? I have, indeed, a grievance,
Being forsaken; you would not let your sister
Companion you in death? You might have called me

949. *invaders:* an allusion to the capture of Carthage by Roman invaders at the
conclusion of the Punic Wars in 146 B.C.

To the same fate; we might have both been taken,
One sword, one hour. I was the one who built it,
This pyre, with my own hands; it was my voice   960
That called our fathers' gods, for what?—to fail you
When you were lying here. You have killed me, sister,
Not only yourself, you have killed us all, the people,
The town. Let me wash the wounds with water,
Let my lips catch what fluttering breath still lingers."
She climbed the lofty steps, and held her sister,
A dying woman, close; she used her robe
To try to stop the bleeding. And Dido tried
In vain to raise her heavy eyes, fell back,
And her wound made a gurgling hissing sound.   970
Three times she tried to lift herself; three times
Fell back; her rolling eyes went searching heaven
And the light hurt when she found it, and she moaned.
    At last all-powerful Juno, taking pity,
Sent Iris from Olympus, in compassion
For the long racking agony, to free her
From the limbs' writhing and the struggle of spirit.
She had not earned this death, she had only sought it
Before her time, driven by sudden madness,
Therefore, the queen of Hades had not taken   980
The golden lock,°, consigning her to Orcus.°
So Iris, dewy on saffron wings, descending,
Trailing a thousand colors through the brightness
Comes down the sky, poises above her, saying,
"This lock I take as bidden, and from the body
Release the soul," and cuts the lock; and cold
Takes over, and the winds receive the spirit.

Aeneas left Carthage precipitously as ordered by Jupiter and Mercury and sailed to his friend Acestes in Sicily. After arranging elaborate funeral games in honor of his father, Anchises—who had died in Sicily on Aeneas' previous visit to the island—Aeneas sailed for Italy. But a number of his companions stayed behind, too weary to face another alien land and further uncertainties. Shortly after his arrival in Italy, Aeneas went to Cumae, near Naples, to consult a prophetic priestess. She guided Aeneas down to the underworld through the entrance at Lake Avernus. Like Odysseus in the Odyssey, Aeneas

981. *golden lock:* Proserpine (Greek, Persephone), queen of the underworld, clipped a lock of hair from a human when his destined time for death had come. *Orcus:* land of the dead; also another name for Pluto, ruler of the dead.

encountered deceased companions and various heroes in the underworld. He
also met his father and, as a distant and solitary compensation, was given a
vision of the future of his own race. The narrative resumes as Aeneas and
the Sibyl enter the underworld.

From BOOK VI

   . . . The Sibyl cried a warning,
"Keep off, keep off, whatever is unholy,
Depart from here! Courage, Aeneas; enter   990
The path, unsheathe the sword. The time is ready
For the brave heart." She strode out boldly, leading
Into the open cavern, and he followed.
  Gods of the world of spirit, silent shadows,
Chaos and Phlegethon,° areas of silence,
Wide realms of dark, may it be right and proper
To tell what I have heard, this revelation
Of matters buried deep in earth and darkness!
  Vague forms in lonely darkness, they were going
Through void and shadow, through the empty realm 1000
Like people in a forest, when the moonlight
Shifts with a baleful glimmer, and shadow covers
The sky, and all the colors turn to blackness.
At the first threshold, on the jaws of Orcus,
Grief and avenging Cares have set their couches,
And pale Diseases dwell, and sad Old Age,
Fear, evil-counseling Hunger, wretched Need,
Forms terrible to see, and Death, and Toil,
And Death's own brother, Sleep, and evil Joys,
Fantasies of the mind, and deadly War,   1010
The Furies' iron chambers, Discord, raving,
Her snaky hair entwined in bloody bands.
An elm-tree loomed there, shadowy and huge,
The aged boughs outspread, beneath whose leaves,
Men say, the false dreams cling, thousands on thousands.
And there are monsters in the dooryard, Centaurs,°
Scyllas, of double shape, the beast of Lerna,°
Hissing most horribly, Briareus,

995. *Phlegethon:* a river of the underworld, flowing with flames instead of water.
1016. *Centaurs:* mythical creatures, half-man and half-horse. 1017. *Lerna:* a
monstrous water snake killed by Hercules (Heracles).

The hundred-handed giant, a Chimaera°
Whose armament is fire, Harpies,° and Gorgons,°   1020
A triple-bodied giant. In sudden panic
Aeneas drew his sword, the edge held forward,
Ready to rush and flail, however blindly,
Save that his wise companion warned him, saying
They had no substance, they were only phantoms
Flitting about, illusions without body.
   From here, the road turns off to Acheron,°
River of Hell; here, thick with muddy whirling,
Cocytus° boils with sand. Charon° is here,
The guardian of these mingling waters, Charon,   1030
Uncouth and filthy, on whose chin the hair
Is a tangled mat, whose eyes protrude, are burning,
Whose dirty cloak is knotted at the shoulder.
He poles a boat, tends to the sail, unaided,
Ferrying bodies in his rust-hued vessel.
Old, but a god's senility is awful
In its raw greenness. To the bank come thronging
Mothers and men, bodies of great-souled heroes,
Their lifetime over, boys, unwedded maidens,
Young men whose fathers saw their pyres burning,   1040
Thick as the forest leaves that fall in autumn
With early frost, thick as the birds to landfall
From over the seas, when the chill of the year compels them
To sunlight. There they stand, a host, imploring
To be taken over first. Their hands, in longing,
Reach out for the farther shore. But the gloomy boatman
Makes choice among them, taking some, and keeping
Others far back from the stream's edge. Aeneas,
Wondering, asks the Sibyl, "Why the crowding?
What are the spirits seeking? What distinction   1050
Brings some across the livid stream, while others
Stay on the farther bank?" She answers, briefly:
"Son of Anchises, this is the awful river,
The Styx,° by which the gods take oath; the boatman

1019. *Chimaera:* mythical fire-breathing monster, the front part of whose body
was that of a lion, the hind part that of a dragon, and the middle that of a goat.
1020. *Harpies:* giant birds with women's faces. *Gorgons:* winged female monsters
with serpents instead of hair.   1027. *Acheron:* a river of the underworld ("River
of Grief").   1029. *Cocytus:* also an infernal river ("River of Wailing"). *Charon:*
the ferryman of Hades.   1054. *Styx:* a third river of the underworld ("Hateful"),
which was believed to flow several times around the perimeter of the underworld.

Charon; those he takes with him are the buried,
Those he rejects, whose luck is out, the graveless.
It is not permitted him to take them over
The dreadful banks and hoarse-resounding waters
Till earth is cast upon their bones. They haunt
These shores a hundred restless years of waiting   1060
Before they end postponement of the crossing."
Aeneas paused, in thoughtful mood, with pity
Over their lot's unevenness; and saw there,
Wanting the honor given the dead, and grieving,
Leucaspis, and Orontes, the Lycian captain,
Who had sailed from Troy across the stormy waters,
And drowned off Africa, with crew and vessel,
And there was Palinurus, once his pilot,
Who, not so long ago, had been swept over,
Watching the stars on the journey north from Carthage.   1070
The murk was thick; Aeneas hardly knew him,
Sorrowful in that darkness. . . .
                              . . . Aeneas, crossing,
Passed on beyond the bank of the dread river°
Whence none return.
                    A wailing of thin voices
Came to their ears, the souls of infants crying,
Those whom the day of darkness took from the breast
Before their share of living. And there were many
Whom some false sentence brought to death. Here Minos°
Judges them once again; a silent jury
Reviews the evidence. And there are others,   1080
Guilty of nothing, but who hated living,
The suicides. How gladly, now, they would suffer
Poverty, hardship, in the world of light!
But this is not permitted; they are bound
Nine times around by the black unlovely river;
Styx holds them fast.
                    They came to the Fields of Mourning,
So-called, where those whom cruel love had wasted
Hid in secluded pathways, under myrtle,
And even in death were anxious. Procris, Phaedra,
Eriphyle, displaying wounds her son   1090
Had given her, Caeneus, Laodamia,
Caeneus,° a young man once, and now again

1073. *dread river:* Styx. 1078. *Minos:* a judge of the dead. 1089–92. *Procris
. . . Caeneus:* a list of disappointed lovers.

A young man, after having been a woman.
And here, new come from her own wound, was Dido,
Wandering in the wood. The Trojan hero,
Standing near by, saw her, or thought he saw her,
Dim in the shadows, like the slender crescent
Of moon when cloud drifts over. Weeping, he greets her:
"Unhappy Dido, so they told me truly
That your own hand had brought you death. Was I—   1100
Alas!—the cause? I swear by all the stars,
By the world above, by everything held sacred
Here under the earth, unwillingly, O queen,
I left your kingdom. But the gods' commands,
Driving me now through these forsaken places,
This utter night, compelled me on. I could not
Believe my loss would cause so great a sorrow.
Linger a moment, do not leave me; whither,
Whom, are you fleeing? I am permitted only
This last word with you."
                    But the queen, unmoving   1110
As flint or marble, turned away, her eyes
Fixed on the ground: the tears were vain, the words,
Meant to be soothing, foolish; she turned away,
His enemy forever, to the shadows
Where Sychaeus, her former husband, took her
With love for love, and sorrow for her sorrow.
And still Aeneas wept for her, being troubled
By the injustice of her doom; his pity
Followed her going. . . .

After his return from the world of the dead, Aeneas began his settlement of Italy. But when the Italian king of Latium, Latinus, gave Aeneas his daughter Lavinia in marriage, the native Italians objected and launched a war against Aeneas and his Trojans. The leader of this Italian resistance was a young king, Turnus. Lengthy and desperate battles followed. As in the battles of The Iliad, gods intervened on both sides. When Aeneas was wounded, for example, his mother, Venus, brought him an elaborate shield made by the god Vulcan on which was carved the future achievements of Rome. After numerous inconclusive encounters, the Trojans and Italians agreed to decide the war by a single duel between Aeneas and Turnus. The narrative resumes after Turnus' initial misfortunes in this duel had been neutralized by the intervention of his divine allies, Juno and Juturna.

From BOOK XII

            . . . And Juno, gazing
From a golden cloud to earth, watching the duel,
Heard the all-powerful king of high Olympus:
"What will the end be now, O wife? What else
Remains? You know, and you admit you know it,
Aeneas is heaven-destined, the native hero
Become a god, raised by the fates, exalted.
What are you planning? with what hope lingering on
In the cold clouds? Was it proper that a mortal
Should wound a god? that the sword, once lost, be given
Turnus again?—Juturna,° of course, is nothing
Without your help—was it proper that the beaten   1130
Increase in violence? Stop it now, I tell you;
Listen to my entreaties: I would not have you
Devoured by grief in silence; I would not have you
Bring me, again, anxiety and sorrow,
However sweet the voice. The end has come.
To harry the Trojans over land and ocean,
To light up war unspeakable, to defile
A home with grief, to mingle bridal and sorrow—°
All this you were permitted. Go no farther!
That is an absolute order." And Juno, downcast   1140
In gaze, replied: "Great Jove, I knew your pleasure:
And therefore, much against my will, left Turnus,
Left earth. Were it not so, you would not see me
Lonely upon my airy throne in heaven,
Enduring things both worthy and unworthy,
But I would be down there, by flames surrounded,
Fighting in the front ranks, and hauling Trojans
To battle with their enemies. Juturna,
I urged, I own, to help her wretched brother,
And I approved, I own, her greater daring   1150
For his life's sake, but I did not approve,
And this I swear by Styx, that river whose name
Binds all the gods to truth, her taking weapons,
Aiming the bow. I give up now, I leave
These battles, though I hate to. I ask one favor
For Latium, for the greatness of your people,

1129. *Juturna:* an Italian goddess of springs and streams; sister of Turnus.
1138. *bridal and sorrow:* a reference to Juno's role in encouraging the affair between Dido and Aeneas.

And this no law of fate forbids: when, later,
And be it so, they join in peace, and settle
Their laws, their treaties, in a blessèd marriage,°
Do not command the Latins, native-born,   1160
To change their language, to be known as Trojans,
To alter speech or garb; let them be Latium,
Let Alban kings endure through all the ages,
Let Roman stock, strong in Italian valor,
Prevail: since Troy has fallen, let her name
Perish and be forgotten." Smiling on her,
The great creator answered: "You are truly
True sister of Jove and child of Saturn,° nursing
Such tides of anger in the heart! Forget it!
Abate the rise of passion. The wish is granted.   1170
I yield, and more than that—I share your purpose.
Ausonians° shall keep their old tradition,
Their fathers' speech and ways; their name shall be
Even as now it is. Their sacred laws,
Their ritual, I shall add, and make all Latins
Men of common tongue. A race shall rise
All-powerful, of mingled blood; you will see them
By virtue of devotion rise to glories
Not men nor gods have known, and no race ever
Will pay you equal honor." And the goddess   1180
Gave her assent, was happy, changed her purpose,
Left heaven and quit the cloud.
                   This done, the father
Formed yet another purpose, that Juturna
Should leave her fighting brother. There are, men say,
Twin fiends, or triple, sisters named the Furies,
Daughters of Night, with snaky coils, and pinions
Like those of wind. They are attendant spirits
Before the throne of Jove and whet the fears
Of sickly mortals, when the king of heaven
Contrives disease or dreadful death, or frightens   1190
The guilty towns in war. Now he dispatches
One of the three to earth, to meet Juturna,
An omen visible; and so from heaven
She flew with whirlwind swiftness, like an arrow

1159. _blessèd marriage:_ a reference to the marriage between the Italian, Lavinia, and the Trojan, Aeneas.   1168. _Saturn:_ Jupiter and Juno, like Zeus and Hera, were husband and wife as well as brother and sister; Saturn was the father of both of them.   1172. _Ausonians:_ Italians.

Through cloud from bowstring, armed with gall or poison,
Loosed from a Parthian quiver,° cleaving shadows
Swifter than man may know, a shaft no power
Has power of healing over: so Night's daughter
Came down to earth, and when she saw the Trojans
And Turnus' columns, she dwindled, all of a sudden,   1200
To the shape of that small bird, which, in the nighttime,
Shrills its late song, ill-omened, on the roof-tops
Or over tombs, insistent through the darkness.
And so the fiend, the little screech-owl, flying
At Turnus, over and over, shrilled in warning,
Beating the wings against the shield, and Turnus
Felt a strange torpor seize his limbs, and terror
Made his hair rise, and his voice could find not utterance.
    But when, far off, Juturna knew the Fury
By whir of those dread wings, she tore her tresses,   1210
Clawed at her face, and beat her breast, all anguish
Over her brother: "What can a sister do
To help you now, poor Turnus? What remains
For me to bear? I have borne so much already.
What skill of mine can make the daylight longer
In your dark hour? Can I face such a portent?
Now, now, I leave the battle-line forever.
Foul birds, I fear enough; haunt me no further,
I know that beat of the wings, that deadly whirring;
I recognize, too well, Jove's arrogant orders,   1220
His payment for my maidenhood.° He gave me
Eternal life, but why? Why has he taken
The right of death away from me? I might have
Ended my anguish, surely, with my brother's,
Gone, at his side, among the fearful shadows,
But, no—I am immortal. What is left me
Of any possible joy, without my brother?
What earth can open deep enough to take me,
A goddess, to the lowest shades?" The mantle,
Gray-colored, veiled her head, and the goddess, sighing,   1230
Sank deep from sight to the grayness of the river.
    And on Aeneas presses: the flashing spear,
Brandished, is big as a tree; his anger cries:

1196. Parthian quiver: the Parthians were a tribe of famous mounted archers
from western Asia (southeast of the Caspian Sea, now the Persian province known
as Khorasan); they inflicted a severe defeat on the Romans in 53 B.C.   *1221. payment . . . maidenhood:* Jupiter had slept with Juturna and given her immortality.

"Why put if off forever, Turnus, hang-dog?
We must fight with arms, not running. Take what shape
You will, gather your strength or craft; fly up
To the high stars, or bury yourself in earth!"
And Turnus shook his head and answered: "Jove,
Being my enemy, scares me, and the gods,
Not your hot words, fierce fellow." And his vision,   1240
Glancing about, beheld a mighty boulder,
A boundary-mark, in days of old, so huge
A dozen men in our degenerate era
Could hardly pry it loose from earth, but Turnus
Lifts it full height, hurls it full speed and, acting,
Seems not to recognize himself, in running,
Or moving, or lifting his hands, or letting the stone
Fly into space; he shakes at the knees, his blood
Runs chill in the veins, and the stone, through wide air going,
Falls short, falls spent. As in our dreams at nighttime,   1250
When sleep weighs down our eyes, we seem to be running,
Or trying to run, and cannot, and we falter,
Sick in our failure, and the tongue is thick
And the words we try to utter come to nothing,
No voice, no speech—so Turnus finds the way
Blocked off, wherever he turns, however bravely.
All sorts of things go through his mind: he stares
At the Rutulians,° at the town; he trembles,
Quails at the threat of the lance; he cannot see
Any way out, any way forward. Nothing.   1260
The chariot is gone, and the charioteer,
Juturna or Metiscus, nowhere near him.
The spear, flung by Aeneas, comes with a whir
Louder than stone from any engine, louder
Than thunderbolt; like a black wind it flies,
Bringing destruction with it, through the shield-rim,
Its sevenfold strength, through armor, through the thigh.
Turnus is down, on hands and knees, huge Turnus
Struck to the earth. Groaning, the stunned Rutulians
Rise to their feet, and the whole hill resounds,   1270
The wooded heights give echo. A suppliant, beaten,
Humbled at last, his hands reach out, his voice
Is low in pleading: "I have deserved it, surely,
And I do not beg off. Use the advantage.

1258. *Rutulians:* the Italian tribe of which Turnus was king.

But if a parent's grief has any power
To touch the spirit, I pray you, pity Daunus,°
(I would Anchises), send him back my body.
You have won; I am beaten, and these hands go out
In supplication: everyone has seen it.
No more. I have lost Lavinia.° Let hatred   1280
Proceed no further."
Fierce in his arms, with darting glance, Aeneas
Paused for a moment, and he might have weakened,
For the words had moved him, when, high on the shoulder,
He saw the belt of Pallas,° slain by Turnus,
Saw Pallas on the ground, and Turnus wearing
That belt with the bright studs, of evil omen
Not only to Pallas now, a sad reminder,
A deadly provocation. Terrible
In wrath, Aeneas cries: "Clad in this treasure,   1290
This trophy of a comrade, can you cherish
Hope that my hands would let you go? Now Pallas,
Pallas exacts his vengeance, and the blow
Is Pallas, making sacrifice!" He struck
Before he finished speaking: the blade went deep
And Turnus' limbs were cold in death; the spirit
Went with a moan indignant to the shadows.

1276. *Daunus:* father of Turnus.   1280. *Lavinia:* Turnus had been betrothed to
Lavinia before her father Latinus offered her in marriage to Aeneas.   1285. *Pallas:*
a young ally of Aeneas; son of Evander, the mythical Greek king from Arcadia
who settled on the future site of Rome some years before the Trojan War.

The New Testament

Dᴜʀɪɴɢ ᴛʜᴇ ʀᴇɪɢɴ ᴏғ ᴀᴜɢᴜsᴛᴜs' sᴜᴄᴇssᴏʀ, ᴛɪʙᴇʀɪᴜs, ᴏɴᴇ ᴏғ the eastern provinces of the Roman empire, Judaea, became increasingly beset by religious and political discontent. One of the events which illustrated this spirit of restlessness was the crucifixion of a young Jewish prophet at the order of a Roman governor. During the young prophet's life he seemed to be proclaiming the impossible and absurd, and his death therefore received little attention. Nevertheless, after his death his teachings continued to spread, first from Jerusalem throughout Palestine, and then through the entire Mediterranean world in the course of the first century A.D. As a result, a new community which knew no geographic boundaries and was held together primarily by his teachings grew up rapidly—the Christian Church. It soon became one of the most powerful forces in Western history.

At least equally significant was the growth, around his teachings, of a remarkable collection of twenty-seven religious treatises written in Greek and known as the New Testament. These treatises were written by a variety of authors who employed different literary forms to give expression to Christian thought. Thus there are, first of all, what we call "Gospels" (the Greek equivalent, *euangelion,* means "good tidings; good news"): four books that describe Jesus' words and deeds as the divine son and servant on earth of an omnipotent divinity. Second, there is an account of the early history of the Christian Church, known as "The Acts of the Apostles." Third, a large number of letters or "Epistles," which use a form of writing that had become popular in the Greek and Roman world in the first century B.C. Finally, there is the book of Revelation, an apocalyptic treatise roughly based on a type that was quite common in Hebrew culture: it makes use of prophetic language and elaborate symbols to reveal the vision of a future age. The selections that follow provide a representative view of most of these literary forms.

The actual writing of the treatises probably extended over a period of about a century, and the selection of these particular works for inclusion in the canon or authoritative writings of the Church lasted almost another three centuries. Thus it was not until the late fourth century A.D. that the New Testament, in its present form, seems to have won general approval in the Church.

Despite differences of literary form and doctrinal emphasis the books of the New Testament display a cohesive unity. This is not due merely to their common indebtedness to the Old Testament, with its promise of a coming Messiah and its emphasis on an all-powerful divinity capable of mercy. The authors of the New Testament also convey different aspects of the same story, and they do so as Roman subjects writing in the relatively homogeneous language of most of the eastern Mediterranean world—Greek.

The New Testament

The Birth and Youth of Christ*

The following two selections illustrate some of the interpretations given to the birth of Jesus in the literature of the early Church. The first is from Luke, who probably used written documents and oral traditions to construct, not later than 75 A.D., a clear account in a somewhat reportorial style. Most critics agree that the author was a cultivated gentile who had traveled widely with Paul and had thus learned about the origin of the Church. The second selection is from the Gospel according to John, which was first circulated at the end of the first century A.D. It does not attempt a detailed factual account, but rather gives a distinct interpretation to the life and being of Jesus as the divine word that took on the appearance of man.

And it came to pass in those days, that there went out a decree from Caesar Augustus,[1] that all the world[2] should be taxed. And this taxing was first made when Cyrenius[3] was governor of Syria. And all went to be taxed, every one into his own city. And Joseph also went up from Galilee,[4] out of the city of Nazareth,[5] into Judaea, unto the city of David, which is called Bethlehem;[6] (because he was of the house and lineage of David:) To be taxed with Mary his espoused wife, being great with child.

And so it was, that, while they were there, the days were accomplished that she should be delivered. And she brought forth her firstborn son, and wrapped him in swaddling clothes, and laid him in a manger; because there

---

* Luke 2:1–52 and John 1:1–18.   [1] Like the subsequent Roman emperors, the emperor Augustus (he ruled from 27 B.C. to 14 A.D.) had the title Caesar. No such decree by Augustus is known from other sources.   [2] The Roman Empire.   [3] Cyrenius Quirinius, Roman governor of Syria who made a census in Palestine for tax purposes in 6 A.D. It is possible that he made an earlier one, but not as governor of Syria.   [4] Territory in northwestern Palestine, west of the Sea of Galilee.   [5] A town in southern Galilee.   [6] A few miles south of Jerusalem.

was no room for them in the inn. And there were in the same country shepherds abiding in the field, keeping watch over their flock by night. And, lo, the angel of the Lord came upon them, and the glory of the Lord shone round about them: and they were sore afraid. And the angel said unto them, Fear not: for, behold, I bring you good tidings of great joy, which shall be to all people. For unto you is born this day in the city of David a Saviour, which is Christ[7] the Lord. And this shall be a sign unto you; Ye shall find the babe wrapped in swaddling clothes, lying in a manger. And suddenly there was with the angel a multitude of the heavenly host praising God, and saying, Glory to God in the highest, and on earth peace, good will toward men.

And it came to pass, as the angels were gone away from them into heaven, the shepherds said one to another, Let us now go even unto Bethlehem, and see this thing which is come to pass, which the Lord hath made known unto us. And they came with haste, and found Mary, and Joseph, and the babe lying in a manger. And when they had seen it, they made known abroad the saying which was told them concerning this child. And all they that heard it wondered at those things which were told them by the shepherds. But Mary kept all these things, and pondered them in her heart. And the shepherds returned, glorifying and praising God for all the things that they had heard and seen, as it was told unto them.

And when eight days[8] were accomplished for the circumcising of the child, his name was called Jesus,[9] which was so named of the angel before he was conceived in the womb.[10] And when the days of her purification according to the law of Moses were accomplished,[11] they brought him to Jerusalem, to present him to the Lord; (as it is written in the law of the Lord, Every male that openeth the womb shall be called holy to the Lord;) and to offer a sacrifice according to that which is said in the law of the Lord, A pair of turtledoves, or two young pigeons.

And, behold, there was a man in Jerusalem, whose name was Simeon; and the same man was just and devout, waiting for the consolation of Israel: and the Holy Ghost was upon him. And it was revealed unto him by the Holy Ghost, that he should not see death, before he had seen the Lord's Christ. And he came by the Spirit into the temple: and when the parents brought in the child Jesus, to do for him after the custom of the law, then took he him up in his arms, and blessed God, and said, Lord, now lettest

---

[7] Messiah; Greek for "The Anointed One." [8] The Old Testament prescribed that both the naming of a male child and circumcision follow eight days after birth. [9] Greek form of "Joshua"; means "The Lord is Salvation." [10] When the angel first announced his coming to Mary. [11] Jewish law of the Old Testament prescribed that a woman shall be unclean for an initial period of seven days after the birth of a male child (Leviticus 12:2ff), i.e., until his circumcision. The next two verses refer to the same passage in the Old Testament.

thou thy servant depart in peace, according to thy word: for mine eyes have seen thy salvation, which thou hast prepared before the face of all people; a light to lighten the Gentiles,[12] and the glory of thy people Israel. And Joseph and his mother marveled at those things which were spoken of him. And Simeon blessed them, and said unto Mary his mother, Behold, this child is set for the fall and rising again of many in Israel; and for a sign which shall be spoken against; (Yea, a sword shall pierce through thy own soul also,) that the thoughts of many hearts may be revealed.[13]

And there was one Anna, a prophetess, the daughter of Phanuel, of the tribe of Aser: she was of a great age, and had lived with an husband seven years from her virginity; and she was a widow of about four score and four years, which departed not from the temple, but served God with fastings and prayers night and day. And she coming in that instant gave thanks likewise unto the Lord, and spake of him to all them that looked for redemption in Jerusalem. And when they had performed all things according to the law of the Lord, they returned into Galilee, to their own city Nazareth. And the child grew, and waxed strong in spirit, filled with wisdom: and the grace of God was upon him. Now his parents went to Jerusalem every year[14] at the feast of the passover. And when he was twelve years old, they went up to Jerusalem after the custom of the feast. And when they had fulfilled the days, as they returned, the child Jesus tarried behind in Jerusalem; and Joseph and his mother knew not of it. But they, supposing him to have been in the company, went a day's journey; and they sought him among their kinsfolk and acquaintance. And when they found him not, they turned back again to Jerusalem, seeking him. And it came to pass, that after three days they found him in the temple, sitting in the midst of the doctors,[15] both hearing them, and asking them questions. And all that heard him were astonished at his understanding and answers. And when they saw him, they were amazed: and his mother said unto him, Son, why hast thou thus dealt with us? behold, thy father and I have sought thee sorrowing. And he said unto them, How is it that ye sought me? Wist ye not that I must be about my Father's[16] business? And they understood not the saying which he spake unto them. And he went down with them, and came to Nazareth, and was subject unto them: but his mother kept all these sayings in her heart. And Jesus increased in wisdom and stature, and in favour with God and man.

*

* *

[12] non-Jews. [13] Simeon is predicting that Jesus' teaching and suffering will divide the Israelites and cause some of them grief. [14] Although it was thus prescribed in the Old Testament only few could make the journey annually; it is a sign of considerable religious devotion. [15] The rabbis or teachers in the synagogue. [16] God; a play on "father" in his mother's preceding reprimand.

In the beginning[17] was the Word,[18] and the Word was with God, and the Word was God. The same was in the beginning with God. All things were made by him; and without him was not any thing made that was made. In him was life;[19] and the life was the light of men. And the light shineth in darkness; and the darkness comprehended it not.

There was a man sent from God, whose name was John.[20] The same came for a witness, to bear witness of the Light,[21] that all men through him might believe. He was not that Light, but was sent to bear witness of that Light. That was the true Light, which lighteth every man that cometh into the world. He was in the world, and the world was made by him, and the world knew him not. He came unto his own, and his own received him not.[22] But as many as received him, to them gave he power to become the sons of God, even to them that believe on his name: which were born, not of blood, nor of the will of the flesh, nor of the will of man, but of God.[23] And the Word was made flesh, and dwelt among us,[24] (and we beheld his glory, the glory as of the only begotten of the Father,) full of grace and truth.

John bare witness of him, and cried, saying, This was he of whom I spake, He that cometh after me is preferred before me: for he was before me. And of his fullness have all we received, and grace for grace. For the law was given by Moses, but grace and truth came by Jesus Christ. No man hath seen God at any time; the only begotten Son, which is in the bosom of the Father, he hath declared him.

The Sermon on the Mount*

Probably some time between 65 and 85 A.D. a Jewish Christian compiled the Gospel according to Matthew. In this work he preserved one of the largest collections of Jesus' sayings, generally known from its opening sentence as "The Sermon on the Mount." These sayings, which are imbedded in the most extensive discourse of Jesus in the Gospels, are attributed to an earlier period of his

---

[17] When God created heaven and earth. [18] Greek, *Logos,* a divine agency through which God created the world. In the Old Testament this is suggested in the repeated "God said" in the story of the Creation. [19] As a creative agency, God's Word is a source of life. [20] The Baptist, appointed by God as a precursor and prophet of Christ's imminent arrival. [21] Word. [22] That is, the Word or Light, in the form of Christ, came to earth and in particular to the Chosen People. [23] Those who accepted the Light were "reborn" into a new family, which was not determined by ethnic identification or human will, but only by the will of God. [24] "Us" refers here to the early apostles who were eyewitnesses of Christ's earthly existence. * Matthew 5:1–8:4.

ministry, when he still worked in Galilee (a northern district of
Palestine where he was born).

And seeing the multitudes, he[25] went up into a mountain: and when he
was set, his disciples came unto him: and he opened his mouth, and taught
them, saying, Blessed are the poor in spirit: for their's is the kingdom of
heaven. Blessed are they that mourn: for they shall be comforted. Blessed
are the meek: for they shall inherit the earth. Blessed are they which do
hunger and thirst after righteousness: for they shall be filled. Blessed are the
the merciful: for they shall obtain mercy. Blessed are the pure in heart: for
they shall see God. Blessed are the peacemakers: for they shall be called the
children of God. Blessed are they which are persecuted for righteousness'
sake: for their's is the kingdom of heaven. Blessed are ye, when men shall
revile you, and persecute you, and shall say all manner of evil against you
falsely, for my sake. Rejoice, and be exceeding glad: for great is your reward
in heaven: for so persecuted they the prophets which were before you.

Ye are the salt of the earth: but if the salt have lost his savour, wherewith
shall it be salted? It is thenceforth good for nothing, but to be cast out, and
to be trodden under foot of men. Ye are the light of the world. A city that
is set on an hill cannot be hid. Neither do men light a candle, and put it
under a bushel, but on a candlestick; and it giveth light unto all that are in
the house. Let your light so shine before men, that they may see your good
works, and glorify your Father which is in heaven.

Think not that I am come to destroy the law, or the prophets: I am not
come to destroy, but to fulfill. For verily I say unto you, Till heaven and
earth pass, one jot or one tittle shall in no wise pass from the law, till all be
fulfilled. Whosoever therefore shall break one of these least commandments,
and shall teach men so, he shall be called the least in the kingdom of heaven:
but whosoever shall do and teach them, the same shall be called great in the
kingdom of heaven. For I say unto you, That except your righteousness shall
exceed the righteousness of the scribes[26] and Pharisees,[27] ye shall in no case
enter into the kingdom of heaven.

Ye have heard that it was said by them of old time, Thou shalt not kill;
and whosoever shall kill shall be in danger of the judgment: but I say unto
you, That whosoever is angry with his brother without a cause shall be in
danger of the judgment: and whosoever shall say to his brother, Raca,[28]
shall be in danger of the council:[29] but whosoever shall say, Thou fool, shall

[25] Jesus.   [26] Interpreters and keepers of records and sacred scriptures, especially
the laws.   [27] Members of an ancient Jewish sect that preached strictest observance
of Mosaic law. They became symbols of a formalist observance of rigid rules.
[28] Obscure term of abuse.   [29] High court.

be in danger of hell fire.[30] Therefore if thou bring thy gift to the altar, and there rememberest that thy brother hath ought against thee; leave there thy gift before the altar, and go thy way; first be reconciled to thy brother, and then come and offer thy gift. Agree with thine adversary quickly, whiles thou art in the way with him; lest at any time the adversary deliver thee to the judge, and the judge deliver thee to the officer, and thou be cast into prison. Verily I say unto thee, Thou shalt by no means come out thence, till thou hast paid the uttermost farthing.

Ye have heard that it was said by them of old time, Thou shalt not commit adultery: but I say unto you, That whosoever looketh on a woman to lust after her hath committed adultery with her already in his heart. And if thy right eye offend thee, pluck it out, and cast it from thee: for it is profitable for thee that one of thy members should perish, and not that thy whole body should be cast into hell. And if thy right hand offend thee, cut it off, and cast it from thee: for it is profitable for thee that one of thy members should perish, and not that thy whole body should be cast into hell. It hath been said, Whosoever shall put away his wife, let him give her a writing of divorcement: but I say unto you, That whosoever shall put away his wife, saving for the cause of fornication, causeth her to commit adultery: and whosoever shall marry her that is divorced committeth adultery.

Again, ye have heard that it hath been said by them of old time, Thou shalt not forswear thyself, but shalt perform unto the Lord thine oaths: but I say unto you, Swear not at all; neither by heaven; for it is God's throne: nor by the earth; for it is his footstool: neither by Jerusalem; for it is the city of the great King. Neither shalt thou swear by thy head, because thou canst not make one hair white or black. But let your communication be, Yea, yea; Nay, nay: for whatsoever is more than these cometh of evil.

Ye have heard that it hath been said, An eye for an eye, and a tooth for a tooth: but I say unto you, That ye resist not evil: but whosoever shall smite thee on thy right cheek, turn to him the other also. And if any man will sue thee at the law, and take away thy coat, let him have thy cloke also. And whosoever shall compel thee to go a mile, go with him twain. Give to him that asketh thee, and from him that would borrow of thee turn not thou away.

Ye have heard that it hath been said, Thou shalt love thy neigbour, and hate thine enemy. But I say unto you, Love your enemies, bless them that curse you, do good to them that hate you, and pray for them which despitefully use you, and persecute you; that ye may be the children of your Father which is in heaven: for he maketh his sun to rise on the evil and on the good, and sendeth rain on the just and on the unjust. For if ye love them which love you, what reward have ye? Do not even the publicans the same? And if ye salute your brethren only, what do ye more than others? Do not even

[30] Here Christ goes beyond the traditional law.

the publicans[31] so? Be ye therefore perfect, even as your Father which is in heaven is perfect.

Take heed that ye do not your alms before men, to be seen of them: otherwise ye have no reward of your Father which is in heaven. Therefore when thou doest thine alms, do not sound a trumpet before thee, as the hypocrites do in the synagogues and in the streets, that they may have glory of men. Verily I say unto you, They have their reward. But when thou doest alms, let not thy left hand know what thy right hand doeth: that thine alms may be in secret: and thy Father which seeth in secret himself shall reward thee openly.

And when thou prayest, thou shalt not be as the hypocrites are: for they love to pray standing in the synagogues and in the corners of the streets, that they may be seen of men. Verily I say unto you, They have their reward. But thou, when thou prayest, enter into thy closet, and when thou hast shut thy door, pray to thy Father which is in secret; and thy Father which seeth in secret shall reward thee openly. But when ye pray, use not vain repetitions, as the heathen do: for they think that they shall be heard for their much speaking. Be not ye therefore like unto them: for your Father knoweth what things ye have need of, before ye ask him.

After this manner therefore pray ye: Our Father which art in heaven, Hallowed be thy name. Thy kingdom come. Thy will be done in earth, as it is in heaven. Give us this day our daily bread. And forgive us our debts, as we forgive our debtors. And lead us not into temptation, but deliver us from evil: For thine is the kingdom, and the power, and the glory, for ever. Amen.

For if ye forgive men their trespasses, your heavenly Father will also forgive you: but if ye forgive not men their trespasses, neither will your Father forgive your trespasses. Moreover when ye fast, be not, as the hypocrites, of a sad countenance: for they disfigure their faces, that they may appear unto men to fast. Verily I say unto you, They have their reward. But thou, when thou fastest, anoint thine head, and wash thy face; that thou appear not unto men to fast, but unto thy Father which is in secret: and thy Father, which seeth in secret, shall reward thee openly.

Lay not up for yourselves treasures upon earth, where moth and rust doth corrupt, and where thieves break through and steal: but lay up for yourselves treasures in heaven, where neither moth nor rust doth corrupt, and where thieves do not break through nor steal: for where your treasure is, there will your heart be also. The light of the body is the eye: if therefore thine eye be single, thy whole body shall be full of light. But if thine eye be evil, thy whole body shall be full of darkness. If therefore the light that is in thee be darkness, how great is that darkness!

[31] Tax collectors for the Romans, objects of hate among the inhabitants of the Roman provinces or colonies.

No man can serve two masters: for either he will hate the one, and love the other; or else he will hold to the one, and despise the other. Ye cannot serve God and mammon. Therefore I say unto you, Take no thought for your life, what ye shall eat, or what ye shall drink; nor yet for your body, what ye shall put on. Is not the life more than meat, and the body than raiment? Behold the fowls of the air: for they sow not, neither do they reap, nor gather into barns; yet your heavenly Father feedeth them. Are ye not much better than they? Which of you by taking thought can add one cubit unto his stature? And why take ye thought for raiment? Consider the lilies of the field, how they grow; they toil not, neither do they spin: and yet I say unto you, That even Solomon in all his glory was not arrayed like one of these. Wherefore, if God so clothe the grass of the field, which to day is, and to morrow is cast into the oven, shall he not much more cloth you, O ye of little faith? Therefore take no thought, saying, What shall we eat? or, What shall we drink? or, Wherewithal shall we be clothed? (For after all these things do the Gentiles seek:) for your heavenly Father knoweth that ye have need of all these things. But seek ye first the kingdom of God, and his righteousness; and all these things shall be added unto you. Take therefore no thought for the morrow: for the morrow shall take thought for the things of itself. Sufficient unto the day is the evil thereof.

Judge not, that ye be not judged. For with what judgment ye judge, ye shall be judged: and with what measure ye mete, it shall be measured to you again. And why beholdest thou the mote that is in thy brother's eye, but considerest not the beam that is in thine own eye? Or how wilt thou say to thy brother, Let me pull out the mote out of thine eye; and, behold, a beam is in thine own eye? Thou hypocrite, first cast out the beam out of thine own eye; and then shalt thou see clearly to cast out the mote out of thy brother's eye.

Give not that which is holy unto the dogs, neither cast ye your pearls before swine, lest they trample them under their feet, and turn again and rend you. Ask, and it shall be given you; seek, and ye shall find; knock, and it shall be opened unto you: for every one that asketh receiveth; and he that seeketh findeth; and to him that knocketh it shall be opened. Or what man is there of you, whom if his son ask bread, will he give him a stone? Or if he ask a fish, will he give him a serpent? If ye then, being evil, know how to give good gifts unto your children, how much more shall your Father which is in heaven give good things to them that ask him? Therefore all things whatsoever ye would that men should do to you, do ye even so to them: for this is the law and the prophets.

Enter ye in at the strait gate: for wide is the gate, and broad is the way, that leadeth to destruction, and many there be which go in thereat: Because strait is the gate, and narrow is the way, which leadeth unto life, and few there be that find it.

Beware of false prophets, which come to you in sheep's clothing, but inwardly they are ravening wolves. Ye shall know them by their fruits. Do men gather grapes of thorns, or figs of thistles? Even so every good tree bringeth forth good fruit; but a corrupt tree bringeth forth evil fruit. A good tree cannot bring forth evil fruit, neither can a corrupt tree bring forth good fruit. Every tree that bringeth not forth good fruit is hewn down, and cast into the fire. Wherefore by their fruits ye shall know them.

Not every one that saith unto me, Lord, Lord, shall enter into the kingdom of heaven; but he that doeth the will of my Father which is in heaven. Many will say to me in that day, Lord, Lord, have we not prophesied in thy name? And in thy name have cast out devils? And in thy name done many wonderful works? And then will I profess unto them, I never knew you: depart from me, ye that work iniquity.

Therefore whosoever heareth these sayings of mine, and doeth them, I will liken him unto a wise man, which built his house upon a rock: and the rain descended, and the floods came, and the winds blew, and beat upon that house; and it fell not: for it was founded upon a rock. And every one that heareth these sayings of mine, and doeth them not, shall be likened unto a foolish man, which built his house upon the sand: and the rain descended, and the floods came, and the winds blew, and beat upon that house; and it fell: and great was the fall of it. And it came to pass, when Jesus had ended these sayings, the people were astonished at his doctrine: for he taught them as one having authority, and not as the scribes.

When he was come down from the mountain, great multitudes followed him. And, behold, there came a leper and worshiped him, saying, Lord, if thou wilt, thou canst make me clean. And Jesus put forth his hand, and touched him, saying, I will; be thou clean. And immediately his leprosy was cleansed. And Jesus saith unto him, See thou tell no man; but go thy way, shew thyself to the priest, and offer the gift that Moses commanded,[32] for a testimony unto them.

The Parables of Jesus*

In his teaching Jesus proved himself a master of the parable. He used these fictitious narratives to clarify, typify, and illustrate moral or spiritual relations. Partially through his influence the parable as a literary form subsequently developed a rich tradition

---

[32] According to Mosaic law, the leper, on the eighth day after he has been declared healed by a priest, must normally bring the priest two male lambs, a ewe lamb, a grain offering, and some oil for a sacrificial rite of purification.   * Mark 4:1–41 and Luke 15:1–32.

in Western literature. The following two samples of Jesus' parables are drawn from the Gospels of Mark and Luke. (The former
is generally considered the earliest of the Gospels and shows traces
of having been written in a cosmopolitan center, possibly with a
non-Christian Greek audience in mind.)

And he began again to teach by the sea side: and there was gathered unto
him a great multitude, so that he entered into a ship, and sat in the sea; and
the whole multitude was by the sea on the land. And he taught them many
things by parables, and said unto them in his doctrine. Hearken; Behold,
there went out a sower to sow: and it came to pass, as he sowed, some fell
by the wayside, and the fowls of the air came and devoured it up. And some
fell on stony ground, where it had not much earth; and immediately it sprang
up, because it had no depth of earth: but when the sun was up, it was
scorched; and because it had no root, it withered away. And some fell among
thorns, and the thorns grew up, and choked it, and it yielded no fruit. And
other fell on good ground, and did yield fruit that sprang up and increased;
and brought forth, some thirty, and some sixty, and some an hundred. And
he said unto them, He that hath ears to hear, let him hear. And when he
was alone, they that were about him with the twelve asked of him the
parable. And he said unto them, Unto you it is given to know the mystery
of the kingdom of God: but unto them that are without, all these things are
done in parables: that seeing they may see, and not perceive; and hearing
they may hear, and not understand; lest at any time they should be converted, and their sins should be forgiven them. And he said unto them,
Know ye not this parable? And how then will ye know all parables?

The sower soweth the word. And these are they by the wayside, where
the word is sown; but when they have heard, Satan cometh immediately,
and taketh away the word that was sown in their hearts. And these are they
likewise which are sown on stony ground; who, when they have heard the
word, immediately receive it with gladness; and have no root in themselves,
and so endure but for a time: afterward, when affliction or persecution ariseth
for the word's sake, immediately they are offended. And these are they which
are sown among thorns; such as hear the word, and the cares of this world,
and the deceitfulness of riches, and the lusts of other things entering in,
choke the word, and it becometh unfruitful. And these are they which are
sown on good ground; such as hear the word, and receive it, and bring forth
fruit, some thirtyfold, some sixty, and some an hundred.

And he said unto them, Is a candle brought to be put under a bushel, or
under a bed? and not to be set on a candlestick? For there is nothing hid,
which shall not be manifested; neither was any thing kept secret, but that it
should come abroad. If any man have ears to hear, let him hear. And he

said unto them, Take heed what ye hear: with what measure ye mete, it shall be measured to you: and unto you that hear shall more be given. For he that hath, to him shall be given: and he that hath not, from him shall be taken even that which he hath. And he said, So is the kingdom of God, as if a man should cast seed into the ground; and should sleep, and rise night and day, and the seed should spring and grow up, he knoweth not how. For the earth bringeth forth fruit of herself; first the blade, then the ear, after that the full corn in the ear. But when the fruit is brought forth, immediately he putteth in the sickle, because the harvest is come.

And he said, Whereunto shall we liken the kingdom of God? Or with what comparison shall we compare it? It is like a grain of mustard seed, which, when it is sown in the earth, is less than all the seeds that be in the earth: but when it is sown, it groweth up, and becometh greater than all herbs, and shooteth out great branches; so that the fowls of the air may lodge under the shadow of it. And with many such parables spake he the word unto them, as they were able to hear it. But without a parable spake he not unto them: and when they were alone, he expounded all things to his disciples. And the same day, when the even was come, he saith unto them, Let us pass over unto the other side. And when they had sent away the multitude, they took him even as he was in the ship. And there were also with him other little ships. And there arose a great storm of wind, and the waves beat into the ship, so that it was now full. And he was in the hinder part of the ship, asleep on a pillow: and they awake him, and say unto him, Master, carest thou not that we perish? And he arose, and rebuked the wind, and said unto the sea, Peace, be still. And the wind ceased, and there was a great calm. And he said unto them, Why are ye so fearful? How is it that ye have no faith? And they feared exceedingly, and said one to another, What manner of man is this, that even the wind and the sea obey him?

Then drew near unto him all the publicans and sinners for to hear him. And the Pharisees and scribes murmured, saying, This man receiveth sinners, and eateth with them. And he spake this parable unto them, saying, What man of you, having an hundred sheep, if he lose one of them, doth not leave the ninety and nine in the wilderness, and go after that which is lost, until he find it? And when he hath found it, he layeth it on his shoulders, rejoicing. And when he cometh home, he calleth together his friends and neighbours, saying unto them, Rejoice with me; for I have found my sheep which was lost. I say unto you, that likewise joy shall be in heaven over one sinner that repenteth, more than over ninety and nine just persons, which need no repentance. Either what woman having ten pieces of silver, if she lose one piece, doth not light a candle, and sweep the house, and seek diligently till she find it? And when she hath found it, she calleth her friends and her neighbours together, saying, Rejoice with me; for I have found the piece which I had lost. Likewise, I say unto you, there is joy in the presence of the angels of God over one sinner that repenteth.

And he said, A certain man had two sons: and the younger of them said to his father, Father, give me the portion of goods that falleth to me. And he divided unto them his living. And not many days after the younger son gathered all together, and took his journey into a far country, and there wasted his substance with riotous living. And when he had spent all, there arose a mighty famine in that land; and he began to be in want. And he went and joined himself to a citizen of that country; and he sent him into his fields to feed swine. And he would fain have filled his belly with the husks that the swine did eat: and no man gave unto him. And when he came to himself, he said, How many hired servants of my father's have bread enough and to spare, and I perish with hunger! I will arise and go to my father, and will say unto him, Father, I have sinned against heaven, and before thee, and am no more worthy to be called thy son: make me as one of thy hired servants. And he arose, and came to his father. But when he was yet a great way off, his father saw him, and had compassion and ran, and fell on his neck, and kissed him. And the son said unto him, Father, I have sinned against heaven, and in thy sight, and am no more worthy to be called thy son. But the father said to his servants, Bring forth the best robe, and put it on him; and put a ring on his hand, and shoes on his feet: and bring hither the fatted calf, and kill it; and let us eat, and be merry: for this my son was dead, and is alive again; he was lost, and is found. And they began to be merry.

Now his elder son was in the field: and as he came and drew nigh to the house, he heard music and dancing. And he called one of the servants, and asked what these things meant. And he said unto him, Thy brother is come; and thy father hath killed the fatted calf, because he hath received him safe and sound. And he was angry, and would not go in: therefore came his father out, and intreated him. And he answering said to his father, Lo, these many years do I serve thee, neither transgressed I at any time thy commandment: and yet thou never gavest me a kid, that I might make merry with my friends: but as soon as this thy son was come, which hath devoured thy living with harlots, thou hast killed for him the fatted calf. And he said unto him, Son, thou art ever with me, and all that I have is thine. It was meet that we should make merry, and be glad: for this thy brother was dead, and is alive again; and was lost, and is found.

Christ's Betrayal, Denial, Trial, Crucifixion, and Resurrection*

As perhaps the earliest extant account of Jesus' last days on earth, the following selection has its own authority and significance. From his early ministry in Galilee Jesus moved on steadily to Jerusalem, where he knew he would have to die. In a straightforward narrative sequence, which is effective because of its apparent restraint, the author of the Gospel of Mark develops the full magnitude of Jesus' crisis and triumph.

After two days was the feast of the passover,[33] and of unleavened bread: and the chief priests and the scribes sought how they might take him[34] by craft, and put him to death. But they said, Not on the feast day, lest there be an uproar of the people.

And being in Bethany[35] in the house of Simon the leper, as he sat at meat, there came a woman having an alabaster box of ointment of spikenard very precious; and she brake the box, and poured it on his head. And there were some that had indignation within themselves, and said, Why was this waste of the ointment made? For it might have been sold for more than three hundred pence, and have been given to the poor. And they murmured against her. And Jesus said, Let her alone; why trouble ye her? She hath wrought a good work on me. For ye have the poor with you always, and whensoever ye will ye may do them good: but me ye have not always. She hath done what she could: she is come aforehand to anoint my body to the burying. Verily I say unto you, Wheresoever this gospel shall be preached throughout the whole world, this also that she hath done shall be spoken of for a memorial of her.

And Judas Iscariot, one of the twelve,[36] went unto the chief priests, to betray him unto them. And when they heard it, they were glad, and promised to give him money. And he sought how he might conveniently betray him. And the first day[37] of unleavened bread, when they killed the passover,[38] his disciples said unto him, Where wilt thou that we go and prepare that thou mayest eat the passover? And he sendeth forth two of his disciples, and saith unto them, Go ye into the city, and there shall meet you a man bearing a pitcher of water: follow him. And wheresoever he shall go in, say

* Mark 14–16. [33] Religious celebration commemorating the liberation of the Israelites from Egyptian captivity. [34] Jesus. [35] Town near Jerusalem. [36] Jesus' disciples. [37] With it started a seven-day period in which only unleavened bread was eaten. [38] Here, the lamb which is killed at the Passover as a traditional symbol of the covenant between God and the Jews.

ye to the goodman[39] of the house, The Master saith, Where is the guest chamber, where I shall eat the passover with my disciples? And he will shew you a large upper room furnished and prepared: there make ready for us. And his disciples went forth, and came into the city, and found as he had said unto them: and they made ready the passover. And in the evening he cometh with the twelve. And as they sat and did eat, Jesus said, Verily I say unto you, One of you which eateth with me shall betray me. And they began to be sorrowful, and to say unto him one by one, Is it I? And another said, Is it I? And he answered and said unto them, It is one of the twelve, that dippeth with me in the dish. The Son of man indeed goeth, as it is written[40] of him: but woe to that man by whom the Son of man is betrayed! Good were it for that man if he had never been born.

And as they did eat, Jesus took bread, and blessed, and brake it,[41] and gave to them, and said, Take, eat: this is my body. And he took the cup, and when he had given thanks, he gave it to them: and they all drank of it. And he said unto them, This is my blood of the new testament, which is shed for many. Verily I say unto you, I will drink no more of the fruit of the vine, until that day that I drink it new in the kingdom of God. And when they had sung an hymn, they went out into the mount of Olives.[42] And Jesus saith unto them, All ye shall be offended because of me this night: for it is written, I will smite the shepherd, and the sheep shall be scattered. But after that I am risen, I will go before you into Galilee. But Peter said unto him, Although all shall be offended, yet will not I. And Jesus saith unto him, Verily I say unto thee, That this day, even in this night, before the cock crow twice, thou shalt deny me thrice. But he spake the more vehemently, If I should die with thee, I will not deny thee in any wise. Likewise also said they all. And they came to a place which was named Gethsemane:[43] and he saith to his disciples, Sit ye here, while I shall pray. And he taketh with him Peter and James and John, and began to be sore amazed, and to be very heavy; and saith unto them, My soul is exceeding sorrowful unto death: tarry ye here, and watch. And he went forward a little, and fell on the ground, and prayed that, if it were possible, the hour might pass from him. And he said, Abba, Father, all things are possible unto thee; take away this cup[44] from me: nevertheless not what I will, but what thou wilt. And he cometh, and findeth them sleeping, and saith unto Peter, Simon,[45] sleepest thou? Couldest not thou watch one hour? Watch ye and pray, lest ye enter into temptation.

---

[39] The householder.   [40] An allusion to the prophetic visions of a Suffering Servant in the Old Testament.   [41] He uses the broken bread as an anticipatory symbol of his broken body and the poured wine as a symbol of his blood that will be shed.   [42] Their usual retreat during the previous week, as Judas also knew.   [43] On the eastern outskirts of Jerusalem.   [44] Bitter and humanly fatal "drink"— i.e., his impending betrayal and crucifixion.   [45] Another name for Peter.

The spirit truly is ready, but the flesh is weak. And again he went away, and prayed, and spake the same words. And when he returned, he found them asleep again, (for their eyes were heavy,) neither wist they what to answer him. And he cometh the third time, and saith unto them, Sleep on now, and take your rest: it is enough, the hour is come; behold, the Son of man is betrayed into the hands of sinners. Rise up, let us go; lo, he that betrayeth me is at hand.

And immediately, while he yet spake, cometh Judas, one of the twelve, and with him a great multitude with swords and staves, from the chief priests and the scribes and the elders.[46] And he that betrayed him had given them a token, saying, Whomsoever I shall kiss, that same is he; take him, and lead him away safely. And as soon as he was come, he goeth straightway to him, and saith, Master, master; and kissed him. And they laid their hands on him, and took him. And one of them[47] that stood by drew a sword, and smote a servant of the high priest, and cut off his ear. And Jesus answered and said unto them, Are ye come out, as against a thief, with swords and with staves to take me? I was daily with you in the temple teaching, and ye took me not: but the scriptures must be fulfilled. And they all forsook him, and fled. And there followed him a certain young man, having a linen cloth cast about his naked body; and the young men laid hold on him: And he left the linen cloth, and fled from them naked. And they led Jesus away to the high priest: and with him were assembled all the chief priests and the elders and the scribes.[48] And Peter followed him afar off, even into the palace of the high priest: and he sat with the servants, and warmed himself at the fire. And the chief priests and all the council sought for witness against Jesus to put him to death; and found none. For many bare false witness against him, but their witness agreed not together. And there arose certain, and bare false witness against him, saying, We heard him say, I will destroy this temple that is made with hands, and within three days I will build another made without hands. But neither so did their witness agree together. And the high priest stood up in the midst, and asked Jesus, saying, Answerest thou nothing? What is it which these witness against thee? But he held his peace, and answered nothing. Again the high priest asked him, and said unto him, Art thou the Christ, the Son of the Blessed? And Jesus said, I am: and ye shall see the Son of man sitting on the right hand of power, and coming in the clouds of heaven. Then the high priest rent his clothes, and saith, What need we any further witnesses? Ye have heard the blasphemy:[49] what think

[46] Either members of the Temple police or an unofficial group gathered by Jesus' leading opponents. [47] Peter. [48] Since the Sanhedrin or Council could not decide a case involving possible capital punishment at night, this was an informal hearing, which had to be confirmed by vote the next morning. [49] The penalty for this would have been death by stoning, but Jesus is eventually charged with rebelling against Rome—hence Pilate and the Roman method of execution: crucifixion.

ye? And they all condemned him to be guilty of death. And some began to spit on him, and to cover his face, and to buffet him, and to say unto him, Prophesy: and the servants did strike him with the palms of their hands.

And as Peter was beneath in the palace, there cometh one of the maids of the high priest: and when she saw Peter warming himself, she looked upon him, and said, And thou also wast with Jesus of Nazareth. But he denied, saying, I know not, neither understand I what thou sayest. And he went out into the porch; and the cock crew. And a maid saw him again, and began to say to them that stood by, This is one of them. And he denied it again. And a little after, they that stood by said again to Peter, Surely thou art one of them: for thou art a Galilaean,[50] and thy speech agreeth thereto. But he began to curse and to swear, saying, I know not this man of whom ye speak. And the second time the cock crew. And Peter called to mind the word that Jesus said unto him, Before the cock crow twice, thou shalt deny me thrice. And when he thought thereon, he wept.

And straightway in the morning the chief priests held a consultation with the elders and scribes and the whole council, and bound Jesus, and carried him away, and delivered him to Pilate.[51] And Pilate asked him, Art thou the King[52] of the Jews? And he answering said unto him, Thou sayest it. And the chief priests accused him of many things: but he answered nothing. And Pilate asked him again, saying, Answerest thou nothing? Behold how many things they witness against thee. But Jesus yet answered nothing; so that Pilate marveled.

Now at that feast he released unto them one prisoner, whomsoever they desired. And there was one named Barabbas, which lay bound with them that had made insurrection with him, who had committed murder in the insurrection. And the multitude crying aloud began to desire him to do as he had ever done unto them.[53] But Pilate answered them, saying, Will ye that I release unto you the King of the Jews? For he knew that the chief priests had delieverd him for envy. But the chief priests moved the people, that he should rather release Barabbas unto them. And Pilate answered and said again unto them, What will ye then that I shall do unto him whom ye call the King of the Jews? And they cried out again, Crucify him. Then Pilate said unto them, Why, what evil hath he done? And they cried out the more exceedingly, Crucify him.

---

[50] Like Jesus, Peter was from Galilee.   [51] Pontius Pilate, appointed procurator of the Roman province of Judaea by the emperor Tiberius in 26 A.D. Although the Romans officially allowed the Jews autonomy in settling all religious disputes, approving a death sentence was always the prerogative of the Roman representatives.   [52] Thus supposedly not recognizing Roman sovereignty and rebelling against the Romans.   [53] To release one Jewish prisoner during Passover as was customary.

And so Pilate, willing to content the people, released Barabbas unto them, and delivered Jesus, when he had scourged him, to be crucified. And the soldiers led him away into the hall, called Praetorium;[54] and they call together the whole band. And they clothed him with purple, and platted a crown[55] of thorns, and put it about his head, and began to salute him, Hail, King of the Jews! And they smote him on the head with a reed, and did spit upon him, and bowing their knees worshiped him. And when they had mocked him, they took off the purple from him, and put his own clothes on him, and led him out to crucify him. And they compel one Simon a Cyrenian,[56] who passed by, coming out of the country, the father of Alexander and Rufus, to bear his cross. And they bring him unto the place Golgotha, which is, being interpreted, The place of a skull. And they gave him to drink wine mingled with myrrh: but he received it not. And when they had crucified him, they parted his garments, casting lots upon them, what every man should take. And it was the third hour, and they crucified him. And the superscription of his accusation was written over, The King of the Jews. And with him they crucify two thieves; the one on his right hand, and the other on his left. And the scripture was fulfilled, which saith, And he was numbered with the transgressors. And they that passed by railed on him, wagging their heads, and saying, Ah, thou that destroyest the temple, and buildest it in three days. Save thyself, and come down from the cross. Likewise also the chief priests mocking said among themselves with the scribes, He saved others; himself he cannot save. Let Christ the King of Israel descend now from the cross, that we may see and believe. And they that were crucified with him reviled him.

And when the sixth hour was come, there was darkness over the whole land until the ninth hour. And at the ninth hour Jesus cried with a loud voice, saying, Eloi, Eloi, lama sabachthani?[57] which is, being interpreted, My God, my God, why hast thou forsaken me? And some of them that stood by, when they heard it, said, Behold, he calleth Elias.[58] And one ran and filled a spunge full of vinegar, and put it on a reed, and gave him to drink, saying, Let alone; let us see whether Elias will come to take him down. And Jesus cried with a loud voice, and gave up the ghost. And the veil [59] of the temple was rent in twain from the top to the bottom.

And when the centurion,[60] which stood over against him, saw that he so

---

[54] Famous palace built by Herod the Great and occupied by the Roman procurator when he visited Jerusalem. [55] "Purple" and "crown" are mockingly used as signs of his royalty. [56] From Cyrene, in what now is Libya. Jews from this part of North Africa soon became active in the early Christian Church. [57] Jesus is thought by some scholars to be quoting part of Psalm 22 in his native Aramaic, spoken by most Palestinian Jews at this time. [58] Famous Old Testament prophet (Elijah). [59] Before the most holy part of the Temple. [60] Roman commander of a company; here in charge of the crucifixion.

cried out, and gave up the ghost, he said, Truly this man was the Son of God. There were also women looking on afar off: among whom was Mary Magdalene, and Mary the mother of James the less and of Joses, and Salome; (who also, when he was in Galilee, followed him, and ministered unto him;) and many other women which came up with him unto Jerusalem.

And now when the even was come, because it was the preparation, that is, the day before the sabbath, Joseph of Arimathaea, an honourable counsellor, which also waited for the kingdom of God, came, and went in boldly unto Pilate, and craved the body of Jesus. And Pilate marveled if he were already dead: and calling unto him the centurion, he asked him whether he had been any while dead. And when he knew it of the centurion, he gave the body to Joseph. And he bought fine linen, and took him down, and wrapped him in the linen, and laid him in a sepulcher which was hewn out of a rock, and rolled a stone unto the door of the sepulcher. And Mary Magdalene and Mary the mother of Joses beheld where he was laid.

And when the sabbath was past, Mary Magdalene and Mary the mother of James, and Salome, had bought sweet spices, that they might come and anoint him. And very early in the morning the first day of the week, they came unto the sepulcher at the rising of the sun. And they said among themselves, Who shall roll us away the stone from the door of the sepulcher? And when they looked, they saw that the stone was rolled away; for it was very great. And entering into the sepulcher, they saw a young man sitting on the right side, clothed in a long white garment; and they were affrighted. And he saith unto them, Be not affrighted: Ye seek Jesus of Nazareth, which was crucified: he is risen; he is not here: behold the place where they laid him. But go your way, tell his disciples and Peter that he goeth before you into Galilee: there shall ye see him, as he said unto you. And they went out quickly, and fled from the sepulcher; for they trembled and were amazed: neither said they any thing to any man; for they were afraid.

Now when Jesus was risen early the first day of the week, he appeared first to Mary Magdalene, out of whom he had cast seven devils. And she went and told them that had been with him, as they mourned and wept. And they, when they had heard that he was alive, and had been seen of her, believed not. After that he appeared in another form unto two of them, as they walked, and went into the country. And they went and told it unto the residue: neither believed they them. Afterward he appeared unto the eleven[61] as they sat at meat, and upbraided them with their unbelief and hardness of heart, because they believed not them which had seen him after he was risen. And he said unto them, Go ye into all the world, and preach the gospel to every creature. He that believeth and is baptized shall be saved; but he that believeth not shall be damned. And these signs shall follow

[61] All the disciples except Judas.

them that believe; In my name shall they cast out devils; they shall speak with new tongues; they shall take up serpents; and if they drink any deadly thing, it shall not hurt them; they shall lay hands on the sick, and they shall recover.

So then after the Lord had spoken unto them, he was received up into heaven, and sat on the right hand of God. And they went forth, and preached everywhere, the Lord working with them, and confirming the word with signs following. Amen.

Saul's Conversion*

One of the most outstanding figures in the Christian Church of the first century A.D. was Paul—known as Saul before his conversion—to whom more than half the letters in the New Testament are attributed. As a result of his travels to Greece, Asia Minor, the Near East, and Rome, he was partly responsible for the spread of Christianity throughout the Mediterranean. His conversion, in which his later activities always remained rooted, is described in the following selection from the "Acts of the Apostles," which is often attributed to the author of the Gospel according to St. Luke.

And Saul, yet breathing[62] out threatenings and slaughter against the disciples of the Lord, went unto the high priest, and desired of him letters to Damascus to the synagogues, that if he found any of this way,[63] whether they were men or women, he might bring them bound unto Jerusalem. And as he journeyed, he came near Damascus: and suddenly there shined round about him a light from heaven: and he fell to the earth, and heard a voice saying unto him, Saul, Saul, why persecutest thou me? And he said, Who art thou, Lord? And the Lord said, I am Jesus whom thou persecutest: it is hard for thee to kick against the pricks. And he trembling and astonished said, Lord, what wilt thou have me to do? And the Lord said unto him, Arise, and go into the city, and it shall be told thee what thou must do. And the men which journeyed with him stood speechless, hearing a voice, but seeing no man. And Saul arose from the earth; and when his eyes were opened, he saw no man: but they led him by the hand, and brought him into Damascus. And he was three days without sight, and neither did eat nor drink.

And there was a certain disciple at Damascus, named Ananias; and to him said the Lord in a vision, Ananias. And he said, Behold, I am here, Lord.

* Acts 9:1-22. [62] Saul was a Jew who had been persecuting the Christian Church throughout Palestine, particularly since he feared that it might mean the end of Pharisaism. [63] of this persuasion, that is, Christians.

And the Lord said unto him, Arise, and go into the street which is called Straight, and enquire in the house of Judas for one called Saul, of Tarsus:[64] for, behold, he prayeth, and hath seen in a vision a man named Ananias coming in, and putting his hand on him, that he might receive his sight. Then Ananias answered, Lord, I have heard by many of this man, how much evil he hath done to thy saints at Jerusalem: and here he hath authority from the chief priests to bind all that call on thy name. But the Lord said unto him, Go thy way: for he is a chosen vessel unto me, to bear my name before the Gentiles, and kings, and the children of Israel: for I will shew him how great things he must suffer for my name's sake.

And Ananias went his way, and entered into the house; and putting his hands on him said, Brother Saul, the Lord, even Jesus, that appeared unto thee in the way as thou camest, hath sent me, that thou mightest receive thy sight, and be filled with the Holy Ghost. And immediately there fell from his eyes as it had been scales: and he received sight forthwith, and arose, and was baptized. And when he had received meat, he was strengthened. Then was Saul certain days with the disciples which were at Damascus. And straightway he preached Christ in the synagogues, that he is the Son of God. But all that heard him were amazed, and said; Is not this he that destroyed them which called on this name in Jerusalem, and came hither for that intent, that he might bring them bound unto the chief priests? But Saul increased the more in strength, and confounded the Jews which dwelt at Damascus, proving that this is very Christ.

The Revelation*

The New Testament concludes with an apocalyptic vision of God's final triumph over the powers of evil. The account of this extraordinary vision was apparently written in the late first century A.D., when Christians were persecuted severely and participation in the worship of the deified Roman emperor was made a test of loyalty to the Roman Empire. With a luxurious richness of detail the powers of evil are symbolized primarily as a dragon or a beast, whereas their conqueror, Christ, is a lamb.

The Revelation[65] of Jesus Christ, which God gave unto him, to shew unto his servants things which must shortly come to pass; and he sent and signified

[64] Town in Cilicia (southeastern Asia Minor). * Rev. 1:1–11, 13:1–18, 19:11–21, 20:1–15, 21:1–27, 22:16–19. [65] Disclosure of God's redemptive purposes reserved for the End or *eschaton*. It originates in God, is made known to Jesus, and then to the author through an angel.

it by his angel unto his servant John: who bare record of the word of God, and of the testimony of Jesus Christ, and of all things that he saw. Blessed is he that readeth, and they that hear the words of this prophecy, and keep those things which are written therein: for the time is at hand. . . . Behold, he cometh with clouds; and every eye shall see him, and they also which pierced him: and all kindreds of the earth shall wail because of him. Even so, Amen. . . .

I John, who also am your brother, and companion in tribulation, and in the kingdom and patience of Jesus Christ, was in the isle that is called Patmos,[66] for the word of God, and for the testimony of Jesus Christ. I was in the Spirit on the Lord's day, and heard behind me a great voice, as of a trumpet. Saying, I am Alpha and Omega,[67] the first and the last: and, What thou seest, write in a book. . . .

And I stood upon the sand of the sea, and saw a beast[68] rise up out of the sea, having seven heads and ten horns, and upon his horns ten crowns, and upon his heads the name of blasphemy. And the beast which I saw was like unto a leopard, and his feet were as the feet of a bear, and his mouth as the mouth of a lion: and the dragon[69] gave him his power, and his seat, and great authority. And I saw one of his heads as it were wounded[70] to death; and his deadly wound was healed: and all the world wondered after the beast. And they worshiped the dragon which gave power unto the beast: and they worshiped the beast, saying, Who is like unto the beast? Who is able to make war with him? And there was given unto him a mouth speaking great things and blasphemies; and power was given unto him to continue forty and two[71] months. And he opened his mouth in blasphemy against God, to blaspheme his name, and his tabernacle, and them that dwell in heaven. And it was given unto him to make war with the saints, and to overcome them: and power was given him over all kindreds, and tongues, and nations. And all that dwell upon the earth shall worship him,[72] whose names are not written in the book of life of the Lamb slain from the foundation of the

[66] A small island off the west coast of Asia Minor. The author was apparently banished to Patmos because he was a Christian. [67] The first and last letters of the Greek alphabet. [68] This chapter has two visions concerning the Christian Church under persecution, which seem to merge into each other. Although no interpretation can claim validity with any certainty, the first beast is often interpreted as representing the pagan state, particularly the Roman emperor, whereas the second beast is thought to represent pagan religion, in particular the priesthood in charge of worship of the Roman emperor. [69] Satan, who cooperates with the pagan authority of the Empire. [70] The heads are sometimes interpreted as representing the deified Roman emperors and the wounded head as representing the emperor Nero. After he committed suicide, it was widely rumored that he had recovered and was alive or would soon return from the dead. [71] His success is temporary, but nevertheless terrifying and vast. [72] Perhaps reflects the almost universal popularity of the emperor cult.

world. If any man have an ear, let him hear. He that leadeth into captivity shall go into captivity: he that killeth with the sword must be killed with the sword. Here is the patience and the faith of the saints. And I beheld another beast coming up out of the earth; and he had two horns like a lamb, and he spake as a dragon.[73] And he exerciseth all the power of the first beast before him, and causeth the earth and them which dwell therein to worship the first beast, whose deadly wound was healed. And he doeth great wonders,[74] so that he maketh fire come down from heaven on the earth in the sight of men, and deceiveth them that dwell on the earth by the means of those miracles which he had power to do in the sight of the beast; saying to them that dwell on the earth, that they should make an image to the beast, which had the wound by a sword, and did live. And he had power to give life unto the image of the beast, that the image of the beast should both speak, and cause that as many as would not worship the image of the beast should be killed.[75] And he causeth all, both small and great, rich and poor, free and bond, to receive a mark in their right hand, or in their foreheads: and that no man might buy or sell, save he that had the mark, or the name of the beast, or the number of his name. Here is wisdom. Let him that hath understanding count the number of the beast: for it is the number of a man; and his number is Six hundred threescore and six.[76]

And I saw heaven[77] opened, and behold a white horse; and he that sat upon him was called Faithful and True,[78] and in righteousness he doth judge and make war. His eyes were as a flame of fire, and on his head were many crowns; and he had a name written, that no man knew, but he himself. And he was clothed with a vesture dipped in blood: and his name is called The Word of God. And the armies which were in heaven followed him upon white horses, clothed in fine linen, white and clean. And out of his mouth goeth a sharp sword, that with it he should smite the nations: and he shall rule them with a rod of iron: and he treadeth the winepress of the fierceness and wrath of Almighty God. And he hath on his vesture and on his thigh a name written, King of Kings, and Lord of Lords. And I saw an angel standing in the sun; and he cried with a loud voice, saying to all the fowls that fly in the midst of heaven, Come and gather yourselves together unto the supper of the great God; that ye may eat the flesh of kings, and the flesh of captains, and the flesh of mighty men, and the flesh of horses, and of them that sit on

---

[73] As seductively as Satan.   [74] Such "miracles" were well-known in pagan magic.
[75] Probably the Christians, who refused to participate in worship of the emperor.
[76] 666; other ancient authorities read "616." The number has been interpreted to signify a vast variety of anti-Christian rulers, ranging from Nero to Hitler.
[77] Whereas the previous passage dealt with the persecution of the Church on earth ("out of the sea"), this one contains a vision of the final victory of Christ over "beasts" and all types of "false prophets."   [78] Christ ready for battle against the Satanic host.

them, and the flesh of all men, both free and bond, both small and great. And I saw the beast, and the kings of the earth, and their armies, gathered together to make war against him that sat on the horse, and against his army. And the beast was taken, and with him the false prophet that wrought miracles before him, with which he deceived them that had received the mark of the beast, and them that worshiped his image. These both were cast alive into a lake of fire burning with brimstone. And the remnant were slain with the sword of him that sat upon the horse, which sword proceeded out of his mouth; and all the fowls were filled with their flesh.

And I saw an angel come down from heaven, having the key of the bottomless pit and a great chain in his hand. And he laid hold on the dragon, that old serpent, which is the Devil, and Satan, and bound him a thousand years. . . .[79] And the devil that deceived them was cast into the lake of fire and brimstone, where the beast and the false prophet are, and shall be tormented day and night for ever and ever. And I saw a great white throne,[80] and him that sat on it, from whose face the earth and the heaven fled away; and there was found no place for them. And I saw the dead, small and great, stand before God; and the books[81] were opened: and another book was opened, which is the book of life: and the dead were judged out of those things which were written in the books, according to their works. And the sea gave up the dead which were in it; and death and hell delivered up the dead which were in them: and they were judged every man according to their works. And death and hell were cast into the lake of fire. This is the second death.[82] And whosoever was not found written in the book of life was cast into the lake of fire.

And I saw a new heaven and a new earth: for the first heaven and the first earth were passed away; and there was no more sea. And I John saw the holy city,[83] new Jerusalem, coming down from God out of heaven, prepared as a bride adorned for her husband. And I heard a great voice out of heaven saying, Behold, the tabernacle of God is with men, and he will dwell with them, and they shall be his people, and God himself shall be with them, and be their God. And God shall wipe away all tears from their eyes; and

---

[79] The millenial reign on earth of the Christian martyrs and Christ.   [80] Symbol of the Last Judgment.   [81] Recording men's deeds.   [82] After all souls have been resurrected for the Last Judgment, neither death nor hell could any longer serve a function, since the unworthy went to a lake of fire (second death) and the Christians to the New Jerusalem.   [83] The New Jerusalem, representing God's new order, from which all that is transitory, deficient, and dangerous is excluded. The Christian Church (Christ's "bride") is compared to this city, a perfect Community. It is perhaps significant that the Bible begins with a vision of a garden (Eden) and ends with a vision of a city.

there shall be no more death, neither sorrow, nor crying, neither shall there be any more pain: for the former things are passed away. And he that sat upon the throne said, Behold, I make all things new. And he said unto me, Write: for these words are true and faithful. And he said unto me, It is done. I am Alpha and Omega, the beginning and the end. I will give unto him that is athirst of the fountain of the water of life freely. He that over-cometh shall inherit all things; and I will be his God, and he shall be my son. But the fearful, and unbelieving, and the abominable, and murderers, and whoremongers, and sorcerers, and idolaters, and all liars, shall have their part in the lake which burneth with fire and brimstone: which is the second death. And there came unto me one of the seven angels which had the seven vials full of the seven last plagues, and talked with me, saying, Come hither, I will shew thee the bride, the Lamb's wife.[84] And he carried me away in the spirit to a great and high mountain, and shewed me that great city, the holy Jerusalem, descending out of heaven from God, having the glory of God: and her light was like unto a stone most precious, even like a jasper stone, clear as crystal; and had a wall great and high, and had twelve gates, and at the gates twelve angels, and names written thereon, which are the names of the twelve tribes of the children of Israel: on the east three gates; on the north three gates; on the south three gates; and on the west three gates. And the wall of the city had twelve foundations, and in them the names of the twelve apostles of the Lamb. And he that talked with me had a golden reed to measure the city, and the gates thereof, and the wall thereof . . . . And the building of the wall of it was of jasper: and the city was pure gold, like unto clear glass. And the foundations of the wall of the city were garnished with all manner of precious stones. The first founda-tion was jasper; the second, sapphire; the third, a chalcedony; the fourth, an emerald; the fifth, sardonyx; the sixth, sardius; the seventh, chrysolyte; the eighth, beryl; the ninth, a topaz; the tenth, a chrysoprasus; the eleventh, a jacinth; the twelfth, an amethyst. And the twelve gates were twelve pearls: every several gate was of one pearl: and the street of the city was pure gold, as it were transparent glass. And I saw no temple therein: for the Lord God Almighty and the Lamb are the temple of it. And the city had no need of the sun, neither of the moon, to shine in it: for the glory of God did lighten it, and the Lamb is the light thereof. And the nations[85] of them which are saved shall walk in the light of it: and the kings of the earth do bring their glory and honour into it. And the gates of it shall not be shut at all by day: for there shall be no night there. And they shall bring the glory and honour of the nations into it. And there shall in no wise enter into it any thing that

---

[84] Christ's wife, i.e., the Christian Church.   [85] The city consists of the redeemed from all nations; the apocalyptic vision of the New Testament transcends the eth-nic boundaries of earlier prophetic visions.

defileth, neither whatsoever worketh abomination, or maketh a lie: but they which are written in the Lamb's book of life.

I Jesus have sent mine angel to testify unto you these things in the churches. I am the root and the offspring of David, and the bright and morning star. And the Spirit and the bride say, Come. And let him that heareth say, Come. And let him that is athirst come. And whosoever will, let him take the water of life freely. For I testify unto every man that heareth the words of the prophecy of this book, If any man shall add unto these things, God shall add unto him the plagues that are written in this book: and if any man shall take away from the words of the book of this prophecy, God shall take away his part out of the book of life, and out of the holy city, and from the things, which are written in this book.

Petronius

FROM *Satyricon*

TRANSLATED BY WILLIAM ARROWSMITH

Petronius (?–66 A.D.)

It is widely agreed but not absolutely certain that the author of a partly extant work called *The Satyricon of Petronius Arbiter* was the Roman aristocrat Caius Petronius, a "Director of Refined Taste" (*arbiter elegantiae*) at the court of the emperor Nero. His suicide at the emperor's order is described in one of the following selections from Tacitus.

The *Satyricon* is a comic narrative, often licentious and always pungently satirical, written in a colloquial style which is unique in all of Latin literature. Although the exact literary form of this work, which originally consisted of at least sixteen books that mixed poetry and prose, remains obscure. However, the surviving fragments suggest that it parodied a number of literary genres. The author seems to have made heroic epic a frequent target of his parodies. For example, just as the god Poseidon in the *Odyssey* haunts Odysseus across unknown seas from adventure to adventure, so in the *Satyricon* the phallic god Priapus chases the narrator, Encolpius, from one lewd adventure to another. A further genre to which there is frequent parodistic allusion is the Greek romance (prose fiction similar to a short novel, frequently about incidents remote from everyday life). In the typical romance, lovers are often unexpectedly separated and then, after numerous and adventurous tests of their love, reunited; so too Encolpius and his beloved are separated and reunited. But unlike the lovers in the romance, who are usually highly idealized, Encolpius is a cynical, realistically portrayed student of rhetoric and literature, and his beloved is a handsome young boy, Giton. Their separation is due to the revenge of Priapus rather than to chance.

The author does not, however, merely parody the conventions of certain literary genres. He also develops his characters brilliantly, as the following selections from the most complete surviving fragment of the work, "Trimalchio's Dinner Party," illustrate. In these passages Encolpius, with coarse realism and unfailing cynicism, describes one stage of his adventurous journey—a dinner given by a grotesque millionaire in an unidentified provincial town in southern Italy. The host, Trimalchio, began as a slave, but through a total preoccupation with money gained his vast wealth and his status as a symbol of parvenu vulgarity. The guests at the dinner are a number of mercilessly satirized characters who display an habitual inclination to deceive, a façade of sophistication which barely conceals their heterosexual and homosexual vulgarity, and an emphasis on living for the transitory sensual experience. The absence of any explicit moralizing on the part of the author makes these characterizations a particularly effective unmasking of an age that found its lasting symbol in the emperor Nero.

Satyricon

Dinner with Trimalchio

At last the third day had come with its prospect of a free meal and perhaps our[1] last meal on this earth. But by now our poor bodies were so bruised and battered [2] that escape, even if it cost us a meal, seemed preferable to staying where we were. While we were gloomily wondering how we could avoid the orgy in store for us with Quartilla, one of Agamemnon's[3] slaves came up and dispelled our despair. "What's eating you?" he asked. "Have you forgotten where you're going tonight? Trimalchio's[4] giving the meal. He's real swank. Got a great big clock[5] in his dining room and a uniformed bugler who blows a horn every hour so the old man won't forget how fast his time is slipping away." Needless to say, we forgot our troubles fast when we heard this. We slipped into our best clothes, and when Giton very sweetly offered to act as our servant, we told him to attend us to the baths.[6]

There we wandered around at first without getting undressed. Or rather we went joking around, mixing with various groups of bathers at their games. Suddenly we caught sight of an old, bald man in a long red undershirt, playing ball with a bunch of curly-headed slave boys. It wasn't so much the boys who took our eyes—though they were worth looking at—as the old man himself. There he stood, rigged out in undershirt and sandals, nothing else, bouncing a big green ball the color of a leek. When he dropped one ball, moreover, he never bothered to stoop for it, but simply took another from a slave who stood beside him with a huge sack tossing out fresh balls to the players. This was striking enough, but the real refinement was two eunuchs standing on either side of the circle, one clutching a chamber pot of solid silver, the other ticking off the balls. He was not, however, scoring the players' points, but merely keeping count of any balls that happened to drop on the ground. While we were gawking at these elegant gymnastics, Mene-

---

[1] Of the narrator Encolpius, his fellow student Ascyltus, and the handsome boy Giton.   [2] On account of exhausting and lewd adventures.   [3] Professor of rhetoric; teacher of Encolpius and Ascyltus.   [4] Trimalchio seems to mean "thrice fortunate" or "great and rich."   [5] A rare luxury item in Rome.   [6] Public baths; popular meeting places of elaborate and luxurious construction.

laus[7] came rushing up. "That's *him!*" he whispered, "that's the fellow who's giving the meal. What you're seeing now is just the prelude to the show." These words were hardly out when Trimalchio gave a loud snap with his fingers. The eunuch came waddling up with the chamber pot, Trimalchio emptied his bladder and went merrily on with his game. When he was done, he shouted for water, daintily dipped the tips of his fingers and wiped his hands in the long hair of a slave.

But the details of his performance would take too long to tell. We quickly undressed, went into the hot baths, and after working up a sweat, passed on to the cold showers. There we found Trimalchio again, his skin glistening all over with perfumed oil. He was being rubbed down, not with ordinary linen, but with cloths of the purest and softest wool. During this rubdown, right before his eyes, the three masseurs were guzzling away at the finest of his rare Falernian wines.[8] In a minute, moreover, they were squabbling and in the next second the wine had spilled all over the floor. "Tut, a mere trifle," said Trimalchio, "they were merely pouring me a toast." [9] He was then bundled into a blazing scarlet wrapper, hoisted onto a litter and trundled off. Before him went four runners in spangled harness and a little wheelbarrow in which the old man's favorite rode, a little boy with a wrinkled face and bleary, crudded eyes, even uglier than his master. A musician with a miniature flute trotted along at Trimalchio's head and during the entire trip played into his master's ear as though whispering him little secrets.

Drunk with admiration, we brought up the rear and Agamemnon joined us when we reached Trimalchio's door. Beside the door we saw a sign:

ANY SLAVE LEAVING THE PREMISES
WITHOUT AUTHORIZATION FROM THE MASTER
WILL RECEIVE ONE HUNDRED LASHES!

At the entrance sat the porter, dressed in that same leek-green that seemed to be the livery of the house. A cherry-colored sash was bound around his waist and he was busily shelling peas into a pan of solid silver. In the doorway hung a cage, all gold, and in it a magpie was croaking out his welcome to the guests.

I was gaping at all this in open-mouthed wonder when I suddenly jumped with terror, stumbled, and nearly broke my leg. For there on the left as you entered, in fresco, stood a huge dog straining at his leash. In large letters under the painting was scrawled:

---

[7] Agamemnon's assistant; the junior rhetorician. These epic names all caricature the characters of—and the relations between—their bearers.   [8] One of the highly esteemed Roman wines; from the Falernian territory in Campania, at the foot of Mount Massicus.   [9] It was customary to pour some wine under the table as an offering to the gods whenever one drank to someone's health.

BEWARE OF THE DOG!

The others burst out laughing at my fright. But when I'd recovered from the shock, I found myself following the rest of the frescoes with fascination. They ran the whole length of the wall. First came a panel showing a slave market with everything clearly captioned. There stood Trimalchio as a young man, his hair long and curly in slave fashion; in his hand he held a staff and he was entering Rome for the first time under the sponsorship of Minerva.[10] In the next panel he appeared as an apprentice accountant, then as a paymaster—each step in his career portrayed in great detail and everything scrupulously labeled. At the end of the portico you came to the climax of the series: a picture of Mercury[11] grasping Trimalchio by the chin and hoisting him up to the lofty eminence of the official's tribunal.[12] . . .

While we were commenting on it and savoring the luxury, a slave brought in a skeleton,[13] cast of solid silver, and fastened in such a way that the joints could be twisted and bent in any direction. The servants threw it down on the table in front of us and pushed it into several suggestive postures by twisting its joints, while Trimalchio recited this verse of his own making:

> Nothing but bones, that's what we are.
> Death hustles us humans away.
> Today we're here and tomorrow we're not,
> so live and drink while you may!

The course that followed our applause failed, however, to measure up to our expectations of our host, but it was so unusual that it took everybody's attention. Spaced around a circular tray were the twelve signs of the zodiac, and over each sign the chef had put the most appropriate food.[14] Thus, over the sign of Aries were chickpeas, over Taurus a slice of beef, a pair of testicles and kidneys over Gemini, a wreath of flowers over Cancer, over Leo an African fig, virgin sowbelly on Virgo, over Libra a pair of scales with a tartlet in one pan and a cheesecake in the other, over Scorpio a crawfish, a lobster on Capricorn, on Aquarius a goose, and two mullets over the sign of the Fishes. The centerpiece was a clod of turf with the grass still green on

---

[10] Minerva (often identified with the Greek goddess Athena) was goddess of crafts and wisdom. [11] Mercury (Greek, Hermes) was the god of commerce and hence Trimalchio's patron god. [12] A throne allotted to officials who supervised the worship of the deified Emperor. [13] A reminder of death was a common part of Roman banquets and of dining room decorations. [14] In the next sentence the relationship between each zodiacal sign and the food above it lies either in a pun or in some associative resemblance. Thus beef for the Bull (Taurus), "twin" kidneys for the Twins (Gemini), and so on. An increasing influence of astrology accompanied the decline of the Roman Empire.

top and the whole thing surmounted by a fat honeycomb. Meanwhile, bread in a silver chafing dish was being handed around by a black slave with long hair who was shrilling in an atrocious voice some song from the pantomime called *Asafoetida*. With some reluctance we began to attack this wretched fare, but Trimalchio kept urging us, "Eat up, gentlemen, eat up!" . . .

By now the astrological course had been removed, the guests were gaily attacking the wine, and there was a loud hubbub of laughing and chatter. My neighbor's pleasant prattle, however, was interrupted by Trimalchio. Lounging back on his elbow, he burst out: "Gentlemen, I want you to savor this good wine. Fish must swim,[15] and that's a fact. But I'd like to know if you were really taken in by that stuff you saw on the top tray. Is that what you think of me? What does our Vergil say?

Is this what men report of great Ulysses? [16]

Not on your life. At dinner, I say, there should be culture as much as food. My old master—may his bones rest in peace—wanted me to be a man of the world and a gentleman of culture. And I think that last course will show you there isn't much that I don't know. Listen now, and I'll explain to you about the zodiac. This heaven, which is where the twelve gods live, changes into twelve signs. Now sometimes it turns into the Ram, that is, Aries. Everyone who gets himself born under the Ram own heaps of sheep and lots of wool; besides, his head is hard, his forehead like brass and his horns like swords. That's why many professors and also muttonheads are born under the sign of the Ram."

We all applauded our droll astrologer and he continued. "After the Ram, the Universe switches over to the Bull, who's sometimes called Taurus. The people who are born under the Bull include bullies and cowboys and people who lie down in soft pastures. Under the Twins, old Gemini, you get two-horse teams, yokes of oxen, lechers who are led around by their balls, and two-faced politicians. Cancer, or the Crab, is my sign; therefore I walk on many legs and my possessions stretch over land and sea, for the crab is at home in both those elements. That's why I avoided putting anything on my sign for a long time: I didn't want my birth-sign queered. Under Leo the Lion you get gluttons and big shots; under Virgo the Virgin you get useless women, deserters, and those who wear chains on their ankles, fetters for men, bracelets for women. Stinger Scorpio has poisoners and murderers. Under Archer Sagittarius you get cross-eyed thieves who cock an eye at the beets but snitch the ham. Under Capricorn, because it means goat-horn, come men who have horns or corns; corn-men are workers who sweat for their wages and horn-men are cuckolds all. Aquarius is a water carrier, so under him you

[15] A fish course had been served.   [16] From *The Aeneid* (II.44).

find innkeepers who water the wine and people who are all wet. But Pisces is for Fishes and he gives us the fishier types of men: gape-mouthed lawyers or just plain fish peddlers. That's why things are as they are. The universe goes whizzing around like a millwheel and is always up to some mischief and people are either dying or just getting born. As for the hunk of earth you saw sitting in the middle, that was packed with meaning too. For dead in the center of everything sits old Mother Earth, as fat as an egg, and loaded with goodies like a honeycomb."

We all cheered and cried "Bravo" and swore that Aratus[17] and Hipparchus[18] were mere amateurs, not to be compared with our host. . . .

Conversation was running along these lines [19] when Trimalchio returned, wiping the sweat from his brow. He splashed his hands in perfume and stood there for a minute in silence. "You'll excuse me, friends," he began, "but I've been constipated for days and the doctors are stumped. I got a little relief from a prescription of pomegranate rind and resin in a vinegar base. Still, I hope my tummy will get back its manners soon. Right now my bowels are bumbling around like a bull. But if any of you has any business that needs attending to, go right ahead; no reason to feel embarrassed. There's not a man been born yet with solid insides. And I don't know any anguish on earth like trying to hold it in. Jupiter himself couldn't stop it from coming. What are you giggling about, Fortunata? [20] You're the one who keeps me awake all night with your trips to the potty. Well, anyone at table who wants to go has my permission, and the doctors tell us not to hold it in. Everything's ready outside—water and pots and the rest of the stuff. Take my word for it, friends, the vapors go straight to your brain. Poison your whole system. I know of some who've died from being too polite and holding it in." We thanked him for his kindness and understanding, but we tried to hide our snickers in repeated swallows of wine.

At long last the tumblers appeared. An extremely insipid clown held up a ladder and ordered a boy to climb up and do a dance on top to the accompaniment of several popular songs. He was then commanded to jump through burning hoops and to pick up a big jug with his teeth. No one much enjoyed this entertainment except Trimalchio who claimed that the stunts were extremely difficult. Nothing on earth, he added, gave him such pleasure as jugglers and buglers; everything else, such as animal shows and concerts, was utter trash. "I once bought," he bragged, "several comic actors, but I

---

[17] Hellenistic poet (third century B.C.) who wrote a famous didactic poem on astronomy, which was translated into Latin by Cicero. [18] A brilliant Greek astronomer of the second century B.C.; through Ptolemy his theories dominated Western cosmological views until the time of Copernicus. [19] Trimalchio had left the room temporarily and the quality of discourse around the dinner table deteriorated relentlessly. [20] Trimalchio's wife.

used them for doing farces[21] and I told my flutist to play nothing but Latin songs, the funny ones."

Just at this point the ladder toppled and the boy on top fell down, landing squarely on Trimalchio. The slaves shrieked, the guests screamed. We were not, of course, in the least concerned about the boy, whose neck we would have been delighted to see broken; but we dreaded the thought of possibly having to go into mourning for a man who meant nothing to us at all. Meanwhile, Trimalchio lay there groaning and nursing his as though it were broken. Doctors came rushing in, Fortunata at their head, her hair flying, a goblet in her hand, and filling the room with wails of distress. As for the boy, he was already clutching us by the legs and begging us to intercede for him. My own reaction was one of suspicion. I was afraid, that is, that these pleas for pity were simply the prelude to one more hoax; for the incident of the slave who had forgotten to gut the pig was still fresh in my mind. So I started to examine the room rather uneasily, half expecting, I suppose, that the walls would split open and god knows what contraption would appear. And these suspicions were somewhat confirmed when they began flogging a servant for having bound up his master's wounded arm with white, rather than scarlet, bandages. Actually, as it turned out, I was not far wrong, for instead of having the boy whipped, Trimalchio ordered him to be set free, so that nobody could say that the great Trimalchio had been hurt by a mere slave.

We gave this ample gesture our approval and remarked on the uncertainties of human existence. "Yes," said Trimalchio, "it would be a shame to let an occasion like this pass by without some enduring record of it." He then called for writing materials and after a brief but harrowing effort produced the following lines:

> We think we're awful smart, we think we're awful wise,
> but when we're least expecting, comes the big surprise.
> Lady Luck's in heaven and we're her little toys,
> so break out the wine and fill your glasses, boys!

. . . Immediately a troupe of rhapsodes[22] burst into the room, all banging away on their shields with spears. Trimalchio hoisted himself up on his pillows and while the rhapsodes were gushing out their Greek poetry with the usual bombast, he sat there reading aloud in Latin. At the end there was a brief silence; then Trimalchio asked us if we knew the scene from Homer the rhapsodes had just recited. "Well," he said, "I'll tell you.[23] You see, there

---

[21] That is, coarse Italian comedy, which would not normally be performed by comic actors of repute. It usually had four stock characters: the clown, the fool, the wise man, and the deceived or stupid father.   [22] Professional reciters of Greek epic poetry, particularly *The Iliad* and *The Odyssey*.   [23] Trimalchio in the following speech completely and ingeniously mutilates Greek mythology.

were these two brothers, Ganymede and Diomedes. Now they had this sister called Helen, see. Well, Agamemnon eloped with her and Diana left a deer as a fill-in for Helen. Now this poet called Homer describes the battle between the Trojans and the people of a place called Paros, which is where Paris came from. Well, as you'd expect, Agamemnon won and gave his daughter Iphigeneia to Achilles in marriage. And that's why Ajax went mad, but here he comes in person to explain the plot himself."

At this the rhapsodes burst into cheers, the slaves went scurrying about and promptly appeared with a barbecued calf, with a cap on its head, reposing on a huge platter—it must have weighed two hundred pounds at the very least. Behind it came Trimalchio's so-called Ajax. He pulled out his sword and began slashing away at the calf, sawing up and down, first with the edge and then with the flat of his blade. Then with the point of the sword he neatly skewered the slices of veal he had cut and handed them around to the astounded guests.

Our applause for this elaborate *tour de force,* however, was abruptly cut short. For all at once the coffered ceiling began to rumble and the whole room started to shake. I jumped up in terror, expecting that some acrobat was about to come swinging down through the roof. The other guests, equally frightened, lay there staring at the roof as though they were waiting for a herald from heaven. Suddenly the paneling slid apart and down through the fissure in the ceiling an immense circular hoop, probably knocked off some gigantic cask, began slowly to descend. Dangling from the hoop were chaplets of gold and little jars of perfume, all, we were informed, presents for us to take home. I filled my pockets and then, when I looked back at the table, saw a tray garnished with little cakes; in the center stood a pastry statuette of Priapus[24] with the usual phallus propping up an apron loaded with fruits and grapes of every variety. You can imagine how greedily we all grabbed, but then a fresh surprise sent us off again into fresh laughter. For at the slightest touch the cakes and fruit all squirted out jets of liquid saffron,[25] splattering our faces with the smelly stuff. Naturally enough, the use of the sacred saffron made us conclude that this course must be part of some religious rite, so we all leaped to our feet and shouted in chorus, "LONG LIVE THE EMPEROR, FATHER OF OUR COUNTRY!" Even this act of homage, however, failed to prevent some of the guests from pilfering the fruit and stuffing their napkins full. And I, of course, was among the chief offenders, thinking nothing in this world too good to fill the pockets of my Giton. . . .

At this moment an incident occurred on which our little party almost foundered. Among the incoming slaves there was a remarkably pretty boy. Trimalchio literally launched himself upon him and, to Fortunata's extreme

24 Son of Dionysus and Aphrodite, god of fertility; usually represented by a deformed anthropomorphic figure with gigantic genitals or by a phallus alone.
25 Often a sacred color, used in ritual.

annoyance, began to cover him with rather prolonged kisses. Finally, Fortunata asserted her rights and began to abuse him. "You turd!" she shrieked,
"you hunk of filth." At last she used the supreme insult: "Dog!" At this
Trimalchio exploded with rage, reached for a wine cup and slammed it into
her face. Fortunata let out a piercing scream and covered her face with
trembling hands as though she'd just lost an eye. Scintilla, stunned and
shocked, tried to comfort her sobbing friend in her arms, while a slave
solicitously applied a glass of cold water to her livid cheek. Fortunata herself
hunched over the glass heaving and sobbing.

But Trimalchio was still shaking with fury. "Doesn't that slut remember
what she used to be? By god, I took her off the sale platform and made her
an honest woman. But she blows herself up like a bullfrog. She's forgotten
how lucky she is. She won't remember the whore she used to be. People in
shacks shouldn't dream of palaces, I say. By god, if I don't tame that strutting
Cassandra,[26] my name isn't Trimalchio! . . . ."

But take my word [27] for it: money makes the man. No money and you're
nobody. But big money, big man. That's how it was with yours truly: from
mouse to millionaire.

"In the meantime, Stichus," he called to a slave, "go and fetch out the
clothes I'm going to be buried in. And while you're at it, bring along some
perfume and a sample of that wine I'm having poured on my bones."

Stichus hurried off and promptly returned with a white grave-garment and
a very splendid robe with a broad purple stripe. Trimalchio told us to inspect
them and see if we approved of the material. Then he added with a smile,
"See to it, Stichus, that no mice or moths get into them, or I'll have you
burned alive. Yes sir, I'm going to be buried in such splendor that everybody
in town will go out and pray for me." He then unstoppered a jar of fabu-
lously expensive spikenard and had us all anointed with it. "I hope," he
chuckled, "I like this perfume as much after I'm dead as I do now." Finally
he ordered the slaves to pour the wine into the bowl and said, "Imagine that
you're all present at my funeral feast."

The whole business had by now become absolutely revolting. Trimalchio
was obviously completely drunk, but suddenly he had a hankering for funeral music too and ordered a brass band sent into the dining room. Then he
propped himself on piles of cushions and stretched out full length along the
couch. "Pretend I'm dead," he said, "say something nice about me." The
band blared a dead march, but one of the slaves belonging to Habinnas[28]—
who was, incidentally, one of the most respectable people present—blew so
loudly that he woke up the entire neighborhood. Immediately the firemen

---

[26] Here as embodiment of insanity (since she prophesied only in a trancelike state).
[27] Trimalchio is still speaking.   [28] An undertaker.

assigned to that quarter of town, thinking that Trimalchio's house was on fire, smashed down the door and rushed in with buckets and axes to do their job. Utter confusion followed, of course, and we took advantage of the heaven-sent opportunity, gave Agamemnon the slip, and rushed out of there as though the place were really in flames.

Tacitus

FROM *The Annals*

TRANSLATED BY ALFRED JOHN CHURCH
AND WILLIAM JACKSON BRODRIBB

Tacitus (about 55–120 A.D.)

ALTHOUGH HE IS BEST KNOWN AS AN OUTSTANDING ROMAN historian, Tacitus was also a famous lawyer and orator, and he had a distinguished political career, culminating in the Roman governorship of Asia in 112–113 A.D. He was married to the daughter of Cnaeus Julius Agricola (who was famous for his success, as Roman governor of Britain, in subduing all of Britain except the Scottish highlands). From early manhood Tacitus continued to count the most distinguished Roman politicians and cultural figures among his acquaintances.

His extant works are *Dialogue on Orators,* a treatise in which the decline of oratory is partially explained in terms of the decline of liberty under the autocratic rule of the Roman emperors; *Agricola,* a portrait of his father-in-law; *Germania,* a valuable ethnographic work on German tribes; *The Annals,* a perceptive history of the Roman empire from the death of Augustus in 14 A.D. to the death of the emperor Nero in 68 A.D.; and the *Histories,* a history of the Roman empire from 68 A.D. to 96 A.D. Parts of the last two works are missing. Although Tacitus, like most historians, did not attain his stated goal of writing history without prejudice, he remains the most reliable witness for the period covered by his works. His method of writing history, which concentrates on outstanding characters and momentous events, often achieving an effect analogous to that of tragedy, has a long tradition behind it. So does his use of irony, which for him is expressive of a serious moral attitude.

The following selections are drawn from one of the last parts of *The Annals.* The first gives an account of the rather unique death of Petronius, and the second describes the notorious burning of Rome in 64 A.D. during the reign of Nero—events that occurred during Tacitus' own childhood. The significance of the second selection is at least threefold. First, it provides a valuable insight into relations between Romans and Christians in the first century A.D. Second, it contains a remarkable characterization of Nero, who was emperor from 54 to 68 A.D. A third significance lies in the undisguised, sober picture it provides of some of the realities of the Roman empire—realities that were concomitants of those aspects of Roman life that Petronius caricatured and satirized some years previously in his *Satyricon.*

The Annals

The Death of Petronius

With regard to Caius Petronius, I ought to dwell a little on his antecedents. His days he passed in sleep, his nights in the business and pleasures of life. Indolence had raised him to fame, as energy raises others, and he was reckoned not a debauchee and spendthrift, like most of those who squander their substance, but a man of refined luxury. And indeed his talk and his doings, the freer they were and the more show of carelessness they exhibited, were the better liked, for their look of natural simplicity. Yet as proconsul [1] of Bithynia[2] and soon afterwards as consul, he showed himself a man of vigor and equal to business. Then falling back into vice or affecting vice, he was chosen by Nero to be one of his few intimate associates, as a critic in matters of taste, while the emperor thought nothing charming or elegant in luxury unless Petronius had expressed to him his approval of it. Hence jealousy on the part of Tigellinus,[3] who looked on him as a rival and even his superior in the science of pleasure. And so he worked on the prince's cruelty, which dominated every other passion, charging Petronius with having been the friend of Scaevinus,[4] bribing a slave to become informer, robbing him of the means of defense, and hurrying into prison the greater part of his domestics.

It happened at the time that the emperor was on his way to Campania[5] and that Petronius, after going as far as Cumae,[6] was there detained. He bore no longer the suspense of fear or of hope. Yet he did not fling away life with precipitate haste, but having made an incision in his veins and then, according to his humor, bound them up, he again opened them, while he conversed with his friends, not in a serious strain or on topics that might win for him the glory of courage. And he listened to them as they repeated, not thoughts on the immortality of the soul or on the theories of philosophers,

[1] Deputy consul.   [2] District of northwestern Asia Minor, stretching east from the Bosporus.   [3] A favorite of Nero's, hated by most of the Roman people; minister to Nero's worst passions; forced to commit suicide by Nero's successor.   [4] Considered a traitor and opponent by Nero.   [5] Southwestern district of Italy; its chief city was Capua in antiquity and now is Naples.   [6] City on the coast of Campania.

but light poetry and playful verses. To some of his slaves he gave liberal presents, a flogging to others. He dined, indulged himself in sleep, that death, though forced on him, might have a natural appearance. Even in his will he did not, as did many in their last moments, flatter Nero or Tigellinus or any other of the men in power. On the contrary, he described fully the prince's shameful excesses, with the names of his male and female companions and their novelties in debauchery, and sent the account under seal to Nero. Then he broke his signet ring, that it might not be subsequently available for imperiling others. . . .

NERO AND THE BURNING OF ROME

The Senate and leading citizens were in doubt whether to regard him[7] as more terrible at a distance or among them. After a while, as is the way with great terrors, they thought what happened the worst alternative.

Nero, to win credit for himself of enjoying nothing so much as the capital, prepared banquets in the public places, and used the whole city, so to say, as his private house. Of these entertainments the most famous for their notorious profligacy were those furnished by Tigellinus, which I will describe as an illustration, that I may not have again and again to narrate similar extravagance. He had a raft constructed on Agrippa's lake,[8] put the guests on the board and set it in motion by other vessels towing it. These vessels glittered with gold and ivory; the crews were arranged according to age and experience in vice. Birds and beasts had been procured from remote countries, and sea monsters from the ocean. On the margin of the lake were set up brothels crowded with noble ladies, and on the opposite bank were seen naked prostitutes with obscene gestures and movements. As darkness approached, all the adjacent grove and surrounding buildings resounded with song, and shone brilliantly with lights. Nero, who polluted himself by every lawful or lawless indulgence, had not omitted a single abomination which could heighten his depravity, till a few days afterwards he stooped to marry himself to one of that filthy herd, by name Pythagoras,[9] with all the forms of regular wedlock. The bridal veil was put over the emperor; people saw the witnesses of the ceremony, the wedding dower, the couch and the nuptial torches; everything in a word was plainly visible, which, even when a woman weds darkness hides.

A disaster followed, whether accidental or treacherously contrived by the emperor, is uncertain, as authors have given both accounts, worse, however, and more dreadful than any which have ever happened to this city by the

[7] The emperor Nero. [8] Probably a pond constructed in the neighborhood of the Pantheon (on the Campus Martius) by Agrippa (about 63–12 B.C.), consul of Rome and expected heir to Augustus. [9] Invariably a male name.

violence of fire. It had its beginning in that part of the circus which adjoins the Palatine and Caelian hills,[10] where, amid the shops containing inflammable wares, the conflagration both broke out and instantly became so fierce and so rapid from the wind that it seized in its grasp the entire length of the circus.[11] For here there were no houses fenced in by solid masonry, or temples surrounded by walls, or any other obstacle to interpose delay. The blaze in its fury ran first through the level portions of the city, then rising to the hills, while it again devastated every place below them, it outstripped all preventive measures; so rapid was the mischief and so completely at its mercy the city, with those narrow winding passages and irregular streets, which characterized old Rome. Added to this were the wailings of terror-stricken women, the feebleness of age, the helpless inexperience of childhood, the crowds who sought to save themselves or others, dragging out the infirm or waiting for them, and by their hurry in the one case, by their delay in the other, aggravating the confusion. Often, while they looked behind them, they were intercepted by flames on their side or in their face. Or if they reached a refuge close at hand, when this too was seized by the fire, they found that, even places, which they had imagined to be remote, were involved in the same calamity. At last, doubting what they should avoid or whither betake themselves, they crowded the streets or flung themselves down in the fields, while some who had lost their all, even their very daily bread, and others out of love for their kinsfolk, whom they had been unable to rescue, perished, though escape was open to them. And no one dared to stop the mischief, because of incessant menaces from a number of persons who forbade the extinguishing of the flames, because again others openly hurled brands, and kept shouting that there was one who gave them authority, either seeking to plunder more freely, or obeying orders.

Nero at this time was at Antium,[12] and did not return to Rome until the fire approached his house, which he had built to connect the palace with the gardens of Maecenas.[13] It could not, however, be stopped from devouring the palace, the house, and everything around it. However, to relieve the people, driven out homeless as they were, he threw open to them the Campus Martius[14] and the public buildings of Agrippa,[15] and even his own gardens, and

---

[10] Two of the seven famous hills on which Rome was built. An important part of the city was on the Palatine.   [11] The Circus Maximus, which by the beginning of the second century A.D. could seat 200,000 spectators, was mainly the scene of chariot races and spectacular imperial shows. It lay between the southwest flank of the Palatine and the Aventine hill.   [12] The modern Anzio, on the coast south of Rome.   [13] Magnificent formal gardens on the eastern outskirts of Rome.   [14] Literally, "field of Mars"; an open space outside the city walls northwest of Rome, dedicated to the god of war, Mars, as a place for military and athletic exercises.   [15] As a high public official (*aedile*), Agrippa in 33 B.C. improved and constructed numerous public buildings in Rome, and as consul in 27 B.C. he built the temple now represented by the Pantheon.

raised temporary structures to receive the destitute multitude. Supplies of food were brought up from Ostia[16] and the neighboring towns, and the price of corn was reduced to three sesterces a peck. These acts, though popular, produced no effect, since a rumor had gone forth everywhere that, at the very time when the city was in flames, the emperor appeared on a private stage and sang of the destruction of Troy, comparing present misfortunes with the calamities of antiquity.

At last, after five days, an end was put to the conflagration at the foot of the Esquiline hill,[17] by the destruction of all buildings on a vast space, so that the violence of the fire was met by clear ground and an open sky. But before people had laid aside their fears, the flames returned, with no less fury this second time, and especially in the spacious districts of the city. Consequently, though there was less loss of life, temples of the gods, and the porticoes which were devoted to enjoyment, fell in a yet more widespread ruin. And to this conflagration there attached the greater infamy because it broke out on the Aemilian property of Tigellinus, and it seemed that Nero was aiming at the glory of founding a new city and calling it by his name. Rome, indeed, is divided into fourteen districts, four of which remained uninjured, three were leveled to the ground, while in the other seven were left only a few shattered, half-burnt relics of houses.

It would not be easy to enter into a computation of the private mansions, the blocks of tenements, and of the temples, which were lost. Those with the oldest ceremonial, as that dedicated by Servius Tullius[18] to Luna,[19] the great altar and shrine raised by the Arcadian Evander[20] to the visibly appearing Hercules, the temple of Jupiter the Stayer, which was vowed by Romulus, Numa's[21] royal palace, and the sanctuary of Vesta,[22] with the tutelary deities[23] of the Roman people, were burnt. So too were the riches acquired by our many victories, various beauties of Greek art, then again the ancient and genuine historical monuments of men of genius, and, notwithstanding the striking splendor of the restored city, old men will remember many things which could not be replaced. Some persons observed that the beginning of

[16] Town about sixteen miles from Rome at the mouth of the Tiber; the port of Rome.   [17] The easternmost of the seven hills.   [18] Sixth king of Rome (about 578–534 B.C.).   [19] The Moon goddess.   [20] In Roman legend a son of Mercury (Hermes), who led a group of colonists from Arcadia in the Peloponnesus to Italy about sixty years before the Trojan War. He was believed to have founded a pre-Roman town at the foot of the Palatine, which was subsequently incorporated into Rome.   [21] Numa Pompilius, the legendary second king of Rome (714–671 B.C.). Tacitus is here enumerating some of the oldest buildings, with associations that belong to legend at least as much as to history.   [22] Roman goddess of the hearth, whose central shrine in the Forum was thought to have been built by Numa. There her fires were always kept burning by six virgin Vestals or priestesses.   [23] The Penates, divinities of the threshold and guardians of the home, brought to Italy with the sacred fire of Vesta by Aeneas; closely associated with Vesta.

this conflagration was on the 19th of July, the day on which the Senones[24] captured and fired Rome. Others have pushed a curious inquiry so far as to reduce the interval between these two conflagrations into equal numbers of years, months, and days.

Nero meanwhile availed himself of his country's desolation, and erected a mansion in which the jewels and gold, long familiar objects, quite vulgarized by our extravagance, were not so marvelous as the fields and lakes, with woods on one side to resemble a wilderness, and on the other, open spaces and extensive views. The directors and contrivers of the work were Severus and Celer, who had the genius and the audacity to attempt by art even what nature had refused, and to fool away an emperor's resources. They had actually undertaken to sink a navigable canal from the lake Avernus[25] to the mouths of the Tiber along a barren shore or through the face of hills, where one meets with no moisture which could supply water, except the Pomptine marshes.[26] The rest of the country is broken rock and perfectly dry. Even if it could be cut through, the labor would be intolerable, and there would be no adequate result. Nero, however, with his love of the impossible, endeavored to dig through the nearest hills to Avernus, and there still remain the traces of his disappointed hope.

Of Rome meanwhile, so much as was left unoccupied by his mansion, was not built up, as it had been after its burning by the Gauls,[27] without any regularity or in any fashion, but with rows of streets according to measurement, with broad thoroughfares, with a restriction on the height of houses, with open spaces, and the further addition of colonnades, as a protection to the frontage of the blocks of tenements. These colonnades Nero promised to erect at his own expense, and to hand over the open spaces, when cleared of the débris, to the ground landlords. He also offered rewards proportioned to each person's position and property, and prescribed a period within which they were to obtain them on the completion of so many houses or blocks of building. He fixed on the marshes of Ostia for the reception of the rubbish, and arranged that the ships which had brought up corn by the Tiber, should sail down the river with cargoes of this rubbish. The buildings themselves, to a certain height, were to be solidly constructed, without wooden beams, of stone from Gabii or Alba,[28] that material being impervious to fire. And to provide that the water which individual license had illegally appropriated,

---

[24] About 390 B.C. Rome was captured by the invading Senones, a powerful Gallic tribe. They were finally expelled from Italy in 283 B.C. [25] Deep lake in the crater of an extinct volcano near Baiae, a fashionable Roman coastal resort in Campania. [26] A marshy plain on the coast between Rome and Lake Avernus, the drainage of which was attempted as early as the fourth century B.C. None of the ancient, medieval, or modern attempts at reclamation of the area was entirely successful until a few decades ago. [27] Senones. [28] Gabii was a town a few miles east of Rome, Alba a few miles southeast.

might flow in greater abundance in several places for the public use, officers were appointed, and everyone was to have in the open court the means of stopping a fire. Every building, too, was to be enclosed by its own proper wall, not by one common to others. These changes which were liked for their utility, also added beauty to the new city. Some, however, thought that its old arrangement had been more conducive to health, inasmuch as the narrow streets with the elevation of the roofs were not equally penetrated by the sun's heat, while now the open space, unsheltered by any shade, was scorched by a fiercer glow.

Such indeed were the precautions of human wisdom. The next thing was to seek means of propitiating the gods, and recourse was had to the Sibylline books, by the direction of which prayers were offered to Vulcanus, Ceres, and Proserpina.[29] Juno, too, was entreated by the matrons, first, in the Capitol, then on the nearest part of the coast, whence water was procured to sprinkle the fame and image of the goddess. And there were sacred banquets and nightly vigils celebrated by married women. But all human efforts, all the lavish gifts of the emperor, and the propitiations of the gods, did not banish the sinister belief that the conflagration was the result of an order. Consequently, to get rid of the report, Nero fastened the guilt and inflicted the most exquisite tortures on a class hated for their abominations, called Christians by the populace. Christus, from whom the name had its origin, suffered the extreme penalty during the reign of Tiberius[30] at the hands of one of our procurators, Pontius Pilatus, and a most mischievous superstition, thus checked for the moment, again broke out not only in Judæa, the first source of the evil, but even in Rome, where all things hideous and shameful from every part of the world find their center and become popular. Accordingly, an arrest was first made of all who pleaded guilty; then, upon their information, an immense multitude was convicted, not so much of the crime of firing the city, as of hatred against mankind. Mockery of every sort was added to their deaths. Covered with the skins of beasts, they were torn by dogs and perished, or were nailed to crosses, or were doomed to the flames and burnt, to serve as a nightly illumination, when daylight had expired.

Nero offered his gardens for the spectacle, and was exhibiting a show in the circus, while he mingled with the people in the dress of a charioteer or stood aloft on a car. Hence, even for criminals who deserved extreme and exemplary punishment, there arose a feeling of compassion; for it was not, as it seemed, for the public good, but to glut one man's cruelty, that they were being destroyed.

[29] Vulcanus is the Roman god of fire (Greek, Hephaestus); Ceres the goddess of fertility and grain (Greek, Demeter); and Proserpina (Greek, Persephone) is the daughter of Ceres who, as embodiment of the seeds of vegetation, spends part of the year under the earth (in the underworld).   [30] Roman emperor from 14 to 37 A.D.

St. Augustine

FROM *The Confessions*

TRANSLATED BY JOSEPH GREEN PILKINGTON

St. Augustine (354–430 A.D.)

AURELIUS AUGUSTINUS, BETTER KNOWN AS ST. AUGUSTINE, was perhaps one of the most striking figures to appear in the early Christian Church after Paul. He was born the son of a pagan father and a Christian mother in North Africa at a time when the Roman Empire was already Christian. Augustine was brought up as a Christian, but during his education in the literary and philosophical traditions of the Greco-Roman world he turned away from Christianity. Inspired by a philosophical treatise of Cicero, he decided to devote his life to the pursuit of truth. He became a teacher at Carthage, Rome, and Milan, and went through a tortuous and troubled spiritual development, including a stage of general skepticism. Finally a prolonged religious crisis led to his conversion to Christianity in 387 A.D. After a period of religious and philosophical contemplation, he returned permanently to North Africa and was later appointed bishop of Hippo, a position he retained until his death.

Augustine's significance, in terms of Western literature, is at least twofold. First, his conversion did not blunt his affection for classical literature or the keen philosophical interest which had been triggered by Cicero; it only made him develop a specifically religious philosophy which always displayed residues of his classical training. Through his assimilation of Greek and Roman thought to Christian dogma, Augustine helped to ensure the survival of classical literature at a time when the ancient era crumbled in a chaotic fury of destruction. Second, some of the subsequent developments in Western literature were strongly influenced by Augustine's voluminous writings. The most influential of these works are his *Confessions* and *On the City of God* (*De civitate Dei*). The latter was inspired by the fall of Rome in 410 A.D. and interprets the earthly and heavenly kingdoms, which grow in this life as an insoluble tangle, as the two forces that determine history.

In his *Confessions* Augustine records the story of his early life and his conversion. He addresses God directly—thus creating a semblance of dialogue—while coming to an understanding of his own emotions, motivations, and psychological development. With this descriptive account he creates a new genre: the autobiographical narrative which transcends a list of one's own achievements. From the very beginning, which gives us the only detailed account from antiquity of an outstanding man's childhood, this autobiography inaugurates the collapse of the relatively unified, anthropocentric Greek and Roman view of man. In its place is presented the distinctively Christian view. Man is no longer at the center and there is no longer magnificence even to his suffering, defiance, and deficiencies; rather, he is henceforth an ignorant and straying child.

The Confessions

But in this my childhood (which was far less dreaded for me than youth) I had no love of learning, and hated to be forced to it, yet was I forced to it notwithstanding; and this was well done towards me, but I did not well, for I would not have learned had I not been compelled. For no man doth well against his will, even if that which he doth be well. Neither did they who forced me do well, but the good that was done to me came from Thee, my God. For they considered not in what way I should employ what they forced me to learn, unless to satisfy the inordinate desires of a rich beggary and a shameful glory. But Thou, by whom the very hairs of our heads are numbered,[1] didst use for my good the error of all who pressed me to learn; and my own error in willing not to learn, didst Thou make use of for my punishment—of which I, being so small a boy and so great a sinner, was not unworthy. Thus by the instrumentality of those who did not well didst Thou well for me; and by my own sin didst Thou justly punish me. For it is even as Thou hast appointed, that every inordinate affection should bring its own punishment. . . .

But what was the cause of my dislike of Greek literature, which I studied from my boyhood, I cannot even now understand. For the Latin I loved exceedingly—not what our first masters, but what the grammarians[2] teach; for those primary lessons of reading, writing, and ciphering, I considered no less of a burden and a punishment than Greek. Yet whence was this unless from the sin and vanity of this life? for I was "but flesh, a wind that passeth away and cometh not again." [3] For those primary lessons were better, assuredly, because more certain; seeing that by their agency I acquired, and still retain, the power of reading what I find written, and writing myself what I will; whilst in the others I was compelled to learn about the wanderings of a certain Aeneas, oblivious of my own, and to weep for Dido dead, because she slew herself for love;[4] while at the same time I brooked with dry eyes my

---

[1] Augustine intersperses his statements with constant allusions to (and quotations from) the Old and New Testament and Virgil's *Aeneid*. Here he quotes from the Gospel according to Matthew 10:30.   [2] Secondary or advanced teachers in the Roman educational system.   [3] A quotation from Psalm 78:39.   [4] A reference to Virgil's *Aeneid*, Book VI, (p. 484).

wretched self dying far from Thee, in the midst of those things, O God, my life.

For what can be more wretched than the wretch who pities not himself shedding tears over the death of Dido for love of Aeneas, but shedding no tears over his own death in not loving Thee, O God, light of my heart, and bread of the inner mouth of my soul, and the power that weddest my mind with my innermost thoughts? I did not love Thee, and committed fornication against Thee; and those around me thus sinning cried, "Well done! Well done!" For the friendship of this world is fornication against Thee; and "Well done! Well done!" is cried until one feels ashamed not to be such a man. And for this I shed no tears, though I wept for Dido, who sought death at the sword's point, myself the while seeking the lowest of Thy creatures— having forsaken Thee—earth tending to the earth; and if forbidden to read these things, how grieved would I feel that I was not permitted to read what grieved me. This sort of madness is considered a more honorable and more fruitful learning than that by which I learned to read and write. . . .

But why, then, did I dislike Greek learning,[5] which was full of like tales? For Homer also was skilled in inventing similar stories, and is most sweetly vain, yet was he disagreeable to me as a boy. I believe Virgil, indeed, would be the same to Grecian children, if compelled to learn him, as I was Homer. The difficulty, in truth, the difficulty of learning a foreign language mingled as it were with gall all the sweetness of those fabulous Grecian stories. For not a single word of it did I understand, and to make me do so, they vehemently urged me with cruel threatenings and punishments. There was a time also when (as an infant) I knew no Latin; but this I acquired without any fear or tormenting, by merely taking notice, amid the blandishments of my nurses, the jests of those who smiled on me, and the sportiveness of those who toyed with me. I learnt all this, indeed, without being urged by any pressure of punishment, for my own heart urged me to bring forth its own conceptions, which I could not do unless by learning words, not of those who taught me, but of those who talked to me; into whose ears, also, I brought forth whatever I discerned. From this it is sufficiently clear that a free curiosity hath more influence in our learning these things than a necessity full of fear. . . .

I will now call to mind my past foulness, and the carnal corruptions of my soul, not because I love them, but that I may love Thee, O my God. . . .

But what was it that I delighted in save to love and to be beloved? But I held it not in moderation, mind to mind, the bright path of friendship, but out of the dark concupiscence of the flesh and the effervescence of youth exhalations came forth which obscured and overcast my heart, so that I was unable to discern pure affection from unholy desire. Both boiled confusedly

[5] Augustine's dislike of learning a foreign language should not be construed as indicating an ignorance of Greek.

within me, and dragged away my unstable youth into the rough places of unchaste desires, and plunged me into a gulf of infamy. Thy anger had overshadowed me, and I knew it not. . . .

Where was I, and how far was I exiled from the delights of Thy house, in that sixteenth year of the age of my flesh, when the madness of lust—to the which human shamelessness granteth full freedom, although forbidden by Thy laws—held complete sway over me, and I resigned myself entirely to it? Those about me meanwhile took no care to save me from ruin by marriage, their sole care being that I should learn to make a powerful speech, and become a persuasive orator. . . .

Theft is punished by Thy law, O Lord, and by the law written in men's hearts, which iniquity itself cannot blot out. For what thief will suffer a thief? Even a rich thief will not suffer him who is driven to it by want. Yet had I a desire to commit robbery, and did so, compelled neither by hunger, nor poverty, but through a distaste for well-doing, and a lustiness of iniquity. For I pilfered that of which I had already sufficient, and much better. Nor did I desire to enjoy what I pilfered, but the theft and sin itself. . . . It was foul, and I loved it. I loved to perish. I loved my own error—not that for which I erred, but the error itself. Base soul, falling from Thy firmament to utter destruction—not seeking aught through the shame but the shame itself!

There is a desirableness in all beautiful bodies, and in gold, and silver, and all things; and in bodily contact sympathy is powerful, and each other sense hath his proper adaptation of body. Worldly honor hath also its glory, and the power of command, and of overcoming; whence proceeds also the desire for revenge. And yet to acquire all these, we must not depart from Thee, O Lord, nor deviate from Thy law. . . .

To Carthage I came,[6] where a cauldron of unholy loves bubbled up all around me. I loved not as yet, yet I loved to love; and, with a hidden want, I abhorred myself that I wanted not. I searched about for something to love, in love with loving, and hating security, and a way not beset with snares. For within me I had a dearth of that inward food, Thyself, my God, though that dearth caused me no hunger; but I remained without all desire for incorruptible food, not because I was already filled thereby, but the more empty I was the more I loathed it. For this reason my soul was far from well, and, full of ulcers, it miserably cast itself forth, craving to be excited by contact with objects of sense. . . . For I was both beloved, and secretly arrived at the bond of enjoying; and was joyfully bound with troublesome ties, that I might be scourged with the burning iron rods of jealousy, suspicion, fear, anger, and strife.

Stage plays also drew me away,[7] full of representations of my miseries and

[6] At the age of 17 Augustine went from his home town, Tagaste, to Carthage for three years.   [7] The early Fathers of the Christian Church vehemently disapproved of theatrical performances. Those who attended plays were excluded from baptism. Here Augustine is arguing with Aristotle's notion of catharsis.

of fuel to my fire. Why does man like to be made sad when viewing doleful and tragical scenes, which yet he himself would by no means suffer? And yet he wishes, as a spectator, to experience from them a sense of grief, and in this very grief his pleasure consists. What is this but wretched insanity? For a man is more affected with these actions, the less free he is from such affections. Howsoever, when he suffers in his own person, it is the custom to style it "misery"; but when he compassionates others, then it is styled "mercy." But what kind of mercy is it that arises from fictitious and scenic passions? The hearer is not expected to relieve, but merely invited to grieve; and the more he grieves, the more he applauds the actor of these fictions. And if the misfortunes of the characters (whether of olden times or merely imaginary) be so represented as not to touch the feelings of the spectator, he goes away disgusted and censorious; but if his feelings be touched, he sits it out attentively, and sheds tears of joy. . . .

Among such as these, at that unstable period of my life,[8] I studied books of eloquence, wherein I was eager to be eminent from a damnable and inflated purpose, even a delight in human vanity. In the ordinary course of study, I lighted upon a certain book of Cicero, whose language, though not his heart, almost all admire. This book of his contains an exhortation to philosophy, and is called *Hortensius*.[9] This book, in truth, changed my affections, and turned my prayers to Thyself, O Lord, and made me have other hopes and desires. Worthless suddenly became every vain hope to me; and, with an incredible warmth of heart, I yearned for an immortality of wisdom, and began now to arise[10] that I might return to Thee. Not then, to improve my language—which I appeared to be purchasing with my mother's means, in that my nineteenth year, my father having died two years before—not to improve my language did I have recourse to that book; nor did it persuade me by its style, but its matter. . . .

I resolved, therefore,[11] to direct my mind to the Holy Scriptures, that I might see what they were. And behold, I perceive something not comprehended by the proud, not disclosed to children, but lowly as you approach, sublime as you advance, and veiled in mysteries; and I was not of the number of those who could enter into it, or bend my neck to follow its steps. For not as when now I speak did I feel when I turned towards those Scriptures, but they appeared to me to be unworthy to be compared with the dignity of Cicero; for my inflated pride shunned their style, nor could the sharpness of my wit pierce their inner meaning. Yet, truly, were they such as

[8] At the age of 19, about two years after his father's death.   [9] A lost introduction to philosophy by Cicero (written about 45 B.C.), which was modeled after an Aristotelian exhortation to study philosophy (*The Protrepticus*).   [10] An allusion to the Gospel according to Luke 15:18 (see p. 503).   [11] Through this "love of knowledge and wisdom" (Greek, *philo-sophia*), which was inspired by Cicero, Augustine now develops an interest in speculation about God and the nature of ultimate reality.

would develop in little ones; but I scorned to be a little one, and, swollen with pride, I looked upon myself as a great one. . . .

By now Augustine was 32 years old and was experiencing the torments of an intellectual and spiritual search for validity. In the intervening period he had in rapid succession become a follower of the rationalistic Manichaean sect, studied Plato and Aristotle, discovered the fallacies of the Manichaeans, taught rhetoric at Rome, and, through the influence of his older contemporary St. Ambrose, started turning to orthodox Christianity. In the following section he describes his conversion to Christianity with a famous display of his powers of psychological perception and vivid description.

Thus was I sick and tormented, accusing myself far more severely than was my wont, tossing and turning me in my chain till that was utterly broken, whereby I now was but slightly, but still was held. And Thou, O Lord, pressedst upon me in my inward parts by a severe mercy, redoubling the lashes[12] of fear and shame, lest I should again give way, and that shame slender remaining tie not being broken off, it should recover strength, and enchain me the faster. For I said mentally, "Lo, let it be done now, let it be done now." And as I spoke, I all but came to a resolve. I all but did it, yet I did it not. Yet fell I not back to my old condition, but took up my position hard by, and drew breath. And I tried again, and wanted but very little of reaching it, and somewhat less, and then all but touched and grasped it; and yet came not at it, nor touched, nor grasped it, hesitating to die unto death, and to live unto life; and the worse, whereto I had been habituated, prevailed more with me than the better, which I had not tried. And the very moment in which I was to become another man, the nearer it approached me, the greater horror did it strike into me; but it did not strike me back, nor turn me aside, but kept me in suspense.

The very toys of toys, and vanities of vanities,[13] my old mistresses, still enthralled me; they shook my fleshly garment, and whispered softly, "Dost thou part with us? And from that moment shall we no more be with thee for ever? And from that moment shall not this or that be lawful for thee for ever?" And what did they suggest to me in the words "this or that"? What is it that they suggested, O my God? Let Thy mercy avert it from the soul of Thy servant. What impurities did they suggest! What shame! And now I far less than half heard them, not openly showing themselves and contradicting me, but muttering, as it were, behind my back, and furtively plucking me as I was departing, to make me look back upon them. Yet they did delay me, so

---

12 An allusion to a phrase in Virgil's *Aeneid* (Book V, line 457).   13 A quotation of a famous phrase from the Old Testament (Ecclesiastes 1:2).

that I hesitated to burst and shake myself free from them, and to leap over whither I was called—an unruly habit saying to me, "Dost thou think thou canst live without them?"

But now it said this very faintly; for on that side towards which I had set my face, and whither I trembled to go, did the chaste dignity of Continence appear unto me, cheerful, but not dissolutely gay, honestly alluring me to come and doubt nothing, and extending her holy hands, full of a multiplicity of good examples, to receive and embrace me. There were there so many young men and maidens, a multitude of youth and every age, grave widows and ancient virgins, and Continence herself in all, not barren, but a fruitful mother of children of joys,[14] by Thee, O Lord, her Husband. And she smiled on me with an encouraging mockery, as if to say, "Canst not thou do what these youths and maidens can? Or can one or other do it of themselves, and not rather in the Lord their God? The Lord their God gave me unto them. Why standest thou in thine own strength, and so standest not? Cast thyself upon Him; fear not, He will not withdraw that thou shouldest fall; cast thyself upon Him without fear, He will receive thee, and heal thee." And I blushed beyond measure, for I still heard the muttering of those toys, and hung in suspense. And she again seemed to say, "Shut up thine ears against those unclean members of thine upon the earth, that they may be mortified.[15] They tell thee of delights, but not as doth the law of the Lord thy God." This controversy in my heart was naught but self against self. But Alypius,[16] sitting close by my side, awaited in silence the result of my unwonted emotion.

But when a profound reflection had, from the secret depths of my soul, drawn together and heaped up all my misery before the sight of my heart, there arose a mighty storm, accompanied by as mighty a shower of tears. Which, that I might pour forth fully, with its natural expressions, I stole away from Alypius; for it suggested itself to me that solitude was fitter for the business of weeping. So I retired to such a distance that even his presence could not be oppressive to me. Thus was it with me at that time, and he perceived it; for something, I believe, I had spoken, wherein the sound of my voice appeared choked with weeping, and in that state had I risen up. He then remained where we had been sitting, most completely astonished. I flung myself down, how, I know not, under a certain fig-tree, giving free course to my tears, and the streams of mine eyes gushed out, an acceptable

[14] An allusion to Psalm 113:9: "[The lord] maketh the barren woman . . . to be a joyful mother of children." [15] A reference to the Epistle of Paul to the Colossians 3:5: "Mortify therefore your members which are upon the earth; fornication, uncleanness. . . ." [16] Alypius had been a fellow student of Augustine at Tagaste and Carthage and had been a close friend of his for a number of years. He later became bishop of Tagaste.

sacrifice unto Thee.[17] And, not indeed in these words, yet to this effect, spake I much unto Thee,[18] "But Thou, O Lord, how long?" "How long, Lord? Wilt Thou be angry for ever? Oh, remember not against us former iniquities"; for I felt that I was enthralled by them. I sent up these sorrowful cries, "How long, how long? Tomorrow, and tomorrow? Why not now? Why is there not this hour an end to my uncleanness?"

I was saying these things and weeping in the most bitter contrition of my heart, when, lo, I heard the voice as of a boy or girl, I know not which, coming from a neighboring house, chanting, and oft repeating, "Take up and read; take up and read." Immediately my countenance was changed, and I began most earnestly to consider whether it was usual for children in any kind of game to sing such words; nor could I remember ever to have heard the like. So, restraining the torrent of my tears, I rose up, interpreting it no other way than as a command to me from Heaven to open the book, and to read the first chapter I should light upon.[19] For I had heard of Antony,[20] that, accidentally coming in whilst the gospel was being read, he received the admonition as if what was read were addressed to him, "Go and sell that thou hast, and give to the poor, and thou shalt have treasure in heaven; and come and follow me." [21] And by such oracle was he forthwith converted unto Thee. So quickly I returned to the place where Alypius was sitting; for there had I put down the volume of the apostles, when I rose thence. I grasped, opened, and in silence read that paragraph on which my eyes first fell, "Not in rioting and drunkenness, not in chambering and wantonness, not in strife and envying; but put ye on the Lord Jesus Christ, and make not provision for the flesh, to fulfill the lusts thereof." [22] No further would I read, nor did I need; for instantly, as the sentence ended—by a light, as it were, of security infused into my heart—all the gloom of doubt vanished away.

Closing the book, then, and putting either my finger between, or some other mark, I now with a tranquil countenance made it known to Alypius. And he thus disclosed to me what was wrought in him,[23] which I knew not.

[17] A reference to a well-known Hebrew doctrine stated, for example, in Psalm 51:17: "The sacrifices of God are a broken spirit: a broken and a contrite heart, O God, thou wilt not despise." [18] The following sentences ("But thou . . . iniquities") are quotations from Psalm 6:3 and Psalm 78:5 and 8. [19] In another part of his *Confessions* Augustine alludes to the fact that Virgil's *Aeneid* too was often consulted in the same way in late antiquity—the power of sheer chance frequently seemed to produce a Virgilian "verse . . . wondrously appropriate to the present business." Indeed, reading random selections from a sacred text was a favorite form of divination throughout the Orient. Later councils of the Christian Church condemned this popular way of reading the Bible. [20] Saint Anthony, an Egyptian monk who became a symbol of ascetic resistance to physical temptations, lived in the third century A.D. [21] From the Gospel according to Matthew 19:21. [22] From the Epistle of Paul to the Romans 13:13–14. [23] Alypius was at the same time experiencing his own conversion to Christianity.

He asked to look at what I had read. I showed him; and he looked even further than I had read, and I knew not what followed. This it was, verily, "Him that is weak in the faith, receive ye"; which he applied to himself, and discovered to me. By this admonition was he strengthened; and by a good resolution and purpose, very much in accord with his character (wherein, for the better, he was always far different from me), without any restless delay he joined me. Thence we go in to my mother. We make it known to her—she rejoiceth. We relate how it came to pass—she leapeth for joy, and triumpheth, and blesseth Thee, who art "able to do exceeding abundantly above all that we ask or think";[24] for she perceived Thee to have given her more for me than she used to ask by her pitiful and most doleful groanings. For Thou didst so convert me unto Thyself, that I sought neither a wife, nor any other of this world's hopes—standing in that rule of faith in which Thou, so many years before, had showed me unto her in a vision. And thou didst turn her grief into a gladness,[25] much more plentiful than she had desired, and much dearer and chaster than she used to crave, by having grandchildren of my body.[26]

How sweet did it suddenly become to me to be without the delights of trifles! And what at one time I feared to lose, it was now a joy to me to put away. For Thou didst cast them away from me, Thou true and highest sweetness. Thou didst cast them away, and instead of them didst enter in Thyself —sweeter than all pleasure, though not to flesh and blood; brighter than all light, but more veiled than all mysteries; more exalted than all honor, but not to the exulted in their own conceits. Now was my soul free from the gnawing cares of seeking and getting, and of wallowing and exciting the itch of lust. And I babbled unto Thee my brightness, my riches, and my health, the Lord my God.

[24] A quotation from the Epistle of Paul to the Ephesians 3:20.   [25] An allusion to Psalm 30:11: "Thou hast turned for me my mourning into dancing. . . ." [26] Augustine's mother, Monica, a devout Christian, had made efforts to arrange a marriage for her son.